MW01675292

The Man Who Killed Apartheid

The Life of Dimitri Tsafendas

New Updated Edition

Harris Dousemetzis
University of Durham

with

Gerry Loughran

Series in World History

VERNON PRESS

Copyright © 2023 Vernon Press, an imprint of Vernon Art and Science Inc, on behalf of the author.

All rights reserved. No part of this publication may be reproduced, stored in a retrieval system, or transmitted in any form or by any means, electronic, mechanical, photocopying, recording, or otherwise, without the prior permission of Vernon Art and Science Inc.

www.vernonpress.com

In the Americas:
Vernon Press
1000 N West Street, Suite 1200
Wilmington, Delaware, 19801
United States

In the rest of the world:
Vernon Press
C/Sancti Espiritu 17,
Malaga, 29006
Spain

Series in World History

Library of Congress Control Number: 2022941596

ISBN: 978-1-64889-696-5

Also available:

978-1-64889-602-6 [Hardback, Standard Color]; 978-1-64889-512-8 [Hardback, B&W];

978-1-64889-697-2 [Paperback, B&W]; 978-1-64889-580-7 [PDF, E-Book]

Product and company names mentioned in this work are the trademarks of their respective owners. While every care has been taken in preparing this work, neither the authors nor Vernon Art and Science Inc. may be held responsible for any loss or damage caused or alleged to be caused directly or indirectly by the information contained in it.

Every effort has been made to trace all copyright holders, but if any have been inadvertently overlooked the publisher will be pleased to include any necessary credits in any subsequent reprint or edition.

For my Maya-Allende

For Krish Govender, Judge Jody Kollapen and Bishop Ioannis Tsaftaridis; men of courage and principle who took a personal and human interest in Tsafendas when to do so risked establishment contumely and possible professional damage. Their commitment to justice and their principles would not allow them to do otherwise.

For Dimitri Tsafendas

Table of contents

	Preface	*vii*
Chapter 1	**The Deed**	1
Chapter 2	**After the Deed**	11
Chapter 3	**The Son of an Anarchist**	35
Chapter 4	**Tsafendas and Verwoerd in South Africa**	73
Chapter 5	**Enter the Tapeworm**	83
Chapter 6	**Redemption**	93
Chapter 7	**Exiled**	99
Chapter 8	**Teacher of English and Bomb-maker**	113
	Figures	*139*
Chapter 9	**Back to Africa**	149
Chapter 10	**Parliamentary Messenger**	183
Chapter 11	**The Outbreak of Torture**	209
Chapter 12	**A Verdict is Arranged**	243
Chapter 13	**A State-President's Patient**	291
Chapter 14	**Justifying the Deed**	323
Chapter 15	**An Unmarked Grave**	363
	Epilogue	*373*
	Notes	*391*

Bibliography 457

About the Authors 479

Index 481

Preface

I first learnt of Dimitri Tsafendas when I came across an obituary shortly after his death in 1999. Although familiar with apartheid and a basic history of South Africa, I had never heard of this man. Since the obituary revealed only some basic facts about him, I decided to find out more. Searching further afield, I discovered Henk van Woerden's *A Mouthful of Glass*, and three other books which mentioned Tsafendas tangentially, Breyten Breytenbach's *True Confessions of an Albino Terrorist*, Dr Peter Lambley's *The Psychology of Apartheid* and Gordon Winter's *Inside BOSS*. Reading these volumes prompted me to investigate further since they contained little or no substantive information about Tsafendas's trial or the long time he spent in prison and detention. Over the following years, I checked the internet regularly for anything new. A few items here and there, occasional articles in the Greek press and two TV documentaries – Manolis Dimelas's *Live and Let Live* and Liza Key's *A Question of Madness* – so intrigued me that I began to think of writing a book about Tsafendas. To do this, I needed to meet people who had known him personally.

In the event, the first five people I contacted turned out to be very important in my work as they had all known Tsafendas well. I spoke to each of them at length and on an ongoing basis, learning facts about Tsafendas, which were not publicly known at the time. The five were Alexander Moumbaris and four Greek Orthodox clerics, Fathers Nikola Banovic, Minas Constandinou, Michalis Visvinis and Bishop Ioannis Tsaftaridis. The three priests had all been close to Tsafendas. Father Minas first met him in Mozambique in 1963 and visited him frequently in prison; Father Nikola shared his home with Tsafendas in Istanbul for more than five months in 1961; Father Michalis called to see him in prison many times over a period of four years. Bishop Ioannis met Tsafendas in prison and although he knew him less well than the other priests, their encounter was a life-changing event for him. As for Moumbaris, he had spent three months in prison alongside Tsafendas in 1973. All of them swore that Tsafendas was perfectly sane and had pretended to be otherwise only to avoid the gallows and that he had killed Verwoerd for purely political reasons. What surprised me was that every one of the five spoke of Tsafendas with unbounded admiration, something I believe would be rare among any random group of five persons commenting on another. Clearly, all of these men, four of them ministers of religion, held Verwoerd's assassin in the highest esteem and invariably spoke fondly of him – not of his deed, but his character. Aware now that Tsafendas was the very opposite of the pathetic figure that had been constructed by South Africa's apartheid authorities and 'sold' to the outside world, I decided I would indeed write a book that would seek to correct the record and right a palpable wrong.

Knowing that Tsafendas had befriended the sailors of the Greek tanker, *Eleni,* shortly before the assassination and aware that these men were central to the police investigation, I procured the crew list from the Greek Ministry of Shipping. I then located and spoke to 17 of the 38 seamen, who all gave me invaluable information about their time with Tsafendas, further confirming the picture of a man who was perfectly sane and deeply political. Over the next few years, I travelled to France, Greece, Mozambique, South Africa and Turkey to speak to more people who had met Tsafendas. I hired private investigators to locate two witnesses I had failed to find, namely Brian Price and Gordon Winter. Their efforts did not bear fruit, but with the help of Dr James Sanders, I was able to interview Winter. Price was the only man I failed to reach. In total, I spoke to 138 people, 70 of whom knew Tsafendas personally, including members of his own family. Some knew Tsafendas exceptionally well and spoke to me formally about him for the first time; five of them had known him since he was a small child. Others included workmates, fellow lodgers, co-prisoners, visitors who talked to him in hospital and prison, clinicians who examined him before his trial, and two of his defence lawyers. Every witness, except for the three members of his defence team, Willie Burger, David Bloomberg and Dr Isaak Sakinofsky, told me exactly the same thing – Tsafendas was a normal, sane person with deep political ideas. My interviewees also included persons related to the judicial proceedings, such as witnesses, lawyers, judges, psychologists, psychiatrists, academics, high-ranking police officers and former secret agents.

Aware that Tsafendas had been politically active in Mozambique, I searched the Portuguese National Archives and discovered that PIDE, the Portuguese secret security police, held a massive file on him (Secret Criminal Record No 10.415 of Demitrios Tsafantakis). What's more, I learnt to my astonishment, that on the day following Verwoerd's assassination, the PIDE, Portugal's International and State Defence Policy, in Lisbon had instructed their counterparts in Mozambique to conceal from the South African authorities any 'information indicating Tsafendas as a partisan for the independence' of Mozambique and that their colleagues in Lourenço Marques had subsequently done exactly that. These were monumental discoveries: I now had in my possession indisputable evidence supporting the testimonies of the witnesses I had interviewed that Tsafendas was a political animal.

By now, I was aware that the National Archives of South Africa contained thousands of documents from the South African police investigations and from the Commission of Enquiry into Verwoerd's death. I was not optimistic as to what I would find since I knew from a number of impeccable sources that Tsafendas's first statement to General van den Bergh, who led the police investigation, had gone missing. It was not unknown for evidence to disappear in cases that contradicted apartheid's official version of various events or was damaging to the regime. I was surprised, therefore, to discover that the archives held more than a hundred statements taken by the police and the Commission of Enquiry, along with other evidence, which in some way contradicted the official version of the assassination and supported the evidence I had already collected from my interviews. With permission from Tsafendas's family, I also obtained his medical records, which included some documents of major importance, such as the Grafton State Hospital report, which revealed that Tsafendas had faked mental illness in 1943 and that the South African authorities were aware of it. In total, about 12,000 pages of documents were discovered and examined, including some from the British National Archives and others from different archival collections in South Africa.

Finally, knowing that the Verwoerd assassination had been a matter of considerable international interest, I went through all the currently available newspapers published at that time, not only in South Africa, but also in Australia, Britain, Canada, France, West and East Germany, Greece, Italy, Mozambique, Portugal, the Soviet Union, the United States and Zimbabwe. The total came to about 120.

The more I learnt about Tsafendas's character, his activism and life-long interest in politics, in particular his loathing of apartheid and colonialism, the more I felt that a major historical injustice had taken place in portraying him to the world as a lunatic and his assassination of Dr Verwoerd as an apolitical and mindless act. I felt a moral imperative to expose one of the greatest cover-ups in apartheid history and reveal the truth about a brave and humble man who was treated so foully by history. At the same time, I concluded that Tsafendas deserved more than just a corrective and extended biography with new information about his life and his motives. It was clear to me that no matter how much evidence I adduced concerning Tsafendas's acts and motivation in my book – and I could not include every single piece – it would not be capable of changing a historical record that had stood for over 50 years. The danger was the book could become simply a matter of debate or dismissed as just another conspiracy theory. I decided, therefore, also to write a detailed report and submit it, along with all of my new evidence, to the South African authorities to request a new official inquiry into the Tsafendas case. My goal was to correct the historical record in such a way that the assassination would not be seen as a mindless political act by someone who blamed a tapeworm, but a political assassination by a perfectly sane person.

A major surprise in the South African archives was the discovery of documents setting out Judge Jody Kollapen's tireless efforts to have Tsafendas released and correct what he saw as a grievous injustice. I was also agreeably surprised to see archived documents concerning Krish Govender's efforts through the Truth and Reconciliation Commission to examine Tsafendas's case. I met with both Mr Govender, Durban State Attorney and co-chairman of the Law Society of South Africa, and Judge Kollapen and told them of my plan to submit evidence to the South African authorities and seek an official inquiry. Both agreed with the idea and offered support. Mr Govender offered to evaluate the evidence, read my report and give me advice. Judge Kollapen, although willing, was not able to participate directly as he still held judicial office. However, he offered invaluable help in various other ways.

Once I had finished collecting evidence and while I was writing my report based on the new evidence, I looked for help from among South Africa's jurists to evaluate my efforts and the evidence I had collected. The first was Advocate George Bizos who happily and immediately agreed to work with me. The second person I contacted was Professor John Dugard, Professor of International Law and a former judge at the International Court of Justice in The Hague. Professor Dugard also happily accepted to look and evaluate the evidence I had discovered and to read my report. Then, Mr Govender introduced me to Judge Yacoob, a retired Constitutional Court judge, who also agreed to evaluate the evidence and co-operate with me on my report. Finally, I contacted Advocate Dumisa Ntzebeza, who also agreed readily to read my report and evaluate my evidence.

To assess Tsafendas's state of mind and properly examine the official diagnosis of schizophrenia, I contacted several prominent psychiatrists and psychologists. The first was Professor Tuviah Zabow, forensic psychiatrist, former head of the forensic psychiatry unit at Valkenberg Hospital and former professor of psychiatry at the University of Cape Town. Professor Zabow agreed to evaluate the new evidence, read my report and offer his opinion, consequently agreeing with my conclusions. I also contacted Professor Alban Burke, head of the Department of Psychology at the University of Johannesburg, to whom I sent some of the evidence I had gathered, along with my report. He, too, provided comments, agreeing with my findings. I also contacted three prominent American scientists, leaders in their fields: Professor Kirk Heilbrun, forensic psychologist and professor of psychology at Drexler University in Philadelphia; Professor Phillip Resnick, forensic psychiatrist and professor of psychiatry at Case Western Reserve University School of Medicine; and Professor Robert L. Sadoff, clinical professor of psychiatry, director of the Center for Studies in Social-Legal Psychiatry at the University of Pennsylvania and chairman of the American Academy of Psychiatry and the Law. Although none felt able to co-operate with me fully, all offered opinions on several matters regarding the case, answered all my questions and allowed me to quote them in my report.

After reading my report and checking the evidence, the five South African jurists agreed to write to the Minister of Justice regarding the case. My report, along with a request to have Tsafendas's case re-examined, signed by Advocate George Bizos, Professor John Dugard, Mr Krish Govender, Advocate Dumisa Ntsebeza and Judge Zak Yacoob, was submitted to the office of the Minister of Justice of South Africa, Advocate Tshililo Michael Masutha on 23 April 2018. The report ran to three volumes, totalling 2,192 pages and 861,803 words, and was accompanied by a 16GB USB memory disc with all the evidence I had discovered – all 12,000 pages of documents from the archives, newspaper articles and other evidence, as well as the recordings of my interviews.

While aware that this report and its submission would hopefully lead to the eventual correction of a long-standing injustice, it was clear to me that the general public would remain largely ignorant of the details of this duplicitous act of mis-government. Believing that the world at large and South Africans in particular should know the truth, I began working on the biography. My aim in writing *The Man Who Killed Apartheid* was to demonstrate that Tsafendas was no tapeworm-obsessed lunatic but a man of hugely generous spirit who laughed easily and cared about those around him; that he knew fear and equivocation; that his deathly deed, 'the execution' as he called it, was rooted in the belief, in his own words, that he could not 'remain silent' in the face of apartheid's crimes. My hope is that the book will finally kill a shabby, old lie from South Africa's darkest time in history.

Working on and researching the life of Tsafendas and his case took me nine years, during which time I conducted formal interviews with 138 people, spoke to hundreds of others and read many documents. To be able to do this required the assistance of people in numerous fields and at every level, and I am very grateful that I was given such co-operation with unstinting generosity. Each person's contribution, no matter how unimportant it may have appeared, played a crucial part in ensuring completion of my project.

I would like to extend, in alphabetical order, my sincerest thanks to the following, whose enthusiastic expertise helped me to set forth Tsafendas's true story: Firstly, however, I must thank Liza Key, who was extraordinarily generous and helpful in numerous ways. Liza gave me a copy of her keynote documentary on Tsafendas, *A Question of Madness*, plus all the information she had assembled, including documents from the South African National Archives and elsewhere. She entrusted me with her personal collection of papers, photographs and the rushes of all her interviews, and allowed me to use her photographs in this book. She put me in touch with several people who were most helpful, including the photographer Ellen Elmendorp and journalists David Beresford and Cheche Selepe. She also secured permission from Helen Suzman's daughter for me to access her mother's archives at the University of the Witwatersrand. I am extremely grateful to Liza and will be forever in her debt.

George Bizos spent countless hours going through my research findings with me, often in his office but also on the telephone. His opinions in several areas were invaluable. He also introduced me to people who were of help in extending my inquiries.

John Dugard participated without reservation, going through the evidence and the outline of my research. He welcomed me into his home in The Hague, where we spent an entire afternoon and evening, some six or seven hours, examining multiple issues. Professor Dugard also wrote the first draft of the letter/request from the five jurists to the Minister of Justice.

Ellen Elmendorp for giving me all the excellent photographs she had taken of Tsafendas and for allowing me to use them in this book.

Krish Govender agreed to meet me immediately when I contacted him, then sought to help me in any possible way. Importantly, he introduced me to a number of people in South Africa, including Judge Zak Yacoob, to whom he outlined the aims of my research project. Krish visited me at my home in England to discuss the project and was helpful throughout the writing of the book in numerous ways.

Judge Jody Kollapen shared his personal memories of Tsafendas with me and further helped by introducing me to Dimitris Skoularikis, who had met Tsafendas in prison; he advised me on my report and arranged its submission to the Minister of Justice. Judge Kollapen also participated in the drafting of the jurists' letter/request to the Minister accompanying my report. By far the most touching moment in this entire project, which made me weep then, and still does, was to read in the archives this passage from Judge Kollapen's memorandum of 24 November 1994 to the regional government of Gauteng:

> *It remains my belief that Mr Tsafendas should not die a lonely man in an institution but should spend the last years of his life in the company of people he knows and perhaps trusts ... In summation, I believe that the man has served his debt to society (if he owed a debt at all in the first place).*

Those words affected me profoundly, making me determined to complete this story, whatever the obstacles.

Solly Mapaila, the Deputy General-Secretary of the South African Communist Party, helped in multiple ways, but mostly by his eager willingness to correct the historical record regarding Verwoerd's assassination.

Manolis Mastromanolis gave me his first-ever interview about Tsafendas, having turned down requests from others several times before. He also introduced me to other crew members of the Greek tanker *Eleni* who knew Tsafendas, and all happily shared their memories with me.

Irini Michaletos and her husband John Michaletos invited me twice to dinner at their home and shared their many intimate memories of Tsafendas; they also let me have the originals of several unpublished family photos with Tsafendas in them.

Alexander Moumbaris was one of those who assured me that Tsafendas was perfectly sane and politically motivated, which he did with passionate conviction. He welcomed me to his house in France, gave me several personal notes about Tsafendas and directed me to other revolutionaries from the anti-apartheid struggle.

Dumisa Ntsebeza, though I gave him very limited time, read sections of my report and checked some of the evidence I had gathered; he also supported the other four jurists' letter/request to the Minister of Justice.

Katerina Pnefma, Tsafendas's step-sister, talked to me endlessly about Dimitri and entrusted me with personal family documents and photographs. Mike Vlachopoulos and Mike Pnefma, Tsafendas's nephews, discussed their uncle at length and gave me family papers and pictures. A particular thank you goes to Mike Vlachopoulos, who has gifted me in his will an expensive coffee table which Tsafendas gave in 1941 as a wedding present to his step-sister, Evangelia!

Researcher and journalist Dr James Sanders entrusted me with personal documents concerning Tsafendas and put me in touch with several resourceful people. However, his biggest contribution was in interviewing Gordon Winter on my behalf. Dr Sanders was one of the few people with whom Winter remained in contact and he agreed without equivocation to interview the former Bureau of State Security (BOSS) agent both then and on an ongoing basis.

Alexandros Tsafantakis, Tsafendas's nephew, along with his family, gave me permission to access his uncle's medical files. Tsafantakis also invited me to stay as his guest in a luxury villa during my stay in Crete, and arranged a massive dinner where 300 to 400 people with the surname Tsafantakis met in the hope of finding some of Tsafendas's relatives. He also took me to Kitharida, the Tsafendas family's village where Dimitri's father was born, to the house of Costas Kargakis, where Tsafendas stayed while in Crete in 1962, and to the places where Tsafendas was trained by Kargakis and his Second World War comrades in bomb-making.

The memories, passion and deep sense of injustice evident in Bishop Ioannis Tsaftaridis's conversations were among the principal reasons I undertook this project. Sharing these feelings with me, Bishop Ioannis invited me to stay in his house in Maputo, introduced me to several people who had met Tsafendas and drove me around the city to meet some of them. He also cooked for me the best lobster and seafood spaghetti I have ever tasted!

Father Michalis Visvinis for his unbelievable hospitality and help. Furthermore, he talked to me at length about his meetings with Tsafendas and introduced me to several members of Pretoria's Greek community, most importantly to members of Tsafendas's family who had previously refused to speak to anyone about the case.

Judge Zak Yacoob agreed immediately to evaluate the evidence I had gathered and to read my report. He also talked patiently and at length with me on the telephone, and was instrumental in finalising the wording of the jurists' letter/request sent to the Minister of Justice.

Particularly supportive were the witnesses I interviewed, who received my questions with exemplary patience many times and on an ongoing basis over the years. Their names are listed in the bibliography and I am eternally grateful to them. In addition to those already mentioned, several contacts entrusted me with documents from their personal collections, thus my sincere thanks go to: David Beresford, a former foreign correspondent of *The Guardian* newspaper in London, who met and talked with Tsafendas; Desmond Blow, a former journalist of the Johannesburg *Sunday Times*, who was a close friend of David Pratt; Graham Blow, Desmond Blow's son, who shared his father's documents, including personal communications between Blow and Pratt; David Bloomberg, Tsafendas's attorney, who gave me a massive file containing photographs and newspaper cuttings from the case, as well as some personal papers and a handwritten note by Tsafendas; Manolis Dimelas, a Greek journalist and filmmaker, who gave me the rushes from his film on Tsafendas and helped with my trip to Kasos; Guy Spiller, who gave me the rushes and a copy of his documentary on David Pratt, *The Liberal and the Pirate*. Spiller also entrusted me with several personal documents as well as others from the National Archives of South Africa regarding Pratt.

A tremendous thank you goes to everyone at the National Archives of South Africa (NASA), especially Ntombizodwa Gumede, Granny Makhubela, Tshepo Malemela, Mary Masango, Sbonile Mbhele and Mavis Xaba, who photocopied some 7,000 pages of documents. In particular, I am extremely grateful to Zahira Adams and Natalie Skomolo, who scanned several thousand extra documents and sent them to me in England. Furthermore, Ms Skomolo, at short notice and without charge, translated a number of documents from Afrikaans to English. Gerrit Wayner was also enormously helpful with all my requests.

Massive thanks are due to the psychiatrists and psychologists I consulted who offered their opinions without demur. Professor Tuviah Zabow looked at my report and the evidence, Professors Alban Burke and Robert L. Sadoff checked some of the evidence and discussed the case with me, and Professors Kirk Heilbrun and Phillip Resnick answered all my questions.

Thank you to all of the following, including everyone at Durham University Library's document delivery service, Northumbria University's inter-library loans team and at the British Library in Boston Spa for providing me with several books and documents; Imraan Abdullah of the South African Historical Archives; Professor Cathi Albertyn of the University of the Witwatersrand, who sent me a copy of her PhD thesis; Beverly Angus and Niklas Zimmer of the University of Cape Town for making copies and sending them to me from Liza Key's archive housed at that university; Akis Apergis for his tremendous help in many ways, especially driving me around Johannesburg to some of my many appointments and for introducing to me Solly Mapaila; June Bam-Hutchison of the University of Cape Town; Terry Bell and his wife Barbara for their hospitality and overall help; everyone at Brooklyn Lodge for their hospitality; Mary Biri and Georgia Maniati of the Greek Ministry of Shipping; Harry Burton and Helen Swainger of *The Guardian* archives; Gavin Cooper, son of Advocate (and later Judge) Wilfrid Cooper who defended Tsafendas, for giving me some of his personal documents; Maggie Davey of Jacana Media for her enthusiasm and her unwavering belief in this book; Jacqui Dorey and Michael Fienberg of Stenham Support Services Ltd; my sister Vasiliki Dousemetzi for her translations; Gerhard Dreyer of City Guns in Cape Town; Michael Dukakis; Toin Eggenhuizen of the ANC who read parts of my report and put me in touch with Denis Goldberg; Barber Ferguson of Ferguson Events; Ana Fernandes and Paula Sereno of the Arquivo Nacional Torre do Tombo; Brian Fobi who sent me a copy of his excellent PhD thesis on Verwoerd; Denis Goldberg for his hospitality and for putting me in contact with Ahmed Kathrada; Shona Hall of Neville Funeral Service; Joe and Julie Horsfield for all their help throughout the years and for being the best neighbors and friends one could hope for; Janice Honeyman receives my sincere thanks for the week's free stay she gave me in her apartment in Sea Point, Cape Town; Francie Jowell, Helen Suzman's daughter, for giving me permission to access her mother's archives; Ronnie Kasrils for his hospitality and willingness to help and for introducing me to people who were of assistance in various ways; Maria Kassimati for all her help; Ken Keable and Bob Newland of London Recruits; Ayten Kececi of Limasollu College, who drove me to meet Mr and Mrs Limasollu at their home and who took me to dinner in

Istanbul; Busi Khangala of the University of Cape Town; Anna Kranz, my colleague at Durham University, who translated a number of newspaper articles from German to English; Anton Krueger who mailed me a DVD of his exceptional play, *Living in Strange Lands*, and met with me to discuss the case; Kyriakos Kyriakou for showing me around his farm outside Pretoria and letting me stay there one evening; Mabel Lewis of the Office of the Secretary to Parliament; Tunc Limasollu and Adviye Vedia Limasollu, son and wife of Limasollu Naci, who welcomed me to their home in Istanbul and gave me pictures of Mr Naci and his college; my very, very good friend Sue Lipschitz for all her help with the publication of this new edition; Benito Madisha; Father Dimitrios Malioglou; Father Georgios Manos; Tsholofelo Masilo, Judge Kollapen's registrar, who submitted my report and the evidence to the Minister of Justice; Sokoyi Masonwabe; Debora Matthews of South African Historical Archives; Michael Meadowcroft, a former British MP with the Liberal Party and honorary president of the National Liberal Club, who scanned documents regarding David Pratt from the Club's archives and shared with me Club minutes which mentioned Pratt; Sandile Memela for his help in trying to locate Mike Phahlane; Gabriele Mohale of the University of the Witwatersrand; Tumi Mokoko of the Legal Recource Centre for printing out thousands of documents I sent to Advocate George Bizos; Naomi Musiker and David Saks of the South African Jewish Board of Deputies; my taxi driver, Samsodien Petersen, for driving me around Cape Town and in particular for the long seven-hour drive to Fraserburg and back to meet Mr Reyner van Zyl; Michele Pickover of the University of the Witwatersrand for scanning documents from Helen Suzman's archive; Piers Pigou; Dimitris Psarras; Simon J Roberts of the National Liberal Club; Tom Schumann from the South African Parliament; Robby Scott; Cheche Selepe for his help to locate Mike Phahlane; Emanuil Selisoglou; Safiye Anil Soylu, head of bilateral relations at the Turkish ministry of education; Maro Spanoudi for putting me in touch with people who knew Tsafendas and for assisting with my inquiries in Mozambique; Brian Stanners; Christodoulos Stavridis; Majid Taghavi; Etienne van Heerden; Hennie van Vuuren; Toerien van Wyk of South African Historical Archives; Marlette van Zyl; Reyner van Zyl, the psychologist who examined Tsafendas, and patiently went through all the evidence I sent him and happily discussed it with me; Gordon Winter not only answered all my questions via Dr Sanders, but also checked several documents I sent him and shared with me some of his own papers on Tsafendas; Nick Whittle of Michael Gamble Funeral Directors for his help in locating Alan Lomas; Dimitris Zitianelis for giving me contacts of several people in Cape Town who had met Tsafendas.

Finally, my heartfelt thanks go to all who assisted me in any way. I believe I have named everyone involved, but if anyone's name has slipped my mind, forgive me and accept that you are also on my list.

Chapter 1

The Deed

'Every day, you see a man you know committing a very serious crime for which millions of people suffer. You cannot take him to court or report him to the police because he is the law in the country. Would you remain silent and let him continue with his crime or would you do something to stop him? You are guilty not only when you commit a crime, but also when you do nothing to prevent it when you have the chance.' – Dimitri Tsafendas

A few minutes before 9 am, central Cape Town was buzzing with rush-hour traffic and hurried office workers. On Hout Street, the weapons shops were not yet open, so Dimitri Tsafendas paced up and down the sidewalk. He was a heavy-set man of middle age, six feet tall and broad-shouldered, with large dark eyes, hard hands and jet-black hair cut short; he wore baggy, grey flannel trousers, a white shirt and a light-coloured jacket. He had risen early, tense and stressed after only a few hours' sleep.

He had left his apartment in the Rondebosch area of the city a few minutes after 6 am to then arrive at the House of Assembly at 6.45 am. This was an hour ahead of his normal start time, but it was important to get his messenger's duties completed before leaving to buy the knives. With time to spare before the weapons shops opened, he took a taxi to the waterfront to enjoy what he expected would be his last sight and smell of the sea. Raising his face to the morning sky, he inhaled the sea air which had been so much part of his life: born in an Indian Ocean seaport, raised beside the Mediterranean, battling the angry Atlantic in the dangerous war years. His dream had always been of another sea, the warm and sparkling Caribbean, and, perhaps naively, of a life of contentment on exotic, socialist Cuba. However, on this fresh, clear morning of Tuesday, 6 September 1966, he knew that would remain forever a dream.[1]

At 9.05 am, Tsafendas entered City Guns, at 57 Hout Street, owned by Tony Harrison, and asked about the sheath knives in the window. Harrison placed two on the countertop. Glancing curiously at his first customer of the day, he thought he might be a fisherman or a merchant seaman. Tsafendas slipped one knife onto his belt and inside his trousers and moved about experimentally. He was comfortable with knives. As a child, one of his favourite possessions was a bayonet from the first Balkan War, a gift from his grandmother, while his father had often hand-crafted blades when he worked for the Iscor Iron and Steel Works in Pretoria. The knife, priced at R3.30, less than US$5 at the time, was a regular, all-purpose product, with a metal scabbard and a spring clip to keep the blade in place. Satisfied, Tsafendas nodded and paid with an R10 note from his wallet. As Harrison counted out the change, his customer pointed to an advertisement for a firearm and asked if a licence was necessary for such a weapon. When told yes, Tsafendas nodded and left.[2]

A few metres down the street was Maurice Klein's hardware store, William Rawbone and Co. Tsafendas wanted a back-up knife in case something happened to the first, but he thought it best not to get both from the same source. He bought the second knife from the store; known as a Black Forest, it was more a stiletto with a patterned aluminium handle, a sheath and a silvered, double-edged blade nearly six inches long.[3]

While Tsafendas was buying the knives, Prime Minister Dr Hendrik Frensch Verwoerd and his wife Betsie were flying into Cape Town airport from Stokkiesdraai, the family's holiday house on the bank of the River Vaal, near Vareeniging in Transvaal, where they had spent a weekend relaxing with family. A waiting limousine sped the couple directly to Groote Schuur, the Prime Minister's official residence in Cape Town. There, Verwoerd began preparing for his scheduled appearance in Parliament that afternoon. It would be his first major speech of the current session and he had his hair cut for the occasion. A morning's work done, the premier and his wife ate a light lunch, then were driven together to the House of Assembly.[4]

Tsafendas turned towards the same destination. A 15-minute walk took him through the public gardens that surrounded the parliament buildings, a neat, well-tended area he had come to know well from his frequent visits there. White people strolled past the lawns and occupied public benches marked 'Europeans Only' and '*Slegs vir Blankes*' (For Whites Only), and children squealed with excitement at the squirrels in the oak trees. There were no black or brown people, for had not Dr Verwoerd specifically declared a few years earlier that such people should not be allowed 'to gaze' at 'the green pastures of European society? There was, he had said, 'no place for them in the European community above the level of certain forms of labour'.[5] Alone in the messengers' dressing room, Tsafendas unwrapped his morning purchases. He slotted the empty sheaths onto his waist belt and slipped in the knives; everything fitted perfectly. He returned the blades to locker, changed into his navy blue messenger's uniform and closed the locker door.[6]

For years, Tsafendas had wrestled with indignation and anger over the systematic degradation of South Africa's black people. Desperately, he hoped that an enraged populace would one day lay siege to Parliament as the French revolutionaries had stormed the Bastille all those years ago. Of course, nothing of the sort had happened and now that almost all internal resistance to apartheid had been crushed, thanks to Dr Verwoerd's brutal efficiency, it seemed clear that it was not going to happen any time soon. The major resistance groups, such as the African National Congress (ANC), the Pan Africanist Congress (PAC), the African Resistance Movement (ARM) and the South African Communist Party (SACP) were banned and their top leaders imprisoned or in hiding or exile. Tsafendas could not get the thought out of his mind: It was Dr Verwoerd, who had turned his country into a police state, his spies and security men hunting down and silencing opponents by the vilest means.

Then one day, it dawned on Tsafendas that a popular uprising was not necessary to remove the most hated man in South Africa. Just one month earlier, on 1 August when he started work at the House of Assembly, he was within fingertip distance of the monster himself. The moment he realised that an opportunity to kill the tyrant had presented itself to him, Tsafendas knew it was his social responsibility, indeed his moral duty, to accept it. If he did not act, he would regret it for the rest of his life; he would consider himself guilty of turning a blind eye to an enormous crime when he had the opportunity to end it.[7]

That is not to say that his determination did not falter at times during the 37 days that he had worked so far in Parliament. Verwoerd was a tyrant, but he was indisputably human, a husband and a father. Tsafendas wondered: Could he find it in himself to deprive this living being of life? During the two wars in which he participated, Tsafendas was secretly glad that he never had to kill nor even shoot at the enemy. He was unsure he could bring himself to pull the trigger simply because an adversary was wearing a different uniform, someone who perhaps did not want to wear the uniform in the first place. Up to now, he could swear he would never kill a human being, not even in self-defence. However, he considered Dr Verwoerd to be not an ordinary human being but a dictator and an oppressor who had enslaved 11 million black, coloured and Asian people so that three million whites could live in comfort. He was someone who, as Nelson Mandela once said, considered Africans to be 'lower than animals'.[8] He was the architect of the world's most ruthless, racist regime since Nazi Germany, a man who had copied several of Adolf Hitler's anti-Semitic Nuremberg laws and applied them to the black people in his own country. That was why Tsafendas had so often, boldly and publicly, denounced Dr Verwoerd as 'Hitler's best student'.

On a few occasions in the course of his duties, Tsafendas had to rein in his desire to punch Verwoerd in the face. The sight of the Prime Minister smiling happily and full of confidence in Parliament with white MPs and ministers cheering him on contrasted painfully in his mind with the plight of coloured and black people he saw on the streets every day. While 79% of the population were suffering, Verwoerd, Tsafendas would tell his friends, was 'laughing and joking with members of his gang'. How he wished to wipe off that self-satisfied smile! He knew, however, that if he did so, he would be arrested and imprisoned and would have achieved nothing. To kill Verwoerd, on the other hand, or to 'remove him' as he put it, would lead sooner or later to the collapse of the racist system. He considered Verwoerd to be the brains of apartheid. By removing the monster's head, he believed the body would soon die. Furthermore, doing the deed in Parliament – the very temple of Dr Verwoerd's power, the place where he had conjured up the loathsome apparatus of race separation – would be a powerful symbol for the oppressed peoples of South Africa and the world! Tsafendas refused to think of it as an assassination; it would be an execution, the killing of a tyrant.[9]

Six years before, at a meeting with members of the British Anti-Apartheid Movement in London, he had publicly declared that he was willing to do 'anything that would get the South African regime out of power'.[10] He now felt that the time had come; he had the means to do it and he was 'so disgusted' with apartheid that he did not care what would happen to him afterwards.[11] He had thought it through many times. He knew that for him there could be no escape. He might reach the monster's lair, but he would never leave it. Infinitely more important if he was to die was that Dr Verwoerd would be dead before him. He found comfort in a verse from *Like Karem (Kerem Gibi)* by Nazim Hikmet, his favourite poet:

> *If I don't burn, if you don't burn, if we don't burn,*
> *how will the light vanquish the darkness?*[12]

If he had to burn so that the light could vanquish the darkness, so be it.

After closing his locker door, Tsafendas mounted to the press gallery on the first floor of the House. He had five hours until 2.10 pm, when the division bell would call MPs and ministers to the Chamber, and he would do the deed.[13] He asked a fellow messenger to change lunch breaks with him so that he could take off between 1 pm and 2 pm instead of his rostered noon to 1 pm. That way, there would be less danger of being ordered on an errand away from the Chamber. The messenger refused. At 1.05 pm, Tsafendas walked into the messengers' room carrying his meal, a plate of curry and rice, which he shared with a colleague. Back in the press gallery after his lunch break, Tsafendas was sent for a plate of curry by a South African Broadcasting Corporation (SABC) staffer, but the reporter complained about the quality and refused to eat it. Needing to return the curry to the cafeteria, Tsafendas said he was 'in a hurry' and asked a colleague to do so. The other messenger refused, saying he was still on his lunch break, so Tsafendas took the plate himself and hurried off. 'I have something to do,' he said. This was around 1.50 pm.[14]

With the division nearing, Tsafendas hurried down to the messengers' room. Alone again, he opened a container of anti-rust solution, which he had brought from his toolbox at home. He doused both blades in the liquid, which he hoped would infect Dr Verwoerd's blood if he survived the stabbing. The label said the solution contained hydrochloric acid, nitrites, oxalic acid and phosphoric acid, so surely, he thought, it would do human harm. He then fitted the sheaths to the waist belt under his uniform and inserted the knives. He checked his watch. There was time. He flipped open his wallet and took out a photograph of his adored late father, Cretan-born Michalis, engineer-cum-revolutionary. Tsafendas wondered if his father would agree with what he was about to do; whatever his reaction, he knew that he would not condemn it.[15] Indeed, only years and circumstances prevented his father from playing the executioner himself. When the white farmer David Pratt shot and wounded Verwoerd back in 1960, Michalis said it was a shame the Prime Minister survived and joked that if he had not had a family, he would himself have taken a gun and shot everyone in the South African parliament. After separating from Marika, his wife and Dimitri's stepmother, Michalis often said that he should never have married, but should have been a rebel, fighting against apartheid and for the independence of Mozambique and other African countries.[16]

Tsafendas smiled wryly at the thought of his stepmother's likely reaction on what he was about to do. She would automatically blame his father – for Dimitri's upbringing and for planting dangerous political ideas in his mind. Michalis would describe himself as an anarchist, his son, more doctrinaire, was an admitted Communist. Despite the strictures of family and friends, there was an unbreakable bond – a blood tie but an ideological one too – between father and son.[17]

Along with his father's photo was another one – of him and Eleni Banovic, the 12-year-old daughter of Father Nikola Banovic, a Greek Orthodox priest he had met in Istanbul in 1961. Tsafendas was a guest in his house for four months and became close to the family, especially their only child, whom he fondly called 'Elenitsa' and loved her as if his own. However, nine months after he left Istanbul, his beloved Elenitsa drowned while swimming. He only learnt this much later, in a letter from her father in response to a gift he had sent her. Reading that letter, he often said, was one of the saddest moments of his life.[18]

Tsafendas slotted the pictures back into his wallet and walked into the parliamentary lobby. One hundred and sixty MPs were taking their places on the green benches of the debating chamber ahead of the 2.10 pm division bell;

officials were rushing to their desks and the public galleries and the diplomatic bays were filling up quickly. There was a sense of expectation in the House because Dr Verwoerd was expected to make an important announcement. After meetings with Leabua Jonathan, Prime Minister of Lesotho, a new foreign policy initiative had been drafted regarding the 'pocket states' of Lesotho and Botswana, which Dr Verwoerd was expected to reveal.[19]

The Prime Minister made his appearance shortly after 2 pm. He was an impressive figure by any standards: tall and broad-shouldered, immaculately suited with his newly coiffed silver hair brushed carefully left to right, he dominated those around him. Blue-eyed and with an upturned nose, he did not have the face of a Roman senator, but authority was evident in the severe set of the mouth and the questing eyes. His public speeches were unhurried, intense and to the point, more the cerebral professor than the rabble-rousing orator.[20] His two bodyguards escorted him to his front-bench place, then left for their usual seats in the public gallery, about 100 feet away.[21] Tsafendas knew that this was the only time the Prime Minister was without a guard.

As he reached his seat, Verwoerd looked towards the spectators' gallery for his wife, but she was not in her usual place, delayed by a crowded elevator. He turned to acknowledge greetings from National Party MPs around him.[22] The Prime Minister was in high spirits, even jaunty, and with reason: the national economy was booming, thanks to cheap black labour, with the highest growth rate in the world after Japan. A few months earlier, his party had comfortably won a new term in office. Commanding the space around him, smiling, nodding, confident, he looked unassailable, a picture of total power. Indeed, he thought, God was on his side. Six years earlier, he had survived the bullets of David Pratt, a sure sign, Dr Verwoerd said, that God approved of his race policies and had spared him to ensure their implementation. Was it this miraculous survival that made him unafraid of assassins? Was it faith in divine protection that emboldened him to remark in 1962, 'If someone really wants to kill you, it's not a very hard job. One thing is certain, there's no point going around worrying about it?'[23] He was about to discover that when it came to his race policies and implementing apartheid, his God had changed his mind.

***

The division bell rang and MP Aubrey Radford walked into the chamber some distance behind Verwoerd. As he did so, he was pushed violently from behind. Spectators saw a burly man in a messenger's uniform plunge past Radford towards the front bench, wrestling with his waist belt. Moving swiftly for a man of his size, Tsafendas strode the last few paces across the floor of the House to the front bench. The Black Forest was now free and he stood over the seated Prime Minister.[24] Verwoerd was idly fingering a small scar on his jaw, a souvenir of Pratt's bullets,[25] when he became aware of the figure before him. Apparently thinking he was about to receive a message, he looked up inquiringly in time to see his assailant raise his right hand holding a knife. Verwoerd thrust up an arm to ward off the blow, but Tsafendas plunged the blade into the seated man's chest, just left of centre. He pulled the knife out and struck again, into Verwoerd's lung. He stabbed twice more, the heart and the neck. Verwoerd slumped forward with blood spurting from his neck and quickly forming a pool on the green carpet.[26]

For nano-seconds, there was stunned silence. In the press gallery, Gerald Shaw, the *Cape Times* parliamentary correspondent, looked at the assembly clock, which was always kept five minutes fast, took out his notebook and scribbled down the time: twenty past two. When MPs realised what had happened, uproar broke out, ending the momentary parenthesis of silence. Frank Walter Waring, aged 58, the Minister for Sports and Tourism and a former member of the South African Rugby team, leapt at Tsafendas from his place behind the Prime Minister. Getting him in a neck-lock, he pulled Tsafendas away from Verwoerd. When his opponent resisted, he dragged him further back, over the desk and on top of himself. Tsafendas slashed blindly with the blade, ripping through Waring's trousers, and somebody shouted, 'Get the knife.' Another MP, Dr W.L. Venter, managed to grab Tsafendas's hand and with the help of others, prised open his locked fingers and seized the bloody blade. MPs formed a whirling scrum around Tsafendas, raining blows and kicking wildly. MP Cas Greyling drove his fist into Tsafendas's mouth, injuring his hand, and a punch from Waring broke Tsafendas's nose. A voice called wildly, 'Don't kill him, remember Oswald.'[27]

With Tsafendas overpowered and pinned to the ground, police Captain Christian Pieter Coetzee searched him and found the second knife on his waist belt. Half a dozen MPs then started to drag him towards the chamber exit, his face streaked with blood and the front of his shirt stained red. As they did so, Tsafendas looked angrily around for the man who had broken his nose, shouting, 'Where is that bastard? I will get that bastard.'[28] Shaw frantically called his news editor, Tom Jessop, and screamed that Dr Verwoerd had been attacked and was bleeding to death. Jessop thought it was a bad joke and put the phone down. Shaw had to call him back to convince him he was serious.[29]

Verwoerd, deathly pale and bleeding profusely, with his left arm hanging limply by his side, was quickly surrounded by MPs, six of them physicians: Radford, who was a surgeon, Venter, E.L. Fisher, G. de V. Morrison, C.V. van der Merwe and Maud Clark. Dr Hilgard Muller, the Foreign Minister, placed a cushion under the Prime Minister's head as Dr Fisher took charge. Swiftly, he tore open the dying man's waistcoat and shirt and noted heavy bleeding from four wounds; he ordered Dr Morrison to perform mouth-to-mouth resuscitation. Fisher kept a medical bag in his office in Parliament, which contained an emergency supply of drugs. He ordered Dr Morrison to fetch the powerful cardiac stimulant, Coramine, and the two doctors injected the contents of two syringes into Dr Verwoerd's heart. MPs were shouting for an ambulance and Felix George Miles, a parliamentary messenger, dialled for one, but found all the lines engaged.[30]

The chamber became deathly silent as Dr Morrison breathed air noisily into Dr Verwoerd's lungs and another doctor rhythmically pressured his heart. The Prime Minister remained inert. Dr Radford felt for the pulse in the victim's left wrist. It was absent and he and Dr Fisher, speaking quietly, agreed that the Prime Minister was dead. Dr Fisher said later, 'We kept on treating him and trying respiratory treatment ... but by then he had no pulse at all. It was hopeless.' Ghostly pale, South Africa's leader lay slumped in his seat, his head tilted back. He had never uttered a word or a sound from beginning to end of the attack.[31]

It was then that MPs, officials and spectators began to realise Verwoerd was dead. Two MPs collapsed in the lobby, others bellowed with rage. Many stood stricken, uncomprehending or unwilling to accept what they had witnessed. Cabinet Minister P.W. Botha, a future Prime Minister, turned to Helen Suzman, the lone MP for the Progressive Party and the only anti-apartheid voice in the House, and shaking his finger in her face, shouted furiously, 'It's you who did this, all you liberals. You incite people. Now we will get you. We will get the lot of you.' Dr Verwoerd's wife, Betsie, came into the chamber. She bent over the lifeless body of her husband, stroked his hair and kissed his forehead. 'God never makes a mistake,' she said a little later, apparently suggesting that there must have been a reason for her husband's death.[32]

At about 2.30 pm, an ambulance crew carried Verwoerd's body on a stretcher out of the chamber and sped to Groote Schuur Hospital. A large crowd immediately gathered outside the hospital, many with radios switched on for emergency news bulletins, and the hospital switchboard was jammed with calls demanding to know Verwoerd's condition. Inside, a hastily assembled team of three surgeons, two physicians and five medical students stood by with emergency equipment. They realised immediately that their skills were not needed.[33] Around 3 pm, some 40 minutes after the stabbing, Barend J. Schoeman, the leader of the House, told those MPs still in the House that he believed the Prime Minister was dead. At 3.05 pm, Groote Schuur Hospital, Dr J.G. Burger, declared that Verwoerd had probably died instantly, and official confirmation came at 3.30 pm in a statement that said the Prime Minister was dead on arrival at the hospital.[34]

As Tsafendas was half-dragged, half-frogmarched out of the Chamber, a young man crying hysterically after witnessing the stabbing from the public gallery tried to attack him, but was fended off by police. Tsafendas was bundled into the back of a police van and on the orders of Captain Genis of the Security Police driven to Caledon Square police station, round the corner from Parliament. Throughout the short journey, the police beat him with fists, feet and batons. Curled into a ball, Tsafendas knew this would happen and that it was only the start. As the blows rained down, he realised that the only part of his body that retained any feeling was one thigh, but through the pain, a single question dominated his mind: Had he dispatched the tyrant? As the blows rained down, he suspected that whether he had succeeded or not, he did not have much of his own life left to live.

Chapter 2

After the Deed

Caledon Square police station was a squat, white-washed, two-storey building with a small formal garden at the front enclosed by an ornamental ironwork fence. A notice above the door in English and Afrikaans said, POLICE STATION/POLISIE KANTOOR. Tsafendas, bruised and bleeding from the assault in the police van, was hustled into the building at around 2.40 pm.[1] Immediately, he demanded a lawyer, specifying George Bizos, whose father he knew well. George Bizos was widely known in South Africa for his defence of prominent anti-apartheid activists, including Nelson Mandela. However, Tsafendas quickly realised that he was not in a position to make demands. A custody officer instructed him to remove his belt and empty his pockets. The officer took the jacket of his messenger's uniform and removed the laces from his shoes, leaving Tsafendas in just his trousers and shirt. When they took his wallet, he thought of asking to keep the photographs, but realised this was not the best time to ask for favours.[2]

After about 15 minutes, Dr Ralph Kossew, the Cape Town district surgeon, arrived to examine him. They had met before. Three months earlier, on 17 June, the doctor had examined Tsafendas with regard to a claim he had made for a veteran's disability grant. Tsafendas recognised him immediately, but Dr Kossew did not. He completed a new form, 'Report on Examination in a Case of Alleged Assault or Other Crime.' Under 'Wounds (if any)', he wrote that Tsafendas had '(1) gaping wound about 1.1/2" in length' extending from the bridge of the nose, which was swollen, and 'laceration about ¼–1/2" in length of lower lip near right of mouth'. He ascribed the prisoner's condition to 'injuries sustained when he was assaulted', and noted that his shirt, vest, underpants and the top of his trousers were blood-stained. The report said Tsafendas answered all questions 'guardedly, but did not appear to be confused'; the doctor did not notice anything wrong with his mental state.[3] The accuracy of Dr Kossew's report has never been seriously questioned, though Tsafendas might be considered lucky to have sustained only a cut lip and a swollen and cut nose from the brawl in Parliament followed by the short, sustained assault by the police.

After Dr Kossew left, Tsafendas was taken to a cell and the beatings began again. When Brigadier Aucamp, a short and heavy-set man[4] in plain clothes, arrived, he began firing questions at Tsafendas as policemen took turns punching their prisoner; when he fell to the floor, he was kicked and pulled up to his feet and punched again; one policeman used a baton. It was in no sense an interrogation; the police did not expect their handcuffed and helpless prisoner to answer questions; it was vengeance. Frequently curled into a ball on the floor, Tsafendas wondered time and again: Had he succeeded? If Verwoerd lived, this pain would be in vain.

Next to arrive at the police station was the chief of the Cape Town Security Police, Major Daniel Jacobus Rossouw. In an informal question-and-answer session, he asked Tsafendas the usual identity questions, including age and nationality. Rossouw then accused him of being 'a horrible murderer'. Hearing those words, Tsafendas knew he had succeeded. Calmly, he replied, 'That is what you think, but the world thinks differently.'[5] He knew that the majority of South Africans would react with joy to the news that their oppressor was dead.

During this time, a police squad led by Captain Genis was searching Tsafendas's room – No 7, Aldor Apartments, Rustenburg Avenue. In a wardrobe drawer, they found a black gas pistol with a white grip, which they confiscated, along with letters, books, papers and a passport.[6]

Meanwhile in Pretoria, Wilhelm Johannes Verwoerd, Dr Verwoerd's oldest son, was in his office at the Geological Survey when he received a phone call from his mother who told him about the attack in Parliament.

> 'Is it serious?' he asked her.
>
> 'Yes, it's very serious,' she replied.[7]

As afternoon turned to evening, Major Rossouw visited Tsafendas again and found him huddled in a cell, bleeding and bruised. Fearful of the scandal if such an important prisoner were to die in custody, the major directed Brigadier Aucamp to have him taken immediately to a hospital. Shackled in handcuffs and leg irons, Tsafendas was brought to Groote Schuur's casuality at 6.30 pm. Under conditions of total lock-down, no outsider was allowed to see the prisoner and plain-clothed policemen never left his side, including when he stripped to be examined and even inside the X-ray theatre. A staff doctor, Dr T.A. Darby, confirmed Dr Kossew's observations as to the two facial lacerations, adding that Tsafendas's nose was broken and blood was obstructing the airways. He stitched the cuts, put the nose in a splint and gave Tsafendas an anti-tetanus injection. The examination lasted about 20 minutes and Dr Darby noted that his prisoner/patient was 'co-operative' and 'composed'.[8]

That Dr Darby's report was so similar to Dr Kossew's might suggest that Tsafendas received no new injuries after being examined at 2.50 pm at the police station. Why then did he need to be hospitalised again four hours after receiving treatment from Dr Kossew? What cannot be ignored is that during apartheid, many doctors, especially those acting for the state, downplayed or ignored evidence of police violence and found dubious causes for deaths in detention.[9] The persistence of questionable reporting by physicians eventually led to the South African Medical Association's expulsion from the World Medical Association.

While Tsafendas was being examined by Dr Darby, the casualty duty doctor telephoned Dr Isaac Sakinofsky, the hospital's head of psychiatry, at his home and he came immediately to the hospital. There he met with the registrar, Dr Hymie Tockar. It was now 7 pm and Dr Sakinofsky wanted to examine Tsafendas, but the room in which he was being held was full of uniformed policemen and plain-clothed security men of all ranks milling about. Since it would be impossible to establish any kind of rapport with Tsafendas under those conditions, Dr Sakinofsky requested that the room be cleared. Brigadier Aucamp refused, citing reasons of security. Dr Sakinofsky contacted the hospital superintendent and upon the superintendent's intervention, Aucamp agreed reluctantly to clear the room, though he stood outside the door with his men posted nearby during the psychiatric check-up. The examination lasted between 30 and 45 minutes and Dr Sakinofsky concluded that Tsafendas was not of sound mind, that he was deluded and could not properly understand what he had done. Noting that he had previously suffered from schizophrenia, the psychiatrist proposed that Tsafendas be detained in a closed mental hospital ward for further investigations while efforts were made to discover his medical history.[10] Tsafendas was not sent to a mental ward, but driven back to the police station in a black American sedan[11] and again roughed up by his guards. Eventually, they left him lying handcuffed on the concrete floor of a windowless cell. There was no bed, only a dirty blanket.[12]

As a detainee under the 180-Day Detention Act, Tsafendas could legally be kept in custody and interrogated without a lawyer for up to 180 days. Having been serially assaulted since 2.20 pm, Tsafendas had a good idea of what to expect in the coming days. By now, he should have been a blubbering mess. In fact, he was relieved that the assaults had not been worse. During past detentions in Mozambique and Portugal, he had been systematically tortured, even given electric shocks. That had not happened, at least not yet. Most importantly, he had done the deed! The architect of apartheid was dead; now, surely, he thought, it was just a matter of time before the system he had created collapsed without him.

***

In the world outside the police station, South Africa's men of power were moving to steady the ship of state. The Minister of Finance, Dr T.E. Dönges, took over as acting Prime Minister and Justice and Police Minister John Vorster ordered the Commissioner of Police, Lt. Gen. John Keevy, to place Major-General Hendrik van den Bergh in charge of the Verwoerd investigation. Deputy Commissioner Van den Bergh was chief of the Security Branch and Vorster considered him the man 'best qualified to get to the bottom of this quickly'.[13] Within hours, Van den Bergh was flying from Johannesburg to Cape Town, accompanied by Brigadier Gideon Joubert,[14] head of the criminal investigation department. His starting point would be an interview with Tsafendas.[15] A few hours later, Wilhelm Verwoerd and his wife Elize flew to Cape Town. 'In the back of my mind we had probably (known) that it was a dangerous job he [his father] has,' he later said.[16]

News of the assassination hit South Africa like a thunderbolt. Cinemas were closed, regular radio programmes and sports events were cancelled and shops pulled down their shutters.[17] The Johannesburg Stock Exchange closed early[18] and markets fell in London and Paris.[19] Newspapers rushed out special editions with huge headlines[20] and, perhaps in an unguarded moment, one South African government official commented about the assassin, 'Thank God he wasn't Coloured. That would have sparked off a reaction that would make apartheid seem like child's play.'[21]

On the notorious Robben Island, where political prisoners were held, the news spread quickly. The inmates were overjoyed and Tsafendas became an instant idol. 'We all saw him as a hero. He was a hero in our eyes. All political, orchestrated persuasions on the island hailed him as a hero,' said Lionel Davis, a prominent anti-apartheid revolutionary prisoner on the island. However, they were careful not to show their delight as they knew what would follow.[22] The next day, the warders took out their anger on the prisoners. Nelson Mandela wrote that 'the authorities began a crackdown against political prisoners as though we had held the knife that stabbed Verwoerd'.[23]

There was shock and outrage in the Afrikaner community, but most black people were delighted and, away from Afrikaner eyes, they celebrated the assassination by singing, dancing and drinking. Some blacks began to call Tsafendas 'Dimitri Defendus'.[24] Blacks and coloureds were not the only ones celebrating. Stanley Uys, the *Sunday Times*'s parliamentary correspondent, revealed many years later that an unnamed member of Verwoerd's cabinet threw a party at his home that night.[25]

Tsafendas's half-brother, Victor, in Pretoria, was the first of the Tsafantakis family to hear of the assassination from a radio broadcast. At first, the news flash did not name the assassin but said he was from Mozambique and was of Greek origin. Victor, well aware of his sibling's political ideas and past activism, feared immediately that this was Dimitri. He contacted no one, but waited in trepidation for confirmation. When Tsafendas's name was revealed soon after, he hurried to his mother, Marika, who was in her home in Pretoria with his sister, Evangelia and Mary Eintracht, Tsafendas's first cousin. They had heard nothing and the women's faces turned pale when Victor delivered the news. Marika's eyes filled with tears and Evangelia burst out in anger: 'Oh my God, what is going to happen to us?' Pity mixed with her terror. 'And what is going to happen to Mimis?' she asked, using the family nickname for Dimitri. Marika covered her face with her hands: 'This boy ... this boy...' she moaned. 'I told Michalis, I told him so many times to stop filling his brain with all this nonsense of revolutions and politics.'[26]

The three were soon joined by another of Dimitri's half-sisters, Eleni, and her husband, Nick Vlachopoulos, along with the family lawyer. They shuttered their windows and drew the curtains and, with the radio constantly updating developments of the assassination, discussed what they should do. Chief among the family's fears was that the police would discover they had bribed a South African Consular official in Lourenço Marques to issue Dimitri an entry visa, the money being provided by Vlachopoulos. It was the only way for Tsafendas to enter the country since he was on the stop list of the Department of the Interior and all his visa requests since the mid-1940s had been rejected because of his communist and anti-colonial activities in Mozambique in the 1930s. The family did not even tell their lawyer about this.[27]

Victor was terrified and blamed Vlachopoulos. Although he personally had played no part in the corruption, indeed had strongly opposed the idea from the start, it was he who had driven Tsafendas back into South Africa in his car. Returning to his house later that evening, he found the windows smashed and red paint spattered over the walls. He seriously considered leaving South Africa and packed a suitcase in case he had to leave suddenly.[28] Eventually, in line with their lawyer's suggestion, the family decided that the best policy was to distance themselves as far as possible from Dimitri. When the police came, they would downplay Tsafendas's political ideologies and declare that they had no knowledge of his activities, that they did not know he was a communist or that he had been banned from entering South Africa; they would claim that they were not close to him and any relations they had with him were strained.[29]

When Marika realised that the police would search her house, she panicked and went through every room looking for anything associated with Dimitri. During a previous stay there, her stepson had brought a suitcase full of books, which she upended. Most were literary classics, but she also discovered some communist and anti-apartheid pamphlets. Tsafendas had also left gramophone records he had bought in the United States and Europe, including a Bob Dylan disc, a record of Soviet communist songs and one of Italian communist songs.

The majority were records by the black American singer-actor and political activist, Paul Robeson, Tsafendas's all-time favourite. Marika knew nothing of Robeson or Dylan, except that Robeson was black and therefore, she concluded, probably illegal in South Africa. She liked both men's songs and had often played them, but now she carried the discs out to a furnace in the back yard and burned them all. She also collected every photo she could find of Dimitri and consigned them to the flames, including a large family photo taken in Lourenço Marques. Vlachopoulos protested that this was unnecessary, but Marika was adamant. Photographs that Tsafendas had sent to her from all around the world went into the furnace, including those of her stepson at anti-fascist and anti-apartheid demonstrations in London. One pictured him wearing the Yellow Star of David, symbol of the anti-racist Yellow Star movement; in another, he carried a placard depicting a Ku Klux Klan man in a white hood and underneath the word VERWOERD. Even her late husband's huge collection of anarchist publications did not escape the flames.[30]

Marika's precautions came none too soon as she was the first of the family to be questioned by the police the day after the assassination. As agreed, she claimed to know nothing about Dimitri's political ideas or activities. She admitted knowing that he had been imprisoned by the Portuguese, but said she knew no details. She also volunteered that when the boy was aged about 15, 'he showed a particular interest in the use of gunpowder and explosives at this stage and at one time nearly blew up our house'.[31] She could not deny knowledge of these two incidents as both were well known, the first to the Portuguese police and the second to the entire Greek community in Lourenço Marques.

Katerina Pnefma, Tsafendas's half-sister, recalls:

> *Remember, these were very difficult times for anyone who was even suspected of being a communist and anti-apartheid. The Communist Party was illegal at the time in South Africa ... my mother had not only known that he was a political animal, but she had helped him to come to South Africa. Can you imagine what would have happened to her and to us if they knew that we knew that he was communist and anti-apartheid and we helped him to come to South Africa? My poor mother was so terrified that they might find out they had bribed this guy in the embassy in Lourenço Marques and that they would all go to jail.*
>
> *None of us told the police that he [Tsafendas] was a communist and anti-apartheid. How could we have said such things then? They might have deported us all or even worse... who knows what they could have*

> *done to us if they had found out that we knew. He [Tsafendas] was saying that the South Africans are Nazis, he was calling Dr Verwoerd Hitler's best student ... he used to say that Jesus Christ was socialist and that if he was alive today he would have been a revolutionary,*[32] *fighting against apartheid and for the independence of Mozambique! How could I have told all these things to the police? They would have said, 'Why didn't you report him to the police since he had such crazy ideas? Didn't you know he was dangerous?'*[33]

The family member who had most to fear from the police investigations was George Michaletos, Tsafendas's uncle in Lourenço Marques, who had arranged the bribing of the passport officer, his friend, J.J. van den Berg. Stricken with terror and unable to sleep, Michaletos wanted to flee immediately back to Greece, but his wife, Artemis, convinced him to remain. However, when Van den Berg was taken in for interrogation, Michaletos's nerve broke and he fled to Zambia, hiding in the house of a relative.[34]

News that Verwoerd's killer was half-Greek shocked South Africa's 40,000-strong Greek community. Most Greeks supported apartheid or at least co-operated with it for commercial, political or personal reasons. Some even gave financial support to the ruling National Party. Opponents of apartheid were widely seen as 'traitors', such as human rights lawyer George Bizos, who was widely shunned by his fellow Greeks.[35] The many Greeks who lived and worked in South Africa sought desperately to distance themselves from Tsafendas, declaring that only a lunatic would murder so popular a leader as Verwoerd. Typical was a certain Charitakis, who declared to the press about Tsafendas, 'He must have been crazy to do such a thing. Dr Verwoerd was very much loved by everyone and was keeping the prestige of the white race in the Dark Continent.'[36] This sentiment was widely shared by Greeks who had no personal knowledge of Tsafendas but were worryingly conscious of their vulnerability as outsiders. One Greek elevated praise for Verwoerd to the level of hagiography. This was George Sakellaridis, owner-editor of the South Africa-based newspaper *Acropolis*, a passionate supporter of apartheid and a financier of the National Party. Sakellaridis, who gave Verwoerd's portrait pride of place on his office wall,[37] published a eulogy for the slain Prime Minister which outdid all other encomiums in its unctuous adoration, including that of the Afrikaners themselves. The article praised him as 'perhaps the greatest son of the South African nation ... a philosopher, an intellectual, a true Christian, a philanthropist, a visionary ... a holy symbol of Christian civilisation and of real patriotism ... who turned South Africa into the only bastion of Christianity in an atheist, godless continent and the only hope of the free people of the continent against the cancer of Communism.' Sakellaridis characterised Dr Verwoerd as a modern 'Prometheus Unbound', who had been 'misunderstood, slandered and wrongfully accused by the unfair and irresponsible international community which was unaware of everything he had done for Black South Africans'.[38]

Sakellaridis also attacked Tsafendas in sneeringly demeaning terms, though conceding he had never met him. He claimed to have made inquiries among some Greeks and discovered that when Tsafendas was a child, he was referred to as 'blackie', causing him to have 'an inferiority complex'.[39] This story was circulated by all South African newspapers and was soon widely accepted as fact, although numerous people who knew Tsafendas personally declared the opposite to be true. For example, a schoolmate of Tsafendas at Middleburg, William Mare Volbrecht, a psychologist, told the police that at the time 'Tsafendas was seen as white and there was never anything that pointed to someone regarding or treating him as a non-white or to him being discriminated against'. Another former Middleburg schoolmate had told the *Rand Daily Mail* that Tsafendas was 'a popular boy and not the least introverted. I particularly remember him singing a Greek song at a school concert. He was very funny and had us all in stitches'.[40] All such evidence was ignored and even today, half a century later, the story persists in some quarters that Tsafendas was called a 'blackie' in boyhood. Sakellaridis also claimed that Tsafendas's family had disowned him,[41] which was entirely wrong, but also came to be widely believed.

The South African government declared that it would not tolerate retaliation against Greeks[42] while Police Commissioner Lieutenant-General John Keevy ordered that no reprisals be taken against them. He said, 'Tsafendas was not and had never been a member of the Greek community.'[43] Even so, this did not protect them from the wrath of Verwoerd's supporters. In Cape Town, Johannesburg and Pretoria, the windows of Greek shops and cafés were smashed, some Greek shopkeepers were verbally abused over the counter and others received threatening telephone calls. The canopy of a Greek shop in Johannesburg was set on fire and an 0.25 ammunition round was fired into a pile of confectionery cans in a café in Cape Town.[44] In Mozambique too, Greeks moved hurriedly to distance themselves from Tsafendas, many claiming he was not a Greek. A widely heard comment from people who did not know him was: 'He must be crazy to kill such a great and good man as Dr Verwoerd.'[45] The tiny Christian sect to which Tsafendas belonged also distanced itself from him, fearing that the negative publicity would hurt their church's image.[46]

Beyond South Africa, national leaders in Europe, the United States, Canada and Australia condemned the assassination and offered condolences. However, not everyone was stricken with grief. Johnny Makhatini, a leader of the banned African National Congress in Algiers, hailed the assassination as 'the beginning of the end for apartheid',[47] and said it would 'help the morale of guerrilla fighters in South Africa (and) increase confusion among whites'.[48] Also in Algiers, Ewald Katjivena, the representative of SWAPO (South West African People's Organization) declared that 'the fascist Verwoerd got what he deserved'.[49]

In Britain, the BBC interrupted its programmes to announce the assassination.[50] Albie Sachs, a well-known South African barrister and freedom fighter, said in an interview with the Corporation that there would be 'jubilation' in the townships that 'a tyrant has fallen'.[51] Asked if he regretted the assassination, he replied that 'assassination never solved problems ... murder is foul, wherever it happens, but I would be hypocritical if I said I had any regrets'.[52] Sachs's comment that 'assassination never solved problems', was omitted from the broadcast.[53] Later that day, an unnamed African appeared on the BBC and stated that Verwoerd's death was the happiest day of his life and he only wished he had done the deed himself.[54] The main BBC news programme in the evening attracted a viewing audience of twelve and a half million, one of its highest ratings for the year.[55]

Elsewhere in London, the satirical magazine, *Private Eye*, in one of its most famous front covers, published a photograph of Africans dancing and leaping in traditional tribal style. The caption, ironically suggesting they were celebrating their Prime Minister's death, proclaimed, 'Verwoerd: A nation mourns'.[56]

There was no mourning in independent African countries. Many were grappling with economic and political problems of their recently acquired independence and South Africa was not a priority. While sympathetic to the sufferings of black peoples, governments knew there was little they could do against the might of their southern neighbour. In many cases, disapproval was conveyed by displays of semantic hostility. In Kenya, for instance, newspapers invariably referred to South Africa as 'the racist regime', resulting in amusing reports on the sports pages as, 'The racist regime lost to New Zealand by an innings and 104 runs.' The *Times of Zambia* ordained that South Africa should be referred to as 'racist' whenever it appeared in the paper and sub-editors fought to write the silliest headline. One outstanding effort was 'Zambia slaps ban on racist vegetables'. So common was the practice that such headlines were accepted without comment by readers.

Verwoerd's assassination opened the floodgates. When the news was announced to the Zambian parliament, there was laughter from some MPs. In Nairobi, the ruling Kenya African National Union characterised the assassination as 'a symbolic and heartening act, from which millions suffering from apartheid would draw hope'. In Lagos, many Nigerians shouted 'Hallelujah' and danced in the streets.[57] Ethiopia's Foreign Minister called Verwoerd's death 'the natural result of apartheid, which breeds blind hate and evil',[58] and in Kampala, Ugandans applauded the killing of the 'hated leader of the persecution of Africans'.[59]

In the United States, the comment by civil rights leader Martin Luther King was more reserved. He said, 'Few individuals in modern times have been so insidious and diabolical in their schemes of oppression as Hendrik Verwoerd, but even in his case, one must deplore the fanatical act of assassination'.[60]

None of the critical statements from around the world was published in the South African press.

As broadcasters around the world reported on the assassination, Tsafendas lay on the concrete floor of his cell, still in blood-stained clothes, trying to sleep as night approached, but the rattle of keys informed him there would be no rest. Kicked to his feet by a policeman, he was led through a succession of locked doors into a windowless room where a man sat at a table with an empty chair opposite. A policeman removed his handcuffs and the man at the table rose to his feet. He was very tall. He introduced himself as Major-General Hendrik van den Bergh.

Van den Bergh, then aged 52, was an imposing figure: 1.96m (6 feet 5 inches) tall, radiating power of command from his many years close to the centre of government. Ruthless in the defence of apartheid, Lang Hendrik (Tall Hendrik), as he was known,[61] was the state's most successful interrogator, equipped with techniques learnt from the CIA's foreign adventures and from the French experience against independence fighters in Algeria in the early 1960s.[62] He was responsible for the extensive use of torture against political dissidents and it was under his command that many prisoners died in detention. Giving evidence before the Erasmus Commission of Inquiry in 1978, he boasted, 'I am able, with my department, to do the impossible. I can today tell you here ... this is not bragging, I have good men, Afrikaners, I don't have weak men ... I have enough men to commit murder if I tell them, "Kill" ... I don't care who the prey is ... these are the types of men I have ...'[63]

As a young man during the Second World War, Van den Bergh was detained as a suspected member of the Stormjaers, the military wing of the pro-Nazi organisation, Ossewabrandwag (OB). One of his fellow detainees was John Vorster and, when the war ended, the two rose in tandem to positions of power.[64] Van den Bergh had a vision that he and Vorster would one day run apartheid and South Africa together. To that end, he pursued suspected anti-apartheid activists with a remorseless tenacity, numbering Nelson Mandela among his countless arrests.

Van den Bergh was responsible for the torture and death in detention of many opponents of apartheid. He was described by the International Aid and Defence Fund as 'a cruel and ruthless man with scant regard either for justice or humanity'.[65] Van den Bergh was also more than a Nazi-style thug. He used his administrative talents to defend the state against accusations of mass murder and infringement of human rights. When the Sharpeville massacre occurred in 1960, he arranged for the wounded victims of the police shootings to be taken from Baragwanath hospital to Boksburg prison, where they were kept under lock and key. This was so that evidence of the police use of dumdum bullets, outlawed by international convention, would be concealed.[66] That those with bullet wounds were dragged from their hospital beds, stripped naked, hosed down and forced to dress again in their blood-stained clothes was of no account to Van den Bergh. Along with the hasty burial of dead victims of the illegal bullets, the removal of wounded protestors was part of a successful and elaborate operation to whitewash the police actions.[67]

In the interview room at Caledon Square police station, the general politely pointed Tsafendas to the empty chair. The prisoner lowered himself gratefully into it, easing the pain in his back from the concrete floor. Speaking softly, Van den Bergh offered him water from a jug on the table. Tsafendas's mouth was dry and he drank greedily. The inquisitor offered him a cigarette, which he declined; Tsafendas disliked the smell of tobacco and had never smoked. Then the questions began – first, his name. Tsafendas said his birth name was Dimitris Tsafantakis, but that the surname had been forced upon the family by the Ottoman occupiers of Crete. He considered this profoundly insulting, like plantation owners giving names to their black slaves. So he changed his surname back to Tsafendas, the family's original appellation.

The general nodded and made an entry in a small notebook. Tsafendas waited for him to finish, then began telling his life story. He stated that he was born in Mozambique in 1918 to a Greek (Cretan) father and a half-Mozambican, half-German mother who belonged to the Shangaan tribe. Van den Bergh appeared taken aback, he had clearly never suspected that the man in front of him was anything but white. He peered closely at Tsafendas and made another note. Tsafendas went on, describing his family, who, with the exception of a half-sister in Rhodesia, all lived in Pretoria. He said his father, Michalis, had died in 1962. After describing his childhood, Tsafendas moved onto his time in South Africa, casually mentioning that he had joined the South African Communist Party in Johannesburg. Horrified, Van den Bergh rested his pen. This was not what he wanted to hear. Tsafendas reassured him: that was 1942, he said, and he had not been in touch since. The statement brought no comfort to the general, who believed that once a communist, always a communist. Tsafendas was lying anyway. He had made contact with former comrades in Pretoria in 1964, soon after he returned to South Africa. He had even been in touch with Rowley Arenstein, a well-known communist lawyer and anti-apartheid activist. Since Arenstein was already in trouble with the police, he made no mention of his name. To the further consternation of his interrogator, Tsafendas then revealed that he had fought with the communists during the Greek Civil War in 1947. That was not all. He declared that he had been arrested five times by the Portuguese because of his anti-colonialist and communist activities and that he had joined the British Anti-Apartheid Movement and taken part in several demonstrations in London.[68] The general's worst nightmare was becoming a reality: Dr Verwoerd's assassin was a committed communist with a trail of political activism going back many years.

In the course of his narration, Tsafendas mentioned being admitted to various hospitals over the years. He was told to name every hospital and the reason for his admission. In one instance, he gave the reason as being a tapeworm infection. This was the first and last time he mentioned a tapeworm, which would subsequently be given huge prominence by the police. Van den Bergh was curious and asked, 'How was it you fell ill so many times?' Tsafendas maintained that it just happened that way. No mention was made of fakery or madness at this point. The general dropped the subject and Tsafendas continued his narration, but when he concluded his life story, Van den Bergh returned to the hospitalisations. Tsafendas suspected that the general wanted him to admit he was mentally ill. He replied that sometimes when he had no money and nowhere to stay, he would pretend to be ill and seek admission to a hospital. There he would get three meals a day, the company of other patients and the attention of nurses and doctors. So why not?[69]

Thus the story unreeled: Mozambique, South Africa, World War Two, Europe, finally back to South Africa and a job as a parliamentary messenger at the very centre of national power. He gave a clear and detailed account of his preparations for the assassination, how first he bought a pistol, then the knives, how he decided where to do the deed and how he approached and stabbed Dr Verwoerd. Finally, Van den Bergh asked the crucial question: 'Why did you do it?' Tsafendas replied: 'I disagreed with his policies.' The general reminded him that the penalty for a capital crime was death by hanging. Tsafendas responded, 'I don't care, kill me.' He said he considered Dr Verwoerd to be a dictator and a tyrant who was oppressing his people, that he was the brains behind apartheid and that without him, he expected apartheid would collapse sooner or later.[70]

The interrogation lasted throughout the night and for many hours the following day. Tsafendas volunteered a detailed account of his life and repeated again and again how he had carried out the deed. He felt he had described his entire life, month by month from birth, but the general insisted that they continue. Eventually, Van den Bergh decided he had heard enough. He walked out of the room and an exhausted Tsafendas never saw him again. He was taken back to his cell. He had lost all track of time. It seemed that aeons had passed since nine the previous morning when he bought the knife that killed Dr Verwoerd.

***

In a private room only metres away, General van den Bergh evaluated the information he had gathered. It could hardly have been worse. The Prime Minister's assassin was not a crackpot or some deranged grudge-bearer, but a card-carrying communist. He had worked openly with the Communist Party in South Africa, fought with the communists in the Greek Civil War and he had been arrested no fewer than five times by the Portuguese colonial police for subversive activities. Yet this man had somehow managed to enter South Africa and, unbelievably, secure a job that put him in the same building as the Prime Minister. More importantly, all this happened while he, Major-General Hendrik van den Bergh, was in charge of national security. He obviously had some hard thinking to do.

Van den Bergh's first action was an order to check whether the Security Police held a file on Tsafendas. He then contacted the Portuguese security police, PIDE, for more information about those five arrests.[71] He ordered his security officers to scour South Africa and find and interview anyone who had ever had contact with Tsafendas, however minimal. He sent Lt. Col. P.J.P. van Wyk of the South African Police to Mozambique to investigate Tsafendas's past and question anyone who knew him or might have information about him.[72] He also asked the Special Branch of the British South African Police in Umtali, Rhodesia, for any information they could find about Tsafendas, preferably from people who knew him.[73]

Van den Bergh then informed Justice Minister Vorster that 'present information indicated that the assassination was the work of one individual'.[74] Later that day, Vorster issued an official announcement to that effect. He also fired the first shot in the official campaign to ensure that no one would ever believe that the 'greatest political crime ever committed in South Africa'[75] might have been politically motivated. Although he must have heard from Van den Bergh of Tsafendas's statements to the police and his long history of political activism, Vorster spread the word that the assassin was 'a simple-minded man whose action could not have political implications of any kind'.[76] Meanwhile, a report was delivered to the Minister on the post-mortem carried out on Verwoerd. This declared the cause of death to be 'multiple stab wounds, one of which penetrated the left ventricle of the heart'. The report added that there were no grounds for a rumour that the assassin was an expert in the use of a knife. The wounds were quite ordinary, said the doctor who performed the autopsy.[77]

***

On 8 September, two days after the assassination, Van den Bergh received a top-secret telegram from the South African embassy in Lisbon. The dispatch confirmed the general's worst fears. It stated that Tsafendas 'has a criminal record in Mozambique, where he is said to have been arrested on several occasions after creating public disturbances, including shouting pro-communist and anti-Portuguese slogans'. However, it also said that he had 'never been convicted as courts have found him to be of unsound mind'. The telegram concluded: 'If information correct, we suspect Portuguese may play down assassin's previous political activities and we would suggest full details in this connection be sought.'[78]

The telegram could not have been more prescient, for on that same day, the Chief Inspector of PIDE in Lisbon sent a secret telegram to the Sub-Director of PIDE in Mozambique, informing him that 'information indicating Tsafendas as a partisan for the independence of your country should not be transmitted to the South African authorities, despite the relations that exist between your delegation and the South African police'.[79]

To guard against any mistakes, the director of PIDE in Lisbon sent to his officers in Mozambique, along with the above letter, a report the Service had compiled the previous day which set out just what should be given to the South African authorities. The report whitewashed Tsafendas's political past, downplaying and even omitting some of his political activities. Some were included, such as his 1964 arrest on accusations of 'making subversive propaganda against the Portuguese government and spreading subversive propaganda among the native masses',[80] because the incident had been reported widely in Mozambique at the time and would have been impossible to conceal. However, important facts not yet mentioned by the press were omitted, including the fact that Tsafendas was banned from Mozambique for 12 years, only being allowed to return after receiving amnesty. Even more significantly that, in 1963, he had convinced Portuguese governmental officials that he was a harmless, reformed person who no longer believed in Communism, the result being that they granted him amnesty after his 12-year exile.

Omissions apart, PIDE lied blatantly to the South African police, claiming they did not have a file on Tsafendas[81] although they had held one for 28 years. Titled, 'Secret Criminal Record nº 10.415 of Demitrios Tsafantakis', it was 130 pages long.[82] Opened in 1938, when the 20-year-old Tsafendas was accused of being 'engaged in disseminating communistic propaganda',[83] it went up to 26 January 1965, the day Tsafendas was released from PIDE custody after spending three months in a police cell in Beira,[84] accused of pretending to be a Christian missionary while actually preaching 'under the guise of religion in favour of Mozambique's independence'.[85]

The report also said that while he was in custody and interrogated by the Portuguese police 'he gave signs of mental disability, which was confirmed by the Hospital do Ultramar'. It added carefully that 'although, Tsafendas is mentally disabled, you do find in him a true spirit of rebellion against the ruling institutions, and a clear adhesion to the independence of Mozambique'.[86] In essence, the report was an attempt to persuade the South Africans that Tsafendas, being mentally enfeebled, was less important than they might believe. Clearly, PIDE felt that it would reflect badly on them if it became known that the man who assassinated Dr Verwoerd was a Portuguese communist with a long history of political activities and arrests. Even more embarrassing for the Portuguese immigration authorities was that Tsafendas had deceived them into believing he was a 'reformed' man, no longer an anti-colonialist and a communist, but now a man without any political interests, thus facilitating his return to Mozambique after 12 years in exile. Serious questions would have been raised about the efficiency of PIDE if it became known that a man they had arrested so many times had returned to the country that they controlled, then used it as a starting point for his murderous journey to South Africa.

On 9 September, three days after the assassination, it was the turn of the South African embassy in Washington to provide Van den Bergh with further revealing information about Tsafendas. A diplomatic cable quoted a 'very reliable source with first-hand knowledge' as saying that the US Immigration authorities had a file on Tsafendas that revealed that he was 'a quarter Negro or African'. The file contained 'full particulars' of his time in the United States. The embassy said, 'He is understood to have shown under psychiatric treatment that he was unstable though (not) insane, but the type of man who would easily be used as an instrument of Communist or hostile organizations. Impression of U.S. Immigration people at the time was that he had been manipulated and was under the influence of someone or some organization. He was subsequently deported to Europe.'[87] The hint in the Washington telegram that Tsafendas might have been a communist stooge was not one that sat well with Van den Bergh.

Along with this cable, it was another document from the United States, a report from Grafton State Hospital in Massachusetts, which seized the general's attention. Tsafendas was admitted to the Grafton hospital on 27 March 1946, remaining there until 31 July 1947. To the five-page hospital report were attached two appendices listing his movements in the United States. Setting out his earlier history, the report noted that, in 1942, Tsafendas had deserted his ship in Canada and had been arrested and imprisoned in the United States at the behest of the US Immigration authorities. While in prison, he had 'showed symptoms of mental disorder', hearing voices talking to him. This resulted in his transfer to the Boston Psychopathic Hospital in 1943. Doctors there were not convinced by Tsafendas's act and eventually, he admitted that he had play-acted to avoid service in the Allied navy and possible death in the Atlantic Ocean. The report said clearly that Tsafendas had 'faked mental illness because he was afraid to ship out because of the numerous leakings (sinkings) of ships'.[88]

Reading on, Van den Bergh discovered another aspect to the story. The report stated that when he was first admitted to Grafton in 1946, Tsafendas 'thought he had a tapeworm' and was 'hardly convinced he hasn't'. He was 'fairly co-operative and in good contact with the environment', but he was diagnosed as suffering from 'schizophrenia, hebephrenic type, with deterioration: prognosis poor'.[89] Thus, the report could be interpreted in two different ways: either Tsafendas had faked mental illness in 1943, but three years later, he was genuinely insane, or in 1946 he had succeeded in fooling the psychiatrists where he had failed three years earlier.

More bad news for Van den Bergh followed when he began receiving accounts of the interviews that his men had conducted with Tsafendas's friends and acquaintances; he began to learn of activities that the Prime Minister's assassin had not mentioned at his own interrogation. In a wide-ranging investigation, the police questioned about 150 people who knew or had associated with Tsafendas, including his family, friends, work colleagues, flatmates, landlords and landladies, even people who had spoken to him for only 20 minutes in their entire lives.

Tony Harrison, of City Guns, was called to an identification parade at Caledon Square police station and he confirmed Tsafendas as the man who had bought a knife from his shop.[90] Some witnesses, especially those who knew Tsafendas well, avoided any mention of his political activities or ideology. They felt that such information might be damaging for him, but also for them for not reporting him as a communist. After all, Communism was outlawed in South Africa. However, there were many witnesses who did state that Tsafendas was a communist and against apartheid. The police discovered that a Greek named Nick (Nikolas) Vergos had described Tsafendas to Johannes Jacobus Botha, a security officer in Mandini, a year before the assassination, as the 'the biggest communist in the Republic of South Africa'.[91] Botha had subsequently reported the accusation to the South African Police in Inyoni.[92] Vergos had also reported Tsafendas to Chrisoffel Johannes van Vuuren, another security officer at Mandini, as a 'dangerous communist' and 'not a Greek, but a kaffir'.[93]

Vergos was not the only person to denounce Tsafendas to the authorities on political grounds. Police discovered that, 18 months before the assassination, a German Roman Catholic priest, Father Probst, had reported Tsafendas as a 'communist and a dangerous person'. The priest further testified that Tsafendas had sworn at the Mozambique government for doing nothing for its black people and that he had learnt many languages from a teacher in Moscow.[94] This latter claim was the last thing Van den Bergh wanted to hear: a possible connection with the Soviet Union and the KGB! It was not the only unwelcome news Father Probst had to offer; he also claimed that, 'during the period he stayed at Mandini, the youngsters in the Mangete Reserve became unruly and aggressive'. He conceded that this was only his suspicion, but pointed out that when Tsafendas was gone, everything became quiet again and the youngsters controllable. The implication was that Verwoerd's assassin was some kind of political agitator.[95]

The political connections continued to build. Kenneth Ross, Tsafendas's landlord in Durban in 1965, told the police that Tsafendas 'was well versed in politics' and that he 'objected to Communists being banished to Robben Island'. He also said, 'In general, Tsafendas opposed every decision taken by the South African government.'[96] Robert Smith, who met Tsafendas in Durban, told his police interviewer that Tsafendas was a 'Communist, a fanatic on politics and seldom spoke of anything else' and that he described both United Party and National Party officials and members as 'capitalistic roughs'. He also testified that Tsafendas had associated in London with Canon John Collins and Solly Sachs, both leading anti-apartheid activists.[97] Jacobus Bornman, a flatmate, testified that Tsafendas 'stood up a lot for the Coloureds' and 'often criticised the South African government and seemed to have a grudge against Verwoerd'.[98]

Worse news began arriving from overseas. Edward Furness, who knew Tsafendas in London, said that Dr Verwoerd's assassin associated there with ANC leader Tennyson Makiwane and other prominent anti-apartheid activists. He said Tsafendas told him that he wanted to 'create a resistance to the regime of South Africa' and that he was willing to do 'anything that would get the South African regime out of power'.[99] A further claim against Tsafendas in London was that he tried to 'recruit people to take part in an uprising in South Africa'. This charge was contained in evidence submitted to the Commission of Enquiry into Verwoerd's death. Tsafendas's response was that yes, he had tried to rally recruits for an uprising, but this was 'confined to the Territory of Mozambique'.[100]

According to Inspector Horacio Ferreira of PIDE, Tsafendas was 'intensely anti-white' and criticised the Portuguese government because it had 'never done anything for its non-Whites'.[101] More unsettling information for Van den Bergh came from six crewmen of the tanker *Eleni*, which had been moored at Cape Town for 43 days, departing only three days before the assassination.

They told the police that in 1947 Tsafendas had joined the Democratic Army of Greece (DSE), the military wing of the Greek Communist Party, fighting the Royalist government forces in the Greek Civil War. Further, six or seven seamen testified that three days before the assassination, Tsafendas had characterised a hypothetical assassination of Verwoerd as being justifiable because he was an oppressive tyrant and a dictator. He had also taken some of the crew to a township in Cape Town to show them the hardships of apartheid and how black South Africans lived.[102]

The police also discovered that Tsafendas received a large amount of correspondence from overseas. Tucked inside a Bible was a letter from a close friend, John Michaletos, a member of the outlawed Greek Communist Party who had recruited Tsafendas to the DSE. The letter did not include Michaletos's address in Athens and although Tsafendas revealed who Michaletos was during his interrogations, he did not disclose his address, either pretending or genuinely not remembering it. This set the South African police on a mammoth attempt to locate the Communist Michaletos and inquire into his relationship with Tsafendas to unearth any possible connection with Verwoerd's murder. First, they contacted people in Cape Town with the same surname. One of these was Costas Michaletos, who had known Tsafendas in Lourenço Marques, but had not seen him since the late 1930s. He told the police that he was aware of two men named John Michaletos, both of whom knew Tsafendas. The first was a doctor with a clinic in Athens. Then he said, 'There is also a Professor John Michaletos in Greece, but I do not know where he currently finds himself. When I visited Greece in 1952, I heard that he was an active Communist.'[103] The professor had been exiled by the government after the civil war and had gone underground for some period. However, he was probably in Athens as Tsafendas had spent the Christmas of 1961 at his home there. The South African police contacted their Greek counterparts, but they failed to locate the professor. The South Africans then contacted PIDE and inquired if they had a file on him. On 17 November 1966, PIDE replied, 'There are no records of John Machletos in the registries of this police.'[104] That both the Greek and the Portuguese police failed to locate Michaletos may have been because the South African police had misspelt his name as Machletos.

As the investigation went on, the general received unfavourable news almost every day. Although Tsafendas had not revealed his association with Rowley Arenstein while in Durban, this became known to the police. Esperanza Theron, a white woman who was working as secretary to her lawyer husband and whose offices were next to Arenstein's, had seen Tsafendas entering Arenstein's office, and walking and talking with him on several occasions. She testified to the police:

> *During 1965 or late 1964 I observed a White or Coloured male whom I have since identified from photographs in the newspapers as Demitrio Tsafendas, frequenting the offices of Rowley Arenstein. Demitrio Tsafendas used to pay visits to Arenstein's office regularly and on occasion he would greet me. I observed Demitrio Tsafendas actually entering the general office of Rowley Arenstein but am unable to state for what purpose he visited Arenstein. I am unable to state the period of time that he used to visit Arenstein, but the visits were very regular. I have also observed Demitrio Tsafendas in the presence of Rowley Arenstein walking down the corridor from Arenstein's office.*[105]

Theron was not the only witness who linked Tsafendas with Arenstein; Robert Smith, the night clerk at Durban Men's Home where Tsafendas stayed, told the police that Verwoerd's assassin had asked him if he knew Arenstein's residential address.[106] Arenstein's name, his relationship with Tsafendas and possible involvement in the case were important to the police, as the lawyer was a very well-known communist and anti-apartheid activist. Tsafendas had admitted being a communist and a former member of the South African Communist Party, but he had not revealed any association with other communists.

The police questioned Tsafendas intensively about Arenstein. He denied ever meeting a person with such a name. However, confronted by Theron's testimony, Tsafendas suddenly 'remembered' that he had visited a lawyer in Durban to make enquiries about buying a translation bureau, but he could not recall his name. This was the best version he could come up with at the time. Tsafendas was then shown a photograph of Arenstein and reluctantly admitted that he was the lawyer he had visited. He insisted that the bureau project was the only reason he had called on him.[107]

Police then questioned Arenstein and his secretary, Thelma Beryl Suddes. The secretary stated that, to the best of her knowledge, she had never seen Tsafendas in Arenstein's office.[108] Arenstein, questioned on 24 September 1966 by Brigadier Baster, denied knowing Tsafendas.[109] The denial was all the police could expect since Arenstein was about to go on trial under the Suppression of Communism Act and the last thing he needed was to be involved with Verwoerd's assassination. On 31 October, he was sentenced to four years' imprisonment for furthering the aims of Communism.[110]

Trawling through the police's own records, Van den Bergh discovered that four files were listed as relevant to Tsafendas and his political activities, but only one could be found. Tsafendas was on the stop list of the Department of Immigration, which held two additional files on Tsafendas.[111] What the police did know, according to the available records, was that in 1938 Tsafendas was dismissed from a job in Mozambique 'owing to his Communist leanings' and that he was suspected of being 'engaged in disseminating Communistic propaganda';[112] that he supported Mozambique's independence from Portugal and wanted to see 'a Mozambique governed by the natives of that Province, be they white or black, and therefore separated from the Mother-nation';[113] that he was in South Africa from 1939 to 1942 and during this time engaged actively in communistic propa-ganda. The reports from Mozambique and Rhodesia further confirmed Tsafendas's political activities and personality. Lt. Col. van Wyk's report from both countries concluded that Tsafendas was 'intensely anti-white' and that 'for all purposes (he) can be seen as a normal, intelligent person'.[114]

At the same time, South Africa's media focused relentlessly on Tsafendas, reporting any scrap of information they could find, doubtful or not. The government further muddied the waters with unofficial leaks and nameless sources belittling Tsafendas and portraying him as an apolitical idiot. Most of the negative stories first appeared in the Afrikaner press. One egregious example of the rumours and stories that were published at the time about Tsafendas comes from *Die Landstem*: 'There were rumours Tsafendas had fled from South Africa, because he was wanted by the police for attempted murder, that he had committed a murder in Mozambique, that he had raped and seriously assaulted a woman in Montreal, that he had raped and assaulted a white woman in Ontario, that he had blown up a ship with dynamite in Boston, that in New York he was found on his way to the docks with explosives, that in Greece he was suspected of murders and rapes, that in Portugal he had strangled and raped a young girl, that in Germany he was suspected of murders.'[115]

Amid the torrent of rumour and misreporting, another example was a story in *Die Vaderland*, the National Party mouthpiece, which said Tsafendas had complained that the government did more for blacks than for whites. The report by the newspaper's Parliamentary correspondent claimed Tsafendas made this remark during his time as a Parliamentary messenger.[116] Since this was the direct opposite of what he believed, it is not surprising that none of his five fellow messengers remembered him saying anything of the sort or Tsafendas discussing politics with them.[117] One, of course, cannot exclude the possibility that Tsafendas made such a remark to the *Die Vaderland* correspondent to protect himself against any suspicion of disloyalty. However, the fact is that this fake news was also widely circulated and accepted while Tsafendas's principled political views were concealed.

On 13 September 1966, exactly a week after the assassination and before Verwoerd's blood had even been cleaned from the carpet in Parliament, John Vorster, an anti-Semite and old-time Nazi, was selected by his party to be the new Prime Minister. Despite being only thirteenth in order of party seniority,[118] he managed to win with the support of the extreme right-wingers in the party – the Broederbond, a secret and powerful Afrikaner organisation of which he was a member (Broeder number 3737)[119] – and the Dutch Reformed Church, where his brother Jacobus was a leading minister.[120] Vorster indicated immediately that he would follow the path laid down by Verwoerd and that the policy of apartheid would remain the nation's guiding principle. Claiming, like Verwoerd, that apartheid was God's will, he declared, 'I believe that we still have a long way to go in the process of fulfilling our calling and that God, who has so called us through His grace, will not abandon us until we have completed our task.'[121] Vorster allotted important security positions to old Nazi comrades from the Second World War camps, including his old friend and adviser, Hendrik van den Bergh, who became head of state security.[122]

Vorster also called for unity between English- and Afrikaans-speaking people, 'for the sake of the fatherland', which was an implicit acknowledgement that he had critics among the non-Afrikaners.[123] Only a year earlier, in 1965, he had been accused of using his powers as Justice Minister to turn South Africa into a police state. His reply was: 'This is no time to be sensitive about principles. In such times, it is the things that weigh heaviest that should count.'[124] In early 1966, Verwoerd had given Vorster the additional portfolios of police and prisons, and Vorster had promptly instructed Van den Bergh that anyone thought to be a threat to the state should 'be taken out of circulation one way or another, if there are valid reasons for not bringing that person to trial'.[125] The diktat was fully compatible with Vorster's personal ideology. One of Vorster's first acts as Prime Minister[126] was to honour his predecessor. On 22 September 1966, just 16 days after the assassination, he announced that the planned new version of the R1 silver coin would bear the head of Dr Verwoerd instead of that of Jan van Riebeeck, founder of the first colony in Cape Town in 1652.[127] The following day, Vorster announced in Parliament that a judicial investigation, a one-member Commission of Enquiry (COE), would be launched immediately 'into all aspects of the assassination of Dr Verwoerd'. Vorster urged anyone with information bearing upon the death of Verwoerd, 'however trivial' to come forward and lay it before the Commission.[128]

General van den Bergh's exhaustive investigation of Tsafendas's past, encompassing police, immigration and diplomatic records, plus face-to-face interviews with numerous acquaintances, demonstrated that the information Tsafendas had volunteered at his 6 and 7 September interrogation represented only a fraction of his political activity over the years. Confronted with this damning array of evidence, Van den Bergh knew that he could not let such facts be publicly known, that he must find a way of suppressing them while presenting Tsafendas as a different person to the committed political activist he clearly was.

It certainly suited the government to portray Tsafendas as an insane person rather than a politically committed communist for various reasons. According to Professor John Dugard, '[Tsafendas was a] politically informed person, angry with apartheid and Dr Verwoerd, determined to make a change, with nothing to lose personally ...'[129] The apartheid regime had two reasons for portraying Tsafendas as insane. First, the regime wished to suggest that no one in his right mind could kill such a wonderful leader as Hendrik Verwoerd. Secondly, the security apparatus, led by the Minister of Justice and Police, John Vorster, wished to avoid accountability for allowing a political revolutionary to be employed in a position close to the Prime Minister.[130]

Gordon Winter, a secret agent of BOSS at the time, was very close to General van den Bergh and co-operated with him in efforts to downplay Tsafendas's communist activities in the media and to have them omitted from evidence placed before the Commission of Enquiry. Winter told Liza Key frankly:

> *Pretoria did not want there to be any suggestion whatsoever that Tsafendas was clever, or programmed, or politically affiliated in any way. It's embarrassing for HJ [Van den Bergh], the supremo of intelligence, for his mob to allow this lunatic – if he was a lunatic – into the House of Assembly, and he then went in with two daggers. That's some security! No wonder they wanted to keep it quiet ... if there was a political motive, it's hardly pro-South Africa. And if it was a political motive, surely wouldn't the Kremlin get some benefit from that? A nice bit of propaganda. You don't want that. The reds under the beds in South Africa were the enemy. We don't let them score victories. Think about it. It's common sense.*[131]

Historian Lulli Callinicos added another reason for concealing Tsafendas's political motivations:

> *At the time [1966] things were hotting up. The ANC and the PAC were banned, they had gone into exile, and they had also of course announced the armed struggle. They were actually scores of, in fact hundreds, going into exile to train for the armed struggle. I think it was a serious threat if it was announced that a member of the Communist Party and of course a man of colour [had assassinated Dr Verwoerd]. [The apartheid authorities feared that] this might actually stimulate and mobilise more blacks to raise up. That was something that was a very real possibility. So it had well suited them to define him as a crazed individual. It was a far better strategy than to find that he had tried to promote a revolution. That's why he was permanently silenced.*[132]

In finding a solution that would meet the best interests of the state, General van den Bergh faced a monumental task of organisation, manipulation and even perhaps persuasion of the stricter kind. He included his own interests in those of the wider objective. Allowing this information to become known would reveal that he, the officer responsible for the nation's security, and his men had allowed a committed communist to cross illegally into South Africa, and then secure a job at the heart of government. His friend, John Vorster, would share the blame as Police Minister. Full disclosure held equally serious implications for the government, the ruling party, the state policy of apartheid and consequently, national stability. It would suggest that there was significant resistance to apartheid inside the country, for which the communists could claim credit around the world. Tsafendas would become an overnight hero for the millions of South African blacks who silently opposed the regime and a totem for the anti-apartheid struggle worldwide.

The best outcome of the investigation for the state would be if Tsafendas could be presented as a madman with no interest in politics, without a motive for killing Verwoerd, simply a lunatic. Much written evidence would have to be suppressed, but that could be done. It would not be the first time Van den Bergh had arranged for testimony to be concealed or manipulated in order to secure a verdict he needed. After all, he had done just that at the enquiry into the Sharpeville massacre and the use of dumdum bullets. The madness aspect was more problematic. Tsafendas was quite firm at his interrogation that he acted from political motives and wanted apartheid ended. Quietly, the authorities began manipulating media coverage with a series of unofficial leaks referring to Tsafendas's alleged mental instability. Editors were not to know that Tsafendas had shown no signs of schizophrenia and had given clear political reasons for his actions. The police had not even appointed a psychiatrist to examine him at this stage, obviously because he appeared perfectly sane to them. Thus what was left was the big question: How could Tsafendas be persuaded to change his tune, to morph from committed activist to apolitical lunatic?

Ten years later, when he was still Prime Minister, John Vorster revealed that General van den Bergh had personally questioned Tsafendas for 48 hours. He then praised his good friend's unique interrogation skills by adding that, 'If a man does not break after forty-eight hours of Van den Bergh's questioning, then you know that he does not know a thing.'[133] Van den Bergh himself, referring to the totality of Tsafendas's interrogation sessions, declared that 'no person in South African history has ever been interrogated as much as Tsafendas'.[134] Vorster's reference to prisoners 'breaking' under Van den Bergh's questioning and the general's statement on the extent of Tsafendas's interrogations, made at a time when torture was widely used against South

African political prisoners, constitute a clear indication of what was to follow in Caledon Square police station for the man who assassinated the architect of apartheid.

Chapter 3

The Son of an Anarchist

In 1918 Mozambique, then a Portuguese colony, it was not unusual for European men to father children with African women. What was unusual was for the men to acknowledge these offspring as their own. When Amelia Williams, Michalis Tsafantakis's housemaid, realised that she was pregnant by her employer, she left his house and disappeared. She assumed Michalis, a Cretan marine engineer, would not acknowledge the child.[1] Amelia herself was of mixed race, her mother an African of the Shangaan tribe, native to Mozambique, and her father a German, supposedly an aristocrat, who disappeared as soon as he learnt of the pregnancy.[2] The name Williams was probably her mother's maiden name. Amelia was born in Namaacha, a town 80 km west of Lourenço Marques on the border with Swaziland, and raised by her mother.[3] She was, by all accounts, a beautiful young woman with skin the colour of ivory and a rounded figure; she dressed like most African women in a print blouse and wide skirt, with a white sash around her body.[4]

Michalis, then aged 27,[5] hailed from Kitharida village, 25 km from Heraklion, the administrative capital of Crete and the island's largest city. His father was a judge, Antonis Tsafantakis, and his mother, Katerina, kept house, although her wide interest in culture and command of languages made her much more than the average housewife.[6] Through many generations, the Tsafantakis family produced rebels who fought the Ottoman occupiers and Michalis was named after the most famous of them, his uncle, Captain Michalis Tsafantakis. The audacious exploits of this dashing rebel chief made him a legend among Cretans and established him as the Turks' priority target. When eventually he was captured, the occupying forces killed him by hurling him from a bridge in Heraklion. The street where he was born in Kitharida was renamed Michalis Tsafantakis Street and all Cretans sang songs of his bravery. Michalis grew up dreaming of following in his uncle's footsteps.[7]

In 1895, Antonis Tsafantakis left Crete with Katerina and young Michalis for the great Egyptian port city of Alexandria, where they settled in the al-Atarine suburb. Antonis was comfortably at home there, having spent his boyhood years in Alexandria after his own father, Captain Dimitrios Tsafantakis, also a Cretan rebel, fled there for safety from the Ottomans. A rare exception in the family, Antonis did not bear arms for the rebels, but pursued a judicial career in Crete. In Alexandria, he found employment as a legal counsel for Fuad I, the

King of Egypt, and would often take little Michalis to the royal palace or to the court, where both wore the traditional fezes and galabeya robes.[8]

By most standards, Antonis was a wealthy man and when Michalis was 18, he paid for him to travel to Italy to study marine engineering at the University of Padua. During his stay in Italy, Michalis became a passionate anarchist, joining an organised group and distributing anarchist newspapers and pamphlets, some of which contained his own articles. Among the journals, he gave out was *l'Università Popolare*, which championed the cause of workers' self-education. The aim was to instruct working men in subjects such as Latin, psychology and physics to widen their horizons as part of a self-emancipation process.[9]

Displaying a natural talent for his subject of study, soon after graduation, Michalis made an important discovery concerning submarine engines. This led to a period working on underwater vessels for the British government, after which he moved briefly to South Africa, then travelled to Mozambique. There, he found work at an engineering company owned by George Voutselatos in Lourenço Marques, which carried out repairs on ships in dry dock. Voutselatos was quick to recognise the new recruit's talents and soon Michalis became a partner in the firm. With his financial situation much improved, Michalis moved into a white two-storey house on 24th of July Avenue.[10]

When Amelia left his house, Michalis was not aware that she was bearing his child, but as time passed and she did not return, he decided to go and search for her. When he tracked her down, he discovered she was several months pregnant. Unlike her own father, he was delighted by the prospect of a child and persuaded her to come back to his house and give birth in a hospital. Amelia agreed and returned to 24th of July Avenue accompanied by a friend from her tribe, Maria, to help out when Michalis was at work.[11]

The baby was born on Monday, 14 January 1918, a boy, which delighted Michalis because he had always wanted a son.[12] The infant's skin was as white as his father's and his hair was just as black. His half-sister, Katerina Pnefma, recalling him as a boy, said, 'He was very white … as white as all the family, but he had different hair. It wasn't so much like the blacks' hair, it was like the coloureds. He did not look black at all, he was much whiter than many 100% whites, especially Greeks, many of whom have this dark complexion. He was as white as any of us [in the family].'[13] Concern about skin colour was not racist but pragmatic. At that time in colonial Mozambique, there were distinct advantages in being white, both for a person's current situation and future prospects.

Proudly, Michalis named his son Dimitrios, informally 'Dimitris' or 'Dimitri', and registered him with the local Civil Administration, naming Amelia and himself as parents. He had long ago decided that he would call his first child

Dimitrios if he was a boy or Dimitra if she was a girl, after his grandfather, Dimitrios Tsafantakis, the famed rebel chief. One of Michalis's loudly and frequently declared boasts was that he was 'Captain Dimitrios's grandson and Captain Michalis's nephew'. When he was old enough, he grew a moustache exactly like his grandfather's.[14]

Michalis had his son baptised Dimitrios by Father Elias Bertolis, a Greek Orthodox priest and a close friend, in a public ceremony in Lourenço Marques; his best friend, John Michaletos, was the child's godfather.[15] Michalis's decision to be open about his son's mixed-race origins incurred the disapproval of many of the city's Greeks. The Hellenic community tended to stick together and resented the prospect of a part-coloured boy joining their ranks. His Portuguese friends, too, argued that Michalis was ruining his life and would never now find a good Greek wife. Michalis ignored them all and a year later moved into a larger, semi-detached house on Rua Andrade Corvo, where he lived happily with Amelia, Maria and his adored baby son.[16]

Interrupting this idyll, sometime in 1919, came a letter from his mother, Katerina, in Egypt. She had found him a marvellous Greek bride with a substantial dowry, she wrote, a beautiful girl from a good family living in Port Said. Like the other family members in Egypt and Crete, Katerina was unaware of the existence of little Dimitri. Michalis did not reply. There had been many such letters and he had ignored them all, reckoning that he should enjoy his freedom as a bachelor before looking for a wife. Of course, there was more to it than that. Michalis knew that much as he loved Amelia, it would not be possible to marry her.[17] In white-ruled, Christian Mozambique, a racially mixed marriage may have been legally possible, but life thereafter would have been difficult for the family, facing curiosity and suspicion from black and white communities alike. The reaction to Dimitri's christening had made that clear. When it came to matrimony, Greek men in Africa invariably took Greek brides and he knew that his deeply traditional mother wanted to follow this path.

Refusing to take his silence for the negative, Katerina insisted that Michalis come meet his bride, Maria (Marika) Sakelis. Unable to resist any longer, Michalis travelled to Egypt to meet Marika later in 1919. He did not tell her nor his mother about the baby, but he did tell his younger sister, Artemis Diana, who lived with their mother. Artemis confirmed his suspicion that their mother would never approve a wedding with Amelia, indeed would rather disown him. She herself thought Marika was a perfect choice and Michalis decided to go ahead with the marriage. He then made a bold proposal: He would tell his mother about the boy, then send him to Alexandria to be cared for by her and Artemis until his marriage to Marika was secured by a child of their own. He would then tell Marika that she had a stepson.[18]

Michalis had no qualms about Dimitri being brought up in Egypt since he had spent some of his own early years there. When Antonis relocated his family to Alexandria, Michalis was four and they lived next to his grandparents, Dimitrios and Victoria. When Crete became safer, his grandparents moved back there and Michalis spent his summers with them. His grandfather was a heroic figure, but Michalis spent more time as a small boy with his grandmother.[19] He therefore knew her better and perhaps loved her more.

Victoria was born in Crete to Greek-Jewish parents. They, too, opposed the Ottomans and paid for it with their lives. Victoria was only nine when her parents were killed and she was left without living relatives. Dimitrios's father, a friend of Victoria's father, decided it was his duty to care for his dead comrade's daughter. However, because he was usually involved in guerrilla warfare in the mountains, he took the little girl to his mother, who lived in Alexandria. Young Dimitrios, who was 14 at the time, told his grandmother, 'Grandma, please look after this girl because I love her and I will be back in five years to marry her.' Five years later, Dimitrios returned to Alexandria and duly married Victoria. They lived happily together until their deaths in Crete. What Michalis loved about his grandmother was the tenderness that underlay her obviously strong will, plus the resilience that helped her survive the loss of both parents at a vulnerable age. Michalis was also in awe of her encyclopaedic knowledge and said she taught him a million things. He planned a similar upbringing for his son, with his mother raising and schooling little Dimitri, just as Victoria had done with him; then, in a couple of years, when he had another child with Marika and Dimitri would be about four, he would bring him back to live with his own family.[20]

With the plan agreed with his sister, Michalis became engaged to Marika and the wedding was arranged to take place in Egypt at Christmas 1920. It was only after the engagement that Michalis told his mother about his son by Amelia. She was shocked but agreed to look after the boy with Artemis until the birth of a child with Marika. Returning to Mozambique, Michalis lived with Amelia and the baby until sometime in 1920 when he steeled himself to inform her of his forthcoming marriage. The wedding was scheduled to take place in a few months and he needed to end his relationship with Amelia as soon as possible. Certainly, he could not wait until just before his marriage. In what must have been a devastating blow for Amelia, he asked her to turn little Dimitri over to him, promising that he would be raised as a loved and equal member of his family when he married Marika. Amelia had probably feared such an eventuality, but she was nevertheless shocked and saddened, and at first, refused. When Michalis finally persuaded her that it would be best for their child's future, Amelia walked reluctantly out of the lives of her lover and their son.[21] Her friend, Maria, remained in the house to look after Dimitri, who was now two years old.[22]

Later that year, Michalis learnt that a Greek woman named Eleni Schinas was about to sail from Lourenço Marques to Athens via Port Said in Egypt. The lady was a friend of his British neighbour Antony Maw's wife, who agreed to ask her, on Michalis's behalf, to take young Dimitri to Port Said. Michalis's mother and sister would travel from Alexandria and receive the boy there. Mrs Schinas agreed and the handover took place sometime in November 1920.[23] Dimitri was now two months short of three. As planned, the wedding of Michalis and Marika took place in Port Said on 5 December 1920, while Dimitri was in Alexandria.[24]

***

Michalis's mother would have been 70 or thereabouts when she agreed to take care of the toddler. Her husband had died a few years earlier, but Katerina was strong-willed and of an independent mind. Born in Crete, she had never finished school, but she was intelligent and pursued a wide range of cultural interests. Both she and her daughter Artemis could speak Greek, Arabic and English, and Dimitri was immediately introduced to a world of multiple languages and exotic cultures. Like two mothers, Katerina and Artemis taught their new charge Greek and Arabic, gave him lessons in Greek history and mythology, and coached him in Cretan and Greek folk songs, such as the romantic epic *Eroticritos*, which Tsafendas often sang in later life. There was always Greek, Western classical and Arab music in the house, with both women singing along, and Dimitri learnt many Greek and Arabic ballads. He also picked up some of the local Cretan dialect.[25]

Katerina was a personal friend of Constantine Cavafy, the most celebrated Greek poet of his time, who was born and lived in Alexandria. Though Dimitiri had no memory of their encounters, they reflected the environment in which Katerina moved. Dimitri's uncontested heroes were his great-uncle, Captain Michalis Tsafantakis, and his great-grandfather Dimitrios Tsafantakis, and Katerina fed him with tales of their heroic adventures. Katerina also told him of his granddad Antonis, the judge and lawyer, and Dimitri would ask her about his life, sorry that he had not known him.[26]

Artemis adored young Dimitri and would take him to the Greco-Roman museum in Alexandria, to ancient buildings and to historic sites. The boy was fascinated by anything from the past, including ruins and especially castles. Artemis would read him stories from Greek mythology, which his quick imagination turned into a personal reality. He revelled particularly in the Trojan War and the Odyssey. Artemis began calling Dimitri 'Mimako', a derivation of Mimis, from Dimitris. Always thereafter he was Mimis to his family and close friends.[27]

Katerina and Artemis were alike in spoiling the boy. When warm, they went to the seaside, where Artemis taught Dimitri to swim. He had a natural ability in the water and learnt quickly – 'He used to swim like a fish', said his step-sister Katerina.[28] Dimitri's love for the sea would come to dominate much of his life, especially his wartime years in the Atlantic. He loved the ocean's smell and its changing moods. In the heat of summer, all three would take their beds onto the open roof of their home and Katerina would serenade the boy with traditional lullabies. What Dimitri loved best was to listen to Artemis talk about the heavens above them, pointing out the planets and the visible stars and constellations.[29] Star-gazing during those warm Alexandrian nights was an experience Dimitri would never forget.

Unlike many children of his age, Dimitri was a hearty eater and his guardians worried, perhaps rightly, that he would become overweight in later life. Nevertheless, growing up, he stayed slim and healthy on his grandmother's meals. He loved fish and seafood but also Katerina's desserts and cakes. His favourites were her concoctions of bitter oranges and sour cherries with a sweet syrup.[30] He sought out these delicacies all his life.

Dimitri quickly made friends with his peers in Alexandria's many communities of Arabs, Christians, Muslims, Jews and Greeks. Most of his friends were Arabs and his guardians would often dress Dimitri in flowing, desert-style Arab garments. The only people he did not have as friends were Turks. His grandmother would not associate with Turks because of past wars but also because of the ongoing conflict between Greece and Turkey, warning the boy about them. Hearing about the Ottoman Empire's occupation of Greece and the Greek War of Independence, and knowing that many of the family had died in the struggle, Dimitri grew up believing that Turks were bloodthirsty monsters.[31]

Katerina was deeply religious and all three would go to Sunday mass at the Greek Orthodox church with Dimitri attending Sunday school afterwards. Katerina taught him to pray in front of an icon of Virgin Mary with infant Jesus before he slept, thanking God for his day and asking for an untroubled night. In the morning, he would thank God for a good night and pray for a safe day.[32]

When he was five, Dimitri gained a first cousin, Mary Vasilogiorgis (later Eintracht). Their homes were close by and they often played together. Dimitri looked upon Mary as his little sister and would take her by the hand to teach her to walk. They remained close all their lives. When he was six, Katerina enrolled her grandson in the Familiadis Community School, a Greek school in their own al-Atarine suburb. He did not take to the discipline of lessons, but he responded to the sociability of school life. During National Day celebrations or sports days, Aunty Artemis would dress him in a fustanella, a traditional Greek kilt-like garment, with a bolero, waistcoat, embroidered leather belt and a soft cap or fez with a long single tassel.[33]

One of his treasures was his great-grandfather's flintlock pistol that hung on the wall in the living room. Katerina would take it down and let him play with it – it had no ammunition – but she would not let him take it outside. There was also a bayonet that belonged to Katerina's father from his army and war years. She refused to let Dimitri play with this because of the obvious dangers to himself and others, but she promised to give the boy both the pistol and the bayonet when he was older.[34]

Clearly, Dimitri was a happy and well-adjusted boy, loved and protected by his grandmother and aunt, but there was something missing from his life which all his playmates had – a mother and father. True, Katerina and Artemis were generous with their love, but Dimitri's instincts told him that this was not how it should be. At least he received letters and gifts regularly from his father, with visits from Mozambique once or twice a year. But his mother ... why had she left him and where was she now? Katerina offered an explanation: His father's work involved him in a great deal of travelling and his mother had to go with him. Things were to change soon, however, and his dad would come to take him to Mozambique and then he would see his mother. Thus, young Dimitri waited for the day his father's travels would end so that he could see his mother. Katerina and Artemis read books about Mozambique and talked to him often about the country where his father lived, such a different Africa to Egypt, full of dangerous lions, massive elephants, clever monkeys and zebras with dark stripes. The young exile dreamed of the day he would see all these things for himself.[35]

In 1922, Michalis and Marika started their own family when Evangelia, nicknamed Vangela, was born. Two years later came a boy, Victor, named after Victoria, Michalis's cherished Jewish grandmother. Alongside his Arab sympathies, Michalis was proud of the Jewish heritage and would talk to his children at length about the Hebrew people and their history. Even though Michalis had planned to tell Marika about Dimitri after the first baby was born, he could not bring himself to do so. For one thing, he feared her reaction, as their marriage had not gotten off to a positive start because of differences in their characters and socio-cultural beliefs. Although Michalis was progressive, sometimes even extremist, in politics, when it came to family matters, he was strict and conservative. Described by Mike Vlachopoulos, his grandson, as 'a Victorian man', Michalis believed the husband was the head of the house and the woman's position was in the kitchen, her main responsibility being to bring up his children. Marika was not happy with this, but there was not much she could do, since she had married Michalis freely and was living in a foreign country with her own family thousands of miles away. In addition, the fact that Dimitri was happy in Egypt, loved and cared for, made Michalis continue postponing the revelation.[36]

This is not to say that Dimitri was absent from his thoughts. Michalis sent him parcels of toys and other gifts almost every month, along with letters to Katerina and Artemis asking for full details of what his son was doing. He asked for a detailed diary to be sent to him once a month. The boy's carers responded willingly, but never as frequently as Michalis wanted. Marika was completely in the dark – all the letters and parcels to and from Egypt were handled at Michalis's work and his bi-annual trips to Alexandria were under the pretence of visiting his mother. He would spend two or three weeks with Dimitri before returning to Mozambique, telling Marika all about his mother and nothing about his son. In his heart, Michalis felt guilty about the subterfuge and kept promising Katerina that the next time he visited, he would take Dimitri back to Mozambique.[37]

Amelia, too, was deceived by Michalis because he had promised he would bring Dimitri back to Lourenço Marques when he and Marika had their first child. Eventually, Amelia discovered that Michalis and Marika had had two children but that Dimitri was still in Egypt. She had not forgotten her baby and began pestering Michalis to bring the boy back to Mozambique and give him to her, since he was not looking after him.

In 1925, Marika began to notice a young Mozambican woman with a baby in a shawl on her back, African-style, lingering outside their home in Lourenço Marques, apparently trying to peek through the windows. Then she spotted her on a few occasions talking to Michalis and wondered if they were having an affair and if Michalis was the father of the baby she was carrying. In her forthright way, Marika confronted her husband and demanded to know his connection with the part-African girl. Michalis temporised at first but eventually told the truth. As for the baby Amelia was carrying, Michalis said the child was not his and he knew nothing about it. Marika had heard nothing of the affair from the local Greeks, who had kept silent out of respect for Michalis, and she was shocked. She was also disappointed with Michalis for lying to her and even more with his mother for conniving in the deception. However, she accepted the situation and agreed with Michalis that the boy should be brought home to live as part of their family.[38]

Later that year, Michalis travelled to Alexandria and came back with Dimitri. Katerina packed Dimitri's favourite sweets and the Marian icon, but most importantly, the portrait of his great-uncle and great-grandfather's flintlock pistol and bayonet. Dimitri's departure left Katerina deeply depressed. The house seemed empty without a noisy and rambunctious seven-year-old. Her health deteriorated rapidly and she died a few years later.[39]

In Mozambique, the young arrival from Egypt quickly settled into his new surroundings as a full member of the family. The first thing he did was to hang Captain Michalis's portrait above his bed. When, a few years later, an earth tremor hit Lourenço Marques and everyone fled the house in panic, Dimitri ran back inside, ignoring Marika's cries. When he emerged, he was carrying the portrait of his hero.[40]

The lack of maternal influence was quickly resolved when Dimitri was introduced to Marika. She hugged him warmly and he had no difficulty in accepting she was the mother he had longed to know and that Evangelia and Victor were his siblings. The children knew nothing of Dimitri's origins and considered themselves natural brothers and sisters.[41] A very good friend of the family, Costas Michaletos, testified to the South African police in 1966 that Dimitri 'grew up with his half-brothers and half-sisters and was always treated as part of the family'.[42]

When Dimitri arrived, the growing Tsafantakis family was living temporarily in Britannia Hotel.[43] Michalis had sold his old house and was building a larger one to accommodate everyone. His partnership in Voutselatos's ship repair company was thriving and the future looked good. At 33, Michalis was beginning to assume the image of a successful businessman – dark-suited, heavy-set and bespectacled, with a small moustache and fleshy facial features, much as his son came to look in later years. However, there was much more to Michalis than his business associates might suspect. He was an educated and well-rounded man and a deeply knowledgeable lover of literature and the arts, particularly music. Western classics, including opera, were passions that he passed on to Dimitri, but it was Arabic music that he loved above all. A gramophone, which he had bought during his student days in Italy, and a radio were the most important items in the house. His friends used to say he was an Arab at heart, but since the Arabs translated many Greek texts and developed the musical theory of the Greeks, Michalis's attachment may be more easily understood. Dimitri, too, with his experience in Egypt, could sing in Arabic and he taught his siblings many songs. Evangelia was the family's best singer. Dimitri's voice was pleasant enough, but he tended to sing out of tune, making everyone laugh.

Michalis's overriding interest was politics. Successful small businessman apart, he remained at heart an anarchist, still receiving revolutionary literature from his contacts in Italy and elsewhere. He was not an outgoing man and would never proclaim his views publicly, but unrestricted political discussion would quickly reveal that he was a deeply committed radical: anti-racist, anti-royalist, anti-fascist and anti-colonialist. His commitment had a practical side, and sometime during the mid-1930s he made a large donation to an organisation that helped Jews to flee from Nazi Germany, while he also made frequent donations to the anti-Francoists in the Spanish Civil War.[44]

Michalis was well-read on international affairs and fascinated by the great political shifts around the world, such as national wars of independence and especially the French and Russian revolutions. He gave Dimitri stories about the ancient Greeks but also books on international revolutionary movements. Michalis admired the writers and philosophers of the Age of Enlightenment, such as Jean-Jacques Rousseau and Voltaire, as well as the Greek philosophers Plato and Aristotle, though his favourite was Honoré de Balzac. He communicated his literary preferences to the young Dimitri, and in time, Balzac became one of Dimitri's favourite authors too, quoting him often during his lifetime. For his tenth birthday, Michalis bought his son a multi-volume encyclopaedia, which so entranced the boy that for weeks, he scarcely left the house. When Michalis gave him money, Dimitri would spend some of it on ice cream, but most would go to books, which he would read to the younger family members.[45]

An early discovery, also a gift from his father, was *Uncle Tom's Cabin,* Harriet Beecher Stowe's seminal novel about slavery in the United States. Having grown up in a multi-cultural society in Egypt and nurtured in the belief that all men were equal, including, as his father regularly insisted, Greeks and Turks, the story of racial discrimination and violence in America shocked the boy deeply and had a tremendous effect on him. Weeping, he ran to his parents and implored his father to tell him if such things really happened. Michalis took him to his bedroom and quietly, at length, opened his eyes to racial and other injustices taking place right then in America and elsewhere. This was the moment when the United States became a hate figure for the young Dimitri. Unaware of his own black origins, he felt a deep need to fight for equality for all, if only to prove that he was not like the whites in the book. Equally, he never hid his mixed origins during his time in apartheid South Africa, determined to dissociate himself from the racist rule around him. The need to isolate himself from any taint of racism stayed with Dimitri throughout his life and he would often weep when he told of reading *Uncle Tom's Cabin* for the first time. It proved to be a small leap from an American social critic to an English one in the person of Charles Dickens, in whose novels about the poor Dimitri saw what he came to perceive as communist themes. While growing up, he began reading adult material such as Shakespeare's plays and Dostoyevsky and later studied historical and political works.[46]

Soon after his arrival from Egypt, his father proposed a target that Dimitri followed enthusiastically into adulthood, which was to read at least one book every week. He did this without fail until his arrest for Verwoerd's assassination.

The book-reading sessions were conscientiously supported by Marika to ensure that Dimitri felt part of the family. Marika, too, played a part in the boy's literary formation. Although deeply religious and instinctively conservative, she sympathised discreetly with some of her husband's radical views and, though not highly educated, she read the classics for pleasure. Marika and her stepson read Russian novels together and soon, Dostoyevsky became his favourite too, like Marika's. This became evident many years later when he was discussing Dr Verwoerd's assassination. He remarked, 'To paraphrase Dostoyevsky in *Demons*, "It's easy to condemn the offender, the difficulty is to understand him."'[47]

His early heroes from Greek mythology were replaced as he grew older by fighters in the Greek Revolution of 1821–32, who toppled the Ottoman Empire and won Greeks their independence. It was during his father's talks about the war that Dimitri learnt that the family's real name was not Tsafantakis, but Tsafendas. The Ottoman rulers had decreed the change a hundred years ago to belittle the Cretans, whose rebel activities were causing them so much trouble. They declared that '*akis*', a suffix indicating smallness, as in a child, should be added to every Cretan family name, sought of as a way to mock the Cretans by suggesting they were little people of no account. The Cretans opposed the change furiously, but the rule prevailed. Excited and indignant, Dimitri beseeched his father to change the family name back to Tsafendas, for it was humiliating to accept a name forced upon them, something he likened to US plantation owners naming their African slaves according to their whim. For weeks, Dimitri pressed his father; Michalis sympathised, but said it would be difficult since everyone knew him as Tsafantakis personally and in all official documents. Dimitri told his father that when he reached maturity he would get the family name back. In the meantime, he began using the surname Tsafendas whenever possible.[48]

Filled with dreams of exotic Africa, Dimitri found Lourenço Marques deeply disappointing with no sign of the lions, monkeys, zebras and especially his favourite elephants that he had been told about. Michalis told him they lived far beyond the city, promising to take him one day, but never did.[49]

Michalis was strict with his children, making sure they followed his rules, something Dimitri was not used to. His two stand-in mothers had catered to his every whim and apparently, he expected the same from his new family. Although his father was initially lenient, he soon realised that Dimitri was out of control and began to discipline him to bring him into line.[50] Even so, Dimitri managed to get away with things that Victor and Evangelia could not. Despite his best intentions, it was difficult for Michalis to hide his partiality for his first-born son and this caused constant friction with Marika.[51]

Michalis took Dimitri almost everywhere – shopping, coffee shops, even backgammon with his friends. Clearly, he was trying to make up for the time lost between them, but it was obvious to the other children that he never spent so much time with them. After a long day at work, Michalis would relax on his balcony with Dimitri, enjoying the evening breeze from the ocean, and the two would chat about their day, read books or skim through the daily papers. Michalis favoured Dimitri also because he was his first-born son, a matter of great importance for Greeks, especially Cretans. Michalis wanted to spend time with his son, he said, to make him 'a useful member of society', someone who would care for others' welfare, not just for his own. Although irritated by the obvious nature of Michalis's favouritism, Marika was conscious of the boy's stepson status and was often more lenient with him than with her own children. It was only when she feared Dimitri might be a bad influence on Victor that she became strict.[52]

Because of this social exposure, almost everyone in the Greek community in Lourenço Marques got to know the young Tsafantakis. When Marika went out with Dimitri, people would call out and wave to her stepson but rarely to her. She spent much of her time on housewifely duties and was not well known. Passers-by would shout '*Geia sou Dimitri*' (Hi Dimitri) or '*Geia su Mitsara*' (Hi Mitsara). Mitsaras is a popular nickname for those named Dimitri, conveying familiarity or admiration. Many Greeks in Lourenço Marques called Tsafendas 'Mitsara' all his life.[53]

Not unnaturally, Dimitri worshipped his father and tried to imitate him.[54] Intellectual pursuits – politics and morals apart – included chess and backgammon, which Michalis taught his son and which they would play for hours on the house balcony or in the garden. As for exercise, Dimitri's favourite possession was a bicycle his father bought him, which he rode every day, sometimes only in his own neighbourhood, other times around Lourenço Marques itself, usually with a small sibling as a pillion passenger.[55] The only thing that Tsafendas did not like about his father was that he was a heavy smoker, rarely without a cigarette in his mouth. Young Dimitri detested the smoke and would wave it away with his arms. The dislike of tobacco stayed with him permanently.[56]

In an uncanny pointer to the life he was to lead, Dimitri collected maps and magazines with articles about foreign countries. Whenever he read about a foreign country, he would go to a large, much-prized globe that his father had bought him to locate the country mentioned. Dimitri also read about the lives and exploits of such famous explorers as Captain Cook and Vasco de Gama, but what fascinated him most was polar exploration and heroes like Ernest Shackleton and Robert Falcon Scott. In his dreams, the young Dimitri became an explorer himself, travelling around the world and discovering unknown places.[57]

The family lived in a spacious house with four bedrooms, one for the parents, one for Evangelia and one each for Dimitri and Victor. Dimitri promptly turned his room into a shrine for his heroes. On the walls, he hung pictures of his grandmother and Captain Michalis Tsafantakis, along with the bayonet and a map of the world. By his bed hung the Marian icon and Dimitri prayed before it at bedtime and again when he woke, thus keeping his promise to his grandmother.[58]

Dimitri did most of his reading in bed, but sometimes he would sit with a book by the window, watching the people outside or scanning the starry sky. The largest object in the room was a bookcase his father had built for him, though soon he had so many books he had to store them under his bed and in the living room. Michalis promised to construct a bigger bookcase when they moved to a larger house, but it never happened. Helen Kavadias (later Grispos), a neighbour and friend, remembered that when she saw Dimitri's room for the first time, she remarked that she 'had never seen so many books before, not even at school'.[59] Dimitri lent his books freely and Ira Kyriakakis, also a neighbour and a friend, described him as 'a lending library'.[60] Marika was not happy with Tsafendas for giving out his books, fearing they would be lost or damaged. For his part, Dimitri considered his friends would be worse off for not knowing the contents of his books. He reckoned that by reading them, they would become better people.[61]

An early example of Dimitri's sympathy for others, which may have stemmed from Michalis's admonitions, concerned his young half-brother. Victor had contracted poliomyelitis at an early age and this left him with a disability affecting one of his legs. Dimitri took his young sibling under his wing and made sure he was involved in whatever games were being played. When he suggested that Victor should be moved into his room so he could look after him better, Michalis agreed and since there was not enough space for two single beds, he made a double bed for the two brothers.[62]

Another example was his interactions with a young, black Mozambican boy who was blind or partially sighted. The boy's mother worked at another Greek home and was bringing her son up alone. Dimitri read stories to the boy and often took him home to join the Tsafantakis family around the table. He even took the boy to the sea to teach him to swim. The lessons went well but one day, the boy got into difficulties and panicked. Dimitri hurried to his assistance but found that he, too, was out of his depth. Both boys were in serious trouble until a group of men rescued them. Though he was an expert swimmer and taught all his siblings to swim, Dimitri was deeply frightened by this incident and, for a long time, would not go near the sea. Ironically, it was the boy who persuaded him to try again, and eventually they resumed their frolics in the water.[63]

In 1927, now aged nine, Dimitris began classes at the Anglican Mission School in Lourenço Marques[64] where his teacher was Costas Michaletos, a young Greek, whose uncle, John Michaletos, was Dimitri's godfather.[65] However, soon Michalis decided that he owed his first-born son a formal secondary education and that he could get that in white-ruled South Africa better than in Mozambique.[66] Accordingly, in 1928, Dimitri joined Middleburg Primary School in the Eastern Transvaal. Arriving in July, he became a boarder in the Nelson House hostel, which was used mainly for Greek and Portuguese boys who were not influent in English.[67]

Having lived in Egypt and Mozambique, he was not intimidated by travelling to another country and experiencing a new culture. He was happy at school and accepted by boys and staff, without anyone suspecting his mixed origins. Shortly after Verwoerd's assassination, a former classmate, William Mare Volbrecht, by then a psychologist, testified to the South African police that 'At that stage Tsafendas was seen as white and there was never anything that pointed to someone regarding or treating him as a non-white or to him being discriminated against. I cannot remember whether he was ever guilty of misconduct ... he was never a loner and mingled freely with us.' Volbrecht also said that Dimitri participated without excelling in school activities and sports and was a keen soccer player.[68] Another former classmate, Dr Samuel Schmahmann, by then a physician, recalled Dimitri as a 'popular boy who was not the least introverted'. He said, 'I particularly remember him singing a Greek song at a school concert. He was very funny and had us all in stitches.'[69]

Some tension between the home-based South African boys and the Portuguese, who came mostly from Mozambique, was inescapable. Usually, the rivalry focused on sport, when teams were invariably chosen on a national basis. Dimitri was taller and stronger than most boys of his age and was admired by his Portuguese classmates, especially for his football skills. The South Africans' best footballer was Jack Cox, slightly older than Dimitri and the son of the school principal. Rivalry between these two on the playing field often escalated afterwards into generalised fist fights and racist name-calling. The Portuguese would call the South Africans 'Boers' and the South Africans would chant 'half-castes' at the Portuguese. In Mozambique, interracial marriages were legal and the South Africans' implication was that all the Portuguese boys were of mixed race. Indeed, no one at the time had any idea that Tsafendas was of mixed race since,[70] as William Volbrecht said, he looked white and was accepted as such. This was when Dimitri heard the word 'half-caste' for the first time.

Miss Peters and Mrs Loock were two of Dimitri's teachers, while Mr J. Martindale was the housemaster at Nelson House.[71] Dimitri's favourite teacher was an English woman, Irene Walker, who invariably gave him good marks in History and English. One day he asked her what half-caste meant and she explained. Dimitri accepted the answer with a shrug of indifference; his mother and father were both white Greeks, so he was clearly no half-caste and therefore, the issue was irrelevant. It was just South African boys hurling insults at the Portuguese because they came from Mozambique.[72]

***

Every six months, Dimitri would travel home to Lourenço Marques on holiday. In Christmas 1928, the family had expanded with the arrival of Katerina (nicknamed Bushia). For Dimitri, holidays were an opportunity to spend time with his dad. Michalis was a keen amateur fisherman and they often went fishing in his small rowboat, although Dimitri did not enjoy it much. He hated seeing the fish flapping and dying in the bottom of the boat and pleaded with his father to return them to the water, which Michalis did. However, the boy's sensitivities did not preclude him from eating fish and seafood, particularly his favourite, lobster, in generous proportions. Dimitri was a hearty eater all his life; Katerina described him as a boy who could 'eat the table'.

His sister Katerina's earliest memories were of touring Lourenço Marques on the back of Dimitri's bicycle when she was around three and he 14, running errands and making trips to the grocery store. As Dimitri grew older, he was allowed to cycle further from the house and the city and he would often head to the city outskirts, to 'explore' them, he would say. There, he began to learn how poor Mozambicans lived, in sharp contrast to his own comfortable life in the city. He got to know every inch of the city, but also its outskirts, and he made friends in many places.[73]

Dimitri was very intelligent. Psychologists who examined him after the assassination calculated his IQ as 125,[74] placing him in the 'superior' or 'gifted' category, one level above that of university students and well above the average IQ of 90–110. His father hoped that he would become a marine engineer like himself or at least study to degree level at university, though he never pushed him. Native intelligence apart, Dimitri became remarkably knowledgeable, carefully stowing away everything he had learnt from Katerina, Artemis, Marika and Michalis. Not only was he a voracious reader, he became fluent at a very young age in Greek, Portuguese, Arabic and English.

In Lourenço Marques, the Greek community celebrated its National Day on 25 March and all the big religious feasts with parties when everyone dressed in the traditional fustanella. Dimitri was taught Greek dances, especially the pentozali, the trademark, five-step folk dance of Crete, by his grandmother. His father was an exceptional dancer who showed his skills in tsamikos, zeimbekiko, hasapiko and syrtaki dances. Dimitri's favourite was the zeimbekiko, performed by a single dancer while everyone surrounds him clapping hands, and would often perform it at Greek celebrations. At the Greek celebrations, Dimitri would proudly thrust Captain Michalis's flintlock into his belt with all the boys around him wanting to hold the gun. Once, Dimitri accidentally broke the hammer on the caplock mechanism. He was devastated, but his father managed to repair the damage and told him, as he invariably did, 'It doesn't matter, Mimako.' This attitude began irritating Marika because Dimitri, growing apace, often ran wild, causing mayhem in the house. She urged Michalis to discipline his son, but he rarely did,[75] his guilt for sending the boy away in his early years never seeming to leave him.

After books, Dimitri's favourite pastime was the cinema and in that, he was joined by his stepmother. Dimitri liked dashing period-film pirate movies starring the likes of Douglas Fairbanks, and he would often say he wanted to be a pirate when he grew up. Marika did not care for sword-fighting swashbucklers but would go along for Dimitri's sake. In later life, Tsafendas said his best memories of his stepmother were their visits together to the movies.[76] Dimitri's imagination was so vivid that he would act out scenes from movies or even books that he had read. He would give roles to his parents and siblings and many Sunday afternoons were spent by the family acting out a drama on the orders of the director Dimitri, who, of course, was the star of the show.[77]

When asked about his adult ambitions, Dimitri would say he wanted to become an actor, although he admitted that theatre seemed mundane and restrictive compared to film. He did, however, love Laurenço Marques's only theatre, the magnificent Teatro Gil Vicente, named in honour of the Portuguese playwright Gil Vicente. An outstanding building by any standards, not least those of colonial Africa, the thousand-seater theatre boasted an ornate, balconied façade with velvet-cushioned seats bearing the playwright's monogram inside. Opened in 1913, it was a gathering place for the wealthy and powerful, whether drama lovers or not; a place to see and be seen. Dimitri was taken there often by his parents – Michalis preferred theatre to cinema – and usually, he would rush to the huge balcony, looking for beautiful girls, greeting friends and soaking up the pre-performance atmosphere.[78]

Besides drama, Dimitri and Katerina shared a love for animals and Dimitri often toured the neighbourhood with a bag of bread scraps, feeding stray cats and dogs, which he would name for his heroes. When he acquired a dog of his own, he named it Bolivar after the Venezuelan revolutionary who led many South American nations to independence from Spain in the 18th century. It wasn't only cats and dogs for Dimitri. When a bird flew into a window of their home, he took it to his room and tended it for days, though eventually it died. Another time, he chased a cat with a mouse between its teeth until it dropped the tiny animal. Dimitri took the mouse home, but it, too, died.[79]

Like boys everywhere, Dimitri loved swords and Michalis had fashioned a toy sword from a piece of aluminium pipe. When playground fencing bouts began and the children decided which character they would be, most plumped for Robin Hood or the French musketeer d'Artagnan. Dimitri always chose Simon Bolivar. One of his sword-fighting opponents (Dimitri persuaded Michalis to make a sabre for him, too) was also his best friend. Manuel was a black Mozambican boy whose mother, Maria, occasionally helped Marika with housework. Maria often brought Manuel along so the boys could play together. Manuel had a fine, light voice which Dimitri much admired. Certainly, it was the exact opposite of Dimitri's boyish gruffness. Undaunted, Manuel taught Dimitri dozens of Mozambican children's songs, which they would sing together on the house balcony. In return, Dimitri taught his friend many of the Greek children's songs he had learnt. The two boys were inseparable, often spending nights in each other's house, sharing beds, playing and talking endlessly.[80]

Among Dimitri's other friends were his neighbours, George Grispos, Andrew Kavalieratos, Andreas Babiolakis, Tamos Tamburazis, plus a gang of local Mozambicans, including the blind boy who shared his swimming excursion. Dimitri would leave the house immediately after breakfast with specific orders from Marika as to how far he could go and to be back for lunch at 1 pm. Both instructions were regularly transgressed. One reason he did not rush home for the appointed hour was that his father was often late and while the family waited, Dimitri would steal a little more play time outside.[81]

Dimitri was a practical joker, which often got him into trouble. The Great Egg Joke was one which the family, and particularly Marika, would never forget. A Greek friend of Marika bought some hens, but, disappointingly, the hens appeared reluctant to reward their owner with eggs and she frequently complained to Marika about them. Having listened to this tale of woe several times, Dimitri stole one of his mother's shop-bought eggs, and with Victor and Evangelia acting as lookouts, he snuck the egg into the barren henhouse. When the neighbour returned that night, she found the egg and delightedly informed Marika. A day or two later, Dimitri planted another egg, and a few days later, a few more. The neighbour was so pleased she took a couple of the eggs to Marika as a gift.

The trouble was that Dimitri did not know when a joke had run its course. Preparing for their fourth sortie, the children saw the woman leave her house. Victor and Evangelia moved towards their lookout posts, and Dimitri had just opened the henhouse door, when the neighbour reappeared. Victor and Evangelia were her prisoners, they had not seen her return and had no time to warn Dimitri, who stood transfixed with eggs in his hands. Now it dawned on her why she was getting so few eggs – Dimitri was stealing them!

Furious, the woman began hitting Dimitri with her bag. He tried to explain, but she would not listen and, taking him by the ear, dragged him to Marika. Dimitri's stepmother was deeply embarrassed and joined in slapping Dimitri, while the other children wailed. It was when Dimitri began crying and swearing before God that he had not stolen the eggs that Marika's onslaught slackened. Victor and Evangelia confirmed that Dimitri wasn't stealing eggs but was putting them there, as he had the others, as a joke. Marika knew that the previous day she had bought ten eggs. She went immediately to her kitchen and discovered that five of the ten were missing and she knew she had used only one. The woman told Marika that Dimitri was caught with four eggs in his hands. Marika asked Victor and Evangelia to swear to God that they were telling the truth, a serious matter for a religious woman like Marika. The children duly swore and a swift calculation revealed that the number of eggs missing from her larder over recent days was the exact number found by the neighbour since her hens allegedly began laying. Convinced now that the three children were telling the truth, Marika nevertheless delivered a few final swipes at Dimitri, not so much for stealing her eggs as for making her look a fool in front of her neighbour.[82]

Another of Dimitri's pranks, though Marika did not think so, was to tie his own siblings to the pillars that supported their house. Letting down car tyres was a regular escapade and a particularly fine diversion, the Tsafantakis children thought, was to lob eggs and tomatoes from the balcony or the roof of their house onto people walking beneath. When Marika discovered that Dimitri had enrolled Victor as his assistant in this enterprise, she was furious and berated her husband: Victor was such a quiet boy and here was Dimitri leading him astray![83]

In his more innocent years, Dimitri demonstrated a marked propensity for malingering. He would fake illness to escape school or church and he showed his siblings how to do it by warming the thermometer so as to raise the mercury. Once when Dimitri complained that he was sick, a Greek doctor who was a friend of the family examined him. He concluded that the boy was perfectly fine. However, because he was fond of his young patient, he went along with the pretence.[84]

Around Dimitri's tenth year, his beloved Aunt Artemis arrived in Lourenço Marques from Alexandria. Dimitri was overjoyed and for some time, Artemis lived in her brother's house and spent a great deal of time with her former charge, who she had not seen for about three years. Eventually, Artemis moved out and married George Michaletos, the son of John Michaletos, Dimitri's godfather. All his life, Dimitri adored Artemis for her kindness to him in Egypt, and often visited her and ate at her house.[85]

Returning to Middleburg, Dimitri, a B-group boy, passed the Standard Three examination in December 1930. Two months later, his father applied to the South African Office of the Commissioner for Immigration and Asiatic Affairs for permission to send his four children, including Dimitri, to Transvaal for their education, to be accompanied by his wife. However, he withdrew his application[86] when he experienced serious financial problems. His partnership in Voutselatos's engineering firm ended, primarily as a consequence of the Great Depression then stalking the world. A little later, he would also lose his house, forcing the family to move to a much smaller one that he owned. In 1932, Dimitri had to leave the Middelburg school[87] because his father could no longer afford the fees. He had reached Standard Six, the first year of high school.[88]

Returning to Mozambique in his mid-teens, Dimitri enrolled again at the Anglican Mission School in Lourenço Marques, but he was bored and often skipped classes.[89] He told his father he wanted to quit school, get a job and earn his own money like his friends. Michalis was furious, perceiving the money he had spent sending him to school in South Africa as cash down the drain. Worse, Dimitri did not want to learn a trade but to get a casual job such as that of a waiter. Michalis offered him two choices: academic study or learn a trade. Dimitri opted for the second, but he also agreed to finish school, thus continuing evening classes at the Portuguese Mission School while working in the mornings.[90]

With his son's future earning power in mind, Michalis apprenticed Dimitri to a friend who owned an industrial workshop, the Vulcan Iron Works. There, he trained as an oxy-acetylene welder.[91] However, it quickly became clear that Dimitri did not like the job. His boss told Michalis that Dimitri was lazy and showed no interest in learning the trade. When Michalis remonstrated with his son, Dimitri replied that he was planning to get married to a rich woman in Mozambique so he would not have to work. Michalis was not amused, although, as it turned out, Dimitri was quite serious as he had drawn up a list of all the wealthy girls he knew in Lourenço Marques who were around his age. Michalis insisted that Dimitri must remain at Vulcan while also continuing at school.[92] He graduated in 1935, aged 17, and worked on and off at Vulcan until 1939. Eventually, to his boss's surprise, he mastered the trade of his apprenticeship and became a more than competent welder.[93]

Progressing beyond his infantile ambitions to be a pirate, Dimitri's dreams created the self-image of a rebel leader, a heroic figure battling for the underdog, a 'revolutionary rebel' as he called himself, righting wrongs in just wars. Simon Bolivar was a constant reference point. One day, his loyalty to the

South American freedom fighter caused panic. Asked by his class teacher what his plans were after leaving school, he said, 'I would like to liberate Mozambique from the Portuguese, just like Simon Bolivar liberated Latin America from the Spanish.' This remark, in Portuguese-ruled Mozambique, terrified his teacher, who hurriedly informed the family. 'Never mind,' the boy's father reassured her, 'he is young, he will mature.' Michalis was actually proud of his son's declaration, though he never told him so.[94]

At that time in Mozambique, it was traditional for Greek boys when 15 years old or thereabouts to visit a brothel for their first adult sexual encounter. Often the parents would give their sons the money and send them off with their blessing. Michalis was not one of these parents. When the issue arose among his teenage contemporaries, Dimitri was keen to go, but he dared not ask his father for the money and had to save up for the occasion. On the day agreed, Dimitri and his friends met outside a brothel near the harbour, which was frequented mostly by seamen. Although initially enthusiastic, Dimitri and the teenage gang lingered uneasily outside, debating whether to go ahead. At that point, a woman came out and invited them inside. The woman whistled and more women emerged. One took Tsafendas by the hand and led him to her bedroom. She was Portuguese with long black hair, but in Dimitri's eyes, elderly and unattractive. He was earlier told by his friends that he could choose someone else, but he was too shy to do so. The woman asked for money, which Dimitri gave her, then she began taking his clothes off. Deeply uncomfortable, unexcited by the woman and put off by her direct demands as to his preferences, Dimitri's first adult sexual encounter was a disaster. The woman's determined employment of her sexual skills to bring him to arousal only embarrassed him and finally, he leapt from the bed, hurriedly pulled up his trousers and, muttering 'Thank you, thank you', fled the brothel for the harbourside.[95]

Needless to say, the wonderful encounter he described to his friends was diametrically opposite to what had transpired. A few weeks later, when the other boys went back to the brothel for a second round, he declined to join them. It was Tsafendas's first and last encounter with a sex worker. When the question of prostitutes came up in the future, he would joke that he was too good-looking to need their services. The truth was he did not like the idea of paying for sex, believing that any woman who had sex with him should really like him. Further, it is difficult not to think that his first disastrous bordello experience never quite left him. It was many years later before Tsafendas felt he could reveal the true events of that night in Lourenço Marques.[96]

Michalis bought a newspaper every day, as well as historical and political magazines, which Dimitri, by then in his mid-teens, read from cover to cover. He would then cut out articles of particular interest and assemble them methodically in a series of scrapbooks. One volume held biographies and articles about people he admired; another contained accounts of historical events; two were dedicated to Greece and Mozambique, respectively, and a fifth consisted of contemporary articles about the modern world. Each volume was meticulously titled on the cover and the articles were illustrated by relevant images. These included photographs and drawings of Lenin, various heroes of the 1821 Greek Revolution, illustrations from the French and Russian Revolutions and, from more modern times, headshots of Sacco and Vanzetti.[97]

Michalis had talked to Dimitri about politics from an early age and translated several of the Italian texts for him. Among these was *Anarchy* by Errico Malatesta, one of Michalis's most admired thinkers. Dimitri also read some of his father's literature in English. He became familiar with the anarchist idea of 'propaganda of the deed', which advocated acts of violence, including bombings and assassinations. He absorbed the writings of Italian-American anarchist Luigi Galleani, which affirmed violence, including murder, to secure the removal of tyrants and oppressors. Galleani's American followers, *i Galleanisti,* had carried out a series of bombings and assassination attempts over the previous 20 years. Michalis agreed with most of Galleani's ideas, though he was becoming a little more conservative as he got older.[98]

Dimitri did not confine his political obsessions to his scrapbooks, however, and his loose tongue became a cause of friction with Marika. He would take his younger siblings to coffee shops for sweets and cakes, but then would become involved in political arguments with other patrons. The children would become embarrassed and his stepmother infuriated. Thereafter when they set off for the café, Marika would demand of Dimitri to keep his mouth shut, threatening to cut off his pocket money, though she never did. She feared that, as he became more independent, Dimitri would influence her younger children. She begged Michalis not to talk constantly to their son Victor about history and politics, as he did with Dimitri. Michalis agreed.[99]

Living under Portuguese rule, colonialism was the political imperative that dominated Dimitri's mind. Subject to its diktats and confronted with the visible manifestations of its power in the colonial offices in Lourenço Marques, he longed for Mozambicans to rebel against the system, often declaring that his great desire was to dynamite those very offices. When it came to blowing things up, the United States of America was never far from Dimitri's mind. From his first, painful venture into *Uncle Tom's Cabin,* America featured high on his list of political *betes noires.* He considered the 'Land of the Free' to be a myth and that freedom and democracy existed for white Americans only. He believed that white settlers had stolen the country from the Native Americans, forced them to live in locations and racially oppressed them like the Jews, blacks and other minorities. 'Liberation' was always the answer Dimitri gave when he was asked about his adult ambitions, clearly dreaming of becoming a revolutionary like Bolivar and his Cretan forebears and freeing Mozambique and other white-ruled African territories from the colonialists. His stepmother nervously warned him to keep such notions to himself because they would cause problems for them all if overheard by some Portuguese people.[100]

Michalis maintained a small workshop in the house where he worked on his ideas for new inventions or made toys for the children. He kept it locked because of the dangers the implements posed to his young family, and even Marika was not allowed to enter the workroom. However, as Dimitri grew older, Michalis invited the boy inside and taught him how to use his bench lathe and other cutting tools for dressing metals. What interested Dimitri more were the many books and newspapers that made the room as much a library as a workshop. Most of the books were about anarchism, politics and history. The majority of the books came from Italy and were in Italian. There were also newspapers that Michalis had brought from his time long ago in Padua, including copies of *l'Università Popolare,* and anarchist literature, which he received at home by mail. The workshop walls were hung with the portraits of prominent anarchists, including Mikhail Bakunin, Emma Goldman, Errico Malatesta and Peter Kropotkin, as well as the American anarchists Sacco and Vanzetti. Dimitri knew no Italian, but he was fascinated by this treasure trove and spent a lot of time in the workshop deciphering whatever he could.[101]

Dimitri knew that if one day he decided to blow up the Portuguese administration offices in Lourenço Marques or the Statue of Liberty in New York, knowledge of how to make the bombs would be essential. Thus when he was about 16 or 17, he spotted a manual on bomb-making in his father's workshop and became extremely excited. The book was in Italian and, knowing that his father would never translate it for him, he bought an Italian dictionary and tried to work out the instructions himself. Secretly, he began to experiment in the manufacture of bombs, including some filled with nails which he tested in a field near their house. One day something went wrong and an explosion destroyed a large part of the workshop. Marika ran screaming from the house with the toddler Katerina in her arms, and Dimitri, amazingly, escaped the blast without a scratch. What he did not escape was Marika's wrath. Setting Katerina down, she began furiously slapping him, but Dimitri accepted the blows silently. Katerina remembered the explosion clearly 80 years later even: 'He would make bombs stuffed with nails and so on and explode them. We could have been killed.'[102]

On learning that her stepson had set up the explosion following one of her husband's books, Marika seized the book and hurled it into the backyard furnace. When Michalis arrived, she berated him for filling his son's mind with what she believed were dangerous political ideas. 'He could have killed us all,' she shouted repeatedly. Finally, Marika threatened to leave Michalis and Dimitri and return to Egypt with the other children unless Michalis agreed to three demands: throw away all the anarchist material and stop receiving anarchist newspapers and literature from overseas; ban Dimitri from entering the workshop ever again; and stop talking and giving books to Dimitri about anarchism and politics.

Michalis tried to argue that the bomb manual was the only dangerous book, but Marika was adamant. Eventually, he agreed to stow all his anarchist literature in a storage room, to stop receiving anarchist literature from overseas and to cease speaking to Dimitri or giving him books on the subject.[103]

The promises were honoured only in part. Michalis made arrangements with his best friend, Dimitris Spanos, a Greek communist who owned a publishing company and a bookshop, to receive the anarchist literature there. Michalis did remember to scold his son for taking the book without permission and setting off explosions. However, the pair continued talking about anarchism and politics when Marika was not around.[104] The workshop blast was the explosion that Marika referred to in her statement to the police after Dr Verwoerd's assassination when she said Dimitri 'nearly blew up our house'.[105] The incident became widely known within the Greek community in Lourenço Marques, although Michalis always said it was an accident that happened while the boy was playing unwittingly with some of his workshop materials.[106]

As an older teenager, Dimitri began to take a less romantic view of politics and his growing awareness of the political realities was to become markedly enhanced when he got a job selling books and newspapers at Spanos's bookshop. Spanos was to become an enduring influence in Dimitri's life and worldview. Michalis met with his best friend almost every day, at the bookstore or in a café, where they talked and argued about politics, and young Dimitri was frequently an avid listener to their debates.

It was Michalis who insisted on his son getting this serious job so he could realise the responsibilities of earning a living. However, Dimitri came later to believe that his father had another aim in mind when he arranged for him to work for Spanos. He suspected that because they could no longer talk politics at home, Michalis sent him to Spanos to continue his 'education' along the 'correct' political path, and for his father, the correct path was anti-authoritarian. He had warned Dimitri many times, half-joking, half-serious, that he could do whatever he wanted in his life except become a fascist or a royalist. As to professions, he could be anything he wanted, even nothing at all, but he must never become a professional soldier or a policeman! Dimitri was warned that if he did, his father would immediately disown him.[107]

Spanos was a former miner who tried and failed to form a labour union in Johannesburg in 1902. Within a year, he was forced to flee the country because of his political activities and he relocated to Mozambique. As a member of the International Socialist League, he was well connected with socialists around the world, including notably William H. Andrews, a pioneer trade unionist and communist who was the first chairman of the South African Labour Party and later General-Secretary of the South African Communist Party.[108]

With financial assistance from Michalis, Spanos opened a general interest bookshop but, as the business flourished, again with financial help from Michalis, he started a news distribution agency, the first of its kind in the region, which funnelled magazines, newspapers and foreign publications, many with socialist content, to bookshops and kiosks throughout Portuguese East Africa. In time, Spanos expanded into printing and publishing, and his company, D. Spanos, Sucras., LDA., became the leading publishing house in Mozambique. Between 1915 and 1921, Spanos published *The International,* the International Socialist League's organ, and distributed it throughout East and Southern Africa. His socialist contacts would ship literary material to him from around the world, including the United States, and he would send Tsafendas to the port and airport to pick up the bundles, which would then be duplicated and distributed across the south of the continent, including South Africa.[109]

As for his new employee, the elder Greek's uncompromising, leftist ideology fitted perfectly with the youth's vision of how the world should be. It was a short step for Dimitri to a life-long conviction that Communism was the weapon that would bring this about. Happily surrounded by books in his new job, Tsafendas lost no time in familiarising himself with the contents of as many as he could handle. Some he read at work between attending to customers, others he took home and put back on sale when he had finished them. Thus he made intellectual discoveries denied to him by his truncated education. The first book Spanos gave his young employee was Emil Zola's *Germinal,* published in 1885. This was a fact-based novel of the harsh conditions faced by coal miners in 1860s France, their exploitation by mine owners and how they tried to improve their working conditions through industrial action. Spanos told Dimitri that similar situations were faced by miners all over the world and that he believed through Communism, and not anarchism, the international working class could improve its conditions. Spanos added strength to his argument by recounting his personal experiences in the mines of South Africa and of his failed attempt to form a labour union. *Germinal* quickly became Tsafendas's favourite book, surpassing *Uncle Tom's Cabin,* and played a hugely important role in turning him from anarchism to Communism.[110]

Another book from Spanos that became a favourite of Tsafendas was *The Home and the World,* the 1916 novel by Rabindranath Tagore. This story of a political awakening in colonial India, with its ever-present threat of violence, seized Tsafendas's imagination, and one character, Sandip, became an enduring inspiration in his courageous rejection of white power in the sub-continent. Thereafter, Tsafendas read anything he could find by Tagore and Zola and he often gave copies of *The Home and the World* and of *Germinal* to friends.[111]

Tsafendas's worldview widened further when Spanos introduced him to political theatre. One day, the Teatro Gil Vicente came up in conversation and Tsafendas remarked to his boss, 'You are the only Greek I know who doesn't go there.' Spanos explained that he refused to cross the threshold because the theatre's image was exclusively 'white' and it was heavily patronised by local colonials. Native Mozambicans wouldn't dream of going there, even if they could afford it. What's more, he said, he did not like the plays the management put on. Instead, Spanos read, and thrust on Dimitri, the political writings of dramatists such as Henrik Ibsen (*An Enemy of the People*), Eugene O'Neill (*The Emperor Jones*) and the stage plays and screenplays of Bertolt Brecht, Germany's leading critic of the capitalist world. Tsafendas particularly admired *The Emperor Jones,* O'Neill's 1920 exploration of the American occupation of Haiti, whose leading character, the African-American Brutus Jones, became another of his literary heroes.[112] Tsafendas was not to know this at the time, but the part of Brutus Jones had been played to huge acclaim by another of his heroes, the black American singer and actor, Paul Robeson. Robeson, the son of an escaped slave with roots in Nigeria, was a passionate socialist, a generous supporter of labour unions and workers around the world and later a leading member of the civil rights movement. In December 1934, he visited the Soviet Union and said, 'Here, I am not a Negro but a human being for the first time in my life. I walk in full, human dignity.'[113] This was headline news in the left-wing press, which reached Spanos's company. As for Tsafendas, Robeson's words hardened his hostility to the United States and further strengthened his conviction that Communism was the way forward.

Tsafendas worshipped Robeson as 'a giant', both in physical stature and for his courage and political influence. That he supported the Republicans in the Spanish Civil War fitted perfectly with Tsafendas's conception of the anti-imperialist. Later, wherever he travelled, Tsafendas would search for the great man's records. A particular favourite was 'Sometimes I Feel like a Motherless Child', though he was quick to point out this was not connected with his personal situation, that he was simply moved by the music and the lyrics about slavery. Best of all was the 'Song of Freedom', which he whistled, hummed and sang constantly, trying to imitate Robeson's dark, bass voice. He scoured Spanos's bookshop for news of Robeson and when he spotted a newspaper photo of him singing to workers, he snipped it out for his bedroom wall. He would continue singing Paul Robeson's songs until he died.[114]

Tsafendas admired Spanos hugely, but the boss had to make a living and Dimitri was not helping. With books and newspapers from floor to ceiling, his young assistant spent too many of his working hours reading instead of selling. Besides, he took to arguing with the customers. Ignoring his boss's complaints, Dimitri would challenge shoppers who bought right-wing newspapers and urge them to buy liberal journals instead. Early every morning, he would check the papers for the latest political developments so that he could argue more effectively with his opponents.[115] Another problem was Dimitri's laziness. The manager would ask him to deliver a batch of newspapers, but Dimitri always had an excuse, usually that 'Mr Spanos told me to read this book and I have to return it to him today'. His superior, a Portuguese man, knew of Tsafendas's 'privileged' relationship with Spanos, but would complain nevertheless. Spanos always said, 'It's OK, yes, I told him to read the book and return it today.' One of Dimitri's tasks was to distribute newspapers and magazines in Lourenço Marques. Mounted on a new bicycle his father had bought him for his 15th birthday and with a sack of papers hanging from his neck, he would speed around the city, in the centre and the outskirts. Some of his friends began calling him 'the postman'.[116]

Much as he admired Spanos, Tsafendas did not agree with him on everything. Firstly, his employer was an atheist and the two argued frequently about religion. Tsafendas would often seek Father Bertolis's help to counter Spanos's arguments. One day, Spanos gave his young employee a book entitled *Treatise of the Three Impostors*, a volume of uncertain origin and authorship, which denied the three Abrahamic religions. The 'three impostors' in the title were named as Moses, Jesus and Mohammed. The book disturbed Tsafendas and he began reading about other world religions. His faith was rocked, but he remained a Christian, arguing that even if God did not exist, Jesus was a wonderful man. A second disagreement concerned violence. In his youth, Spanos supported strong-arm tactics as a means of achieving political change, but later came to reject the use of force. Tsafendas, for his part, believed violence was sometimes necessary to bring about essential change.[117]

Despite their disagreements, it was Spanos who brought about a life-changing experience in his young assistant. On a regular basis, Spanos distributed books and newspapers in villages outside Lourenço Marques and in the rural areas. Not only did he carry socialist publications, he often delivered medication on request and supplied them free of charge. Sometimes, the locals would ask him to bring particular items from the capital, which he did on his next visit. Spanos, by then in his 60s and in failing health, began to reduce his rural trips to occasional weekends. One day, Tsafendas asked his employer to take him along on a visit to the villages. When Spanos drove up in his van, Dimitri was surprised to see him wearing old and shabby clothes. He was soon to realise why. Conditions in the villages were shocking – mud huts and hovels for houses, open sewers, no toilets, often no clean water, raggedly dressed people. It was then, to his embarrassment, that he realised why Spanos dressed as he did. And there stood Dimitri in neat, clean clothes! Impulsively, he seized a can of water and handfuls of mud and smeared the mess over his clothes, making them look old and dirty, too. Tsafendas, like most Europeans in Mozambique, had never visited the rural areas. He had been to poor parts of Lourenço Marques, but they were nothing compared to this. He felt ashamed that he lived in a large, clean house with electricity and running water when a few miles away, people were subsisting in tin shacks and cardboard hovels. He was further shamed by the hospitality of the rural poor, who shared with him what little food they had.[118]

The whole experience shook young Tsafendas to the core. The two slept that night in one of the villages, except that Tsafendas lay awake most of the time, pondering how he could assist these poverty-stricken people. In the morning, he told Spanos that he would persuade his father to buy food and he would bring it every week along with the books. Spanos smiled and patted Tsafendas on the shoulder. 'You can't feed all of them Dimitri,' he said, 'not even the government can.' What was needed, he said, was a socialist type of system, like that in the Soviet Union, where conditions of such poverty, he claimed, did not exist. Spanos then said something that stayed with Tsafendas forever: 'Give a man a fish and you feed him for a day, teach a man to fish and you feed him for a lifetime.' Spanos argued that the best way to get people out of poverty, especially the youngsters, was to educate them. That, he said, was why he brought literature to them. Eagerly, Tsafendas offered to teach the Mozambicans, especially the children, English and History. Spanos liked the idea and offered to help with books and teaching aids, and so Tsafendas began travelling to the villages each weekend, instructing the children and distributing Spanos's literature. Spanos often followed him and they spent many nights sleeping in the villages before returning home the next day. If Spanos could not go along, he paid one of his employees to drive Tsafendas there. Sometimes, the driver was Tsafendas's friend, George Grispos, who was also employed by Spanos. Convinced by Spanos's arguments, Tsafendas moved ever closer to a belief in the Soviet system. Further reading, talks with Spanos and encounters with Soviet seamen in Lourenço Marques strengthened his belief that Communism was the way of the future.[119]

Tsafendas needed no convincing that, as Spanos repeatedly said, education was the best route out of poverty to full freedom. He believed that all his life.[120] Thus, he determined to extend his teaching to Lourenço Marques. He contacted Father Bertolis, who promptly agreed, and poor youngsters from Lourenço Marques and the outlying villages began gathering regularly for lessons in the Anglican church. Dimitri was popular with the students because he made them laugh, and soon other pupils joined his class, including the children of Greek parents who wanted their young ones to learn English for free. Dimitri began teaching English, but soon added History to the curriculum. Spanos provided some books. Michalis was proud of his son's initiative and occasionally slipped into the class and observed him teaching.[121] That Dimitri had a talent for instruction is hard to dispute. In later life, he did the same thing at a higher level and was much prized by his employer. The fact is he enjoyed teaching and said he was happy to do it without payment.

One of the Greek pupils at Dimitri's lessons was Helen Kavadias. Their families were friends, she was eight or nine when Tsafendas first met her. Helen was friendly with the Tsafantakis girls and so got to know Dimitri outside of the classroom too. Dimitri would often take her along with his young sisters on trips for ice cream and to the beach.[122]

In 1935, Spanos died. Tsafendas was devastated by the loss of this man who was not only his mentor but his very good friend, an employer who did not just pay his wages but helped guide him towards his political destiny. To his surprise, he discovered that Spanos had told his wife to give him several books and publications that he knew he liked. Tsafendas treasured these forever, but after Spanos's death, he left the bookshop. The partners who took over the business did not share Spanos's leftist ideology and put an end to the trips to the villages. Grispos would drive Tsafendas there from time to time, but eventually, without funds or transport, the lessons and the literature deliveries ended.[123]

Tsafendas did not remain jobless for long, securing work almost immediately at a coffee shop, the Chai et Kiosk, owned by Peter Sideris, a friend of his father. Unsurprisingly, he was soon in trouble with the boss, a conservative Greek loyal to the Portuguese government, for arguing with the customers about politics. More than that, he turned the premises into a virtual distribution centre for communist literature. Every day he would turn up to work with a sack full of such publications which he got from various friends and associates of Spanos. He would start political conversations with customers and, if he perceived a positive response, he would offer the customer a book or pamphlet, some for sale, others free.[124]

Around then, Tsafendas began flirting with Sideris's oldest daughter who was slightly younger than him. He insisted that he was genuinely fond of the girl and that she was not on his hit list of wealthy Lourenço Marques girls, although she could easily have been since her father was one of the richest Greeks in the city. It was mission impossible anyway. The girl's mother suspected that something was going on because Dimitri frequently found an excuse to go to his boss's house, usually volunteering to bring the family groceries. She knew about

Tsafendas's racially mixed background and was horrified at the thought of having such as person as a son-in-law. Time after time, she told her husband not to send young Dimitri to their house because she did not want him around their daughters, but Sideris ignored her. He had enormous respect for Tsafendas's father and he liked Dimitri personally. Although he supported the Portuguese colonial government, Sideris was not racist and kept Tsafendas on his payroll despite the arguments with customers.[125]

Eventually, this was bound to end in disaster and it happened when Dimitri confronted a wealthy Portuguese businessman and city councillor. Dimitri denounced the man to his face as a fascist and accused him of exploiting Mozambicans. He told him, 'One day the Mozambicans will rebel against the Portuguese and take back everything you stole from them.' The outraged councillor, aware that Tsafendas was distributing communist literature from there, complained to Sideris and said he intended to inform the police because he considered his assistant a 'dangerous communist'. Reluctantly but feeling he had no choice, Sideris fired Dimitri. He knew that if he did not do so, he would be in serious trouble with the colonial authorities.[126] Portugal's security police, the International and State Defence Police (PIDE), recorded that Dimitri was dismissed for 'voicing Communist ideas'.[127] As for the fledgling romance with Sideris's daughter, without access to the house and the mother's implacable opposition, this relationship withered on the vine.

Although Spanos had died, Dimitri frequently visited Lourenço Marques harbour, no longer to collect books and magazines, but to check if any Soviet ships had docked. If one had, he would ask permission to board, then chat to the seamen, asking about life in the Soviet Union. Much to Marika's dismay, he would also bring crew members back home for lunch. Once, a Soviet mariner gave Dimitri a hat which he said was similar to one worn by Lenin. Dimitri wore the hat constantly, proudly proclaiming that it was identical to that worn by the leader of the Russian revolution. Slowly, Dimitri began to pick up some of the Russian language and he bought a Russian dictionary to expand his vocabulary. His exposure to the Soviet seamen was a further step on his path to a passionate belief in Marxism.[128]

After being dismissed by Sideris, Tsafendas applied for work at the Imperial Airways factory in Quilemane, Mozambique. In order to complete his application, he needed his birth certificate, which he collected from the offices of the Civil Administration. He was paralysed with shock when he saw that his mother's name was given not as Marika Tsafantakis but as Amelia Williams, described as a native Mozambican woman. He complained to the administrator that there must be a mistake, but the official double-checked the files and insisted that Amelia Williams was named as his mother. Shocked, confused and panicky, Dimitri raced home to see his father. Michalis was in the living room with Father Bertolis, Marika was in the kitchen and Katerina was upstairs. Neither Victor nor Evangelia were in the house. Michalis and the priest rose to their feet when Dimitri stumbled in, weeping and distraught. Dimitri went straight to the point and demanded to know if 'Mama' (Marika) was his real mother. Crying and wailing, he begged Michalis not to lie and to tell the truth.[129]

Michalis was stunned and, suspecting someone in the Greek community had revealed the hidden truth, asked what was he talking about. Who had told him otherwise? Certainly, Marika was his mother. When Father Bertolis supported Michalis, Tsafendas reacted furiously and accused them both of lying. He then collapsed into a chair at the table, his head in his hands, sobbing and hyperventilating in grief. Katerina, who was seven or eight at the time, heard the uproar and emerged from her room. Stricken, Michalis cradled his son's head in his arms. 'Mimako mou (*my Dimitri* in Greek) what's wrong?' he whispered. 'What happened? Who told you this?' Still sobbing, Dimitri retrieved the crumpled birth certificate from his pocket and handed it to his father. Michalis glanced at the birth certificate, then signalled to his wife, who had come in from the kitchen, the priest and Katerina to leave them. Marika and Father Bertolis went to the kitchen and Katerina, curious, stayed out of sight on top of the stairs.[130]

Alone with his son, Michalis hugged Dimitri tightly, then quietly, he began to tell the boy the truth, weeping softly himself as he did so. He said Dimitri's mother, Amelia Williams, was his housemaid, half-German and half-Mozambican from the Shangaan tribe, and that they had lived together and were lovers before he met Marika. He assured Dimitri that he and Marika loved him just as much as they loved their own children. Dimitri listened with his head lowered, eyes averted from his father. Dimitri then wanted to know where his mother was now. Sadly, Michalis said Amelia had died some ten years earlier. The boy stared, devastated. Where? How? Michalis could only say she died of tetanus, but he knew no more since he had only heard of her passing long after the event.[131]

Dimitri asked for a picture of her. His father shook his head, but described Amelia as he remembered her from those years as a beautiful, kindly, quiet and good person. He said he had loved her, but it was simply impossible for them to marry. He told how he had begged her to give up their child, promising that he would always look after him and bring him up as a full member of the family he started with his Greek wife. Dimitri could not hear enough: What clothes did she wear? What did she look like? What was her character? Michalis told his son everything he could remember about his mother, including, smiling as he said it, that she could not cook Greek food very well although she made very good tzatziki. Dimitri asked where she was buried, but Michalis did not know that either. He said he had tried to find her grave, but Amelia had left the village that Michalis knew and moved to another. No one could tell him anything more.[132]

Dimitri was saddened that Marika, who he loved, was not his mother, but devastated that he would never know his birth mother. Marika returned to the living room, hugged Dimitri, tossled his hair and kissed him. Calling him Mimako, she assured him that she loved him 'very, very much', that he was her son and would always be her son. Dimitri looked at her for the first time as his stepmother. He nodded his understanding of her love and they clung to each other, weeping softly. Father Bertolis knew it was time to leave and walked out without a word.[133]

Dimitri never referred to Marika as his stepmother; it was always mama, either directly to her or in conversation concerning her. When asked about his mother, he would say he had two, named Amelia and Marika. He considered Marika to be his mother, along with Amelia, until he died.[134] Michalis and Dimitri never spoke of his origins again. Katerina, although she had witnessed the scene, was not sure what had happened. Her parents did not tell her at the time and took the same approach with their other children, feeling they were too young to hear the whole story.[135]

Hoping against hope that she might actually be alive somewhere or at least that he might learn something more, perhaps the location of her grave, Dimitri asked the registrar of births and deaths in Lourenço Marques if they had a death certificate in her name. They had, and his last hope of her being alive vanished. The certificate said she died on 12 January 1927,[136] just two days before his ninth birthday. They would both have been in Lourenço Marques, perhaps only miles apart. For many weeks, Dimitri sought desperately to learn more about Amelia, particularly the location of her grave.[137] He visited Namaacha, her birth village, and several neighbouring Shangaan villages, and spoke to many of her tribespeople, but all they could say was that she was dead, no one knew where she was buried. Amelia's own mother had died many years earlier and Amelia apparently was her only child. Amelia left the village soon after her mother died and had no known living relatives. One thing Dimitri did discover was the home in Namaacha in which his mother was born and raised before she left to seek a better life with Michalis in Lourenço Marques. It was a simple mud hut.[138]

Despite the lack of knowledge about his mother, Dimitri continued to visit Shangaan villages, seeking to learn as much as possible about his origins and ancestry and the history and customs of his mother's tribe. He managed to pick up enough of the language to communicate and build the beginnings of a friendly relationship with the villagers. He even started teaching English and History to children there. Tsafendas went on visiting the village until he left

Mozambique and whenever he was back in Lourenço Marques, he would always return to the village and spend some days there.[139]

After the discovery of his origins, Dimitri decided to get away from Mozambique for a while. Thus, he did not pursue his job application at Imperial Airways, but on 9 August 1935, sought permission to enter South Africa. On 12 December 1935, the interior ministry refused his application, then confirmed the refusal on 24 April 1936.[140] No explanation was given, but the likeliest cause was his mixed-race status and his dismissal from Sideris's kiosk 'on account of his Communistic leanings', two of the reasons cited for later refusals.

Surprised and angry, Dimitri decided to slip across the porous Mozambican–South African border anyway and in 1936 found work at the Fountain Café near Pretoria railway station. He served customers and scrubbed tables there for two or three months, then travelled to Johannesburg and worked in three eating places, the City Tea Room, the Elgin Café and the Cosmopolitan Restaurant.[141] He also joined the South African Communist Party, although some resident party members considered him too young for political activism. Joining the party was Dimitri's first proud public statement of political principle and he was unhappy that some comrades did not share his enthusiasm. He paid his membership dues – two shillings and six pence per month – at a party office at the Trades Hall and joined eagerly in party activities, attending meetings and volunteering for duties such as distributing leaflets.[142] After a few months, Dimitri returned to the family home in Lourenço Marques to meet his new half-sister.[143] The baby was Eleni (Helen), who would become the closest of his siblings. Big, shambling teenager though he was, Dimitri loved children, and neighbours and friends of the family frequently called on him for baby-sitting duties. He responded gladly, always refusing to take money for his time.[144]

Back in Mozambique, Dimitri renewed his application for work at Imperial Airways and was accepted.[145] With his own money in his pocket, 18-year-old Dimitri played the part of teenager to the full, partying constantly. Before long, he was flirting again with Sideris's daughter. Soon afterwards, the girl's mother returned home and found him dancing with her daughter to music from a gramophone. Outraged, she berated him about his behaviour, stating, among other things, that he had the manners of his mother, making clear that she did not mean Marika, but his Mozambican mother. She was the first person ever to mention his real mother to Dimitri. Although everyone in the Greek community knew the circumstances of his birth, no one ever referred to it. Despite his anger at the abuse, Dimitri was so desperate to learn about his mother that he asked Mrs Sideris if she knew her. Angrily, the woman retorted, 'How could I have known your mother!' implying that they did not move in the same circles. Dimitri restrained his desire to punch her, lowered his head silently and left the house. Both Sideris and his daughter later apologised for Mrs Sideris's behaviour, but Tsafendas never approached the Sideris girl again.[146]

Michalis believed in the dictum *mens sana in corpore sano* (a healthy mind in a healthy body), but he had not managed to convince his son of the merits of athletic endeavour. However, Tsafendas had read somewhere about Jack Johnson, the first African-American heavyweight boxing champion of the world, and he took a sudden interest in that sport. Thus, he enrolled at the Teatro Varieta gymnasium, which was owned by a good friend and former business associate of his father, Willie Conte. Although no athlete, Dimitri took immediately to the noble art and, for some time, he dreamed of becoming a boxer.[147] At boxing, he got to know Reuven Levy, an older Jewish boy and a communist who acted as his trainer, and the two became close friends. Reuven had his own car and used it to teach Tsafendas to drive, and sometimes he even drove him on his teaching trips to the villages.[148]

Tsafendas won prizes at local boxing tournaments[149] and when his pugilistic prowess made him popular with girls, he had his first serious relationship. This was with a Mozambican girl named Stella. She was not on his list of wealthy women, in fact she was very poor, but he fell in love with her from the moment they were introduced by his friend, Manuel. Years later, Tsafendas said he had his first real sexual experience (he never considered his encounter with the prostitute to be such an experience) when he was 18, but he did not mention the name of his partner. He merely said she was 'a beautiful Mozambican girl' who he used to date. The assumption must be that this was Stella in 1936. When asked by his friends Manuel and Grispos how far he had gone with her, Dimitri would shake his head and say, 'A gentleman does not reveal such things.' He dated Stella for more than a year.[150]

When the Olympic Games came to Berlin in 1936, Tsafendas added a new addition to his pantheon of heroes, namely the black American athlete Jesse Owens, whose triumphs, which so angered Adolf Hitler, he followed closely. Although his practice of collecting newspaper cuttings had waned and he had little interest in athletics as such, Tsafendas searched everywhere for stories about Owens, creating a special biographical file for him and placing his picture on his bedroom wall.[151] About then, Tsafendas was ordered to report for military service in the Portuguese army. He attended the interview and a medical examination in Lourenço Marques and was found fit to serve, but was rejected because of his racial origins. Sons of European fathers and African mothers were not accepted for the military at that time. Dimitri was delighted. He had no wish to serve in a colonial army.[152] Sometime later, he fell victim to appendicitis and was hospitalised for the first time in his life, soon recovering full health.[153]

It was that same year, when Dimitri was just 18, that the Spanish Civil War broke out. Michalis had become very passionate about the conflict, searching for whatever news he could find of its progress. He told Marika that if he did not have children, he would have left her to go and fight with the International Brigades in Spain, as some of his anarchist friends had done. It was a remark he quickly regretted because Dimitri promptly expressed his desire to join the anti-fascist forces. Horrified to hear this, Michalis tried desperately to change his son's mind. He argued that he was too young and inexperienced and that he would have many opportunities to join a just cause in the future. Michalis said that he would surely die if anything happened to his son.[154]

Girls and cars were fine, natural interests for growing teenagers, but for Dimitri, in reflective mood, politics was rarely far from his mind. By this time, Dimitri was widely considered by the Greek community to be a communist and was often referred to as 'The Red'. In case there was any doubt, Dimitri made sure when he went out to wear a red carnation or a red rose in his lapel. After dark, he daubed communist and anti-Portuguese slogans on the walls of the city. His father was secretly pleased by this evidence of his son's political commitment, but Marika was terrified, fearing that he would get them into trouble with the colonial police.[155]

One day, not long after Mussolini invaded Ethiopia, Dimitri, along with George Grispos and Manuel, carried out what they considered to be a campaign of 'revolutionary acts' in 'solidarity with Ethiopia'. Using metal forks, they scored deep scratches into the paintwork of cars belonging to members of the Portuguese government in Mozambique and workers at the German and Italian embassies. The three friends would observe their targets until the coast seemed clear; two would then keep guard while the third, usually Dimitri, scraped the automobiles and often deflated the tyres. They only stopped after a story about MPs' cars being vandalised appeared in a local newspaper. No one ever discovered they were the culprits.[156]

In 1937, worried by his deteriorating financial situation, Michalis took a major decision; that he and his family should move to South Africa. His arrangement with his engineering partners in Lourenço Marques had broken down and he concluded that there was no realistic future for him in Mozambique. South Africa, on the other hand, appeared better equipped to survive the economic storms. Besides, it was familiar territory to him, since he had worked briefly in Pretoria after leaving Alexandria as a young man and before he moved to Mozambique in 1916.

On 17 July 1937, Michalis applied for permanent residence status in South Africa. The application was for himself, Marika and their four children; Dimitri was not included.[157] Michalis was aware that his oldest son had been denied entry to South Africa two years ago. Add to this that Dimitri was of mixed race and suspected by the Portuguese authorities of being a communist, and so he feared that including his son in the application could result in refusal for all of them. What he planned was to invite Dimitri to South Africa after he had settled there. If Dimitri were to not be involved in any new political confrontations, Michalis thought that subsequently, he might be able to secure a visa for him. Michalis was not comfortable with this plan, but believed that he had no other choice. He hoped also that leaving him behind might make Dimitri more mature.[158]

The family's application was accepted, and Michalis, Marika and the four children moved to Johannesburg later that year.[159] Michalis had not forgotten Dimitri, however. Quietly, he asked Artemis and Gerry Kyriakakis, a friend, to keep a watching brief on his son and to contact him if he got into trouble in any way. Dimitri still wanted to go to Spain and fight General Franco, and father and son often argued heatedly about it, something they rarely did otherwise. Eventually, with persuasion from Aunty Artemis, Dimitri agreed to drop his plan. Michalis feared that Dimitri might be tempted to renege on his promise and so before he left, he made his son swear to him that he would not go to Spain.[160]

Michalis retained ownership of the house in Lourenço Marques and Dimitri enjoyed his new role there as lord of the manor, living in spacious quarters where he could do whatever he wanted, whenever he wanted. Michalis had shipped his gramophone and radio to South Africa, but friends supplied musical replacements for the many noisy parties Dimitri organised. His male friends brought their girlfriends and the house was almost constantly occupied. Manuel had practically moved in with him. The two were virtually inseparable. Social lives apart, both worked for Imperial Airways after Tsafendas had intervened to get Manuel a job there. Tall, slim and good-looking, a lively talker and a fine singer and dancer, Manuel was very successful with the ladies. Dimitri soon found that being a friend of Manuel was a useful factor in his own search for success with the opposite sex and he admitted openly that if it was not for his friend, he probably would not have had a girlfriend at all. He was not alone in benefitting from Manuel's aura. Another Greek in the group, Andreas Babiolakis, told, 'We were all hanging around with Manuel hoping to get some of the bones he left. We were all ugly, especially in comparison with him, particularly Dimitri!'[161]

Tsafendas agreed with Babiolakis's comment and happily compared Manuel to Paul Robeson and himself to Quasimido. However, their friendship went much deeper than seeking girlfriends together. They had known each other since childhood, long before girls were an issue, and they would always remain friends. After leaving Mozambique in 1939 and throughout the following years, Tsafendas wrote and sent gifts to Manuel from many of the places he visited. Often the presents were items of clothing because Manuel always had an eye for fashion. For Manuel's wedding, Tsafendas sent his friend a suit, and, through his aunt Artemis, a bouquet of red roses. Whenever Tsafendas returned to Lourenço Marques, Manuel was one of the first persons he visited.[162]

On 17 January 1938, Dimitri, now equipped with a Portuguese passport, applied for an entry visa into South Africa. He wanted to see his family, perhaps get a job and eventually relocate there. In July, his application was rejected. He was given no explanation, but it appears from police documents that the refusal was based on a description of him by the South African Consul-General in Lourenço Marques as a 'half-caste', suspected of being 'engaged in disseminating Communistic propaganda', who was dismissed by Sideris 'owing to his Communist leanings'.[163]

Later that year, Dimitri came to the authorities' attention again when a dispute arose over a decision by the Lisbon government to require Mozambique to grow cotton for the Portuguese textile industry. The effect was to send the Mozambican economy and workers into free fall. Tsafendas was outraged and, full of Marxist zeal, he handed out copies of the Communist Manifesto to cotton workers and to his colleagues at Imperial Airways and spoke out publicly against the new order. Making no secret of his disdain for the Portuguese government, he scribbled his views on city walls, proclaiming his support for an independent Mozambique based on majority rule. Manuel accompanied and assisted his friend in all of these activities.[164] Reports that Tsafendas was 'spreading Communist propaganda' soon reached PIDE.[165] The security police investigated the claims but did not arrest him on grounds that the accusations were 'never proven'. Presumably, none of those who accepted Dimitri's literature told the police who had given it to them. In stilted formal language, a PIDE report said it was 'quite possible' Dimitri was 'engaged in disseminating Communistic propaganda', but there was 'not sufficient evidence in substantiation of this belief'.[166]

Nonetheless, this incident dogged Dimitri for the rest of his life since it was the first item in a PIDE file titled, 'Secret Criminal Record nº 10.415 of Demitrios Tsafantakis'.[167] The file got steadily fatter as the years passed and by the time of his arrest in 1966, it totalled some 130 pages, containing a detailed account of his life and identifying him as 'a partisan for the independence of Mozambique'.[168] In a report written in 1961, PIDE stated that while Tsafendas was 'residing in that Province (Mozambique), he was twice a suspect of Communist activities, but evidence of such activities was never found'.[169] This was a reference to his dismissal by Sideris. Clearly, PIDE was by then keeping a close watch on Tsafendas, seeking an opportunity to catch him in communist or anti-Portuguese activities.

Having lost his job at the airline factory because of his suspected involvement in disseminating communist propaganda, Dimitri was hired, after a word from Michalis, by Gerry Kyriakakis, who owned Olympia café, as a waiter. As a result, he became close to the Kyriakakis family, particularly the youngest daughter, Ira, the one who had attended his English classes. However, once again ignoring all warnings, Dimitri argued with the patrons about politics, particularly on the cotton issue, and pressed communist publications on the customers. Eventually, Kyriakakis decided that Dimitri was jeopardising his business and, despite his friendship with Michalis, he dismissed his young waiter. Ira Kyriakakis saw Dimitri as someone who was 'very passionate about politics'. She said, 'He was a communist and very much against the Portuguese and colonialism generally … he did not speak about anything else, only politics.'[170]

Dimitri now turned his attention to South Africa again. Having been refused a visa, he decided that having entered that country illegally once before, in 1936, he would do the same again, and in 1939 he did just that, slipping across the Mozambique border. He did not know it at the time, but he was not to be allowed to return to Mozambique, the land of his birth, for 24 years, banned and rejected time after time because of his political activities. A 1953 PIDE report stated that, before leaving for South Africa, Tsafendas had 'voiced Communist ideas' and 'distributed such propaganda in the Portuguese colonies', actions that led to his ban.[171] His numerous applications to return were invariably refused. For now, Tsafendas had his eyes turned to the south of the continent.

Chapter 4

Tsafendas and Verwoerd in South Africa

Widely perceived as the embodiment of South African nationalism, Hendrik Frensch Verwoerd, the second child of a deeply religious Dutchman, Wilhelmus Johannes Verwoerd, and Anje Strik, was born near Amsterdam, Netherlands, at 4 pm on 8 September 1901. Both Wilhelmus, a partner in a grocery business, and his wife felt a strong emotional attachment to the Boers fighting the British in faraway South Africa and in 1903, they left Holland and moved to Cape Town. Hendrik was 18 months old.[1] In later years, the very fact of his being foreign-born prompted Verwoerd to identify fiercely with the land of his adoption, constantly seeking to prove his loyalty by being more Afrikaner than the Afrikaners.[2] In 1912, Wilhelmus Verwoerd took his family to live in Rhodesia, but they returned to South Africa in 1917.[3]

A clever and pious youth, Hendrik's first career thoughts were directed towards the Dutch Reformed Church and life as a minister, but in the event, he chose the world of academe.[4] A star student at the highly rated Afrikaner seat of learning, Stellenbosch University, he wrote his master's thesis on psychology and philosophy in 1922.[5] Within a year, he became a lecturer in psychology at Stellenbosch[6] and in 1924, Verwoerd attained his PhD, publishing the first such thesis written in Afrikaans. He entitled it, 'An experimental study of the blunting of emotions'.[7] It was at Stellenbosch that Dr Verwoerd met Elizabeth (Betsie) Schoombee, a fellow student the same age as himself, who was to become his wife. Betsie's specialist subject was Afrikaans Nederlands literature and she became one of the first women in South Africa to obtain a master's degree at a time when few women aspired to a university education.[8] She was also a founding member of the Student Women's League.

Three years after starting his career as a lecturer, Dr Verwoerd was offered a scholarship worth R1800 by Oxford University, but he preferred Germany as his next arena of study. Rejecting Oxford's dreaming spires, he accepted a German scholarship worth half as much and during 1926 and 1927 studied psychology at the universities of Hamburg, Leipzig and Berlin.[9] This was a time in Germany when national socialism was acquiring recognition as a growing political force. In 1925, Adolf Hitler had just been released from prison, having published *Mein Kampf* outlining his life and political ideology. It was in Germany that Verwoerd married Betsie.[10] During a visit to the United States in December 1927, Dr Verwoerd learnt that he had been offered a professorship in applied psychology and psychotechnics at his alma mater, Stellenbosch University.[11] Returning to South Africa in 1928, Dr Verwoerd became the chair in applied sociology and social work at Stellenbosch.[12] Betsie, turning her back on a teaching career, devoted her life to her husband's professional advancement and to their growing family, giving birth eventually to five sons and two daughters.[13]

Twenty years before apartheid became national policy, the Verwoerds practised race segregation in their own home. They refused to employ black workers[14] and Betsie educated their children at home to isolate them from contact with 'inferior negroes'.[15] There was gossip at the time that Betsie herself might have a black bloodline in her ancestry.[16] As well as caring for the children, Betsie expressed her personal support for her husband's work and policies, arguing on his behalf with vigour and intelligence.[17]

During the 1930s, Verwoerd demonstrated his concern for poor, working-class Afrikaners by searching for ways of improving their status, while simultaneously campaigning in the harshest terms against Jews fleeing Nazi Germany for refuge in South Africa.[18] In 1936, a chartered ship, the SS *Stuttgart*, reached Cape Town with 500 German Jewish refugees. It was the last large refugee vessel to leave Germany before the outbreak of war in 1939.[19] Billed as a Stellenbosch professor, Verwoerd led an impassioned campaign to keep the *Stuttgart* refugees out, arguing that Jewish immigration would lead to the 'downfall' of South Africa.[20] As well as addressing large anti-Semitic protest rallies in the Cape area with other Stellenbosch professors,[21] Dr Verwoerd presented a formal case against the refugees' admission to the Hertzog-Smuts government.[22] His arguments were accepted and the government denied the refugees permission to land.[23] Later that year, 75 German Jews arrived aboard the ship *Guilio Cesare* and Dr Verwoerd protested successfully again.[24]

The year 1937 was a key one for Verwoerd with him joining the Broederbond, swiftly becoming one of its leading figures. In 1940, he was voted onto its executive council, of which he remained a member until his appointment in 1950 as the country's Minister for Native Affairs.[25] The chairman of the Broederbond for many years and a close friend of Dr Verwoerd was Piet Meyer, a Nazi fanatic who had named his son 'Izan', which is 'Nazi' spelt backwards.[26] When Verwoerd became Prime Minister, he lost no time in appointing Meyer as chairman of the SABC.[27]

It was also in 1937 that Johannes Strijdom, the nationalist leader in the Transvaal, offered Dr Verwoerd the post of editor of *Die Transvaler*, a newly established Afrikaans-language newspaper which would become the mouthpiece of the National Party.[28] Verwoerd accepted the offer with alacrity and piloted the newspaper along hyper-nationalist lines, promoting the prospect of a South African republic and regularly attacking blacks and Jews. Verwoerd invariably referred to black Africans as 'kaffirs'[29] and believed that God made the black man to be in perpetuity a 'hewer of wood and drawer of water' for the white man.[30] He also denounced Jews as an obstacle to the Afrika-ners' economic well-being.[31] Raucous in tone and making no attempt to disguise its race hatred while simultaneously praising Hitler, *Die Transvaler* was often likened to Nazi hate sheets.[32]

Dr Verwoerd's first editorial on 1 October 1937 was an anti-Semitic tirade that sought to present the 'Jewish issue' not as a race problem but as a question of economics. Dauntingly entitled 'The Jewish problem regarded from a nationalist point of view: A possible solution: Proportional distribution in trades and businesses the first great necessity',[33] the article proposed a solution. Verwoerd suggested that because the involvement of Jews in business harmed Afrikaners economically, there should be a quota system that would bar Jews until they comprised not more than 5% of South Africa's commerce and industry (*eewewigte verspreiding*). This prompted Jewish businesses to pull their advertising from the paper, resulting in another anti-Semitic tirade from Verwoerd.[34]

In 1937, the Nationalist Party called on the government to withdraw recognition of Yiddish as a European language and to bar Jews from certain professions.[35] At a crucial time in world history, Dr Verwoerd, in his role as editor, began to give form and content to nationalist ideas concerning the separation of races, which were to become systematised in due course as the policy of apartheid. From his *Die Transvaler* soapbox, Verwoerd attacked not only Jews and blacks but the British, too.[36]

Tsafendas entered South Africa for the second time, probably by hitch-hiking or stowing away on a freight train, and moved in with his family in Johannesburg. It was the year the Second World War broke out. His father was employed by the South African government, which declared war on Germany shortly after Britain's declaration on 3 September 1939. Michalis never spoke about his job, but the family assumed it was with submarines again since his work trousers were always wet to the knees.[37] Tsafendas began looking to develop his career skills and signed on for welding classes at Progress College.[38]

South Africa was many miles from the roar of the guns in continental Europe. Johannesburg's cinemas and bars were open and nightlife was in full swing, all entertainment enjoyed by Dimitri and his sisters and friends, some of the latter acquaintances from his 1936 stay. One of Michalis's good friends, the Egyptian Consul in Johannesburg, came to dinner. Michalis would put on Arabic music records or tune the radio to Arab stations and he, the Consul and Dimitri would sing Arab songs together. The diplomat was impressed that Dimitri knew so many Arabic melodies and often brought him gifts. He would also ask him to translate Greek documents for the consulate, which Dimitri did free of charge.[39]

With Dimitri, however, politics was never far away and he quickly renewed his links with the Communist Party. He attended meetings on the steps of Johannesburg City Hall addressed by leaders he named as Wolfson and Joffe, joined the boiler workers and welders union, delivered party leaflets to coffee shops and under cover of darkness smeared anti-Nazi slogans on city walls, often with money from Michalis to buy the paint. There was strong opposition to Communism in South Africa and not only did Tsafendas argue with the party's opponents, he fought them in the streets. More than once, he ended up with his face bruised and his clothes torn after brawling with thugs of the Ossewabrandwag and other extreme right-wing organisations. He always said his side won. Because of his heavy build, he provided security at party meetings and acted as a bodyguard for local communist leaders.[40]

Tsafendas stored many communist documents at the family home in Johannesburg and invited party members there to make political placards. Although Communism was not illegal at the time in South Africa, Marika was terrified that her stepson's activities would bring trouble on the family and she often wailed that 'he will send me to my grave before my time'.[41] She was right that Dimitri's unconcealed activism, notably leaflet distribution, would soon be noted by the authorities.

There was romance in his life too. Sarah[42] was a South African Jewish girl, the older sister of Evangelia's friend. They met when Dimitri accompanied Evangelia to Sarah's house. He was immediately stricken. Sarah was slightly younger than he was, soft spoken and very beautiful. Both were shy, Dimitri to such an extent that he could say little more than hello and goodbye. Evangelia tried to discourage him, saying Sarah was 'a very serious girl' from a strict family who would marry a Jewish boy someday and would have no time for him. Nevertheless, Tsafendas wrote a letter to Sarah and asked Evangelia to take it to her. Sarah showed Evangelia the letter, which said how much Dimitri liked her, how beautiful she was and that he would very much like to meet her privately as he had never felt this way before. Sarah sent a reply via Evangelia and so it remained for several months. They only saw each other when Evangelia was present and all they ever said was hello and goodbye, although the letter exchanges went on every four or five days.[43]

Eventually, Dimitri found the courage to speak to Sarah and discovered to his surprise that she liked him and wanted to continue seeing him. It seems he had impressed her with his knowledge of literature and with the many books she had seen in his room when she visited Evangelia. What impressed her most was his knowledge of Hebrew history and his story of being raised by his grandmother, who was Jewish. Obviously, this was a gloss on the truth because it was his great-grandmother Victoria who was Jewish and she had raised his father, not Dimitri. Sarah later discovered the error, but Dimitri managed to convince her it was a misunderstanding and he meant to refer to his great-grandmother.[44]

Sarah's father did not allow his daughter to go out with boys and she only saw Dimitri when her older sister or Evangelia or both were present. Thus the father did not know of the feelings they had for each other. Hemmed in by chaperones, the relationship lasted a little over a year, ending in 1941 when Evangelia moved out of the Tsafantakis family home to get married in Pretoria. This made it impossible for the would-be lovers to meet, although by then, the relationship had begun to cool.[45]

Soon after the family moved to South Africa, Michalis Tsafantakis met a Greek man in his early-mid-30s named Charles (Harilaos) Nissiotis. Finding him to be hard-working, kind and honest, Michalis thought he would make a good husband for his eldest daughter, Evangelia, although she was then only 16. Meeting Evangelia for the first time, Nissiotis was delighted to find such a beautiful prospective bride. They became engaged, with the wedding itself planned within the next couple of years. Tsafendas strongly opposed the proposed marriage, pointing to the difference in ages and arguing with his father that Evangelia should be allowed to find a husband for herself. However, he changed his mind when he met Nissiotis, who not only had the qualities his father had noted but was also politically liberal and anti-Nazi, fitting perfectly with Tsafendas's worldview. The two men spent a lot of time together, indeed more than Evangelia and Charles did, and Tsafendas got along with Nissiotis better than he did with his half-sister. As for Evangelia, she was very fond of Charles and happy with the wedding plans, while knowing she had to do what her father decided for her anyway.[46]

In August 1939, the signing of the Molotov–Ribbentrop Non-Aggression Pact between the Soviet Union and Nazi Germany caused Dimitri and his father to have one of their rare arguments. Michalis was deeply upset that Stalin should consort with the Nazis, while Dimitri, perhaps blinded by his juvenile passion for Communism, defended the Soviet leader. However, in time he changed his position, sharing his father's disappointment that the Soviets had sided, even briefly, with Hitler's Germany. Dimitri's avid interest in the progress of the war was reflected in his consumption of newsprint. He bought two or three newspapers every day, spending hours following the latest developments.[47]

In May 1940, Tsafendas secured a job as a welder with the British Mining Supply Company in Johannesburg,[48] a crucial move since the company was engaged in war work – the production of armoured vehicles – and this prevented Tsafendas's immediate deportation when it was discovered he had entered South Africa illegally. What happened was that Tsafendas applied for permanent residence in 1941, whereupon investigations revealed that he had crossed into South Africa without a residence permit, thus contravening Article 2(a) of the Aliens Act No. 1 of 1937. On 6 August 1941, at 'H' Court in Johannesburg, a magistrate fined him £12.10s or one month of hard labour. Tsafendas paid the fine and was released and given a residence permit valid for a single year.[49]

As a known communist, Tsafendas remained under the watchful eye of the South African authorities. His official position and the authorites' suspicions were set out in a letter dated 13 October 1941 from the Commissioner for Immigration and Asiatic Affairs to the Commissioner of Police in Pretoria. This document stated that Tsafendas received permission for temporary residence because his job with the British Mining Supply Company was 'controlled labour', that is, essential war work. However, the letter pointed out that Tsafendas had been refused an entry visa for South Africa when he made earlier applications from Mozambique. The Commissioner for Immigration also noted the report from the South African Consul-General in Lourenço Marques that Tsafendas was a 'half-caste' who had been dismissed by a newspaper distributor for 'Communist leanings'. In conclusion, the letter said: 'The above information is passed to you in order that the activities of Tsafendas may be watched, and I will be glad if you will advise me in due course should anything to his detriment become known.'[50]

One week later, the Pretoria Police Commissioner was sent a reassuring letter by the Deputy Commissioner of Police, Witwatersrand Division, which included Johannesburg where Tsafendas was working, The letter, dated 20 October, stated that 'from a security point of view, nothing detrimental to Tsafendakis (Tsafendas) is known in this division and so far there is no evidence that the man has shown any Communist tendencies since he entered the Union'. Noting that Tsafendas was employed on 'essential war services as a welder on army filter plants',[51] the letter added that he had registered as required under the Aliens Registration Act, that his parents lived in Pretoria and his father was employed by Iscor Iron and Steel Works as a fitter and turner. It seems that, for once, Tsafendas had let his head rule his heart and gave no sign of his communist leanings while at work.

***

In the early years of the war, Dr Verwoerd's *Die Transvaler* editorials invariably hailed Germany's battlefield victories while playing down Nazi losses, but his handling of news dispatches in support of the swastika led to a significant personal defeat. In 1941, the Johannesburg newspaper, *The Star*, accused Dr Verwoerd of falsifying the war news in Germany's favour. The editorial making this charge was headlined 'Speaking up for Hitler'.[52] Verwoerd sued for defamation, demanding damages of £15,000. In his judgment, Judge Phillip Millin painstakingly itemised ten occasions on which, he said, Verwoerd had manipulated the news. He said:

> *There have been proved two very grave cases of the publication of false news in reckless disregard of whether it was true or false; six cases, on the whole less serious but still clear cases of falsification, where news, originally correctly reported, was falsely restated for the purpose of editorial comment; and two cases in which news was falsified by means of misleading headlines. On the evidence, he, Dr Verwoerd, is not entitled to complain. He did support Nazi propaganda, he did make his paper a tool of the Nazis in South Africa, and he knew it.*[53]

The judge dismissed the case and awarded costs against Dr Verwoerd. Supporters of Verwoerd said the judge ruled as he did because he was Jewish.[54] Verwoerd was not the only member of his family who supported the Nazis during the war. His wife Betsie was a member, indeed a section commander, of the Ossewabrandwag.[55] Voerwoed did not join for fear membership might compromise his position with *Die Transvaler* and the National Party. However, he fully supported his wife's activities for the organisation.[56] Many years later, Betsie claimed that the Ossewabrandwag had attempted to kill her husband on 22 October 1941, because he opposed the group.[57] However, she produced no feasible evidence for this and what seems likelier is that she wanted to remove the stain of her husband being a Nazi supporter during the war. She did much the same in 1960 when Verwoerd's standing was at a nadir after the Sharpeville massacre. Again she claimed that her husband had received threats to his life, but that he ignored them. According to two leading South African journalists, David Beresford, correspondent of the British newspaper, *The Guardian*, and Desmond Blow of the *Sunday Times*, as well as Gordon Winter, former agent of the South African secret services, Betsie made up the 1960 story in an effort to boost her husband's waning popularity and endow him with a heroic status.[58]

In 1941, with the war machine rolling through Europe, Dr Verwoerd wrote, 'The Afrikaner honours Germany's achievements in many fields.'[59] By 1943, however, as the German forces began suffering major losses, he toned down his editorials. This change of stance came too late to redeem his reputation, however, as he was by then firmly established in the eyes of his critics as a 'tool of the Nazis'.[60] In 1943, the National Party offered Dr Verwoerd a safe seat in that year's elections, but he decided to remain editor of *Die Transvaler*.[61]

***

In late 1941, Evangelia and Charles Nissiotis were married. Tsafendas helped enthusiastically with the preparations and gifted the newlyweds an expensive, modern coffee table made of wood with a cigarette holder and an astray. The table is still being used by Mike Vlachopoulos, the son of Dimitri's half-sister, Eleni.[62] Nevertheless, Dimitri undermined his generous gesture by starting a huge political row at the wedding. Overhearing two Greek guests at a nearby table talking in supportive terms about Hitler and the German victories in Europe, he rounded on them, denouncing them as 'Nazis and fascists', whereupon arguments erupted. Michalis and Charles had to be called on to calm things down. Tsafendas's step-sister Katerina said, 'He was always doing things like this. You couldn't take him anywhere, he would always embarrass us. He couldn't keep his mouth shut, he would always find someone to fight with. If he overheard a conversation about something he disagreed with, he would enter the conversation and turn it into an argument. Fascists and colonialists were like a red flag for him, especially the Nazis. When he saw one, oh my God what could he do! It was like a red rag to a bull.'[63]

In the aftermath of the wedding row, some guests attempted to console Evangelia by telling her that Dimitri was not her full brother anyway. This was the first she had heard of Dimitri's origins. She was shocked and at first, refused to believe it. However, her parents confirmed the story and also revealed the truth to their younger children. The siblings were surprised but reacted in a matter-of-fact way and nothing changed in their relationship with their half-brother.[64] Soon after, Dimitri left South Africa and despite many dogged efforts, he was not able to return for 21 years.

Tsafendas's employment with the British Mining Supply Company ended during the first half of 1942, when he was fired for 'irregular attendance and loafing'.[65] He told his parents he was leaving for Cape Town because he wanted to join the navy and fight the Nazis.[66] On 18 April 1942, the authorities wrote to Tsafendas at his father's house in Johannesburg requesting that he apply for an extension to his temporary residence permit, due to expire on 6 August 1942. There was no reply because Tsafendas was already in Cape Town.[67]

On 8 June 1942, Tsafendas applied for a permit to leave South Africa by sea for the United Kingdom. The Witwatersrand police official who had reported favourably on Tsafendas in October 1941 now told the Commissioner for Immigration that no reports of subversive activities had been received and the police had no objection to an exit permit for Tsafendas. However, when Tsafendas's political beliefs and activities in Mozambique were made known to the British High Commissioner, Mr Cockram, he declared himself to be 'not in favour of this type of man being granted facilities to go to England'.

The refusal was conveyed to the chief immigration officer in Cape Town on 18 June in a letter that reiterated the original description of Tsafendas as a 'half-caste' but which added that Tsafendas was 'engaged actively in Communistic propaganda' not only in Mozambique, but also while in South Africa. The letter said he had only been allowed to stay in South Africa because he was engaged in crucial war work and it concluded, 'As he has now been discharged from his employment, he should be ordered to return to Lourenço Marques forthwith'.[68]

In the event, the order came too late. On 13 June 1942, five days before his deportation was requested, Tsafendas left Cape Town aboard the Greek freighter SS *Eugene Livanos*, on which he was employed as a mess boy. He was 24 and his destination was Canada.[69] It was the start of an odyssey that would take him through many countries and across miles of oceans. This would be the last time he would see his father and he was not to see the rest of his family for more than two decades. The last thing his father told him was to become 'a useful member of society'. The words stayed in Dimitri's mind for the rest of his life.

Chapter 5

Enter the Tapeworm

Avoiding deportation to Mozambique by a matter of days, Tsafendas embarked on a journey to North America to fight the Nazis, brimming with anti-fascist zeal and eager to add his name to the roll of family heroes. It never happened. The *Eugene Livanos* was a Greek merchant ship crewed largely by roughnecks lacking the discipline of a naval vessel. Throughout the 81-day voyage from the Cape of Good Hope through the Atlantic Ocean to Canada there was the constant, nerve-wracking fear of U-boat attacks, but just as upsetting for Tsafendas was persistent below-the-deck violence. The men smoked marijuana and fought continually among themselves.[1] Some of them heaped constant abuse on the few black seamen. Tsafendas was angered by this, but since he was alone, he did nothing. Later, he felt ashamed that he did not have the courage to stand up and defend his black shipmates.[2]

Worse was to come when some of the crew wanted to have sex with Tsafendas. Two men tried to rape him, but he beat the younger one and the other backed off. Furious, Tsafendas reported the attack to the second officer, who lectured the two assailants and assured Tsafendas that it would not happen again. It never did happen again, but most of the crew turned against Tsafendas for what they saw as a betrayal of his fellow crewmen to their superiors.[3]

The freighter reached its destination, Saint John in New Brunswick, on 1 September 1942.[4] Here was a small town where a native of Lourenço Marques should have felt at home since its economy was based on shipbuilding, with a dry dock that was among the biggest in the world. However, all Tsafendas could think of was getting away from his crewmates. Disembarking as soon as the ship docked, he reported to the Canadian immigration office and naively declared that he did not want to go back to the *Eugene Livanos* and wanted a transfer to another vessel. When officials said he must return to the *Livanos*, Tsafendas refused and so was arrested as a deserter. He was taken first to a detention barrack for seamen in Montreal, then sent back east to Halifax, Nova Scotia, where he was held for many weeks while the authorities debated his future.[5]

It was during those empty days behind bars in Halifax that Tsafendas heard endless horror stories from his fellow detainees about Allied ships being torpedoed by German U-boats, which were then ranging freely through the North Atlantic. Some vessels exploded and sank within minutes, others were badly damaged and foundered slowly with many casualties, a few managed to limp to safety in a friendly port. Tsafendas had always been comfortable with the sea, swimming in it or sailing upon it, but the thought of struggling to stay alive in burning, freezing or oil-covered waters appalled him. His worst fears were realised when the Canadian authorities assigned him to serve aboard a weapons carrier, which would form part of a convoy supplying war material to Allied troops in Europe. Terrified at the prospect, Tsafendas decided to escape and flee to the United States.[6]

Curious to see if any other prisoners would be interested in joining him, Tsafendas brought up the subject light-heartedly and four men gave him positive signals. Another inmate was being released at the time and Tsafendas jokingly asked him to get them a hacksaw blade so they could cut through the bars to freedom. A short time after his release, the ex-prisoner managed to smuggle to them a small hacksaw blade.[7] By now, it was winter and Halifax, on the exposed north-eastern seaboard, was hit by a remorseless cycle of rain, sleet and heavy snow, with temperatures rarely above freezing, often registering around minus 8°C. Tsafendas was not prepared to wait the winter out.

Knowing that January would be even colder, the group of five made its bid for freedom on 10 December 1942.[8] Using the hacksaw blade, the men cut through the bars of a toilet and lowered themselves to the ground using three bedsheets tied together; they then scaled the wall of the detention centre. Three men followed Tsafendas over safely, but the rope of sheets suddenly unravelled and the last man fell inside the wall and broke a leg. With the injured man lying screaming and prison warders racing towards them, Tsafendas and his companions took flight. The escapees got away and the prisoner survived his fall, but Tsafendas was deeply upset. It was he who had thought up the escape plan and he who had tied the sheets together. When he learnt that the man's leg was paralysed, he suffered from guilt for many weeks. His remorse was heightened when he acknowledged to himself that the whole enterprise was an attempt to evade service in a war that he had once been so keen to join.[9]

Turning towards the United States, the four escapees were to endure three weeks of serious physical deprivation. They were on foot in the depths of winter with no extra clothing and very little food; they had only a few dollars between them and had to be constantly alert for police or military uniforms. Their target was the 71-mile-long St. Croix River, which formed part of the US–Canada border between Maine and New Brunswick. Knowing that fording the river in sub-zero temperatures was not an option, they were relieved to discover that the waterway was frozen from shore to shore. Thus they slid, ran and skated across this last icy obstacle into the United States. Exhausted and nearly starving, Tsafendas and his friends made no attempt to escape, indeed were probably thankful, when they were arrested by the American Coast

Guard in Maine on New Year's Eve, 1942.[10] It had been a heroic journey by any standards, demonstrating a physical toughness in Tsafendas.

The four were charged with contravening US immigration laws and imprisoned in Bangor, Maine.[11] The American penitentiary was altogether tougher than the seamen's detention centres in Canada, and Tsafendas and his friends were targeted by both their fellow prisoners and the warders, especially when the word got out that they were naval deserters. At one point, the US authorities gave Tsafendas a choice: Stay in prison or rejoin the navy. Under other circumstances, he would probably have taken the second option, but with further news of the torpedoed and sunk ships coming out, he was terrified to ship out and kept putting off a decision. However, after some three months behind bars and under pressure to decide, he took the only way out: he went mad. That is to say, he refined the shamming skills he had used as a child and pretended to lose his mind; he told the warders that he could hear voices from the radiators. The prison officials called a doctor, who concluded that Tsafendas 'showed symptoms of mental disorder'. He was taken to the Boston Psychopathic Hospital, 235 miles away, and on 23 April 1943, after putting on a performance several times, transferred to Metropolitan State Hospital, the largest and most modern facility of its type in the state of Massachusetts. He was initially diagnosed as having 'psychoneurosis – mixed type' plus 'many psychopathic traits'.[12]

A fellow patient there was a young Irishman named Tom Tuff, also a merchant seaman, who had been diagnosed as schizophrenic. Tom, in his early 20s, was the skinniest person Tsafendas had ever seen, who claimed this was because there was a tapeworm in his stomach eating his food. Tom regularly asked for extra food portions to 'feed the worm' and, because he was so thin, the cooks always gave him more. Everyone seemed to be interested in Tom's tapeworm and, apart from the extra food, Tom clearly enjoyed the attention he received, especially from the female nurses. Tsafendas was deeply impressed.[13]

The two young men became friends and spent many hours chatting. Tsafendas was intensely curious about the tapeworm and wanted to know everything about it. Tom never suggested the worm had a personality or that it talked or influenced him, just that it consumed his food. He said that he became infested with the worm when he was a child. A doctor gave him a purgative and though parts of the creature emerged, most of it, including the head, stayed inside. Further doses had no effect and the boy believed the tapeworm was hiding deep in his body, where the strongest medicines could not reach it. Tom's behaviour was otherwise perfectly normal and Tsafendas suspected that the boy was pretending to be insane so as not to be drafted into the US military. He noted that the tapeworm only made its appearance after Tom received his army call-up papers. Tsafendas asked Tom many times if he was making it all up, pleading with him to reveal the truth, but the young Irishman held to his story.[14]

Tom was a missionary member of a Christian sect that did not have a name.[15] He referred to it as the Christian Church, but it was also known as the No-Name Church and sometimes as Two by Twos.[16] Tsafendas had never heard of the sect, but was impressed by Tom's knowledge of Christian theology and his philosophical take on the world and life. Tom explained that his church's mission was primarily evangelical and that it was guided by the Bible. The church had members all over the world and its financial needs were met by their offerings. It had no church buildings or other property and prayer meetings and scripture studies were held in members' homes on Wednesdays and Sundays. Could such a man really be schizophrenic, Tsafendas wondered.

As for his own beliefs, Tsafendas considered himself a nominal Christian, having been baptised and gone to church services and Sunday school under the stern eye of Marika. Until meeting Tom, Tsafendas had not given much thought to religion. He had an instinctive tendency to believe, but he opposed many aspects of the official church, which he saw as a wealthy and conservative power, a pillar of colonialism with close ties to repressive governments. Instead of defending the powerless and the oppressed, he believed the church in colonial territories helped to perpetuate an unjust system of foreign rule, partly in order to protect its own position. Thus for someone like Tsafendas, who saw the institutional church as part of the establishment, Tom's simple, independent Christian sect held great appeal. It did not have churches or temples, Bishops or priests and it had no connection with established authority. Its members were ordinary, apolitical people who believed in God and gathered together to pray to Him. This was exactly how Tsafendas believed Christianity should be and Tom's sect resonated with both his religious and political instincts.[17]

Tsafendas soon learnt that while faking illness might have got him off school, claiming to hear voices did not convince psychiatrists at the Metropolitan State Hospital that he was insane. When challenged directly, Tsafendas confessed that 'he had faked mental illness because he was afraid to ship out on account of the many sinkings of allied shipping by the U-boats'. The hospital referred his case to the US Immigration and Naturalization Service (INS). Tsafendas was now caught between the devil and, literally, the deep blue sea. Officials of the INS gave him an ultimatum: 'Deportation back to Africa or work for the Merchant Marine.' He chose the second option.[18]

Tsafendas was discharged from the hospital on 24 June 1943, but remained in detention until he received orders to ship out. On 14 August, he was released on a $1,000 bond[19] and directed to present himself on 2 September to the SS *Pillory*, which he boarded under a warrant of deportation. The ship sailed to Greenland then returned to the United States, docking in Boston. Tsafendas moved to the SS *Benson,* then served on a series of merchant vessels and Liberty ships aiding the Allies' efforts.[20] Liberty ships were low-cost cargo vessels of simple construction that were built in huge numbers in American yards. Intended to replace cargo ships torpedoed by U-boats, they were capable of carrying ammunition, tanks, food, even troops. Manned by merchant seamen, they served in all theatres during the war but were used primarily to guarantee that Allied forces in Europe received war materiel from North America.

As for Tsafendas, nervously but stoically, he endured these voyages until the day his worst nightmare became reality and his ship was torpedoed.[21] Flames spread through the cargo hold and Tsafendas joined the crew in manning pumps to stop the blaze from spreading. Eventually, the fire was contained and the stricken vessel limped back to port in the United States. That was enough for a terrified Tsafendas. Once again, he pretended to be mad, and from then to the end of the war, he was involved in a bewildering series of transfers between Liberty ships and hospitals as he tried desperately to avoid further service at sea. Although he had dreamed since childhood of fighting in a revolution or in a just war with a great cause, now that he had the chance, he was frankly afraid. Having come close to death, the last thing he wanted was to go to sea again while the war still raged. He had his life ahead of him, he argued; he was too young to die.[22]

After returning to Boston from service at sea sometime in early 1944, Tsafendas travelled to New York and checked into the Seamen's Convalescence Home in Oyster Bay, Long Island. On 9 May of that year, he left aboard the SS *John Holmes* for Liverpool, England, from where in June he found his way to the US Army 96th General Hospital in Worcestershire, seeking admittance on the grounds of mental ill health. Tsafendas stayed in the hospital until shipping out on the US Army hospital ship *Wisteria* to Charleston, South Carolina, where he arrived on 12 August 1944. Upon examination, doctors concluded he was suffering from an unspecified type of psychosis and he was admitted to the Roper Hospital in Charleston. There, on 2 September, a board of inquiry ruled that Tsafendas was 'insane at the time of arrival' in Charleston. The board also found that he had been excluded from the United States as an insane person under the 1917 Immigration Act and was thus ineligible for a visa. Given that he had been ruled insane, however, a decision was taken that he should remain in the Roper Hospital *pro tem.* Later in September, while pretending to be recovering from illness in Roper Hospital, Tsafendas was given orders to ship out again. He promptly took to his heels, only to be apprehended on 5 October in Boston. Taken to prison, he staged the mad act once more and was transferred to another public health facility, on Ellis Island, New York.[23]

As the war neared its end, the American authorities became engaged in what looked like a game of ping-pong with Tsafendas as they tried unsuccessfully to remove him from the country. On 25 February 1945, he was deported aboard the Greek vessel, SS *Maria Nicolao*. However, on 3 December 1945, with the war now over, he managed to re-enter the United States in New York, as a mess waiter on the SS *Robin Locksley*. In January 1946, he was arrested at St Bernard's Home on West 95th Street in New York City, where he had been living since his arrival. He was charged with violating the 1924 Immigration Act by remaining longer in the United States than permitted as a seaman and on 10 February was deported again aboard the SS *Hood Victory*. Once more, however, Tsafendas managed to return to New York aboard the same ship on 10 March 1946. He then travelled to Medford, Massachusetts, to meet Tom Tuff. Tom had recovered from his tapeworm problem as soon as the war ended and was discharged from hospital. The two men met up on 13 March 1946 and, for the first time, Tsafendas attended a meeting of the Christian sect. Tom urged Tsafendas not to mention his 'tapeworm problem' to anyone, saying he had been ill during the war but now was cured and had come to the conclusion that he never had a tapeworm. He said he would be embarrassed if his fellow believers found out about it. Tsafendas agreed to stay mum about the tapeworm but repeatedly urged Tom to admit that he had made it up to avoid the draft. Despite Tsafendas's pressure, Tom held his ground and said it was simply a coincidence that he recovered when the war ended. Tsafendas was not convinced but let the matter drop. Meanwhile, in a letter addressed from 42 Alexander Avenue, Medford, Tsafendas wrote to President Roosevelt complaining that he had been granted leave in the United States of only 29 days. He cited his service in the US Merchant Marine and asked to be considered for additional free time.[24]

Now penniless and unable to find work due to his illegal status, Tsafendas admitted himself to the Boston Psychopathic Hospital on 19 March 1946. This was the hospital where he had first staged his lunatic act in April 1943. Back again, he tried the voices-from-God trick once more, but it took the doctors less than a week to conclude that he was an impostor and discharge him. By now, it was clear to Tsafendas that if he was ever to make his madness act work, he had to do more than claim he heard voices. Thus, when he soon afterwards admitted himself to the Grafton State Hospital in Massachusetts,[25] he staged a much more elaborate charade.

Not only did he claim to hear voices from the radiators, he also smeared the walls of his room with his faeces and pulled crazy, leering faces at the staff. When the doctors did not seem convinced, he decided to steal Tom's tapeworm. He claimed that an insatiable tapeworm lived in his belly and ate his food, which was why he was often hungry. It worked. This was something the medics had never heard of and it piqued their curiosity. Like Tom before him, Tsafendas enjoyed the attention the story brought him, particularly from the female nurses who wanted to know all the details of his strange problem. Tsafendas would talk happily about the tapeworm, adding elements to the story that he had heard from Tom. Better still, he was given extra food portions.[26] In combination with his other 'symptoms', the doctors concluded that Tsafendas really was mentally sick and he spent 16 months in the hospital as they sought to discover the source of his illness. He was finally discharged from Grafton on 31 July 1947 with the notation, 'schizophrenia-hebephrenic type, condition Improved'.[27]

Tsafendas spent the next few weeks travelling up and down the American East Coast between Boston and New York. He fell in love with jazz, which he was hearing for the first time, and sought out clubs where the best bands and soloists could be heard. He also visited every music shop he could find looking for Paul Robeson's records. When he came across a four-disc album by Robeson, *Songs of Free Men,* containing revolutionary, communist and anti-fascist songs, he bought it immediately. The problem was he did not have a turntable to play it on and, worse, he did not have the money to buy one. Eventually, he spotted an old-fashioned, portable graphophone in a second-hand shop. He was desperate to have it as there was only one left and it was by far the cheapest he had come across. However, he had less than half the price the shopkeeper was asking. He suggested a bargain: he would give the owner what money he had, promising to return with the balance in a week. Knowing that the man was highly unlikely to accept such a deal, Tsafendas offered to hand over his passport and his overcoat as collateral. The shopkeeper agreed and gave Tsafendas the graphophone. A week later, as promised, Tsafendas returned with the money and retrieved his coat and passport. The deal was well worth it. He liked the album so much that later he bought two more copies as backups and also sent one to his father in South Africa. Very soon he could sing most of the songs. They included the 'Song of the Plains', a Soviet partisan melody which Tsafendas often whistled, 'The Four Insurgent Generals' about the Spanish Civil War, and 'Joe Hill', about the Swedish-American labour activist and songwriter, who was wrongfully convicted and executed for murder and who became a heroic symbol for labour unions all over the world.[28]

Tsafendas also visited theatres and opera houses. A play that moved him was Ben Hecht's *A Flag Is Born,* a drama about a homeland for Jews in ancient Israel, a cause which Tsafendas, ever conscious of his Jewish ancestry, supported enthusiastically. He was so impressed by the play that he kept his ticket in a safe place. Later, when he came across fundraisers for the creation of Israel, he gave them all his spare cash and even sold some of his clothes for the cause.[29]

As someone who considered himself a born revolutionary, it was inevitable that Tsafendas should turn his enquiring intellect to the American Revolution. He visited historic sites in Massachusetts, Pennsylvania and New York, and devoured books on all aspects of the subject. Up until then, it was the French and Russian revolutions that were of interest to him, but a major reason for this was his early antipathy to modern United States prompted by the whites' treatment of the Native American and the African-American peoples. Now he acknowledged the courage of the American rebels and the sagacity of the Founding Fathers and he was ready to compare them to the Bolsheviks and the French revolutionaries. Tsafendas became fascinated in particular with Benjamin Franklin, his favourite among all the rebels and one of the political philosophers he most admired. He travelled to Philadelphia to visit the Benjamin Franklin National Memorial and he paged through his written works. What fascinated Tsafendas was Franklin's justification of tyrannicide, the argument that it was morally justifiable to kill a tyrant or dictator. The phrase 'Rebellion to tyrants is obedience to God', would become a favourite quote. Exploring the issue further, Tsafendas discovered that its roots lay in ancient Greece, while several important religious and political thinkers like John of Salisbury and Saint Thomas Aquinas had also declared tyrannicide to be justifiable.[30]

Tsafendas's persistence in returning to the United States time after time seemed at odds with his frequently voiced dislike of its treatment of minorities. What he told friends was that he admired the United States as a modern and technologically advanced country. He loved the social life, theatre and music; he was particularly fascinated by the New York subway and used it often to explore the city. Now with experience, his harsher views began to soften. He had long believed that the Founding Fathers would be ashamed to see how the United States treated some of its people, with economic and social freedom being merely theoretical for blacks, Native Americans, Jews and other minorities. Certainly, discrimination existed and he read about it in the newspapers often, but he had to admit he had not personally seen evidence of it. Besides, the longer he stayed, the more he liked Americans, finding them open and outgoing, and some of them politically very progressive. He always stated freely that he was a communist, as he did at the hospital, and no one seemed particularly bothered.[31]

Shortly after the end of the war, Tsafendas was at a cinema when a newsreel was played, titled *Nazi Murder Mills.* These were the first newsreel pictures of the liberation of the Nazi death camps, depicting piles of naked dead Jews in mass graves. Tsafendas was devastated and stumbled weeping from the movie house. Like most people around the world, this was his first glimpse of the horrors of the genocide and he found it hard to believe what he had seen. Sleepless all night, he pondered how humans could do this to other humans. He had always considered the Nazis to be disgusting, but he had not guessed at the depths of their evil. The newsreel was a life-changing moment and slowly there grew in him feelings of guilt and deep-seated shame for his behaviour during the war.[32]

As further news films and survivors' accounts emerged from Europe, Tsafendas, with painful honesty, re-examined his conduct during the war. Now he accepted the truth: he had been a coward. True, he had spent much time in peril at sea in support of the fighting forces and had even been torpedoed, but he had been forced into such a role by the authorities while doing everything possible to avoid it. He had rationalised his stance by arguing that he was not afraid to fight, but he did not want to do so at sea because there was little chance of survival. It was the same with the air force; he had a deep-seated fear of flying – he never once flew – and he calculated that if his warplane was hit by enemy fire, he would almost certainly die. Now, ashamed and humiliated, Tsafendas accepted that he had sought consistently to avoid combat with those same fascists he had so smugly denounced in the safety of civilian life. What particularly embarrassed him was that he had besmirched the family honour. What would those Cretan heroes, his great-grandfather and his great-uncle, think of him, if they knew? Indeed, what would his father think if he discovered that his son had shirked an honourable call to arms? Such thoughts made him desperate to redeem his honour by finding and fighting bravely for a cause he believed in. He made a resolution: he would take the 'straight road' and make his family proud, he would voluntarily fight in the next just war or revolution, wherever this might be. Now, however, his stay in America was coming to an end. When picked up by the police, the only question for the INS was to which particular country he should be deported. This was something of a problem since he had a residential history in Mozambique and South Africa and he held both Greek and Portuguese passports. Tsafendas asked to be sent to South Africa, but a decision was taken on 22 August 1947 to deport him to Greece, despite his protests that he knew no one in Greece. Tom Tuff furnished him with contacts for Christian Church members in Europe and on 27 September, Tsafendas travelled to Piraeus, the port city of Athens, aboard the steamship, *Marine Jumper*.[33] He had two suitcases with him, one containing his clothes and the other his books and his records.

As for Tom Tuff, Tsafendas never saw him again; they stayed in contact by correspondence until Tsafendas's arrest for Verwoerd's assassination. There was no contact after that and Dimitri never learnt what became of his friend, but he never forgot him. In later life, he would happily tell stories of Tom, this kindly and clever young man who evaded the draft by creating the unique spectre of a giant tapeworm lodged inside him and stealing his food. Dimitri admitted his own imagination would never have stretched to such a feat, but he was the first to acknowledge that by stealing the tapeworm for himself, he avoided the gallows. In the most fundamental sense, nice Tom Tuff saved his life.[34]

Chapter 6

Redemption

Desperate to redeem himself by fighting for a just cause, stepping onto the docks at Piraeus, Dimitri Tsefandas found a country embroiled in civil war. When the Second World War ended, many officials who had collaborated with the Nazis, instead of being put on trial, were given positions in the police force, the army and even the government. Soon began what became known as the White Terror, when the wartime collaborators hunted down former members of left-wing resistance groups. This led to the organisation of the Greek Democratic Army (DSE), the military wing of the Greek Communist Party, and the beginning of civil conflict. The government and its army were supported by pro-royalist Greeks but also had the backing of the United States and Britain. It was not difficult for Tsafendas to choose a side.

Still, though, Athens in October 1947[1] was not where Tsafendas wanted to be. A complete stranger to the country of his paternal ancestors, he had never been to mainland Greece and could find no work. Just to survive, he sold the clothes he brought with him from America.[2] Desperate, he applied for permission to return to South Africa, where his family lived and where he now considered to be his home. The application was rejected without explanation. Unknown to Tsafendas, some anonymous immigration official forwarded the application to his superior with a note saying, 'He is a Communist, a half-caste and a previous illegal immigrant. Refusal strongly recommended.'[3]

Tsafendas turned to the local Christian Church sect and a member gave him lodgings in his house, so at least he had a roof over his head.[4] After much searching, he located John Michaletos, a good friend from Lourenço Marques and nephew of George Michaletos who was married to Tsafendas's aunt, Artemis. John Michaletos was now a teacher of Greek literature and a member of the Greek Communist Party. When Michaletos introduced other party members, Tsafendas declared that he dearly wanted to join the Democratic Army and fight the Greek fascists. His wish was passed on and very soon he found himself with his rebel comrades in the mountains. Tsafendas was excited and relieved at this early opportunity to fight for a cause he believed in and hopefully expunge memories of his behaviour during the Second World War.[5]

In the mountains around Athens and in Central Greece, Tsafendas received basic training in guerrilla warfare. Although he had never handled firearms, he was pleased to discover he was a talented marksman. All his new comrades had fought the Germans during the Nazi occupation of Greece and Tsafendas was thrilled to join them. When the fighters moved through the mountains, they were welcomed by villagers, who gave them food and a place to sleep. Villagers and fighters knew each other well since, during the occupation, it was the armed men who handed out food in the villages. Being feted as part of a brave band of resisters was a proud experience for Tsafendas. Not only was he accepted by everyone as an equal, the fact that he was from Africa made him stand out in his unit. For protection against spies and betrayal, they all used *nommes de guerre* and Tsafendas called himself Michalis, after his ancestor hero. As to the dark spot in his past, Tsafendas told his comrades only that he had served in the US navy, principally on Liberty ships ferrying war materiel to the Allies.[6]

Tsafendas was in the mountains for a few months, always on the move with his unit, but never involved in combat. That he had no opportunity to demonstrate his shooting skills in an authentic firefight was deeply disappointing, but then came a new twist in a life that was proving to be full of surprises. Tsafendas's team included a number of women partisans who had taken up arms against the Germans during the occupation and then continued fighting the Royalist forces. One in particular attracted Tsafendas. Her name was Zoe[7] and she had long, red hair. Conditions were not ideal for romance and flirting among partisans was frowned on, but Tsafendas managed to spend a lot of time chatting with Zoe, hoping that one day better opportunities would open up.[8] Such hopes were dashed, however, when his commanding officer decided to send him on a special mission. The officer observed that since Tsafendas had served in the American navy, held a Portuguese passport and was not known to anyone in Athens, he was perfectly placed to work in the capital as a clandestine informant for the DSE. The idea appealed to Tsafendas's conspiratorial sense of adventure and his ever-present need for redemption. He agreed eagerly and was instructed to proceed to Athens and wait to be contacted. Leaving his unit after tearful embraces with his comrades, Tsafendas buried his uniform near a tree, leaving a mark for the day he would hopefully retrieve them, then travelled on to Athens.[9]

His contact in the capital turned out to be a teenage waiter who worked in a coffee shop in Plaka, a historic district in Athens. The young man told Tsafendas that the comrades wished him to apply for work with the American Reconstruction Mission, which was set up under the US Marshall Plan to help the war-torn nations of Europe get back on their feet. Among the items provided by America were arms and weapons for the Greek army and for British and American forces in Europe. It was made clear to Tsafendas that information on what sort of war materiel and how much of it was going to the DSE's enemies would be of great value to the men in the mountains.[10]

Tsafendas duly applied for work with the Mission and was taken on[11] because of his experience with the US Navy and the fact that he was fluent in Greek and English. He had also impressed his American interviewers with his knowledge of and admiration for the American Revolution.[12] He was employed as an interpreter and quickly found himself in the position he had targeted, namely the section responsible for delivering supplies to the American and British forces.[13] Not only was he now able to provide his comrades with important logistical information in relative safety, he was also generously rewarded by the enemy itself – insofar as the United States backed the Greek government – with a generous salary of 30,000 drachmas per day.[14] It was no surprise that he thoroughly enjoyed his time there.

With his financial situation much improved, Tsafendas contacted John Michaletos and together, they explored Athens, which Dimitri soon knew like the palm of his hand. Michaletos was widely known in literary circles and had written a well-received book about Constantine Cavafy, the Greek poet from Alexandria who Tsafendas had met as a boy when the writer visited his grandmother. One of their favourite spots was the Plaka coffee shop where Tsafendas's spy-contact worked. They would sit for hours at a table under the trees, enjoying the Athenian sky. Tsafendas often said he felt like a tourist. As Athens moved slowly towards post-war normality, he explored the city's nightlife and renewed his interest in theatre. He had adored ancient Greek drama since he was a child and now was his chance to see the great plays performed, often going to watch after work.[15]

During the day, he visited many of the ancient sites he had been told of and read about and for which Greece was justly famous. With Michaletos, he was a regular at coffee shops such as the Dexameni, the patisserie Floka, and very often, the Brazilian Café, famous for its high-quality coffee and the place where espresso was first introduced to Athens' coffee lovers. Sitting in comfort, enjoying the sun and watching people pass by, it was as if the civil war did not exist. Customers scarcely mentioned it and the staff just got on with their jobs. Tsafendas himself was careful not to talk about the conflict or give any hint of his political beliefs.[16]

Meanwhile, memories of Zoe began to fade when he met Marina at one of his Christian Church prayer meetings. Marina was from a small village in the Peloponnese area of Greece and had come to Athens looking for work, which she found as a domestic servant in a wealthy man's family home. Marina's father had died during the war and her family relied on her for money, which she sent regularly. Tsafendas often offered assistance for her family, but she never accepted his money. In time, seeing each other regularly, they fell in love. Marina was deeply religious and refused to have sex before marriage, which did not please Tsafendas. She was not interested in politics except insofar as she was anti-communist, as were her relatives and the family she worked for in Athens. She told Tsafendas that she was afraid of communists. She did not know that Tsafendas was one, something he kept quiet about, knowing it would jeopardise his work for the DSE and could even place him in grave danger if it became known. In the several months they saw each other in Athens, Tsafendas never revealed his political views or mentioned his time in the mountains.[17]

Marina wanted to get married, but Tsafendas felt he was too young. Besides, he wished to return to Africa while Marina did not want to leave her family in Greece. Then suddenly Marina disappeared. Tsafendas tried desperately to locate her. At the house where she worked, he asked about her, pretending to be a relative. He was told that she had left abruptly to go to her village over a family health issue. People from their church knew no more than Tsafendas – that she had simply vanished without a trace. It was several years later that John Michaletos, in response to repeated requests from Tsafendas, disclosed in a letter that Marina had died from natural causes. However, he did not know where or when or why she left Athens so suddenly without saying anything to anyone. Years later, Tsafendas also made inquiries about Zoe, but he received no replies and never did discover what became of her.[18]

In South Africa, meanwhile, 1948 was a landmark year for the National Party as it won the 26 May general election under the leadership of D.F. Malan. During the campaign, the Nationalists made great use of the term 'apartheid'[19] and Malan suggested that the whites had a choice: 'integration and national suicide' or 'apartheid' and the protection of a 'pure white race'.[20] The National Party, in coalition with the Afrikaner Party of Nicolaas Havenga, won the election with 41.2% of the vote.[21] Dr Verwoerd had finally resigned his post as editor of *Die Transvaler*[22] so that he could enter politics full time as a National Party MP. In the event, he lost by just 171 votes to the United Party candidate.[23] However, with the support of the Broederbond and at the insistence of Strijdom, Prime Minister Malan appointed Verwoerd as a senator instead.[24]

With the National Party in power, Malan's[25] first step was to install apartheid as national policy and thus 'safeguard the racial identity and dominance of whites'. He did this by writing into law long-accepted race-separation practices that already served the economic interests of whites and overseas investors. The effect was to elevate and enrich Afrikaners at the expense of blacks and coloureds, depriving them of opportunities to advance economically. At the same time, Malan released a number of fascists who had been jailed for supporting the Nazis during the war, an action which enraged South African veterans who had fought with the Allies.[26]

Economics apart, Malan's policies systematically eroded the political rights of black people while placing power into ever fewer, invariably Afrikaner, hands. Africans watched helplessly as the demands of their leaders for national political representation were denied, while coloureds were put on a separate voters' roll, which was abolished a few years later. Black communities were physically re-ordered to serve the economic interests of the whites, squatter camps were destroyed and black townships created where families would live and provide cheap labour in the urban areas. Apartheid swiftly became an integral part of South African daily life, based entirely on white domination of black people. African lives were organised, ordered and controlled so as to supply white-owned industry and agriculture with cheap labour and thus boost economic development.[27]

That the system should provoke violence between whites and blacks was inevitable and when Dr Verwoerd gave his first speech as a senator late in 1948, he argued that there should be no retreat from apartheid, which was the only way to deal with unrest stirring all over the country.[28] In a speech of undisguised racism, he declared that South Africa was 'a white man's country and we must remain master here'. He described blacks, coloureds and Indians as 'swarming everywhere, uncounted and uncontrolled' and 'taking possession of the theatre and the streets'. His only slightly mollifying observation was a vague suggestion that blacks at some point could be masters of their own homelands.[29]

Remorselessly, apartheid took control of every aspect of life in South Africa, to the gratification of Dr Verwoerd, who declared that his ultimate aim was a complete separation between whites and Africans, for the good of both.[30] As the Nationalists bedded in, Dr Verwoerd began to emerge as a leading figure in the new government, possessor of one of the sharpest minds in politics, and perhaps the hardest working politician.[31] He began to highlight issues about the black population in the areas of labour, settlement, education and elsewhere, proposing radical changes and new legislation. In his eyes, black workers were simply units of labour, a perception that would persist throughout the apartheid years.[32]

Back in Athens, sometime near the end of 1948, Tsafendas called in at the Plaka coffee shop to pass on some information to the young waiter, but he was not there. Following standing instructions, he did not ask about him, but went back the next day. There was still no sign of him and again, he left without saying anything. Two days later, he returned to the café and this time, ignoring orders, he asked the other waiters where their young colleague was. He had been arrested as a communist, they said, and they had no idea what happened to him. Shocked, Tsafendas left and never returned. The fate of the waiter remained a mystery to him and the DSE never attempted to re-establish contact with Tsafendas. His days as a spy were over.[33]

The timing was appropriate, since his job with the American Reconstruction Mission ended in December 1948. Tsafendas spent Christmas in Michaletos's house and in the new year found work as an interpreter with an American company, Messrs. Steers-Grove. He worked there for three months, during which there was no word from the DSE.[34] This did not surprise him because, by April 1949, it was clear that the communists were losing the war. This happened officially six months later and Tsafendas decided that it would be best for him to leave the country.

On 12 April, Tsafendas penned yet another appeal for permission to return to South Africa, which he described as 'the country I was brought up in and the country of my mother, Amelia Williams'. The letter gave Tsafendas's home address as Box 80, Central Post Office, Athens, and was addressed to the Department of the Interior in South Africa, where it was date-stamped received on 26 April. Tsafendas pointed out that he did war work in Johannesburg between 1940 and 1942, then 'joined the Merchant Navy voluntarily and risked my life in submarine-infested seas all over the South & North Atlantic'. He concluded, 'I am here a man without a country, living in strange lands with people who have different ways of living, customs & languages.'[35] There was no known response, but almost certainly, his application was turned down, for the usual reasons – Communist/half-caste/illegal immigrant.

Among the few people Tsafendas got to know during his time in Greece were members of the Christian Church sect. Because they had helped him when he first arrived in Athens, homeless and penniless, he felt an obligation towards them and continued to attend their prayer meetings. At one of them, he was asked if he wished to be baptised since this was necessary to become a full member. He was uncomfortable about such a ceremony and questioned whether it was necessary since he had been baptised into the Greek Orthodox Church as a baby in Mozambique. However, shortly before he left Greece, he agreed and asked that John Michaletos[36] perform the ceremony, which involved whole-body submersion. The baptism took place sometime in early 1949 on a remote Athens beach. The sea was freezing, but the service did not last long.[37]

Later that year, through the offices of the Greek Red Cross, Tsafendas obtained an official document known as a refugee passport. He quit his job with Steers-Grove and approached a shipping company in Athens, citing his maritime experience. The company allowed him to work his passage to Europe aboard the Greek cruise ship, *Corinthia*. Destination: France.[38] His plan was to travel from France to Portugal and then to Mozambique.

Chapter 7

Exiled

Stepping onto French soil, Tsafendas knew there was only one place he wanted to be: Paris, home of the French Revolution. Slipping off the ship in Marseille, he travelled by train to Paris,[1] presented himself to the authorities and legalised his presence in the country.[2] He then hastened to the sites he had read about so often: Place de la Concorde, once the Place de la Revolution, where the anti-monarchists set up a guillotine and beheaded King Louis XVI and Queen Marie Antoinette, then Danton, Robespierre, Corday and 1,200 others; Place de Bastille, site of the infamous political prison stormed on 14 July 1789; the Palace of Versailles, ten miles west of Paris, once the home of the royal family. The idea of mobs attacking the strongholds of authority excited Tsafendas. As a child, he had dreamed that one day the exploited Mozambicans would besiege the Portuguese administration in Lourenço Marques, and later, he fantasised of a siege in Cape Town, with the South African parliament and apartheid falling to the forces of good. In Paris, he bought two *bonnets rouges,* the soft, conical red caps worn by the revolutionaries; he mailed one to his father and kept the other for himself.[3]

With a return to Africa ever in his mind, Tsafendas acquired a 90-day visa for Spain, but spent only three days there, travelling towards Portugal.[4] It was there that his problems began. On 8 November 1949, he was arrested at the Portuguese border post of Barca d'Alva. He showed immigration officers his Athens-issued refugee passport[5] but they doubted his claim to be Portuguese.[6] When they contacted Lourenço Marques, Tsafendas knew the game was up. Police there confirmed he was registered Portuguese, but added that he was a suspected communist, that he had been fired from his job for that reason and that he was suspected of distributing communist propaganda and of 'voicing Communist ideas'.[7]

He was detained at the Barca d'Alva for three months, then moved to the notorious Aljuba Prison in Lisbon, where most political suspects were incarcerated.[8] Conditions were bad, brutality reigned and at times, he feared for his life. For six months, he was kept in a small cell, painfully restrictive for such a big man, and sometimes left without food or water for days. Worst of all were the guards. Though he was not physically tortured, the warders were cruel, pushing and screaming at the prisoners, and at one point, he thought they were going to put him against a wall and shoot him.[9]

To keep his spirits up, he would softly whistle lesser-known revolutionary songs or play them through in his mind, careful never to enunciate the lyrics. When anyone asked what he was whistling, he said they were Mozambican folk tunes, but he did not know the words. Two favourites were Paul Robeson's 'Song of Freedom' and 'Zot Nit Keynmol' (Song of the Warsaw Ghetto). The latter was one of the best-known songs to come out of the Holocaust, was written in Yiddish, but also had English lyrics. Tsafendas spoke no Yiddish, but he learnt the lyrics perfectly in that language.[10]

In his darkest moments, Tsafendas wondered if he would ever be free of this hell hole. His chance arrived in the most unexpected of ways. The authorities discovered that he had never completed his compulsory service in the Portuguese army and brought him before a military board of inspection in Lisbon. Tsafendas explained that he had appeared for an interview in Lourenço Marques as ordered, but had been rejected for military service because his mother was a Mozambican African. Contacted about this, the colonial administration in Mozambique confirmed Tsafendas's story.[11] However, there had been a significant change in the law four years earlier, when it was decreed that all male Portuguese of the appropriate age must fulfil the requirements of military service, whatever their racial origins. Thus Tsafendas was exculpated from suspicion of being a deserter but was told he must nevertheless do his army time.[12]

Trapped and determined not to serve 'the Portuguese dictatorship' as he called it,[13] Tsafendas decided once again to play the mad man. Having observed Tom Tuff closely and noted the doctors' reaction to his 'tapeworm problem', he decided to use his story again, claiming that it lived inside him, consumed his food and controlled his life, that it had been there since childhood, avoided all purgatives and refused to leave. Psychiatrists swiftly concluded that this man must surely be insane.[14] His military obligation was swiftly cancelled and he was set free upon payment of 1,200 Portuguese escudos.[15]

After months in a brutal prison system, Tsafendas now found himself penniless and jobless in Lisbon, where he did not know a soul. A situation that would overwhelm anyone, Tsafendas demonstrated a resourcefulness that was to assist him so often on his travels. He applied for and was granted a police permit to work as a maritime salesman,[16] and promptly began hawking embroidery, postcards and watches, mainly to holidaymakers on cruise ships.[17] This was the perfect avocation for Tsafendas, something he could turn his hand to whenever necessary. He was his own boss and could operate wherever he wanted and for as long as he wanted. During subsequent travels in Europe, he often traded as a hawker, visiting places that aroused his curiosity, including the historic sites he had read about as a boy, talking to people and insistently asking questions. The only drawback was that the job was physically arduous, at least for someone like Tsafendas with a tendency to physical laziness. If it wasn't for that, he said, he would have done it permanently.[18]

Tsafendas applied in turn for visas to Mozambique, South Africa and the United States, but all were turned down. Listed communists were not welcome in any of these countries. Now with money for postage, Tsafendas wrote to his father in South Africa about his experiences, including his time in prison. The letter worried Michalis, but he could not resist a feeling of pride at the political path his son was pursuing. Tsafendas corresponded regularly with his family, especially with Michalis, to whom he wrote almost every month. He often sent them gifts, as well as photographs of himself, invariably smiling and wearing a clean suit.[19] Whatever his circumstances, financial or personal, he did not want his loved ones to worry that he was having a difficult time. In every letter his father wrote, he would ask if Dimitri needed anything, especially money, and in every reply, Tsafendas assured him he was fine. His only regret was that he was not allowed back in South Africa to be with the family.[20] If he had been, he would have found that 1950 was a landmark year.

The most significant event of the year was Malan's appointment of Dr Verwoerd as Minister of Native Affairs.[21] This Ministry was the frontline department dealing with the implementation of apartheid, and Verwoerd thus became the driving force behind the policy of race segregation. NP supporters greeted his appointment with delight, convinced that the new Minister would 'save Afrikanerdom from being swamped with blacks in its own country'.[22] Dr Verwoerd was not about to disappoint them and moved quickly to achieve his long-sought aim: total separation of Africans from whites, including living space, which he argued would be good for both groups.[23]

In October 1951, after he had saved enough money to buy a ticket and accrue some extra cash, Tsafendas sailed from Lisbon to Lourenço Marques aboard the ship *Save*.[24] Since he was a Mozambican, he did not expect any problems to return to the country of his birth. However, when his passport was checked, it was discovered that the police had a file on him relating to his past communist and anti-colonialist activities, and he was refused entry.[25] He knew that pleading would not work, so he resorted to his tried and tested acting skills – he groaned loudly, clutched his stomach and dramatically doubled over, apparently stricken by acute appendicitis. He was rushed off the ship to a hospital in the city but, less than an hour later, he miraculously recovered and slipped away to freedom.[26] Very soon, the Greeks in Lourenço Marques learnt of Tsafendas's appendicitis trick and it became the sensation of the day. Even years afterwards, people were still talking about how Tsafendas had managed to pull off such an act. Not impressed, however, was Tsafendas's father. His daughter Katerina Pnefma said that Michalis 'almost died of shame' when he heard about it.[27]

Back on home ground, and with the police now after him, Tsafendas headed straight to his boyhood friend, Giorgos Grispos, who welcomed him delightedly and volunteered to hide him temporarily.[28] Aware that his Portuguese passport would always betray his communist background, he had concluded that if he was ever to get to South Africa, a virgin Greek passport was needed to solve this problem. Optimistically, he presented himself at the office of the honorary Consul for Greece, the Englishman, Anthony Maw, his father's old friend and neighbour. If he thought the family connection would assist him, he was wrong. Well aware that Tsafendas was a communist and suspected of political subversion, Maw received him coldly and refused to issue him with any kind of travel document.[29]

Tsafendas then called on Manuel, who by now was married with children and employed as a transport worker, and found refuge at his house while rethinking his plans.[30] However, before he could move, the police tracked him down and once again, he was behind bars, this time in the civilian prison in Lourenço Marques.[31] If there was one advantage for Tsafendas about being jailed in his home town, it was the presence of his beloved aunt. Artemis visited Tsafendas every day, along with her son, John, bringing him delicious home-cooked food. She always gave some to the guards in the hope that they would treat her nephew kindly.[32] On 15 December 1951, Deputy Police Chief António Fernandes Roquete, with Mário Figueira, agent and clerk, interrogated Tsafendas at length.[33] A few days later, Tsafendas was released without charge,[34] but he was informed that he was banned from Mozambique, that he would be deported and that he must not attempt to return.[35] The officer gave no reason for the ban. Tsafendas protested furiously, but to no avail. When the authorities told him he would have to pay for his return ticket, Tsafendas exploded, demanding to know why he should buy a ticket for a journey which he did not wish to make. Fare or no fare, the authorities wanted Tsafendas out of Lourenço Marques, so on the day after Christmas in 1951, he was put aboard the ship *Angola* for the voyage back to Lisbon.[36] What Tsafendas did not know at the time was that because of his political activities and outspokenness during the late 1930s, he was destined to spend his next twelve years in exile from Mozambique.

In January 1952, the *Angola* reached Lisbon. Tsafendas was reminded that the law required him to pay the Portuguese authorities for his return journey. Furious, he refused point-blank, pointing out that he had been forced onto the *Angola* against his wishes when he wanted to stay in Mozambique, where he was born. Hearing this, the Portuguese authorities asked PIDE in

Mozambique to provide them with Tsafendas's file. This told them that Tsafendas was believed to be a communist and had been investigated for 'unclear activities' when he lived in Mozambique. The Portuguese security authorities, seeking more information on these issues, promptly took Tsafendas into custody for interrogation.[37]

Tsafendas sought to convince his interrogators that he was no longer a communist, nor a member of any subversive organisation and that the accusations of involvement in subversive activities in Mozambique during the late 1930s were mistaken. His efforts were in vain and the PIDE decided to detain him for further interrogation. Accordingly, soon thereafter, he found himself behind bars in the Cascais Fort,[38] as notorious for its treatment of political prisoners as the Aljuba Prison. Both prisons were controlled by PIDE. A decree of 13 June 1949 specifically provided that it was the duty of PIDE to apply or extend 'security measures', namely internment, to suspect persons 'as long as they show themselves dangerous'. In other words, they could keep prisoners in custody indefinitely.[39] There were times when Tsafendas believed that was to be his fate. Though in the event his time in Cascais Fort lasted only a year,[40] but unlike in Aljuba, he was subjected to crude and systematic torture.[41]

The first time Tsafendas was tortured, he thought the guards were going to play music for him. They carried into his cell a wooden box that looked exactly like an American phonograph his father owned, known as a graphophone. It was only when he saw that it sprouted electric cables of different colours that he realised this was no musical device. He was then stripped naked, the wires were attached to parts of his body and the current turned on. The pain was indescribable. What the torturers wanted was information about his activities in Mozambique and any other communist associations he might have; they also pressed him to change his political beliefs. At times, involuntarily, a prisoner would urinate. This would always prompt the guards to turn up the current. It was not long before the pain became unendurable and Tsafendas resorted to the tapeworm story. He babbled that he was not a communist, that a tapeworm that lived inside him was the communist and controlled his actions. His torturers just laughed.[42]

As he had in Aljuba, Tsafendas sought relief with Paul Robeson, humming or whistling the tune of 'Song of Freedon' aloud. When asked what the song was, he gave the same explanation as before. Somehow, he felt that his secret knowledge gave him a measure of authority over the guards, a badly needed feeling of control. He spent months in solitary confinement in a windowless cell, not knowing if it was night or day. He saw no one and talked to no one. He would sit for hours by the door trying to hear sounds, for sound gave hope; deprived of sight, it was the only sense he could use. It assured him that he was still alive. When the guards did remove him from his cell and allow him a few minutes in the prison yard, the daylight hurt his eyes so badly he thought he was going blind.[43]

About 12 months later,[44] his interrogators began to accept that Tsafendas was not a member of any secret organisation and that the actions that brought him to the attention of the authorities – a protest against Portugal's new cotton policy towards Mozambique and the distribution of communist publications – were two where he had acted alone. Even so, they rejected his claims that he was no longer a communist and facing what looked like an indefinite future in solitary confinement, Tsafendas began truly to fear he would not survive. Reduced physically by the minimalist prison diet, lack of exercise and deprivation of daylight, and deeply fearful of further electric torture, he decided his only route to freedom lay in convincing his captors he was insane. To do this, he would resurrect the tapeworm but this time with a measure of sophistication. Claiming to hear voices had not worked and he knew there was no point in shouting, 'I have a tapeworm, I have a tapeworm.' In solitary confinement, he was no longer being interrogated and so needed to raise the issue of his intestinal lodger in a more subtle fashion. Accordingly, he began asking the prison guards for more food. When they said, 'You already had your plate', Tsafendas would reply that the tapeworm had eaten the food and his stomach was empty. Although the guards laughed, Tsafendas repeated this move several times, always claiming the tapeworm had eaten his food. Then, one day, a doctor visited and Tsafendas explained his 'tapeworm problem' with unprecedented sincerity.[45]

The doctor concluded that the case needed further examination and ordered that Tsafendas be taken to the Instituto de Medicina Tropical and to the Hospital do Ultramar for physical and psychiatric examinations. A PIDE report said that 'during his interrogations he gave signs of having some sort of mental disability, which was confirmed by the Hospital do Ultramar'. What the hospital report said was that Tsafendas was a victim of 'intestinal parasitosis (and) manic-depressive psychosis' and, importantly, that he was not dangerous.[46] After more than a year in prison, he was released on 23 April 1953, and found a place in Albergue da Mitra (Hostel Mitra) in Lisbon, a hostel for the aged and destitute.[47]

As the months passed and Tsafendas recovered slowly from his prison experience, it became obvious that he must move on. In Portugal, he was harassed frequently by PIDE and the police with house searches and identification demands, and he was clearly liable to re-arrest at any time.[48] Doggedly, he reapplied for admission to South Africa and then the United States, and when he was routinely rejected, he decided to change his surname. He had long intended to make the change because of the Ottomans' belittling *akis* suffix. Now, he also entertained a slight hope that a new name might escape the attention of the South African and Portuguese authorities in Mozambique and allow him entry into those countries.[49]

As it turned out, this would not be the only time he would use another name. In the following years, he often registered himself for work, as a guest in hotels and certainly at Portuguese governmental departments under a slightly different surname to obscure his past. He was in possession of a birth certificate written in Greek and he would often change or replace one or two letters, while retaining a resemblance to his real name. The name was written as 'Τσαφαντακης', so he would keep the Greek letters similar to English letters, such as T, a, t, k, but substitute some with his own, thus getting names such as Tcamantakis or Tralaitakis. On several occasions, he even used the surnames Stafendas, Tsascadeskis and Tsafedis. Having legally changed his surname, he then sought and received a new Portuguese passport and on 8 January 1954, armed with this valid document, crossed into Scandinavia.[50]

Born and bred in Africa, Tsafendas was shocked by the winter cold in Denmark and Sweden, where he worked as a carpenter and got on well with the local people.[51] Not able to bear the weather, when he heard there were good jobs in West Germany, he decided it would be his next destination and bought a German dictionary to study the language. Tsafendas was curious about a nation that had fallen so completely under the spell of Adolf Hitler. Late in 1954, he made his move. Crossing into West Germany, he made some initial contacts with Christian Church members then settled in the port city of Hamburg on the River Elbe.[52]

Tsafendas's first discovery was that in less than a decade since the war ended, huge strides had been made towards rebuilding the country. As for anti-Semitism and Nazism, he could find no trace of the old ideologies. Ordinary people were welcoming, even to foreigners like himself, and he associated with more communists than any country after Greece. During the two years in West Germany, he found not a hint of the fascism of old and enjoyed exploring the country and getting to know its people.[53] With Tsafendas, Mozambique was never far from his mind and he applied again through the Portuguese embassy for permission to return. Again he was refused for the usual reasons.[54]

Finding a job in Hamburg was not easy because he did not have the necessary papers and his German was still inadequate. Unemployed, homeless and penniless, he needed respite and relief, and so he decided to follow a well-worn route. He presented himself to the Tropen Krankenhaus Hospital in Hamburg, claiming to suffer from tapeworm trouble. He was sloppy, though, and made a mistake which he was careful never to repeat. Instead of contacting the psychiatric department, he reported to general enquiries and was sent to a gastroenterologist, who examined him and found nothing. Despite his protests, a dismayed Tsafendas found himself back on the streets.[55]

Hamburg boasted a fine Greek Orthodox church, St. Nicholas's, where Tsafendas became friendly with the pastor, Father Damaskinos Doxiartis. The priest gave him some small jobs around the church to earn some money. Tsafendas also got in touch with some German communists. Most were students and among them was a German university girl in her early 20s. The girl immediately fell in love with this large, good-natured, clever man from Africa, who had actually fought with the communists in the Greek Civil War. It was not long before Tsafendas moved in with her. Not everything was plain sailing, however. Father Damaskinos was not happy with Tsafendas for associating with communists and often scolded him about it.[56] Worse, Tsafendas made no progress in securing a work permit and while his relationship with the student vastly improved his German, he was embarrassed to live in a young woman's house at her expense. Feeling like a kept man, he finally broke off the relationship and moved out.[57]

The next step, inevitably, was to a hospital. Not for rest and recreation, but to gain some time while he looked for work. On 11 February 1955, Tsafendas went to Ochsenzoll Krankenhaus Hospital in Hamburg, pretending that he had taken 20 sleeping tablets. Doctors pumped his stomach and found nothing and, realising that he would be discharged, Tsafendas started talking about his tapeworm and faking symptoms of depression and torpor. This intrigued the medics, who detained him for further investigation. Tsafendas made use of the time to apply for jobs and to write to his family in South Africa. He was not considered by the doctors to be dangerous and was allowed outside to walk in the hospital's garden. He became friends with the nurses and did small jobs for them, helping distribute patients' meals and bringing needed items from the hospital stores.[58]

Tsafendas had not told anyone about his hospitalisation, thus, a few weeks later, Father Damaskinos was surprised to see him as a patient when he visited sick church members. The priest spread the word about Tsafendas and people started dropping in on him, including Swiss, Greek and American preachers from his Christian Church sect. One of the sect's leaders, an American, Ralph Daniels, who was a good friend of Tsafendas, travelled from Karlsruhe to see him. However, another member of the sect told the doctors that he was suspicious of Tsafendas and did not trust him because he had admitted to being a communist and said he had deserted during the Second World War.[59]

His former girlfriend also visited when she heard about him and they resumed their relationship. Father Damaskinos came with a priest he said would succeed him at St Nicholas's, Father Efthimios Eleftheriadis, and the three chatted. Father Efthimios found Tsafendas to be 'well-mannered ... a very educated and intelligent person'. When friends remarked to Tsafendas that he seemed perfectly well, he appeared embarrassed and said he had just been depressed by his inability to find work. He made no mention of the fake suicide attempt or the tapeworm.[60]

After nearly six months in the hospital, a useful stay as far as Tsafendas was concerned, doctors discharged him on 6 June 1955. A report by two hospital physicians, Dr Bieser and Dr Schmidt-Janssen, said their patient had improved gradually with care, suffered a setback at one point requiring further treatment, but eventually 'was quieter, had no complaints and no more paranoid ideas'. The diagnosis of Dr Bieser, a senior physician, was 'mixed-pictured phasic psychose' while that of a psychiatrist, Dr Nachtwey, was 'endogenous depression, mixed-picture'. Their report added that Tsafendas was picked up by a female friend, who intended to accommodate him.[61] This was the student, with whom Tsafendas stayed happily for the next few weeks.

With the help of his communist friends, Tsafendas eventually found a labourer's job in Hamburg harbour. He was employed illegally as he was still without a work permit. He was surprised to find out that many of his new colleagues were Turkish immigrants. This was his first exposure to Turkish people and, as someone of Greek descent, he was cautious. His grandmother in Egypt forbade him to play with Turkish children, saying they were not good people. Tsafendas, however, believed in the saying 'Take as you find', and in time he became extremely close to many Turks, especially the communists, and found that Greeks and Turks had more in common than separated them. He wished forlornly that he could tell his much-loved grandmother how wrong she was about Turkish people.[62]

Working illegally and still without a work permit despite his dramatically improved language skills, Tsafendas knew he could not continue living like this in West Germany. He lodged yet another application to return to Mozambique and, when it was turned down yet again, he set Plan B in motion. He accepted that colonial Portuguese officials could prevent him from entering Mozambique, but, as a citizen, they could not bar him from Portugal from where he thought he could convince the authorities to remove the ban and allow him to enter his homeland. Thus he applied at the Portuguese Consulate in Hamburg for his 'urgent repatriation' to Portugal and, on 11 June 1955, he returned on board the Portuguese ship, *India*.[63]

Back in Lisbon, Tsafendas resumed life as an itinerant hawker, while associating, though mostly just attending meetings, with leftists, communists and other opponents of the regime.[64] Portugal's dictatorial Prime Minister Antonio de Oliveira Salazar was at the height of his powers and employed a ubiquitous secret police force to spy on perceived enemies of the state, particularly communists. Accordingly, Tsafendas was once again targeted by PIDE and often subjected to house searches and identification inquiries. However, he had long ago learnt how to spot PIDE agents: they all wore the same type of overcoat, in the hot months as well as the cold ones, they carried handguns at the waist which bulged under their clothing, and they pulled down their hat brims like movie gangsters.[65] The truth, of course, was that PIDE were the real gangsters.

For the next three years, Tsafendas badgered the Portuguese for permission to return to Mozambique, but after PIDE supplied information regarding his 'political and professional activities', all his requests were turned down.[66] A typical appeal he hoped might end his exile was a letter he wrote in March to the President of the Portuguese Republic, which said:

> *I am writing to inform you that I have been exiled in Portugal since 1951. I do not know why I am here, since there are no charges against me, and I have not been judged. I wish, according to the law of amnesty, to go back to my homeland, or to be judged before a court so I am at least aware of the motives of my situation, and of who wishes me harm.*[67]

On 18 April, he wrote a similar letter to the Minister of the Interior. The appeals proved fruitless; the PIDE reports on his political past ensured that the ban remained.[68]

In 1957 and 1958, Tsafendas was granted permission to board ships lying in the River Tagus and sell his souvenirs and embroideries.[69] Then spotting a money-making opportunity, he travelled to Belgium for the widely publicised Brussels World Fair (Expo 58), hoping to make a decent profit from sales of his embroidery.[70] The fair was an extraordinary undertaking. Thousands of workmen laboured for three years to prepare a two-square-kilometre site north of Brussels which hosted the pavilions of 44 participating nations. Dedicated by King Baudoin to world peace and economic and social progress, the fair attracted 41 million visitors between April and October of 1958 and was accounted an extraordinary success. Tsafendas did not see it that way.

On arrival, he was as impressed as any other visitor, but then he came across an ethnological exposition that claimed to show a typical village in Belgium's African colony, Congo. Behind a 5ft-high wooden stockade, Congolese families lived on bare earth among mud huts, acting as they were thought to behave in their so-called primitive state in Africa. To his horror, the village was labelled a 'Human Zoo'. The 'human zoo' phenomenon was popular in the late 1800s, when white western people were curious about foreigners, often natives of territories colonised by their own nations. They had heard about them, but before the arrival of cinema, they had no notion of what they looked like.

Tsafendas was outraged by the exposition for the way it exploited, demeaned and humiliated Africans. He found it incomprehensible that a so-called civilised nation could treat its fellow human beings in such a degrading manner. In a typical, spontaneous gesture, he protested angrily to the Expo officials. However, other visitors to the fair seemed to find nothing wrong with the 'zoo' and when Tsafendas's agitation came to the attention of the police, they threatened to arrest him if he continued making a disturbance. Tsafendas's attitude towards the Belgian authorities was already negative because of their reported brutality to the indigenous people in their African colonies, and for a time, he thought of planting a bomb in the fair. It was only a passing thought because he knew that innocent people would die, but the 'Human Zoo' remained a deeply shocking memory. When the first independent Prime Minister of the Congo, Patrice Lumumba, was assassinated three years later with Belgian and US involvement, Tsafendas's antipathy for the Brussels government turned to lifelong anger. He did not blame the ordinary Belgian, who he knew had nothing to do with the country's colonial practices, but he was so angered he decided he could stay in Belgium no longer.[71] As it happened, the Belgian exhibit was among the last of its kind. By then, *tableaux vivant* of primitive peoples were being seen widely as degrading and racist and were banned by many countries. The saddest part of the Brussels story is that of the 297 Congolese who populated the 'zoo', an unknown number died during the show and were buried in a mass, unmarked grave.

With some money in his wallet, Tsafendas decided to bypass Portugal and its persistent harassment and try his luck once again in West Germany. He arrived there in September 1958 and registered at the Aliens Office in Frankfurt. Soon afterwards, he received a work permit.[72] The first thing he did was to celebrate by buying a second-hand automobile from an American soldier. It was a vast, flashy, Detroit specimen, not in great shape but a bargain price because the owner was anxious to get rid of it before returning to the United States.[73]

Tsafendas quickly found a job as a welder at the heavy engineering company of Fries & Son in Frankfurt. Eight years later, Horst Hartmann, senior personnel officer at the company, remembered Tsafendas's arrival for work clearly:

> *He drove up in a big, battered American car. I thought he was more likely to apply for an executive job than as a welder. He was well-dressed and well-mannered and was extremely courteous … a very pleasant man. He*

> *looked like a satisfied, successful businessman, and his looks certainly didn't fit the job he wanted. But he spoke good German, so I took him on.*[74]

Six weeks later, Tsafendas quit Fries & Son, saying the job was a bit too energetic for him, but in his briefcase was an excellent reference from his boss. Hartmann said: 'We liked him … he was always laughing, a good worker. He left of his own accord … we would have liked to keep him.'[75] Short as his tenure was, it is clear that Tsafendas was not forgotten by his workmates. Interviewed eight years later, Guenter Haafe, 57, the factory gatekeeper, remembered the jovial greeting Tsafendas gave him every morning. He said: 'He was a jolly man, always smiling and friendly. He would almost always come into my locker room to say hi. He was really one of the friendliest workers I have met and trust me, in my twelve years as a doorman I have seen thousands and thousands of faces coming in and out. This man was courteous, they do not make them like that anymore.' Three other workmates, questioned about Tsafendas shortly after he had killed Verwoerd, said, 'He was a nice guy', 'He was a good comrade' and 'He left me with a good impression.'[76]

***

In September 1958, while Tsafendas was working for Fries & Son, Dr Verwoerd was elected Prime Minister of South Africa in succession to Strijdom. Malan had retired in 1954 and was succeeded by Strijdom, who died on 24 August 1958. As a minister under Malan and Strijdom, Dr Verwoerd had earned a name for himself as the author and enforcer of a series of bold racial policies. The opposition United Party characterised him as an 'evil genius' but his devoted National Party followers fondly dubbed him 'Oom (Uncle) Henny'[77] and *Die Rots* (The Rock). What they were saying was that Verwoerd was the bedrock required for the continuance of nationalist rule, indeed for the future of white rule in black Africa.[78]

Despite his standing in the party, Dr Verwoerd's rise to ultimate power was no shoo-in. When Strijdom died, there was a short but intense struggle for leadership of the National Party involving Dr Verwoerd, Dr Eben Dönges [79] and Strijdom's Justice Minister, Charles Swart.[80] Party elections took place on 2 September 1958 and Verwoerd won the first round with 80 votes against 52 for Dönges and 41 for Swart. Short of an outright majority, a run-off took place between the two front-runners and Dr Verwoerd crossed the line with 98 votes to Dönges's 75. Verwoerd attributed his victory to the will of God and celebrated with his supporters by singing the traditional Dutch anthem, 'Let God's Blessing on Him Fall'.[81] After his victory, Verwoerd stepped up the segregation of the races in almost every aspect of their lives. By now, he believed that he had been chosen by God to lead the Afrikaners and thus perceived himself as a man with a divine mission.[82]

The *New York Times* characterised Dr Verwoerd's victory as 'bad news', predicting that

> *there will be no rejoicing anywhere, not even among the majority of the South African people, that Hendrik Verwoerd has been chosen Prime Minister. This is an affliction which the unhappy people of South Africa will have to bear for a while ... Dr Verwoerd is an outstanding example of a gradually disappearing breed – the racist. In Hitler's days he was pro-Nazi and anti-Semitic. His passion and his role in South Africa today is that of the champion of an extremist white supremacy. He is the most fanatical exponent of apartheid.*[83]

For black South Africans, Dr Verwoerd's ascendancy turned out to be very bad news indeed. Quickly he replaced moderate MPs with extremists, often pro-Nazis and members of the Broederbond.[84] He then began transforming the comparatively mild form of apartheid which had existed for the last ten years into a system of complete segregation, causing the political atmosphere in the country to take a significant turn for the worse.[85] Focusing on rigorous controls of urban blacks and the creation of 'homelands', Dr Verwoerd's measures involved no less than the massive restructuring of an entire society and the movement of enormous numbers of people at great expense.[86] Verwoerd-style apartheid sought to control every single aspect of inter-racial relations in the country. At the same time, he moved ruthlessly to crush any opposition to his policies. According to the *Cape Times* in 1958, 'banishments, deportations, shootings, burnings, arson, closing of schools' were the order of the day in what it called 'Verwoerd's Native Empire'.[87]

While Dr Verwoerd was working effectively to turn South Africa completely white and segregated, Tsafendas was finding out about West Germany, where he was to spend a year in two well-paid jobs. For six months, he worked for Anglo-American Fashions and Designers in Frankfurt, and the rest at a US Army printing works in Hochst, a district in Frankfurt.[88] Salaries were good and Tsafendas was living a comfortable life. He toured the country with his car and visited the birthplace of Karl Marx in Trier.[89]

Tsafendas also applied yet again to return to Mozambique and was again turned down. As for getting back to South Africa, that now seemed impossible. The apartheid government had passed the Suppression of Communism Act and was enforcing it vigorously. Tsafendas knew that as a former registered member of the South African Communist Party and well known to PIDE for his communist activities, he would never be permitted legal entry to the country. He therefore decided to visit Britain, a country he had always wanted to see. First, though, he returned to Hamburg to bid farewell to his former girlfriend and his friends. He tried to sell the big American car but received no decent bids. Friends offered to sell it on his behalf and send the money to England, but in the end, he decided to give the vehicle to his former girlfriend in gratitude for the love and generosity she had shown him.[90] She was delighted and on 15 May 1959, she drove Tsafendas from Hamburg to Calais in France, from where he took the ferry to Dover, England.[91]

Chapter 8

Teacher of English and Bomb-maker

Tsafendas's official welcome to Britain was casual by any standards. In Dover on 16 May 1959,[1] he showed his Portuguese passport to an immigration officer and asked for a work permit, genially suggesting that because of his many languages, he might get a job as a hotel porter. His request was stonily refused. He then asked if he could remain in Britain as a student. Negative! Instead, he was given a tourist visa expiring on 2 September and told that he must not take employment and must leave on or before the appointed date.[2] With his usual insouciance, Tsafendas thanked the official and boarded a train to London without the slightest intention of leaving the UK until it suited him.

In London, he got a room in a cheap hotel and began exploring the city he knew so well from his reading: the famous red buses and telephone boxes, the underground train system which Londoners called The Tube, Trafalgar Square with Admiral Nelson atop the pillar and Piccadilly Circus with the statue of Eros suggesting love might be in the air. The capital city was a few years away from the fabled Swinging Sixties, but London's Soho district was not short of jazz clubs, pubs and discos, and Tsafendas lost no time in making their acquaintance. He listened to speakers at Hyde Park Corner, placed flowers on the grave of Karl Marx in Highgate Cemetery and sent souvenirs to his family in South Africa.

Perhaps through force of habit or in a surge of optimism, Tsafendas also applied once again to enter South Africa on 4 August 1959. Had he known the contents of his immigration file, he might not have bothered. It stated that he had sought permanent residence status in South Africa numerous times without success, that in 1941 he entered illegally and was fined; it said he had communist leanings and had threatened to enter without permission if he was denied again. The clerk dealing with this latest application wrote sarcastically, 'Refusal is suggested!' The following month, on 11 September, Tsafendas, named officially as 'Demetrio Tsafandakis, alias Demetrio Tsafendas', was placed on the stop list of the South African Department of the Interior. This signalled that the department's head office needed to be consulted in the event of any new application by Tsafendas.[3] The department noted that he had made no fewer than nine applications to be allowed into South Africa (1935, 1936, 1938, 1941, 1946, 1947, 1948, 1950 and 1959), all of which had been rejected.[4]

Although he looked for work in London in defiance of his visa conditions, with Tsafendas, politics was never far away, and when he discovered the Anti-

Slavery Society on Vauxhall Bridge Road, he visited its offices frequently. Sometimes he spoke at its meetings about the treatment of Mozambicans and black South Africans in their respective countries. He became friendly with the secretary of the society, Commander Thomas Fox-Pitt, a former colonial officer in Northern Rhodesia and a leading figure in the modern anti-slavery movement. Fox-Pitt often acted as a tour guide for Tsafendas, who helped to translate documents for the society and occasionally acted as an interpreter for African immigrants. He also participated in any demonstrations which the society organised or supported.[5]

One aspect of London life which Tsafendas happily embraced was its multiculturalism. It was the first time he had seen so many people of different races mixing freely. He formed the opinion that black immigrants in Britain, nearly all of them recent arrivals from the Caribbean, were treated better than African-Americans in the United States. He found ordinary Britons welcoming to foreigners such as himself. His prejudice against Britain because of its long record of colonialism and its support for the royalists in the Greek Civil War began to soften.[6]

Through the Anti-Slavery Society, Tsafendas met members of the nascent Anti-Apartheid Movement, which was to become the strongest international opposition to the apartheid regime in South Africa. Tsafendas took part in many meetings and the fact that he was seen as a white with South African links condemning apartheid was important for the movement. He also met and worked closely with the ANC representative in London, Tennyson Xola Makiwane, who he came to admire deeply. He gladly helped with tasks such as putting up posters and distributing leaflets.[7]

Tsafendas also attended political rallies in Hyde Park, Labour Party meetings at London's Caxton Hall and events organised by the Committee of African Organisations.[8] His personal belief was that most Western governments, whatever their rhetoric, in practice supported the white regime in South Africa, and that violence would be needed to bring down apartheid. He desperately tried to recruit people to take part in an uprising in South Africa, but none of his London comrades agreed to do anything violent; however, they gave their support to the stance of the ANC, which was then one of non-violence.[9]

With his money running out and without a work permit, Tsafendas was offered illegal employment as a waiter in a restaurant owned by two Greek-Cypriot brothers. When one of them discovered that Tsafendas was an exceptional dancer, he asked him to perform for the customers, which he did, to much applause, especially from the lady diners. One night, a young woman asked Tsafendas to teach her the zeibekiko, a supposedly strictly masculine solo routine. Tsafendas said he would be happy to do so, but the restaurant dance floor was too small. When the lady said he could come to her home and give a lesson, her partner intervened and said thank you, but no thank you and pulled her away. Next day, the second brother told Tsafendas, 'I pay you to wait tables, not to dance.' The two had already disagreed on politics and an argument erupted. Tsafendas had had enough. Soon afterwards, he quit the job and walked away.[10]

By now, money was a serious problem and Tsafendas sold some of his clothes for cash. When Fox-Pitt heard of this, he gave him an old grey flannel suit he owned and arranged for him to stay at a hostel in Victoria, owned by a member of the society, which housed indigent immigrants without charge until they were settled. Tsafendas was deeply embarrassed by Fox-Pitt's generosity and gave him one of his treasured copies of Paul Robeson's album *Songs of Free Men,* which he had brought from the United States. Tsafendas never forgot Fox-Pitt and considered him one of the finest men he ever met.[11] For his part, Fox-Pitt characterised Tsafendas shortly after Verwoerd's assassination as 'very simple-minded and not at all sinister'.[12]

Eventually, Tsafendas left the hostel, unwilling to accept charity any longer. Not only was he now jobless and penniless, he was also illegal. The date for his departure had passed and Tsafendas assumed he was on the British police's 'Wanted' list as an illegal alien. His solution? To take refuge in a hospital until he could find work that would pay him enough money to leave Britain altogether. Tsafendas went to St Pancras Hospital in central London, said he was not well and blamed a tapeworm. By now, he had refined the tapeworm pitch so that he knew exactly what to say, how to look and, most importantly, how to answer the doctors' questions. Thus he had no difficulty in securing admission to the mental ward.[13]

Tsafendas did not like St Pancras, where he was treated for depressive psychosis. The building was cold, he hated the food, there were lots of rules and he was not allowed outside of his ward. He spent much of his time reading newspapers, checking the jobs columns and writing many letters to potential employers.[14] This voluminous correspondence roused the curiosity and suspicion of the hospital staff. To allay this, and reinforce the belief that he had mental problems, Tsafendas wrote a jumbled, crazy letter that made no sense at all and addressed it to Harold Macmillan, the British Prime Minister.[15] He did not post it, but made sure that the doctors would see it. It ended up in his medical file as evidence that he was not entirely sane. More importantly for Tsafendas, he was left undisturbed to continue applying for jobs and sending letters to friends.

One day, he heard about an island off the south coast of England named the Isle of Wight, where there was a marvellous psychiatric hospital that looked more like an ancient castle. He had loved castles since childhood and decided this was a place he had to see.[16] On casually inquiring, he discovered that the hospital was rated as one of the best psychiatric institutions in Britain, but it only accepted patients on transfer from other hospitals. Typically concluding that this was a problem that could be solved by direct action, Tsafendas checked himself out of the St Pancras Hospital and headed for the Isle of Wight. On 4 October, penniless and by now illegal for over a month, Tsafendas secured admission to the Whitecroft Mental Hospital, claiming he had problems with a tapeworm.[17] The hospital staff were suspicious. Patients invariably arrived from other medical institutions by agreement, nobody just turned up on the doorstep. Tsafendas claimed that he was a tourist and had fallen ill suddenly. Once again, he convinced the medical experts and he was admitted.

It did not take Tsafendas long to realise he was onto a winner and the hospital was the best he had ever known. The food was good, the rules were relaxed and many of the patients were there voluntarily. It was like living in a luxury hotel. Tsafendas was allowed to leave the ward and stroll in the gardens without supervision and, before long, he was slipping away from the hospital to explore the island. He even visited some pubs and chatted with the locals about their experiences during the Second World War. One night, to his consternation, he spotted one of the hospital psychiatrists walking towards him accompanied by a woman. There was no way he could avoid them. The doctor greeted Tsafendas with a simple 'good evening'. Tsafendas responded and they passed by. Had the doctor recognised him? Why else did he greet him? Tsafendas could not sleep that night, but next day, the psychiatrist spoke normally when they met and Tsafendas realised he had not been identified.[18] This was probably because he had been wearing a hat the previous evening and it was already dusk. As for the greeting, this was a rural area where people acknowledged passers-by whether they knew them or not.

The Isle of Wight idyll did not last. On 3 December, police turned up at the hospital and arrested Tsafendas for outstaying his visa. He was not surprised. He suspected that his tapeworm story had never really convinced the doctors and eventually, they decided to check with the authorities. The hospital issued a medical certificate which described his mental condition as good enough for him to travel to any country and a swift deportation hearing was held. The immigration lawyers argued for his removal to Portugal, but Tsafendas said he feared arrest and harassment there and asked to be sent back to the country from which he arrived, West Germany. This was agreed and, within 24 hours, Tsafendas was on his way to Frankfurt.[19]

***

Soon after arriving for his third sojourn in West Germany, Tsafendas was given a work permit and settled down to a job at a tractor factory in Munich.[20] However, he kept a close watch on events in South Africa and it was these which were to lead him to his fateful rendezvous with Dr Verwoerd six years in the future. The early months of 1960 were some of the most turbulent in South Africa's history as angry protests against increasingly tough apartheid restrictions raged all over the country. They took place in the Zeerust area, in Sekukuniland, at Virginia, Kroonstad, Pietermaritzburg and Harding, as well as in several districts in Natal.[21] A peaceful protest at Sharpeville, a black township south of Johannesburg, on 21 March 1960, was transformed into a massacre when police opened fire on the crowd, killing 69 black South Africans and wounding 180. A pivotal event in the history of apartheid, the Sharpeville massacre shocked the world and caused an outcry of international proportions. The police had used the banned dum-dum bullets, which split and expanded upon impact, causing a larger wound. When casualties were taken to local hospitals, the police warned medical staff, who had seen the injuries, that it would not be in the national interest for them to make 'exaggerated' disclosures.[22] Police at the hospitals removed bodies that had been badly damaged by the dum-dums, and an estimated 24 such corpses were buried in secret to avoid post-mortems.[23] General van den Bergh, then a police captain, ordered officers at the Baragwanath hospital to drag wounded blacks from their beds, irrespective of their condition. They were taken in handcuffs to Boksburg Prison, where they were stripped naked, hosed down and ordered to dress again in their bloody clothes. To punish them for their 'agitation', they were forced to wear the same clothes unwashed for months afterwards.[24]

As news of the massacre spread, the government accused a bizarre list of culprits, including just about everyone but themselves. Verwoerd blamed anti-apartheid 'propaganda' which, he said, had 'an inciting effect on the Bantus'.[25] He also said Sharpeville had been the result of a communist conspiracy[26] and that it could never be described as a reaction against apartheid[27] but was just a 'periodic phenomenon'.[28] He even claimed that the demonstrators had fired first, although no weapons were found among them.[29] Looking further afield, Verwoerd said British Prime Minister Harold Macmillan was partly to blame[30] for having 'stirred up' black people during a visit to South Africa when he spoke of a 'wind of change' in Africa.[31]

In addition to Sharpeville, there were killings that day at the Langa and Nyanga townships near Cape Town. When some among a crowd of 10,000 marching against the pass laws threw stones at whites, the police opened fire and launched baton charges. Two protestors were killed and 50 injured.[32] After Sharpeville, Verwoerd declared a state of emergency, under which many meetings were banned, people and buildings searched, newspaper editors intimidated, scores of black people killed and thousands arrested.[33] Citizens knew not to say anything that might be interpreted as subverting the government's authority or inciting resistance. Opposition newspapers, fearful of censorship and of action against individual employees, carried no photographs of the massacre victims.[34]

The ANC and the PAC called for a day of mourning and work stoppages, and there were demonstrations all over the country.[35] Police were ordered to beat the strikers back to work.[36] The emergency regulations were so wide-ranging that even a scientific lecture about sex in Witbank was banned.[37] In the 21 days immediately following Sharpeville, some 88 blacks were killed and 365 injured as a result of state violence. In total, 11,729 blacks, 90 Asians, 98 whites and 36 coloureds were detained without being charged or put on trial. As late as 31 August 1960, only 400 of them had been released.[38] Shrugging off international condemnation and calls for reform, Verwoerd instructed National Party leaders not to waver from established race policies.[39]

It was during this period of continuing state violence that Tsafendas decided he must 'do something' to hit back at Verwoerd and the apartheid state. Night after night, he pondered options. Angrily, he considered planting a bomb at the South African Consulate in Cologne, right there in West Germany, but later, he concluded that a better option would be to return to South Africa and take up arms against apartheid on the front line.[40] Unknown to Tsafendas, he was not the only one disgusted by Verwoerd's brutal dictatorship. On 8 April 1960, Verwoerd outlawed the ANC and the PAC[41] and on the following day, David Pratt, a British-South African farmer and millionaire businessman, shot Verwoerd twice in the head at the Rand Easter Show in Milner Park, Johannesburg.[42] Pratt was a man who was deeply upset by the racial injustices he encountered in South Africa and he opposed apartheid fiercely. Concerned by poverty among Africans, he built a school and houses on his farm for black workers and their children. A member of both the South African and British Liberal Parties, Pratt was active in the British Anti-Apartheid Movement, then in its infancy, and a leading supporter of the move to boycott South African goods; he often spoke publicly against apartheid at Liberal party meetings. Pratt moved freely among prominent members of the Anti-Apartheid Movement, including David Ennals, its chairman, and Jeremy Thorpe, MP, later to become Leader of the Liberal Party.[43]

On 11 April, just two days after the shooting, Eric Louw, Verwoerd's Minister of Forreign Affairs, stated that 'in this country there is complete freedom of the Press'. This claim was followed within days by a clampdown on information about Pratt. A few days earlier, Norman Phillips, a Canadian and foreign editor of the Toronto *Daily Star*, had been arrested for filing 'reports critical of the government' which, it was claimed, could damage Canadian–South African relations.[44] Louw said that Phillips would be freed from custody when the police had finished interrogating him on condition that he agreed to quit South Africa immediately. A few days later, in Cape Town, police arrested another foreign journalist, Myrna Mackenzie of the London *Daily Herald* and the *New York Post*.[45] At the same time, the editor of *Africa South* magazine fled the country in fear of imminent arrest.[46] The Pratt blackout was announced the next day by the police, banning the media from publishing anything about him, including his name and photograph, until the end of the emergency.[47] According to a government spokesman, the intention was to avoid ill-feeling 'between the white races'.[48] In reality, the authorities wanted to suppress the picture of Pratt emerging from the foreign press, that of a perfect gentleman, compassionate and concerned about injustice, poverty and inequality, a man who loathed Verwoerd and his policy of race segregation and was an active member of the Anti-Apartheid Movement.

Pratt, an epileptic, who had suffered from depression for many years, was found to be unfit to stand trial and was ordered confined to a mental hospital. In reality, Pratt was perfectly sane, as all of his friends stated before and after his trial. However, his defence team believed the only way he could secure a lighter punishment would be to plead insanity. Convincing the court was not difficult because it was more convenient for the state that he should be found 'unfit' than revealed as a privileged white millionaire who loathed apartheid. This argument held sway despite Pratt ignoring his lawyers and delivering to the court an extraordinary, lucid and logical attack on apartheid. In the course of his peroration, he declared:

> *I don't say it of my own accord, and I don't say it as David Pratt, I say it as a message for every South African, Afrikaner, English South African, Coloured, Indian, Bantu, Malay. Every person in South Africa has got to play his part if we are to build the South Africa that I know can be built … (South Africa) has got to take her rightful place in the community of nations and in particular the continent of Africa. She is the finest country in this continent and there is no better in the world and she is capable of doing it, and she can do it, and she has a great and glorious future, a glittering future waiting for her as long as she observes the basic laws of God and human dignity, which of course, means, in the words, I think, of Macmillan at the time, 'Rule by merit and not pigment of skin.' South Africa has to throw off the slimy snake apartheid which is gripping its throat. Practical apartheid, obviously, cannot go immediately. The principle of apartheid has to be flung off, and then it is out, and then it is up to the Coloured section of the population how rapidly the practical*

> *section is put into effect ... Your future lies before you. If you are worthy of it – this I say to the people of South Africa – you take it.*[49]

Pratt regretted bowing to his lawyers' advice and claiming insanity, which he came to consider an act of cowardice. He determined he would 'set the record straight' with a retrial at which he would accept criminal responsibility for his act. However, the authorities refused his retrial request. They feared, with good reason, that Pratt wanted to turn the new proceedings into a trial of apartheid, with the participation of many prominent people and anti-apartheid activists as defence witnesses such as Jeremy Thorpe, David Ennals, Sir Paul Dukes, former MI6 agent who was a close friend of Pratt, and Harry Oppenheimer, one of South Africa's wealthiest and most influential men.[50] It was soon after this that Pratt was found dead. Attendants who entered his hospital room on 1 October 1961 discovered that Pratt had died of asphyxiation, apparently by tying the ends of his bedsheet to the leg of his bed, then putting his head in the loop and rolling over and over until he ran out of oxygen.[51] Devising such a gruesome but clever method of self-destruction was well within the bounds of Pratt's abilities, but no inquest was held and alternative possibilities were never explored. Pratt's death was arbitrarily ruled as suicide, though doubts must remain considering that many so-called suicides during apartheid proved to be murders by the police or security forces. Pratt died on his 53rd birthday, shortly before he was due for a parole hearing.

Verwoerd's survival, after two bullets were fired into his head, was remarkable. All he was left with was some loss of hearing in his right ear and a small scar on the chin.[52] Naturally, he attributed his survival to divine intervention. Verwoerd's survival appeared to strengthen his self-perception as the man who saved the country's whites and to harden his line on apartheid. Rejecting calls to soft-pedal policy after Sharpeville, he vowed, 'If I cannot save the country, then I would rather resign. I will never be an accomplice in the destruction of our people by abandoning our policy.'[53]

Later that year, in September and October, a series of sabotage attacks swept South Africa, targeting the industrial infrastructure. The most serious targeted a pylon, carrying electricity to Johannesburg, causing a 45-minute blackout to hundreds of houses in the city. The saboteurs were members of the National Liberation Committee (NLC), which turned to direct action after concluding that Verwoerd's government was not only unwilling to negotiate but was resorting to violence against peaceful demonstrators, as at Sharpeville, to crush any resistance to apartheid.[54] Soon afterwards, the ANC took a similar decision and formed Umkhonto we Sizwe (Spear of the Nation) as its military wing.

The key year of 1961 was marked by one further major event, which trained the international spotlight on South Africa and enraged the apartheid government: in October, the president of the ANC, Chief Albert Luthuli, was awarded the Nobel Peace Prize. The first non-Westerner to be so honoured, he was commended for 'his efforts to seek equality by non-violent means'. In what the *New York Times* described as 'a scathing attack', the SABC pointed out that Luthuli had been confined to his home area since 1953 under the Suppression of Communism Act, that he had spent a year in custody on a treason charge, had hailed the Freedom Charter as 'a revolutionary document' and had burned his pass after Sharpeville.[55] The banning order confined Luthuli to his home, prevented him from making statements or receiving visitors and even kept him from church on Sundays. However, fearing international condemnation, the apartheid authorities suspended the ban for ten days in December 1961 and Luthuli travelled to Oslo, where he was feted widely and presented with his Prize.[56]

As for Tsafendas, since it was impossible for him to get back to South Africa or Mozambique legally – and heaven knows he had tried often enough – he decided to take the illegal route, travelling from the north through the heart of the continent to Mozambique and from there into South Africa. It would be a gigantic task, nearly 4,000 miles from Egypt to Johannesburg, through six countries and across as many frontiers, but he was sure it could be done.

Tsafendas took delivery of a temporary Portuguese passport on 25 May 1960 and started his journey on 30 June, leaving Munich by train through Austria and Yugoslavia to Piraeus in Greece. After a few days at the home of his friend John Michaletos, he took the ferry to Alexandria. His beloved grandmother was long dead, but he spent several days visiting old friends and acquaintances. Then came his first bureaucratic hurdle; his temporary passport expired and he was turned down for a new one by the Portuguese Consulate. Undaunted, Tsafendas's thoughts turned to Beirut, capital of Lebanon. There, he had heard, an enterprising traveller could get whatever he wanted, including, he assumed, fake passports. Thus, using a refugee *laissez-passer* document,[57] he rode a ferry to Lebanon. In Beirut, he stayed for a few days with members of the Christian Church, but was unable to get the passport he wanted.[58]

Meanwhile, in South Africa, great changes were afoot. A referendum was set for 5 October 1960 to decide whether South Africa wanted to remain in the Commonwealth of Nations or become a republic. Only the country's 3,067,638 whites could vote, the remaining 12,773,490 blacks being declared ineligible.[59] The call for a republic won by a respectable margin, 52.3% of the votes.[60] To 'sever the British connection' was a popular political catch-phrase among Afrikaner nationalists at the time and the referendum victory fulfilled a dream nurtured by thousands since their defeat in the Boer War.[61] Passage of the referendum gave a huge boost to Dr Verwoerd's standing nationally while confirming his untouchable status among the Afrikaners.[62] Soon after the vote, Nelson Mandela asked Dr Verwoerd to call a national constitutional convention, warning that if he refused, there would be a massive three-day strike. Verwoerd's response was negative, born of his belief that South Africa was a 'white country and any concessions to the blacks only means demands for fresh concessions'.[63] Mandela described Verwoerd's South Africa as a 'grim dictatorship'.[64] Dr Verwoerd responded with a patronising dismissal of the Commonwealth, claiming that those members of the group who attacked apartheid did so as a result of their 'immaturity'.[65]

After spending Christmas of 1960 in Beirut, Tsafendas, although he did not have any valid travel papers, somehow managed to travel to Jerusalem. There, he went to the Consulate of Spain on 20 January 1961, requesting a visa for Israel as a refugee. The Consul-General could not determine if Tsafendas was indeed a political refugee and declined to assist him.[66] Running out of options, Tsafendas contacted the Portuguese Consulate in Jerusalem, but his past came to haunt him once again. A telegram from Lisbon advised the Consul-General of suspicions concerning Tsafendas's communist involvement in Lourenço Marques.

In Jerusalem, Tsafendas was accommodated by the Lutheran Church and took the opportunity to visit the Jordan River and the famed Christian sites of the Holy Land. Acknowledging that his grand plan to walk through Africa was dead, at least for now, he decided to return to Portugal. However, there was to be a lengthy diversion before that ever happened. Travelling through Lebanon and Syria by bus, he crossed the Taurus mountain range into Turkey and arrived in Ankara in May 1961. There he stayed for a month, learning the rudiments of the Turkish language.[67]

***

It was June when Tsafendas reached Istanbul. Penniless once more, he discovered that in Turkey, you could earn money by giving blood at a hospital. He promptly rolled up his sleeve and was 'paid about one pound for a pint of blood',[68] roughly equivalent to a Turkish labourer's weekly wage.[69] Not long after he arrived, he visited the Greek Orthodox church of Panagia in the city's Pera district and met Father Nikola Banovic, the church's 31-year-old pastor. Because he had no steady work, Tsafendas began to help out around the church and the adjoining cemetery. One role he fell into with ease was that of tour guide for Greek visitors. Most were interested only in Greek Orthodox churches from the time of the Byzantium, such as Hagia Sophia, so Tsafendas was comfortable showing them around. He also took the tourists to Greek taverns and Greek souvenir shops. It was Father Nikola who recommended Tsafendas to the visitors and from this association, there began a friendship that was to endure over many years. The priest was impressed by Tsafendas's knowledge of the Bible and scripture, which he could cite by heart, and by his cultivated manner of speaking Greek. He described him as 'a very polite and well-mannered man, a gentleman'. He noted that he always had books with him, some of them in Turkish, and Tsafendas explained that his quick command of the language owed something to associating with Turkish immigrants when he lived in West Germany.[70]

One day, Tsafendas asked if he could rent a small, bare room near the church, whereupon Father Nikola invited him to move into a small spare room in his own home, in a block of flats near the church. The priest wanted no rent and Tsafendas, embarrassed, refused. Eventually, the two agreed that, in return, Tsafendas would help with odd jobs at the church. At that time, a large stray dog lived in the graveyard. Nobody knew where it came from, but the priests and church-goers fed it with bread and water. When he saw it, Tsafendas, the dog-lover, took charge. He cleaned the animal's matted fur, fed it meat and bones, and built it a wooden kennel. He named it Robespierre, after the French revolutionary leader.[71]

Father Nikola was Greek of Yugoslav origin and widely respected by the church. He was married with one child, a 12-year-old daughter, Eleni, who he absolutely adored. Tsafendas and Eleni bonded immediately and spent hours together. She called him Uncle Dimitri and he addressed her by the diminutive 'Elenitsa' meaning 'Little Eleni'. He helped with her studies, taught her rudimentary English and held her spellbound with exotic stories about distant Africa. He taught her African children's stories as well as Mozambican songs, plus one song that she came to love above all – Paul Robeson's 'Canoe Song'.

A favourite pastime for both men was playing chess and backgammon. Tsafendas loved backgammon but had not played it since his father taught him as a boy and he was no match for Father Nikola. Although he lost constantly, Tsafendas always insisted on a new game, which the priest accepted reluctantly because he found Tsafendas easy to beat. After a couple of months, however, the tables turned and Tsafendas won half of their games. They also played chess, where the priest turned out to be no match for Tsafendas, whom he considered to be the best player he ever faced.[72]

The priest was astonished at how fast this Mozambican-Greek man improved his Turkish. Tsafendas said this was mostly because he often visited the Grand Bazaar, where commodities of every description were bought, sold and noisily argued about. Listening to the exchanges and the bargaining and talking to the merchants was a huge help with colloquialisms and the common argot. Hearing about Tsafendas's tutoring skills, the parents of some of Elenitsa's school friends asked him to teach English to their children too and he happily agreed. Before long, he was instructing more than 20 Greek children in one of the church's spare rooms. Soon, Turkish children who lived in the neighbourhood heard about the lessons and Tsafendas scheduled classes for them too, as often as three or four times per week. Some of the Turkish students were Jewish, which made it a unique class for its time, containing Christian, Muslim and Jewish children! The children adored their unorthodox teacher, who made them laugh, told them fascinating stories about Africa and taught them folk tunes from Mozambique.[73]

Because Tsafendas refused to take money for his teaching, some mothers brought food from their own kitchens, most often dolmadakia (stuffed grape leaves), one of his favourite dishes. After a few weeks, Tsafendas had as many as 50 students attending lessons throughout the week, with the main class held in a room at the church after Sunday worship. Tsafendas took his teaching duties very seriously and always wore a suit in front of his classes. Father Nikola's wife laundered and ironed his clothes. Father Nikola remembered Tsafendas saying that 'education is one of the most important things in life'. 'He loved children,' the priest said. 'He was a good-hearted man with high principles.'[74]

One problem which arose from living in Father Nikola's house was that of the Greek Orthodox mass on Sundays, which always took place in the early hours. Tsafendas had firm ideas about sleep. He considered that time spent sleeping was time wasted and he only slept long enough to stay healthy and that six hours was his weekday maximum. However, on Sundays, he liked to give himself two or three hours more. 'Even Jesus rested on Sunday,' he used to joke. Since joining the Christian Church, Tsafendas had stopped his irregular attendance at Greek Orthodox services, but being Father Nikola's guest imposed a certain obligation, he felt. He solved the problem by attending the Greek Sunday mass and shifting his Sunday lie-in to Saturdays.[75]

As Tsafendas grew closer to Father Nikola, he began to tell him about his life, including the circumstances of his birth and how he considered both Marika and Amelia to be his mothers. He said he was devastated that he had never met his birth mother but Marika had always been a real mother to him. He showed the priest a photograph of his stepmother and snaps of his father and his siblings, which he kept in his wallet. Although he had not seen them since 1941, they would always send him pictures of family events. Most of all, Dimitri spoke of his admiration for his father and his sadness that he could not see him in person. He explained why he was banned from Mozambique and South Africa and he even spoke of his arrests and torture by the Portuguese and how he 'played the fool' to make them stop, though he did not mention the specifics of his mad act. The priest said although Tsafendas was saddened by his exile and forced to live 'like a gypsy', he often declared proudly, 'When enemies consider you a threat, then you are on the right path.'[76]

Tsafendas and Father Nikola spent many hours talking about Christianity, but even more about politics. When Tsafendas admitted he was a communist, the priest urged him not to reveal this to anyone because Communism was banned in Turkey. Furthermore, when he discovered that Tsafendas had two records of communist songs, one in Italian and one in Russian, he pleaded with him not to play them. What Father Nikola found strange about Tsafendas was that he was both a communist and a Christian, a devotee of an atheistic philosophy and a believer in an all-powerful, loving God. Tsafendas always gave the same answer: that Jesus was himself a communist, thousands of years before Karl Marx. He was a rebel, Tsafendas said, just like Spartacus, Fidel Castro, Che Guevara, Simone Bolivar, Benjamin Franklin and V.I. Lenin. He argued that Jesus and his 12 apostles were anti-establishment rebels who constituted the first communist movement in history. He denounced the missionary churches in Africa for betraying Christ's revolutionary stance and supporting the European colonialists. Tsafendas's proposition, that if Jesus was alive today, he would have fought apartheid and joined with the rebels in Cuba, did not convince Father Nikola.[77]

One day, while discussing life in Istanbul for Greeks, Tsafendas said he believed it would be better for everyone if there were no religions and nation-states, if there was no distinction between Greeks and Turks and between Muslims and Christians. Father Nikola, who always considered his friend a dedicated Christian despite his occasional criticism of the church, was deeply shocked. This, he thought, was a step too far. It emerged that Tsafendas had been talking recently to both Greeks and Turks about the pogrom against Greeks in Istanbul six years earlier. Turkish mobs had killed several Greek individuals and destroyed Orthodox churches and Greek properties. Although he had grown up believing his grandmother's denunciations of Turks, Tsafendas had since mingled with a lot of Turkish people and found he could no longer hold such opinions. At the same time, although he had made some good Turkish friends in Istanbul, he believed they retained some suspicions about him simply because he was Greek and Christian. For him, Greeks were exactly the same as Turks, that if this barrier of nationality and religion could be lifted, the two peoples could live happily with each other, since they had so much in common. Expounding this view to Nikola, he added that the same thing was happening between Israelis and Arabs, as well as elsewhere in the world. The conversation lasted for at least a couple of hours and the priest listened fascinated to Tsafendas's deeply held but, to him, extraordinary beliefs.[78]

An event that triggered a major disagreement between them was Adolf Eichmann's trial, then taking place in Israel. Following the trial through the daily newspapers closely, when the Nazi architect of the Final Solution was sentenced to death, Tsefendas was overjoyed. Father Nikola, though also anti-Nazi, opposed the death penalty and the two men argued bitterly over the morality of taking a human life. Tsafendas's view was that not only the state but any individual was justified in ending the life of someone like Eichmann. He added that he would personally have hunted down and killed him, or any other Nazi criminal, if he had been given the opportunity. The 'only good Nazi,' he said, 'was a dead Nazi.'[79]

While in Turkey, Tsafendas got in touch with a Greek comrade, a fellow Democratic Army member who soldiered with him in the Greek Civil War. This man was now a dentist, living with his family in Sofia, Bulgaria, where he had fled after the defeat of the communist army, as did most of the communists and Democratic Army fighters. Tsafendas had corresponded with him for years and when they arranged to meet, his comrade travelled to Istanbul. Tsafendas and Father Nikola met the man at the city's main railway station. The priest was nervous about local Greeks learning of these two men's past history, and almost certainly, he winced when the visitor declared flatly at the outset that he was an atheist. Nevertheless, he invited Tsafendas's friend to his home for dinner. There, the two old friends reminisced about their wartime experiences until after midnight, by which time, their hostess, the priest's wife, had gone yawning to bed.[80]

By now, almost every Greek in Istanbul knew of Tsafendas, the teacher the children loved who appeared out of the blue and was commonly known as 'the African'. He could often be spotted in Istanbul's bookshops, obsessively searching the shelves. What he was looking for in all probability were the works, in the original Turkish, of Nazim Hikmet, the Turkish communist poet he had heard about from the immigrants in West Germany. Hikmet had spent much of his life in prison or in exile and his books were not easy to come by. However, Tsafendas found some volumes of his poetry in Turkish, which he read with delight. Hikmet remained a life-long favourite and Tsafendas talked about him and his poetry to anyone who would listen.[81]

One day a beautiful young woman appeared in Tsafendas's English language class. She appeared to be in her early 30s, thus about ten years younger than him, but almost as tall, with black hair, long and straight, and fine, alabaster-white skin. She was dressed mostly in black – ankle-length skirt and long-sleeved top under a long, black woollen coat, and a dark woollen hat. Even her spectacles and handbag were black. She was Turkish and was accompanied by a student's mother. She taught English at Limasollu Naci, the best private language school in Turkey, and because she had heard so much about Tsafendas from the boy's mother, she decided to drop in on one of his classes. By the end of the lesson, she was so impressed that she offered to introduce Tsafendas to the owner and founder of the language college, Mr Limasollu Naci.[82]

After interviewing Tsafendas, Limasollu offered him a one-week trial at the college. Though never professionally trained, Tsafendas's instinct for teaching made him an instant success as he secured the attention of the pupils with a fund of exotic and amusing anecdotes about Africa. Limasollu had no hesitation in making the job offer permanent. Thus, Tsafendas worked five days a week at the college, but also continued with his free lessons at the church.[83]

For Tsafendas, this was one of the happiest times of his life. He was always ready to cover for absent colleagues and spend extra time with pupils who needed more attention. There was no dress code at the college and most of the teachers wore casual clothes, but Tsafendas insisted on wearing suits with shirt and tie. He said that one of the things he liked best about the job was that he could wear a suit without feeling overdressed. Dimitri became popular with some of the students' parents, who came to the school curious to meet the new Greek-African teacher they had heard so much about. He was often invited to their homes for coffee or for dinner. Now with money in his pocket, the new teacher would buy sweets for the children. Between college and church, Tsafendas kept in touch with his family in South Africa, sending photographs showing himself at historic sites, as well as postcards and gifts. Marika got most of the gifts, often Christian icons.[84]

Now earning a regular salary, Tsafendas wished to move out Father Nikola's house and live independently. The priest begged him to stay, if only for the sake of little Elenitsa, and Tsafendas agreed but only if he was allowed to pay rent plus arrears for the two months he had already spent there. An agreement was eventually reached: no back rent, but Tsafendas would be charged for food and lodgings from now on.[85]

Turkey at this time, Muslim but with a secular ethos, was a comparatively easy-going country and Tsafendas explored Istanbul's outstanding restaurants, particularly those in the Sultan Ahmet area and the seafood restaurants overlooking the Bosporus. One welcome aspect was the ease with which he could find someone to play backgammon, with both Greeks and Turks habitually playing in cafés and small eating places. During the first months of his stay in the city, Tsafendas lost most of the games, but he improved quickly and became very competitive. Called the 'master' not because of his skill levels, but because some Turkish opponents considered him very lucky with the dice, Tsafendas would joke that he had a special 'wristy' way of throwing the dice, though he knew it was a matter of luck. He had a particular fondness for suits and hats, and providing he did not feel overdressed for the occasion, he would wear a necktie, too.[86]

Tsafendas was delighted to discover that Limasollu Naci, clever, charming and well-read, was also a communist, though he did not broadcast the fact, and the two quickly developed a good relationship. They shared a passion for politics, history and good food, especially seafood, and would spend hours together in speciality eating houses. Tsafendas could not help thinking how wrong his grandmother was in denigrating the Turks, although he understood the roots of her hostility.[87]

That Tsafendas was from Africa, though he did not look like a typical African, that he had a magic touch with children and that he demonstrated such extraordinary skill with languages bestowed on him an exotic aura in the eyes of many Greek women. However, what impressed them most were his dancing skills, which he showed off at Greek functions. Some of the elderly ladies' interest in Tsafendas clearly went beyond his dancing skills, judging by the number of times he was asked to do small jobs, help them home with heavy bags or translate something that puzzled them. Mostly, they just wanted to spend time with this interesting man, but if Tsafendas scented eroticism in the air, as he indicated to Father Nikola, the age difference ensured that things went no further.

One time, however, things got rather more complicated. Tsafendas was drinking coffee with Father Nikola's parishioners after the Sunday mass when a wealthy Greek widow in her 60s came up and introduced her shyly smiling daughter. What Tsafendas did not know was that the daughter, in her mid-20s, was struggling to find a husband, despite her vast fortune, because she was not very attractive. The mother was searching for a suitable candidate and it did not take long for Tsafendas to realise that he was the object the ladies' attentions.[88] Fighting back an impulse to take flight, Tsafendas forced himself to listen politely as the mother listed the many businesses and properties they owned and explained how difficult it was for two women to look after them. What they needed, she said, was a man to take charge. When Tsafendas prevaricated, she added that they also had a very profitable dry-cleaning business, which needed an owner. Tsafendas joked weakly that he couldn't even wash his own clothes. Undeterred, the mother whispered softly into Tsafendas's ear that her daughter was a refined young lady and, not to put too fine a point on it, a virgin. Although many men were after her, none was good enough; her prospective husband, the mother said, should be someone cosmopolitan, someone educated with a respectable job, 'like a teacher'. The inference was unavoidable and Tsafendas sought desperately for a way of escape while Father Nikola, who had joined them at the table, tried not to smile at his friend's discomfiture. Tsafendas decided that the best he could do was to portray himself as a totally feeble and useless human being. Far from running a line of businesses, he said, he couldn't even fry an egg. Changing tack, he then desperately declared that he was a communist, believing that would frighten off any capitalist matriarch, but the mother was undeterred and said that one of her favourite uncles was also one. Whatever self-disparagement Tsafendas offered was brushed aside until the widow declared how badly she wanted a grandchild and Tsafendas realised his chance had come. Sadly shaking his head, he said quietly that alas he was not capable in that department. Shocked, the widow asked why. It was Africa, he said, a disease he contracted there as a child which rendered him impotent for life. Her expression changing from shock to terror, the widow demanded to know if the condition was contagious. Tsafendas delivered his masterstroke: 'The doctors don't know yet.' He tried to say a little more about this imaginary disease, but the lady had heard enough and seizing her daughter's arm hurried her away. It was the priest who lost control first. Putting his head into his hands, Father Nikola guffawed quietly, saying, 'Oh, my God, forgive me.' Tsafendas joined in, chuckling and patting his friend's back. As for the widow, she never came near Tsafendas again.[89]

After Tsafendas was appointed at the college, he took his beautiful woman colleague, who had introduced him to Limasollu, out for dinner to thank her. They saw each other on a friendly basis, but the relationship deepened quickly and, side-stepping her Islamic principles, he moved into her house. This time Father Nikola could not object to Tsafendas leaving, despite Elenitsa's protests, because he realised this was important for his friend, a matter of the heart.[90] Tsafendas was in love and very happy, but after two or three months, relations began to deteriorate. His colleague wanted to marry, but Tsafendas was not enthusiastic. He did not want to settle in Turkey; he wanted to return to South Africa and Mozambique and fight against the ruling regimes there. Besides, he was Christian and she was Muslim and neither were willing to change religion. Finally, she gave her lover an ultimatum: marry or part. Tsafendas chose the second option.[91]

Around December 1961, Tsafendas obtained a new Greek passport and doggedly applied once more for permission to return to Mozambique. Yet again, he was refused. Perhaps it was securing the Greek passport he had long sought or the break-up with his girlfriend, but Tsafendas now accepted that much as he loved his life in Istanbul, and much as he was loved in return, it was always going to be temporary. Accordingly, after some six months at the college, with the new passport in his possession, he resigned. He had the future all mapped out and he explained the plan to Limasollu and Father Nikola. He would travel to Bulgaria to meet the family of his ex-comrade, the dentist, then go on to Athens and meet up with John Michaletos. Michaletos had already invited him to spend Christmas in Athens with his family. He had spoken with both men and they were expecting him. After that, he would return to Portugal and hopefully persuade the Portuguese to let him return to his beloved Mozambique. If not, he would try the illegal route. One of the Turkish communists he had met in Istanbul had given him the contacts of a man in Brussels who could help get a fake passport. He calculated that it would be useful to have a document in another man's name so that he would not be stopped at the border.[92]

Limasollu tried to change Tsafendas's mind but, realising that was impossible, he gave him bonus money for his journey and handed him a glowing reference, a document which, it could be said, changed the course of South African history when Tsafendas used it to get a job at the House of Assembly in Cape Town. Tsafendas bought parting gifts for every student at the college and every child at the church. He presented a multi-volume, Greek-language encyclopaedia to Father Nikola to give to Elenitsa on Christmas Day. Finally, he asked the priests to be sure to look after the cemetery dog, his friend, Robespierre. His girlfriend was unhappy about their break-up and refused to speak to Tsafendas. After leaving Istanbul, Tsafendas kept in touch with both Limasollu and Father Nikola by letter. Tsafendas remembered Limasollu and Father Nikola until the day he died; he characterised Limasollu as 'a great and very generous man, one of the best men' he ever met,[93] and Father Nikola as a 'saint', an 'unbelievably kind and wonderful man ... exactly as priests should be.'[94] The priest said, 'You don't often meet people like Dimitri, he was special, a man in a million. Honestly, it was a privilege to know him.'[95]

Before the end of December 1961, Tsafendas left Istanbul by train for Sofia to meet his dentist comrade again. Tsafendas had been having trouble with his teeth for some time, so his friend fitted him with a bridge and capped his upper teeth with silver, something that was to be remarked upon by many in the future. Tsafendas took a train back to Istanbul, then hitched a ride on a fish refrigeration truck to Athens, where he spent the Christmas and New Year of 1961–62, as arranged, with the Michaletos family.[96]

Tsafendas loved being back in Athens, a completely different city to the one where he lived for almost two years during the civil war in 1947–49. Like any other modern European capital, Athens was booming and brightly lit, the streets thronged with traffic and boasted a lively nightlife. Although he stayed for only a week, he managed to revisit several of his favourite coffee shops and restaurants and spent hours in taverns which now played live music.

Tsafendas had always wanted to visit his father's birthplace and see the graves of his many relatives in Crete. So, in early January 1962, he took the ferry from Piraeus to the island of Crete. Knowing only the family name and his father's place of birth, Tsafendas initially had difficulty finding his relatives. There were several families named Tsafantakis and many men also named Michalis, but unrelated. When he did get in touch with some distant relatives, he discovered that they had never heard of him and most were dubious about him.[97] However, an uncle, Giorgos Tsafantakis invited him to stay in his house. Giorgos's son, Aris, had moved to South Africa with the help of Tsafendas's father and was now living there permanently. A few months later, Giorgos Tsafantakis received a card from Tsafendas, thanking him for his hospitality.[98]

The family village on Crete was Kitharida and Tsafendas visited all his known relatives' graves, lit a candle at each and said a prayer. His grandparents' house had not been occupied for years and though locked, was in bad shape. Tsafendas took photographs of the village and sent them to his father. In the town of Moires, 60 km south of Heraclion, Tsafendas met a man in his mid-70s named Costas Kargakis (nicknamed Psarocostas), whose granddaughter was married to Tsafendas's nephew, Michalis Tsafantakis. Kargakis had raised the girl on his own after her parents were killed during the Second World War. She and her husband had then moved to West Germany due to their inability to find suitable work in Greece. Kargakis happily invited the uncle of his son-in-law to his home, where he lived alone, and Tsafendas stayed for two to three weeks. He soon discovered that the old man had fought with the Greek resistance during the Nazi occupation of Crete and in one of the most daring exploits of the war. In April 1944, a band of Greek partisans and two British officers kidnapped the German military governor of Crete, General Heinrich Kreipe. Kargakis was one of the bands that marched the general over the mountains to the coast, where he was picked up by a British submarine and taken to Egypt.[99]

Tsafendas spent a lot of time with Kreipe's kidnappers who showed him the spot where the general was taken and explained the details of the operation. They even sang resistance anthems together. Furthermore, Tsafendas was told that one of the kidnappers, George Tyrakis, now lived in Johannesburg and he copied his address so he could call on him when eventually he got back to South Africa. The successful kidnap of a high-ranking army officer sent wheels spinning in Tsafendas's mind. Why not do the same thing with Hendrik Verwoerd and exchange him for a batch of South African political prisoners? In his heart of hearts, Tsafendas knew this would be next to impossible on his own, but from then on, the idea of kidnapping Verwoerd remained at the back of his mind.[100]

Kargakis was an expert bomb-maker, who used natural, readily available ingredients such as fertilizer. Tsafendas was captivated and for days, the two would disappear into the mountains and fire off explosions. Kargakis's comrades would join in, adding marksmanship to Tsafendas's bomb-making lessons. Weapons were no problem since every Cretan household had a gun and almost everyone still does. Tsafendas concluded that he had never fired as many rounds, even when he was with the DSE in the civil war. However, he knew that when he decided to go to war against the fascists and colonialists in South Africa and Mozambique, he would have to rely on his own bomb-making skills. The unexpected stint learning about bombs extended Tsafendas's stay in Crete by a few more weeks. As for Kargakis and his old comrades, they were happy to relieve the boredom and impart their rebel skills.[101]

Tsafendas valued his stay in Crete highly and considered it an important and influential phase of his life, indeed as a wake-up call. His association with the partisans and his admiration for their wartime exploits prompted him to think seriously of undertaking a similar action against apartheid in South Africa and/or the Portuguese colonists in Mozambique. His mind was filled with what he had learnt in Crete and what he would do when he got back to Africa. He mulled over a kidnap-exchange plot many times and pondered where in South Africa and Mozambique he might best place a bomb, not to kill, but to express resistance to oppression, to engineer a sort of symbolic attack.[102]

Before leaving Crete, Tsafendas visited members of the Christian Church in Heraclion and Rethimnon. He then returned by ferry to Piraeus, and, alternating between bus and ferry, travelled to Brindisi in southern Italy.[103] Tsafendas arrived in Brindisi on 31 January 1962. Because of his lengthened stay in Crete, he did not have enough money to complete his return to Portugal. Feeling he had no alternative, he sought admission to the A. Di Summa Hospital on an emergency basis, claiming he was suffering from acute enteritis. He did not want to stay long in the hospital and therefore did not use the tapeworm act, which would certainly have prompted the extended investigation. While in the hospital, he wrote to the Portuguese embassy in Rome, saying he was a Portuguese citizen in poor health and almost penniless and asking for help to return to Portugal. An interview was arranged at the embassy and, after eight days in the hospital, Tsafendas travelled to Rome and presented himself at the embassy on 8 February. A consular statement dated 10 February said, 'His weak health and the fact that he wasn't in possession of any resources made him request repatriation.' The embassy gave him an allowance of 6,000 lire and a Rome–Lisbon train ticket costing 26,000 lire. Tsafendas promised to pay back the money when he got a job.[104]

***

Portugal was intended to be just a way-station on his journey back to Mozambique, but things were not so simple. First, he needed money. The 6,000 lire was spent on his long train ride from Rome, so that when he arrived penniless in Lisbon in February, he took a bed in the Albergue Da Mitra, the shelter for destitute men where he had stayed some ten years earlier.[105] He found work as a welder on a bridge over the River Tejo for 120 escudos per day.

However, Tsafendas was never a fan of hard labour and his lack of enthusiasm eventually cost him his job. He was promptly offered alternative employment at 60 escudos per day, but decided he would rather work again as a hawker.[106]

Tsafendas was not to know it, but it was at this time – 14 February 1962 to be precise – that his father died in Pretoria.[107] Marika wrote immediately to tell Tsafendas, but he had left the Lisbon address she had for him and he did not get her letter.[108] Renewing contacts with his old left-wing friends and chatting and participating in their meetings prompted Tsafendas to submit yet another application for entry to Mozambique. This time, when he received the expected refusal, he visited a police station and asked for clarification of his situation and the reasons for his continued exile from the country of his birth. He declared that he was no longer a communist, that he was a reformed citizen and a loyal subject of the Portuguese government. Suspecting his claims to have turned over a new leaf might not do the trick, he also pretended to be a little mad, though harmlessly so, and in need of family care.[109] The police officer who interviewed him, Captain Cascais, was dubious but sent him for examination at the Institute of Psychiatric Welfare of Lisbon. On 6 April 1962, Tsafendas was examined by Dr Pegado, who concluded that Tsafendas was unstable and needed to be in the care of his family. His report said: 'Demitrio Tsafandakis is fundamentally a psychopath who leads an always unstable and adventurous life. At the moment, he does not show signs of psychosis. I agree entirely with Captain Cascais in that one should wait for information regarding his family before finally deciding what destination he is to be given.'[110]

However, nothing came of Tsafendas's charade, either because of the slow pace of the Portuguese bureaucracy or because the authorities were not convinced by his claims and held back on any action. Deeply disappointed that Africa was out of reach again, Tsafendas turned towards London. He had stayed in touch with his old comrades in the Anti-Apartheid Movement and the Anti-Slavery Society and they told him that opposition to apartheid was growing in Britain. Thus in June 1962, Tsafendas found himself in London for a second time. Knowing that he would not be allowed to enter the country after being expelled three years earlier, Tsafendas used the Greek passport obtained in Istanbul, which gave his name as Dimitrios Tsafantakis, not Tsafendas, the name he was known by when he was deported. It worked and the immigration officers failed to detect that Tsafantakis and Tsafendas were the same person.[111]

Now that he had money from his work in Lisbon, there was no need to take refuge in hospitals. He contacted his old friends and found that the Anti-Apartheid Movement had grown enormously and that calls to boycott South African goods were vigorous and widespread. Working for the anti-apartheid cause brought Tsafendas into contact with such leading figures as Solly Sachs and the radical Anglican priest, Canon John Collins,[112] and he associated closely with David Gardener, a member of the Labour Party, and prominent in the cause.[113] As always, he joined enthusiastically in protest meetings and demonstrations, he helped in organisational issues, put up posters and distributed leaflets. He was also a frequent visitor at the North Middlesex Cricket Club in Hornsey, North London, which was the meeting place for members of the movement. There, he met Edward Furness, a South African living in England, who spoke to the South African police after the assassination. He said that Tsafendas 'was well-dressed and appeared to be wealthy' and that Tsafendas told him that he wanted 'to create a resistance to the regime of South Africa' and mentioned 'civil disobedience'. He said Tsafendas told him that he was willing and ready to do 'anything that would get the South African regime out of power'.[114]

Three years after his 1959 visit, Tsafendas sought to discover if there had been a change of heart regarding violent action against the South African government, especially since the ANC had abandoned its non-violence policy a year earlier and created a military wing, Umkhonto we Sizwe. To his dismay, he realised that still none of the anti-apartheid activists was willing to take up arms.[115]

On 1 July 1962, the newly established British neo-Nazi group, the National Socialist Movement, organised an anti-Semitic rally in Trafalgar Square under the banner, 'Free Britain from Jewish Control'. Some 2,000 anti-fascists, including Tsafendas, occupied the square to forestall the demonstration. The vicar of Holy Trinity Church in Dalston, Reverand Billy Sargent, handed out Yellow Star badges similar to the Yellow Star of David that the Nazis forced Jews to wear in Germany.[116] Tsafendas proudly pinned one to his lapel. The pre-emptive occupation prevented the rally from going ahead, but inevitably violence erupted and Tsafendas happily joined in until the police broke up the fighting.[117]

On 22 July, again in Trafalgar Square, Tsafendas and other anti-apartheid activists fought with members of Sir Oswald Mosley's Union Movement (UM). Mosley, the notorious leader of the long-banned British Union of Fascists, founded the racist UM in 1948 following his release from detention after the Second World War. Mosley was an avid proponent of apartheid, had visited South Africa and enjoyed close ties with Verwoerd's National Party. The UM's agenda included protests against the boycott movement, which invariably ended in violence. Three weeks later, another battle took place. Weapons were not involved and Tsafendas, using his weight and strength, laid waste to the opponents around him. Now he urged his comrades to take the fight to the fascists. Accordingly, he and a few others besieged a UM office in London, smashed the windows and broke into the building. However, Mosley's men produced knives, iron bars and broken bottles and sent the attackers fleeing. Tsafendas was stabbed in the hand and stomach by a fascist wielding a broken bottle.[118]

Although he got out of the building, he was not a good runner and became separated from his comrades. Two young fascists quickly caught up with him and, attacking from behind, hit him across his back with an iron bar. Then two more appeared. Surrounded, Tsafendas tried to take the offensive to his enemies, but they pulled him down and rained kicks on his body from head to toe. His assailants were younger and fitter men; sometimes they let him stagger to his feet, only to punch him to the ground again. A crowd began gathering and shouted at the fascists to leave their victim alone. Seeing the crowds swell, the fascists slipped away and bystanders helped Tsafendas to a nearby pharmacy. He then made his own way to a hospital. His wounds were not life-threatening – a bleeding mouth, many bruises and two knife cuts – but the small scar that remained on his hand he considered thereafter to be a badge of honour.[119] In another demonstration, Tsafendas carried a placard depicting a figure in a Ku Klux Klan outfit labelled 'VERWOERD'.[120] He sent photographs of himself wearing the Yellow Star and carrying the KKK placard to his father, sure he would be proud of him. He still did not know his father was dead.[121] Years later, Tsafendas would recall the fights with Mosley's fascists as among the proudest moments of his life while proudly showing his scar to anyone who would listen,[122] like Shakespeare's soldier who fought at Agincourt for King Henry of England: 'Will he strip his sleeve and show his scars and say, "These wounds I had on Crispin's Day!"'

It was October of 1962, and he was back in Lisbon again working as a hawker, when Tsafendas finally heard from his stepmother that his father had died. Her letter was in response to postcards and photographs he had mailed to his father. What Dimitri did not know was that Michalis and Marika, though still married, had been living separately for the last few years and barely talking to each other. Nobody in the family told Dimitri about the separation because they felt the news would upset him when he was many miles away and could do nothing about it. Michalis in particular often said he did not want to worry his son with his troubles. The fact is he was deeply unhappy that he had not seen his boy for more than twenty years, but Dimitri was banned from the country and Michalis had a deep-seated fear of flying, which posed difficulties for any journey to Europe. Michalis was comforted by the thought that Dimitri was living a good life of his own choice overseas, far from racist South Africa, whose government both he and his son despised. Dimitri ensured his father felt at ease about him by sending regular photographs of himself, always wearing different suits, looking prosperous and smiling happily.[123]

The main reason for his parents' split was Marika's growing frustration over her husband's obsession with politics. She often said he was becoming more like his son every day. Indeed, Michalis talked constantly against apartheid and denounced Prime Minister Verwoerd specifically as 'a bastard' and 'a monster'. That Dimitri was banned from entering South Africa was a huge grievance with him, though he often described the ban as 'a badge of honour'. Michalis was also critical of the ANC and other resistance movements for failing to take direct, physical action against the regime. He was convinced that only violence would bring about apartheid's defeat. Unlike Dimitri, Michalis confided his thoughts to relatives and close friends and did not broadcast them to the world at large.[124]

Upon his retirement as an engineer, Michalis plunged back into anarchism. He opened the boxes of books and pamphlets that he had locked away in Mozambique after Dimitri's workroom explosion, and created a new study filled with revolutionary literature. He had lost touch with his old comrades and had long ago stopped receiving any anarchist literature, but he spent much of his time in the new study, paging through his old books. On the walls he hung photographs or posters of some of his political heroes, including Errico Malatesta and Buenaventura Durruti. Marika was terrified that the anarchist literature would lead their grandchildren towards a passion for politics, like Dimitri, although they were not even ten years old. What upset Marika most was Michalis constantly telling anyone who would listen that he should never have married, but become a rebel instead, fighting in revolutionary wars. Naturally, she found this a hurtful and insulting comment. When Michalis died, Marika threw away most of his books and all of the posters to keep them out of the hands of her grandchildren.[125] Tsafendas was devastated to hear that his adored father had died and he became determined to return to South Africa at all costs to visit his grave. He knew the South Africans would never give him permission and the best route would be from neighbouring Mozambique if he could persuade the Portuguese to end his long exile and allow him to return. Tsafendas was sure it was not beyond his acting abilities to convince officials behind their desks, even medics, that he was no longer a communist, that he held no subversive ideas and he did not care about independence for Mozambique. In other words, he was a man reformed, a loyal supporter of Salazar. Tsafendas then put his plan into motion. He stopped associating with leftists while brazenly spouting off in public against the evils of Communism and the virtues of Salazar. He hoped that when the secret police inquired about him again, they would hear all this and might consider backing him for amnesty. He even found a girlfriend and moved in with her in her house. He believed that being in a 'serious relationship' would act to his favour with the Portuguese authorities.[126]

Tsafendas's offensive began on 27 October 1962, when he entered a police station in Lisbon and meekly asked for permission to return to Mozambique, assuring them that he was no longer a communist and had rejected his former anti-colonialism. It didn't work.[127] Desperate and knowing he would be rejected again, in November 1962, he nevertheless submitted yet another visa application to the South African embassy in Lisbon. In January 1963, the immigration attaché wrote to Tsafendas urging him not to incur any further expense in connection with his application. In other words, to not bother to ask again.[128] With no alternative possible, Tsafendas kept up the anti-communist, pro-Salazar charade, sure that sooner or later in this security-ridden nation, the all-seeing PIDE would learn of his change of heart and investigate.[129]

In the summer of 1963, Tsafendas made a formal application to Portugal for amnesty covering his previous behaviour and asked that he be interviewed personally. When this request was granted, Tsafendas used his considerable powers of persuasion to argue that his subversive ideas belonged 25 years in the past when he was young and immature. This time, he also pretended to be slightly, harmlessly mad. He produced documents from hospitals where he had been treated, which confirmed periods of mental infirmity. These, he said, were responsible for his radical ideas. But now, after the treatment he had received, especially while he was in prison in Lisbon, he had changed his ideology altogether. He gave them Dr Pegado's report of April 1962, stating that he was psychopathic and needed to be in the care of his family. Of equal, if not greater, importance, PIDE had contacted Tsafendas's old associates and confirmed that he was now a loyal supporter of the Portuguese dictatorship.[130]

This time it worked. In August or September of 1963, after twelve years of exile, the Portuguese authorities, convinced by his act and the information it received from PIDE, decided to extend its powers of amnesty to Tsafendas and permit him to return to Mozambique.[131] Although he could afford the fare, Tsafendas preferred to save the money and buy presents for his family, so he asked the social services to pay for it. It was his way of wreaking some small vengeance on the Portuguese for his many years of exile and his many rejections. A few weeks later, Tsafendas received the fare from the government and, in October 1963, he sailed to Mozambique aboard the *Princippi Perfecto*.[132] With him were two large suitcases which contained his personal effects and gifts for friends and family, but also forbidden anti-apartheid and communist literature.[133] Tsafendas had taken the precaution of replacing the books' dust jackets with innocent, apolitical covers.[134]

Figures

TOP: Dimitri Tsafendas (second from right) with (left to right) his step-sister Evangelia, step-mother Marika, step-brother Victor and his father Michalis (courtesy of Irini and John Michaletos).

BOTTOM LEFT: Dimitri Tsafendas in his grandmother's house in Egypt, aged four or five (from Liza Key's *A Question of Madness*, courtesy of Liza Key).

BOTTOM RIGHT: Dimitri Tsafendas (top of photo) with (left to right) his step-sister Evangelia, step-sister Katerina (bottom), step-mother Marika and step-brother Victor (courtesy of Mike Vlachopoulos).

TOP LEFT: Costas Kargakis, the Greek partisan whose grand-daughter was married to Tsafendas's cousin. Tsafendas stayed for about a month in Kargakis's house in Crete in 1962 and was trained by him and other partisans in bomb-making (courtesy of Alexandros Tsafantakis).

TOP RIGHT: Captain Michalis Tsafantakis, Tsafendas's great-grandfather and prominent rebel of the Great Cretan Revolution against the Ottomans (1866-1869). Tsafendas's father was named after him. Tsafendas worshipped his great-grandfather and during an earthquake ran back into the family home to rescue his portrait (courtesy of Alexandros Tsafantakis).

BOTTOM: Patrick and Louisa O'Ryan (courtesy of Liza Key).

TOP: Tsafendas at an identification parade in Caledon Square Police Station shortly after the assassination (from Liza Key's *A Question of Madness*, courtesy of Liza Key).

BOTTOM: Police photo of Tsafendas in Caledon Square Police Station shortly after his arrest for the assassination (from Liza Key's *A Question of Madness*, courtesy of Liza Key).

TOP: Tsafendas at Sterkfontein Hospital in the mid-1990s, aged around 77 (from Liza Key's *A Question of Madness*, courtesy of Liza Key).

BOTTOM: Father Nikola Banovic (left). A close friend of Tsafendas; Father Nikola shared his home with Tsafendas for about five months in Istanbul in 1961 (courtesy of Father Nikola Banovic).

ABOVE: Tsafendas behind a bullet-proof window in the Maximum Security Section of Pretoria Central Prison, photographed by Gordon Winter during his October 1976 visit (courtesy of Gordon Winter).

TOP: Tsafendas in late October 1997 at Sterkfontein Hospital (photo courtesy of Ellen Elmendorp).

BOTTOM: Tsaflndas and Liza Key at Sterkfontein Hospital (photo courtesy of Liza Key).

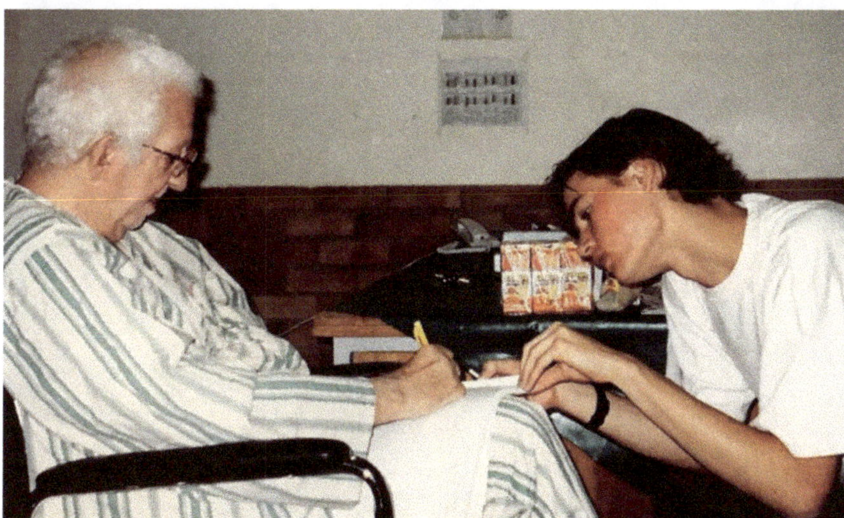

TOP: October 9, 2021, Maputo, Mozambique. His Grace Ioannis Tsaftaridis, Archbishop of Zambia and Malawi and Deputy of the Orthodox Diocese of Mozambique, and liaison between the Inter-parliamentary Assembly on Orthodoxy and the Pan African Parliament, holds a memorial service at the Greek Orthodox Cathedral of the Archangels Michael and Gabriel to honour Tsafendas and his memory.

BOTTOM: Fifteen-year-old Joris Beresford talks to Tsafendas regarding a school essay he had written about him. The photograph was taken at Sterkfontein Hospital in April 1998, five and a half months before Tsafendas died, and is the last known photograph of him (courtesy of Liza Key).

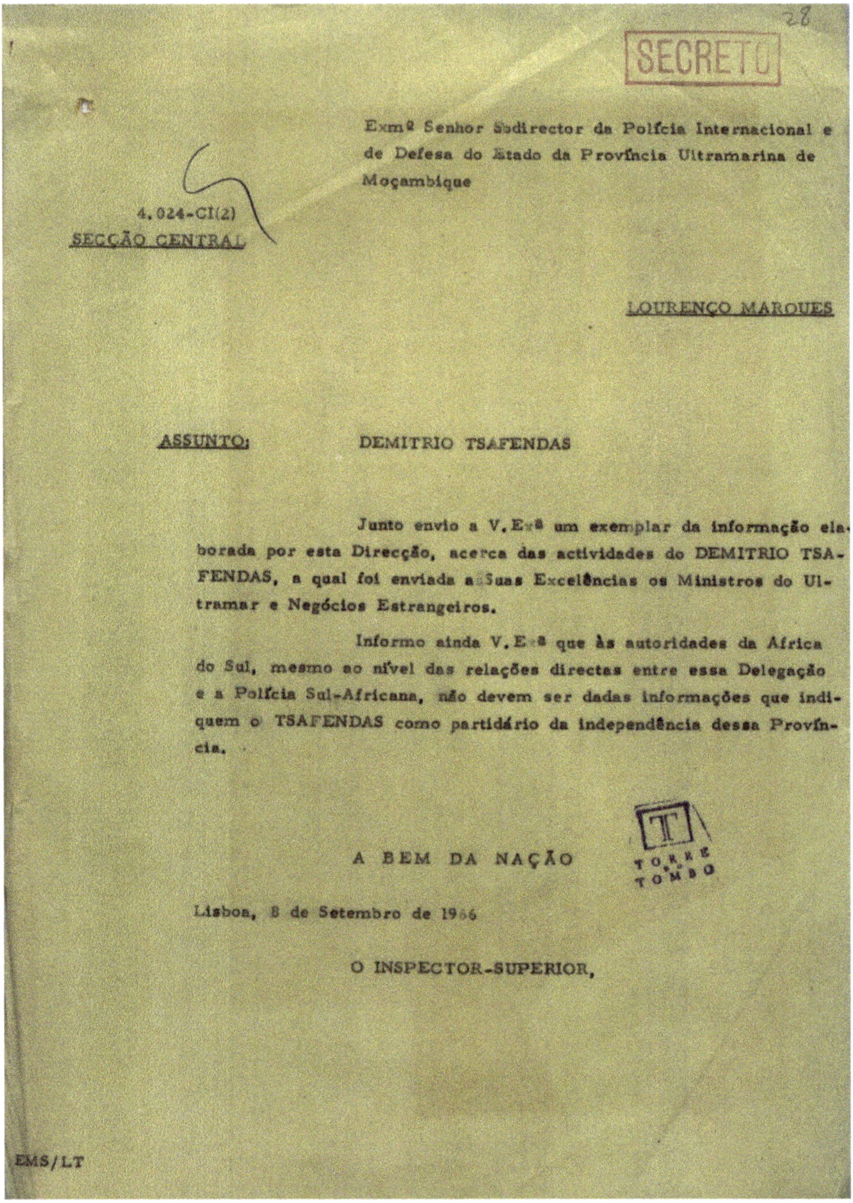

28

SECRETO

Exmº Senhor Subdirector da Polícia Internacional e de Defesa do Estado da Província Ultramarina de Moçambique

4.024-CI(2)
SECÇÃO CENTRAL

LOURENÇO MARQUES

ASSUNTO: DEMITRIO TSAFENDAS

Junto envio a V.Exª um exemplar da informação elaborada por esta Direcção, acerca das actividades do DEMITRIO TSAFENDAS, a qual foi enviada a Suas Excelências os Ministros do Ultramar e Negócios Estrangeiros.

Informo ainda V.Exª que às autoridades da Africa do Sul, mesmo ao nível das relações directas entre essa Delegação e a Polícia Sul-Africana, não devem ser dadas informações que indiquem o TSAFENDAS como partidário da independência dessa Província.

A BEM DA NAÇÃO

Lisboa, 8 de Setembro de 1966

O INSPECTOR-SUPERIOR,

EMS/LT

ABOVE: Two days after the assassination, PIDE's chief inspector in Lisbon issued the above secret order, instructing the sub-director of the force in Mozambique that "information indicating Tsafendas as a partisan for the independence of your country should not be transmitted to the South African Authorities, even despite the relations that exist between your Delegation and the South African Police." The order was followed and PIDE downplayed and omitted some of Tsafendas's political activities (Processo de Demetrio Tsafendas. PT/TT/PIDE/D-C/001/6818. 'Imagem cedida pelo ANTT').

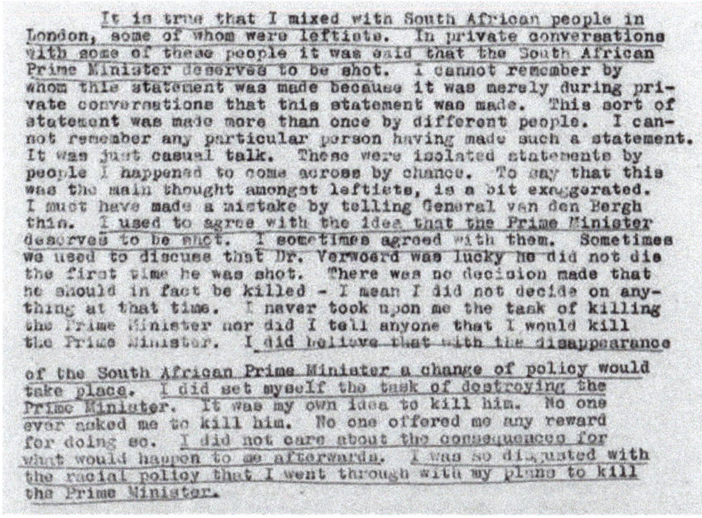

It is true that I mixed with South African people in London, some of whom were leftists. In private conversations with some of these people it was said that the South African Prime Minister deserves to be shot. I cannot remember by whom this statement was made because it was merely during private conversations that this statement was made. This sort of statement was made more than once by different people. I cannot remember any particular person having made such a statement. It was just casual talk. These were isolated statements by people I happened to come across by chance. To say that this was the main thought amongst leftists, is a bit exaggerated. I must have made a mistake by telling General van den Bergh this. I used to agree with the idea that the Prime Minister deserves to be shot. I sometimes agreed with them. Sometimes we used to discuss that Dr. Verwoerd was lucky he did not die the first time he was shot. There was no decision made that he should in fact be killed - I mean I did not decide on anything at that time. I never took upon me the task of killing the Prime Minister nor did I tell anyone that I would kill the Prime Minister. I did believe that with the disappearance of the South African Prime Minister a change of policy would take place. I did set myself the task of destroying the Prime Minister. It was my own idea to kill him. No one ever asked me to kill him. No one offered me any reward for doing so. I did not care about the consequences for what would happen to me afterwards. I was so disgusted with the racial policy that I went through with my plans to kill the Prime Minister.

TOP: A portion of Tsafendas's statement to the police on 11 September 1966 (courtesy of National Archives of South Africa, Pretoria). Nowhere in the statement does he mention the tapeworm or say anything which could conceivably suggest that he might be a schizophrenic. Professor John Dugard said this statement 'confirms the view that Tsafendas was not insane. It reads like a very normal story of a politically informed person, angry with apartheid and Dr Verwoerd, determined to make a change with nothing to lose personally – really an incredible statement which was carefully concealed' (Professor John Dugard in a personal interview, 7 February 2016).

BOTTOM: At the book launch of *The Man who Killed Apartheid,* November 8, 2018. From left to right, Reneva Fourie, member of the Central Committee of the SACP; Akis Apergis, anti-apartheid activist; Advocate George Bizos; Minister of Justice and Correctional Services Michael Masutha; Constitutional Judge Jody Kollapen, who gave the keynote address; Attorney Krish Govender, former Durban State Attorney and co-chairman of the Law Society of South Africa; and Harris Dousemetzis.

Chapter 9

Back to Africa

Mozambique, 1963

There is something uniquely physical about Africa, a combination of heat, light and smells, and the Africa-born Tsafendas recognised it the moment he set foot back in Lourenço Marques. In Lisbon, he was some 12,000 km from Johannesburg, but now in Lourenço Marques it was just 500-plus, a mere six or seven hours by road. South Africa was almost within touching distance.

The first person to welcome Dimitri after his years of exile was Artemis, his favourite aunt. From her house, Dimitri spoke to Marika and his half-sister Eleni, announcing his arrival in Mozambique and wanting to know how soon they could meet. He was banned from South Africa, but the family could get together where they all once lived. When Marika asked how he had been allowed to return to Mozambique when he was banned, he simply said he made an application which was accepted, mentioning nothing about the 'psycho' act. His stepmother said they would drive up from South Africa just as soon as they could.[1]

While waiting for them, Tsafendas visited some of his old friends, including Ira Kyriakakis, to whom he gave a hat he had bought especially for her in Lisbon.[2] Top of the list, naturally, was Manuel, still good-looking and physically fit. Tsafendas had kept in touch with him throughout the long years of exile, writing often and sending gifts for his children. The two friends now spent at least part of almost every day together, usually sitting on the balcony of Artemis's house, filling the gaps in the past twelve years. They would also sing as they did in Tsafendas's family home when they were boys.[3]

Tsafendas also discovered and fell in love with a seafood restaurant some 10 km out of Lourenço Marques called the Costa Do Sol. Owned by a Cretan named Petrakakis, it offered spectacular views of palm trees, sandy white beaches and distant ocean rollers, the perfect backdrop as Tsafendas consumed his favourite saganaki prawns. There almost every night, either with Aunt Artemis or Manuel,[4] he met George Liberopoulos and George Ananiadis, who found much to enjoy in Tsafendas's company, considering him, as they told the South African police after Verwoerd's assassination, to be someone of 'very high intelligence'.[5] Very importantly, he also spent time with a young Greek Orthodox priest, Father Minas Constandinou, mostly discussing Christianity. Father Minas was deeply impressed by Tsafendas's extensive knowledge of Christianity, but also his grasp of other religions, too.[6]

On the day of the great family reunion,Tsafendas, who had been watching from the balcony all day, ran from the house, arms wide like an excited child, and yanked the passenger door open before his half-brother Victor had brought their car to a stop. He seized Marika in a bear hug and the pair wept and embraced for long minutes while the relatives and neighbours watched, smiling and tearful. Victor hugged him, then introduced his wife, Anna, who had never met Dimitri. As Tsafendas moved forward, smiling widely, Anna momentarily stepped back, frightened by the sight of his metal teeth. Also in the car was Nick Vlachopoulos, the businessman husband of Eleni. He, like Anna, had never met Tsafendas but was eager to do so because he was intrigued by the family stories of Tsafendas's rebellious character and quietly sympathised with what he had heard of his political ideas. Eleni had been desperate to come too, but had to stay behind to look after their two little boys, aged four and six, and the family's café business. The plan was that she would travel to Lourenço Marques to see him in a couple of weeks, along with her sister, Evangelia, and her sister's husband, Charles Nissiotis.[7]

Tsafendas's situation had been thoroughly discussed on the long drive north. Everyone knew he was *persona non grata* in South Africa and they also assumed from the photographs he had sent his father of the anti-apartheid and anti-fascist demonstrations in London that he was still politically active. The family also knew that he had entered South Africa illegally once before and Marika in particular was nervous that he might be thinking of trying something like that again. All affirmed that they would do nothing illegal to help him enter South Africa and, if he pressed, they would kindly but firmly dissuade him. What they planned was a reunion, a tearful one no doubt, with much gossip and conversation and filling the gaps in the missing years, some convivial meals, the giving and receiving of presents, then back to their homes in South Africa while Tsafendas remained in Lourenço Marques.[8]

Certainly, there were many presents. Dimitri excitedly distributed those he had brought from Europe (always more for Marika) and then the visitors settled on the balcony and listened to Tsafendas add colour and detail to stories he had told in his many letters – his experiences in the war years, protests, imprisonments, the journeys through Europe, teaching in Istanbul, fighting with the communists in the Greek Civil War. Finally, there arose the question of his future, the issue that Marika feared. Tsafendas spread his arms and said how nice it would be if he could move to South Africa, just to lead a quiet life there near his family. Bluntly, as was her style, Marika asked if he had now 'put some sense into his brain', meaning, if he had realised that he was no longer in Europe, where he could say what he liked about governments and leaders. Did he accept that carrying placards and shouting anti-establishment slogans in South Africa would get him into serious trouble, and probably the family, too? Had he forgotten that cast-iron rules were in place and that these were enforced by a vigilant and violent police force and its agents? Tsafendas assured everyone that he was well aware of these dangers, but stressed that he was no longer a member of the South African Communist Party or any other political organisation. He side-stepped questions as to his precise political beliefs and reiterated that all he wanted was to settle down, get a job and live peacefully as part of the family in Pretoria. He looked hopefully around for support, but Marika, much as she loved her stepson, shook her head: Dimitri was banned from South Africa, she said, and that was final. What's more, if he tried to enter illegally, as he had done in the past, he must expect no help from the family. 'Don't knock on my door if you do such a thing,' she said.[9]

However, Tsafendas had no intention of sneaking across the border; what he had in mind was entering through a frontier post with a legitimate visa in his passport. It was Artemis's idea, which she had discussed with Dimitri soon after he arrived. She said her husband, George Michaletos, was friendly with a passport officer at the South African Consulate in Lourenço Marques, who might be willing to turn a blind eye if they persuaded him that Dimitri was a good man and no security threat. Her husband was against the idea but agreed to talk to the diplomat, J.J. van den Berg. He showed him a sheaf of positive references that Tsafendas had collected from employers all round the world, and Van den Berg said he would check with his office. Next day, he told Michaletos that he could not help because Tsafendas's name was on the government stop list and this was impossible for him to ignore. South Africa was beginning to look out of reach for Tsafendas until Artemis asked the question: Would a financial inducement change Van den Berg's mind? George Michaletos said he wanted no part in any such deal and anyway he did not have the funds to spare. It was decided that the idea should be put to Marika and the others when they arrived.[10]

The family was opposed, Victor so strongly that he threatened at one point to drive back home and leave them all behind. Tsafendas pleaded his personal cause, saying he was a changed man and promising that he would not get involved in any political activity that might endanger them. He found an unexpected ally in Nick, Eleni's husband, whose intervention turned out to be crucial. Nick appealed to Marika's and Victor's finer feelings, stressing how marvellous it would be if all the family was reunited now that they were getting older and Michalis had died. In a private conversation in the evening, he reminded Marika and Victor that Dimitri had lived away from them for 22 years and had never asked for anything. He then volunteered to take the whole matter upon himself, including making the payment, relieving them of all responsibility. Artemis also spoke in favour of the bribe plan. After much pressure, the family agreed and reluctantly Michaletos said he would introduce Vlachopoulos to Van den Berg.[11]

The following day he did so, then walked swiftly away as Vlachopoulos delivered the proposition. Van den Berg responded in the negative. Vlachopoulos pressed, knowing the diplomat was personally opposed to apartheid, and assured him that no one would ever know. The South African remained unmoved. A larger sum was mentioned by Vlachopoulos, but Van den Berg's reply remained firm. Vlachopoulos realised that money was not going to be a motive for the official and appealed to his humanity, stating again that Tsafendas was a reformed man and that all he wanted in South Africa was to see his father's grave. He insisted that a temporary permit would be fine and that Tsafendas would be out of the country quickly and no one would ever know. Eventually, Van den Berg agreed to issue Tsafendas with a temporary visa. It is difficult to know precisely what transpired between Vlachopoulos and Van den Berg. Although Van den Berg had refused the offer of money, Vlachopoulos contacted his wife Eleni in Pretoria and she wired a cash sum to him and he gave the money to Van den Berg. This exchange happened after the visa was issued.[12]

While unclear as to why Vlachopoulos gave money to Van den Berg when the diplomat had already issued the visa without a bribe, it seems very likely that this was a kind of reward, common among Greeks, known as a 'fakelaki'. Vlachopoulos was known to be a very generous man and was known to have given a few 'fakelakia' in his life, thus it seems likely that he gave the money as 'reward' for his 'service', despite the diplomat's professed reluctance.

On Saturday, 2 November 1963, Tsafendas appeared before Van den Berg at the South African Consulate and applied for a temporary entry into South Africa. Van den Berg issued the visa.[13] The day before they left, Artemis prepared a huge farewell meal to which Tsafendas also invited Manuel and his family. As the evening concluded, Tsafendas and Manuel started singing and were joined by others in the family. It was the last time the two best friends saw each other.[14] Two days later, Tsafendas and his family re-entered South Africa by car via the Komatipoort border point.[15] The atmosphere in the automobile was tense. Throughout the journey, Marika agonised that they would be found out and Victor had kept his wife in the dark, believing it best she did not know what they had done. They had reason to be worried. The international community was waking up to the evils of apartheid and South Africa was looking ever more embattled and repressive. A year earlier, the United Nations had called for political and economic sanctions. Then African nations began closing their airports and harbours to their white-ruled southern neighbour, and just three months earlier, the UN Security Council called for a voluntary arms embargo against South Africa. Dr Verwoerd's government reacted by tightening internal security even further and cracking down on any signs of opposition. Passing the Sabotage Act allowed it to remove freedom of speech from opposition publications and place the internationally known anti-apartheid activist, Helen Joseph, under house arrest. Simultaneously, in Pretoria, the family's destination, the infamous Rivonia Trial was underway, in which ten leading anti-government activists, including Nelson Mandela, Walter Sisulu and Denis Goldberg, were accused of sabotage.

However, it was family, not politics that preoccupied Tsafendas upon arriving in Pretoria and the first thing he did was visit his father's grave. Michalis was buried in the Rebecca Street Cemetery, where a few years earlier, he had bought a large plot for his entire family. He was the first to be interred there. Lighting a candle, Tsafendas placed flowers in a vase and knelt for at least 15 minutes, weeping, gazing at Michalis's picture and stroking it gently as one would a pet kitten. He took two photographs from his wallet, those he had sent his father from London, unaware that he was already dead. One showed Dimitri with the Yellow Star pinned to his coat and in the other he carried the KKK placard of Verwoerd. Marika and Nick looked on in silence, moved by Dimitri's grief, as he held the photographs up to his father's graveside picture, as if for him to see.[16]

Marika wept too, but her relationship with her dead husband was more complicated. True, she had separated from Michalis, but she never stopped loving him. In truth, she thought he was a great man. The problem was they were diametrically different: in politics, she was a conservative and he was a rebel, even an anarchist; at home, he was the conservative, an old-fashioned believer that the husband was head of the house, that Marika had no say in the big decisions, her duties being to feed the family and bring up his children. One thing that became apparent was that the older Michalis got, the more he became like his first-born: open, uninhibited, demonstrative. From being careful not to reveal his radical political ideas, Michalis took to criticising apartheid openly, and particularly Dr Verwoerd. He celebrated the attempted assassination of the Prime Minister in April 1960 by David Pratt and expressed disappointment that Verwoerd survived.[17]

Putting down his photographs, Dimitri took a handkerchief from his pocket, cleaned and polished Michalis's photograph, then used it to sweep the grave. 'Has he gone mad,' Marika wondered, 'cleaning the grave with a handkerchief?' Dimitri complained that there were no flowers, the candles were old and dirty and he didn't like the picture of his father. Marika protested that she visited the grave as often as she could, but she had to look after her grandchildren when their parents were at work. Dimitri later replaced his father's graveside photo with one he liked better and from then on, he visited the grave at least once a week, tidying it, leaving flowers and lighting a candle.[18]

A joyful family reunion was organised at the home of Nick and Eleni. Dimitri was delighted to meet their two small boys, Michalis (Mike), aged six, and Dinos, seven. He extended his arms for the boys to run and embrace him, but when he opened his mouth and smiled, Michalis screamed and fled in terror from his uncle's ghastly, metal-toothed smile. 'It's a monster, it's a monster,' he cried to his mother. Tsafendas's teeth were to become a kind of horror movie leitmotif.[19]

Tsafendas was saddened and embarrassed about the teeth incident, but the children's fear did not last and soon they were begging to hear his stories. Tsafendas was intrigued to discover that one of their favourite toys was a miniature Katyusha rocket, the weapon used widely by the Soviets during the Second World War. He had sent it to his father from somewhere in Europe years ago.[20]

Some relatives had gathered to greet Dimitri, among them his cousin, Mary Vasilogiorgis, who had grown up with him in Egypt and Mozambique. Her surname was now Eintracht, after she married a German Jewish man. Mary also lived in Pretoria and insisted that he come to dinner at her house the next day. Tsafendas had a gift for everyone, including his other half-sister, Evangelia, and her husband, Charles Nissiotis. His third sister, Katerina Pnefma, who was married and living in Rhodesia, was absent. Some other new family he met were Fotini Gavasiadis, Vlachopoulos's sister, her husband Markos and their three-year-old son, Nick. She had heard a lot about Tsafendas and was looking forward to meeting him.[21]

Tsafendas spent his first few days in Pretoria at Evangelia's house. There, Marika, in her efficient, no-nonsense way, explained the disposition of his father's estate. She said although they were separated, Michalis had left all of his money to her. It was not a large sum, but he wanted to be sure that as a widow she could survive without the humiliation of begging from their children. At the same time, he asked her to help any family member who might fall on hard times. He specifically mentioned Dimitri. Tsafendas did not pretend he was not disappointed to receive nothing from his father's will, but he understood his thinking and, upon reflection, agreed with its fairness. After all, none of his siblings had benefitted either.[22]

Anxious to regularise his status, Tsafendas gratefully accepted an offer from Charles to work at their café while applying to the authorities for permanent residence. Charles believed it would help Tsafendas's application if he showed that he had a steady job. He even gave Tsafendas a letter naming himself as his 'guarantor' and accepting financial responsibility for him while in South

Africa.[23] On the application form, Tsafendas lied flatly that 'he had never previously applied for permanent residence in South Africa, had never been found guilty of a criminal or unlawful action, had never been refused entry to any South African harbour and had never been deported from South Africa or any other country'. He was required to attend three interviews with three different officers of the Department of Immigration and he made a good impression on all of them. Taking note of his evident politeness, the fact that he spoke so many languages and his glittering references from Limasollu Naci and Fries & Son, they recommended approval. None of them checked their government's stop list to see if Tsafendas's name was there.[24]

Further hurdles awaited him, however, including convincing two different state doctors that he was sane and capable of working and supporting himself. For Tsafendas, with his extensive experience of hospitals and medics, this was the easy part. On 11 November 1963, he was examined by Dr C. Been and found 'not to be mentally or physically defective in any way' and 'generally in a good state of health'.[25] Three days later, the second state physician, Dr A.C. McDonald, saw nothing wrong with Tsafendas and also wrote a favourable report.[26] The final act was an interview with a senior immigration officer. Noting the positive reports by his colleagues and the doctors, this officer issued Tsafendas with a certificate for permanent residence.[27] None of the officers checked the government's stop list carefully, where they would have found Tsafendas's name. Presumably, they felt that anyone with a valid visa issued by the South African Consulate in Lourenço Marques plus a briefcase full of glowing references presented no threat to the nation.

After 21 years away, Tsafendas was bewildered and disturbed by what he saw in Pretoria and Johannesburg. Where, he wanted to know, were the Africans? Pretoria was the country's capital and Johannesburg its financial hub, two teeming, densely populated metropolises, but there was scarcely a black person to be seen in their central areas during the day and none at all at night. The few Africans he saw in the streets were labourers making deliveries or sweeping the roads. Tsafendas had followed developments in the country closely from Europe, but press accounts gave no indication of how apartheid had been entrenched. The government's propaganda machine had surpassed itself in producing filmed advertisements showing South Africa as a happy, sun-filled nation where all the races lived comfortably, separate but supposedly equal. Tsafendas was quick to make comparisons with pre-war Germany when the Nazis presented the concentration camps as akin to country houses, with slides and swings where children played happily and their parents looked on indulgently. Not taken in by official propaganda, his contacts in the British Anti-Apartheid Movement and his father's letters had kept him abreast of the situation. Even so, the cityscapes were a revelation.

Entire black communities had been forcibly removed from central city areas to the urban outskirts and the rural areas beyond. Usually, the vacated space was zoned for the use of whites. Tsafendas realised this was Dr Verwoerd's conception of how apartheid should work.

By steering the necessary legislation through Parliament,[28] Verwoerd had managed to deny 79% of South Africans full access to their basic human rights and their rights as citizens, effectively turning the black population into servants of the whites. Black people, though born in the country, had no land rights, were forced to live in designated areas[29] and were forbidden to enter 'Whites Only' territory; at the same time, whites, who constituted 21% of the population, owned 87% of the land, forcing the 79% of blacks onto the remaining 13%.[30] Govan Mbeki said these policies of Verwoerd closely resembled the model for Jewish ghettos under Nazi Germany.[31]

Racial discrimination was particularly evident in the disbursement of health resources. Care standards for whites were among the best in the world, with many patients suffering from illnesses associated with affluence, such as coronary heart disease. Blacks were largely victims of poverty, suffering from malnourishment, TB, pneumonia, typhoid and gastroenteritis. In 1964, life expectancy for whites averaged 70 years, while for blacks it was 40. Infant mortality rates were even worse. In 1960, the death rate per 1,000 live births for whites was 29.6, for blacks 95. Challenged about the disparities, Dr Verwoerd stated that in 1958 South Africa spent $8.61 per head per year on the health and education of Africans, while governments in Belgian Congo spent $1.30 and India 3 cents on their people.[32] However, Verwoerd failed to mention that unlike the countries he compared it to, South Africa was the richest state on the continent and one of the richest in the world.

Child mortality among blacks was so bad that only 55% lived to the age of 16, at which point they were required to obtain a life-long pass controlling where they could travel, live and work.[33] Dr Verwoerd's infamous Pass Laws Act sought to control the movements of black people by requiring all Africans aged 16 and over to carry a passbook when in a white area. The 92-page book, in effect an internal passport, stated where and during which hours the holder could remain in a white area, invariably an urban neighbourhood. Even those few Africans officially permitted to remain in the cities were required to stay in their homes after 9.30 pm or face arrest. A warning siren was sounded at 9.00 pm to remind them. The passbook became the South African version of the Star of David which Jews in Nazi Germany were forced to wear. Blacks loathed the passbook and named it the Dompas (Stupid pass).[34] Failure to carry the document carried a fine of R20 or immediate imprisonment. Apartheid was the worst form of capitalism and one of its main purposes was to provide cheap labour for the white community; indeed, the need for this labour was the only reason that all blacks were not driven out of the cities and into the rural reserves. The providers of this essential labour were treated as slaves, however, and paid contemptible wages by their white employers. Figures from the year 1960 showed that the average African wage was £13 a month and an appeal for a minimum wage of £1 a day was rejected. The average white wage at the time was £68 per month. In 1965, only 20% of the country's middle-level workers, such as clerks and artisans, were black; a third of blacks lived and worked as labourers on white farms (the rest were divided equally between the cities and the reserves). By 1970, 17% of the population that was white earned 72% of all annual paid income while 70% of Africans earned 19%. As early as 1957, Dr Verwoerd, who earned £4,500 per annum as Minister of Native Affairs, made no secret of his belief that apartheid would fail if blacks were allowed to improve their skills and earn higher wages. For the wellbeing of whites, wages of black labour had to remain low and strict controls maintained on the movement of the black population.

Rigorous application of the pass laws under Dr Verwoerd led to the imposition of forced labour and the disappearance and deaths of uncountable numbers of black workers. Special police units known as Ghost Squads launched lightning, night-time raids up and down the country and arrested thousands of pass law offenders.[35] Because the Native Commissioner's Court could not handle the huge numbers, police quietly bypassed the court system and press-ganged many men into working on white farms. The lie they were told was that they would be free of trouble if they did some farm work, whereas they were liable to five years in jail if they appeared in court.[36] Some hijacked workers were traced to potato farms in the Eastern Transvaal, while others were killed by farm foremen and buried under ploughed land. When reports began circulating of black men going missing, Dr Verwoerd blamed communist propaganda. Then when evidence was found, he blamed 'the Jews', stating that the farms in question were Jewish-owned.[37]

Over the years, South Africa's treatment of its lowest-paid workers was denounced by international organisations as 'forced labour' and 'slavery'.[38] As far back as 1953, a UN agency, the Independent Labour Organisation, defined South Africa's system as forced labour and, in 1965, the International Agency for Employment declared that the 'state of African labour forces, bound to a South African economy under the principles of white supremacy' could 'barely be differentiated from slavery'.[39]

Perhaps the most sinister aspect of Dr Verwoerd's apartheid policy was that it aimed not only to keep Africans subservient but to ensure that they would never aspire to be anything better. The Bantu Education Act was designed to teach Africans that they were 'not allowed to gaze' at 'the green pastures of European society' and that there was 'no place for them in the European community above the level of certain forms of labour'. Furthermore, the Act was designed to prevent blacks from learning about such dangerous

'European values' as 'freedom' and 'equality' that were not for them. Verwoerd's own words about the Act and its aims speak for themselves:

> *Natives will be taught from childhood to realise that equality with Europeans is not for them ... People who believe in equality are not desirable teachers for Natives... The Bantu must be guided to serve his community in all respects. There is no place for him in the European community above the level of certain forms of labour. Within his community, however, all doors are open. For that reason, it is of no avail for him to receive a training which has as its main aim absorption in the European community, where he cannot be absorbed. Until now he has been subjected to a school system which drew him away from his own community and misled him by showing him the green pastures of European society in which he was not allowed to graze... if the Native in South Africa today in any kind of school in existence is being taught to expect that he will live his adult life under a policy of equal rights, he is making a big mistake. The Native who attends school must know that he will be the labourer in the country.*[40]

This was a time when the government spent $180 per year on the education of every white child and $25 on each black child.[41]

When South Africa's racial policies prompted criticism from abroad, Verwoerd blamed foreigners for failing to understand apartheid. It was, he said, a 'domestic affair', and people who did not live in the country could not understand its nature and background. Apartheid was something good and he was trying to do his best for all sections of society.[42] He also characterised his overseas critics as 'the ducktails (young hoodlums) of the political world' and insisted that 'We in South Africa are trying to do our level best for all portions of our population... we have been misunderstood... we are not the barbarians we are supposed to be, we are Christians ourselves...'[43]

Another thing that foreigners did not know, according to Dr Verwoerd, was that whites lived in southern Africa before blacks. Expounding on this unique perceptive, he claimed that what was now the nation of South Africa was vacant land until settled by whites from Europe.[44] The truth, as all recognised scholars agree, is that blacks occupied the land, farmed it and raised cattle on it for thousands of years before any white man arrived. The early white settlers were so unprepared for the rigours of Africa that they often had to beg the indigenous herders to sell cattle to them to prevent them from starving.[45]

Dr Verwoerd's race theories were difficult to credit 15 years after a war in which six million Jews had died on the altar of race theory. 'We whites must rule the blacks', he declared in 1960.[46] In an interview published by the German magazine, *Die Zeit*, on 20 October of that year, he declared that South Africa's Africans should be grateful that their European colonisers did not murder them as American whites had done with their Native Americans. He said:

> *The experiences of our ancestors in this country were rather similar to those of the Americans and the Indians. But while the Americans annihilated the Indians as they advanced through the continent, the Boers allowed the blacks to live. Should we now suffer because our ancestors behaved in such a Christian and humane fashion? No, I tell you, this is a white country and any concessions to the blacks only means demands for fresh concessions. It would be absurd to turn the blacks into imitations of Europeans and force a Western-type democracy upon them. We plan to develop them along their own lines, using their own traditional communities and tribal chieftains.*[47]

What all this meant in reality was that blacks lived as if under martial law, with the police and security services operating in a way that, according to South African writer Hans Pienaar, was 'more reminiscent of an occupying army', judging by the extraordinary levels of violence they meted out to terrified blacks.[48] More than one observer saw reflections of 1930s Nazi Germany in the new South African order.[49] Every night pass raids took place all over the country and armed patrols were visible at each street corner. Verwoerd's newest innovations were 'machine-gun belts', which were open areas where blacks could be gunned down should they appear to threaten White areas in the course of a riot.[50] The law was weighted entirely against accused persons. Prisoners awaiting trial could be held for up to 180 days without access to a lawyer, then, when that term ran out, the 180 days could be re-imposed, not just once but indefinitely, or as Vorster boasted when he was Minister of Prisons, 'until this side of eternity'.[51] It was impossible for families, reporters or lawyers to discover who had been arrested or where a person was being held. No such information was ever divulged. Detainees would simply disappear.[52]

Punishments for active opponents of apartheid were severe, up to and including execution, though long jail terms were more usual. A common measure was the imposition of banning orders, a traditional method in South Africa for dealing with perceived political troublemakers, under which offenders were banished or restricted as to where they lived and banned from making public utterances. Bannings had been in use since at least 1927, but they escalated sharply under Dr Verwoerd, resulting in thousands of families being rendered destitute in the absence of the bread-winner.[53] Celebrated recipients of banning orders included Albert Luthuli, Nelson Mandela and Elizabeth Mafekeng, the first black woman to be punished in this way.[54]

The ultimate punishment for opposing the apartheid regime was execution. South Africa at the time was 'the world's busiest hangman', as Albie Sachs named it, executing around one hundred people a year. The 194 men hanged between July 1963 and June 1965 represented 47% of the world's executions over that period. Almost all were convicted of anti-government resistance.[55] Hanging may have been the ultimate deterrent, but flogging, by whip or cane, also increased sharply during the 1950s and after.

Verwoerd's government was simultaneously engaged in a campaign of state terror that included murder, bombings and extra-territorial abductions. Kenneth Abrahams, Anderson Ganyile and John Lyati Pokela were among those who were kidnapped on foreign soil and smuggled back into South Africa. Activists were then interrogated and usually sentenced to long terms of imprisonment.[56] Bombings included the 1963 destruction of an East African Airways Dakota aircraft sent to pick up four members of the ANC who had broken out of a Johannesburg prison, and the blowing up of a hostel for South African refugees.[57]

State terror was not the only threat to blacks in South Africa, where paramilitary groups or packs of white racists regularly went on the rampage, their atrocities ignored by the authorities. For example, in Cape Town in 1961, hooligans hurled a petrol bomb through the window of an Indian family's home after the son of the house was arrested for distributing anti-republic leaflets. Also, in Cape Town, the windows of three leaders of the Coloured People's Congress were shattered by rocks. Lawyers known to defend blacks were constantly threatened and often attacked. In Natal, the veteran Boer nationalist and racist Raymond Kirch Rudman led a group of home-grown white thugs who called themselves the Ku Klux Klan.[58]

The rules of apartheid often led Verwoerd's South Africa down strange and embarrassing legal pathways, demonstrating the absurdity of many racial rules. For instance, the traditional Christmas performance of Handel's great oratorio, *Messiah,* was banned because the choir was black, but the orchestra and conductor were white.[59] In the world of popular entertainment, Louis Armstrong was refused a visa because the authorities did not want audiences to see a black man who was admired worldwide;[60] when the movie *Othello* was released with the white British actor Laurence Olivier playing the African name part, Verwoerd opposed it as inappropriate;[61] and when *Oceans 11* came round, the African-American actor Sammy Davis Jr's photograph was removed from the publicity material.[62] In 1963, a South African Indian won the Natal Golf Open competition, beating 113 white players. Because rules barred black people from entering the clubhouse, the winner was awarded his prize outside in the rain.[63] Vividly aware of these nonsensical situations, and of the pain which, in many cases, they caused, Tsafendas redoubled his intention to fight apartheid in any way he could.

Although Tsafendas lived at first at Evangelia's house, No. 1 Fatti's Building, Paul Kruger Street, he spent a lot of time in his stepmother's house. Tsafendas was surprised and pleased to see that Marika had kept all the files he had created from newspaper cuttings and magazines when he was a boy. More than that, she had placed them in plastic sleeves to protect the covers from dust and sunlight. Dimitri was touched by this unexpected gesture of affection and embraced and kissed his stepmother with that bear hug that the family was to know so well. As always with Dimitri, however, there were problems. Among the personal possessions, he brought into South Africa were two long-playing records of communist songs, one in Italian and the other Russian, several records by Paul Robeson, and a collection by Bob Dylan. The album covers depicting the massive, handsome, black Robeson terrified Marika, especially one showing him about to hurl a spear, a still from his movie, *Sanders of the River*. Marxism was illegal in South Africa and Marika pleaded with Dimitri not to play the communist songs, then, when he did, often singing along with them, at least to lower the volume. Exasperated and fearful, she would tell him, 'You are going to get us all put in jail.' Tsafendas rated *Bella Ciao*, one of the Italian communist anthems, as one of his all-time favourites and he whistled it throughout his life. Marika, to her surprise, discovered that she liked both Robeson and Dylan and would sing along to some of Robeson's more popular songs, but softly.[64]

If the domestic disagreement about the records could be rated a squall, a full-scale storm erupted when Marika and Evangelia discovered that most of Dimitri's books had been about Communism or left-wing politics disguised with phoney covers as literary classics. Among them were anti-apartheid pamphlets and a poster honouring Patrice Lumumba. Dimitri was out of the house at the time and Marika looked fearfully at a second suitcase that he always kept locked. When he returned, she demanded that he open the suitcase. Tsafendas refused, protesting that he was too old to be ordered about by his mother, but, when Marika insisted, he unlocked the case, which was filled with Marxist and anti-apartheid pamphlets. It was then that Marika realised that Tsafendas had lied to her and the whole family when he assured them that he would not be involved in politics back in South Africa. Already terrified that the police might find out about the bribe they paid to J.J. van den Berg, Marika urged Eleni, Charles, Nick and Victor to convince Tsafendas to destroy the books. Instead, starved of anything but pro-apartheid propaganda, they looked through the proscribed literature with interest.[65] The chances are their curiosity turned to serious apprehension when Tsafendas handed them the most notorious document of apartheid South Africa, The Freedom Charter.[66]

This document, which Mandela once described as 'the most radical proclamation ever made by the national movement in South Africa',[67] was the product of a 1955 meeting of anti-apartheid activists in Kliptown, near Johannesburg. Known as the Congress of the People, the meeting set out the dissidents' core democratic demands as 'the right of the people to govern; freedoms regardless of race, colour or sex; equality before the law; and equal access to education, housing, and medical care.'[68] It enshrined these elements in a declaration that became known as The Freedom Charter. The government viewed it as a treasonable, revolutionary tract and responded by arresting more than 500 people in September 1955.[69] The Charter became a central issue in the notorious Treason Trial which started the following year, when 156 people, including Mandela, were accused of treason.

Hastily setting aside the Charter, Dimitri's relatives discovered two books that intrigued them because they were not about politics but medicine. One featured insanity and psychiatry, the other concerned intestinal disorders. Clearly, Tsafendas had read them to perfect his acts, but when asked about them, he just smiled and said, 'I like reading medicine ... it could save your life.' However, the discovery that Tsafendas had smuggled proscribed literature into the country angered and worried his family, who felt he had betrayed them and placed them in personal danger.[70]

The situation boiled over as a result of Tsafendas's behaviour at church soon afterwards. It was a Sunday and the whole family attended the Greek Orthodox morning service. At one point, the priest welcomed a family newly arrived from Greece and praised South Africa and its policy of apartheid and the opportunities for people to come and work. He then criticised communists, 'terrorists' and other 'enemies' of the country. Tsafendas was furious and only Victor's intervention stopped him from interrupting the priest. However, when the time came for communion, Tsafendas refused to take the sacrament or to kiss the priest's hands, as was customary. Instead, he began arguing quietly with him while puzzled communicants lined up behind them. Tsafendas told the priest that Jesus would have been ashamed to see men of God supporting a regime that oppressed the people. Politely, the priest replied that Greeks should be grateful for South Africa's hospitality and should not bite the hand that fed them. By now, Nick and Victor were trying to pull Tsafendas away and members of the congregation began shouting in support of the priest. Tsafendas stayed calm, repeating what he had said and denouncing apartheid, until Victor and Nick managed to drag him bodily back to their pew.[71]

Once back at Evangelia's home, the family turned on Tsafendas, reminding him he was no longer in Europe, where he could say what he wanted. Marika moaned that it was a mistake to bring him back to South Africa, which she now deeply regretted; she had only done it because he assured her he had changed when obviously he had not. Why couldn't he just be a law-abiding citizen like all the other Greeks? Victor complained that he had embarrassed them in front of the whole church and now the entire Greek community would hear about it. Tsafendas apologised and promised to be discreet in future and once again, Marika blamed her late husband for planting silly ideas in him. Evangelia, fearing that they would lose Greek customers, asked Tsafendas to stop working at their café.[72]

In order to escape the tense family situation, Nick Vlachopoulos suggested that Tsafendas move out of Evangelia's home and occupy an apartment he owned, where he could stay rent-free. Vlachopoulos had taken a great liking to his brother-in-law and shared most of his political views. Because the apartment would not be available for a few days, Markos and Fotini Gavasiadis, who also admired Tsafendas, invited him to move into an empty room in their spacious house at 568 Church Street, West End, Pretoria. Tsafendas formed a close friendship with both his hosts, especially Fotini, and since there was a further delay in the apartment's availability, he ended up staying there for a few weeks. Vlachopoulos's apartment, coincidentally next to Fotini's house, became Tsafendas' home for the next eight months. He filled it with the paraphernalia he had brought from Europe, mostly books and political posters depicting internationally known revolutionaries such as Ahmed Ben Bella, Fidel Castro and Lumumba.[73]

Tsafendas's move led to another hugely important friendship, one which linked two men regarded as outsiders by many of their own people. The apartment had previously been let rent-free by Vlachopoulos's father to Antonis Bizos, father of the stormy Greek human rights lawyer and anti-apartheid activist George Bizos. Nick Vlachopoulos was a friend of Antonis and introduced him to Tsafendas at a Greek wedding in Johannesburg. Both Tsafendas and Antonis often wore carnations in their coat lapels and the flower came to represent a familial link. Nick's children often delivered a carnation from their mother to Antonis at his old apartment and, when Tsafendas got to know Antonis, Eleni would also give him a carnation to give to their old friend. Tsafendas met and talked with Antonis often during his time in Pretoria and visited him frequently in Johannesburg. He did not mind the journey, since he considered Antonis to be the only Greek with whom he could have a serious political conversation, indeed one of the few Greeks in South Africa who was not racist or a supporter of apartheid.[74] Antonis and his son George were considered to be an embarrassment, indeed traitors, by most of the Greek community because of their public stance against apartheid.[75] 'Traitor' was also a favourite label that expatriate Greeks in Mozambique pinned on members of their community who supported independence for the country in which they lived; Tsafendas was one of them.

Vlachopoulos owned the Proclamation Hill Café, also on Church Street, a few metres from the apartment he had given to Tsafendas. Fotini worked there full time and Tsafendas began going daily for coffee and to read the newspapers. Markos helped out when he was not busy with his full-time job as a plumber and Nick ran the café late afternoons and evenings. Very often the café filled up quickly in the mornings and, seeing Fotini struggling, Tsafendas would come to the rescue. He was adept at all the service tasks, helping to serve, cook, pour coffees and do anything else that was needed. Fotini suggested that Nick hire Tsafendas full-time but her brother was doubtful, fearing that Tsafendas would talk politics with the customers, but in the end offered him a permanent position on good wages. Tsafendas declined, however, and insisted on continuing to help out when needed in part payment for his rent-free apartment.[76]

As for talking politics, Tsafendas never argued with the customers about anything while working at the café. He was polite and respectful, but also joked with customers as appropriate and in time became so popular that some patrons, especially older people, would come to the café just to talk to him. Even when he secured work full-time, Tsafendas would help out at the café, much to the delight of Nick and Fotini. They found Dimitri physically lazy when it came to mopping tables and clearing up, but he was quick with the bills, working out prices and change in his head, and his PR value to the café was inestimable.[77]

Fotini found Tsafendas to be 'fiercely anti-Afrikaner', often equating Afrikaners with Nazis and Verwoerd with Hitler. He never read Afrikaans newspapers, declaring that 'the only truth you can read in an Afrikaans newspaper is the obituaries'. He refused to speak in Afrikaans either, on grounds that it was the language of the oppressor.[78] This is not to say he considered all Afrikaners to be racists and he was certainly happy to associate with the likes of Hendrik Johannes van Loggerenberg, a Pretoria businessman, who knew many Greeks and was a good friend of Marika. He would often eat at her house, which is where Tsafendas met him. The Afrikaner and the mixed-race rebel socialised for close to nine months and they got on perfectly well.[79]

During his time in Pretoria, Tsafendas became very close to Fotini and Markos. As neighbours, they saw each other every day for nine months, often for a meal in the couple's home or to talk and hear about Tsafendas's travels and adventures, as well as his political views. Fotini thought of him as a 'philosopher'. In addition to meals, she often washed and ironed his clothes, while Tsafendas helped with the shopping and cleaning in the house and the café. One aspect of his behaviour that never failed to impress her was Tsafendas's politeness. He would always open doors for her, carry her bags and offer to help with any heavy task. Fotini 'loved him' in a sisterly way and considered him to be 'a real gentleman', describing him as one of the 'kindest, funniest and most openly generous men' she had ever met. As for Tsafendas, he always counted Fotini as one of his greatest friends.[80]

Above all, Fotini was impressed by Tsafendas's quick mind. She said, 'Dimitri could buy you and sell you any time he wanted and as many times as he wanted, he was so clever. He would find a way to convince you that he is right and that you are wrong – even if you *know* that you are right and that he is wrong! He would turn things upside-down and at the end, he would even make you apologise to him!' Tsafendas gave Fotini numerous books to read, more literary classics than politics, and Fotini considered their times together as tantamount to a personal education. He also gave her and her husband The Freedom Charter, which made a profound impression on the young couple and their understanding of apartheid in South Africa.[81]

Eleni agreed with Fotini about Dimitri's intelligence. He was, she said, 'very, very clever, cleverer than any of us'.[82] An area where Eleni and Dimitri disagreed was music. Eleni adored the Beatles, but Tsafendas did not. He gave her his Robeson records and others he brought from Europe and, though she liked some, she still preferred the English group. Tsafendas criticised the Beatles as superficial and their songs as meaningless and repetitious with ridiculous lyrics full of 'na, na, na' and 'yeah, yeah, yeah'. [83] However, it is probable that he would have changed his mind had he learnt of the group's later development under the influence of the rebellious John Lennon.

Before he even met Tsafendas, Nick Vlachopoulos knew they had much in common, judging by what he had heard from his wife, and so it proved as their relationship in Pretoria deepened. They spent hours talking politics and mulling over Tsafendas's past political activities, including his battles with fascist thugs in London. Tsafendas would invariably display the bottle scar he received in Trafalgar Square. As for South Africa, Tsafendas went close to the edge when, loudly and frequently, he used his trademark description of Verwoerd as 'Hitler's best student'.[84]

During Christmas 1963, Katerina, known in the family as Bushia, travelled to Pretoria from Rhodesia to see Dimitri and to introduce her two little boys to him. It was yet another tearful family reunion and Bushia asked Dimitri to visit Rhodesia and meet her husband, Gerry Pnefma (Pnefmatikos), when he was settled. However, things turned sour when Tsafendas started an argument about arranged marriages. Bushia was extremely beautiful and had lots of suitors in South Africa, but she married Gerry Pnefma by arrangement. Tsafendas opposed these old customs, especially prevalent in Africa, where expatriate Greeks invariably married other Greeks. He declared that young people should meet and marry whoever they fell in love with. Bushia was deeply hurt by his attack on her marriage and began to regret inviting him to her home. Marika was furious, but also taken aback by the vehemence of her stepson's argument. Tsafendas's thinking on this matter extended to interracial marriage too. He argued that Greeks, if they wished, should marry non-Greeks, even 'non-whites'. Having seen many happy mixed-race couples in Europe, he denounced South Africa's Immorality Act, which prohibited sexual relations across the races. Such legislation, he declared angrily, was similar to the Nuremberg Laws of Nazi Germany, which were drafted to preserve Aryan racial purity against contamination by Jews. Marika and Victor thought this was nonsense, but Eleni, Nick and Fotini agreed with most of what he said. Being in race-conscious South Africa, however, they urged him to keep such ideas to himself.[85]

At Christmas, Tsafendas sent a gift to Elenitsa Banovic, the daughter of Father Nikola and his favourite among all the children. To his horror, some weeks later, a letter from the priest informed him of Elenitsa's drowning in the sea in September 1962, just nine months after Tsafendas had left Istanbul. She was only 13. Devastated, he wept for days, saying it was the saddest moment of his life. It was almost a year before he found the courage to express his sorrow on paper. The priest replied that he understood his reaction and he should not feel guilty. Father Nikola heard nothing more of Tsafendas until Verwoerd's assassination.[86]

On 9 December 1963, Tsafendas got his first paid employment since returning to South Africa, doing maintenance and development work for City Engineering and Carron Limited.[87] He got the job just before his savings ran out and now, with money in his pocket, the first thing he did was buy a bicycle. He used it constantly, mostly to go to work, but for short distances, too. 'It is good exercise,' he said, and taught Fotini and the small son of Marika's black domestic worker how to ride it. Although he was paid well, Tsafendas rarely had money to spare because he spent so much on books and food, but when he did, he was generous with it. Fotini said, 'If he had only one rand in his pocket, he would give it without hesitation to someone who needed it.' The most frequent recipients of his generosity were his nephews and Fotini and Markos's son, Nick, for whom he bought toys, chocolates and sweets.[88] What Tsafendas most enjoyed was babysitting his adored nephews, Nick, Michalis and Dinos, which is when he taught them children's songs from Mozambique, as well as Paul Robeson's famous 'Canoe Song'. They too called it the 'Ah yee oh koe song', just like Elenitsa had in Istanbul.[89]

Pretoria's neon-lit nightlife was lively and uninhibited, equal to most capitals in Europe but the polar opposite of his memories from the past. Needless to say, these activities were only for whites. Social life for Tsafendas in Pretoria was an eclectic affair, ranging from prayer meetings with members of the Christian Church to visits to theatres, cinemas, restaurants and nightclubs, often with Fotini or Eleni. Sometimes his Christian friends in Pretoria or Johannesburg would go searching for a bride for Tsafendas, but he was never impressed and failed to rise to the bait. The three women closest to him at this time of his life were Fotini, a good quarter-century his junior, Eleni, his half-sister, and Mary, his cousin. All found much to admire about Tsafendas. When he took the ladies out, he insisted on paying, though Fotini and Eleni constantly urged him to stop spending and start saving. His invariable answer was 'I can't!' He said, 'Saving money is like holding my breath. I can't live like that. We only live once, I want to enjoy it while I can.' It might have been different were he married with a family, he said, but, being single, he could always find a job and survive, so why save? 'And when you are too old to work?' they asked him. 'I will retire to Cuba,' he said. 'I won't need much there.' Tsafendas believed that as a former member of the South African Communist Party and a DSE fighter in Greece, he would be welcome in the socialist paradise of Cuba. He insisted that he always had enough to get by on, often quoting Epicurus that 'being self-sufficient is the greatest wealth'.[90] What astonished everyone as they got to know Tsafendas was the size of his appetite. Some of his friends calculated that he ate as much as two to three normal adults. However, though he was a big man, he was not fat and Tsafendas attributed this to a good metabolism, drinking plenty of water and walking a lot.[91]

Whatever the fun distractions of Pretoria, nothing could keep Tsafendas from politics. He contacted old comrades from the South African Communist Party, but it became clear they had no wish to become involved in anything risky; he suspected they did not fully trust him because he had been away from South Africa for so long. He even tracked down George Tyrakis, the Cretan rebel who had participated in the kidnapping of the Nazi general, only to find that not even he was interested in any spectacular act of opposition.[92]

On 3 February 1964, Tsafendas's work contract expired,[93] but four days later he started with F.A. Poole Engineering Pty. Ltd. There, he encountered serious trouble. Tsafendas was taken on as a welder but was later transferred to the fitter-turner department, working 45 hours per week at 77 cents per hour. He was put in charge of the removal of machinery from the old factory to the new one and, according to his bosses, he 'did this work well'. [94] The problems began when his foreman, Albert Vercoueil, began receiving complaints that Tsafendas bullied white Portuguese and South African workmen, though there were no such complaints concerning black and coloured workers.[95] Tsafendas became very unpopular among white workers because he backed the black staff if he thought they were being mistreated. It was clear, too, that his political opinions were involved because almost all the white workers supported apartheid and the Portuguese dictatorship.[96]

Tsafendas was particularly disturbed and angered when he learnt that one of the men, Antonio Texeira Da Silva, had served with the Portuguese army in Mozambique. When questioned about Tsafendas's sanity during the course of the assassination investigation, Da Silva saw Tsafendas's attitude as a difference of political opinion and nothing abnormal. 'He never behaved as an insane person whilst employed here,' Da Silva said.[97] Tsafendas also crossed swords with 34-year-old Nikolaas Jacobus Nel. He objected to the way Nel was talking to black workmen and an argument erupted. According to Nel, Tsafendas threatened to stab him, although he had no knife at the time. Nel found Tsafendas to be unpopular among the white workers, but popular with the black workforce, and he never spoke to him again.[98]

Soon after he started working for the company, Tsafendas was involved in an accident, which he believed was caused deliberately by white South Africans with whom he had argued earlier. A machine malfunctioned while Tsafendas was working on it and he suffered burns to his body. He was taken to a hospital, where he was treated, by Dr Been, the doctor who had approved his health status for permanent residence. It is not known how Tsafendas suspected sabotage, but his injuries kept him off work for several days.[99]

Vercueil found Tsafendas to be an 'intelligent person and completely mentally balanced', someone who quickly grasped his duties but was 'untidy and lazy in rounding off his work'. On 10 July 1964, Vercueil admonished him for this. When Tsafendas responded by mumbling, Vercoueil ordered him into his office and told him, 'Dimitri, you are no good to me, you are always causing trouble and your work is no good. You must leave today.' According to Vercoueil, Tsafendas responded in anger, 'You are like your bloody government, but I will get you, and I will get your Prime Minister, too.'[100] Out of work and at a loose end, Tsafendas decided to accept Bushia's invitation to visit her and her family in Rhodesia.[101] Thus, later that day, he applied in writing for a return visa to allow him to visit Mozambique and Southern Rhodesia. Ms J. Markram, an assistant in the Department of the Interior, did not notice Tsafendas's name on the national stop list,[102] thus the fourth government official to overlook it. The likeliest explanation is that Markram did not even check, since Tsafendas held a permit for permanent residency and a valid Portuguese passport. Thus Tsafendas waved goodbye to his family, indicating to Fotini that he would be back sooner or later. He put his furniture in storage and gave his bicycle to the little African boy he had taught to ride.[103]

Tsafendas crossed the border from South Africa on 19 July 1964, on a temporary tourist permit valid until 9 August, and travelled to the small town of Marandellas, where Bushia and her husband, Gerry, ran a grocery store.[104] From the start, relations were difficult. In his usual way, Tsafendas railed against colonialism in Africa, including Rhodesia, at a time when negotiations with Britain were taking place to decide the colony's future. Hoping to stop him talking about politics, Gerry asked Tsafendas about his time in Europe. To their dismay, Tsafendas told them about his time in the Greek Civil War and then showed them photographs of himself taking part in anti-apartheid demonstrations in London. His frightened hosts realised that as well as being an anti-colonialist, he was still a communist, not a comfortable discovery in Marandellas with its history as a centre for white settlement.[105]

There were other irritations. Bushia was disappointed that her half-brother had changed his surname from Tsafantakis, and she thought it absurd that he had deserted the Greek Orthodox church to join the Christian Church, a sect of which she had never heard. However, the final straw came when Tsafendas accused his hosts of under-paying and exploiting their black domestic staff. He said that from what he had seen so far in Rhodesia, most whites, including Greeks, took advantage of the Africans they employed. A bitter argument broke out and Tsafendas left the next day. Bushia later regretted shouting at Dimitri, but she knew that if he had remained, he would have got into a political argument with someone and, in such a small town, this could have cost them customers. Looking back, she wished she had spent more time with him as she was not going to see him again.

Leaving Marandellas, Tsafendas took an apartment in Avondale, a suburb of the capital, Salisbury. He applied for employment as a linguist with the Public Services Board, but was turned down. He then travelled to Lake Malawi in neighbouring Nyasaland in search of work, but returned within weeks.[106] Jobless in Salisbury, Tsafendas was pleased to receive an invitation from a good childhood friend, George Grispos, who lived in Umtali, some 200 km from the capital. They had not seen each other since 1939 and when Tsafendas arrived on 20 August 1964, it was as if he was attending a reunion of Lourenço Marques exiles. Grispos's wife, Helen Kavadias, had attended his English classes all those years ago and in the house next door was Helen's mother, Sophia Kavadias, who remembered Dimitri from the time she and the Tsafantakis family were neighbours. For the two nights of his stay in Sophia's house, the little group did little but talk politics and listen about Tsafendas's adventures round the world. One thing they noticed in particular was his anger about racism in colonial Africa.[107]

At one point, Helen reminded him of how years ago they used to call him a 'lending library' and she asked him to suggest a good book he had read lately. Tsafendas went to his battered suitcase and gave her his copy of the *Invisible Man*, Ralph Ellison's acclaimed story of how it felt to be black in America. He said everyone in Africa, black and white alike, should read it. Helen assumed from the title that it was science fiction, only to discover after he left that it was the story of an African-American man, who, being black, assumed an aura of invisibility to the white people around him, a typical Tsafendas read. Tsafendas had just two days with his old friends before he was arrested because his 9 August tourist permit had expired. He was deported immediately to Mozambique by train from Umtali.[108]

Back in Mozambique, Tsafendas lived in a boarding house, the Pension Gloria in Beira, from 28 August to 8 October 1964.[109] The house was owned by a Greek, Stelios Marangos, and most of the tenants were Greek. The large Greek community in the area regarded him, rather nervously, as a political celebrity. One of the tenants, a young man from Crete called Nick Papadakis, knew about Tsafendas's reputation as 'the Red' and had heard of his arrests by the Portuguese police and his long exile, but he had never seen him. Now here he was in the flesh! Papadakis promptly arranged to share a two-bedroom house with him. For a month, he listened to Tsafendas propound his views and found himself deeply impressed by his idealism and determination to fight for a just cause. He considered him to be 'a man of revolutionary zeal, eager to fight apartheid and for the independence of Mozambique ... He was very polite and open-hearted, very witty and sarcastic ... a gentle giant with a big heart who was helping everyone around him ... poor but very generous ... very clever with a very fast brain'.[110]

Among Tsafendas's best friends at the time were Xenofon and Marika Contis, whose 21-year-old daughter Irini was engaged to John Michaletos, Tsafendas's cousin and Aunt Artemis's son. Irini admired Dimitri immensely and said, he was 'very, very clever and he knew a lot. He was very well-read ... very friendly and talked a lot, mostly about Communism and Christianity. He had very strong political convictions and nobody could change his ideas. He was very staunch in what he believed.'[111]

Unable to find work, Tsafendas left the Pension Gloria and tried to get back to Umtali through the Forbes Border Post. He did not have the necessary visa and was declared a prohibited immigrant and returned to Mozambique.[112] Soon afterwards, he landed a job with the Hume Pipe Company in Gondola, a city some 150 km from Beira.[113] He spent the next four weeks in Gondola, returning to Beira most weekends.[114]

On Tsafendas's recommendation, Nick Papadakis applied for work at Hume Pipe and was duly accepted. However, Tsafendas made it an uncomfortable experience for him[115] by frequently and loudly declaring that colonial Portugal was exploiting Mozambique's oil resources.[116] He had frequent arguments with Portuguese and other whites on the workforce, charging them with maltreating the black co-workers. He even urged the blacks to go on strike, but this was a step too far for them. As for Papadakis, much as he admired Tsafendas, he was afraid to spend a lot of time with him while at work, fearing his outspokenness would get them into trouble. He urged

Tsafendas repeatedly not to talk politics at work, but his friend would not listen. After work, they spent their free time together and Papadakis looked on Tsafendas as a big brother.[117]

Like many Greeks in Gondola, Tsafendas frequented two cafés, Scala Café and John Verghis's café shop.[118] At first, the Greeks kept their distance – most of them supported the colonial status quo – but slowly, they came to realise that far from being a sinister troublemaker, Tsafendas was polite and open-hearted and a teller of jokes with a quick and clever mind. The Greeks always sat together and when Tsafendas came in, he would be promptly invited to join them. The group often sang together and Tsafendas impressed everyone, especially the ladies, with his dancing skills. One of the reasons that led to his growing acceptance was that, as in Lourenço Marques in the 1930s and Istanbul in 1961, he organised free English and history lessons for poor local children at a local Catholic church.[119]

The most common topic of conversation in the cafés was politics and none of the Greeks sympathised with Tsafendas's ideas, no matter how popular he was, which did not bother him. A frequent topic was Tsafendas's theory to make the world a better place by eradicating racism, conflicts and wars. Tsafendas believed that conflict and tension would never cease as long as the world was made up of nation-states with different religions and races, each with its own beliefs, ambitions and desires. The world would become a better and safer place and peace would reign only if individual countries and all religions ceased to exist; an alternative, he said, would be if everyone believed in one, single religion and if all peoples were the same colour. His listeners wondered how everybody could become the same colour? Half-joking, half-serious, Tsafendas replied, 'Well, everyone should have sex with someone of a different colour so that a new race will be created with everyone the same colour or at least all mixed. Only then will there be no racism and discrimination anymore.' His listeners laughed and this remark was discussed for a long time in Beira.[120] Although Tsafendas spoke light-heartedly about the sex part, he truly believed that racism and conflict would be eradicated only if his three elements (no nation states, no religious beliefs and everyone of mixed race) were present. He held to this view, which he reiterated many times, until the day he died.

Sir Antony Sher, the British-South African actor and playwright, considered Tsafendas's theory about the races a 'rather wonderful ideal for the future'.[121] In 1998, the American actor and film director Warren Beatty produced, wrote, directed and starred in a film titled *Bulworth*. The movie's hero, US Senator Bulworth, played by Beatty, declared that in order to eradicate racism, '[we should] eliminate white people, black people, brown people, yellow people ... get rid of 'em all! All we need is a voluntary, free-spirited, open-ended programme of procreative racial deconstruction. Everybody just gotta keep fuckin' everybody till they're all the same colour.' This is effectively what Tsafendas said 35 years earlier.

With Tsafendas, however, when politics was involved, trouble was never far away and not all of his listeners found his beliefs amusing. One day, speaking generally, he accused the Greek community of exploiting Mozambicans. Somebody responded angrily that he was an embarrassment and a traitor to his fellow Greeks. Tsafendas replied that most of the Greeks in Mozambique were an embarrassment to the human race and that he was proud to be considered a traitor by such people as it meant he was politically correct. There was laughter at this riposte, but one of the younger Greeks moved furiously to attack Tsafendas physically and had to be held back by his friends. Not everybody in the community held these views and Tsafendas had some very good Greek friends who were fair and open-minded, such as Babiolakis and Papadakis.[122]

With non-Greeks, it was different. At Hume Pipe in Gondola, Tsafendas worked with an elderly Indian man. He learnt that the man's daughter was planning to marry and he was building an extra room onto his own small house for the girl and her husband. However, the work was moving very slowly because of the father's age and lack of money. So each day after work, Tsafendas joined the old man and they laboured together on the room until the job was finished. When the wedding took place, Tsafendas was the only non-Indian invited.[123]

Many of the Greeks who listened to Tsafendas's lectures could not comprehend the visionary nature of his thinking. One of these was Andreas Babiolakis, someone he had known back in their early days in Lourenço Marques. Babiolakis's political ideas were the exact opposite of Tsafendas's, which he considered unacceptably extreme. For instance, one day Tsafendas declared that 'Verwoerd and [Portuguese Prime Minister] Salazar are fascist dictators and should be executed like Mussolini'.[124] Years later, Babiolakis conceded that Tsafendas was 'ahead of his time'. He said: 'Everything he was saying then about Africa and Mozambique was correct and came to happen. He was telling us [the Greeks], including me, to take our money and leave while there was time, because sooner or later, the Portuguese would be kicked out and everything we had "stolen" from the Mozambicans would be returned to them. We should have heard him, but none of us did … he was a good and bright man. The things he was saying at the time seemed wrong and stupid, but we couldn't see beyond our noses … he was right about everything.'[125]

Tsafendas and his good friends, Nick Papadakis and Andreas Babiolakis, often went to the bar of the Gondola Hotel, which was popular with Greeks. Again, the usual topic of discussion was politics and Tsafendas enjoyed arguing with people he considered to be fascists and colonialists. On 12 November 1964, Tsafendas was again talking politics as usual with some Greeks and 'various native races', as a PIDE report put it. At one point, he said something like this: 'This land is not called Portugal, it is called the United States of Mozambique; our flag has the colour blue and a rainbow, that rainbow that represents all of the colours ... We already have money, what we need is not to be mistaken by saying that we are Portuguese. No! We are Africans! Some day this will be over, I am sure that it will be over. Check my face in front of everyone, I don't like the Portuguese flag. Long live our land, the United States of Mozambique. Do not be fooled by my colour, my mother was African, I am also African.' [126]

Tsafendas had often talked of a flag for an independent Mozambique and a democratic South Africa containing all the colours of the rainbow representing the country's different races and minorities.[127] It would not take long for PIDE to hear about Tsafendas's flag comment. Thirty years later, Archbishop Desmond Tutu and Nelson Mandela used the term 'Rainbow Nation' to describe post-apartheid South Africa after its first fully democratic general election in 1994.

One of Tsafendas's best friends in Gondola, a workmate at Hume Pipe named Vittorio and an Italian communist probably from Naples, invited Tsafendas and some other Greeks to his wedding. As the celebrations proceeded, guests rose spontaneously and proposed toasts to the bride and groom. Tsafendas, too, stood, raised his glass and spoke briefly in honour of the happy couple, but then launched passionately in his rough baritone into his favourite Italian communist anthem, 'Bella Ciao'. The Greeks listened speechless, but Vittorio and his Italian friends joined in eagerly, clapping and pounding the tables with fists and spoons. When Tsafendas finished, he received a huge ovation and Vittorio called for another song. Tsafendas obliged with a second communist number, 'Fischia il Vento'. This time, many Greeks, though not communists, joined in the rhythmic applause.[128]

Joking and talking politics in bars and cafes was customary for Greeks, but the cause closest to his heart – independence for Mozambique – Tsafendas knew could only be achieved among the peasants in the villages. The armed struggle against the colonialists, led by FRELIMO, was at an early stage and Tsafendas knew he could not join it because of the physical demands, being too heavy to run or walk long distances. Instead, every weekend, he went to the rural areas where he chatted with villagers in their local dialects and urged them to join the independence fight with FRELIMO. He showed them books on Mao, Castro and other Cuban and Russian revolutions, holding them up as heroes of the proletarian struggle. The star among his cast of international revolutionaries, however, was Frantz Fanon. His custom was to write quotes from Fanon's works on the backs of the photographs, then give them away to local Mozambicans; he believed that the people would be more impressed if they see that these nicely spoken revolutionary words were the thoughts of a black man.[129] When his Greek acquaintances asked where he disappeared to at weekends, he said he was visiting friends. Not everyone believed him, but they said nothing, believing the less they knew about Tsafendas's activities the better.[130]

In odd juxtaposition with the communist literature that Tsafendas carried were copies of the Bible. If challenged by the authorities, he could claim he was teaching the Biblical precepts of peace and non-violence and, should this fail, he calculated he could fall back on his 'insanity' act. He believed that the Portuguese would not harm him since he had been diagnosed as insane in Lisbon and, to prove it, he always carried the medical certificate with him too. When Ira Kyriakakis once warned him against criticising the Portuguese, Tsafendas told her smiling, 'But I am crazy, I can do what I want,' and showed her the hospital certificate. Tsafendas later said this was a tactic dating back to the early years of Christianity, known as 'being foolish for Christ', when Christian believers would pretend to be mad so that the Romans would spare their lives.[131]

Inevitably, Tsafendas's evangelising trips to the countryside came to the attention of the Portuguese authorities. After learning of his comments about a rainbow flag and the exploitation of Mozambique's oil by the Portuguese, the police watched him closely and, on 16 November 1964, he was arrested in Maforga, a small town five miles from Gondola. He had been heard talking about independence and urging the villagers to join the struggle against the Portuguese colonialists. His suitcase was found with a large amount of communist and anti-fascist literature. As a result, the police accused him of 'making subversive propaganda against the Portuguese government and spreading subversive propaganda among the native masses' and took him in for interrogation.[132] When asked about the contents of his suitcase, Tsafendas said he used the Bibles to preach Christianity while the political books were for his personal use and not to conduct subversive propaganda. This excuse cut no ice with the police, who were well aware of what he was doing in the villages. Tsafendas was then thoroughly interrogated and eventually formally charged with pretending to be a missionary spreading the word about religion, while in reality preaching 'under the guise of religion in favour of Mozambique's independence'. The following is an extract from PIDEs' Confidential Report Regarding Demetrio Tsafendas: no: 2707/64/SR, dated 25 November 1964:

> *When asked to describe all of the subversive activities that he has been developing against the Country and in favour of Mozambique's independence, he answered: That, he hasn't been developing any kind of such subversive activities against the Country neither in favour of*

> *Mozambique's independence. However, wishes to clarify that he supports, as a Mozambican, the idea of Mozambique's independence, governed by the natives of that Province, whether they are black or white.*
>
> *When asked to say the reason why, on the last day, twelve, in Gondola, he was, together with various black nationals, advertising in favour of Mozambique's independence, saying the following phrases: 'This land is not called Portugal, It is called United States of Mozambique; our flag has the colour blue like the rainbow, that rainbow that represents all of the colours: we already have money, what we need is not to be mistaken by saying that we are Portuguese. No! We are Africans. At any day this will be over, I am sure that it will be over. Check my face in front of everyone else, I don't like the Portuguese flag. Long live to our land 'United States of Mozambique'. Do not be fooled by my colour, my mother was African, I am also African.' He answered [sic]: That, in fact, when the respondent found himself, together with the other black nationals, at the bar in Gondola Hotel, in the middle of that uplifting environment and already with a 'few glasses,' he pronounced those words. His attitude is due to his ideas, already mentioned before, about Mozambique's independence. That he wishes to clarify that, although he agrees with Mozambique's independence, he doesn't belong, however, to any subversive party or organisation that works in this sense.*
>
> *When asked to say what was his religion and if it was true or not that he has dedicated himself to preach as a missionary and, under the guise of this same religion, advertised in favour of Mozambique's independence, he answered: That he is a Christian and considers himself a representative of God on earth, a missionary, that wishes he could preach the Christian religion but that he is not allowed to because, on this earth, there is no freedom of expression. That is not, then, true that, under the guise of the religion, he has been advertising in favour of Mozambique's independence. That, being a Christian, he is not, though, Roman Catholic.*[133]

Tsafendas's alleged offences were so serious he was consigned the following day to the PIDE sub-delegation in Beira.[134] For the first 14 days, Tsafendas was locked up in a police cell, interrogated by PIDE's Sub-Inspector Joaquim Piçara Sabino, PIDE's brigade chief Augusto de Sousa Maia and PIDE agent Francisco Virgílio. Inspector Horacio Ferreira, the officer in charge of the cells, described Tsafendas as being 'intensely anti-white' and convinced that 'the Portuguese Government has never done anything for its non-Whites', adding that Tsafendas was 'normal' and 'very intelligent'. Furthermore, according to

Ferreira, during his detention, Tsafendas was often seen to read books written in 'Bantu languages, but never the Bible'.[135]

What particularly concerned the police at this time was the FRELIMO and they were anxious to know if Tsafendas was a member or if he had made contact with them. They found it difficult to believe that he knew nothing about the group when he was urging the country people to join it, and he was beaten sporadically. The interrogators were well-informed about Tsafendas's day-to-day movements and asked again about the Gondola Hotel incident four days earlier when he spoke of a United States of Mozambique and a rainbow flag. Tsafendas claimed as an excuse that he had taken 'a few glasses', but he did not deny the remarks, which, he said, represented the truth of his ideas about an independent Mozambique. Obviously, he could not have done otherwise since so many people had heard him. To make things clear, he outlined again his idea of an independent Mozambique as 'a Mozambique governed by the natives of that Province, be they white or black, and therefore separated from the mother nation'. However, he denied belonging to any party or subversive organisation or promoting subversive activities against the security of the state.[136]

On 25 November 1964, the Sub-Director of PIDE in Mozambique sent the transcript of Tsafendas's interrogation along with request No. 2707/64-S.R for additional information about Tsafendas, to the General Director of PIDE in Lisbon.[137] While waiting for a response and since it had by now been ascertained that PIDE had maintained a file on their prisoner since 1938, Tsafendas was transferred to PIDE's headquarters in Beira, where he was interrogated and kept in solitary confinement. Christmas of 1964 came and went without Tsafendas knowing about it since he had no access to the news and lost all track of time. His physical treatment, including occasional beatings, was nothing like the horrors he had suffered in the past, but he was now 46 and felt he could no longer endure physical maltreatment. Eventually, he decided to go back to his old method of securing his release, i.e. to pretend lunacy, but this time without the tapeworm. Appropriately, since he was accused of pretending to be a Christian missionary and since he carried Bibles and other holy books, he decided he would indeed pretend to be a missionary. Not just any missionary, though, but the most famous of them all, the apostle Peter. This would not be a problem, he reckoned, since he knew St Peter's life, he could quote lengthy passages from the Bible and he was well aware of what to say and do when faced with a psychiatrist. More importantly, he knew what *not* to say and what *not* to do.[138]

Thereupon, whenever his guards brought his food to his cell, Tsafendas assumed his most sanctimonious demeanour, made the sign of the cross over them and raising his eyes to heaven prayed unctuously, 'Forgive them Lord, for they know not what they do.' When asked what he was doing, he said they would be forgiven because they did not know who he truly was. Asked who he was, Tsafendas said he was Peter. 'Peter who?' the guards asked, puzzled. 'Peter from Bethsaida,' he replied, indicating that the guards must have heard of him. With his captors still looking blank, Tsafendas continued, 'I am prepared to be sacrificed like my Lord Jesus Christ.' He then quoted Christian scripture to them at inordinate length. In truth, Tsafendas was finding it difficult to keep a straight face, seeing the guards' baffled reactions. Fearing he was about to giggle, he turned his back on his captors, knelt in a corner of his cell and pretended to be deep in silent prayer. At this point, the guards called a doctor. Tsafendas insisted that he was St Peter, the first of Jesus's 12 apostles, and repeated his willingness to die for his Lord. The deception worked with the doctor and he had the prisoner taken to the government hospital in Beira for further examination. This was in January 1965 and, once again, Tsafendas had escaped going to prison by pretending to be crazy. Tsafendas later admitted that he never had so much fun as when he pretended to be St Peter. He would laugh out loud when describing the guards' reactions.[139]

While Tsafendas was in custody, all his Greek friends and acquaintances in Gondola were questioned by the police. Asked if Tsafendas talked politics with them, they replied in the negative because they did not want the police to think they knew about his political ideas and had not informed the authorities. The Greeks, probably to their puzzlement, were also asked if Tsafendas was insane. Of course, they said no. His new friend Papadakis was later stunned when a Portuguese policeman told him that Tsafendas was released from custody because he was insane and thought he was St Peter. When he saw Tsafendas and asked him about it, Tsafendas appeared to be deeply embarrassed. He said he had a nervous breakdown in custody but was okay now, and changed the subject. Papadakis and all the other Greeks concluded that Tsafendas made up the apostle act to secure his release.[140]

Tsafendas's journey to freedom lasted many weeks and revealed the extensive knowledge the police had of him, but in the end, his release owed everything to his acting skills. On 18 December 1964, the PIDE General Director in Lisbon had sent to his colleagues in Beira a report on Tsafendas's activities after he had left Mozambique in 1939. The report said this was 'a story of what his life had been, an authentic adventure novel, peregrinating around the world' and that after he was arrested by the Portuguese police, 'in the course of inquiries, he demonstrated signs of mental illness, a fact that was confirmed by Ultramar Hospital'.[141]

On 19 January 1965, while Tsafendas was still in hospital, Francisco Bartolomeu da Costa Lontrão, a PIDE officer in Beira wrote to the Sub-Director of PIDE in Lourenço Marques that 'the defendant Dimitrius

Tsafendakis is a supporter of the independence of this Province, without however being a militant for any of the clandestine and subversive organizations that strive for it'. Noting that Tsafendas had 'a certain abnormality', the police added that 'it is convenient that all investigations stop and the files be handed to the Sub-Director of the Delegation, so that they can be assessed and he can decide what should be done with them, as well as with the defendant'.[142]

On 23 January 1965, Alberto Henriques de Matos Rodrigues, a PIDE officer in Lourenço Marques, made the following suggestion to the Sub-Director of PIDE in Mozambique:

> *Having seen the archives, it is remarked with a minimal margin of error, that the defendant Demítrio Tsafendas is mentally ill and therefore not chargeable at a juridical or penal level. Given this, it seems to us a pure waste of time to continue working on these files, since we already know what their end will be. Therefore, considering the probable fact that the defendant cannot be charged, and he is not at all dangerous, I propose the release of the defendant, and closure of the archives.'*[143]

The Sub-Director agreed and Tsafendas was officially freed on 26 January 1965,[144] but remained in the hospital in Beira for further treatment. A PIDE report stated: 'Analyzing his declarations, and taking into account that he was mentally ill – and therefore not imputable in the juridical system – his case was archived and he was freed, since he was not considered dangerous.'[145]

A few days after being informed of his official release, Tsafendas miraculously became sane again and told the doctors he no longer believed himself to be St Peter. Happy that its treatment had worked, the hospital discharged him.[146] Once again, Tsafendas had managed to convince the Portuguese that he was mad but harmless.

Penniless and homeless, Tsafendas contacted his last employer, Hume Pipe Company, for wages unpaid because of his abrupt arrest and also asked his stepmother to sell some furniture he owned in Pretoria. Unwilling to embarrass or compromise his good friends Babiolakis and Papadakis by asking for refuge, he went to Beira's fire department, where they gave him a bed for ten nights while he looked for work. He made sure to be around at mealtimes, knowing he would get a plate of food, but relations soon broke down over the firemen's support for the Portuguese government. By then, Hume Pipe had paid him for four days owed, the equivalent of R41 and Tsafendas promptly left the firehouse, according to fireman Jose Lopez Baltazar, without even thanking them. A few days later, Marika sent him R20 from the sale of his furniture.[147]

Through the offices of Gerry and Katerina Pnefma, Tsafendas was taken on as an interpreter at the Beira docks. However, he lasted only a few days before he was fired. He had denounced the manager and the company as 'capitalists exploiting the workers' and had urged his colleagues to strike for higher wages and better working conditions. The manager told Gerry Pnefma that the 'only reason he did not call the police was that he did not want to cause his family problems'. He urged his friend not to help Tsafendas again because he was 'a dangerous Communist' who could get him into trouble.[148]

Sometime in February came another crisis. Tsafendas was at a café owned by John Verghis along with a crowd of Mozambicans and Greeks, again including Babiolakis and Papadakis. The drink was flowing and, at one point, Tsafendas bought beer for everyone, then paraphrasing Mark Antony in Shakespeare's *Julius Caesar,* happily called out, 'Friends, countrymen, lend me your glasses.' They all dutifully raised their glasses. However, when Tsafendas called on them to drink to a recent attack by FRELIMO, everyone froze and lowered their glasses untouched as Tsafendas downed his beer. Verghis politely asked Tsafendas to leave, which he did, never to return. The next day, Tsafendas was arrested again by the police, who had learnt of his rebel-rousing at the docks and his remarks at the café. He was interrogated and severely beaten, but he was freed a few days later because by now, the police accepted that he was mentally ill and not chargeable at a juridical or penal level.[149]

Soon after his release, Tsafendas entered a café that he normally did not frequent but popular with Greeks. His face bruised and shirt torn, it was obvious he had been roughed up. He looked like a broken man and appeared deeply embarrassed to be seen in such a condition. All the Greeks in the café knew about Tsafendas, but not all had met him. Many assumed he was drunk and most who recognised him, aware that he had been in police custody, turned their backs and walked out. Tsafendas had gone to the café to look for Andreas Babiolakis, a regular there, but he was not in that night. Only three Greeks remained in the café: Costas Poriazis, a man named Polakis and Giangos Babiolakis, Andreas's older brother. The three knew of his arrest, but they were surprised to see him looking such a mess. Tsafendas asked after Andreas and Giangos told him that he was in Lourenço Marques and not expected to return for a few days. He then asked Tsafendas what he wanted from his brother. Tsafendas said vaguely, 'I don't want anything, just to see him.' He then acknowledged the three men and walked out.[150] Poriazis went after him and asked if he needed anything. Tsafendas insisted that he did not. 'Do you need some money?' Poriazis asked, but before Tsafendas could answer, Giangos intervened and asked quietly, 'Do you have a place to stay?' Then, before Tsafendas could answer, he said, 'Come with me, you can stay in my house.' Giangos asked Poriazis and Polakis to stay in the café and not to mention that he was taking Tsafendas home. Giangos disagreed with Tsafendas about politics but was a generous and caring host. Tsafendas spent the next few days in the comfort of Giangos's home, often visited by Poriazis, Polakis and his host's brother, Andreas.[151]

By now, Tsafendas had decided that he had no future in Mozambique because PIDE would always be watching him. Having escaped twice, he knew he could not continue living there and decided to return to South Africa. The problem was that he had no money for the fare. Meanwhile, his half-sister Katerina was coming to Beira in a few days for the wedding of George Galanakis, who knew the Tsafantakis family well. He telephoned Katerina and suggested they meet before the wedding, but she refused, saying his arrests and particularly his rabble-rousing at the docks had humiliated her husband and herself. 'When are you going to understand that you are not in Europe to go around saying whatever you like?' she stormed. 'I can't go anywhere without people asking me about you and your arrests.'[152]

Any hopes he had of changing Katerina's mind went up in smoke when Galanakis met Tsafendas in a café. After a few moments of small talk, Galanakis, appearing deeply uncomfortable, asked Tsafendas to step outside for a private word, as other customers had joined their table. Before he could say anything, Tsafendas guessed he was being disinvited to the wedding for which he had received an invitation three months earlier. Apologising profusely, Galanakis said his wife-to-be and her family would feel very uncomfortable if he was there. They did not know him personally, but they had heard of his arrests. Some high-ranking Portuguese police officers would also be there, making things doubly awkward. 'I understand,' Tsafendas said, and then to lessen his friend's discomfort, lied that he had suspected such a situation and had decided not to come anyway. He assured Galanakis that he understood. Tsafendas did not attend but sent a wedding present to the newlyweds with Andreas Babiolakis.[153]

After a few days, Tsafendas decided it was time to start back to South Africa, hitch-hiking first to Lourenço Marques, then crossing the border into South Africa. Giangos offered him money so that he could sail to Lourenço Marques rather than hitch-hike. Tsafendas was reluctant, but he knew this would make his journey much easier. Contributing 500 escudos each, Giangos, his brother Andreas, Nick Papadakis, Costas Poriazis and three of their Greek friends handed Tsafendas 3500 escudos, about 1000 Euros at today's rate. Tsafendas promised to pay them all back, though the men said the money was a gift. He returned all the money in the course of the next few months, sending sums in instalments to Babiolakis and asking him to distribute them among the others. With cash in his pocket, Tsafendas bought a suit, some clothes and a suitcase.[154] He then decided to go by ship directly to Durban, believing that the immigration checks on ships from Mozambique would be less thorough than the checkpoints on land. Although he had a valid visa for South Africa and a legitimate Portuguese passport, Tsafendas was well aware that he was banned from entering the country. On 5 March 1965, Tsafendas bought a passage aboard the *Karanja* and left Beira for Durban.[155] It was to be his last ocean voyage. He would never see the land of his birth nor leave South Africa ever again.

Chapter 10

Parliamentary Messenger

Arriving in Durban on 8 March 1965, the *Karanja*'s passengers were checked by immigration officers who arrived on board with the official stop list of banned persons. Tsafendas was named on the ship's passenger manifest as Tsafendas Dimitrio. The stop list included a certain Tsafendakis Dimitrio alias Tsafendas Demetrio. Amazingly, the similarity was missed by the official concerned, the fifth government bureaucrat not to spot Tsafendas's name on the official list of banned persons.[1]

Stepping ashore, Tsafendas discovered a South Africa that had changed little since he had left it two years before. The major difference was that in that short period, Verwoerd had crushed or neutralised any significant opposition to apartheid. A series of draconian laws had led to the exile, imprisonment or death of most of his serious opponents. Tsafendas's first act on his return was to explore Durban, a city unlike any he knew in South Africa. Third in size after Johannesburg and Cape Town, Durban had an unmistakeably British feel to it and English was widely spoken. Its position on the Indian Ocean made it a mecca for tourists and its beaches attracted thousands of pleasure seekers each year. Soon after he settled in the city, Tsafendas called on Rowley Israel Arenstein, a well-known advocate, banned from practising law because of his known Communism and opposition to apartheid. Tsafendas had been given Arenstein's contacts by a member of the Anti-Apartheid Movement in London and the two met often and discussed politics endlessly. A major point of disagreement was the use of violence against apartheid, which Tsafendas supported and Arenstein rejected. When Arenstein referred to his favourite political thinker, Thomas Aquinas, Tsafendas confessed ignorance and Arenstein gave him a book on the Christian saint and philosopher. Tsafendas read it immediately and discovered to his excitement that Aquinas considered tyrannicide, the killing of a ruling tyrant, to be morally justifiable. Arenstein said that was the only part of Aquinas's philosophy which he disagreed with, but for Tsafendas, if he was ever told that to kill was a sin, he knew Aquinas had argued to the contrary.[2]

Arenstein suggested that since Tsafendas could speak so many languages he should apply at the city's court where they were always looking for interpreters. Tsafendas had good references, not least from the Limasollu language school in Istanbul, but Arenstein suggested he get an endorsement from someone local. So Tsafendas approached Antonis Kalogirou, a Greek friend of his father's and someone who had known the family in Lourenço Marques. Kalogirou was everything Tsafendas was not, being very wealthy and a member, indeed a financier, of the National Party, with close ties to some of the party's MPs. He was unaware of Tsafendas's political ideology since he had not seen him since he was a boy and happily agreed to provide a reference.[3]

Tsafendas was interviewed for the job by the head interpreter at Durban Magistrate's Court, Cornelius Johannes Rudolph, and worked there when needed. Rudolph found him 'normal' and 'intelligent',[4] a colleague considered him a 'whiner' who complained about working conditions and his lack of money,[5] while other interpreters had him down as 'the chatty Greek'.[6] Socially, Tsafendas loved Durban's beaches as much as anyone and often patronised the widely popular Cuban Hat tea room on the North Beach, colour bar notwithstanding. This was a combination of café, drive-in and takeaway, owned by Kyriakos Skordis, president of the Greek community in Durban. Drive-in customers would give their orders to the all-Indian staff, who would clip a food tray to the window of their car door and relay their requirements to the kitchen. It is possible that Tsafendas was given Skordis's contacts by a fellow Greek, but if not, the reference to Cuba in the name of the tea room would certainly have caught his attention. Whatever brought him there in the first place, he returned frequently, though he gave Skordis the impression that he was 'in a poor financial situation'.[7]

Another Greek café Tsafendas liked to visit was owned by a former Greek army officer, Peter Pappas, who quickly became a friend. When out of work, Pappas gave him free meals, usually curry and rice, which Tsafendas paid for when he got a job. What struck Pappas was that Tsafendas, although poor himself, often gave small sums to poor whites in the area. As an ex-soldier, Pappas was intrigued by Tsafendas's physical proportions. Six feet tall himself and superbly fit, he challenged Tsafendas one day to demonstrate his strength. In response, Tsafendas put his arms round Pappas and picked him up like a baby.[8]

Between stints at the court, Tsafendas worked for South African Railways at Umbilo, Durban. He was medically examined on 15 March 1965 and pronounced fit after declaring that he had never suffered from any 'disease, disability, illness or injury, nervous breakdown, psycho-neurosis or mental disease'.[9] Since he had no money to travel to work and had not yet found a place to stay, Garnet Vincent Muller, the senior foreman, organised a staff collection and gave Tsafendas some two rand while he also arranged accommodation for him at the E.R. Carney Hostel at Montclair. Tsafendas worked 12-hour day shifts, 6 am to 6 pm, with a night shift, 6 pm to 6 am, every other week, removing and replacing jumper cables. Muller found him to 'possess intelligence above that of the average person',[10] while Tsafendas's immediate boss, Johannes Jacobus Uys Aurets, found him to be 'a good worker', 'well-mannered, well-spoken and good-natured'.[11] However, it was not long before he got into arguments with some Afrikaner workers about politics. One night, around 2 am, as Tsafendas was resting on a bench, one of the Afrikaner workers, P.A. Louw, threw a paper bag full of water at him, then ran off. Tsafendas stood up angrily, dripping with water, then went home to take off his wet clothes. A few days later, he resigned, saying the work was 'unsuitable to him'.[12]

On 19 April 1965, Tsafendas started work as a fitter and turner with Fraser and Chalmers Ltd, at Mandini, a town about a hundred kilometres north of Durban. His boss, Charles Edwin Woods, found him to be a 'good tradesman',[13] 'a very good worker, far from being a crank. He seemed to be a fairly intelligent man, but he was a violent type and we couldn't keep him.'[14] Among the employees was Nick Vergos, known as 'Nicky the Greek'.[15] If there was one man with whom it was inevitable that Tsafendas would quarrel it was Vergos, a fascist and a racist who regularly bullied the African workers, often ordering them to run personal errands for him, such as fetch cigarettes. When Tsafendas praised Communism and criticised apartheid, Vergos told him to shut up because he could get them all fired or arrested. That Vergos supported the royalists during the Greek Civil War was a particular provocation for Tsafendas and they argued frequently.[16] Vergos urged Woods to get rid of Tsafendas because he was a communist,[17] later describing Tsafendas to Jan Johannes Albertus Fourie, a police sergeant, as a 'communist bastard'.[18]

Vergos had arranged for two of the company's African workers to do some work in his house, then refused to pay them, claiming that they had done a poor job. When they protested, he threatened to get them fired, and since the work was strictly illegal, they could not complain. Just 20 days after Tsafendas had started working there, on 7 May, Tsafendas intervened in an incident where the workers confronted Vergos in the canteen. He asked Vergos to pay the men but Vergos refused and swore at Tsafendas. Tsafendas slapped him twice on the face and Vergos fell to the ground. Both men were separated and Tsafendas went to his room, but shortly afterwards, Vergos appeared with a knife in his hand. Tsafendas told him to 'get out' but Vergos slashed at him with the knife, cutting Tsafendas's hand as he tried to ward off the blade. Vergos then aimed at his opponent's stomach, but Tsafendas jumped back and the blade only scratched him. Tsafendas then wrestled with Vergos and managed to disarm him by twisting his arm. Near breaking point, he let go and Vergos fled from the room.[19]

Tsafendas was treated for the slash wound in the company's emergency medical room, then was taken to the hospital, where, for the next two months, he received follow-up treatment.[20] Undeterred, Vergos continued to campaign for Tsafendas's dismissal and told Johannes Jacobus Botha, the company's security officer, that Tsafendas was 'the biggest Communist in the Republic of South Africa', a remark Botha later shared with the police in Inyoni.[21] Vergos also asked the company boss, Christoffel Johannes van Vuuren, to fire Tsafendas because he was 'not Greek but a kaffir and a Communist'.[22] When the police stepped in to investigate, neither Vergos nor Tsafendas revealed the reason for the fight, Vergos because he had illegally employed the two Africans for personal work and Tsafendas because he would get the two workers into trouble by disclosing the illegal arrangement.[23] Tsafendas subsequently took Vergos to court over the attack. He was found guilty and slapped with a fine, which he paid.[24] For Tsafendas, it was the end of his short stay with Fraser and Chalmers Ltd as he was fired. Vergos, who had been working there for many years, kept his job.

Soon after this incident, Tsafendas was sitting on a public bench outside Mandini Store, a local grocery, when a German-born priest, Father Hanno Probst, who ran the Mangete Catholic Mission in Zululand, about 14 km from Mandini, asked about his bandaged arm. Tsafendas explained that he had been stabbed. Noting Tsafendas's dark hair and complexion, the priest observed that he was not a white South African but probably from Mozambique. When Tsafendas expressed surprise that the priest had spotted it, Father Probst said he had travelled a lot and could usually guess where people came from. Tsafendas then remarked that he had travelled widely too and could speak eight languages. The priest tried him and found he could speak Spanish, Czech, Italian and English. When Tsafendas mentioned he had been to Munich, the German tried him in the Munich dialect and was astonished to find that Tsafendas spoke it very well. Aware that very few people who were not from Munich could speak or understand the Munich dialect of German, Father Probst became suspicious and the conversation took a cooler turn. He said, 'You must have had a very good teacher in Moscow to be able to speak these different languages so well.' According to the priest, Tsafendas agreed that he had. Why he lied about this when he had never been to any such school is unknown; perhaps he was simply being mischievous.[25]

It was then Tsafendas's turn to ask questions and the first one naturally was, 'Which church do you belong to?' When he heard it was the Roman Catholic Church, he turned on Probst, claiming that Catholic nuns in Mozambique hospitals injected fatal poisons into natives with the approval of the Portuguese government. Angered by such an extraordinary accusation, Probst told Tsafendas he was spreading propaganda, in the way that criticism was being directed at that time against Catholic nuns in the Congo, accusing him of being a communist and reminding him that Communism was outlawed in South Africa. 'I think it would be better for you to return to Mozambique,' the priest said.[26] The next day, Father Probst decided it was his duty to report his encounter with Tsafendas, though he did not know his name. He returned to Mandini from Mangete and called Van Vuuren. The priest outlined his conversation of the previous day, describing the heavy-set Mozambican with the bandaged arm as 'a Communist and a dangerous person'.[27]

After his ill-fated venture to Mandini, Tsafendas returned to Durban. Between June and August of 1965, he lived at the Durban Men's Home at 160 Queen Street, whose employees and residents remember him talking loudly and often against the Verwoerd government. A staff member, Kenneth Heugh Ross, found Tsafendas to be 'very fond of discussing politics', a subject that he thought he was 'well versed' in; he 'blatantly opposed to the National Party policy, decried every decision taken by the South African Government' and 'was definitely pro-Russian'.[28] The night clerk, Robert Harpur Smith, recalled Tsafendas saying that if South Africa was a communist state, 'there would be no need for a Durban Men's Home because everybody would have sufficient', that he considered the government's policies 'rotten' and the members and officials of the United Party and the National Party 'capitalistic roughs'.[29] Both Smith and Ross were also impressed by the large amount of literature Tsafendas had in his possession.[30]

While in Durban, Tsafendas regularly attended Christian Church prayer meetings in members' homes. At one such service, a preacher handed Tsafendas a letter from Helen Dorothy Daniels, 36, a coloured woman from Cape Town and also a minister of the church. Although she had never met him and did not know what he looked like, the letter said that she wanted to meet and marry him. He had been recommended highly to her by a coloured family named Tillik in Benoni or Brakpan, and by other church members who had known him during his nine-month stay in Pretoria a year earlier. Tsafendas, who was 12 years older than Daniels, replied cautiously in early July 1965 that he would prefer to meet her before responding to the marriage proposal. Helen sent him four more letters and a photograph of herself. Tsafendas replied to the letters but did not enclose a photo. Eventually, they arranged to meet in Cape Town.[31]

Tsafendas got a lift to Port Elizabeth and then caught a train to Cape Town. On 28 August, after almost 24 hours of travel, he arrived at Helen Daniels's home in Belleville,[32] carrying two suitcases, a load of pots and pans and a large bundle of dirty laundry. His clothes looked dirty and neglected and Helen Daniels was unimpressed.[33] His explanation that he had travelled for a day non-stop, much of it in the back of a dirty van, did little to assuage her disappointment, but she hid her feelings and invited him to take the spare bedroom. Perhaps he might turn out better than first impressions suggested.

However, it was soon apparent that there was no romance. Tsafendas found Helen attractive, but he quickly acknowledged that their personalities were incompatible and he knew it would be impossible to live with her for the rest of his life. Consequently, he made no attempt to establish any kind of relationship and became essentially a house guest. Helen was disappointed that Tsafendas made no effort to discuss a relationship and, on another level, she was disturbed by some of his personal habits – helping himself to food from the stove and the refrigerator, eating in a messy way, and sometimes lying down with his shoes on the bedspread. They respected each other, though. Tsafendas considered Helen 'one of the nicest ladies' he had ever met and she found him to be 'a good person with a good heart' and his travel stories interesting. However, this was not the stuff of true love, and they knew it.[34]

On 1 September 1965, Tsafendas surrendered the identity card identifying him as white and applied for reclassification as a coloured person.[35] The Department of the Interior official dealing with his case, a certain Mr Rossouw, was astonished that anyone classified as white, and therefore a member of the privileged race, should want to be re-classified. He repeatedly asked Tsafendas where he was staying and whether the people he was staying with were white or coloured. Tsafendas was eventually given a blank identity card, but Rossouw later asked for it back and the case stalled.[36]

When Tsafendas arrived at the Daniels household, Helen's father declined to take rent from him, regarding him as his potential son-in-law. To make up for this, Tsafendas bought food for the household, and when on 13 September, he got a job at the Table Bay power station as a fitter, he increased his purchases, in particular buying large amounts of meat. The family thought he was overdoing it and it was not necessary to eat meat all the time. At this stage, Tsafendas was still expected to become part of the family and Helen's mother would cook the food, wash and iron his clothes and make sure he was comfortable. She seemed genuinely fond of him and Tsafendas reciprocated. Tsafendas attended all their religious services, sang and prayed with other church members and received communion. He met many of Helen's friends, who were invariably impressed by his kindness and politeness and the fact that he could speak so many languages.[37] Helen's best friend, Joyce Dick, described him as a 'very well-dressed gentleman', an improvement on when he knocked on the Daniels' door.[38]

Eventually, Helen's parents realised that Tsafendas and Helen had no intention of marrying each other and so Helen's father asked Tsafendas to start paying rent. Tsafendas did not take this too well, especially since he believed the food he was buying cost more than rent would bring in. He agreed, but decided to look for another place to live. On 16 October 1965, Tsafendas left the Daniels' house and Helen never saw him again.[39] On 25 October, he received seven days' notice of termination from the power station on grounds of unsatisfactory work. He resigned on the same day to avoid being officially dismissed.[40]

Tsafendas moved into a boarding house owned by Violet Manning at No. 7 Prince Street, where he rented room No. 3, next to a couple from Portugal, the Ferreiras. Tsafendas made a good impression on Mrs Manning. He paid his rent from a large bundle of notes and, since he was well-dressed and well-spoken, she took him for a successful businessman, 'a man of means'. Although he took a serviced room, Tsafendas always made his own bed – a habit he pursued even in hotels and hospitals since he considered it rude to leave the task for others. This impressed his landlady even more. However, Tsafendas did not get along with his neighbours, mainly because Mr Ferreira was a supporter of the Portuguese dictatorship, but also because Mrs Ferreira complained that he spilled water on the kitchen floor. Mrs Manning asked Tsafendas not to go into the kitchen again, but when Mrs Ferreira complained once more, she gave Tsafendas notice to leave at the end of the month, two days later. Tsafendas returned the keys and left on 30 November 1965.[41] Ironically, his expulsion led Tsafendas into the warmest friendship of his life.

Earlier that month, Tsafendas was at a conference of the Christian Church in Durbanville, when he mentioned to a minister that he had to move out of his lodgings. Patrick O'Ryan, a Coloured teacher of English and Art at Bishop Lavis High School, was present and was told by the minister about a 'highly cultured gentleman, a very refined gentleman who speaks seven languages' looking for accommodation. O'Ryan met Tsafendas and said later that 'a single glance was enough to tell he was a good man'. He had no hesitation in inviting him to stay with his family, his wife Louisa and eleven children, at 9 Westminster Street, Lansdowne. When asked about rent, O'Ryan said he would not ask for any until Tsafendas got a job. This was agreed and Tsafendas moved in with the O'Ryans as soon as he left Mrs Manning's house.[42]

Patrick O'Ryan was tall, slim, elegant and well-educated and had a refined way of speaking. His small house was already bursting at the seams, yet finding space for Tsafendas was a decision that came to delight everyone involved. The new lodger quickly became part of the family; 'Uncle Dimi' to the children, who adored this huge, jolly man who would play with them, pick them up from school, help them with their studies and babysit the younger ones. After school and on holidays, he took them to the beach and taught the younger ones to swim. Tsafendas often bought sweets and toys for the children as well as food for the whole family and this embarrassed Patrick, as head of the household. Uncle Dimi then told the children he and their dad had bought the sweets together. From the oldest child to the youngest, they could not get enough of him. Tsafendas, in turn, adored all the children, but his favourite was the youngest, four-year-old Enid. He taught her nursery songs and at night sang her to sleep. Watching Tsafendas interacting so happily with the children, Patrick and Louisa got the impression that their guest would have loved a family of his own. 'This man has never had the opportunity to know much about home life. This is probably the first home where he is at home,' Louisa told her husband. They tried to ensure he felt as much part of their family as possible.[43]

Tsafendas loved Cape Town; it was beautiful and had a cosmopolitan feel to it, though doubtless, this perception was reinforced by the absence of black people from the central area and the better beaches. As in Durban, Africans, coloureds and Indians were forced to live in or beyond the city's outskirts and out of sight of tourists. Thus like everywhere else in South Africa, vibrant and culturally significant native areas were destroyed, the most infamous example being District Six, which by the late 1950s had been depopulated in a bid to eliminate permanent black residency and obstruct the development of black radicalism.

On 19 November, Tsafendas was hired by City Tramways after he was medically found fit to work there.[44] He asked O'Ryan how much rent he wanted, as per their agreement, but his host said it was against church rules to charge a fellow member. When Tsafendas said he must leave then, his host mentioned how disappointed the children would be. Eventually, and much against O'Ryan's will, the two agreed that Tsafendas should meet the family's food bill, which he did many times over, as well as buying treats for the children.[45] Reuben O'Ryan, who was closer to Tsafendas than any of the other children, was 16 at the time. He said, 'We all loved him ... he was an adorable man ... he was the answer to our prayers. We were poor and he brought food to our house.'[46]

Patrick O'Ryan spent a lot of time listening to Tsafendas's adventures around the world. He did not have any particular interest in politics, but he could hardly avoid the subject as Tsafendas delivered regular denunciations of how official South Africa treated its blacks and coloureds. One day, Tsafendas told him, 'If I ever got hold of Dr Verwoerd, I would bash his skull.' Plus, as with so many others, he endlessly reiterated his verbal portrait of Verwoerd as a tyrant, dictator and Hitler's best student.[47]

Tsafendas talked openly to many people, but certain things he confided only to Patrick O'Ryan, and one of these was the tapeworm story. He described how he became involved with the Christian Church through Tom Tuff in an American hospital, how Tuff claimed to have a tapeworm inside him, and how he used Tuff's story to convince the Portuguese police that he was mad, escaping further torture and receiving amnesty back to Mozambique. Up until Verwoerd's assassination, O'Ryan was the only person Tsafendas told about the origins of the tapeworm story.[48]

Astonished one day to see Tsafendas start on his second or third plate of food, one of O'Ryan's sons inquired how he could eat so much. Jokingly, his father said Uncle Dimi 'has a tapeworm inside him which eats his food'. He warned the boy that if he did not eat his food, Uncle Dimi would take it and give it to the worm. Patrick immediately regretted his words, expecting Tsafendas to get angry at his secret being revealed. Far from it, Tsafendas got into the act, as the boy began asking him a question, most fascinated. Popping a piece of bread into his mouth for the tapeworm, he paused momentarily, then opened his eyes wide and breathed heavily, claiming that this is what happened when the tapeworm was eating. The children were amazed and continually asked about the tapeworm, whereupon Tsafendas would repeat his terrifying performance. If a child was dawdling over his food, he would tell him to eat it up quickly or he would give it to the worm.[49]

After Tsafendas's first performance, which she watched, Louisa told her husband, 'that figures' as an explanation for their guest's gargantuan appetite. Patrick did not tell her the real story and Louisa assumed that Tsafendas really believed he harboured a tapeworm. Sometime later, at a prayer gathering in a church member's house, little Enid O'Ryan gave Tsafendas a piece of bread and loudly asked him to feed the tapeworm to show their friends what happened when the tapeworm ate. Deeply embarrassed, Patrick told everyone it was just a joke and there was no tapeworm, but Uncle Dimi, quite untroubled, launched into his act. When the astonished hosts looked to the O'Ryans for an explanation, Louisa said he did indeed have a tapeworm, but Patrick brushed this aside, insisting it was all a joke. Tsafendas himself appeared entirely untroubled by the affair and would launch happily into the tapeworm drama whenever the children asked.[50]

Although his confrontations with officialdom often made things worse for him, in November 1965, Tsafendas embarked on a legal action against the American government. In a four-page affidavit drawn up by a Cape Town lawyer, Ismail Essop, Tsafendas charged that he had been deported against his will by the US Immigration and Naturalisation Service to Greece in 1947 and he claimed compensation to the tune of £100,000. His claim, sent to the US Consulate in Cape Town, pointed out that he had served on US Liberty ships carrying war materiel to America's World War allies from 1941 to 1946. Tsafendas complained that although he wished to be sent to South Africa, where he had friends and family, he was forcibly transported to Greece, where he knew no one. He claimed $50,000 for the effects on his health and $50,000 for loss of income.[51] Tsafendas was interviewed in the US Consulate in Cape Town by the American Vice-Consul, John Hurley, and the affidavit was forwarded to the State Department in Washington. In January 1966, the state replied that all such claims must be taken up by the individual's embassy in Washington or through federal court. A footnote to this story: Vice-Consul Hurley was present in the House of Assembly when Tsafendas assassinated Verwoerd.[52]

Tsafendas soon got to know the Greek cafés in Cape Town and met many Greeks. However, he was shunned by most of them as they were supporters of apartheid and withdrew when they discovered his political beliefs. Many of the city's Greeks owned restaurants and coffee shops. Tsafendas's habit was to visit an establishment and discover the prevailing political opinion and, if it was racist, which it usually was, he would not go back. The Belgravia Café, however, was owned by Costas Hagios, who held firm anti-racist and anti-apartheid opinions, and the two became firm friends. Tsafendas became a regular at the café, always smartly dressed in a suit and often wearing one of his many hats. Greeks filled the café and Tsafendas's arrival was invariably acknowledged, but no one ever invited him to sit with them. Some were from Mozambique and had heard of his imprisonment and communist activities. Hagios considered Tsafendas to be 'a gentleman, very polite, with delicate manners and very well-read', 'a clever and witty man', but he also suspected that at heart he was sad. Tsafendas never said anything to indicate what the cause of this might be, but Hagios believed he saw it written on his face.[53]

Sometime in December, O'Ryan asked Tsafendas to move out temporarily because some family members were coming to visit and there was not space for everyone. It was arranged that he would move to the house of Richard Poggenpoel, a coloured friend of the O'Ryans and a fellow member of the Christian Church. Poggenpoel's wife and his widowed daughter lived with him. About two weeks after Tsafendas had moved in, Poggenpoel received an anonymous letter saying that his daughter could get a bad reputation because an unmarried man was living with them. Poggenpoel was ready to ignore the letter but Tsafendas insisted on leaving. Despite Poggenpoel's protests, Tsafendas paid him R4 in rent, and since the O'Ryans' guests had gone anyway, returned there. Patrick continued to refuse rent money.[54]

Tsafendas was required to report for training at City Tramways on 24 November, but he failed to do so. He did turn up on 29 December, whereupon he was hired as a trainee bus conductor (No. 10236). His career collecting fares did not last long, however, and he resigned on 12 January 1966. His supervisor, Johannes Christiaan Oosthuizen, found him to be 'slow and lazy' but 'mentally normal', while Tsafendas decided conducting buses was not his metier. 'This is too much for me,' he said. 'I cannot do it and I will resign,' and he resigned.[55]

On 13 January 1966, Tsafendas applied for work at the Marine Diamond Corporation and was medically examined the same day. Completing a company questionnaire, Tsafendas ticked the 'No' box to an inquiry whether he ever had 'any mental complaints'. He did not mention any health issues, presenting himself as a fit and healthy person, while the doctor who examined him concurred and found him perfectly capable of working for the company.[56] When he joined, Tsafendas associated mostly with the coloured workers, although everyone assumed he was white. Carel van Heerden, the company's senior security officer, described Tsafendas as 'friendly, outgoing, and not aloof ... I noticed that his eating was messy. Otherwise, he was completely normal.'[57] Tsafendas was initially employed as a machine operator under the maintenance foreman, Reginald Spence, but after a few weeks, supervisor Ralph Lighton decided that while Tsafendas had 'excellent reasoning powers', he was 'lazy and inefficient', so he put him in charge of two suction-dredge pumps, which entailed less work and responsibility.[58] However, the change of jobs did not improve Tsafendas's work rate and another employee, Keith Martincich, described him as one of the laziest persons he had ever seen.[59] Tsafendas often visited the company's offices and on occasion, spoke to a personal secretary, Gillian Lieberman. It became apparent to her that Tsafendas was someone who did 'not agree with authority, governmental or other'. She found him to be 'intelligent, someone apparently able to reason in conversation, but a strange person, a unique character'.[60]

On the afternoon of 14 January, Tsafendas arrived home at the O'Ryans' and was immediately surrounded by the children, hugging and kissing him and begging him to play with them. Little Enid asked Uncle Dimi to put a hair-band around his eyes as she wanted to show him something special. Tsafendas obliged and she led him to another room. When Tsafendas removed the blindfold, he was stunned to be greeted by a chorus of 'Happy birthday to you, Happy birthday dear Dimitri, happy birthday to you ...' from a room packed with well-wishers. Apart from the O'Ryans, there was Richard Poggenpoel and his wife and other friends and members of the Christian Church. Tsafendas could not stop the tears as one after the other, the guests hugged and kissed him and wished him well. It was his 48th birthday, but how did O'Ryan know? Smiling, his host and party organiser confessed that he had seen it on one of his job applications. Tsafendas joked that usually the only true information on his job applications was his date of birth. The party went on for more than two hours and it was the happiest birthday Tsafendas ever had as an adult and he expressed his everlasting gratitude to Patrick.[61]

For some time, Tsafendas had had some breathing difficulties and so on 25 February 1966 he went to Groote Schuur Hospital. Tsafendas complained of a blocked nose and was found to have a deviated nasal septum blocking his left nostril. On 19 April, Dr Leon Goldman performed a surgical resection of the septum and Tsafendas was discharged on 22 April. Four days later, he was treated for a recurrence of bleeding, then checked on 3 May and discharged as fit on 17 May 1966.[62] Meanwhile, in March, he resigned from the Marine

Diamond Corporation. He told supervisor Leighton he considered the small transfer craft that took workers to their transport boat dangerous, while a co-worker, Hulse,[63] who often discussed politics with him, said Tsafendas told him he quit because 'the work was too hard for an old man like him'.[64]

In April, Patrick and his wife began preparing for some members of the extended O'Ryan family to come and stay for a few months, whereupon Tsafendas said he would move out so they could have more room. Patrick insisted he stay, but Tsafendas had made up his mind, promising to come back once the guests left. The children cried when he left but, as assured, he returned at least once every week, bringing meat for the pot, and sweets and toys for the children. By the time Patrick's guests left, Tsafendas had settled in a house that was more convenient for the commute to his new work at the House of Assembly, so he never did return to live with the O'Ryans. However, he visited, on occasion, in the evenings and his conversations with Patrick invariably lasted long into the night. There is no doubt that Tsafendas was rarely happier than when he stayed with the O'Ryans. He loved the children as his own and, as for Patrick, he considered him to be the best person he ever met, a 'saint', he said. The two men remained close friends and met often, if not in Patrick's house, then socially in cafés or at church gatherings.[65]

It was also in April 1966 that the first recipient of the newly established Dr Verwoerd Award was announced as Dr Verwoerd himself. The award had been set up to mark the failed assassination attempt on the Prime Minister by David Pratt in April 1960. Its aim was to recognise 'exceptional service' rendered to the state by one of its citizen. Dr Verwoerd declined to accept the cash that went with the award, asking that it be used to establish a medical scholarship instead.[66]

After leaving the O'Ryans and for the next six to seven weeks, Tsafendas stayed at a home kept by Elizabeth Magdalena Groves, who quickly noted that her newest arrival had nothing good to say about Afrikaners. The other tenants complained to her that Tsafendas was argumentative and persistently denounced Afrikaners as backward people. Groves, a former nurse who had worked in mental institutions and was experienced with mentally ill people, said she found Tsafendas to be a 'very good eater' but 'besides his rough table manner', she had 'nothing against him'. She said, 'He was completely normal ... a normal person to the best of my knowledge.'[67]

Sharing accommodation with Tsafendas at Groves's house was a German man named Fischer and a young Afrikaner traffic policeman, Jacobus Johannes Bornman, aged 22, who became friends with him. Bornman found Tsafendas to be 'normal', 'intelligent', 'a friendly and plausible person', but also thought that he was 'lazy'. Bornman was not seriously political and Tsafendas tried to 'educate' him on the subject. According to Bornman, Tsafendas 'stood up a lot for the Coloureds' and 'talked about Russia but not as if he had ever been there'. He often criticised the South African government and seemed to have a grudge against Dr Verwoerd. He was neat in his person but his eating habits were messy.' Bornman also testified to the police that Tsafendas 'left the impression that he really liked me. On one occasion, I had no money and then Tsafendas gave me five cents. I later wanted to return the money to him, but he would not take it.'[68]

Unable to find a job that suited him, Tsafendas applied for a veteran's pension/disability grant from the government on 7 May 1966. The Department of Social Welfare referred him to the district surgeon's office; under 60, in order to qualify for the grant he needed to be found 'unable, owing to infirmity of mind or body' to undertake regular work. An examination was arranged for 17 June.[69]

On 11 May, still out of work, Tsafendas offered his services as a Portuguese interpreter for British ships on the Beira patrol.[70] Rhodesia had declared independence from Britain on 11 November 1965, but the white minority was still ruling the black population. The United Nations approved a regime of sanctions, including an oil embargo. However, it soon became apparent that Rhodesia was getting crucial oil supplies from South Africa and independent ship magnates, who saw quick profit by breaking the sanctions. Tankers were quietly unloading in Mozambique, from where the oil was fed into Rhodesia by pipeline. Britain attempted to stop this manoeuvre by blockading the Mozambique Channel with Royal Navy frigates and destroyers. A job with the patrol looked like an appropriate follow-up for Tsafendas from his experiences with the US navy, but nothing came of it.

Dr Verwoerd's practical support for the racist regime in Rhodesia strengthened Tsafendas's determination to take action against him and apartheid. He considered going back to Beira to blow up some of the oil pipelines. The idea excited him; he knew how to make bombs from natural ingredients and he knew where the pipelines were, having worked there less than two years earlier. Knowing that he would need money to meet travel and living costs and to buy the bomb ingredients, he decided to start saving immediately. He was sure he could re-enter Mozambique easily enough but he would need to get out as soon as the deed was done, in which case, he concluded, his escape should be to Zambia. He therefore applied for permission to reside in that country, but was refused. The idea remained with him, however, and he decided to save cash to bankroll the project if it proved feasible at some point in the future.[71]

As planned on 17 June, Tsafendas was examined by the district surgeon, Dr Ralph Kossew. Tsafendas was in no doubt that he would fulfil the conditions for a grant. It was the reference to 'infirmity of mind' that caught his attention. He knew, and later admitted, that when he wanted to be found sane, he would be found sane, and when he wanted to be found insane, he would be found insane. When Tsafendas entered Dr Kossew's consulting room, he immediately started talking about things that made no sense, claiming that in the boarding house where he lived, they murdered people with poisoned food. 'Twenty people died in a year that way,' he told the doctor. Although not a psychiatrist, Dr Kossew decided within ten minutes that he had heard enough and declared Tsafendas to be schizophrenic, having delusions of a persecutory nature, and therefore 'unable owing to infirmity of mind' to do any work. He signed his application to receive the grant, but it was a hollow victory for Tsafendas. His application was turned down by the Department of Social Welfare on the grounds that he 'had not rendered war service as defined in the Act'.[72]

Needing a job, Tsafendas became a constant visitor to the Department of Employment, where he was interviewed seven times by government officers – thrice by Ian Boswell, twice by Gideon Cloete and twice by Pieter Benjamin Geldenhuys. Polite, well-spoken and well-dressed, he made a good impression on all of them. In Boswell's opinion, Tsafendas 'was at all times neatly dressed and never gave the impression of being destitute',[73] while Cloete described him as 'perfectly normal', 'neat' and 'clean' and apparently 'eager to get employment';[74] Geldenhuys also thought that Tsafendas was always 'neatly dressed' and 'never got the impression that there was mentally anything wrong with him or that he acted abnormally'.[75]

On 4 June 1966, having left Grove's house, Tsafendas rented a room in Woodstock from Wilhelmina de Vos, with whom he quickly crossed swords. When he mentioned that he was thinking of joining the British navy on the Beira patrol, De Vos was outraged. 'You can't go against your own people,' she said, meaning the Rhodesians and the Portuguese. 'You are a traitor!' Tsafendas walked away without reply. Shortly afterwards, she asked him to leave because, she told the police later, she 'could not endure his messy ways any longer'.[76]

Tsafendas's next domicile was a rented room in the house of Alice Theyer, also in Woodstock, where he stayed until 30 August 1966. There, apparently because of his bearing, a neighbour said he was nicknamed 'The Texas Millionaire'. Theyser told the police that she 'never got the impression in any way that he [Tsafendas] might be mentally unbalanced. To me, he appeared a quite normal person.'[77] She did, however, have problems with his domestic behaviour. One day he left water on the bathroom floor and another time he forgot to switch off her electric kettle and Theyser made him pay for a new one. She also took badly to his outspoken declarations of his opinions and finally asked him to leave.[78] It was at this time that Tsafendas frequented Barling's Tea Lounge nearby. He would go there for tea or coffee and write letters to his friends. When questioned by the police, its owner, Herbert Summers, said that he 'never had reason to even suspect that he [Tsafendas] could be mentally unbalanced. He acted quite normal'.[79]

During June and most of July, Tsafendas ate his meals at Mary Scott's boarding house in Woodstock. Scott was Greek, married to a white South African; she often cooked Greek food and many Greeks came to eat there. Unimpressed by Tsafendas's table manners, Scott told the police that she used to call him the 'Pig',[80] but never in front of him nor other guests. Other visitors and tenants, such as Panagiotis Peroglou and his fiancé Pamela Abrahams, Elias Constantaras and Stratis Vamvarapis, found Tsafendas to be very polite and well-mannered, especially with the ladies. Tsafendas would always stand up to greet Pamela or other ladies when they entered the room and would always offer his seat if another one was not available.[81] When lodgers complained that they suspected he was a communist and that he was constantly talking against white South Africans and apartheid, Scott asked Tsafendas's good friend Constantaras to beg him to stop. Not only was she concerned about losing trade, she feared she might even get a visit from the police. Constantaras spoke to Tsafendas, who was not happy that Scott did not ask him herself, but complied with her request. Tsafendas and Constantaras got on well and talked politics constantly. Once when Constantaras visited Tsafendas in his room, he was astonished by the number of books he had. When he asked to borrow one, Tsafendas gave him Jean-Paul Sartre's *Anti-Semite and Jew,* which he had just finished and considered exceptional. Much as he liked politics, Constantaras found the book boring and returned it; he had really been looking for an adventure story. What impressed Constantaras most about Tsafendas was his friendliness and how easily he could talk to all types of people.[82]

In July, Tsafendas visited N.D. Hartford, a reporter for the *Cape Argus.* Earlier in the year, he had asked Hartford if there was any news of the freedom fighters in Mozambique, describing himself as a rebel from Mozambique. Hartford thought Tsafendas might provide material for a magazine article. During a subsequent 75-minute interview, Tsafendas described how he entered South Africa illegally from Mozambique in 1936 when he was a teenager; he did not criticise South Africa but denounced Portuguese rule in Africa and said he still suffered from headaches as a result of the electric shocks when he was arrested in Lisbon in 1949 and 1952.[83]

The most talked-about sporting event of the year was the 1966 football World Cup, taking place in England from 11–30 July. White South Africans were mostly divided between two of the favourites: England, generally supported by English-speaking citizens, and West Germany, backed by Afrikaners. This World Cup was of special interest to Africa because 16 African nations boycotted the competition in part-protest against South Africa's re-admission to FIFA in 1963 after being expelled in 1958. As for Tsafendas, although he loved playing football as a child, he had given it up long ago and now believed, in true Marxist style, that it was the opium of the masses, that dictators and authoritarian regimes followed the principle of 'bread and circuses', using the game to keep ordinary people distracted from serious issues. Tsafendas held to this belief until he died. As for his team of choice, it was neither England nor West Germany, but the Soviet Union. [84]

What was extraordinary about such a high level of interest was that there was no television coverage of the competition in South Africa because there was no national television. While African countries such as Nigeria, Rhodesia, Kenya and the Congo had enjoyed television services for years, Verwoerd said 'No'. On the one hand, the Prime Minister denounced the medium in extravagant terms as 'corrupting', 'noxious' and akin to 'atomic bombs and poison gas', on the other hand, he used it to propagate abroad an image of South Africa as some kind of sun-soaked paradise where friendly whites and blacks lived cosily side by side, separately but happily. High-quality programmes were commissioned to show the country in these glowing terms on overseas stations.[85] However, at home, Verwoerd did not want a window through which South Africans could view the rest of the world, perhaps causing citizens to question apartheid and the repression involved in its implementation.

The SABC was headed by pro-Nazi Piet Meyer, a long-standing friend of Verwoerd and a dedicated Afrikaner, who saw the broadcaster's role as simply to support and assist the National Party and its policy of apartheid. Meyer also acted as a barrier against incoming news that might embarrass the regime. For instance, by switching to FM broadcasting, the Corporation ensured that few radio listeners could hear the international outcry that followed the Sharpeville massacre. Besides, the SABC had no qualms about distorting the news, something it could achieve as a result of its monopoly. Two years on, when Martin Luther King Jr. was assassinated, the Corporation presented his death as follows: 'Widespread rioting has broken out in the United States following the assassination of the Negro civil rights agitator, Martin Luther King.'[86]

One day in July, while walking past the House of Assembly, he remembered his early plans to kidnap Verwoerd and exchange him for political prisoners or simply to bomb Parliament. He was only metres from the main entrance and he could see white politicians arriving in their limousines. Without any clear idea of what he intended, Tsafendas started observing parliament buildings and quickly realised that the kidnapping or bombing would be impossible to carry off without help. Tsafendas also knew an explosion in a confined space would kill good people too. Nevertheless, something about the idea stuck:

Parliament was where Verwoerd could always be found and that surely would be the killing ground.[87]

Tsafendas knew his problem would be access, how to reach a head of state protected by an iron-clad security system. For a couple of weeks, he lingered outside Parliament, not every day so as to avoid suspicion, but often enough to memorise the layout, entrances, exits, guards, passes, procedures, opening and closing hours. One mid-day, he sat on his favourite public bench feeding the seagulls from a bag of fish and chips he had bought from the Portuguese shop across the road. This was another tactic he employed to avoid suspicion, just in case some sharp-eyed policeman wondered why he came to sit outside Parliament so often. After all, he was a big man and hard to miss. As the gulls soared away with the last fishy scraps, a small, white man came and sat next to him. They chatted and the man mentioned that he was a messenger in the House of Assembly. Asked if there were any jobs there, the man replied that they were desperate for messengers, that if he were to apply, he would surely be taken on. Tsafendas said good day to the messenger, walked casually into the House of Assembly and filled in an application form for employment as a parliamentary messenger.[88]

Over the next few days, Tsafendas bought a new suit and paid for a shave and a haircut at a barber's shop. On 16 July, armed with three references, from Limasollu Naci College in Istanbul, from Fries & Son in Frankfurt and from Antonis Kalogirou, the member of the National Party, he reported to Parliament for an interview. He was questioned by the chief messenger, Piet Burger, and two senior messengers, Piet Schuin and Sydney Wiehand. The interviewers were impressed. The candidate was neatly dressed, well-spoken and well-mannered. All went smoothly until Wiehand noted that, since Tsafendas had even taught English in Istanbul, surely he could get a better job than that of a messenger. Tsafendas replied that he had searched unsuccessfully for work for several months. 'I can't find any work at the moment, and I must fill my stomach,' he told them.[89] He even said he would work for R100 per month rather than the normal messenger salary of R238. The interviewers appreciated his honesty and determination to get the job and, two days later, Tsafendas was notified in writing to report to Parliament for duty on 1 August 1966. He was in and his salary was to be R238 per month.[90]

By now, however, his savings had almost run out and his imperative was to survive. He found some temporary work that would cover him up to 1 August and perhaps even after on a part-time basis. Tsafendas visited Mike Augustides, owner of a men's clothing store, Mike's Outfitters, in Woodstock and told him that for an agreed commission, he could bring crews to his shop from the ships at Cape Town docks. Augustides agreed and when Tsafendas brought the first customers, he paid him commission of about R10.[91] Augustides found Tsafendas to be 'overly talkative and sociable'.[92]

On 24 July 1966, a Greek tanker, the *Eleni*, docked in Cape Town for repairs to its rudder, damaged while the vessel was en route to the Persian Gulf.[93] Tsafendas visited the ship as soon as it arrived and every day thereafter. The *Eleni* had a crew of 38, of whom 34 were Greek, nine of them from the tiny Greek island of Kasos.[94] This was where the parents of Tsafendas's stepmother came from. Other crew members were a Portuguese, an Austrian and a Spaniard, and the final person was Maria Glinatsis De Fountotos, the Argentine wife of Captain Michalis Fountotos, who often accompanied him on his voyages. Tsafendas told the men he was a former seaman and his origins were also in Kasos. The crew were sceptical at first, thinking that he was simply trying to impress them, but when he named his relatives on the island, who were all well-known to the nine seamen, he was welcomed with pleasure and became immediately popular with the crew.[95]

On his first visit, 24-year-old Emanuel Tsabouniaris gave Tsafendas money to buy him short-sleeved T-shirts and cigarettes ashore. It was late at night and when Tsafendas left, the crew made fun of Tsabouniaris, saying, 'Don't expect to see him or your money again.' To everyone's surprise, Tsafendas arrived with the items early next morning and handed over the change but Tsabouniaris told him to keep it. Tsafendas insisted he take it. Like the crew, Tsabouniaris became very fond of Tsafendas, but he found it very strange that he was a hawker; he thought he was very educated, well-spoken and polite for such a job. Some of the men suspected Tsafendas was more than a hawker and only used the job for cover so that he could walk freely around the harbour.[96]

Generally, however, the crew and Tsafendas felt comfortable with each other and he became a regular visitor to the *Eleni* over the next six weeks. Most of the Greeks were left-leaning, some of them even communist, but a few were royalists. The two groups knew where everyone's loyalties lay and kept aloof from each other. That period, mid-to-late 1966, was a tense one in Greek politics. The wounds of the Greek Civil War had not healed and the nation was only months away from a military coup that would herald a seven-year military dictatorship. Moreover, the Greek Communist Party was illegal, informers were everywhere and anyone suspected of communist sympathies was watched and sometimes prosecuted.

The tanker crew were all much younger than Tsafendas and, though travellers themselves, they listened fascinated to the stories of his adventures around the world. Since Tsafendas had started his job as a parliamentary messenger, which required that he work in the mornings, he visited the seamen mostly late afternoon and night, though occasionally at lunchtime. The unofficial leader of the group was the boatswain, Manolis (Emanuil)

Mastromanolis, one of the Kasos islanders. At 30, he was older and more experienced than most of the crew and was seen by many of them as a father figure. Tall and slim with a dark complexion and black hair, he was very popular and most of the crew wanted to go ashore with him because he always attracted a bevy of beautiful women.[97]

The crewmen asked Tsafendas which the best shops and restaurants in Cape Town were and his advice was to keep their wallets closed for they would simply be boosting the economy of a despicable regime. None of the men had visited South Africa before and they had only the crudest idea of what apartheid was. To help them understand the situation, he took at least eight of the crew to a black township in Cape Town. He explained that the people there had been displaced from their original homes because the government wanted the land for whites. Now they needed passes to travel from one place to another and they were forbidden to enter some areas at all. Some of the township Africans knew Tsafendas and greeted him warmly and he took the seamen to a black family's house. Tsafendas knew the family and had brought presents and sweets for their three young children. The family gave their visitors tea, but they had to borrow cups from neighbours and there were not enough chairs for everyone, not even space for everyone in the living room, so some of the men stayed outside, playing with the children. The Greeks were embarrassed by the difficulties they had caused and urged Tsafendas to leave, but he said that would be an insult to their hosts. The house was a typical township shack made mostly of scavenged wood and cardboard with a sheet of corrugated iron for a roof. They were certainly a strong wind would blow the top off this family's house and, even with a roof, water would simply pour in when it rained.[98]

Their experience in the township shocked the seamen. Dimitris Zafiriadis, the tanker's 'donkeyman', remarked angrily that the ruling Afrikaners 'should be taught a lesson' and Mastromanolis declared that 'the South Africans need a good whipping'.[99] A 40-year-old stoker, Michalis Vasilakis, who was from Kasos, likened the conditions to those in Greece during the Second World War occupation by Germany when people starved to death.[100] Vasilakis, along with Zafiriadis, both communists, would become Tsafendas's closest friends among the seamen. Seeing ragged, skinny children in torn clothes, dull-eyed parents and their pathetic hovels was 'like a fist in our bellies', said Nikolas Kambouris, the 23-year-old assistant cook.[101] Zafiriadis wept openly, asking Tsafendas, 'What kind of people are these?' meaning the South African whites.[102] None of the men ever forgot their visit to the township; they refused thereafter to spend any money in whites' shops in Cape Town and urged crews from other vessels to do the same.[103]

Some afternoons, Tsafendas would take groups of *Eleni* seamen on tours of Cape Town, sometimes including Mike's Outfitters, and at least once to a Greek Orthodox Church service. He also taught three men, Tsabouniaris, Panteleimon Aspiotis and Ioannis Speis, how to fish for lobster. He would then give their catch to the head chef, Dimitris Stavrianos, to cook for everyone. However, he warned the sailors to keep quiet because it was illegal in South Africa to catch lobster. Once, the men asked Tsafendas to take them to a good Greek restaurant, which he did and, despite their protests, paid for all of them. He argued that they were 'strangers in his town' and he should pay. The restaurant owner was not an apartheid supporter, which is why he used his establishment. This was the only time they ate out, as they all followed Tsafendas's advice to keep their money in their pockets.[104]

Many nights aboard the tanker were spent singing Greek songs, even communist and revolutionary ones. Seated on chairs on the deck, the men gazed at the starry night sky or the harbour full of lights, enjoying the smell of the sea. Tsafendas knew all the songs and surprised the men by singing them with evident passion, often weeping during the anthems. From time to time, he would talk cautiously of the hidden areas in his past. He told some of the group that, like many of their family relatives who were arrested, jailed or exiled by the Greek Civil War, he, too had been involved. He had fought in the hills with the DSE, he said, but had shot no one because he was re-assigned to Athens to do intelligence work. He even told them about his arrests and detentions by the Portuguese and how he had pretended to be crazy to avoid service in the Portuguese army. However, he never referred to the tapeworm or gave any specifics. His dream, he told them, was to retire and live the rest of his life in Fidel Castro's socialist Cuba.[105]

In conversations on the *Eleni*, Tsafendas denounced the government incessantly as a bunch of Nazis and Verwoerd as the 'bastard', 'tyrant' and 'monster' who 'created it all'. Once, Vasilakis showed Tsafendas a newspaper with Verwoerd's photograph on the front page and Tsafendas spat at the floor, a classic Greek demonstration of contempt. When Kambouris said he should be careful, Tsafendas said 'I will be fine' and, smiling, pointed to his head, meaning he had the brains to stay free. The seamen were surprised by the extent of Tsafendas's knowledge, but they admired his soft-spoken manner and some of them began calling him 'Professor', which made Tsafendas laugh out loud.[106]

At work in Parliament, Tsafendas quickly discovered that his duties as a messenger were far from onerous, mostly running errands for the correspondents in the press gallery, taking orders for the kitchen and bringing their meals. At the same time, his application for reclassification was being considered by the authorities.

As a result of the scrutiny of files and the exchange of correspondence between departments, it was discovered that Demitri Tsafendas was the same as Demitrio Tsafantakis who had entered South Africa illegally in 1939 and had been on the national stop list since September 1959. In hindsight, this was a crucial discovery which might have changed South Africa's history. On 9 August 1966, on the recommendation of the secretary of the interior, a warrant was issued for Tsafendas's deportation, but bureaucratic dilatoriness meant the document was never acted upon.[107]

Exploring the House of Assembly and its procedures, Tsafendas concluded that while it would certainly be possible to plant a bomb inside the building, it was also possible to kill Verwoerd alone. He would shoot the Prime Minister in the lobby outside the debating chamber, run from the building to the docks and hide aboard the *Eleni.* If he acted shortly before the tanker's scheduled departure following its repairs, he could be out of the country within hours. First, however, he needed a firearm. He knew a licence was necessary but he also knew seamen often carried guns, so he approached Vasilis Perselis, the *Eleni*'s 34-year-old steward, for a weapon for protection because he lived in a rough area. Tsafendas lied that he had been attacked and robbed a few weeks ago and needed a firearm 'to scare people off in case of another attack'. Perselis referred Tsafendas to Mastromanolis, who told him that he could sell him a Beretta and a springleaf knife for US$80. Mastromanolis did not possess either weapon, but he knew crewmen who did; his plan was to buy the weapons and sell them on to Tsafendas for a quick profit. The boatswain pointed out that there were no bullets for the Beretta, but Tsafendas assumed they could be bought locally. Tsafendas did not have the money just then, so they agreed to wait until he got his wages at the end of August.[108]

Meanwhile, Tsafendas scoured the tanker for a hiding place. When a couple of seamen found him near the engine room, not where he would normally be, he simply said he was lost. Not long after, Tsafendas found his ideal refuge and decided to test it. One evening after dinner, he pretended that he was leaving, but instead hid in the secret place. He took a can of beer with him, so that if he was found, he could say he got drunk. The rehearsal worked and nobody noticed him. He did the same thing three times and was never found; when he left his hiding place in the morning, everyone assumed he had just arrived. Tsafendas was equally careful with the House of Assembly, finding the quickest and easiest way out of the building and calculating how long it would take him to get to the tanker. He practised his preferred route several times, always making allowances for the traffic.[109]

Sometime in late August, Tsafendas visited the O'Ryans and as usual, brought presents and sweets for the children. At one point, he told young Reuben that if anything happened to him, he wanted him to have his toolbox containing his welding equipment. Reuben did not see anything untoward about Tsafendas's wish at the time. However, he never did get the toolbox, which is assumed to have been confiscated by the police.[110]

Tsafendas spent the following days waiting for the repairs to the *Eleni* to be completed, so he could put his assassination plan into effect. On 30 August, the perfect opportunity seemed to arrive when a senior messenger, Fred Feinauer, asked Tsafendas to work as a waiter at a function in the House of Assembly organised by the parliamentary correspondents, which Verwoerd was scheduled to attend. The event was set for Friday, 2 September, one day before the *Eleni*'s scheduled departure, and Tsafendas was one of seven messengers asked to serve drinks.[111] Verwoerd would finally be in a social milieu, shaking hands, moving about and sipping drinks. One careful shot from a uniformed waiter would do it. Quickly he worked out the details. There would be instant and total chaos, he would flee the building in the confusion and disappear onto the *Eleni*, leaving the following day.[112] The timing was right, the planning fireproof.

On the day before the function, a letter was typed up by a clerk requiring the police to serve the deportation order on Tsafendas. Once typed, however, the letter remained in an office 'out' tray and the police remained ignorant of the order.[113] That same day, Tsafendas bought US$80 from Barclays Bank on Adderley Street, paying R57.78 mainly in used R2 notes. According to the teller, Brenda Jessie Nicholson, he said he was going to Mozambique.[114]

Tsafendas then took a taxi to the *Eleni*. When he appeared on board asking for the Beretta, Mastromanolis realised he had forgotten all about it. He hurried to see Nikolas Mavronas, the 17-year-old galley boy and the youngest member of the crew, knowing that he had bought a Beretta in Cape Town for US$15 or US$20. What Mastromanolis did not know was that the firearm was a replica. Even Mavronas did not discover that the weapon was not genuine for several days, giving the crew much fun at the boy's expense. 'All of us thought it was real when we first saw it,' Mastromanolis said. Somehow, unlike the others, Mastromanolis had not discovered the truth about the weapon until he went to see Mavronas with Tsafendas waiting.

Eager to get his money back, the galley boy suggested that they should sell the gun to Tsafendas anyway because he would probably not spot it was fake and they could share the money. Mastromanolis demurred, but when Mavronas pointed out that Tsafendas had said he only needed the weapon to 'scare people off' and the replica was good enough to do that, the boatswain agreed. He wrapped the replica gun in a newspaper, put it in a plastic bag and took it to Tsafendas, who was eating with the crew. Tsafendas glanced inside and saw a glint of metal. Excellent! Mastromanolis charged him US$30 instead of the amount first quoted. He kept ten and gave Mavronas twenty. Tsafendas still wanted a springleaf knife for back-up, and Mastromanolis referred him to Tsabouniaris, who had one. However, Tsabouniaris refused to sell the knife because it was a souvenir. It was only when he got home late that night that Tsafendas discovered to his fury that the so-called Beretta was only a gas pistol.[115]

The following day was the day of the function and Tsafendas was without either gun or knife. As soon as he finished work, he hastened to the ship, found Mastromanolis and Mavronas in the galley and angrily demanded another gun or his money back. The men said they had no more guns and they had spent the money.[116] Mastromanolis said the gas pistol would be adequate to frighten malefactors off, which is what Tsafendas said he wanted, 'not to kill anyone'. Mastromanolis then talked about repaying some money, but Tsafendas angrily said, 'I don't care about the money' and insisted he wanted another gun. Tsafendas's insistence prompted Mastromanolis to tell him, 'Oh leave me alone, do you think I'm a cowboy?'[117]

Vasilis Perselis jokingly handed Tsafendas a butcher's knife from the kitchen and Tsafendas picked it up and momentarily smiling, said, 'That would certainly do the job, but unfortunately I can't go out in the street with this.' Still angry, Tsafendas barged into the captain's cabin and rudely demanded that he intervene. After learning the details, the captain said he had known his boatswain for more than ten years, that Mastromanolis was an honourable man and would never knowingly cheat him. He was sympathetic but said there was nothing he could do.

Disappointed, Tsafendas returned to Parliament and that evening helped to serve drinks at the reception where he had planned to kill Verwoerd. Ironically, the disaster of the gun turned out to be irrelevant because the Prime Minister failed to appear at the party. It was then that Tsafendas realised there was only one place Verwoerd was certain to be and where he, too, could gain access: the debating chamber of Parliament. That, he knew, was where the deed must be done. He also decided that in order to be totally sure and reliant on no one but himself, the weapon would have to be a knife.[118]

After the function, Tsafendas returned to the *Eleni* for a 'Farewell to Cape Town' dinner party organised by the crew. The dining room had been decorated by the wives of Captain Fountotos and Chief Officer John N. Toutountsoglou with flowers and stylish napkins. Other non-crew members included two ship's chandlers men who Tsafendas knew, Peter Protoulis and Antonis Nichas, who had brought their girlfriends, and Maria Kokkinidou, a middle-aged woman from the Greek island of Kilimnos, also the home of Captain Fountotos's family. Maria had visited the tanker often with a Greek friend, Nikolas Christodoulou, after she called on the captain and they discovered their common roots. Her son, Costas Kokkinidis, 25, also visited the vessel, and a few days before it left Cape Town, Captain Fountotos hired Costas as a temporary crew member.[119]

For the dinner party, Tsafendas sat with those he had got to know best during the last 42 days, namely Nikolaos Billis, Giorgos Kantas, Cleanthes Alachiotis, Nikolaos Kambouris, Michalis Vasilakis, Dimitris Zafiriadis and Grigoris Pouftis. Embarrassed by the gun issue, he and Mastromanolis avoided each other. Another crewman who was little known to Tsafendas was Ioannis Xexenis, the ship's carpenter. At 57, Xexenis was the oldest of the crew, a very quiet man who kept to himself. Xexenis sat on one side of Tsafendas for the dinner, with Vasilakis on the other. The crew were astonished at how the taciturn Xexenis spoke happily and volubly to Tsafendas throughout the meal, although previously they had scarcely exchanged a word. At one point, Xexenis told Tsafendas about a Greek village, the birthplace of one of his parents. Also from the village, he said, was Ioannis (Jean) Karageorgis, a Greek man who, on 13 October 1961, had assassinated Prince Rwagasore, the first elected president of independent Burundi in central Africa. Xexenis had never met Karageorgis but knew members of his family. He wondered what Tsafendas knew about the assassination since he had lived in Africa for so many years. The other men were entirely ignorant of the affair, so Tsafendas explained that Karageorgis was hired by Belgian colonialists, Burundi's former rulers, to perform the assassination. Tsafendas condemned him angrily and said he was rightfully executed after his arrest.[120]

There followed a discussion among the men about high-level assassinations, including those of John F. Kennedy and King George I of Greece. Bored by this, some of the men left the table, but others found Tsafendas's views fascinating, especially when he raised the question of whether assassination could ever be condoned. He argued that if Karageorgis had assassinated Verwoerd instead of Prince Rwagasore, he would have been entirely justified because the South African Prime Minister was a tyrant and a dictator who oppressed millions of South Africans. Tsafendas said that in ancient Greece, it was a democratic citizen's duty to kill a tyrant or a dictator and Verwoerd fitted both categories. A lively argument ensued, with some men accepting Tsafendas's justification, while others, shocked, disagreeing violently. The spirited debate went on long into the night. This dinner party conversation about justifiable homicide would become a major issue in the police investigation that followed the assassination and by the Commission of Enquiry that was appointed to investigate the circumstances of Dr Verwoerd's death. After the dinner, guests changed tables and the men began singing and playing guitars.[121]

The next morning, Saturday 3 September, Tsafendas took some of the crew for a last look around Cape Town, then went home for a nap. At about 3 pm, he returned to the tanker to say a final goodbye to his friends. The *Eleni* had been moved to a new mooring from where it would leave. He spent a couple of hours aboard ship, speaking to everyone, including Mastromanolis who greeted him warmly. He apologised for the Beretta dispute, but pointed out that Tsafendas had only asked for a gun to scare people off. He also promised to repay the money to Tsafendas when they docked in Venice since he had to wait for his wages at the end of the month. Tsafendas did not seem to care about the gun any longer and even told him not to bother sending the money. Mastromanolis found this strange after the fuss Tsafendas had made about getting his money back. Nevertheless, he said he would send it, then they hugged and said goodbye.[122]

Contact details were passed on so the men could call on Tsafendas when they were next in Cape Town and his closest friends wanted his mailing address to correspond with him. Alachiotis, Billis, Kantas, Kambouris, Vasilakis, Pouftis and Zafiriadis were touched when they saw that Tsafendas had brought them two plastic bags filled with cigarettes and snacks. To Kambouris, Vasilakos and Zafiriadis he gave anti-apartheid and communist pamphlets, reminding them that they were banned in South Africa.[123] Then Tsafendas stood at the dock until the *Eleni* weighed anchor and slipped away between 5 pm and 5.30 pm.[124]

The next day was a Sunday and Tsafendas attended a prayer service at a Mr Hall's home in Pinelands.[125] Monday, 5 September, happened to be a public holiday, so Tsafendas did not make his usual journey to Parliament. At one point, his landlady, Rosamund Popkiss, saw her lodger pacing back and forth outside her house. He looked worried and when she asked if he was all right, he said he had something on his mind, giving no hint as to what it was.[126] Almost certainly, Tsafendas was struggling with his assassination plan, since shooting was no longer an option. He knew now that he must kill Verwoerd with a knife, in which case it would be impossible to escape. It was a momentous decision but one he could not avoid. He was so disgusted with apartheid that he did not care about the consequences. He believed it was his social responsibility to act because he was perfectly positioned to do so. He had the chance to rid South Africa of its tyrant and if he did not take it he would regret it all his life. Indeed, he believed that if he rejected this opportunity, he would share responsibility for the crime of apartheid, whereas if he killed the architect of the system, a more humane policy would sooner or later emerge.[127] It was time to change the history of South Africa.

Chapter 11

The Outbreak of Torture

On the afternoon of Thursday, 8 September 1966, shackled by handcuffs and leg irons, Tsafendas was sleeping fitfully on the concrete floor of a cell in Caledon Square police station. The pitch-black space had no window, bed or furniture, only a stained woollen blanket that he had pulled around his shoulders for warmth. The cell, he guessed, was eight feet by six – with his legs extended, he could just about touch the walls, and was painted black two-thirds of the way up, then merged into a dirty grey. The door was metal and had no inside handle. He had been here since the early hours, when General van den Bergh finally ended an interrogation that lasted a day and almost two nights, so when he slept, it was through sheer exhaustion. He was still clad in the white shirt, now stained with his blood, and the trousers of his parliamentary messenger's uniform, but the waist belt had been removed and there were no laces in his shoes. Waking abruptly, he realised policemen had entered his cell. He had not heard the rattle of the keys. A uniformed officer stood at the door while another abruptly deposited a tray of food and a glass of water on the floor. Both left without speaking. Tsafendas ate and drank, not ever expecting it; what he expected was violence. True, he had been deprived of sleep during the general's seemingly endless interrogation, a form of torture, and he had been beaten frequently on the day of his arrest, but was that not to be expected? After all, he had killed their god. Surely the real retribution was still to come.[1]

Soon after, the police came again and unlocked the cuffs and leg irons. Then they handed him shampoo and a towel and led him to a cubicle where he showered while they watched. What was going on, he wondered? Was he being prepared for sacrifice, like the Biblical fatted calf? In his mind, over and over, he sang Robeson's 'Song of Freedom' and the 'Zog Nit Keynmol' to keep up his courage. As he finished towelling himself dry, one of the policemen walked towards him holding an open razor. Tsafendas backed away. The officer smiled a smile without warmth and opened his other hand, which held shaving cream. Carefully, Tsafendas shaved the dark growth from his jaws. Led back to his cell, he found a hanger with clean clothes and he slipped on the sleeveless vest, a white, open-neck shirt and grey flannel trousers. Not a word had been spoken, but he knew now that violence was not imminent, that he was being prepared to meet someone important or be taken to some public place.[2]

At 2.15 pm, exactly 48 hours after he had plunged a knife repeatedly into Hendrik Verwoerd, Tsafendas was brought before Cape Town Chief Magistrate C. Willman. Eight armed police officers stood around the walls of a cramped, improvised courtroom above his cell in the police station. A high-ranking official told newsmen that it was 'in the interests of the accused' that proceedings were taking place in the police station and not the magistrate's court. 'We did not want a repetition of what happened between Lee Harvey Oswald and Jack Ruby in Texas,' he said.[3]

Tsafendas answered firmly when addressed. He was not handcuffed and he had no lawyer. The charge sheet described him as a male adult, aged 48, a messenger of Portuguese nationality. H.C.F Jacobs, senior public prosecutor, asked that Tsafendas be remanded in custody until 6 October. He submitted a certificate from Attorney-General Willem van den Berg, which stated that Tsafendas had been arrested on a charge of murder and that he should not be allowed bail. Magistrate Willman asked Tsafendas if he understood the application. Tsafendas said, 'I understand, my lord.' Willman then ordered that the prisoner be detained in the station police cells until the date requested. The hearing lasted five minutes and he was taken back to his cell.[4]

It was later that afternoon that the violence began, but not the crude pummelling by fists or blows from a baton which he had expected, but modern torture at an entirely different level. Uniformed policemen, no longer silent but shouting and kicking, ordered their prisoner to his feet and pushed him along a corridor to a cell with a heavy, fitted door. Waiting inside were three or four men in plain clothes. There was no window, just a table and one wooden chair. On the table was a polished, wooden box trailing coloured wires. When he saw it, Tsafendas's heart shrivelled within him because he remembered the device the Portuguese police had used on him in 1952. This time, however, he knew it was no Graphopone but an instrument to elicit music of a different sort. Without a pause, the men in plain clothes slammed Tsafendas onto the chair and violently pulled off his clothes, leaving him naked except for a vest. In what seemed like a single movement, an officer yanked his hair back, another pulled a burlap sack over his head and a third tied his legs together from behind. With a precision clearly gained from practice, they attached electric cables to his testicles and Tsafendas felt water being poured over the sack. Immediately, unbearable pain seared through his groin, as if his testicles were exploding. His large frame jerked and spasmed from the waves of pain, and losing all sense of dignity, he screamed again and again, simultaneously fighting for breath under the water-soaked hood. Tsafendas had been abused and tortured before, but this was at a level he had never experienced.[5]

The manually operated torture machine worked like a generator. Cables could be attached to testicles or ear lobes, fingers or nostrils, then the operator would turn a brass handle to start the current flow, which rang two bells atop the box, providing a hideous musical accompaniment to the torture. The operator could change the rate at which the current was applied, varying the levels of pain. Mostly he would turn the handle 20 or 30 seconds before his captor lost consciousness. Then would come more water and the torture process again.

For the next 20 days, Tsafendas was abused by electric shock treatment or some other form of violence. Sometimes, as they ratcheted up the power, the police would tell him, 'This is for Doctor Verwoerd.' At other times they would shout words he could not understand. If they wanted information, he could not hear their questions. He tried to blot out the noise of the machine's ringing bells by singing Robeson's 'Song of Freedom' and 'Bella Ciao' in his head, but so intense was the pain that he found himself howling instead. The torturers gagged his cries by stuffing a towel into his mouth, removing it and reapplying it until his screams stopped. Tsafendas prayed silently to God that he would die so that the torture would end, and when death did not come, he prayed that he would black out, which frequently he did. Often, coming to on the concrete floor, he pretended to be still unconscious until boots and a bucket of water in the face brought him choking back to life. More than once, Tsafendas lost control of his bladder and urinated over himself, which always made his torturers laugh.[6]

On one occasion, Tsafendas vomited onto his belly and the floor. His captors told him to clean the floor by eating his vomit. He pretended to do so but the vomit remained and they kicked him repeatedly. 'You did it, clean it up, you bastard,' they shouted. Tsafendas lowered his head to the floor, among the malodorous contents of his stomach, tears rolling from his eyes. Never had he suffered such humiliation. Violently, a hand grabbed his hair and forced his head into the pool of slime, scraping it from side to side. 'Eat it, you pig, eat it,' a voice said. The torture only ended when he was pulled onto a chair, a tear-stained robot flecked with regurgitated food, with no further power to resist. After this, Tsafendas fought desperately not to throw up. He could never face such a disgusting horror again.[7]

The torture sessions commonly ended with Tsafendas waking up on the rough concrete floor of his own cell, wet and half-naked, his trousers and shoes flung next to him. Despite the pain he endured, his body showed little visible trace of ill-treatment, one reason that electric shock torture had become standard practice against most political prisoners in South Africa. Lyttelon Mngqlikana, who was held in Vooruitsig Prison in 1964, stated that the warders were 'careful not to hit a prisoner on parts of the body which would show. It was futile to complain about a beating unless a prisoner could show marks.'[8]

Justice Minister John Vorster had essentially legalised torture four years earlier with passage of the Sabotage Act of 1962. This law made sabotage a capital crime, hugely widened its definition and required accused persons to prove their innocence. No limits were placed on police methods to secure a confession and crude beatings gave way to more sophisticated methods to secure information. Numerous political prisoners at this time described experiences similar to those of Tsafendas.[9] There can be no doubt that throughout the 1960s and up to the fall of apartheid, torture by electric shock was routine, and it is no surprise that, in 1966, Tsafendas did not escape it.

In the period following his remand, a routine developed whereby Tsafendas was interrogated with violence on a daily basis. The questions put to him arose from evidence then being uncovered by police investigating his past. As for the beatings and electric shocks, they came in no set pattern and slowly Tsafendas came to realise that it was possible to cope and survive, that the torture had limits. He knew when the machine was turned on that after a certain time, it would be turned off. What he must do, he told himself, was grit his teeth and wait it out. He was convinced that they wanted to punish him but not kill him, at least not yet.

At one point, Tsafendas received an unexpected visitor, an Italian Roman Catholic priest. Baptised into the Greek Orthodox Church and a believer in God but not organised religion, Tsafendas was unsure of the priest's role. Had he come on a routine visit, as Catholic prison chaplains did with new inmates, or did the authorities want him to see a priest for their own reasons? If so, they could have arranged for a minister of his own Christian Church sect or a Greek Orthodox priest. Perhaps they could find no one else willing to meet Tsafendas, since neither church in South Africa wanted anything to do with him. Tsafendas wondered if it was General van den Bergh's idea, perhaps to find out more about him, using religion as a probe. If so, he could not believe the visits helped the general, since he and the priest talked mostly about theology, not about himself. He did wonder sometimes if the priest was filling the role that clergymen traditionally played for the condemned man, seeking a confession or offering words of consolation. Whatever the reason, chatting to the priest was a welcome break from the torture and the interrogation. However, after a couple of visits, the priest failed to show up and Tsafendas never saw him again.[10] He did have other visitors, though these were strictly unofficial. Some of the guards would allow their girlfriends to take a quick look at Tsafendas in his cell.[11] Everyone wanted to see what the Prime Minister's assassin looked like.

On the day of Tsafendas's remand, Verwoerd's body, accompanied by his bulldog Punch, which refused to leave his side, was flown from Cape Town to Pretoria, the administrative capital of South Africa.[12] Verwoerd's eldest son Wilhelm wanted a small, family funeral, but the government insisted that a state funeral was necessary and eventually, he agreed.[13] Two days later, on Saturday, 10 September, a funeral of grandiose proportions took place before the biggest crowd ever seen in South Africa, estimated at 250,000, while unknown numbers followed proceedings by radio. The principle ceremony was a religious service before some 10,000 mourners in the vast amphitheatre of Pretoria's Union Buildings. The service was led by State President Charles Robert Swart and attended by many diplomats in formal attire. Among the VIPs was Ian Smith, Prime Minister of Rhodesia, who was the only national leader present. Also there were Paramount Chief Kaiser Matanzima, some 20 Africans representing seven ethnic groups, and representatives of South Africa's Indian and coloured communities. The SABC described the ceremony in English, Afrikaans and nine other languages.[14]

When the service concluded after just over an hour, a vast cortege escorted Verwoerd's casket solemnly towards its final resting place in Church Street cemetery. Thirty-eight policemen on horseback led the procession, followed by motorised army detachments and 400 marching soldiers. The day was bright and sunny and flights of Harvard aircraft formed the letters 'HV' in the clear, blue sky. Church Street cemetery, established in 1867, was a Christian burial ground, thus all the graves were oriented towards the east. At its centre was Heroes' Acre, containing the graves of renowned public figures, and this was where Verwoerd was interred. The committal ceremony was restricted to family and members of the cabinet, with thousands gathered in silence outside. As the coffin was carried to the graveside, artillerymen fired 19-gun salvoes from the hills surrounding the city.[15] The National Party newspaper, *Die Vaderland,* reminded loyal readers in a front-page editorial that Verwoerd may have gone, but 'his message remains'.[16]

The day after the funeral, the Afrikaner newspaper *Die Beeld* reported that the Security Police had a file on Tsafendas. However, 24 hours later, John Vorster, on his last day as Minister of Justice, Prisons and Police before becoming Prime Minister, declared that the police had no such file. He described the report as 'devoid of all truth', adding that many published reports at this time were unduly sensational. He promised that a complete statement would be made when the time arrived. 'The whole matter is still being investigated continuously and after the trial it will, as is proper, be disclosed to the public.'[17]

Vorster was either misinformed or lied knowingly because the Security Police did hold a file on Tsafendas. Indeed, three further files on Tsafendas had been created by the Security Police, but only one could be found in 1966. According to the subsequent Commission of Enquiry into Verwoerd's death, Tsafendas was named on the national stop list of banned persons in 1959, a copy of which had been in the possession of the Security Police since 1964. The lone surviving file was described by the Commission as 'an old police file, W.D. 10/10/4102, bearing the name Demetrios Tsafandakis'. The Commission gave details of three others: one had been opened in 1941 by the Commissioner of Police in Pretoria, bore the file number 6/1835/3697 and the name Demetrios Tsafendakis, but was destroyed in 1963; and there were two files of the Witwatersrand Division, W.D. 10/3/305 and W.D. 2/2078/366, but the former could not be traced and the latter was destroyed in 1946.[18]

In Cape Town on Sunday, 11 September, Tsafendas gave his first formal recorded statement. It was taken by Major Daniel Jacobus Rossouw, head of the Cape Town Security Police, who had interrogated Tsafendas briefly in the hours after the assassination and disclosed to him, inadvertently or otherwise, that Verwoerd had died. Major Rossouw was an experienced interrogator, having questioned front-line political prisoners such as John Harris, Stephanie Kemp and several leading members of the resistance movement and the ANC.[19] Tsafendas could not make his mind up about the major. He was invariably polite and appeared better informed about world affairs than General van den Bergh, such that Tsafendas did not have to explain, for example, what happened during the Greek Civil War.

Furthermore, Tsafendas was surprised and grateful when the major handed him a pamphlet that the Christian Church had mailed to him and which Rossouw had retrieved from the post office. At times, exchanges between the two appeared more like a friendly conversation than an interrogation session. On the other hand, Harris, Kemp and the others had been tortured during their interrogations and Rossouw must have known of this, as surely he knew of Tsafendas's own torture. Yet he did not intervene. The best Tsafendas could hope for was that he would be spared violence during the course of this interrogation, as proved to be the case, though this was no pointer as to what might happen in the future at the hands of others.[20]

Tsafendas began his statement by declaring:

> *I have been warned by Maj. Rossouw that he is investigating a charge of murder against me arising from the death of the late Prime Minister, Dr H. F. Verwoerd. My rights have been explained to me and I understand the warning given to me. I am in my sound and sober senses and I have not been influenced in any way to make this statement. I am prepared to make a statement.*[21]

Tsafendas then talked freely about his life, his early years in Egypt, his return to Mozambique to join his father's family, his schooling in South Africa, then, as an adult, his travels around the world; he spoke of his many arrests and hospitalisations, the Portuguese amnesty that allowed him entry into Mozambique, his slowly growing anger over South Africa's racial policies, his decision to 'remove' Verwoerd and his purchase of a gun and then knives to that end. Rossouw's interrogation, though not as long as Van den Bergh's, lasted more than 24 hours and spilled into a second day. However, he allowed Tsafendas to sleep for a few hours after the first long session.[22]

On 12 September, the *Pretoria News* reported that rumours that Tsafendas had hanged himself in his cell 'spread today like wildfire'. A police spokesman dismissed the report with a laconic, 'We know nothing about it.'[23] The same day, the second day of Rossouw's interrogation, Tsafendas confirmed the information the South African police had discovered about his political activities. He affirmed that when he was in London, he attended political meetings, explaining that

> *they were anti-colonial meetings, anti-apartheid meetings and anti-racial meetings ... I did take part in a protest and propaganda meeting at Trafalgar Square, anti-colonial protests. I was holding the posters up but I did not speak at those meetings ... I was anti-colonial, against slavery and in favour of all colonies controlled by Belgium, France and Portugal being afforded self-government. I was in sympathy with the people fighting racialism, hence the reason for attending the meetings mentioned above ...*[24]

Tsafendas was also asked about his association with Tennyson Makiwane and other anti-apartheid activists in London. He said:

> *It is true that I mixed with South African people in London, some of whom were leftists ... in private conversations with some of these people it was said that the South African Prime Minister deserved to be shot. I cannot remember by whom this statement was made because it was merely during private conversation that this statement was made. This sort of statement was made more than once by different people. I can-not remember any particular person having made such a statement. It was just casual talk. These were isolated statements by people I happened to come across by chance. To say that this was the main thought amongst leftists is a bit exaggerated.*[25]

As for the killing of Verwoerd, he said:

> *I used to agree with the idea that the Prime Minister deserved to be shot. I sometimes agreed with them. Sometimes we used to discuss that Dr Verwoerd was lucky he did not die the first time he was shot. There was no decision made that he should in fact be killed – I mean I did not decide on anything at that time. I never took upon me the task of killing the Prime Minister nor did I tell anyone that I would kill the Prime Minister. I did believe that with the disappearance of the South African Prime Minister a change of policy would take place. I did set myself the task of destroying the Prime Minister. It was my own idea to kill him. No one offered me any reward for doing so. I did not care about the consequences, for what would happen to me afterwards. I was so disgusted with the racial policy that I went through with my plans to kill the Prime Minister ... I wanted to see a government representing all the South African people. I do not think the Nationalist government is representative of the people and I wanted to see a different government.*[26]

Tsafendas denied that he had returned to South Africa with the specific aim of killing Verwoerd. He said that he got the idea 'some days after' he had 'started working in the House of Assembly' when 'all kinds of thoughts came to my mind about murdering the Prime Minister. I saw an opportunity of shooting the Prime Minister from the lobby.' As with his previous statements, there was no mention of a tapeworm and nothing to suggest that he was insane. Tsafendas was determined not to use his trick this time, no matter what they might do to him, since that would undermine his act of assassination and would be a victory for apartheid. Like Van den Bergh, Rossouw asked Tsafendas about the absence of an escape plan. He replied, 'I did not think I would get away after murdering the Prime Minister. I did not care what happened to me.'[27]

Professor John Dugard told the author that Tsafendas statement 'confirms the view that Tsafendas was not insane. It reads like a very normal story of a politically informed person, angry with apartheid and Dr Verwoerd, determined to make a change with nothing to lose personally -- really an incredible statement which was carefully concealed'.

After giving his statement, Tsafendas was returned to his cell and Rossouw took the document to Van den Bergh. He found the general beleaguered by a seemingly endless flow of unwelcome reports about his prisoner. Checking through Tsafendas's newest statement further dismayed Van den Bergh, who knew he faced serious problems if he wished to present Verwoerd's murder as a random, non-political act. Tsafenda's latest statement gave no comfort to

Van den Bergh, who was trying to put together a case for court. The fact that Tsafendas was a communist, that he killed Verwoerd because he was a tyrant and a dictator who was oppressing his people, that he hoped that by killing him, a change of policy would take place in South Africa. Tsafendas simply could not be allowed to say this in open court! Nor could much of the police evidence be permitted. That a committed communist had been allowed to work in Parliament would deeply embarrass Van den Bergh himself as well as Vorster with his responsibility for security; worse, it might suggest that there was significant resistance to the ruling regime and certainly, it would be a huge propaganda victory for the communists, with Tsafendas proclaimed a hero, a martyr and symbol of resistance to apartheid. Van den Bergh concluded that all this information must be concealed and Tsafendas must be presented not as a political warrior, but as a madman, a loose cannon, a weirdo, a wanderer, a man with mental problems and without a cause. The embarrassing evidence could be suppressed, as that had been done often enough. The problem was Tsafendas because the picture the general wanted to present of him could only be achieved with the assassin's 'co-operation'. How could you make a man with deeply held political convictions change his tune? Van den Bergh knew exactly how and within 24 hours what Tsafendas later called his 'living hell' began.

Every day from 13 September, the day after Tsafendas had given his statement to Major Rossouw and also coincidentally the day that John Vorster was chosen as Prime Minister, he was subjected to extraordinary violence. The police, never in uniform, would force him to remove his clothes and then they would attack his naked body with their batons. Frequently, they ridiculed his appearance and made his belly and groin particular targets for their blows, which Tsafendas tried to ward off by tightly crossing his legs. They also laced him into a straightjacket and used him like a boxer's punch bag. Invariably he fell, and when he could not move, they kicked him angrily. Often they failed to remove his handcuffs or leg irons after the punishment session and he was left shackled in his cell.[28]

One evening, trying to sleep on the floor of his cell, the silence was broken by the sound of keys rattling in the lock. Tsafendas reflexively curled into a ball, pulling his legs close to his body in anticipation of police boots thudding into his groin. The blows did not come. Instead, two policemen, shouting in Afrikaans, yanked him to his feet and dragged him out of his cell. In a room on the second floor, they raised a window and forced him out, head first, with a policeman holding each foot. Then they began shouting questions at him. If he gave an answer they did not like, they would lift a leg as if to jettison him into space. One question was whether he was a communist. He replied, 'Yes, I am' and immediately one of his captors jerked his foot upwards so that he hung perpendicularly. They said they would let him drop and claim he had tried to escape. Frequently, the same question would be repeated and his answer, if it displeased them, would bring a torrent of screams and threats. Eventually, he was dragged back into the room and, lying helpless on the floor under the window, was thrashed by the policemen with fists, boots and batons.[29]

Thus psychological torture and the threat of defenestration was added to the violence of electric shocks and physical assault. After this, whenever Tsafendas was taken from his cell, he shook with fear, sweat coursing down his face and spine. Desperately, he tried to hide his terror by biting his lip and singing revolutionary songs in his head. Sometimes, uniformed policemen would enter his cell just to check that he was alive. They never spoke. If he was sleeping or pretending to sleep, which was most of the time, they would kick him to secure a response. There were times when Tsafendas daydreamed of going up against the guards in a one-on-one confrontation. He was confident they would have no chance against him. They were big, strong men with well-trained bodies, but he reckoned he would win because they did not have his nerve and determination. However in reality, his will by now was weakening along with his body and he feared that to resist or defy his captors would only make matters worse. As for protesting, that was out of the question.[30]

As well as growing evidence as to Tsafendas's widespread political activities and arrests and his pro-communist and anti-apartheid ideology, Van den Bergh had just received a disturbing new claim. Maria Kokkinidou, the Greek woman who periodically visited the *Eleni* to see her son, newly hired as a crew member, had told the police that Verwoerd's death was discussed on the tanker the day before it left, that is, three days before Verwoerd died.[31] Her statement was confirmed by two South Africans working on the *Eleni* at the time, security guard Reginald Maile and watchman Edmund Stollenkamp.[32] Tsafendas was known to have visited the vessel every day of the 42 days that it was docked in Cape Town and had already told Van den Bergh and Rossouw that he bought a gun on the *Eleni* and, at one point, had planned to escape aboard the tanker.

Maria Kokkinidou's claim meant that the entire *Eleni* crew, now on the high seas, must be questioned. The South African government contacted their Greek counterparts for permission to question the men at a convenient point. Obligingly, Greek officials contacted Captain Fountotos, who was skippering the *Eleni* towards the port of Mina al-Ahmadi in Kuwait. The Greek Ministry of Shipping asked Fountotos to return to Cape Town, with the approval of the *Eleni*'s owner, the Mavroleon Company. Fountotos pointed out that it would take twice as long to return to Cape Town as to reach Kuwait and suggested that the questioning take place in the Arab port. South Africa agreed.[33]

The news that Tsafendas had killed Verwoerd shocked the *Eleni* crew, who feared that their association with him could somehow implicate them in his crime. Most fearful were those men who had gone with him to the township and young Mavronas. The crew did not know how Verwoerd had been killed and some made cruel fun of Mavronas, suggesting Tsafendas had somehow got the fake Beretta to fire and so he, Mavronas, would be charged as an accessory to murder. Kambouris and Vasilakis collected the banned books about apartheid that Tsafendas had given them and threw them overboard. Zafiriadis thought they were overreacting and just hid his own. He also suggested that the crew should refuse to give evidence about Tsafendas for fear they would incriminate or endanger him. The captain learnt of this suggestion and ordered otherwise, arguing that the police would already know everything pertinent. More importantly, he relayed to the crew a message from the Greek Ministry of Shipping, ordering them to co-operate fully with the South African authorities.[34]

The crew met several times among themselves to discuss what they would tell the police. Quickly, they determined to distance themselves from Tsafendas as far as possible; however, they calculated that they could not stray too far from the truth because he was likely to have told the police everything under torture. What's more, there were plenty of witnesses who had seen them with Tsafendas every day, often laughing and joking and clearly on friendly terms. In the end, the men decided to be open about everything except two things: singing communist songs and having sex with African women. Tsafendas's friends such as Alachiotis, Aspras, Kantas, Billis, Pouftis and Zafiriadis reasoned that if they admitted to singing Red anthems with Tsafendas, they would be exposed as communists and probably fired by their employer. Since that sing-song had taken place when none of the crew's right-wingers was on board and the police could not possibly know about it, they decided to stay quiet. As for the sex, some seamen had slept with African women, a forbidden act under apartheid, despite Tsafendas warning that the police had 'ears and spies everywhere'. However, the crew guessed that the police would be more interested in politics and murder than in pursuing infractions of the sex laws, and therefore they would take their chances and not mention the sex. Regarding the visit to the township, it was agreed that this was probably known to the police and so they decided that, if asked, they would say they went there as tourists, just to see how the people lived.[35]

When the *Eleni* reached Mina al-Ahmadi, the crew discovered, to their surprise and relief, that no South African police were waiting for them on the dockside. Upon leaving Kuwait, still without sign of police, formerly heated arguments as to their best defence fell into abeyance since it seemed that the police were no longer interested in them. They were wrong. On 12 October, when the *Eleni* docked in Venice, three South African policemen came on board. They wore civilian clothes and were accompanied by an official from a Greek Consulate somewhere in Italy who translated for those who did not speak good English. Captain Fountotos told his crew that he had only just been informed of the police's visit and asked them to co-operate. Some of the crew believed they had been kept in the dark so that they could not prepare their answers.[36]

The consular officer advised the crew to tell the truth and disclose everything they knew about Tsafendas. He stated repeatedly that the case was almost closed and the investigators knew everything about Tsafendas anyway. He said Tsafendas had told them about his time on the tanker, and he warned the men that they would be in trouble if they lied or held anything back. He said the Greek government was co-operating fully with the South African authorities and the government was asking them to do the same. Some of the men felt that their consular representative appeared more 'threatening' than the policemen. Consistently refering to Tsafendas in negative terms, he said Tsafendas was not Greek, but Mozambican, and that he had caused Greeks in South Africa to be attacked by local people, who considered them all responsible for Verwoerd's death.[37]

All of the crew were questioned by the police, including Captain Fountotos and the four non-Greek seamen. They were asked standard questions, such as, 'How did you meet Tsafendas? What did he do? What did he talk about? What was your impression of him? Did he discuss politics? Did he say anything about the Prime Minister? When did he come to the tanker and why? They wanted to know everything Tsafendas had said to them and they also asked about the sale of the gun. The questioning lasted from around 9.00 am to 4.30 pm. The only crew member who refused to make a statement was Zafiriadis, although he volunteered a very short and unimportant comment regarding the sale of the gun. The men revealed that Tsafendas had taken them to the township, that he told them he had fought in the Greek Civil War with the communists and that he had faked mental illness to avoid service in the Portuguese army. As for Verwoerd, they said Tsafendas characterised the Prime Minister as a tyrant, a dictator, 'Hitler's best student' and the brains behind apartheid.[38]

To the men's surprise, the police showed little interest in the sale of the gun; they were more keen to learn how it was that Verwoed's death was discussed three days before it happened? The men had no idea what the police were talking about and a number of them assumed this was a reference to the conversation when Tsafendas had spoken of a hypothetical assassination of Verwoerd as being justifiable on grounds he was a tyrant and a dictator oppressing his people. Six or seven men told the police about this incident and insisted that it was the only time that Verwoerd's death was discussed on board. They insisted that Tsafendas was speaking in hypothetical terms and not about any real murder plan. They guessed that this was the conversation referred to by Maria Kokkinidou. The men assumed that Kokkinidou's son, Costas, had overheard, and misunderstood, parts of their conversation, which he passed on to his mother.[39]

It must have been around mid-September when Tsafendas received an unexpected visitor. Although he wore civilian clothes, he introduced himself as a member of the Security Police in Pretoria. He looked about the same age as Tsafendas. The policeman said he was half-Greek, half-South African. Tsafendas was surprised. Tall and well-proportioned, a blond Nordic type though with black beady eyes and a thick brown moustache, he looked more like a Scandinavian athlete than a Greek or South African.

'My mother was Greek, but my father was South African,' he said. 'That's why I have an Afrikaner name.'

Tsafendas addressed him in Greek, but his visitor could manage only a few words. The policeman claimed he had taken an interest in Tsafendas's case after reading that he was half-Greek. He also said he had visited his family in Pretoria. Tsafendas had heard nothing of them since his arrest and immediately asked about them. The policeman replied that it had been very hard for them and for the whole Greek community.

'Afrikaners have gone wild,' he said, attacking Greeks all over the country. He stressed that Tsafendas's family was safe, at least for the time being.

'What's going to happen to them?' Tsafendas asked. 'I don't know,' said the policeman. 'They are still under investigation ...'

Tsafendas insisted that his relatives had nothing to do with the assassination and would totally disapprove of it. He lied that the family were devoted supporters of apartheid and had grown away from him because they opposed his political views. As he had done with Van den Bergh and Rossouw, he distanced himself from his family, highlighting what he said were their strong political differences.[40]

The half-Greek policeman did not make a good impression on Tsafendas, who found him superficial with a hint of sleaze, while at the same time seeming to show off his authority. As with the Catholic priest, Tsafendas wondered about the motive for his visit. In time, he came to feel that the policeman was trying to find out more about him and his story, using a different approach to those of Van den Bergh and Rossouw. He asked Tsafendas about his treatment and encouraged him to tell the truth. Tsafendas told him the truth. The policeman asked why Verwoerd's death was discussed on the *Eleni* the night before it sailed, three days before the assassination. Tsafendas insisted that he had said nothing about his assassination plan to anyone. The policeman also had some advice: 'You should not aggravate them,' he said. 'Communism is the last word they want to hear. What is the point of insisting you are a communist?' He also advised him to stop calling Verwoerd a tyrant and a dictator because that only angered his inquisitors, when he should be trying to pacify them. Before leaving after his first visit, he asked Tsafendas if he needed anything. When he replied, 'water', the policeman asked the guard at the door to fetch a glass, and Tsafendas drank it at once.[41]

Between the policeman's visits, the torture continued, sometimes the window, often the electric shock machine. When Tsafendas did not have the strength to walk to the 'torture chamber', as he called it, the policemen dragged him, feet trailing. If he urinated involuntarily, he was forced to stay in his sodden underwear so that he would not wet the floor. Tsafendas was wearing the same clothes he had been given on 8 September for the remand hearing, which were now stiff with sweat, dirt, urine, mucus and blood. He was repelled by his own body odour and his torturers often shouted that they were beating him because he smelled like a pig.[42]

The only policemen he ever saw in uniform were those who brought his food. They never spoke. He would always say 'thank you', but all he received was stony silence. Adding to his agony was hunger and what seemed like endless thirst. Tsafendas was usually given one meal and a single glass of water per day. Frequently, the police spat into the dishes and cups. Seeing the spittle and the phlegm, he could not bring himself to touch the food or the water. It was water he craved most. His mouth became so dry that he coughed in wrenching spasms and was unable to talk. He considered pleading with the guards, but pride forbade it. He realised that he had not experienced a bowel movement since his arrest and, considering the minuscule nature of his rations, he was not surprised.[43]

The Greek-South African policeman began visiting almost daily, always bringing with him a glass of water. He would stay for at least 30 minutes, sometimes as long as an hour, discussing Tsafendas's past and what the guards were doing to him, urging him to stop aggravating the police by insisting he was a communist and Verwoerd a dictator. Considering the drift of the policeman's questions, Tsafendas became convinced that he was an emissary of General van den Bergh, sent to probe his state of mind and assess any changes in his attitude. He appeared to be the classic 'good cop', suggesting ways he could behave to lessen his torment from the 'bad cop' torturers. Tsafendas was not impressed and, in his mind, labelled him as 'pathetic' and 'Van den Bergh's lackey'.[44]

On 14 September, his first full day in office, Prime Minister Vorster announced that a Commission of Enquiry would be held 'into all aspects of the assassination of Dr Verwoerd'. The process would be led by Justice Jacques

Theodore van Wyk, South Africa's representative at the World Court in The Hague. Vorster urged anyone with information about the matter, however trivial, to come forward and place it before the Commission. He also announced that the hearings would take place behind closed doors. Clearly, the government was determined that no one would be allowed to hear witnesses describe Tsafendas as a passionate communist and anti-apartheid activist. Nor did it want any unpleasant surprises from new evidence that might be volunteered spontaneously. With Van Wyk, a National Party member and a committed supporter of apartheid, chosen to control proceedings, the enquiry was guaranteed to follow the path the regime planned.[45]

It was at this point that the South African police learnt that Tsafendas had told the Portuguese about a tapeworm. Clearly, this excited his interrogators and they asked eagerly if the worm had told him to kill Dr Verwoerd or if it was connected in some way with the assassination. Not so, said Tsafendas. His persistent denials only increased the pressure and now they were not asking but insisting, putting words in his mouth: 'You are mad, the tapeworm made you do it, didn't it?'[46] Tsafendas held his ground, declaring repeatedly that the tapeworm had nothing to do with the assassination. At one point, certain that when apartheid collapsed his act would be viewed very differently in South Africa, he declared, 'History will prove whether I am right or wrong for killing Dr Verwoerd.'[47] This statement did not go down well with his interrogators.

On 19 September, Tsafendas gave a second statement to Major Rossouw. Most of the questions concerned his involvement with the South African Communist Party and whether he was in touch with communists elsewhere in the world. He was asked to name all the hospitals to which he had been admitted and the reasons. He complied. He also named the languages he could speak. Major Rossouw asked him, 'Were you ever indoctrinated by any person to commit the unlawful act for which you are now charged?' Tsafendas replied, 'No, I was not. I did not do it at the instigation of anyone. I did it on my own because I thought it was the right thing.' Tsafendas then described how he schemed to kill Verwoerd, how at first he bought a gun and planned to escape aboard the *Eleni* and later bought two knives. This exchange ensued:

'Did you know that the *Eleni* had sailed before you attacked the Prime Minister? If so, what were your plans to get away?'

'Yes, I knew the ship had already left. I never thought about hiding if I had to do the job with a knife. I didn't have much of a chance of getting away when using a knife. I didn't care much and didn't give it a second thought that I would be caught. I just happened to do it that way. I always had a grudge against the South African Government on account of its racial policies and I hated Dr Verwoerd because he was a foreigner, a Hollander.'[48]

In referring to Verwoerd as a foreigner, a Hollander, Tsafendas was expressing his conviction that all colonialists in Africa were foreigners, people from other parts of the world illegally occupying African land. He perceived apartheid as a form of colonialism. The Portuguese in Mozambique and those who formed and supported the white governments in Rhodesia and South Africa were all foreigners in Tsafendas's eyes, and he considered all three countries to be 'occupied lands'.[49]

The statement was read over to Tsafendas, who acknowledged that the contents were correct and that he had answered freely and voluntarily.

'Are you prepared to sign this statement?' the major asked him.

'Yes, I am prepared to sign it.'

At no point did Tsafendas make any mention of the tapeworm. All his replies were clear and articulate.

Shortly after the interrogation ended, Tsafendas was visited by a doctor in his cell. His medical report said, 'He (Tsafendas) complained of mild breathlessness at times and a feeling of discomfort in the throat. On examination, he appeared in good physical condition and nil abnormal was found in the chest. His temperature was 98.0 F. I came to the conclusion that he was suffering from hyperventilation at times and prescribed a multivitamin tablet containing phenobarbitone gr 1/2.'

Naturally, he was given no tablets.[50]

By now, time was running out for Van den Bergh to construct a case accusing Tsafendas of the assassination for reasons free of all political motivation. The attempts to have him admit that a tapeworm had something to do with the assassination had failed, and here he was, in his latest statement, reasserting that he killed the Prime Minister because he considered his policies racist. To admit the existence of serious opposition to apartheid would be a huge blow to the ruling regime and to let it be known that a communist had penetrated the inner sanctum of Parliament would be catastrophic for the general personally. Although the state was within its rights to detain Tsafendas for 180 days, such a long stretch would be impractical in the face of liberal pressures from outside. It was time to take drastic measures against Tsafendas.

Sometime after his second recorded statement to Major Rossouw, the state's most important prisoner was trying to sleep when his cell door slammed open and a plain-clothed policeman kicked him in the stomach and shouted, 'Your time has come, you bastard.' A second policeman followed with his boot as

Tsafendas tried to rise. 'Get up, you communist pig,' he grunted. Shouting continually, the two guards grabbed Tsafendas and pulled him to his feet. Two more men stood at the door and Tsafendas feared something dreadful was about to happen to him. Amidst a cacophony of shouts and insults, he was quickly handcuffed. Then suddenly his world turned black. He hadn't seen it coming but a hood had been pulled over his head. Half-carried out of his cell, Tafendas was forced into a half-run. 'Faster, faster,' they yelled, but, half-starved as he was, his legs could not respond. Under the hood, sweat began coursing down his face, his heart pounded and he gasped for breath. 'Your time has come, you fucking bastard,' they shouted repeatedly, 'Now you're going to pay, you communist pig.' Suddenly, they stopped and Tsafendas understood he was in a new room. Three or four men were pulling at him, positioning him precisely, it seemed. Tsafendas knew this is where it would happen, whatever it was.

The next thing he knew, hands were pulling at his leg, tugging upwards, lifting it onto a higher surface, a chair surely or perhaps a stool; then the other leg and then suddenly his whole body was raised, hands holding him in place. He was still handcuffed. It was when a voice said, 'Do you have a last wish, you bastard?' that he felt a rope slide over his head and settle around his neck. He was seized with terror, he had not expected this. Unbidden, unexpected tears coursed down his face, mixing with the perspiration. Irrationally, he felt glad that his executioners could not see the shame of his tears. Now Tsafendas had no doubt he was about to die and, with a fervour he had never known, he begged God to forgive his sins. 'Do you have a last wish?' a harsh male voice repeated. Someone else said, 'Let's get this over with' and the rope was jerked tight around the hood. Hyperventilating, Tsafendas prayed to not suffer. 'Last time, any last wish you fucking bastard?' a voice said. Seconds seemed like an hour. Then came the other voice, venomously, 'This is for Doctor Verwoerd,' and the noose turned into an iron band and Tsafendas's large body was somehow freed and he knew he was hanging, strangling. Deprived of oxygen, all he heard was a roaring noise in his head, as if all the voices in the cell had joined together. He did not struggle, he had no hope.

In the past, he had wondered about death, assuming a million thoughts would crowd his brain and that his life would flash before him. Nothing like that happened. His mind was blank. He had no sense of time. All he could think as he hung choking, his face suffusing, was that it would be over when everything went black. He longed for that moment. But blackness didn't come. What happened next was the crash of his body hitting the floor. He tried to understand. Was he even alive? The terrible roaring noise continued in his ears and he realised it was the sound of voices, the policemen yelling in Afrikaans. The noose was still around his neck, but slack now. He drew huge gasps of air into his starved lungs and he knew then that he was alive. He remained motionless, his head drooping like a beaten dog. The policemen laughed at him, almost hysterically, about their hanging joke, pointing and mocking like children bullying the weak kid, but their words were not for children. 'Did you think that this is all you are going to get? ... your time is coming, but not today … maybe tomorrow, maybe the day after, who knows?' Repeatedly, he heard, 'Be sure, you're not getting out of here alive.' He was left on the floor, still handcuffed, with the hood and the rope around his head. As they left, the policemen flung a reminder at him: 'Maybe tomorrow, maybe the day after …'[51]

After that, the mock hangings took place daily, sometimes twice a day. The ritual was always the same. He was cuffed and hooded with extreme violence, then dragged to the hanging room as his torturers yelled the same threats in his face, 'Now, you bastard, your time has come … a last wish … this is for Doctor Verwoerd.' Sometimes he resisted getting onto the chair but they beat his shins with batons until he lifted his legs. If he contrived to fall off the chair, they beat and kicked him back into place. The fearful moment came when the rope turned into an iron band and then the terrible, hanging time – he had no idea how long – when he dangled, suffocating, before his release. At first, he convinced himself that this was just torture, physical and psychological combined, that they were making him suffer, but they would not kill him. But each time, they left him hanging for longer and longer and he was not sure anymore.

His life was full of torture. Electric shocks, beatings and mock hangings took place every day and often, between them, it was the window or the straightjacket. The guards pursued their task of delivering pain with an almost religious dedication, sometimes changing the sequence of the tortures so that he would not know what to expect next. Despite the pain and humiliation, the thought of suicide never crossed his mind. 'Only a brave man could kill himself,' and he did not consider himself one. The fact was he no longer cared what would happen to him. He knew he would die, but it did not matter for he had achieved his goal, he had done something worth doing, he had killed the tyrant and they could not take that away from him. During his previous arrests, he had resisted his jailers because he would be freed sooner or later. He knew a future was waiting for him. Now, he knew he had no future but he consoled himself with the thought that whatever they did, he was their victor. He reminded himself of this often to boost his spirits. He had beaten them; they were hurting him because he had won and however much they tortured him, they could not change that. After some time, he even assisted his torturers. He went straight to the designated chair for the electric shocks, positioned himself at the window when they wanted to dangle him outside and lifted his leg for the chair in the hanging room. He began to feel like a trained animal in a circus, anticipating orders from these new masters to whom his life now belonged. It would not last long; of that he was certain. Death, which had always terrified him, was now, he believed, an imminent certainty. The prospect was as fearful as ever, but he bowed to its inevitability. What he found unbearable to contemplate was the *process* of his killing: how it would happen (by what method?), when (today, tomorrow, next week?) and how much torture would he endure before his bloodied body and his wracked heart gave out.[52]

Among the worst aspects of the prison regimen was that the torture often took place at night. Sometimes the night-shift policemen would just beat him in his cell. At other times, they would wake him, then do nothing, letting him suffer by waiting for violence that never came, which was almost as bad as the violence itself. The fear-filled expectation of these nocturnal visits made it impossible for Tsafendas to sleep for any length of time, with him closing his eyes usually in the early hours through sheer exhaustion, which would be when he would be led away for hangings or shocks. His only thought each dawn was how to survive another day.[53]

The *Eleni* discussion was probably not the last piece of undesirable information to reach General van den Bergh. Almost certainly, the police found out about the bribe that J.J. van den Berg, South Africa's passport control officer in Lourenço Marques, had accepted from the Tsafendas family. The circumstances are unknown and it is very possible that Tsafendas named the man under torture. What is known is that Van den Berg was arrested at his home and driven away by security officers who refused to tell his family where he was taken. He was subjected to serious violence, questioned for hour after hour and not allowed to sleep. His son said later that his father's ribs were broken and he was made to stand naked for long periods in his own urine and ordure. He was eventually released but had great difficulty finding work, moving from job to job as his children moved from school to school. At one time, the family was reduced to living in a relative's garage.[54]

The extraordinary severity of J.J. Van den Berg's treatment strongly suggests that the police had learnt about the bribe. However, the fact that a South African diplomat had accepted money to assist the man who killed the Prime Minister was so scandalous that it could never possibly be revealed. A major pointer to the bribe having been discovered was the lack of action against other erring government employees. At least seven known officials missed the fact that Tsafendas's name was on the stop list of the Department of the Interior – three immigration officers who separately interviewed Tsafendas for his permanent residency permit in Pretoria in 1963, Miss J. Markram, the assistant in the Department of the Interior where Tsafendas applied for a return visa to visit Mozambique and Southern Rhodesia and the three messengers who approved Tsafendas's application to work in the House of Assembly. Add to these the officials who cleared Tsafendas when he arrived in Durban aboard ship on 8 March 1965.

Often between the torture sessions, Tsafendas was visited by the Greek-South African policeman. He asked Tsafendas if he seriously thought he would be allowed to stand up in court and declare that he was a communist, and had killed Verwoerd because he believed he was a tyrant and a dictator. He hinted strongly that David Pratt had not committed suicide but had been murdered by the police and he implied that exactly the same scenario was planned for him. There were already rumours that he had hanged himself, the policeman said, and showed him a copy of the *Pretoria News* of 12 September.[55] The report had been planted as part of the police strategy, he implied. He would be found 'hanged with a plastic wire around his neck in his cell', if he maintained his stance with regard to Verwoerd, Tsafendas was told.[56]

Aware of Dr Sakinofsky's examination of Tsafendas and his diagnosis, General Van den Bergh appointed Professor Adolf Johannes van Wyk, an experienced psychiatrist, to examine the prisoner. Professor van Wyk, a loyal supporter of the apartheid government who knew which way the political winds blew, was a professor of psychiatry at the University of Pretoria, senior psychiatrist at Pretoria General Hospital and Deputy Commissioner of Mental Health of South Africa. He was also involved in the case of John Harris, anti-apartheid rebel and member of the African Resistance Movement who planted a bomb in a Johannesburg railway station in 1964. The professor had diagnosed him as sane and Harris was hanged. Professor van Wyk examined Tsafendas in his cell in Caledon Square for the first time on 23 September and then again the following day. He found Tsafendas to be perfectly sane and capable of following the trial proceedings.[57]

By 25 September, 18 days after he had killed Verwoerd, Tsafendas could barely walk and had to be dragged to the torture chambers. He was certain that time was running out and any time now his large frame would be left hanging until he choked to death or until his neck snapped; if he did get out, it would be as a crazy man. The only question was whether he would be crazy and alive or crazy and dead. The pain was now unbearable and he no longer had the strength to comfort himself with revolutionary songs. What he found agonising was the thought that he could be hanged in his cell and the world would believe he had committed suicide; the police could portray him any way they wanted, as they did with Pratt, and the world would accept their story, as they did with Pratt. He was determined to remain alive.

The idea that he could get out as an insane man seemed burned into his brain. He resisted its implication, he defended the assassination as a heroic political act for almost 20 days of constant psychological and physical torture, but eventually, he admitted that he could take no more. There was no more fight in him. The prospect of spending the remaining years of his life in a psychiatric hospital as the price for escaping 'death by suicide' seemed a deal worth accepting. Seeing no possible alternative, Tsafendas decided that for one last time he would play the fool. It would not be a problem; he had deceived the Portuguese police and medical experts with ease. Besides, he felt his present captors would prefer to dispose of him as a madman rather than a suicide. Perhaps they were feeling some measure of public scepticism about the frequency of 'suicides' among political prisoners. Thus it should not be difficult to convince them he had lost his mind. He consoled himself with the thought that this was as much a victory as a surrender. He had killed the tyrant and managed to stay alive. He was convinced in his heart that apartheid would collapse sooner or later without Verwoerd's brains behind it. And then he might even be paroled. If not, why, there was always the possibility of escape from a hospital and even from a jail, providing he got out of his police cell alive.

***

Having decided that a lifetime in a mental hospital was preferable to a short trip to the mortuary, and with plenty of practice behind him, Tsafendas began acting the madman once again. Having used the tapeworm story before to his advantage, but also having been caught faking mental illness, he refined his performance to a level he believed Tom Tuff himself would have admired. We are not in position to know exactly which fiction Tsafendas concocted this time, but we do know that once his new performance began, torture stopped, and soon afterwards, he was being seen by his state-appointed lawyers.[58] General van den Bergh had presumably concluded that his prisoner had committed wholeheartedly to his madman role and that it was safe for him to be seen by defence counsel. Although he could lawfully be held without legal representation for another 160 days, the general and Vorster knew that it would be in the best interests of the state to present Tsafendas as receiving a 'fair trial' as soon as possible, which would conclusively wrap up proceedings. Tsafendas needed to be tried with dispatch and found insane.

Without delay, General Van den Bergh contacted Judge Andries Beyers, Judge President of the Cape, and informed him that Tsafendas was now 'ready' to be seen by lawyers. Acutely conscious that the trial proceedings, including the conduct of Tsafendas's defence, could not be left to chance, he probably did not tell the judge of the accused's wish to be represented by George Bizos. Tsafendas's preferred choice was already *persona non grata* with the government, having defended headline dissidents Nelson Mandela and Bram

Fischer, among others. Only recently, Vorster's personal lawyer, by name of Krueger, had conveyed a warning from his employer to Bizos that his 'leash is getting shorter'.[59] One is not certain as to what transpired between the general and the judge, but the fact is that Beyers was asked to appoint himself Tsafendas's defence counsel.

On coming to power back in 1948 and laying the foundation stones of apartheid, the National Party took care to appoint judges who supported its policies. One of these was Justice Andries Beyers, who was a National Party member and a committed supporter of apartheid. He had also represented the government in a number of important legal proceedings, including the *Harris* case in 1951, when the government succeeded in removing the coloured voters from the electoral roll. It was no surprise therefore that Judge Beyers, then aged 63 and at the height of his powers, was chosen to preside over Tsafendas's trial.[60] Although a believer in the basic tenets of apartheid, Beyers was not blind to the problems thrown up by the policy of race separation. When asked to represent the Cape Supreme Court at Verwoerd's state funeral in Pretoria, aware that he was to preside over the trial of Tsafendas, Beyers feared that his attendance could compromise his impartiality in the eyes of the public and so sent Judge Marius Diemont in his place. People who were close to Beyers described him as a compassionate man of 'pronounced personality and sometime humanity'. He was known to oppose the death penalty, a rather unusual stance among South Africa's men of power.[61] On 25 September, Judge Beyers appointed David Bloomberg, aged 34, as the lawyer to lead Tsafendas's defence team. Bloomberg's father, Abe Bloomberg, was an MP for the United Party, and a good friend of Beyers, as well as chairman of an equine club of which the judge was a board member. Gossip had it that Abe's relationship with the judge was the reason David Bloomberg was appointed.[62] The fact that Bloomberg was a loyal servant of apartheid, as he had already proved and was going to do again later, and he was not going to make waves, would probably also have counted in Judge Beyer's decision.

It was obvious that such a case could be a career-maker for an ambitious young lawyer. Although David Bloomberg was not a member of the National Party, just a year earlier, he had publicly and controversially signalled his loyalty to Verwoerd and the apartheid regime. In a *New York Times* article, Bloomberg seemed more concerned about the South African theatre than his black fellow citizens. Boldly, he denounced Arthur Miller, Edward Albee and other American writers for refusing to allow their works to be performed in South Africa unless before mixed audiences, which had recently been prohibited. Bloomberg described racial separation as 'South Africa's answer to the problem of achieving peaceful coexistence of different people at different stages of their development ... it is designed to make it possible for various racial groups to enjoy the full privileges of a free society, each in their own area, unhampered by the strains imposed by a multiracial society. Apartheid is not a political ruse, but merely a notion that people get on best with their own kind.' He wrote that the government, 'in its wisdom', had decided that separate development was 'a more harmonious and peaceful solution than enforced integration' and was 'in the best interest of the non-white population'.[63] As events would show, this was not the only time Bloomberg defended apartheid.

Later that day, Judge Beyers appointed Wilfrid Cooper as a defence advocate and the young Willie Burger as Bloomberg's junior. Beyers made clear to Cooper that he only had one line of defence for Tsafendas, which was insanity, and that if Tsafendas was not found to be insane, he would 'swing'. Cooper got the message. The trial was to commence on 17 October and Beyers made clear that he would accept no requests for a postponement. The state wanted to close the case as soon as possible.[64] Cooper was nicknamed 'The Tiger' by the legal fraternity for his aggressive cross-examination skills and was building a reputation as an excellent advocate. Cooper's political position was presumably unknown to Beyers at the time since the young advocate had only recently begun his career. However, Cooper was a critic of apartheid and would turn out to be one of the few South African lawyers willing to defend anti-apartheid activists, taking the cases of Jeremy Cronin, David and Susan Rabkin, Steve Biko, Imam Abdullah Haron and Mapetla Mohapi.[65]

On the morning of Monday, 26 September 1966, Bloomberg became the first in the defence team to visit Tsafendas. Led by a police officer through a series of locked and barred doors, he came to a large cell guarded by an armed policeman. Inside, sitting huddled in a corner, he found Tsafendas. He said Tsafendas wore 'a dazed expression and seemed uninterested in his visitors' and when he got slowly to his feet, Bloomberg saw that he had 'some facial injuries'. Major Cerff, the police officer accompanying the lawyer, quickly claimed that they had occurred when MPs brought Tsafendas down in Parliament as he attacked Verwoerd. Bloomberg doubted the major's explanation since it was 20 days since the assassination, but did not ask Tsafendas about them or other possible wounds, nor did he order treatment. He claimed later that he did nothing because the injuries 'appeared superficial'.[66]

Later the same day, Tsafendas was visited by Wilfrid Cooper, who described him as being a 'bundle in the corner' of his cell. When Cooper told him he had been appointed to represent him, Tsafendas went into an act which he had started a few days earlier, protesting that according to the tenets of his religion, he did not need a legal defence. When Cooper argued that it was in his best interest to be defended, Tsafendas responded, 'I don't know why the good Lord should have chosen such an infirm person like me.' Cooper asked Tsafendas straight out why he had killed Verwoerd, but rather than answering the question frankly, as he had done with the police, Tsafendas embarked on a long and irrelevant story about horse-racing. After several unsuccessful attempts to get a sensible answer from Tsafendas, Cooper gave up. However, he had noticed what he described as a strong 'incongruity' about Tsafendas. This was that 'he had the appearance of a hobo, a rough-looking individual, yet when he spoke, he described his feelings with a certain measure of delicacy'.[67]

On the afternoon of 26 September, Bloomberg, Cooper and Burger saw Tsafendas together. Bloomberg thought he 'looked tired and somewhat dazed and at first spoke slowly but coherently'. Though polite and co-operative, he showed no interest in the questions put to him. When the lawyers tried to extract hard facts about his past, Tsafendas would meander away from the subject, appearing not to remember which question he had been asked. At one point, he made the extraordinary remark: 'I suppose when this whole thing is over, it will be difficult for me to live in Cape Town. Oh, well, I suppose I will have to live elsewhere!' Then later, he said, 'You know, I didn't really like my work in Parliament. I don't think I will apply again for a job there.'[68] Clearly, Tsafendas was enjoying his much-practised role of a person without a serious grasp upon reality.

To ensure that his defence team was on the right track, Tsafendas listed all the hospitals where he had been treated or admitted while studiously omitting the examinations he underwent for reasons of employment and residential status when he was found to be perfectly sane and healthy. When asked why he was hospitalised so many times – which was the chance he was waiting for – Tsafendas said he had a tapeworm in his stomach that made him feel 'unwell and nervous' and controlled his life.[69]

Asked if he remembered what had happened in Parliament on 6 September, Tsafendas offered a deliberately hazy account, with none of the details he had given to the police. As for motive, he made no mention of his political convictions but talked vaguely of 'frustrations' in his life and concerning heads of state. Then Tsafendas made a serious mistake. According to Bloomberg, he said he had worked in the Houses of Parliament in London but could not get close enough to Prime Minister Harold Macmillan to attack him. Bloomberg here demonstrated an extraordinary lapse in his work, failing to double-check such a significant remark. Although he sought to confirm everything Tsafendas told him, including all his overseas hospital admissions, he failed to ascertain if the London parliament story was true. Had he done so, he would have discovered that Tsafendas was lying, since he never held such a position. This misstep apart, Tsafendas played the role of an insane person throughout the interview with complete conviction, and Bloomberg and his fellow lawyers simply accepted what he told them.[70]

Convinced of their client's insanity, the defence lawyers decided that their next step should be to appoint psychiatrists to examine Tsafendas, to confirm he was treated at the hospitals he had named, and to find people in Cape Town who knew him and could speak of his state of mind. All of this was going to be difficult to accomplish in the three weeks until the trial. Wasting no time, Bloomberg and his associates began their search.

To serve as the defence's chief expert witness, Bloomberg named Dr Harold Cooper, who had worked in psychiatric hospitals in Johannesburg and Cape Town and then gone into private practice. He was an unexpected choice, given that in a 1951 murder case, *Rex v. Kennedy,* the court rejected a psychiatric evaluation made by him.[71] To strengthen the defence's case for insanity, Bloomberg appointed two other experts – Dr James William MacGregor, a specialist psychiatrist and neurologist who practised in Cape Town and Dr Aubrey Zabow, a psychiatrist in private practice in Cape Town and a part-time consultant in psychiatry at Groote Schuur Hospital and Somerset Hospital. Dr Cooper advised Bloomberg also to appoint his good friend and colleague, Mr Reyner van Zyl, a clinical psychologist, who was working at Grand Parade Centre in Cape Town, to carry out psychological tests on Tsafendas. The defence team was unaware that Tsafendas had already been examined by a state psychiatrist and had been found to be perfectly fit to stand trial.

A few days later, Bloomberg visited Tsafendas in his cell. Again, he found his client 'huddled in a corner and badly bruised'. Tsafendas told him that a policeman and a man in civilian clothes had entered his cell during the night and that the latter had beat him. Bloomberg questioned the duty officer, who denied that such a thing ever happened, saying it was impossible for any man in civilian clothes to get into Tsafendas's cell. Later, Bloomberg claimed that he personally investigated the cause of Tsafendas's injuries and discovered that he had been beaten by a famous horse trainer who was friendly with a high-ranking police officer. Apparently, the two men were out drinking and the policeman thought of introducing Tsafendas to his friend, who in turn saw it as his patriotic duty to beat up Verwoerd's assassin![72] Bloomberg never revealed their names, but what he did though was attribute Tsafendas's injuries to an unnamed individual, thus absolving the police of blame.

Advocate George Bizos and Professor John Dugard believe that it was impossible at that time for an outsider to walk into the high-security section of a police station and beat up a prisoner, especially the man who had just assassinated the Prime Minister. Both men believe the story to be a lie.[73] As for Bloomberg, he demonstrated an extraordinary naivety in accepting such a story, assuming that he genuinely believed it, at a time when the police were well known to do violence to inmates in prisons and police stations. More important from Tsafendas's point of view, Bloomberg again failed to protest about Tsafendas's injuries or appoint a doctor to examine and treat him. Instead, he approached Dr Isaac Sakinofsky, after learning that he had examined Tsafendas only hours after the assassination and diagnosed him as deluded and not of sound mind. Bloomberg asked the doctor to examine his mental state again for the defence.

In the course of their consultations, Tsafendas told Bloomberg that he had applied for a disability grant and that he had been diagnosed as schizophrenic. He omitted the fact that he had been medically examined on ten other occasions since returning to South Africa and was found to be sane and healthy. Bloomberg confirmed from records at the Department of Social Welfare that Tsafendas was examined for ten minutes by the district surgeon of Cape Town, Dr Ralph Kossew, who, like Sakinofsky, had also examined him on the evening of the assassination. Bloomberg asked Dr Kossew to testify for the defence with regard to these two encounters with Tsafendas.[74]

At the same time, the state appointed Jacobus Erasmus, a clinical psychologist at Weskoppies Hospital in Pretoria, to examine Tsafendas. Erasmus carried out a series of psychological tests on him on 28 and 29 September and testified on Tsafendas's summary trial that the tests indicated 'clear signs of schizophrenia'.[75]

Dr MacGregor was the first of the defence psychiatrists to examine Tsafendas, which he did in Bloomberg's presence on 29 September. Tsafendas responded to the doctor in much the same way as he did with his appointed lawyers. An hour and a half later, Dr MacGregor declared that he had no doubt Tsafendas was mentally disordered, but said he needed to see him again before he could offer a final opinion. Further 90-minute consultations took place on 4 and 11 October in the presence of Dr Zabow and Dr Cooper. Aware that his only information about Tsafendas came from Tsafendas himself, Dr MacGregor said he needed additional information about the accused from other independent sources. However, he was told this was not possible due to lack of time and the reluctance of the police to provide further information about the accused. Dr MacGregor thereupon confirmed his original opinion that Tsafendas was schizophrenic, based on what he had heard from the accused.[76] Tsafendas enjoyed talking to the 'Scottish' doctor; he said he liked his style and thought he was good man.[77]

The second defence psychiatrist to examine Tsafendas was Dr Zabow, first on 30 September with Bloomberg present, then on his own on 4 October and finally with the other psychiatrists on 11 October, with each consultation lasting 90 minutes. Dr Zabow, too, asked for third-party information about Tsafendas, but he did not receive any. Thus he based his diagnosis of schizophrenia on what he was told by Tsafendas himself, which, like Dr

MacGregor, he took at face value.[78] Tsafendas also became fond of Dr Zabow and thought he was a kind and good man.[79]

Dr Cooper was the third to examine Tsafendas, the first time in the presence of Bloomberg on 1 October. Dr Cooper concluded immediately that Tsafendas was a schizophrenic, but asked to see him more times to be sure. Wanting to know more about Tsafendas's background, his medical history and his movements shortly before the assassination, he contacted the police. However, the answer he received was that it was the job of the police to find out more about Tsafendas's past; he was told that his responsibility was to assess his state of mind at the present time, not at the time of the assassination. He was assured by both the police and the defence lawyers that this was a straightforward case of a schizophrenic with a long history of mental illness that his medical records, which they were about to receive, would confirm. Dr Cooper had serious misgivings about all this and suspected that the police wanted an insanity declaration to cover up their security failures, including allowing Tsafendas to get so close to Verwoerd.[80]

Nevertheless, Dr Cooper examined Tsafendas again on 4 October, then again on 11 October along with the two other defence psychiatrists, and a final time on 14 October. In all, he spent six hours with Tsafendas and without any third-party information about him, he maintained his diagnosis of schizophrenia. The opinion was based entirely on what he heard from Tsafendas, which he had no opportunity to cross-check.[81] One oddity about the examination process was that all three psychiatrists examined Tsafendas for the second time on 4 October, each on his own. He was also seen that day by the state psychiatrist, Professor van Wyk.[82] Each examination lasted 90 minutes, thus, for six hours Tsafendas had to go over the same areas and answer similar or identical questions. Upon being informed by his defence team that they would plead insanity on his behalf, Tsafendas shrugged and said, 'Well, you just do whatever you think is best.'[83]

Dr Sakinofsky, for his part, moved quickly on his own to find information on Tsafendas's medical past. Assuming he would be required to testify as a medical witness because he had examined Verwoerd's assassin on the evening of the assassination, he contacted the medical director of the Ochsenzoll Krankenhaus Hospital in Hamburg and asked him to send the hospital's account of its dealings with Tsafendas. The hospital sent its record, with a diagnosis of *'endogenous depression, mixed-picture'* by Dr Nachtwey,[84] on 3 October, and copies were given to Attorney-General van den Bergh and to the police. Dr Sakinofsky also telephoned Judge Beyers inquiring about his own 6 September report on Tsafendas. The judge referred him to the office of the Attorney-General, from where he learnt that 'his evidence had been allocated to the defence'. Subsequently, he was asked by Bloomberg to examine Tsafendas again, which he did on 6 and 14 October.[85]

According to the remand order made by Chief Magistrate C. Willman on 8 September Tsafendas appeared on Thursday, 6 October before a specially constituted court in Caledon Square police station. The makeshift courtroom measured some 15 feet by 15 feet and held seven policemen and four reporters, as well as court officers, including Mr Willman, who presided. Also present was Bloomberg, on behalf of Tsafendas (though Wilfrid Cooper was named as defence counsel), and Mr H.C.F. Jacobs, senior prosecutor. Tsafendas was not cuffed and stood with his hands clasped behind his back. He wore a creased brown suit and a white shirt without a tie; he had no waist belt and hitched up his trousers from time to time. At 10.30 am, magistrate Willman was ushered into the room and the proceedings began. Prosecutor Jacobs stated that a preparatory examination had been opened against Tsafendas on 9 September 1966 and now asked that the accused be remitted for trial. He said an indictment had been served on Tsafendas and that Wilfrid Cooper had been informed of today's proceedings.[86]

Addressing Tsafendas, Willman said he was being held for summary trial and would remain in the police station cells. Speaking publicly for the only time, leaning forward slightly, Tsafendas said, 'My lord, I do not understand the word summary.' Willman replied, 'It means that you will be tried without preparatory examination.' Tsafendas responded, 'Yes, my lord.' Tsafendas was remanded for summary trial on 17 October at the Criminal Sessions, Cape Town, on a charge of murder. The hearing lasted four minutes and fifty seconds. With policemen holding onto his jacket sleeves, Tsafendas was escorted across a narrow passage to a lift to the cells.[87]

Later that day, at Dr Sakinofsky's request, Tsafendas underwent an electroencephalogram (EEG) at Groote Schuur Hospital. An EEG detects electrical activity in the brain and assists in the diagnosis of conditions such as seizures, epilepsy, brain tumours and the like. Tsafendas's EEG was perfectly normal. Sakinofsky saw Tsafendas again on 14 October, after which he reaffirmed his original diagnosis that he was schizophrenic.[88] On a personal level, Tsafendas became very fond of Dr Sakinofsky. The doctor was just 30 years old and Tsafendas found him to be a 'very kind, good and intelligent boy'. Tsafendas felt bad about lying to convince him he was insane, but he knew he had no choice.[89]

The last doctor Bloomberg chose for the defence was Dr Hendrik Muller, a specialist physician who was also Judge Beyers's doctor; he knew the judge was unlikely to question his findings. The particular task allotted to Dr Muller was to ascertain whether Tsafendas could really be harbouring a tapeworm.

Muller saw Tsafendas on 12 October, but did not physically examine him, having concluded from their discussions that the tapeworm was a delusion.[90]

The last medical specialist to examine Tsafendas was Reyner van Zyl, the psychologist. As with the psychiatrists, Van Zyl was briefed verbally by the defence team and the police about Tsafendas's past and his long history of what appeared to be schizophrenia. Van Zyl said:

> *We were told, or I was told, the group of guys that examined him, that he had been in various mental hospitals all over the world ... we were given this information, that he was a disturbed, schizophrenic man. And that was the background that we had available, and nothing else. The third part [the medical reports] was given to us almost in summary: He has been to this hospital, that hospital, that hospital ... I think three or four were mentioned, various hospitals overseas.*[91]

Van Zyl examined Tsafendas twice on 13 October, first for two hours, then for 90 minutes. He also presented Tsafendas with a series of psychological tests similar to those of Erasmus earlier. Van Zyl concluded that Tsafendas was schizophrenic, but that his intelligence resulted in his schizophrenia not being as 'florid' as was often seen in mental hospitals. Tsafendas rated the psychological tests as 'childish stuff' and sometimes he struggled not to laugh at the nonsense he was talking and which the doctors were taking seriously.[92]

The many hours that Tsafendas spent with the psychiatrists and the psychologists were a welcome intellectual break from the boredom of incarceration. Besides, he was getting three meals a day and was allowed to have a shower regularly. Above all, the torture sessions ended, or at least were suspended. As for the interaction with his examiners, Tsafendas found it easy to convince the medics that he was insane, even easier than other times. He got the impression that he was pushing at an open door, that his examiners were actually keen to find him insane. There were times, Tsafendas thought, when the psychiatrists could have cornered him with tough questions, but they seemed to avoid such possibilities and accepted what he told them. The problem for the psychiatrists was that they had no access to information about Tsafendas except what he chose to tell them. Tsafendas's favourite medic was Dr Sakinofsky, who, though younger than the rest, appeared the more professional. He also received the impression that Sakinofsky wanted to protect him and at least save him from the gallows.[93] He was surprised by the comparative lack of professional experience of his examiners. Van Zyl, Erasmus, Dr Zabow and Dr Sakinofsky were all in their early thirties and had very little, if any, practice in examining serious criminals.

Meanwhile, Bloomberg and his assistants were contacting hospitals in Europe and the United States in search of any medical records pertaining to Tsafendas. With the 17 October trial date looming ever closer and restricted by the limited technology of the time, the researchers managed to track down at least four hospitals. They also located several people from various walks of life who knew their client. However, because their names were on the state's witness list, the defence could not consult them without the state's permission and this was refused by Attorney-General van den Berg. The defence took their case to Judge Beyers, who gave the lawyers permission to speak to witnesses on the state's list, and this the defence proceeded to do.[94]

However, any elation Bloomberg may have experienced at this victory swiftly disappeared when he spoke to the witnesses. Confidently expecting them to support the defence's line that Tsafendas was a lunatic, he found instead that none of them considered Tsafendas to be out of his mind; no one had heard him talking the way he did with the lawyers and the psychiatrists and, importantly, no one had ever heard him talk about a tapeworm. When Nick Vlachopoulos, Tsafendas's brother-in-law, called to enquire about the case, he was told he would not be needed. There was no explanation, but the other family members were also removed from the list of defence witnesses, evidently because of the testimony they gave to the police supporting Tsafendas's sanity and declaring no knowledge of a tapeworm. Certainly, it would have sounded strange in court to hear that his family knew nothing of a tapeworm that had supposedly dominated their half-brother's life since he was a child. Non-family witnesses who testified to the same effect were also crossed off.[95]

Then came Patrick O'Ryan, Tsafendas's best friend, who, when asked by advocate Cooper if he knew about the tapeworm, hesitated. Of course, he knew all about the tapeworm. Tsafendas had told him he claimed to have a tapeworm in the past to stop the Portuguese police from torturing him. But what did this lawyer know about the tapeworm? Was he suggesting that Tsafendas really believed he had a tapeworm or was his good friend pretending to be mad again to escape from his predicament? Aware of the gravity of the situation, O'Ryan decided to move cautiously in order to not harm his friend. 'Yes, I know about it ...' he told Cooper slowly. The lawyer could not hide the relief that spread over his features.[96]

O'Ryan was the only person out of 50–60 potential witnesses interviewed by the defence lawyers who had heard Tsafendas mention such a creature. Cooper told O'Ryan flatly, 'You have to mention this in the court. It is the only way to get him free.' Without even asking O'Ryan what he knew about the tapeworm, he said he must highlight to the court the importance of the tapeworm in Tsafendas's life. O'Ryan then understood that Tsafendas had indeed used the tapeworm to pretend insanity. Cooper, in fact, asked O'Ryan to 'exaggerate' some stories and incidents about Tsafendas, so as prove he was insane.[97]

A deeply religious man, O'Ryan felt uncomfortable about lying under oath. He knew that Tsafendas did not really believe he had a tapeworm, but he agreed without hesitation to testify as Cooper asked, in order to save his friend's life. However, there was one problem. When questioned by the police on 17 September, O'Ryan had testified that Tsafendas 'was not spiritually or mentally disturbed ...' More importantly, he had not mentioned the tapeworm in his lengthy statement. Cooper acknowledged the difficulties this statement could cause O'Ryan, but the defence was desperate to have someone confirm the existence of the tapeworm and O'Ryan was the only one who could do so. They decided to call him as a witness in the hope that his testimony to the police might not be brought up or might be somehow glossed over.

In selecting their list of defence witnesses, Bloomberg and Cooper named only nine from the many they had interviewed. These were: Peter Daniels, Helen Daniels's brother, and his wife Merle Daniels, Patrick O'Ryan and his wife Louisa, Gerald Shaw, James Johnston, Owen Smorenberg, Gillian Lieberman and Gideon Cloete. The line-up demonstrated the desperation of the defence team. None of these witnesses, with the exception of O'Ryan and his wife, knew Tsafendas well, but each was seen as being able to support a specific part of the defence strategy.

At first glance, the strangest choice for a witness was James Johnston, a preacher in the Christian Church. Johnston had told the police, 'I do not know Tsafendas very well and the longest discussion I had with him was for about ten minutes on each occasion.' They had met a few times but had spoken only twice, thus, a man who had talked with Tsafendas for 20 minutes in his entire life was called to testify, while people who had known him for years or lived in the same house with him for months were rejected. A closer look at his statement to the police indicates why Johnston was chosen. He had stated in his statement, 'I did think Tsafendas to be slightly unbalanced and that he seemed to have a mysterious background, but otherwise he appeared to be all right.'[98] This was the closest statement the defence found that cast doubts about Tsafendas's sanity.

Assured by the opinions of the defence psychiatrists that Tsafendas was schizophrenic, Bloomberg and Cooper met with the prosecutor, Attorney-General van den Berg, and stated that insanity would be the main plank of their defence. Van den Berg acknowledged that Tsafendas had many strange ways and beliefs, but he did not accept that he was insane or so mentally impaired that he could not understand court proceedings and instruct his lawyers accordingly. To back this up, he gave the defence lawyers a copy of a report by Professor van Wyk, the state psychiatrist he had personally appointed to examine Tsafendas. That Van Wyk had already examined Tsafendas three times surprised the lawyers because they were not aware of it and the examinations had taken place without their consent.

Professor van Wyk's report read:

> *He is orientated. He gives a good account of himself. His comprehension is good and his answers are relevant. His emotional responses are adequate and apt. His discourse is coherent. At times he is discursive, but not vague and he never strays from the main point of conversation. The tests indicate that his intellectual abilities are above average. He maintains that he is infested with a tapeworm, and that this influences his life. He denies that he suffers from hallucinations. I have found no indications that he is incapable of following the court proceedings or that he is unable to exercise his rights and privileges and instruct his legal advisers and assist them in the conduct of his defence.*[99]

Bloomberg and Cooper wondered whether their three psychiatrists and Professor van Wyk had examined the same man. What was more surprising about Van Wyk's report was the reference to the tests and Tsafendas's intellectual abilities. However, Erasmus, who carried out the tests, although he confirmed in the court the result about Tsafendas's abilities, also said that he had found 'clear signs of schizophrenia'.[100] Such information is absent from Van Wyk's report, despite the fact that Erasmus must had given him his results since they were co-operating state witnesses and he was appointed to complement and support the psychiatrist's diagnosis.

Greater surprises were to come, with Professor van Wyk changing his mind within ten days of his first examinations. After examining Tsafendas on 4 October, he 'definitely decided' that Tsafendas was schizophrenic.[101] The Attorney-General must have been aware of Van Wyk's new diagnosis when he met Bloomberg and Cooper after the 6 October hearing. Also, Jacobus Erasmus, the psychologist appointed by the Attorney-General himself, after his examination of Tsafendas on 28 and 29 September, concluded that there were 'clear signs of schizophrenia', which makes the Attorney-General 's contention in his meeting with the defence that Tsafendas was sane appear absurd. The only explanation might be that he was not aware of his two experts' findings.

Five days before 'The Trial of the Century' as it was being hailed by the press, two assessors were named to sit with Justice Beyers – a psychiatrist, Dr P.H. Henning, medical superintendent of the Fort Napier Hospital in Maritzburg, and an advocate, Peter William Edward Baker, a senior counsel from Cape

Town. Presenting the state's case would be Cape Attorney-General Willem van den Berg, assisted by Donald B. Brunette.[102]

Outside of the courts, the assassination was taking its place in popular culture, replayed and bowdlerised with little decorum. Youngsters play-acting with knives, yelled at each other, 'I'll Demitrio you' or 'I'll Tsafendas you!' A much-quoted joke in reference to Tsafendas's employment in Parliament was set in heaven, where St Peter asks Dr Verwoerd upon his arrival, 'How did you get here?' and he replies, 'A messenger sent me.' There was also a 'knock-knock' joke which signalled that Dr Verwoerd was already becoming history:

> 'Knock, knock.'
>
> 'Who's there?'
>
> 'Hendrick.'
>
> 'Hendrick who?'
>
> 'Have you forgotten already?'[103]

Chapter 12

A Verdict is Arranged

The assassination had a devastating effect on Tsafandas's family, both emotionally and practically, prompting anger, bitterness and accusations that he ruined their lives and careers. Half-brother Victor Tsafantakis claimed he never received a promotion he was due from his employers, Iscor in Pretoria, because of his link to Tsafendas, and half-sister Katerina Pnefma experienced endless bureaucratic difficulties in seeking to relocate from Rhodesia to South Africa. There was worse: finger-pointing, whispering, rejection, insults, even physical attacks. Perhaps the angriest sibling was Katerina:

> *It took another twelve years before our application to reside permanently in South Africa was accepted. We had to hire lawyers and appeal several times. We spent a fortune … He [Tsafendas] had ruined my life. I knew he had the moment I heard about it [the assassination]. I knew the destruction he had caused us. We had to be protected from reporters. My sister-in-law – my brother's wife – and my two sisters at their businesses, the Afrikaans people would come and spit at them. Their houses, their windows were broken. They used to throw stones. We suffered an enormous amount. I lived in a small town and people would turn around to see me, to look at me, because I was Tsafendas's sister … I had this community, in which I was very high up in business, and we knew the whole little town, in which, of course, after that, I never felt the same. And, as I said before, we never went anywhere, anyway. And, after that, we were all stigmatised. My sister, Michalis's mother, also never went anywhere. My poor sister that is now alone, she also … none of us, we were all totally destroyed. From then on my brother's career was at a stop. He never went higher; he remained as he was. So he destroyed my brother's career. He destroyed us as a family, because wherever we went, they knew who we were.*[1]

Although the family sought to distance themselves as far as possible from Tsafendas, they followed his case closely, buying all the English-language daily papers and listening to the radio constantly. The police and Tsafendas's defence team advised that their presence at court would not be necessary, but Nick Vlachopoulos and his sister Fotini Gavasiadis held the view that some of the family should attend. They quoted two reasons: to provide some moral support for Tsafendas and just to see and remember him since they were certain he would be executed. Vlachopoulos suggested that he and Marika should go, but Tsafendas's stepmother refused. She had blamed her late husband for leading Dimitri astray and poisoning his mind with politics. 'Where is he now [Michalis],' she asked sarcastically, 'to see his much beloved's [Dimitri's] *achievement*?'[2] Marika was not alone. Pnefma and her siblings also blamed their father for politicising Dimitri in a way that led to his killing of Verwoerd: 'You can't imagine how many people had told my poor father to do something with him and his crazy political ideas. You can't imagine how many! Even my poor mother told him to talk to him because he would get us into trouble someday, as he was often doing, but my dad did nothing. It was actually all his fault. He taught him all these things, but my father was a cautious man, he was not like Dimitri; he wouldn't go around saying all these stupidities. His son was the opposite; he couldn't keep his mouth shut ...'[3]

Constantly wailing 'Oh my God, he has ruined us, he has ruined us all,' Marika would nevertheless pray for Dimitri every night, as did the others. Vlachopoulos, however, argued that Dimitri 'was not a common criminal' and they should not be ashamed of him because the assassination was a political act, that Tsafendas was 'a freedom fighter and a political prisoner'. Vlachopoulos made it clear that while he personally did not agree with the assassination, he believed Tsafendas was correct when he referred to Verwoerd as a tyrant and a dictator, adding that the majority of South Africans, that is, the black population, applauded the act. Hearing these remarks, Marika crossed her breast again and fanned herself furiously, saying, 'I'm not well, I'm going to faint.' The fan she used was one that Tsafendas had sent from somewhere in Europe. Eleni gestured to her husband to stop talking.[4]

Vlachopoulos tried to change Marika's mind, but she remained unmoved and launched into a litany of the disasters that would now befall them: their lives would never be the same again, everyone knew who they were, there would be whispers wherever they went, their businesses would suffer and they might even have to leave Africa and go and live in Greece. Although before the assassination, Marika always referred to Dimitri as her son, he had now become her stepson and it was all her late husband's fault for making him a communist and an anarchist. For Marika, anarchism and Communism were the same. What angered her in particular was that Dimitri had lied to her in Lourenço Marques when he said he was no longer a communist, that he wanted to settle down and that he was not going to get involved again in politics. He had 'betrayed her trust', she said and she was never going to forgive him for this. She said she would never have brought him to South Africa if she knew that he still held the same old political ideas.[5]

Evangelia and Victor agreed totally with their mother. Dimitri now was no longer their brother, but a half-brother with an African mother and they did not want to see him again. Eleni was softer, worried about Dimitri's future not about what people might say, but she, too, thought that none of their family should go to the court. However, when Vlachopoulos suggested that he should go to Cape Town for the trial, she reluctantly agreed. Nick's decision provoked furious opposition from Marika, Victor and Evangelia, who argued that if Nick was recognised his presence would be taken as a sign of their support for Dimitri.

For his cause, Vlachopoulos found an unexpected ally in Charles Nissiotis, Evangelia's husband, who had always liked Tsafendas. He had known him in the early 1940s in Johannesburg and then in Pretoria in 1963–64. Their friendship would have been even closer were it not that Evangelia did not get along well with her half-brother. Charles gave his views for the first time during a heated argument in his own house. He said that Vlachopoulos was right and that someone should go to the court. Stressing that he did not condone Tsafendas's action, he reminded everyone that, like it or not, Dimitri was part of the family, that he was a good and generous man and that what he did, he did for the public good and not for himself. Shocked by his words, Marika crossed herself many times and cried, 'Help me God, what else will I hear, the poor woman!' Nissiotis then carefully pointed out that Marika and her children had been constantly talking about what would happen to them, but no one had mentioned what was going to happen to Dimitri. This observation seemed to strike a chord. Eleni cried, 'Oh, Mimako,' using his childhood diminutive, 'why did you have to do such a terrible thing?' Marika looked heavenwards and whispered, 'Please help him God.'[6]

Nissiotis said he would go to the trial whether the family liked it or not. Not only did he want Tsafendas to see someone from his family in the courtroom, but he wanted his brother-in-law to see him, Charles, in person and know that he had not forgotten him and that he was there for him at this dreadful time. Nissiotis wept while he said this, convinced, despite his hopes, that his friend would be hanged and seeing him in court would be the last time. Thus, he and Vlachopoulos decided to go to Cape Town for their brother-in-law's trial, starting on 17 October. They arranged to arrive a day early and to be back in Pretoria on 20 October. They could not have stayed any longer as the Tsafantakis family was required to give evidence to the Commission of Enquiry into Verwoerd's death on 21 October in Pretoria.[7]

At 10.03 am on Monday, 17 October 1966, Judge Beyers entered Court No. 1 of the Supreme Court building in Cape Town, and Tsafendas's summary trial began. The court, the biggest available, was packed with 300 spectators. Forty reporters from South African and foreign newspapers sat at specially erected tables and even occupied the jury box, which would not be needed for the trial. Flanking the judge were the two assessors and opposite and below him, in the dock, stood Tsafendas, hands behind his back, wearing a double-breasted suit, a light-coloured shirt and a maroon tie. He had been brought to the court from Caledon Square earlier that morning.[8]

Attorney-General Willem van den Berg stood ready to lead the case for the state, while advocate Wilfrid Cooper and his junior, Willie Burger, occupied the defence lawyers' seats along with their instructing senior, David Bloomberg. The court building was situated only a few hundred yards from Parliament, where Verwoerd had died 41 days earlier, and security was total. Inside the courtroom, plain-clothed police officers lined the walls and guarded both entrances, while reinforcements surrounded the building outside and police marksmen occupied strategic positions on nearby rooftops. Hundreds of spectators, both men and women, mostly white, jostled in Keerom Street, having failed to gain entrance to the court, and press photographers mingled with the crowd. The precautions were the most stringent for any case heard at the court and lasted for the duration of proceedings.

Among the spectators were Nick Vlachopoulos and Charles Nissiotis. They had flown in the previous day and were staying at a friend's house. They agreed that while in Cape Town they would make no contact with the family in Pretoria. They did not want the police to know they were attending the trial and they feared the family's phones might be bugged. Since neither man had the Tsafendas family surname, they felt sure their presence would go unnoticed. There were other Greeks at the trial, but almost certainly, they did not know Tsafendas or anyone else in the city. They were there simply out of curiosity. Vlachopoulos and Nissiotis were convinced that at some point in the proceedings, Tsafendas would deliver a political manifesto characterising Verwoerd as a tyrant and dictator and as Hitler's best student, and would therefore be sentenced to death. They got seats in the middle of the crowded courtroom where it was almost impossible for Tsafendas to notice them. This could only possibly happen if they stood up while everyone else was seated and Vlachopoulos attempted on a few occasions to make eye contact with Tsafendas, but his brother-in-law did not look in his direction. Both men wanted to make Tsafendas aware of their presence, but that turned out to be impossible.[9]

When the case was called, Advocate Cooper rose and, addressing the judge, said that, in the view of the defence, the accused was mentally disordered in terms of Section 28 of the Mental Disorders Act of 1916 and was therefore unfit to plead. The relevant section states that 'if a court finds a person to be mentally disordered, he must be committed for detention in a mental institution until the State President orders his release'.[10] The advocate reminded the judge that according to the Act, a person was mentally disordered if he was incapable of managing himself or his affairs, or was a danger to himself or others. He then stressed that the Act referred to the mental condition of the accused at the time of his arraignment or during his trial, that being 17 October; the court should not be concerned with his mental condition at the time of the alleged offence. Cooper said, 'This, my Lord, is on the basis that this court cannot and will not try an insane person, irrespective of his culpability. I accordingly apply to your Lordship at this stage to hold an enquiry into the accused's mental condition.' [11] Attorney-General van den Berg raised no objection and the judge ruled that such an enquiry would now take place, a process described by David Bloomberg as, in effect, 'a trial within a trial'.[12] Advocate Cooper said the defence would offer evidence that Tsafendas was suffering from schizophrenia and was mentally disordered. He then called his first witness, Dr Harold Cooper, the psychiatrist.

Dr Cooper testified that, 'I made a diagnosis of schizophrenia on the basis of my interviews with him [Tsafendas], but in order to try and add either supportive or negative evidence towards this diagnosis, I felt it essential to elicit a history from him and try and decide whether the history I obtained from him was consistent with my impression of him suffering from schizophrenia.'[13] What Dr Cooper was saying, in essence, was that he formed his conclusions in the first place on what Tsafendas told him, and that to seek confirming or contrary evidence, he went back and asked his patient himself. Thus, instead of seeking the views of third parties or assessing his patient's medical or criminal records, he based his diagnosis entirely on what Tsafendas told him and had no way of knowing whether what he said was true or not. Although hampered by a shortage of time and a rebarbative attitude by the police, this seemed a haphazard method of forming a diagnosis, particularly in a case of such huge importance.

The most important part of Dr Cooper's testimony was his claim that Tsafendas began to believe he had a tapeworm that controlled his life in 1935 or 1936. The doctor said that Tsafendas spoke to him about it at length and that he 'is quite likely to refer to his tapeworm in his everyday life but not every time he is confronted by anybody, not constantly in conversation'. However, Dr Cooper was unaware that Tsafendas had never spoken about the tapeworm to anyone except Patrick O'Ryan, to whom he had confided the truth of the story. He was also unaware that not one of approximately 200 people questioned by the South African police and the Commission of Enquiry in connection with Verwoerd's death had ever heard Tsafendas talk about a tapeworm. Renowned forensic psychiatrists and forensic psychologists interviewed during the course of research for this book, including Professors Alban Burke, Kirk Heilbrun, Robert Sadoff and Tuviah Zabow, all found it hard to believe that someone who was convinced he harboured a life-controlling tapeworm for 30 years should never mention it to any of his friends or acquaintances. Professor Heilbrun told the author, 'It is exceedingly unlikely that an individual would have a delusion about a controlling tapeworm for thirty years and nobody around him ever heard or noticed anything to that effect.'[14]

Dr Cooper's testimony regarding the assassination was also puzzling. He said that Tsafendas

> *didn't know why he killed the deceased … he knows he did it but he doesn't know why… he was extremely vague in his attempts to explain why he killed Dr Verwoerd. He told me that he had a great deal of difficulty in understand-ing and explaining why he did, but one thing was quite definite, he said the tapeworm was right in the middle of it. I am quoting his words. I asked him whether the tape-worm actually told him to kill Dr Verwoerd. He said: 'No, that is not so.'*

Dr Cooper then said that Tsafendas 'felt that the reasons underlying his killing of Dr Verwoerd were far too complex. He couldn't explain to me why. And then he started talking about frustration, frustration, and the tapeworm, and not holding jobs, and having nowhere to live, and the whole thing became jumbled in his mind.'

In contrast to Dr Cooper's testimony, Tsafendas had given perfectly clear reasons to the police for killing Verwoerd, without any of the complexities or frustrations mentioned by the doctor. He had said specifically that he did not consider the Prime Minister 'to be the real representative of all South Africans' and wanted 'to see a government that will represent all South Africans', that he was 'disgusted with his policies' and that he hoped that by killing him 'a change of policy would take place'. Extraordinarily, this detailed statement was not used by the Attorney-General to challenge the doctor's testimony.

As to the planning and execution of Verwoerd's assassination, Dr Cooper testified that Tsafendas was 'unable to describe how he had planned and carried out the killing'. However, Tsafendas had explained to the police how he planned and carried out the attack in such detail his account covered almost two pages. Again, the Attorney-General, who should have been in possession of Tsafendas's statements to the police, did not use them to challenge Dr Cooper.

Dr Cooper then stated that Tsafendas talked in a disjointed manner, that he was 'unable to function at a reasonable level', that he was 'unable to follow a conversation after fifteen minutes', that he was unable to keep a job for more than two months and that he was 'rather isolated from his surroundings, in the sense that he tends to not make any close friends, nor maintain any close friendships, he does not really concern himself terribly with any intimate relationship and is quite unable to form and maintain any intimate relationships'. Although the police had assembled a wealth of evidence from witnesses describing Tsafendas as being exactly the opposite, the Attorney-General allowed all of Dr Cooper's claims to go unchallenged. For example, the charge that Tsafendas could not hold down a job for more than two months was contradicted by his six months as a teacher of English in Istanbul. Professors Alban Burke, Robert Sadoff and Tuviah Zabow believe it would have been impossible for a man with Tsafendas's reported level of schizophrenia to hold down such a job for such a length of time. Tsafendas also worked for nearly two years as a welder with the British Mining Supply Company in Johannesburg, five months at F.A. Poole Engineering in Pretoria, nine months at his brother-in-law's coffee shop in Pretoria, five to six months as an interpreter at Durban Court, and six months at a tractor factory in Munich. None of his workmates at any of these places saw anything odd about a man taking a job as it became available and many praised Tsafendas for his work and character. The Attorney-General himself wrote in a memorandum on 3 October, 14 days before the trial, that 'for 6 years he worked at the Vulcan Iron Works, General Engineers, as an oxyacetylene electrical welder. According to testimonials from this firm, he had performed his duties in a satisfactory manner. These testimonials were included with his application for permanent residence in South Africa.'[15] Yet in his role as state prosecutor, the Attorney-General did not use his own evidence to question the witness.

The police had numerous statements depicting Tsafendas as a totally different person to the one outlined by Dr Cooper. For example, Gillian Lieberman, personnel secretary at the Marine Diamond Corporation, whose office Tsafendas often visited, told the police: 'I had various discussions with him. I found him intelligent, someone apparently able to reason in conversation.'[16] Ralph Lighton, who worked with Tsafendas for nine to ten weeks at the Marine Diamond Corporation, said in a statement that he 'never got the slightest impression that he was mentally unsound. He had excellent reasoning powers.'[17] J. Willemse, Tsafendas's landlord in 1965, characterised him as a 'sophisticated, friendly and well-spoken man.'[18] None of these, nor several similar statements, were used by the Attorney-General.

Dr Cooper also testified that Tsafendas appeared to be 'unconcerned' about his future and he took this as a sign of schizophrenia. He testified that 'this type of emotional reaction is frequently seen and completely consistent with a diagnosis of schizophrenia'. What the psychiatrist did not know, because he did not have access to the accused's statements, was that Tsafendas had told the police he did not care about what would happen to him. It is clear that fear of the consequences came second to his determination to kill Dr Verwoerd. This could hardly be described as schizophrenia-induced indifference. Many men, confronted with the probability of death, have acted with the sort of equanimity demonstrated by Tsafendas.

Further evidence of Tsafendas's schizophrenia, according to Dr Cooper, were his 'aimless ramblings, wanderings around the world, from one country to another with an apparent inability to find any sort of niche for himself, an inability to adjust himself to any one fixed abode'. However, Tsafendas had not wandered around the world for the sake of it. What the doctor did not know was that Tsafendas was banned from Mozambique and South Africa and that he was constantly persecuted and harassed in Portugal, and further that when he was granted amnesty by the Portuguese government in 1963, he had immediately returned there. There was nothing aimless about Tsafendas's movements. He travelled either to seek a better life or because the countries he passed through were on the way to his destination, many of them as he tried to return to Mozambique illegally from exile. Tsafendas characterised his travel as 'forced globe-trotting' and said he had to live 'like a gypsy' because of the bannings and his persecution in Portugal.

One of the most astonishing claims by Dr Cooper was that Tsafendas was 'unsympathetic' towards 'Coloureds and Natives' and that he wanted to develop 'a new race'. Presumably, Dr Cooper based his 'new race' claim on a misreading, intentional or otherwise, of Tsafendas's theory that racism, wars and conflicts would only be eradicated if all people were the same colour, and there were no nation-states or religions. His claim about a 'new race' was taken out of context, nor was it stated that the race idea was one of three factors he declared necessary to eradicate racism and wars. The theory of a 'new race' to eradicate racism permanently was applauded when it was proposed by Warren Beatty in the 1998 movie, *Bulworth*, but Tsafendas was ridiculed for saying the same thing 32 years earlier.

Questioned by the Attorney-General, Dr Cooper confirmed that Tsafendas told him that history would prove whether he was right or wrong for killing Dr Verwoerd. The psychiatrist commented, 'I don't know what he means. It is a funny sort of answer to give, that history is going to prove whether he is right or wrong.' It is possible that Dr Cooper's failure to understand the obvious meaning of Tsafendas's remark may have had more to do with a wish to avoid its political implications. Tsafendas was well aware that his deed would find only condemnation in South Africa under the current regime, but he believed it would be hailed when apartheid fell. The 'time will tell' observation is one that has been widely used by leaders defending a crucial action or decision. When Fidel Castro went on trial in 1953 for his revolutionary activities against the Cuban dictator, Fulgencio Batista, he concluded his testimony by saying, 'History will absolve me.'[19] The British Prime Minister Tony Blair and the American President George W. Bush both said, 'History will judge' when criticised for their decision to go to war against Iraq in 2003.[20] They were not considered to be schizophrenic and nor was their sanity questioned. Tsafendas, too, believed he had done the right thing and that history would justify him. In his 19 September statement to Rossouw, he said that he killed Dr Verwoerd because he 'believed it was the right thing to do'.[21]

Dr Cooper ended his testimony by stating, 'My final assessment of this man's mental condition is that he is suffering from a mental illness known as schizophrenia; that I feel I have good reason to believe that he has been suffering from this mental illness for probably at least 20 years, and that this mental illness is of such a degree as to make him certifiably mentally disordered in terms of the Mental Disorders Act.'

The Attorney-General then launched into what appeared to be a vigorous attempt to challenge Dr Cooper's testimony, something he did not do with any subsequent witness. However, his questions were mostly irrelevant and often led nowhere. Sometimes, he managed to do a disservice to his own arguments. What seemed evident was that Van den Berg was either incompetent or he did not have access to evidence gathered by the police.

Most astonishing was his attempt to challenge Dr Cooper's belief that the killing was not politically motivated. Van den Berg claimed that Tsafendas had given political reasons for killing Dr Verwoerd. However, instead of using Tsafendas's statements to the police, which gave logical political reasons for his act and which could easily overturn Dr Cooper's argument, he used a report produced by Dr Sakinofsky. In this, Sakinofsky stated clearly that he had found Tsafendas to be a schizophrenic based on what was told by him. That consisted of ideas which purported to be political but which were obviously not those of a sane man and were far from Tsafendas's real political ideas. Van den Berg's move was to further reinforce the idea of Tsafendas as a schizophrenic, but, perhaps more importantly, to signal that he did not have any clear political thought. The damage the Attorney-General was doing to his argument could have been bigger, but he was stopped by Judge Beyers from proceeding further with the report.

In the defence's view, however, the judge himself had been overly aggressive in his questioning of Dr Cooper. He referred to schizophrenia derisively as 'skyzophrenia' and at one point asked the psychiatrist, 'Does he know he's being tried for murder and does he know that for murder he can swing?' Fearing that they were facing a belligerent judge, advocates Cooper and Burger saw Beyers in chambers and complained that he was creating an impression of being hostile to the defence. According to Cooper, the judge replied gruffly that he did not accept that as a judge, he could not enter the arena. However, Cooper said, there were no further acerbic exchanges.

Vlachopoulos and Nissiotis were stunned by the day's proceedings. No political manifesto was delivered by Tsafendas, there was no denunciation of

Verwoerd as tyrant and dictator, even the words 'communist' and 'Communism' were never uttered. Often the pair gave each other sidelong looks of surprise, but they were both so absorbed by what they heard that they hardly spoke throughout the whole day. Whenever they did, they used English as they did not want anyone to realise they were Greek. Their immediate joint conclusion was that Tsafendas had lied to the doctors. They knew him well – he did not talk in a disjointed manner, he was more than capable of following a conversation for more than 15 minutes and, above all, they knew he was perfectly sane. Their only question was how he made up the story about the tapeworm. Some things, especially hearing Dr Cooper recite Tsafendas's alleged words, would have made them laugh had the circumstances been different. Depressed and pessimistic before the trial, the two men found their mood was changing. By now, they believed that Dimitri was going to pull it off and escape execution by pretending to be insane. Vlachopoulos admitted later to being a little disappointed that Tsafendas would not claim responsibility for his act, but Nissiotis said he would have done the same. The men were desperate to call their wives in Pretoria and tell them the news, but they stuck to their no-contact plan. Anyway, the family would hear the news on the radio and in the newspapers soon enough.[22]

Nissiotis and Vlachopoulos were not the only ones sympathetic towards Tsafendas in the court that day. When proceedings ended, cleaners found a middle-aged, soft-spoken, neatly dressed white woman, sitting in the dock opposite the bench which Tsafendas had occupied just hours earlier. The cleaners asked her to leave, but she refused, saying she was praying for the accused. Around 5 pm, a court official spoke to the woman and she said that Tsafendas needed prayer and love. She asked the official to hand to the accused's defence team a book she was carrying. Its title was *Love Can Open Prison Doors.*[23]

Headlines across the world after the first day of the trial were that Dr Verwoerd's assassin believed he had a tapeworm that was responsible for the killing. Even though Dr Cooper quoted Tsafendas as saying specifically that the tapeworm did *not* tell him to kill Dr Verwoerd, the widespread perception of the time was that this was the case. Most surprised of all were Tsafendas's family. Marika and Dimitri's siblings and in-laws were astonished to learn about Dr Cooper's testimony. Marika, crossing herself many times as usual, asked her children if she had heard correctly. The family immediately said that Tsafendas said all this to Dr Cooper to pretend he was insane and to escape the death penalty. The person worst affected by Tsafendas's arrest was his half-sister Katerina in Rhodesia. She had not left her house and spoke to no one in the neighbourhood except her husband, Gerry Pnefma, and barely to him. She had talked by telephone to her family in Pretoria but only twice or thrice since 6 September and her house was as quiet as a cemetery. They bought no newspapers and did not listen to the radio.[24]

The day after the trial opened, Gerry Pnefma returned to his house less than an hour after leaving for work. Katerina was surprised but assumed he had forgotten something. She was aware that the trial had started the previous day, but she did not want to hear about it, fearing it would bring more pain and embarrassment. She knew what her half-brother would tell the court about Dr Verwoerd; she had heard it so many times. Like the rest of the family, she expected the trial judge would hear him voice his political manifesto.

'Bushia, Bushia,' her husband shouted excitedly, using his wife's pet name, out of breath and waving a newspaper. 'Come see what he said, Bushia,' he shouted. Reading the front-page headline, Katerina put her hand to her mouth in surprise. Speed-reading the story, she began giggling, then laughing so hard she could scarcely breathe. 'Read the rest, read the rest' Gerry told her. 'How did he think of it? A tapeworm! A tapeworm? A tapeworm?' Bushia was still laughing, a woman who had not smiled for 41 days. Gerry was curious. 'But does he believe all this?' he asked his wife cautiously. Although he had spent only a few days in his brother-in-law's company, his impression was that Tsafendas was a very intelligent person and thoroughly political. He had never heard any mention of a tapeworm from Tsafendas, Bushia or any other relative and no one had ever raised a question about his sanity. His wife shook her head in disbelief and admiration. 'He was always very, very smart, a devil, but how on earth he thought of this tapeworm story?' Slowly, as her laughter dissipated, a wave of sorrow overwhelmed her – what was going to become of Mimis now. She had been furious with him when he was named as Verwoerd's accused assassin, believing he had ruined her life, but when she read about the tapeworm, she wondered if he had been severely tortured to make up something like that. She had no doubt then and none until she died in 2016, 50 years later, that her half-brother invented the tapeworm to escape the gallows.[25]

Putting down the newspaper, Bushia telephoned her sisters in Pretoria. Their reaction had been the same; everyone in the family had laughed, wondering how Dimitri had come up with such an outrageous idea. When she heard the news,Tsafendas's favourite aunt, Artemis Michaletos, feared the worst for her nephew. Her husband had fled Lourenço Marques to Zambia out of fear that the police might discover he had arranged the bribing of the consulate official for Tsafendas's visa to South Africa. Artemis was in Lourenço Marques when she read about the tapeworm and reacted exactly as had the rest of the family. She later told her husband, 'I knew it, I knew he would find a way not to be hanged.' She was sure now that he would escape execution.[26]

On the second day in court, for Nissiotis and Vlachopoulos, the dread of the first day had been replaced by a surging hope that their brother-in-law would escape the death penalty. However, they were anxious as to what else would be said and what else Dimitri had told the doctors. The first witness of the day was Dr Muller, the personal physician of Judge Beyers, flatly contradicting some of Dr Cooper's testimony from the previous day. According to Dr Muller, Tsafendas was able to understand what was said to him, had no problem communicating with him and was not 'particularly disturbed'. More importantly, Dr Muller contradicted Dr Cooper's beliefs that Tsafendas was not able to hold down a job and unable to follow a conversation after 15 minutes.[27]

Following Dr Muller on the witness stand was Dr Kossew, the district surgeon who examined Tsafendas regarding his disability grant application. The doctor testified that Tsafendas told him that in the house where he lived, people were being murdered by poison in their food. Though he was not a qualified psychiatrist, Dr Kossew testified that he was able to determine, after an examination which lasted 'a little bit longer' than ten minutes, that Tsafendas was a schizophrenic with ideas of a 'per-secutory nature'. He considered him incapable of working in the 'open market' or in 'sheltered employment' and therefore eligible for the disability grant he had applied for. The doctor testified that he had 'no idea' and 'no means' of verifying Tsafendas's statements. He stressed that his responsibility was mostly to make a determination of his physical condition and not his mental state.[28]

What was extraordinary about Dr Kossew's role in the case was that no one raised the fact that Tsafendas had sought a disability grant, having been referred by the Department of Social Welfare. In order to qualify for such a grant, an applicant had to be found 'unable, owing to infirmity of mind or body, to undertake regular work'.[29] This is exactly what happened to Tsafendas; had he been found sane, he would not have qualified for the grant. During the previous two and half years, however, on those occasions when Tsafendas needed to prove he was healthy and sane, all five doctors who examined him found him to be so. Indeed, another five doctors who examined him at various times all had considered him to be fit and healthy. These examinations, just like Dr Kossew's, were known to the police, but were not brought up in court.

Another important fact that apparently went unnoticed was that Tsafendas did not mention the tapeworm during Dr Kossew's examination. The police were also aware that about a year before this examination, Tsafendas had told doctors that he was St Peter. Thus over a period of one and a half years, Tsafendas was apparently suffering from three different delusions, not to mention his claim that in the early 1940s, he heard voices from radiators. These different claims seemed like Tsafendas's flippant choices, but this was not picked up by any expert, including the police, who possessed all his medical files. According to Alban Burke, head of psychology at the University of Johannesburg, to claim two delusions at the same time, or to have delusions coming and going, stretches credulity: 'It's not impossible, because the human brain is difficult to understand, but it is unlikely. It's possible, but it's improbable.'[30] Reyner van Zyl, the psychologist who examined Tsafendas for the defence, agrees that it is next to impossible: 'Yes, one [delusion] may disappear, and the other one may then appear. But two at the same time? I don't think so, because these delusions are usually very powerful.'[31] At the time of Tsafendas's examination by Dr Kossew, he was living at Wilhelmina de Vos's hostel. The fact that he said nothing about poisoned food to any of his friends and kept on living there and eating her food were other important points not raised at the trial.

The third witness of the day was Peter Daniels, Helen's brother, who lied flatly about Tsafendas's relationship with his sister, reversing the roles they played. He claimed that Tsafendas wrote to and pursued Helen, wanting to marry her, and that he was allowed to stay in their house only because it was their Christian duty as members of the same Christian sect.[32] Once again, the Attorney-General failed to point out these departures from the truth. Helen Daniels had told the police in her statement of 15 September that she approached Tsafendas and asked him to marry her: 'I wrote my letter during the June holidays in 1965 and received a reply from him on July 10, 1965. I wrote in my letter that I would like to meet and wanted to marry him. His answer was that he wanted to meet me first before giving me a positive answer. I wrote to him again – four letters – all of which he answered. I sent him a picture, but he did not send me one in return.'[33]

Tsafendas had then travelled to Cape Town from Durban to meet her and was invited to live in her house as her family expected him to marry their daughter. Although Helen had told all this frankly to the police, Van den Berg failed to use her statements to disprove her brother's testimony. Peter Daniels clearly testified as he did to protect his sister's reputation, which would have been destroyed if it became known that she, a minister in their church, had proposed marriage to the man who killed South Africa's Prime Minister.

When asked by advocate Cooper, 'What then is your overall impression that you have of Tsafendas?' Peter Daniels replied, 'Well, my own words at one time were, "this man is mad."' Daniels claimed Tsafendas had many strange habits and described several incidents which made him believe Tsafendas was insane. At seven o'clock one morning, he said, Tsafendas arrived at the house with a parcel of meat, eggs and 'some other victuals', unconcerned that blood was dripping from the meat. This turned out to be 'approximately two to three pounds of T-bone steak', which Tsafendas cooked and ate. There was also chicken and Daniels thought that it was very strange that their guest did not wash the chicken before cooking it. He also found it strange that Tsafendas had such a big meal so early in the day. What Daniels did not mention was that Tsafendas had just returned from working his night shift. What may have looked like breakfast to Daniels was Tsafendas's dinner. Just as when he lived with the O'Ryans, he had his main meal in the morning when he got back from work. As for not washing the chicken, it seems the well-travelled and knowledgeable Tsafendas was aware that it is healthier not to wash a chicken before cooking to avoid the spreading of bacteria from the splashing water.

Other oddities in Daniels's view were Tsafendas not removing his hat during a social visit to a relative, and how 'one hot day he tried to cool the fowls off, which proves to me that he was also mentally deranged'. Advocate Cooper asked, 'How did he try to cool the fowls off?' Daniels replied, 'He got hold of the hosepipe and tried to cool the fowls down, because he thought that they were hot, too.' Loud laughter in the court was interrupted by Judge Beyers who said seriously, 'One does it with fowls when it gets hot. I keep fowls. When it gets very hot, you may have to do it. They die if you don't, sometimes.'

As with Daniels's testimony about his sister, Attorney-General van den Berg failed to push him on Tsafendas's so-called insanity, raising instead a series of aimless questions that offered nothing to the state's case. This failure seemed all the more extraordinary because Helen, who lived under the same roof as Tsafendas and her brother, had told the police that she had not 'noticed anything abnormal about him [Tsafendas]. There was never any indication that he was mentally abnormal'.[34] Unsuitable to support the defence's line, she would have made an excellent witness for the state to break her brother's testimony. Although the Attorney-General did not have the opportunity to question her, he could have used her statement to the police to point to her brother's lies and inaccuracies, but he did not do so. One important statement Peter Daniels made which contradicted Dr Cooper's testimony of the previous day was that Tsafendas wanted 'to be among the Coloured community, make himself a Coloured man' and that he 'preferred to be a non-European'.

After Peter Daniels came Merle, his wife, who said her impression was that: 'By the things that he did and the strange way that he acted sometimes, we felt that he wasn't all there.' What did Tsafendas do to make her feel this way? He sometimes lay on the bed with his shoes on and spoke about 'the different preachers he had met all over the world from the same faith'. Cross-examining her, Donald Brunette, assistant to the Attorney-General, did not seem to find these things very strange. He asked if she thought Tsafendas was 'a bit eccentric?'

Mrs Daniels replied, 'Could you explain that word to me?' 'Well, I mean he did strange things here and there, but it wasn't anything in particular.' Merle insisted that Tsafendas was not eccentric, but definitely strange.[35]

The evidence of the Daniels couple seemed more like a description of Tsafendas's everyday conduct, exaggerated in an attempt to save his life. Patrick and Louisa O'Ryan were urged to do exactly this by advocate Cooper, so it is likely that the Daniels were also asked to do the same thing. Indeed, Patrick O'Ryan was next to take the stand, the fifth witness of the second day, the defence's main witness and the man Cooper relied on to talk about the tapeworm. O'Ryan acknowledged in his testimony that he had taken a 'deep liking' to Tsafendas, that he had 'confidence in him' and considered him a 'very kindly man' with 'a good heart'.[36] As requested by Cooper, he spoke extensively and untruthfully about the tapeworm. However, when asked for his opinion of Tsafendas's mental state, he stated that he 'never actually doubted his mental state'. He could not have testified otherwise as he had made a similar statement to the police. Surprisingly, O'Ryan was never asked how a person claiming to host a massive and voracious tapeworm that controls his life could possibly be sane. However, it was during O'Ryan's testimony that for the first and last time during the proceedings, the Attorney-General made use of evidence collected by the police to challenge a witness's statements. Van den Berg asked him the obvious question, the one which O'Ryan and the defence team most feared: 'Why didn't you mention anything about this worm to the police in your statement?'

O'Ryan panicked. This was his worst nightmare. He had feared he would be asked such a question but advocate Cooper assured him and told him to say that he had indeed mentioned the tapeworm, but the policeman taking his statement had not written it down. Cooper had calculated that it would be impossible to ascertain the truth or otherwise of his witness's statement, since the policeman could not possibly remember everything he had said, especially if he did not record it. O'Ryan had talked for almost an hour and the policeman wrote down only a few of the things he said. Now though, O'Ryan's mind was in turmoil. As a God-fearing Christian, he had never lied before and he began to perspire and wondered if he was going to faint. Eventually, he produced a mumbled answer: 'The police mentioned, number one, that that was not necessary, I must just leave it.'

> 'So you say that you mentioned this worm to the police?' Van den Berg asked him.

'Yes. Not necessary, they mentioned. And I also made a statement about this treatment [Tsafendas's treatment] and the police said it is common in the papers.' His last comment should have made things worse since up until the trial, nothing had been reported in the press about the tapeworm. Fortunately for O'Ryan, Van den Berg failed to pick up on his slip. However, O'Ryan was not out of the woods since Van den Berg had something else in mind. Pointing to a police officer in the first row of the court, he said, 'This gentleman here, Mr Troost, took the statement, not so?'

It was only then that O'Ryan recognised the policeman who had taken his statement. Feeling the perspiration under his collar, O'Ryan moved to take a handkerchief and mop his neck, but then changed his mind, thinking it would be better not to show that he was sweating heavily. He identified Troost as the policeman who had taken his statement. 'That is right.'

> 'So you tell me that you told Mr Troost about this worm?'
>
> 'Yes, I said he mentioned the worm.'
>
> 'And Mr Troost said it was not necessary to make any mention of it?'
>
> Knowing now that he could not continue the lie in front of the policeman, O'Ryan went back to the original excuse advocate Cooper had thought of using, 'No, he just brushed it away.'
>
> 'What exactly did you say to Mr Troost?'
>
> 'I just said he mentioned the worm and also the third degree.'
>
> 'Just give us your exact words that you used to Mr Troost?'
>
> 'Mr Troost spoke to me in the form of questions, which I answered, but in between I mentioned these two things that I noted were not noted.'
>
> 'You told Mr Troost that this man has on many occasions mentioned to you ...'
>
> 'No, no, I did not say on many occasions.'
>
> 'What exactly did you say to Mr Troost?'
>
> 'I said he mentioned a worm, and the brainwashing.'
>
> 'What did Mr Troost say to that?'
>
> 'Well, in writing – he just continued to write and ...'
>
> 'So in spite of the fact that you mentioned something about the worm, he did not take that down in writing?'
>
> 'No.'

> Obviously, O'Ryan was not in position to know what Troost was writing from the things that he was saying, but this question was never raised. Van den Berg then started reading out extracts from O'Ryan's statement to the police, putting O'Ryan in an even more difficult spot: '"His spiritual view seemed confused, but he was not spiritually or mentally disturbed." You said that?'
>
> 'Yes.'
>
> '"I never got the impression that something was wrong in his mind?"'
>
> 'That is correct, yes.'
>
> 'Did you say that?'
>
> 'Yes.'
>
> 'Why then did you not say anything about the worm in the statement?'
>
> O'Ryan had no choice now and could no longer continue claiming that Troost had told him it was not necessary to mention it. 'It was so commonplace, most likely, that I did not want to draw any more attention to it. I only mention it casually.'
>
> 'You said you told Mr Troost?'
>
> 'Casually, yes.'
>
> 'You told him about the worm?'
>
> 'Yes.'

Surprisingly, the subject ended there, without anything else being said about it. Despite his panic, O'Ryan stood his ground and let it sound like he had told the police about the tapeworm, but the policeman did not write it down. Obviously, Van den Berg could not prove otherwise.

Those were not the only lies O'Ryan volunteered to save his friend's life, as he also told the court that he and Tsafendas did not discuss politics. He had been asked by advocate Cooper to make such a claim since it would not help Tsafendas for the court to hear his real beliefs. The truth was Tsafendas had spoken at length and excitedly about politics, expressing his opinion that Dr Verwoerd was a tyrant and 'Hitler's best student', and if he ever got hold of him 'he would bash his skull'.[37] However, O'Ryan was caught out again by the Attorney-General during the cross-examination when he read extracts from his statement to the police. Without disclosing the extent of their discussions, he had mentioned that Tsafendas opposed apartheid and the Portuguese colonialists in Mozambique. Van den Berg asked him: '"He read the newspaper and it was apparent that he was against the state policy of both South Africa and Portugal." Did you say that?'

'Yes.'

'"He made the impression with me that he was favourable towards the Coloureds and he repeatedly applied to be classified as a Coloured." Did you say that?'

'Yes.'

'He labelled the apartheid policies as unfair?'

'Yes.'

'"I did not encourage him, because we advocate the Biblical idea of subservience to a Government." Is that right?'

'Yes.'

O'Ryan also lied that Tsafendas talked in a disjointed way in an attempt to support Dr Cooper's claim that his friend spoke like that. However, this was also caught out by the Attorney-General! He read again from his statement:
'"He was well-spoken and had good vocabulary"?'

'That is right.'

'"I never got the impression that something was wrong in his mind"?'

'That is correct, yes.'

Inexplicably, the Attorney-General did not ask O'Ryan why he told the police that Tsafendas was 'well-spoken and had good vocabulary' when he told the court that he spoke in a disjointed manner.

O'Ryan later said that giving evidence at Tsafendas's trial was the most frightening experience of his life. He felt as if he was walking through the 'fiery furnaces of hell'. He had lied for the first and, as it turned out the last time in his life, and he considered that to be a great sin. However, he did not feel guilty; he believed he had done a good thing and that God understood. Thirty years later, O'Ryan said he had no regrets about lying as he had done it to save his friend's life.[38]

The sixth witness of the day was Louisa O'Ryan, Patrick's wife. Her testimony was the shortest of all. She, too, spoke about the tapeworm, but unlike her husband, she did not lie, as she really believed that Tsafendas had one or thought he had one. She also exposed a discrepancy which went unnoticed.

She testified that Tsafendas had told her he had the tapeworm since he was a small boy and that his stepmother had not dealt with it adequately.[39] However, Dr Cooper had told the court that Tsafendas said to him he had had it since 1935 or 1936; Tsafendas would have been 17 or 18, not a little boy. Tsafendas had also not mentioned his stepmother to Dr Cooper and had attributed it to witchcraft.

Owen Smorenberg, a work colleague of Tsafendas at the Cape Town City Council Power Station, was next, who astonishingly said he 'got the impression' that Tsafendas was a supporter of Verwoerd, Vorster and apartheid, and that he did not like the coloureds,[40] although he had testified to the police earlier that Tsafendas 'never discussed politics with me'.[41] None of the huge amount of indisputable evidence gathered by the South African police which proved Smorenberg's 'impression' totally wrong was used by the Attorney-General to challenge this testimony. Also ignored was the evidence given earlier by Peter Daniels and Patrick O'Ryan, who stated the exact opposite.

Smorenberg was used by the defence to strengthen its claim that the killing was not political because Tsafendas favoured Dr Verwoerd, and that he was simply insane. Smorenberg was well-spotted among some 200 witness by the defence team since he was the only one to get the 'impression' that Tsafendas was an apartheid supporter. Witnesses who formed exactly the opposite impression to Smorenberg were many. They included Jacobus Bornman, who told the police that Tsafendas 'stood up a lot for the Coloureds',[42] Father Hanno Probst, who said he heard Tsafendas 'swearing at the Mozambique government, saying it did nothing for the black people',[43] and Inspector Horacio Ferreira, of the Portuguese Security Police in Mozambique, who testified that Tsafendas was 'intense anti-White' and had told him that 'the Portuguese Government has never done anything for their non-Whites'.[44] Tsafendas himself had admitted to the police in a recorded statement whose transcript was in the Attorney-General 's possession that he had become a member of the British Anti-Apartheid Movement, that he was in 'sympathy with the people fighting racialism' and that he was 'anti-colonial', 'against slavery' and 'against apartheid'.[45] If nothing else, the fact that Tsafendas wanted to be reclassified as coloured instead of white should have been enough to discount Smorenberg's impression. However, none of this evidence was called upon by the Attorney-General and Smorenberg's testimony went unchallenged, to be accepted by the court as reliable.

Smorenberg also testified to some 'odd incidents' involving Tsafendas, though it required some determined prodding by advocate Cooper to focus him on two in particular at work.

> 'Was there any other incident which stands out in your mind as being odd?' the defence counsel asked him.
>
> 'From what point of view?'
>
> 'Just odd incidents. Things that you thought were strange conduct on the part of Tsafendas?'
>
> 'Regarding his conduct?'
>
> 'Yes?'

Smorenberg gave two examples of what he considered to be strange conduct. First, when Tsafendas asked about eight rusted bolts, Smorenberg told him to order new ones; later, he noticed that the old bolts had been put back while the new ones lay to one side. The other incident involved Tsafendas complaining that he had been underpaid by a half-hour. The discrepancy, Smorenberg said, was due to there being a public holiday in the week, Kruger Day on 10 October; when that happened, some overtime payments were delayed until the next payday. Smorenberg said, 'He had great difficulty in understanding why he had to wait an extra week for his money.'

To describe these two incidents as 'strange' is to exaggerate the sort of mishaps and misunderstandings that occur during busy working days everywhere. If Tsafendas, and not someone else, put back the old bolts, it could have been absent-mindedness or momentary lack of concentration. As for the overtime payments, Tsafendas's anxiety about a system which apparently was new to him seems natural. Smorenberg appeared to struggle in court to recall evidence of Tsafendas's strange behaviour and a short time later he contradicted himself by saying he considered Tsafendas's intelligence to be 'perhaps a little bit higher than normal'. As for the two 'strange' incidents, he had mentioned neither in the statement he made to the police less than two weeks earlier.

When asked directly about Tsafendas's mental state by advocate Cooper, Smorenberg replied, 'Well, I wouldn't say he is mad, but he seems a little bit barmy.' This was an opinion that could have been voted down overwhelmingly had other witnesses' evidence been called. What was sad in retrospect was that Smorenberg presented Tsafendas as a man who did not like coloured people and who supported Dr Verwoerd, Vorster and apartheid, and the fact that these claims went unchallenged meant that the world was left with the impression that these were Tsafendas's genuine beliefs, when the exact opposite was true. Finally, Smorenberg told the court that Tsafendas was a 'friendly type of man' who spoke 'fairly freely' to him, thus contradicting testimony by Dr Cooper and other psychiatrists that he was unsociable and withdrawn.

An example of a witness who could have been used by the state to challenge the defence line that Tsafendas had no interest in politics, liked Verwoerd and did not care for coloureds, was Nick Vergos with whom Tsafendas had fought physically at Mandini. Believing that Vergos had 'vital information' regarding Tsafendas, the Chairman of the Commission of Enquiry into Verwoerd's death, Judge J.T. van Wyk, appealed for him to come forward. Six hours later, on 12 October, Vergos, surprisingly and at his own will, walked into the Johannesburg office of the *Rand Daily Mail* and offered to give an interview to the newspaper. Characterised as a 'key witness' by the *Daily Dispatch*[46] and an 'important witness' by the *Cape Times*,[47] Vergos was subsequently questioned by the police and testified before the Commission, but he was not called to give evidence at Tafendas's summary trial.

The reason? His testimony would have contradicted what was heard in Court. Tsafendas and Vergos worked at Fraser and Chalmers, where Vergos had asked his superiors to dismiss Tsafendas because he was 'a kaffir and a Communist',[48] describing him as 'the biggest Communist in the Republic of South Africa'[49] and a 'Communist bastard',[50] even reporting him to a security officer as a 'dangerous communist'.[51] The two had fought over Vergos's refusal to pay two African workers he had employed illegally.[52] All this evidence was in the possession of the South African police. Clearly, Vergos would have been the perfect witness for the state if it really wanted to challenge the defence position.

The eighth defence witness of the day was Dr Sakinofsky, who recalled his examination of Tsafendas on the evening of the killing. He testified that Tsafendas voiced several 'delusional ideas' such as that he was imprisoned by the Portuguese for 14 years and that they had tried to kill him with electric shocks, that Verwoerd was 'in league' with Salazar the Portuguese dictator and that he was also a 'foreigner'.[53] Dr Sakinofsky had no way of knowing that Tsafendas had indeed been submitted to electric-shock torture by the Portuguese on two different occasions, that he was also imprisoned by them for almost three years and that he had to spend another 12 years in exile from Mozambique due to his political activities there. As for calling Verwoerd a 'foreigner', this was no delusion; it was the way Tsafendas referred to the Portuguese in Mozambique and the whites ruling Rhodesia and South Africa. Tsafendas considered these three countries to be 'occupied lands' ruled by 'foreigners' and 'colonialists'. Tsafendas was not referring to the nationality stated in Dr Verwoerd's passport, but to the fact that he was illegally occupying a post in an entity that was illegally ruling a country. Tsafendas, as he told the police, wanted to see a government that would represent South Africans of all colours, not just the whites. He had also told PIDE when they arrested him in 1964 that he wanted 'a Mozambique governed by the natives of that Province, be they white or black, and therefore separated from the mother nation'.[54] Tsafendas was not the only one who saw the white rulers of South Africa as foreigners. Dr Verwoerd, in a speech on 8 February 1961, which might have been entitled, 'How others see us', said, 'There are people who are far away and do not understand us. They see this southern point of Africa only as a white-dominated country in a large continent with over 200 million people who are black. And then they say we do not fit here, we are foreign to the body of Africa.'[55] It is very possible that Tsafendas did not explain his belief in full to Dr Sakinofsky, but the Attorney-General was well aware of Tsafendas's political ideas and what he meant. However, he did not challenge Dr Sakinofsky.

Dr Sakinofsky told the court about other 'delusional ideas' held by Tsafendas, for example, that Dr Verwoerd opposed the British Commonwealth and had been against the idea of a 'Cape to Cairo Union', Cecil Rhodes's plan was to connect adjacent British-ruled territories in Africa through a continuous line from South Africa to Egypt. Dr Sakinofsky was the only person to hear this particular claim and it was obvious that Tafendas was lying. None of the other witnesses and nothing from the vast quantity of additional evidence made any mention of Tsafendas favouring ideas such as a Cape to Cairo Union. On the contrary, he was a committed anti-colonialist and a critic of Britain because of its support of the royalists during the Greek Civil War and its colonial policy in Africa. However, the Attorney-General made no attempt to challenge Dr Sakinofsky's testimony.

The psychiatrist also testified about something he called a 'graphanola', which Tsafendas told him was a 'radio' that was used to torture him. Dr Sakinofsky did not know the word and when he failed to find it in several dictionaries, he concluded that Tsafendas made it up. He argued that this was also a sign of mental ill health because 'some schizophrenics manufacture words'. Clearly, Dr Skinofsky had not explored enough. True, there was no 'graphanola', but there was a 'graphonola' (in English 'grafonola'), a 1907 improved version of the graphophone, itself a prototype of Columbia's original phonograph. Tsafendas likened the wooden box the Portuguese used to torture him with his father's graphophone in Lourenço Marques.[56] Tsafendas was right, as the electric shock equipment used against South African and Portuguese prisoners looked like the graphophones of the 1930s, but presumably ignorant of the equipment, Dr Sakinofsy and the court could hardly envisage it looked 'like a graphophone'. They were also clearly unaware that the 'graphonola'/grafonola' and the 'graphophone' were effectively the same device.

An important part of Dr Sakinofsky's testimony was his claim that Tsafendas did not have any 'passivity feelings' during this first interview. He said, 'A passivity feeling is another very important cardinal feature of schizophrenia, whereby an influence on the patient is interpreted, by the patient, as being due to an external agency. For instance, if a patient believes that his body had been changed by hypnosis or by computers or something like that, or by an enemy, this would be passivity.' Thus Tsafendas did not believe at the time that he had a tapeworm and it obviously made its appearance later while he was in custody. Dr Sakinofsky then testified that Tsafendas told him about the tapeworm during their second interview on 4 October: 'He never said to me that the tapeworm, as one perhaps might have expected, that the tapeworm had told him to kill Dr Verwoerd, but he said that the tapeworm, being a demon inside him, had taken him over, and he remembered another case, when he had blurted out in Lisbon that he was a Protestant, he felt here again the tapeworm was responsible.'

Dr Sakinofsky also made an important recommendation to the court – that, for a criminal case such as this, a forensic psychiatrist to be called to examine Tsafendas. As an independent evaluator and someone with a sophisticated understanding of the interface between mental health and law, a forensic psychiatrist is able to work with law enforcement to determine if a suspect is able to stand trial. However, Dr Sakinofsky's recommendation was ignored.

Finally, Dr Sakinofsky testified that Tsafendas told him he 'couldn't remember what had happened at the time of the killing', that 'I fell on him [Verwoerd], people tell me, and it is probably true, but I don't remember a thing about stabbing him. I could have stabbed him a thousand times without knowing it'; he said it was as if he 'had been hypnotised'. This bit of information was revealed in an interview on 14 October. Twice, just a month earlier, on 11 and 19 September, Tsafendas had described perfectly well to the police how he killed Dr Verwoerd, but also how he planned it. Nothing about being hypnotised or his mind going blank. The Attorney-General did not find it necessary to question the doctor of these discrepancies in Tsafendas's accounts. This was one of the clearest examples of Tsafendas lying to Dr Sakinofsky. The doctor's diagnosis of Tsafendas as schizophrenic was inevitably based on the evidence available to him. Although Dr Sakinofsky conceded that 'in psychiatry, after one has interviewed a patient, it is best practice to seek collateral information from family, friends, and medical records', he was not in possession of any information when making his diagnosis.[57] The single medical record in his possession stated that Tsafendas was diagnosed as suffering from 'mixed – pictured phasic psychose'[58] and not schizophrenia.

The ninth and last witness of the second day was Gillian Claire Lieberman, personnel officer in the Marine Diamond Corporation. She said little about Tsafendas except that he was not happy with the working conditions and that he was 'rather untidy, sloppy'. That was all the defence needed as they were trying to portray Tsafendas as someone unable to look after himself and hold onto a job. Lieberman also testified that Tsafendas seemed 'odd' to her, but she did not elaborate and neither the Attorney-General nor the judge asked what she meant.[59] Leaving the statement hanging gave the impression that Tsafendas was mentally peculiar. Lieberman's statement to the police on 9 October, however, was that she found Tsafendas to be 'intelligent, someone apparently able to reason in conversation, but a strange type of person, a unique character'.[60] She also said she got the impression that Tsafendas did 'not agree with authority [Governmental or other]', but she did not repeat this statement in court and the Attorney-General did not mention it. Although the police had questioned four other colleagues from the Marine Diamond Corporation, all of whom knew Tsafendas better than Lieberman as they worked alongside him, neither their presence nor their statements were used at the trial. Not only had they no complaints about Tsafendas's ability to perform his duties, one had told the police of an incident which demonstrated his calmness and ability to adjust. Carel Sebastiaan van Heerden, the company's senior security officer, told the police of an occasion when 'we were transferred from the marina on a small outboard boat to the Colpontoon. It was terrible, rough seas, so much so that almost all of us old hands got seasick. It struck me that Tsafendas adapted well. He was one of the few who was not seasick. Upon landing, he filled the mess basin on the lower deck with water and started shaving. His calm way struck me that he must know the sea. He was friendly, outgoing, and not aloof. I noticed that his eating was messy. Otherwise, he was completely normal.'[61]

The first witness on the third day of the summary trial was Reyner Johannes van Zyl,[62] the clinical psychologist, who testified that he had organised a series of tests, though at times Tsafendas seemed uninterested in doing them. The tests were: the new South African standardisation of the Wechsler Bellevue Adult Intelligence Test; the Thematic Apperception Personality Test; and the Rorschach Personality Test. Van Zyl explained that the Wechsler Bellevue Adult Intelligence Test was an 'intelligence test consisting of ten sub-tests, and testing different aspects of intelligence'. Tsafendas's results in the tests were the following, where the average score is 10:

Information sub-section: 11.5

Comprehension test: 14.5, 'a very high score,' Van Zyl said.

Arithmetic: 9

Digit span: 12.5

Similarities: 8.5

Picture completion: 13

Object assembly: 10.5

Block design: 10

Digit symbol substitution: 8.5

Picture arrangement: 15.5

Van Zyl then scored Tsafendas as follows: 'Full I.Q. tests at 113.5. His verbal I.Q. tests at 125.00.'

In 1970, Dr Peter Lambley, a British psychologist at the Valkenberg Psychiatric Hospital in Cape Town and for some time a colleague of both Dr Cooper and Van Zyl, followed the case closely. He wrote in his acclaimed 1980 book *The Psychology of Apartheid*:

> *The evidence from the IQ testing indicated a temporal impairment – shown by only two low scores out of ten – rather than a major impairment of functioning. Truly hebephrenic schizophrenics show the reverse: impairment on all but one or two tests. Tsafendas's scores showed him to be withdrawn and cut off – interpreted in court as schizophrenia – but not demented in anything like the degree claimed. Anyone, in fact, any normal-neurotic person in the same frightful and shocking situation, would show the same kind of fall-off in performance. If you took Tsafendas's IQ test results (ten sub-tests) and asked a clinician to evaluate them blind, that is, without knowing who he was, they would say, and I quote: 'Highly intelligent, creative adult male with some personality problems.*[63]

Dr Lambley did in fact give Tsafendas's results to other clinicians to rate blind. He said, 'No one said he was schizophrenic or even severely disturbed. They noted that in some instances, his sub-test results showed an extremely high level of intellectual functioning.'[64]

Van Zyl then spoke about the Rorschach Personality Test, 'a series of ten standardized ink blots which is shown to the patient'. He testified that on the Rorschach Test, Tsafendas 'showed some typical signs of schizophrenia' and that he had 'very poor human contact'. Van Zyl said, 'He showed me eyes where I could not possibly see eyes and a nose and a mouth which were just not there.' This seemed to amuse Judge Beyers. 'Modern paintings?' he enquired, to dutiful smiles around the court.

Fifty years after the trial, in 2016, Van Zyl was given several of the statements taken by the police from people who knew Tsafendas. Upon reading them, he acknowledged that their opinions were diametrically opposed to his diagnosis of 1966, adding that his diagnosis would have been different if he had seen them at the time. He said, 'Yes. Look, obviously, that is important information, and information that influences one's findings in the end. There is no doubt about it.'[65]

Dr Lambley described Van Zyl as inexperienced at the time and not formally trained in the Rorschach Test procedure. He said Van Zyl 'could not formally score an ink blot protocol, his grasp of psychotic signs was superficial, and he was unfamiliar with the research literature pertaining to Rorschach scores and schizophrenia, then, as now, still in its infancy. Examination of Tsafendas's responses and the interpretations given in court demonstrated clearly that the testers were inexperienced.'[66] Van Zyl himself admitted in 2016 that he was indeed inexperienced and not fully acquainted with the Rorschach literature and some of the other tests he performed on Tsafendas and that he was better with the Thematic Apperception Test.[67]

According to Professor Alban Burke, 'Back in those days, the psychological tests were very unsophisticated. So you could have results and it could have been argued one of two ways, to say it proves or disproves. It was never an exact science. Whether the interpretation was right or wrong, the Rorschach inkblot test was never a scientific tool, it was mainly a projective test ...The fact is that those tests and the interpretation of those tests, were always open to interpretation ... The test could, at most, say that there is a possibility of schizophrenia, at the very most, but you could never make an accurate diagnosis. There are people who would argue that you could, but you could never make an accurate diagnosis of schizophrenia based on that test, or on any test for that matter.'[68]

Van Zyl also testified, like the psychiatrists, that he 'got the impression' that Tsafendas was 'vague in thinking and difficult to communicate with at a personal level. I felt that he was in a world of his own. In his talk, he was circumstantial and often went off the point. His thoughts were constantly blocking and he was very poor in abstract thinking.' It seemed to him that Tsafendas was a withdrawn man who 'lived only to eat and to sleep'. Van Zyl was unaware of any of Tsafendas's numerous political activities or that he had voluntarily taught English to poor children in Mozambique and in Turkey. Unlike Van Zyl, the Attorney-General was well aware of Tsafendas's political and educative activities, but did nothing to challenge Van Zyl's incorrect diagnosis.

Van Zyl testified that Tsafendas was 'a completely withdrawn and isolated' person, 'completely in-capable of caring for himself, even to a small extent'. Again, there was enough evidence in the police's possession that showed Tsafendas as quite the opposite, but none of it was used. For example, Keith Martincich, a fellow worker at the Marine Diamond Corporation, testified that Tsafendas 'spoke to me every day and I got the impression that he was a sociable type'.[69] Hulse, from the same company, told the police that Tsafendas was 'very talkative',[70] while Pieter Geldenhuys and Ian Boswell of the department of labour testified that 'he was very talkative'.[71] Smorenberg, despite his statements on the witness stand, told police that 'Tsafendas was very talkative and gave the impression that he was very friendly. He wanted to talk to everybody and it became known to me that he was able to speak different languages'.[72] Albert Vercueil, Tsafendas's boss at F.A. Poole Engineering for five months, found him to be a 'very friendly, social and talkative person'.[73] Jacobus Bornman, Tsafendas's flatmate for two months, characterised him as 'a friendly and plausible person'.[74] Guenther Haafe, doorman at the Frankfurt factory where Tsafendas worked in 1958, said, 'He was a jolly man, always smiling and friendly. He would almost always come into my locker (room) to say Hi. He was really one of the friendliest workers I have met and trust me, in my twelve years as a doorman I have seen thousands and thousands of faces coming in and out; this man was courteous, they do not make them like that anymore.' Horst Hartmann, Tsafendas's boss at that job, said Tsafendas was 'well-dressed and well-mannered, he was extremely courteous ... a very pleasant man. He looked like a satisfied, successful businessman ... we liked him ... always laughing, a good worker.'[75] Again, the Attorney-General did not use any of these comments to challenge Van Zyl.

Van Zyl stated that he would not have certified Tsafendas based on the tests if he was not aware of what he described as his 'previous impulsive actions and behaviour', although such behaviour was not evident during his examinations, when Tsafendas, he said, seemed to be 'such a harmless person'. Van Zyl did not tell the court who told him about Tsafendas's 'impulsive actions and behaviour', his source being David Bloomberg, the other psychiatrists, mainly Dr Cooper who had learnt about such behaviour from the accused himself, but primarily the police. Fifty years later, Van Zyl recounted to the author how he was given a 'short summary' of Tsafendas's alleged medical history and hospitalisations, but that he had never seen the actual medical reports or any other document relating to Tsafendas's past. Dr Cooper and the other psychiatrists were also told verbally about Tsafendas's alleged 'impulsive' past behaviour, although none of them witnessed such behaviour in their own examinations of Tsafendas.[76]

Van Zyl concluded at the time that his tests clearly showed that Tsafendas was 'suffering from schizophrenia' and that he was certifiable. He also testified that the accused was of above-average intelligence, and he conceded that his 15.5 score for the 'Picture arrangement' test was inconsistent with a person who had allegedly been a schizophrenic for some 20 years. Once more, no recourse was made to the abundant evidence held by the police which could very easily have broken down Van Zyl's diagnosis.

The twelfth witness in the trial was James Johnston,[77] the Christian Church minister who had told the police that he had only seen Tsafendas 'periodically and had no discussions with him'. In fact, he had met Tsafendas twice. His statement said, 'I do not know Tsafendas very well and the longest discussion I had with him was for about 10 minutes at each occasion.'[78] In his testimony before the court, he stated that his impression was of an 'odd man, a strange man, because any discussion that we entered into he could never follow it fully'. Johnston had not mentioned anything like this in his statement to the police and the Attorney-General did not ask Johnston if he considered two 10-minute conversations with a man he scarcely knew enough to make these conclusions. Johnston also testified that he found Tsafendas strange after hearing about his travels, but he did not state what was strange about them. The Attorney-General, of course, did not find it necessary to ask.

In his cross-examination, Van den Berg referred Johnson to two contradictory statements made during his interview by the police:

'Did you say this to the police?: "The Sunday night before the assassination of Dr Verwoerd I saw Tsafendas at a service in Mr Hall's home in Pinelands, but he did not discuss anything or take part in the service that night. He appeared to be perfectly normal."'

> 'That is correct.'
>
> 'You said that?'
>
> 'That is correct.'
>
> 'Then you added to this?: "I must say I did not speak to him apart from saying good-night." Did you say this: "I did think Tsafendas to be slightly unbalanced and that he seemed to have a mysterious background, but otherwise he appeared to be all right."'
>
> 'I did say that, yes.'

This is how Van den Berg closed his cross-examination; without challenging the contradiction, nor did he raise the fact that in the course of his life, Johnston had only two 10-minute conversations with Tsafendas. The weakness of Johnston's testimony demonstrated the difficulty Bloomberg faced in finding suitable witnesses to support the defence's line.

Next on the witness stand was Gideon Jacobus Cloete, an employee at the department of labour who had met Tsafendas thrice in his office. Cloete testified that Tsafendas was actively seeking work, which might be taken as confirming Dr Cooper's diagnosis that, although Tsafendas looked for work, he was unable to hold a job down. However, in cross-examination by the

Attorney-General, Cloete contradicted the picture of Tsafendas being given to the court when he described Tsafendas as someone who was 'well-dressed' and of 'neat appearance' and who showed no signs of 'abnormality'.[79]

Gerald Shaw,[80] the *Cape Times* political correspondent at the House of Assembly, was the 14th defence witness. He described two incidents in the press gallery which were clearly intended to support the defence claim that Tsafendas could not hold down a job, even a menial one of a parliamentary messenger. In one incident, Shaw said that Tsafendas gave him the wrong change and in the other that he delivered a hamburger he had ordered to the wrong room. These seem like errors which anyone could make, wrong change, wrong recipient, and hardly indicative of schizophrenia or even serious incompetence. A significant factor that went unmentioned was the timing of the two incidents. Tsafendas gave the wrong change to Shaw on 6 September, only a few hours before the assassination; he had already bought the knives and was waiting for the right moment to strike, as he explained in his statement to the police. With something like that on his mind, it is hardly surprising that he mixed up the reporter's change. The hamburger incident took place on Friday, 2 September. This was the day Tsafendas was scheduled to work as a waiter at a function organised by the parliamentary correspondents,[81] at which he intended to kill Dr Verwoerd. Although the plan was aborted when Verwoerd failed to attend, Tsafendas's mind earlier would surely have been on his preparations for the attack, which would explain his absent-mindedness. The Attorney-General surely knew that both incidents took place on days when Tsafendas was planning to kill Dr Verwoerd, yet he did not raise any concerns. Forty-one years later, Shaw wrote that he had only a 'brief acquaintanceship' with the accused and that he 'had never found Tsafendas to show signs of insanity'.[82]

With the next witness, the trial moved into handwriting. Appearing for the defence was Felix Bernheim,[83] a graphologist,[84] appointed to examine a letter allegedly written by Tsafendas in 1959 to the British Premier Harold Macmillan from the St. Pancras hospital in London. Judge Beyers's comment, after glancing briefly at the letter, was, 'I cannot make head nor tail of it. Which of course is the purpose of giving it to me.'[85] Bernheim testified that Tsafendas was the author of the letter, but since the authorship was never contested, the expert's evidence seemed unwarranted. The letter was offered for the nature of its contents, as evidence of the work of a deranged person.

The penultimate defence witness was Dr Zabow,[86] who brought the trial back to psychiatry. His testimony proved very similar to that of Dr Cooper and Dr Sakinofsky. Like Dr Cooper, he testified that he came to a diagnosis of schizophrenia based entirely on what Tsafendas told him during three meetings each lasting 90 minutes and without any additional information. He argued that Tsafendas suffered from 'thought disorder' and was unable to deal with questions he was asked. He said Tsafendas was 'unable to care for himself' and 'live adequately on his own', that he needed control and treatment, that he was a 'drifter', that he could not relate to people around him and that there was very little chance of his recovery.

The Attorney-General 's incompetence or his determination to picture Tsafendas as a schizophrenic was obvious in Dr Zabow's testimony. The psychiatrist testified at length that he was unable to get a coherent account from Tsafendas about the killing. He also read long, verbatim excerpts from his examination of Tsafendas, which showed the accused talking in a disjointed manner and giving irrelevant answers. As if not present during the testimony, the Attorney-General then asked whether Tsafendas was able to give 'a good account of his actions'. Judge Beyers broke in, reminding Van den Berg that 'the witness has told us at length about the garbled, nonsensical, stupid, disjointed account which the accused did give him when he asked him the question. He has read out at length the account he gave him when he asked him: "Did you kill the Prime Minister, and why?" He read pages of the account.' The Attorney-General dropped the subject without another word.

What was even more extraordinary about the Attorney-General 's approach to Dr Zabow's testimony was that once again, he did not use any of the evidence in his possession, including Professor van Wyk's report, his own expert witness, which flatly contradicted Dr Zabow's assessment.

The 17th and final defence witness was Dr MacGregor,[87] who also found Tsafendas to be schizophrenic. Like his confreres, he stated that he based his diagnosis on what Tsafendas had told him, without the opportunity to check whether or not his statements were true. He told the court, 'I thought I had to – time was a little bit precious – I had to take shortcuts. I accepted what was given to me about this man's life history, various dates and to which countries he had been. I told him that I was a psychiatrist and I wished to see what his mental state was. I then divided my psychiatric interview up in the usual way. I asked him questions about his childhood; asked him questions about his adult life, his interests, his views on life, his aims, his religion, his political views; and then, finally, coming down to the murder, the motives for the murder and his feelings about the murder.'[88]

At one point, the defence counsel referred to the contradictory statements regarding Tsafendas's feelings about race, where all the witnesses declared that Tsafendas preferred coloureds to whites, except Smorenberg, who testified to the contrary. Dr MacGregor responded, 'I think this shows an ambivalence, a variation, a plus and minus sign, so to speak, about his attitude towards the coloureds. And this kind of ambivalence is very typical of the attitudes of schizophrenics. They are inconsistent in their attitudes and outlooks.' However, it was not Tsafendas who was inconsistent; the only inconsistency was Smorenberg's statement, alone in contradiction to the views of 200 others. What Dr MacGregor saw as 'ambivalent' behaviour by Tsafendas was in fact Smorenberg's misunderstanding of Tsafendas.

Dr MacGregor also told the court that Tsafendas had no aim in life, that he had achieved nothing worthwhile and that he had no friendships of lasting depth. The psychiatrist was not aware of Tsafendas's long-standing political activism or his stints teaching poor children unpaid, but the Attorney-General knew all this, though he did not challenge the witness's testimony. Advocate Cooper addressed Tsafendas's characterisation of Dr Verwoerd to Smorenberg as the 'right man', interpreting this as meaning a 'good man!' Thus when the lawyer asked how Tsafendas could have killed someone he thought was a 'good man', Dr MacGregor, unaware of Tsafendas's feelings concerning Dr Verwoerd, attributed his action once again to 'ambivalence', 'when a schizophrenic swings from one extreme to the other'. That Smorenberg's statement might have been inaccurate was apparently never considered. Dr MacGregor concluded his testimony by saying his prognosis was that Tsafendas's condition was 'hopeless' and he doubted treatment would help him. He also suggested that given Tsafendas's past escapes, 'I don't think any ordinary asylum would hold this man for any length of time'.[89]

An intriguing aspect of the trial came towards the end of the defence case when the assistant to the Attorney-General, Donald Brunette, cross-examined the doctor. He asked MacGregor whether he was aware that Tsafendas in the past had 'simulated abnormality', referring to the time when Tsafendas had pretended he attempted suicide in Hamburg. The doctor replied, 'I know nothing in the reports that say that he simulated abnormality.'

Although Dr MacGregor had no knowledge of this reported simulation, it seems impossible that the Attorney-General was unaware of such evidence in Brunette's possession. The question must be asked why Brunette or the Attorney-General himself did not ask the other defence psychiatrists about simulation and why Brunette waited for the last defence witness to raise the issue. Even stranger is that Brunette dropped the subject once Dr MacGregor stated that he was not aware of the incident. After such a revelation, one would have expected the state to produce the evidence of Tsafendas's simulation and continue the cross-examination. However, Brunette just let the matter drop. The fact that Tsafendas had 'faked mental illness' in 1943, something known to the police, was never brought up in court.

Thursday, 20 October was the fourth and final day of Tsafendas's summary trial. It was now the turn of the state to present its case. The first witness for the prosecution was Jacobus Erasmus,[90] the clinical psychologist the Attorney-General had appointed to examine Tsafendas on behalf of the state. His testimony followed Van Zyl's professional line, including conducting some of the same tests as his colleague on Tsafendas. He testified that Tsafendas 'is unable to direct his thoughts to one subject only', that he 'cannot strive towards adult objectives and often resorts to fantasy', shows a 'stereotypical tendency towards a general withdrawal from reality' and sets extremely high ideals for himself, but is unable to take positive steps to achieve them, and rather believes in his own fantasy world and that his ideals would be achieved through supernatural or magical means'. He also said Tsafendas 'shows a strong tendency towards withdrawal from his surroundings'.

The defence was stunned by Erasmus's testimony, having expected the state to claim that Tsafendas was perfectly sane and capable of following the trial. However, the most important factor here was not Erasmus's testimony as it was given to the court, but the fact that he said he had diagnosed Tsafendas as schizophrenic from 29 September. The importance of this revelation would become apparent after the testimony of the second of the state's two witnesses.

Professor van Wyk[91] was the 19th and last witness to testify. Like Erasmus, he stated that he had found Tsafendas to be schizophrenic and that he agreed with the other psychiatrists' opinions. He said he wanted to know more about Tsafendas's background and 'motivation for the act'. However, like the defence's medical experts, Van Wyk failed to search for third-party opinions of or experiences with Tsafendas, and made his diagnosis of schizophrenia based entirely on what he heard from the man himself. As a state-appointed expert, he could easily have found what he was looking for in the two statements Tsafendas gave to the police, not to mention the 200 or so statements taken from Tsafendas's friends and acquaintances.

Professor van Wyk told the court that his diagnosis of schizophrenia 'is not a conclusion which I have only reached today. I came to that conclusion before.' This was another surprise for the defence since the Attorney-General had given them Van Wyk's report on 6 October, which must have been written some time before that, which stated that he had 'found no indications' that Tsafendas was 'incapable of following the court proceedings'. The other state witness, Erasmus, had testified just a few minutes before Van Wyk that he had examined Tsafendas on 28 and 29 September and his tests had revealed 'clear signs of schizophrenia'. However, Van Wyk's report said nothing about schizophrenia and stated the tests showed that Tsafendas was 'very intelligent'.

Professor van Wyk's conduct raised a number of questions. Firstly, why did his initial report not mention that Erasmus, the other state witness, had detected signs of schizophrenia? It was the psychologist's duty to support the psychiatrist's diagnosis and the pair must have discussed the tests Erasmus organised which led him to his conclusion. The second question concerned the conduct of the Attorney-General. Professor van Wyk later changed his mind about Tsafendas and diagnosed him as schizophrenic, thus agreeing with the defence experts. The state knew of the defence line since 6 October when Bloomberg and Cooper had shown their hand to the Attorney-General, and knew of Van Wyk's diagnosis reversal since 4 October. The question therefore is, since the state's own witnesses had come to the same conclusion as the defence team as to Tsafendas's mental state, why did Van den Berg's questioning appear to take a sceptical attitude to the first defence witnesses and why did he stand by while Judge Beyers submitted the experts to an aggressive cross-examination after they testified as expected? If the Attorney-General did not agree with his witnesses' findings, he could have appointed new experts to examine Tsafendas, yet he did not do so, which suggests that he agreed with their findings.

David Bloomberg wrote later: 'One presumed that the Attorney-General knew what evidence his psychologist and psychiatrist would be giving. If that was the case, why did he challenge, in cross-examination, the evidence of the defence witnesses, when he knew that his own witnesses agreed with them, and allow Dr Harold Cooper, in particular, to be tested so vigorously and sceptically by the judge?'[92] Gavin Cooper, son of Wilfrid Cooper, also wrote about his father's surprise: '… they were left puzzled as to why, if the State had known what their experts were going to say when they took the stand, the Attorney-General had cross-examined Dr Cooper so aggressively on the first day of the inquiry to try to prove that Tsafendas was able to stand trial. Was the State as surprised as the defence with the testimony of their key witnesses?'[93]

Is it possible that the state did not know what its main witnesses were going to tell the court? That would explain the Attorney-General 's behaviour, but common legal practice made such a situation impossible, according to Advocate George Bizos and Professor John Dugard.[94] There remains three apparent explanations:

> The Attorney-General was totally incompetent.
>
> He was not given the Verwoerd investigation evidence gathered by the police and thus, he could not challenge all the defence witnesses.
>
> He acted as he did to portray the proceedings as a fair trial as though the state was genuinely trying to prove that Tsafendas was sane. In other words, he was pretending to challenge the defence, while in reality, he was strengthening its case.

Combining aspects of all three elements could also explain the Attorney-General 's behaviour. According to Dugard, 'prosecutors were never independent' during apartheid and he was 'quite sure' that Van den Berg knew what he had to do in this case and it is possible that he 'could have suppressed' the evidence.[95] Advocate Bizos also concurred that during apartheid the 'public prosecutor was the last wheel of the car'.[96] Whatever his motive, the fact is that the Attorney-General single-handedly turned what should have been a straightforward summary trial, since both state and defence agreed that the accused was insane, into a show trial.

After Professor van Wyk gave evidence, the Attorney-General stated that he had concluded the state's case. Judge Beyers then adjourned the hearing until 10.45 am, pending a decision on whether he would give judgment then or announce it later. Bloomberg and Cooper were shaken by what both described as the 'abrupt end' to proceedings.[97] When Judge Beyers re-appeared in court it was to deliver his verdict,[98] which he began by declaring that South Africa was a 'highly civilised' country for giving Tsafendas a fair trial. Judge Beyers's next sentence was: '(If) a man is charged on a capital charge, this country sees to it that, at the expense of the State, he is represented.' Tsafendas was indeed defended at the expense of the state. However, he had asked to be represented by George Bizos, but the state-appointed lawyers of its own choice. A truly civilised country would have complied with the accused's request and given him the lawyer of his choice. It must be noted, however, that Judge Beyers was possibly unaware of Tsafendas's request for Bizos when he named his defending lawyers.

Judge Beyers then referred to the tapeworm and the medical experts' examinations. He made a hugely inaccurate statement when he said that 'ordinary everyday people with whom he came into contact did not take long before they could see that this man was mentally affected'. The fact is that of the 200 or so people questioned, only four commented negatively on Tsafendas's mental state and none of them knew Tsafendas well. Of course, Beyers was not aware of this fact and had based his opinion merely on the evidence presented to him.

Judge Beyers never kept notes at his trials, relying on what was said to be a photographic memory. However, his powers of recall failed him on at least two occasions during the Tsafendas trial. Referring to Smorenberg, he said, 'I shall not forget that when he was asked: "What did you think of this man?", his answer was: "I don't like to call any man mad, but he is *definitely* barmy."' What Smorenberg said was, 'Well, I wouldn't say he is mad, but he seems *a little bit* barmy.'[99] The judge also characterised Smorenberg's testimony as 'the strongest piece of evidence'. The fact is Smorenberg's testimony was well off the mark; none of the other witnesses had said anything that bore the slightest resemblance to Smorenberg's statements, while the vast majority contradicted his claims. It was a pity that the Attorney-General did not use any of the evidence gathered by the police in court, thus leaving Judge Beyers to take Smorenberg's remarks seriously.

Judge Beyers also said Tsafendas's madness was 'obvious to Daniels and his wife. Daniels said that this man is mad. It was obvious to O'Ryan and his wife. It was obvious to Mr Johnston that this was a queer, strange man.' Patrick O'Ryan never said that Tsafendas was mad. On the contrary, he said, 'I never actually doubted his mental state, since to me he had a mind that the majority of people have.'[100] The court also heard O'Ryan's statement to the police where he said that Tsafendas 'was not spiritually or mentally disturbed ... I never got the impression that something was wrong in his mind'.[101] This, the judge seems to have overlooked. Judge Beyers said it was obvious to Johnston that Tsafendas was a strange man, but was unaware that Johnston had spoken to Tsafendas for only 20 minutes in his life.

Peter Daniels did indeed characterise Tsafendas as 'mad' but due to actions which most people would not consider crazy. After all, it was Peter Daniels who thought that Tsafendas was 'mentally deranged' because he 'tried to cool the fowls down' with a hosepipe. Judge Beyers himself retorted that this was the right thing to do in hot weather. Although all the other incidents described by the Daniels couple were of a similar, debatable type, the Judge mostly took their testimony seriously, mostly due to the Attorney-General 's failure to successfully challenge them.

Judge Beyers concluded that Tsafendas was a schizophrenic and unfit to stand trial. He said:

> *It became clear, as psychiatrist followed psychiatrist, that there can be no doubt whatever in this case that the man before me is a schizophrenic, that he is a lunatic – in more direct terms – or, as Roman Law would have had it, that I have before me a furiosus. A furiosus is something which I cannot try. I can as little try a man who has not got at least the makings of a rational mind as I could try a dog or an inert implement. A man who is mentally disordered can perform no legal act. He couldn't possibly plead.*

The judge concluded: 'It is therefore my duty to recommend that the person, Dimitri Tsafendas, be taken from here to a prison and that he is detained there, pending the determination of the State President of this country.'

Tsafendas was legally entitled to be remitted to a psychiatric hospital where he could receive treatment as a certified schizophrenic. David Pratt, in similar circumstances six years earlier, had gone from court to a psychiatric hospital. For Judge Beyers specifically to order Tsafendas into a prison, pending the State President's decision, was yet another contradiction of South Africa's perception of itself as a highly civilised country. True, Dr MacGregor had commented that 'no ordinary asylum' could keep Tsafendas for long,[102] but this was no habitual escape artist as that remark implied. Certainly, Tsafendas had left or 'escaped' from a psychiatric hospital, but then he was a patient and free to come and go. It was not as if South Africa lacked the appropriate facilities for a schizophrenic. The Fort, at Bloemfontein, was a maximum security mental institution, and if Tsafendas was considered to be particularly dangerous, special facilities could easily have been created in a secure hospital environment.

Another difference with the earlier case was that Judge President Frans Rumpff sent Pratt for 14 days of psychiatric evaluation at Weskoppies Hospital for mentally disturbed persons.[103] There, he was monitored on a daily basis by a doctor charged with evaluating his mental state.[104] No such observation was accorded to Tsafendas, although the longest total time that any individual psychiatrist spent with him was six hours. There was also a significant difference in the environment for examinations. Pratt was observed in the clinical surroundings of a hospital, while Tsafendas was seen in a cell in Caledon Square police station. The important question of third-party opinions also came into play. Professor Austin Lamont, the state psychiatrist who examined Pratt, interviewed six people who were well-acquainted with the patient, including relatives, friends and an employee.[105] As has been well established, none of the medical experts who examined Tsafendas spoke to a single person who knew him. It is noteworthy, too, that none of the five psychiatrists who examined Tsafendas was a forensic psychiatrist, simply psychiatrists with different types of expertise.

When the summary trial ended, Tsafendas's defence team spelt out to him the 1944 Amendments to the Criminal Procedure Act, which ruled that since mental illnesses might prove temporary, the charge in cases such as his could never be abandoned or withdrawn. This meant that Tsafendas could be tried again if his mental state was deemed restored.[106] Tsafendas got the point; he had to remain insane at least for as long as apartheid existed.

As for Nissiotis and Vlachopoulos, despite their efforts, they were never able to make eye contact with their brother-in-law. Hearing the judge's verdict left them with a bittersweet taste in their mouths. Although Tsafendas was not sentenced to death, Vlachopoulos believed that the authorities would never forgive him for what he had done, that they would be outraged that he 'got away with it' and that they would have him killed in prison. As the men watched Tsafendas being marched out of court, they felt certain they would never see him again. Vlachopoulos wept quietly and, outside the court, Nissiotis patted him on the back and said, 'He will be fine, he will manage …' A tearful Vlachopoulos still looked worried and Nissiotis added, 'He will be fine, you will see. He is too clever for them.'[107]

Seen from an historical perspective, Tsafendas's summary trial was more like a Soviet-style show trial of the 1930s than an interested search for truth in the Anglo-Saxon juridical tradition. The aim was clearly to reassure South Africans that there was no threat to law and order or to the ruling regime because the man who killed their beloved Prime Minister was just a wandering lunatic who believed a tapeworm in his stomach ruled his life. That Tsafendas gave the police perfectly lucid political reasons for killing Dr Verwoerd while stating repeatedly that the tapeworm had nothing to do with the assassination were lost in the welter of sensational headlines and the eagerness of the public to believe 'the tapeworm made him do it'.

Those with their hands on the levers of power, such as General van den Bergh, knew they would need to move astutely if they were to achieve the result they wanted at Tsafendas's trial, namely branding the assassin as an apolitical lunatic and excusing the authorities of any perceived security errors. A quick disposition of the case was deemed necessary, with the only possible outcome being a declaration of insanity. Thus a trial for murder became an investigation of Tsafendas's mental state. The defence lawyers received minimal co-operation from the police when they made requests for statements or documents that might suggest anything other than insanity. Consequently, an abundance of evidence, including the statements of witnesses, pointing overwhelmingly to Tsafendas's normality, as well as his political commitment, remained unknown to the Bloomberg team. One who was well aware of the police cache, however, was the Attorney-General, whose behaviour throughout the trial varied from the odd to the inexplicable, assuming that as chief prosecutor, he was genuinely seeking to prove Tsafendas was fit to hang.

The evidence gathered by the police in their investigation of Verwoerd's murder was enough not only to challenge but to break down every single defence witness, including the psychiatrists. However, the Attorney-General did not use any of it. Questions concerning the Attorney-General 's role in the case, as well as his personal honesty, arose ten days after the trial ended. On 30 October, *The Post* reported in a front-page story that Tsafendas had been a member of the South African Communist Party and wondered whether the Attorney-General was aware of this. At that time, it was not known to the press or public that Tsafendas was a former party member and the word communist was not even mentioned during the summary trial. The Attorney-General 's reply to the journalist was: 'This is news to me. I certainly had no knowledge of it until this very moment when you brought it to my notice.'[108] This was an outright lie. In the detailed memorandum that he wrote about Tsafendas on 3 October, two weeks before the start of the summary trial and 27 days before this interview, the Attorney-General recorded in the third paragraph: 'In a statement to the South African Police on 19 September 1966, Demitrio Tsafendas admitted that he had joined the Communist Party shortly before World War II.'[109] Why did Van den Berg lie? The likeliest explanation seems to be that if he had admitted knowledge of Tsafendas's membership, he would have been asked why this was not brought up at the summary trial, which then would have led to the next question: 'Was other important information suppressed?' Whatever the Attorney-General 's reasons were, the fact that he lied about such an important fact regarding Tsafendas raised serious questions as to his integrity and created further suspicion about his role at the trial.

What cannot be overlooked is that during apartheid, it was not unusual for the state to lie and fabricate evidence in judicial proceedings. The Theron trial was taking place in Johannesburg, where Johannes Andrias Theron, a head warder at the Cinderella Prison in Boksburg, was accused of 12 charges under the Commissioner of Oaths Act and the Prisons Act, two of which were publishing information about prisons in a newspaper and two were inciting people to do so.[110] Theron had revealed to newspapers some of the tortures used to extract information from prisoners, including electric shocks.[111] The prosecutor was the infamous Percy Yutar, the Deputy Attorney-General of the Transvaal who blindly supported apartheid.[112] According to Benjamin Pogrund, the *Rand Daily Mail* journalist who covered the trial, Yutar's 'unscrupulous alliance' with the police turned 'day into night',[113] so the defence team described the state case as being 'riddled with perjury from top to bottom'.[114] Yutar's behaviour was even worse during the Rivonia Trial, when he was again the prosecutor, Denis Goldberg recalled that Yutar 'would actually make false statements! The prosecutor would make false statements deliberately.'[115]

Tsafendas's family and friends were delighted he had escaped execution and were unanimous that he had invented the tapeworm for that reason. Many, including his priest friends Minas Constandinou in Mozambique, Nikola Banovic and Agathagelos Vaporidis in Turkey, Damaskinos Doxiartis and Efthimios Eleftheriadis in West Germany, had been praying for him. Father Nikola even mentioned his name during Sunday mass. Tsafendas's aunt, Artemis, lit a candle in thanksgiving, as she had promised when praying for his safe delivery. Relieved, Artemis's husband left Zambia where he had been hiding and returned to Lourenço Marques. Even then, he remained nervous for years, fearing that one day he might be called to account for the bribe.[116]

While the Minister of Justice, P.C. Pelser, declared that the government accepted the trial findings and urged the public to do likewise,[117] he also announced the appointment of a Commission of Enquiry to 'thoroughly investigate the effectiveness of the existing legal rules applicable to cases of this type'.[118] While the summary trial was taking place, the Commission of Enquiry had begun and was collecting further evidence about Tsafendas, his movements and contacts. The Commission began hearings behind closed doors on 5 October 1966 in the Thomas Boydell Building in Cape Town.[119]

Commissions of Enquiry were common under apartheid and were usually set up to investigate scandals arising from state violence in an effort to win back the public's confidence.[120] Part of the powerful system of repression and propaganda, they often concealed more than they revealed, where their work and inquiries regularly blocked evidence of state crime and closed down public discussion. Thus the Commission of Enquiry into the Sharpeville massacre of 1960, presented as a fearless, fact-finding operation, was in reality a 'whitewashing' machine.[121] Professor John Dugard said:

> *One of the most disgraceful things about South Africa during this period was the way in which judicial commissions were manipulated, and also the way in which inquest inquiries were conducted and the magistrates just ignored the evidence. And it was quite clear that the Sharpeville Inquiry and the Langa Inquiry ... they were both conducted by judges who were political appointments. And they knew how to make a finding that would help the government. That was very clear.*[122]

When the Commission into Verwoerd's death was announced, information about Tsafendas was sought from the public through newspapers and the radio, which publicised a detailed questionnaire. Anyone with any information was required to get in touch and embassies, banks and businesses, as well as government departments were paged. Police made the statements given by Tsafendas and the many witnesses they interviewed available while ordinary citizens sent in affidavits and numerous letters. All government departments declared their files open for inspection. One hundred and five people, including Tsafendas, gave evidence before the Commission, [123] but because it was a closed-door hearing, the public had no idea what was said. Prime Minister Vorster argued that the case was too serious to be conducted in public, declaring that the integrity of Judge van Wyk, named to lead the enquiry, was sufficient guarantee that the people would hear the truth, the whole truth and nothing but the truth.[124]

Whether 'integrity' was the correct word to describe Judge van Wyk's conduct would have been a matter of debate among knowledgeable South Africans, as well as some outside the country. A good friend of Vorster and Verwoerd, Van Wyk was a dedicated supporter of apartheid and of the National Party,[125] and he did not hide his racist views. In the early 1950s, there was just one black member of the Cape Town Bar, a lawyer called Ndhlovu. Because the Group Areas Act had just come into force, he was prohibited from taking chambers as his building was in a 'white' area. On those occasions when Ndhlovu was present in the common room, Van Wyk ostentatiously refused to enter.[126]

Van Wyk represented the government successfully in a number of prominent cases and ascended the legal ladder with unusual dispatch. In 1949, he became South Africa's youngest King's Counsel, aged just 36, and in October 1955 was promoted to judge.[127] A notable success was representing the apartheid government on the *Harris* case, when the government moved to strike coloured voters from the common electoral roll.[128] One of Van Wyk's co-counsels was Andries Beyers. The conduct of both men angered the opposition law team. In a letter to United Party leader J.G.N. Strauss, the voters' attorney, Pilkington-Jordan, complained that both Beyers and Van Wyk had treated the court with 'scant courtesy' and that they had been 'thoroughly rude' to Graeme Duncan KC, the leader of the legal team representing the voters. He said: 'They really are monkeys in dinner jackets and the sartorial elegance of that garb does not in the least conceal the barbarian beneath ...'[129] In January 1962, Van Wyk was elevated to the Appellate Division and rewarded for his services to apartheid with a position as an *ad hoc* member of the International Court of Justice in The Hague. There, he heard a keynote case, *Ethiopia and Liberia v. South Africa*, in which the two independent African nations claimed collectively to have a mandate to control South West Africa.[130] On 16 July 1966, the Court ruled in South Africa's favour. This was a triumph for Van Wyk, whose provocative manner of celebrations, however, infuriated many African states.[131]

By 1966, Van Wyk had established a reputation as a legal professional of proven loyalty to the government, someone who could be relied upon to produce the judgment it favoured. Beyers and Van Wyk were appointed to oversee their individual proceedings in a move that Professor Dugard interprets as the government guaranteeing it would get the outcome it desired, 'I suspect that the government was very careful when it came to appointing judges to hear the Tsafendas case, and so that would explain why both Beyers and Van Wyk were involved.'[132] A scalding assessment of Van Wyk was penned by Dennis Davis, a High Court judge in South Africa, and Michelle le Roux, an advocate of the High Court of South Africa, as follows: 'Whereas Beyers was a man of pronounced personality and sometimes humanity, Van Wyk possessed none of the latter. He did have a formidable intellect, which was evenly matched by a parsimonious and mean-spirited view of the world, a true apartheid ideologue. Unlike Beyers, he never showed an inch of compassion when confronted by the inhumane consequences of apartheid.'[133]

It goes without saying that the enquiry into Verwoerd's death hid more than it revealed and excused the police and bureaucracy failures that allowed Tsafendas to enter South Africa and get a job near the Prime Minister when he was banned from the country. It further strengthened the idea that the assassin was a hopeless lunatic by obliterating Tsafendas's intelligent, generous and politically committed character and presenting him as an unsociable, crazy loser, thus ensuring that the assassin would find no sympathy from the public and history would not associate Verwoerd's assassination with any political motive.

To a great extent, it succeeded. For more than half a century, history books have written off Verwoerd's murder in a single line as the work of a crazed assassin: *A History of South Africa* by Frank Webb (updated edition 2000) – '... the Prime Minister was stabbed to death on the floor of Parliament by a deranged Parliamentary messenger'; *A History of South Africa* by Leonard Thompson (2014) – 'A deranged attendant stabbed him to death'; *Mandela: A Biography* by Martin Meredith (2010) – Verwoerd was 'assassinated in the National Assembly by a deranged Parliamentary messenger'; *Mandela: The Authorised Biography* by Anthony Sampson (2011) – 'Mandela was ambivalent when he heard Verwoerd had been stabbed by a deranged Parliamentary messenger'. Occasionally Tsafendas's name would actually be published: *Longman's Chronicle of the 20th Century* recorded that Verwoerd was '... assassinated by a Bible-quoting Parliamentary messenger', naming him correctly but misidentified his parents as Greek and Portuguese.

The report of the Commission of Enquiry into Dr Verwoerd's death was tabled in Parliament and published on 24 January 1967.[134] It achieved its main goal, to confirm the trial verdict and assure nervous South Africans as to the apolitical and deranged nature of the assassination by an unlikeable, apolitical and unsympathetic outsider. Commenting on Tsafendas's evidence to the Commission, the report accepted that Tsafendas was capable of pretending to be mad:

> *The Commission was aware that he was quite knowledgeable about mental disorders – he also ad-mitted to the Commission that he had read fairly extensively on the subject in order to determine what was wrong with him – and therefore adopted a somewhat sceptical attitude towards him. It is clear that his word cannot be relied upon, and that he is sufficiently intelligent to put on a fairly good act.*[135]

The report referred to some of Tsafendas's political activities and movements in an authoritative and evidently well-informed way, but it soon became apparent that such references were only to those activities which were already known to the public while the dominant feature of the report was what it withheld. The 'revelations', such as Tsafendas's membership of the Communist Party, were already known to the public through the press; the only real disclosure by the

Commission was Tsafendas's attempt to recruit people while in London for an uprising in South Africa. Absent were Tsafendas's 12-year exile from Mozambique, his armed combat in the Greek Civil War, and some of his arrests and detentions by the Portuguese police. Generally, the Commission omitted most of Tsafendas's political activities and downplayed the rest.

More importantly, Tsafendas's characterisations of Verwoerd as a 'tyrant', 'dictator' and oppressor of his people, which were known to the Commission, did not make it into the report. Nor did the fact that Tsafendas had associated with leading members of the British Anti-Apartheid Movement such as David Gardener, Solly Sachs and Canon Collins, and that he was a friend of the ANC representative in London, Tennyson Makiwane. Naturally, the Commission did not want Tsafendas to be associated with the ANC in any way.

However, there were three particular omissions which clearly demonstrated that the Commission's goal was not to reveal the truth, but to give credence to the government version of the assassination. The first was Tsafendas's motive for killing Verwoerd, a crucial question which it sidestepped. Although the Commission had in its possession Tsafendas's statements to the police in which he gave clear political reasons for his action and it itself had questioned Tsafendas, the report omitted all of his explanations. Whereas in other areas of the investigation, the Commission quoted large chunks of Tsafendas's statements verbatim, when it came to motive, it used none of his own words. Instead, it speculated at length about what his motive might have been, having stated pointedly in its first paragraph that Tsafendas was not a 'normal person'. The question of motive is dealt with in one of the report's shortest chapters, a mere nine paragraphs, mostly portraying him in an entirely negative light, for instance, as 'maladjusted, rejected, frustrated, feckless rolling stone ... boastful, selfish, unscrupulous and crafty'. Only four obscurely worded and suppositional sentences directly address the question of motivation, as follows:

> *Although there were exceptions, he almost invariably displayed strong feelings against the present South African Government. During the Second World War, he was a member of the Communist Party in South Africa; in England he made contact with extreme leftists, and even tried to find support for an uprising against the present Government in South Africa. It is probable that while he was working in the House of Assembly his interest in politics and his condemnation of the present Government became more intense. The discontent of the crew of the Eleni about the Im-morality Act probably had a profound effect on his already receptive mind. In the clouded mind of this outcast, who was a com-plete failure, whose life meant practically nothing to*

> *him, was born a cunning plan to make use of his power to destroy the head of a Government which he hated.*[136]

Anyone reading this might conclude that Tsafendas had no real motive for his action, since only hatred for the government is mentioned, along with some vague speculation as to what might have triggered his hand. Although the chapter was titled 'Demetrio Tsafendas's motives', the greater part of it was dedicated to discrediting and belittling Tsafendas, as in the excerpt quoted above which employs eight disparaging adjectives.

The main conclusion of the chapter is that Tsafendas killed Dr Verwoerd because he hated the government. This was certainly true, but the specific reasons for his action were not mentioned, namely that he believed Verwoerd to be a dictator and not the real representative of all South Africans, and that he hoped a change of policy would take place after the assassination. Although known to the Commission, through the statements Tsafendas had given to the police and were in its possession, these reasons were not included in the report, obviously because they were incompatible with what was heard about him at the trial. Besides, his lucid, three-point explanation as to how to eradicate wars and racism (no nation states, no religion and all people of the same colour) did not sound like the madman the Commission wished to portray. This chapter of the report offered convincing proof that the Commission did not want to give the real answers to the questions it posed, but, like so many other inquiries during apartheid, sought simply to present a picture that was convenient for and favoured by the government. Despite the report's efforts to present Tsafendas as mentally disordered, it made no mention of the tapeworm, whereas at the summary trial, the tapeworm was said to have played a major part in the assassination.

The second important omission concerned the discussion of Verwoerd's death on board the *Eleni* three days before the assassination. The Commission discussed this question in Chapter IIC, paragraphs 77–87 in great detail in its report, with particular attention that there were rumours about the death on the ship days before it occurred; what was omitted was any sort of explanation as to how this might have come about, as well as significant details relating to Tsafendas and his background and activities. Reginald Robert Maile, a South African security guard on the *Eleni,* told the police that three days before the assassination, he was asked by Maria Kokkinidou, who often visited the *Eleni,* where her son worked on a temporary basis, 'Is Dr Verwoerd dead?' Edmund George Stollenkamp, the ship's night watchman, was also involved in these exchanges about Dr Verwoerd having died. Judge van Wyk had raised the question with Major Rossouw when the latter gave evidence before the Commission:

Judge Van Wyk: Another thing is that there is a lot of evidence that on the Friday morning BEFORE the murder people had been running back and forth screaming to one another that Dr Verwoerd had been murdered – are you aware of this?

Major Rossouw: Yes I am aware of that ...[137]

Although the Commission referred to 'a lot of evidence', its report contains very little of this evidence and fails to explain what happened. The Commission concluded:

It is impossible to establish with any certainty exactly what was said. However, there is no doubt than Dr Verwoerd's death was mentioned on that morning three days before his death. What makes these incidents more than a coincidence is the fact that this was said at the ship which was visited daily for almost 40 days by the man who killed Dr Verwoerd, where he bought a pistol and tried to buy a knife which he wanted to use – according to at least one statement made by him subsequently – to kill Dr Verwoerd. The fact that Dr Verwoerd's death was mentioned at that ship was probably more than pure coincidence ... What could have happened is that the discontented crew of the Eleni might, on the numerous occasions when they condemned the State's colour policy, have wished for Dr Verwoerd's end. Something of this kind could have had a profound effect on the feelings of resentment Tsafendas already had. It might also have been that Tsafendas had on some occasion or other intimated that it was his intention to murder Dr Verwoerd, and that for obvious reasons those who heard this do not now wish to make any admission in this regard.[138]

The fact is that at least six of the *Eleni* crew had plainly told the police how talk of Verwoerd's death had occurred. This was when Tsafendas had characterised a possible assassination of the Prime Minister as justifiable because he was a tyrant and a dictator as compared to the 1961 assassination of Prince Rwagasore of Burundi, which was to be condemned because he was democratically elected. Naturally, the Commission could never reveal Tsafendas's argument – that killing Verwoerd was justifiable because he was an oppressor – so Judge van Wyk dreamed up a scenario replete with phrases such as 'what could have happened' and 'it might have been' to show that he was attempting to find out what had happened.

The 'justifiable assassination' discussion was not the only important information omitted in retelling the *Eleni* issue. The known facts that Tsafendas had taken some of the crew to a township in Cape Town and that he had made a spitting gesture against Verwoerd, who he constantly characterised as 'Hitler's best student', are also omitted.

In its determination to present Tsafendas as a madman, the Commission distorted, manipulated and ignored the evidence of witnesses on a comprehensive scale, omitting from its report anything positive, while including everything negative. Of the 200 witnesses interviewed by the police and the Commission, 44 made positive statements about Tsafendas's character or in some way contradicted the report's negative picture. Of the rest, six made negative comments, while the remainder had nothing to say, either positive or negative. In percentage terms, that means 22% of statements were positive, 3% were negative and 75% were neutral. However, the Commission used only one of the 44 positive comments (2.2%), but 100% of the negative. The single positive reference, by Bornman, that Tsafendas was 'good-natured',[139] represented a mere fraction of the many positive things Bornman had to say about Tsafendas.

Although the report seemed to suggest that the Commission had some doubts as to the extent of Tsafendas's alleged insanity, accepting that he was clever enough to put on a good act, it goes to great pains to press its case for insanity. For instance, only four witnesses out of some 200 thought there was something mentally wrong with Tsafendas and none of the four knew him well or had more than minimal contact with him, that is 2% of the total. One of them was Wilhelmina de Vos, his landlady. The Commission wrote in its report that De Vos's 'impression was that he was mad'.[140] However, De Vos had testified to the police a couple of weeks earlier that she had found him to be 'a completely normal person',[141] the fact that she gave a different statement to the Commission was almost certainly not unconnected with the outcome of Tsafendas's summary trial. The other three were Caroline Barbeau, Keith Martincich and James Johnston, none of whom knew Tafendas more than superficially. The Commission used three of these four, thus 75% of the negative statements. On the other hand, 51 of the 200 witnesses, that is 25.5%, had commented that Tsafendas was perfectly normal, while the rest made no comment, presumably because Tsafendas seemed perfectly normal to them or they would have mentioned it. However, the Commission used only six of the 51 positive statements, thus only 11.7%. Negative statements were used, positive evidence ignored; whatever supported the theory that Tsafendas was mad or as described by the psychiatrists at his summary trial is included, while contradictory evidence fails to see the light of day. In distorting Tsafendas's character and intentions, the Commission used unfounded characterisations and misrepresented some incidents. As to the evidence about Tsafendas's character and mental state, it omitted 90% of what was positive.

The primary aim of the report was to discount suggestions that there might be serious political opposition to the apartheid regime or that the assassination was part of a wider plot. It sought to do this by portraying the assassin as a wandering lunatic who killed Dr Verwoerd out of a vague hatred for the government. To that end, it suppressed crucial evidence showing Tsafendas as a politically motivated person who killed the Prime Minister because he considered him the brains behind apartheid. In this way, it reassured a nervous public, at the same time presenting Tsafendas in such an ugly light as to ensure there would be no sympathetic public demonstrations when his fate was announced. The Attorney-General at Tsafendas's summary trial might not have had access to all the police evidence and Judge Beyers certainly did not, but this was not the case with Judge van Wyk. He was in possession of a wealth of evidence making clear that Tsafendas was not as described at the summary trial, and he omitted much of it to present the distorted picture of Tsafendas that he required.

Professor John Dugard says that he believes Judge van Wyk would never have contradicted Judge Beyers's trial verdict, no matter what evidence he had collected. His conclusions had to be similar to those that led to his colleague's verdict and in line with what was already heard in court because he needed to present Tsafendas and the assassination in a way that suited the government. That is why he was chosen in the first place.[142] The only difference between Beyers and Van Wyk was that Beyers had judged Tsafendas based on the evidence presented to him, while Van Wyk had access to evidence showing a completely different Tsafendas, one which he deliberately concealed. The way the Commission of Enquiry into Dr Verwoerd's death was conducted places it in the dishonourable line of Sharpeville, Soweto, Langa and other discredited apartheid Commissions. Nevertheless, historians, journalists and academics have tended to go to the Verwoerd enquiry as a source of information about Tsafendas and the assassination, taking its contents at face value, without challenging it.

Undisguised evidence as to the government's true beliefs concerning the assassination came a few months after the trial from Dr J.D. Vorster, the Prime Minister's brother, when he addressed an anti-communist symposium in the United States sponsored by the Church League of America. Vorster said, 'Your President Kennedy and our Dr Verwoerd were both killed by Communists.'[143] On 19 March 1967, the *Sunday Times* front-paged Vorster's statement next day under the headline, 'Premier's brother drops a bombshell'.[144] Where was the wandering, hopeless, apolitical schizophrenic with a tapeworm portrayed in the trial? It seems that Dr Vorster was fully aware of Tsafendas's communist beliefs, most probably thanks to his brother.

As for Tsafendas, immediately after the trial he was taken back to the Caledon Square police station pending the decision of Charles Robert Swart, the state president. It did not take long to arrive and it surprised nobody. Although declared to be a state president's patient, Swart, most likely with Vorster's encourangement, ordered Tsafendas to be held indefinitely in prison and, specifically, on Robben Island. His prison service file, A5078, described him as 'a person of Colour, an extremely resourceful and cunning individual who is physically and mentally able to plan and execute escape'.[145] This is hardly the man described by the psychiatrists at his summary trial, i.e. someone unable to function at a reasonable level. However, the description is just the way Tsafendas was described by people who knew him well. Vorster's remark and Tsafendas's prison file are just two more indicators that those in authority were well aware of what Tsafendas was really like, and that he was not the caricature that was put on trial and described so vividly and maliciously by the Commission of Enquiry.

Chapter 13

A State-President's Patient

Sometime in early November 1966, Tsafendas was taken under heavy guard from his cell in Caledon Square police station to Cape Town harbour, where a small boat was waiting for him. Some four miles out in Table Bay, he could see his destination clearly: Robben Island, the notorious penal institution for black political prisoners. Tsafendas was about to make history as the only prisoner classified as 'white' ever to be held there. Apart from the clothes he was wearing, his entire personal belongings were contained in an envelope provided for him by his interrogator in Cape Town, Major Rossouw. They were four photographs that the major had found in Tsafendas's wallet after his arrest: a picture of his father, a family portrait taken in Lourenço Marques, a shot of Elenitsa and a picture from Egypt showing Tsafendas as a small boy dressed in Arab garments. The major had also included Tsafendas's birth certificate, which the police had confiscated from his apartment. Tsafendas was grateful for Major Rossouw's gesture, having resigned himself to never seeing the photographs again.[1]

Robben Island, a little more than two and a half miles long and scarcely a mile wide, had a long, dark history as a place of detention. First used by the Dutch almost 400 years earlier to imprison rebellious Africans, it later played exactly the same role for the British. At one time, the prison fortress was a lunatic asylum in which the races were segregated[2] and it had also done time as a leper colony.[3] The island's role as a holding place for opponents of government was accelerated in the early 1960s under Verwoerd as large numbers of political prisoners were consigned there. By 1964, Robben Island held hundreds of ANC, ARM and PAC members and unaffiliated dissidents, as well as a few non-political prisoners.[4] Notable detainees when Tsafendas arrived included Eddie Daniels, Walter Sisulu, Nelson Mandela, Raymond Mhlaba, Govan Mbeki, Jacob Zuma, Ahmed Kathrada, Lionel Davis and Robert Sobukwe. All the prison guards were white, and all the prisoners were black or coloured. Initially, there were some coloured warders, but they were withdrawn for fear they would be sympathetic to the prisoners.[5]

Like the Nazi death camp Auschwitz, above whose main gate a sign declared *Arbeit Macht Frei* (Work Sets You Free), the entrance to Robben Island prison displayed the equally ironic claim *Ons Dien Met Trots* (We Serve with Pride).[6] The prison regime was based on violence, imposed by racist, baton-swinging warders, many of whom revelled in the infliction of pain. Indeed, many guards were hired because of their 'inhumane cruelty'.[7] The merest signs of defiance provoked brutal punishment. When Johnson Mlambo, a political prisoner serving a 20-year sentence, argued with a warder, he was buried up to his neck in the prison compound in the middle of the day. When, after several hours, he pleaded for water, the warder he had 'offended' opened his pants and urinated on his head.[8] It was common practice for the warders to urinate on detainees and in their food. Prisoners were forced to work long hours in a rock quarry and were subjected to frequent, violent strip searches. The 'politicals' were allowed to send just two letters and receive two visits a year. Petty apartheid was observed even here, with coloured prisoners, for example, being given more sugar than blacks.[9] Detainees went barefoot and their heads were shaved. Mandela and other senior prisoners fought to improve conditions, but the only response possible for most detainees was to sing defiant protest songs in languages the warders did not understand.[10]

Upon arrival, the photographs were immediately confiscated and Tsafendas was taken directly to the punishment wing of B section. There he was locked into a cell 6'6'' long and 6' wide. For a man of his bulk, it was more like an undersized animal's cage in a cheap zoo.[11] There was no bed, just a sisal mat on the bare ground, a bucket for a toilet and an electric light that never went out. Some daylight filtered through a skylight set behind metal bars. Tsafendas was given the two-piece 'uniform' all prisoners wore – baggy white shorts and a shirt. Outside the cell door was a plate with his name and reference number.[12] Although he was declared to be a victim of mental illness and placed in the unique category of a 'State President's patient', he received no medical attention or medication and was treated as the alleged most dangerous of all the prison's inmates.

The punishment wing was a solitary-confinement zone for prisoners who violated regulations. Tsafendas had violated no regulations, thus there was no justification for his incarceration there. Indeed, as an adjudged mental case, he should not have been in a prison at all but in a psychiatric hospital. This was irrelevant to the authorities, in whose eyes he had committed the most serious crime of all. The prison guards were instructed to act as if he was 'the invisible man', never to speak to him and to ignore him if he spoke to them.[13]

News of Tsafendas's arrival spread quickly through the prison population. Verwoerd's assassination had been celebrated joyfully by most of the political prisoners, but they were curious: Who was this man with a Greek name, apparently white but unknown to any of the opposition movements, who appeared suddenly out of nowhere and dispatched their hated enemy at the very heart of government? Desperate though they were to talk to him, Tsafendas's isolation made this impossible. He was the lone prisoner in a cell block opposite theirs but with no sightlines and beyond the reach of sound. It was only on the very rare occasions when Tsafendas was allowed into the exercise yard that he became visible to the other inmates from their cell windows. Defying the guards, they would shout, 'Hey, Tsafendas' and wave frantically or pump a clenched fist in honour of their hero. Infrequently, when his guards were out of sight, Tsafendas snatched the chance to raise his clenched fist in the traditional gesture of solidarity and salute his fellow inmates.[14]

Tsafendas had a horrendously hard time on Robben Island; his body a daily target for violence, his mind crucially denied the sustenance of human communication. It was testament to his mental strength that he survived the remorseless cruelties of incarceration without descending into despair and madness. He had no access to books, newspapers or radio, and on most days he was given only a single meal, which he rarely ate because he knew the guards, had spat or urinated in it. Sometimes, they did this in front of him. Disgusted, he would take only the bread that came with the plate of food. If he had not eaten for several days, he would force himself to put aside the phlegm-spattered portion and eat what seemed to be clean. He never drank soup because it was impossible to remove the sputum or urine he was sure was in it. He reflected that although he was tortured viciously by the Portuguese in prison, at least they gave him food and water.[15]

As so often in past detentions, Tsafendas's custodians, especially the younger ones, treated him like a punch bag. 'This is for Dr Verwoerd, you fucking pig', they would shout as they kicked and punched him. They said they were avenging Verwoerd's death, but Tsafendas believed they were really demonstrating their loyalty to the apartheid authorities. In such a post, the tougher you acted, the better for your career. Piet van Rensburg, a Nazi fanatic with a swastika tattoo on his wrist, was the terror of all prisoners. Tsafendas was no exception. Night-time cell searches targeting Tsafendas were common. Shouting and screaming, the guards would crash his door open and shove Tsafendas up against the wall, then violently take his tiny living quarters apart, throwing everything moveable to the floor. This was standard procedure for the political prisoners, with the guards ever alert for hidden books and subversive material. However, Tsafendas was in solitary confinement without access to any other prisoner or to a single printed word. There was nothing to be found, the search was simply another form of psychological torture.[16]

Without events to differentiate them, the days felt endless and awfully long. Tsafendas realised quickly that a life without news or books or music or any meaningful exercise of the mind would lead eventually to lethargy and despair, even madness. He decided that he must fill his many vacant hours with exercises for the mind. His brain must remain sharp. To think was to live. He started with music. The ballads of revolution had always given Tsafendas the power to survive, anthems such as 'Song of Freedom', the 'Zot Nit Keynmol' (Song of the Warsaw Ghetto), 'Bella Ciao' and various Greek songs. The lyrics emboldened him, gave him renewed strength. He sang them softly, standing close to the skylight, looking up and out. The warders soon realised what he was doing and ordered him to stop. 'No singing' was one of the prison's rules. Tsafendas complied, but inside his head, he continued making music. He would sit for hours with his back against the wall, his eyes closed, melodies running free. It was like listening to the radio, except that his unheard voice sounded better in the mind than his real-life singing voice did in his ear.[17]

Music filled many an empty hour, but Tsafendas longed for books. Reading had been his major love, along with music and good food, and the lack of literature forced him to seek an alternative. Ever resourceful, Tsafendas decided that since he was not able to read new material, he would 're-read' the books from his past. Lying on his sisal mat, he would bring to mind a particular book he had enjoyed and reconstruct it in as much detail as possible. It was like making pictures out of words and turning them into movies in his brain. In this way, he managed to replace another cultural artefact he missed so badly, the cinema. Realistically, Tsafendas acknowledged that remembering old classic stories would not be enough to keep him sane, so he started 'writing' his own books. For many long hours, he would ponder ideas, dream up plot lines and create characters. At night, as he fell asleep, he would hold the story in his mind and sometimes find that the plot had developed further in his dreams. This would go on for days until the story ended, complete with title. Another diversion, during the evenings before he slept, was to picture his life if he had not killed Verwoerd, that is, where he might now be and what he might be doing; it was not an exercise in regret, simply another way of passing the time. Tafendas determined early in captivity that keeping his brain active was a priority and for this, he devised various exercises in mental arithmetic. He would add, subtract, multiply and divide large numbers by other large numbers without the aid of pen or paper. He enjoyed this enormously and dedicated an hour every day to such brain teasers.[18]

Within a few weeks of arriving on Robben Island, Tsafendas had created a detailed daily roster of mental activity, which he followed religiously. Included, for the first time in his life, was an afternoon nap, a useful means of passing time but also of finding stories in dreams. Tsafendas believed silent singing gave him strength for the rest of the day, so that was how the daily discipline began. Thus the daily curriculum panned out as follows: singing, reading (turning books into pictures in his mind), mathematics, writing, napping, singing, movies, writing and sleeping. This routine proved to be the bedrock of his sanity and he would follow it not only during his time on the island, but also during the long, hard years he would later spend in Pretoria Central Prison.

In the present reality of Robben Island, however, Tsafendas was aware of the danger of fiction and fantasy dominating his mind. While replaying scenes from his much-loved classics, dissecting old movies and devising stories of his own, life outside of prison walls was never far from his thoughts. Many years ago he had fled from a Canadian prison in the depths of winter. Was it not possible that he could do something similar again? Systematically and unobtrusively, he explored every possibility of escape, the movements of guards, the openings and closings of gates. However, Robben Island was unlike any of the prisons he had been held in before, a sea-girt fortress from which, he concluded, getting away was simply not possible. Did this mean that he was condemned to spend the rest of his life behind bars? Tsafendas was not optimistic that he would ever be officially released; he believed that even if apartheid collapsed, he would remain in jail because he had murdered a man. However, he did nurture the hope that he might be paroled one day, even after 25 years, to live out his life in socialist Cuba or perhaps in a democratic South Africa or Mozambique.[19]

When Christmas 1966 arrived, Tsafendas asked that he be allowed to spend his permitted exercise hour on 25 December with the other prisoners. The authorities' response was to deny him even the regulation hour out of his cell.[20] He remained there all day. Not a person spoke to him and he was given no food. Two years earlier in Beira, he had also spent Christmas Day alone in his cell, but at least there, he was given food.

In February 1967, after more than three months on Robben Island, a transfer order arrived[21] and a few days later, Tsafendas was taken from his tiny cell in handcuffs to the island's harbour, where he was put aboard a vessel for Cape Town. During his time on the island, he had never glimpsed the waters surrounding the prison, and disembarking in Cape Town, he took a deep breath and a long look at the Atlantic Ocean. He feared he would never smell or see the sea again. He was right. A police escort took him to Ysterplaat, the South African Air Force (SAAF) base, from where a military plane flew him to the SAAF base of Waterkloof, on the outskirts of Pretoria. Under tight security, he was then driven swiftly to Pretoria Central Prison.[22]

This vast, four-storey facility housed an estimated 7,000 prisoners, including robbers, rapists and murderers, as well as white political activists. During apartheid, black political prisoners were mostly held on Robben Island with whites in Pretoria Central. The most prominent political prisoners there at the time were Denis Goldberg,[23] a Rivonia trialist and a member of Umkhonto we Sizwe and the Communist Party, who was serving four life sentences for 'attempting to overthrow the state' and David Kitson,[24] a leader of the Communist Party, as well as a bomb instructor of the Umkhonto we Sizwe.[25]

The prison was notoriously overcrowded, with inmates clad in identical knee socks and khaki shirts and shorts, sharing communal cells. The prison was the official site for the nation's executions. Prisoners were known as *eenhede*, or 'units', effectively objects whose management was in the hands of their warders.[26] Here, too, as on Robben Island, apartheid ruled, with white prisoners, including the politicals, treated better than the black inmates.

Tsafendas arrived to find that, just as on Robben Island, special arrangements had been made for him; in this case a purpose-built cell not only on the death-row section of the prison but close to the hanging room itself. His guards called it 'a flat' and it became Tsafendas's personal torture chamber.[27] South Africa at that time was executing about one hundred people a year. To handle such numbers, special gallows were constructed at Pretoria Central which permitted warders to hang several men at a time.[28] Each hanging caused Tsafendas at least a week of mental torture. This would begin with the condemned man or men being moved into the nearby execution cell seven days ahead of the due date. Over the next few days, the hanging machinery was tested, including the loud, sudden operation of the trap doors, noises that were impossible for Tsafendas to blot out. The day before the executions, other prisoners on death row would begin to sing and lament. The hangings always took place at dawn and Tsafendas, tortured by what he could hear, would weep and wail throughout.[29] Tsafendas would often shout at the warders, 'You murderers, you're doing it again.'[30] He believed he was placed so close to the execution chamber and exposed to the noisy ritual of hanging as a warning of what waited for him if ever he became 'sane' again. A fellow inmate and anti-apartheid activist Professor Renfrew Christie was also close enough to hear the hangings. He remembered later that:

> *we were also put as close to the gallows as possible … we listened to about three hundred hangings … you would hear the sound of the trapdoors opening and half an hour later you would hear the sound of nails being driven with a hammer, which meant the people were dead and were being placed into coffins.*[31]

The authorities had screened off the landing in front of Tsafendas's cell to provide an area for him to exercise out of sight of his fellow prisoners. The screen also allowed the warders free reign to dispense bodily punishment to Tsafendas, which they did on a daily basis. A guard would stand at each corner and they would push Tsafendas from one to the other, forcing him to run and jump to avoid their blows.[32] Even worse was the daily violence that took place in a small laundry room to which Tsafendas would be walked as part of his official morning 'recreation'. Potgieter, a huge warder and a former rugby player, would walk behind Tsafendas on the way to the laundry, aiming baton blows at his head and frequently drawing blood. Once inside the laundry, two prison officers would punch and kick their helpless prisoner around the walls and use their truncheons on his knees. The pain from the knee blows was excruciating and the attacks left Tsafendas with permanent mobility problems. Often, the guards would lace him into a straight jacket and attack his exposed body parts with fists and batons until he lost consciousness.[33]

What always made the guards laugh was when a blow brought a yelp of pain from Tsafendas. However, there was one Afrikaner warder, Potgieter's assistant, who would often intervene if his boss was not present. 'That's enough! That's too much,' he would say, and his colleagues would desist. When the beatings ended, Tsafendas could scarcely move. He said, 'I couldn't stand up straight. I couldn't walk straight. I was bent over at the waist.' The compassionate warder would help Tsafendas back to his cell, a courageous gesture given the attitudes of his fellow guards. Tsafendas never forgot the name or face of this officer.[34] He later said, 'He was good to me. He sympathized with me and protected me whenever possible, when I was beaten on the skull ... completely different [to the other Afrikaner warders], very good-natured.'[35]

Tsafendas was subjected to constant solitary confinement, an especially painful restriction for a man with a naturally gregarious nature. Fraternisation with other inmates was impossible and, for the first five years, Tsafendas did not speak to a single fellow prisoner. Officially, he was entitled to 60 minutes a day exercise out of his cell, but often this did not happen, sometimes for days at a time. On other occasions, the hour-long 'exercise' became a visit to the laundry room, where he was subjected to yet another beating.[36]

Two of the worst things Tsafendas suffered on Robben Island were replicated in Pretoria Central, namely lack of access to the printed and spoken word and the constant befouling of his meals. Warders frequently urinated or spat into his food.[37] Sometimes, thinking it was a huge joke, they would bring him a single carrot for dinner, supposedly for the tapeworm, and nothing else.[38] The fact is for Tsafendas, Pretoria Central was to become a years-long, living hell. Nothing he endured on Robben Island or in the two most notorious political prisons in Portugal, the Cascais Fort and the Aljuba, compared with the psychological and physical cruelty meted out to him in Pretoria Central.

Unknown to Tsafendas, on 3 December 1967, apartheid-ruled South Africa hit the world's headlines for an entirely positive reason, when a team of University of Cape Town medics, led by cardiac surgeon Dr Christiaan Barnard, carried out the world's first successful human heart transplant.[39] Naturally, the recipient was white and the heart he received came from a white donor, in accordance with apartheid's ruling that donations be carried out on strictly racial lines.

In January 1968, some eleven months after his transfer to Pretoria, Tsafendas received what would be his first and only visitor for eight years: David Bloomberg, his attorney at his summary trial.[40] Bloomberg was no longer Tsafendas's lawyer and had no legal responsibilities for him. He later claimed that he visited him because he had 'retained an interest' in Tsafendas's 'mental condition and welfare' ever since he defended him.[41] According to Bloomberg, Tsafendas had lost weight and his hair was turning grey, but 'his mental condition seemed unchanged and the tapeworm was still paramount in his thoughts'. Bloomberg said Tsafendas expressed satisfaction about his food and treatment, and when asked if he wanted to send a message to his friends, he wrote, 'I wish to thank you. I always think of everybody, and especially Judge Beyers. I don't know how to thank you all. Demitrio Tsafendas.'[42]

After the meeting, Bloomberg wrote to Brigadier Floris Coetzee, who had arranged the visit:

> *Physically, Tsafendas seems to be very well indeed. He has obviously lost an enormous amount of weight, which is satisfactory as he was previously grossly overweight. He told me that he has been well treated by the prison authorities, and certainly he has a much happier and friendlier disposition than when I last saw him. As to his mental condition, you will of course appreciate that I am really unqualified to express an opinion. However, through Tsafendas and other legal matters, I have picked up a fair amount of lay knowledge concerning mental conditions. My impression of Tsafendas at the present time is that outwardly he has improved, but that basically he still has the same obvious symptoms which resulted in his being diagnosed as a chronic schizophrenic. My view, for what it is worth, is that he is still mentally disordered in terms of the Mental Disorders Act.*[43]

Bloomberg did not seem to notice that Tsafendas had been tortured and was detained next to the execution chamber on death row. Tsafendas had lost close on 25 kg in 14 months, hardly the healthily positive development Bloomberg considered it to be. That Tsafendas continued to maintain the tapeworm fiction is not surprising. Throughout his years of incarceration, he was careful to play the role of lunatic, aware that he would be liable to capital punishment if the authorities decided retroactively that he was sane. As for the note of thanks to his lawyers and the judge, it is difficult not to suspect that a calculated sense of irony inspired Tsafendas to write in such laudatory terms.

The first hint of Tsafendas's inhumane treatment to reach the outside world came in December 1968, when Bernard Mitchell, a former inmate, gave an interview to the British daily, *The Guardian*. Mitchell revealed that a special cell had been constructed for Tsafendas and that he was tortured regularly. 'We used to exercise in the yard below his cell and you could hear him screaming,' he said.[44] Mitchell was not the only one to hear the torture. Fellow prisoners Denis Goldberg, David Kitson and John E. Matthews all stated later that they heard him howl in pain under the warders' blows.[45]

In 1970, Dr Peter Lambley, a young British psychologist who arrived in South Africa to work, took an interest in Tsafendas's case, having heard about him from Dr Harold Cooper. Dr Lambley also worked with Reyner van Zyl, who had also examined Tsafendas back then. Dr Cooper admitted to Dr Lambley that he had 'several misgivings about the proceedings' and that 'he thought perhaps the authorities were covering up their own lax security procedures and having Tsafendas declared insane helped them avoid being responsible in any way for the assassination'.[46]

While working at the Valkenberg Psychiatric Hospital in Cape Town and living in the city, Dr Lambley met people who knew Tsafendas. An opinion he often heard, from staff who had dealt with Tsafendas, but also from those who were friends and acquaintances, was that he was 'shamming, that he was able to appear insane any time he felt like it but otherwise functioned well. There were various "explanations" as to why he was shamming, most of them nonsensical, but there was common agreement that he was shamming.' By now deeply curious, Dr Lambley took the results from Tsafendas's psychological tests and gave them to several clinician colleagues to evaluate, without naming the patient. None of them found any signs of schizophrenia while noting that the patient was 'highly intelligent'.[47]

Reports of Tsafendas's violent treatment continued to surface throughout the 1970s. In 1971, the Progressive Party MP Helen Suzman, at the time the only opponent of apartheid in the South African parliament, became aware of the situation. Professor of law and critic of apartheid Barend D. van Niekerk[48] was told of Tsafendas's treatment by a former Pretoria Prison inmate. Van Niekerk wrote to Suzman and to Justice J.F. Ludorf[49] that 'Tsafendas is being subjected to the cruellest possible treatment. Perhaps you may raise the question of his treatment in the Justice vote. I think it is shocking that he should at all be detained in gaol, where he probably does not get the psychiatric treatment he needs.'[50] Around the same time, Suzman also received similar information from A.M. Towert, a civil servant, who informed her that Tsafendas was being held in the 'execution block at Central Gaol, Pretoria'.[51] Suzman, an experienced parliamentarian, thought there was a 'chance something might be done' if she reported the issue privately to the

Minister of Justice and the Commissioner of Prisons, whereas to go public would probably result in 'a flat denial'.[52] Subsequently, there was some amelioration in Tsafendas's treatment, probably because of her efforts, but in the long run, the brutalisation continued through the seventies.

In late 1971 or early 1972, after four years within earshot of the gallows and subjected to violence on a daily basis, Tsafendas was moved to the maximum security section of Pretoria Prison, which housed about a hundred prisoners. Colloquially referred as 'Maximum', it was also known ironically as 'Beverly Hills' for its 'luxurious' conditions and treatment of the prisoners. Though designated for white political offenders, many of the inmates were black or coloured men with death sentences, although about half of them had had their sentences commuted to life imprisonment. 'Maximum' accommodated political prisoners, usually while they awaited trial, but also young prisoners to protect them from the threat of rape, though in some cases, the minors appeared more dangerous than the mature prisoners.

As for Tsafendas, though still nominally on death row, he no longer had to endure the sounds of men being hanged and Potgieter's attentions; he was allowed to have a Bible. He also received visits from the prison's Reformed Church pastor, though his attitude towards Tsafendas was no more compassionate than the environment. Tsafendas was also seen by a psychiatrist, not to treat his proclaimed schizophrenia, but to confirm, for legal reasons only, that he remained schizophrenic. This procedure came to be repeated every two or three years. There was never any medication or treatment, he was simply interviewed to confirm he was unable to stand trial, a conclusion Tsafendas deftly assisted with his 'lunacy' act.

In 'Beverly Hills' Tsafendas was detained in an area comprising three cells, a bathroom, a chapel and a small exercise yard. There was also a toilet and a tap activated by a button. He was the only prisoner there, not to enjoy the comforts of so much space, but to be isolated from the other prisoners. The cell was a little more than the length of a bed, thus walking was restricted to two steps forwards and two backwards. To reach the cells he had to ascend a large wide staircase with 15–20 steps.

Although he was no longer close to the gallows, Tsafendas did not quite get away from the executions, which often took place twice every week. From his new quarters, he got a glimpse of the condemned men being led to their deaths. What was unavoidable was the singing by fellow prisoners, intended to give comfort and bolster courage, through the night, up to the moment of execution. From time to time a singing voice could be distinguished and recognised and then one day it would vanish. The vast majority of those executed were blacks. One of the very few white men to be hanged in Tsafendas's time was an Afrikaner policeman who had murdered the husband of a woman with whom he had an affair. He had initially managed to escape with the help of a warder but was spotted in a taxi rank next to the city railway station and re-arrested. Tsafendas heard him screaming '*Nee, Nee*' as he was dragged back to his cell. He was hanged the next morning. This is how it was for Tsafendas, where he spent 22 years of his life.

About a year after Tsafendas's relocation to 'Maximum', a prisoner was moved into the cell next door, one of the two empty cells in his section. He was Alexander Moumbaris, a Greek-Australian citizen and a member of Umkhonto we Sizwe. He had been arrested on the South Africa–Swaziland border, with his pregnant French wife, Marie-Jose, as they smuggled MK fighters into the country.

Placed in neighbouring cells, Tsafendas and Moumbaris could not see each other, and although they could speak, they did not do so for fear an unseen warder was listening. During Moumbaris's time there, he once witnessed Tsafendas being beaten outside his cell with a section of hosepipe by a group of warders. He had infringed no rules, the beating was just 'for fun'. Moumbaris knew who Tsafendas was and was eager to talk to him. Tsafendas, on the other hand, had no idea of his neighbour's identity and, ever-cautious, responded to Moumbaris's overtures with small talk and general topics. They talked, generally in Greek, when their cell doors were unlocked at mealtime and exercise sessions in the tiny yard. Initially, Tsafendas talked to Moumbaris about his life and his travels. He said he had a deep desire to visit Jericho in the Holy Land, but he acknowledged that it would never happen. Moumbaris once asked him what his Christian denomination was, meaning Orthodox or Roman Catholic. Tsafendas replied: 'Just Christian.' The two also talked about the Bible, which Moumbaris, although an atheist, had read twice in jail because there was nothing else to do! At one point, Tsafendas asked Moumbaris to teach him algebra. Moumbaris began the teaching, but when he took a pen and a piece of paper to demonstrate, the warders rushed in to see what they were doing. Confronted with numbers, diagrams and mathematical symbols and probably fearing these were secret codes or something, they confiscated the paper. Despite Moumbaris's insistence that it was merely a form of mathematics known as algebra, the warders were not convinced and forbade any more maths lessons.[53]

It was obvious to Moumbaris that Tsafendas did not completely trust him, so he avoided asking him about politics and the assassination. Gradually, however, Tsafendas began opening up about his life and ideology, so one day, quietly and proudly, he said in Greek, 'I got τον Νταή τους' ('their tough-guy' or 'their champion', but in a pejorative sense). Soon after this, a prisoner was placed in the third empty cell in their section. The prisoner was not political and rumour was that he had a lengthy criminal record, including beating his girlfriend. Both

Tsafendas and Moumbaris concluded that the new man had been placed to listen in and report on any conversations they might have. Although they continued talking, they became very cautious, Tsafendas in particular, and Verwoerd, the assassination and politics were never mentioned again.[54]

Moumbaris was fortunate to have George Bizos as his lawyer, widely celebrated in South Africa as a human rights champion and an opponent of apartheid who had defended several prominent opposition activists. During Bizos's first visit for consultations with Moumbaris at 'Maximum', there was constant singing because of a forthcoming execution. Bizos complained to the authorities that such conditions were unbearable, not only for consultations but for his client to live there. After about three months as Tsafendas's neighbour, Moumbaris was moved to the European section of the prison known as Pretoria Local, where he could prepare for his trial. Bizos secured a 12-year sentence for Moumbaris, but he completed only seven years before escaping in December 1979, along with Tim Jenkins and Stephen Lee. The escape was a huge embarrassment for the state and a major coup for the MK and the ANC. Moumbaris continued his struggle against apartheid by opening and running an ANC office in Paris. Later, Moumbaris was given two medals by the democratic government in recognition of his bravery. As for Tsafendas, Moumbaris told the author, 'I not only regard Dimitri Tsafendas as a sane man but also as the bravest and the most ill-treated man I have ever met.'[55]

In the early and mid-1970s, a series of high-profile political prisoners was incarcerated in 'Beverly Hills', such as Antony Holiday, Breyten Breytenbach, Jeremy Cronin, Denis Goldberg, Tim Jenkin, Stephen Lee, Hugh Lewin, David Rabkin and Raymond Suttner, all prominent anti-apartheid activists and rebels. Some were in the same section as Tsafendas but too far away to communicate, and when the other prisoners were allowed out for exercise, Tsafendas was kept locked inside his cell. Isolation was not the only punishment. Breytenbach said that the warders

> *were martyrizing [Tsafendas]. There was no doubt about that ... throw out his food, throw it on the floor, walk in it, have him clean it up ... throw a bucket of water on his floor and get him to dry it ... this seems to be a continuing and ongoing sport amongst the warders ... They felt personally responsible or called upon to punish him for what he had done. He was never going to be tried and he was never going to be executed ... they were really egging one another on to see who could be the most awful. Some of them felt that they personally had to take it out on him for having killed Dr Verwoerd. He had to be punished day after day ... 'you killed our leader' kind of thing ... although they themselves*

> *had never known Dr Verwoerd, they were much too young to be concerned with that ... but there was this kind of revenge ... generally using him as a punching bag.*[56]

In 1976, ten years after the assassination and despite the government's efforts to consign Tsafendas to oblivion, his name surfaced prominently in South Africa in three different contexts. Firstly, William Tanner, a South African playwright, director and designer who had been living in self-exile in England because of his opposition to apartheid, wrote a play entitled simply *Tsafendas,* which was staged in London. Tanner based his script on the report of the Commission of Enquiry, press reports from the time of the assassination and research by John Nankin, a South African stage designer, actor and director. Nankin visited newspaper libraries, the South African archives and the government printer; he was also introduced to members of the Greek community at a get-together organised for him by a friend of the owner of Mike's Outfitters, for whom Tsafendas once worked. Soon after this, the Security Police visited Nankin's father and questioned him about his son's enquiries regarding Tsafendas. Nankin was unconcerned and continued with his research.[57]

Tanner was not convinced that Tsafendas was insane, but since his play was based largely on the report, it portrayed Tsafendas as he was presented there. Tessa Marwick, who directed the play, told the author that Tanner's intention was not to highlight the assassination but to throw light on Tsafendas's character and his troubles, his 'odyssey around the world'. According to Marwick, their intention was for Tsafendas not be seen as a madman, 'but as a disorientated man', a 'displaced person', 'always looking for a safe place to live'.[58]

In the programme note, Tanner wrote although his play was 'built entirely from material publicly available, it is not a documentary ... the characters are in no way meant to represent actual persons, living or dead. Likewise, the dialogue in the trial scene is no mere verbatim reconstruction of what passed between the erudite and painstaking men who appeared, and does not reflect their individual professional contributions. While there is nothing in the text that is not drawn from an "actual" source, dramatic context may render events or speeches unfamiliar. This is intentional.'

The play opened on 16 February 1976, in the Almost Free Theatre in London's Soho district, where patrons were invited to 'pay what you can afford'. It was a one-hour, lunchtime production and several South African actors who would rise to prominence in the future filled roles, including Bill Flynn as Tsafendas.[59] London's critics were not overwhelmed by the play, seeing Tsafendas haunted by a tapeworm, a failure with women and mocked and cheated by whites. *The Times* critic, Ned Chaillet, argued that 'Mr Tanner has written part of an interesting play but needs more leisure to develop his story'.[60] B.A. Young of the *Financial Times* described the play as a 'documentary hagiography', which showed Tsafendas as 'a pathetic little figure ... his action in stabbing Verwoerd was no gesture of defiance to tyrants ... he was a madman'.[61]

Patrons arriving for the play found an actor at the door of the theatre dressed in a South African police uniform, giving orders. There was also a visual display created by the actor Stefan Bubenzer, who was playing a policeman in the play, which featured a live tapeworm, alongside photographs of Tsafendas and Verwoerd and of the knife which Tsafendas used to kill the Prime Minister. Described by one critic as 'totalitarian paraphernalia', the display intended to reflect the authoritarian nature of the South African state.[62] The play ran for two weeks and was generally well received by London's midday audiences. There were reports in South African newspapers, but the authorities ignored the play and its actors. Nevertheless, Tanner decided there was enough interest to stage the work in his home country. Dorrian McLaren would direct and Charles Comyn was to play Tsafendas at The Space Theatre Club in Cape Town. The Space was an alternative theatre venue rated as a 'theatre club', which allowed it to evade apartheid legislation and admit racially mixed casts and audiences.

Like Tanner, McLaren was not convinced that Tsafendas was insane. Eager to portray him as close to reality as possible and in order to 'get a clear picture of Tsafendas's personality, physical characteristics and mannerisms', McLaren and some of her actors spoke to several people who had met him in Cape Town. The picture of Tsafendas that emerged from their interviews was completely different to the one portrayed in court, the Commission's report and Tanner's play. McLaren said, 'The various people I spoke to who knew Tsafendas in any way told me that they wouldn't have said he was "mad" or that different from other people. A number of people said he was a "character" on account of his clothes, social etiquette, his habit of reading the Bible and telling religious stories.'[63]

One of those they spoke to was Rosamund Popkiss, Tsafendas's landlady at the time of the assassination. Popkiss said Tsafendas 'had an enormous appetite and shovelled his food'. She also said that 'he appeared to be religious in a hearty way', invariably dressed in a dapper fashion with a suit and a broad-brimmed hat, and that he was always courteous to her. However, she was not keen to elaborate further about her infamous lodger's character or his mental state. When McLaren pressed her, she asked her to drop the subject. Seeing how 'frightened and adamant she was', McLaren and her colleagues left, 'puzzled'. Ten days later, as McLaren and her actors were rehearsing the play at The Space, a young woman appeared. She told McLaren that she was Mrs Popkiss's daughter and that she 'wanted to explain about Tsafendas and her mother'. She said that since their visit, she had become 'upset and very anxious', explaining that at the time of the assassination, their house was besieged by reporters and sightseers and that her mother had been threatened. When McLaren asked her by whom, Popkiss looked away for a while and then said, 'My mother doesn't talk about it to me. But she is very frightened; she doesn't want you to mention her name.' This was because McLaren had told her that she would acknowledge her in the play programme.[64]

Among others McLaren spoke to were Mike Augustides and Neville Judson of Mike's Outfitters, where Tsafendas had worked in the two months before the assassination. Both men said that they found Tsafendas to be 'competent at his job but overly talkative and sociable'. Augustides said Tsafendas left the job on good terms with him and fellow workers and that he quit because he had 'better things to do'. However, he added that sooner or later he would have dismissed him because 'overall, he was not selling enough'.[65]

McLaren talked with Tanner about making changes to the play. She wanted to make the assassination central to the action and to mention Tsafendas's past political activities and some of the new information she had gathered from his past acquaintances. Tanner was open to some changes, but he disagreed with making the assassination central to the play and still wanted to portray Tsafendas as a misplaced person, down on his luck. McLaren eventually agreed, mostly because she feared the authorities would censor the play if it was rewritten along the lines she suggested. The play opened at The Space to an enthusiastic reception from the audience and to overwhelmingly positive reviews from critics. The authorities made no attempt to censor the script, which portrayed an apolitical Tsafendas, and those involved were never harassed. Tsafendas was never aware of the play at the time.[66]

On the morning of 16 June 1976, students streamed out of numerous high schools in Soweto to demonstrate against a decision to impose Afrikaans as the official medium of instruction in schools. With up to 20,000 students marching in the streets, armed police reacted with brutal force. This led to ever larger protests as schools in other townships joined the protest.[67] Tsafendas's name was acclaimed passionately by thousands of anti-government protestors. They ritualised their hatred for the government in a series of anti-Vorster chants, three of which hailed their hero Tsafendas. One chorus asked, 'Where are you now that we need you, Dimitri Tsafendas?' This was an adaptation of an anti-Nixon chant during Watergate, 'Where are you now that we need you, Harvey Oswald?'[68] By chanting the name of Oswald, the man who killed President Kennedy, the implication was that the American protestors would have liked him to do the same to President Nixon. The South Africans for their part were expressing a similar longing to have Vorster dead. The other slogans were '*Tsafendas Inyanga Yezizwe*' (Tsafendas, Healer of the

Nation)[69] and one which translated as 'Tsafendas's poison being stronger than Verwoerd's'. The protests continued off and on until early 1978 and caused the deaths of many students. The initial government claim was that 'only 23 students' were killed by police, but the true figure was between 600 and 700.[70]

Tsafendas's torture became an issue once again when *The Observer* of 1 August 1976 published an article headlined, 'Horror in black and white'. This was essentially a personal view of life in Pretoria Central Prison by Brian Price, a Briton who escaped while serving an 11-year sentence for dealing in LSD.[71] His cell was close to Tsafendas's and they had spoken a few times, usually when Price cut Tsafendas's hair. *The Observer* said its editors 'closely cross-examined' Price and checked his allegation as far as they were able. They decided to publish because the story was 'consistent with reports from other sources'.[72]

Price said Tsafendas 'was treated with gross inhumanity and was a broken man'. The guards urinated in his food, then forced him to eat it and kicked and beat him routinely. 'For the first five years or so, the warders used to lay into Tsafendas. He was a plaything for sadists,' he told *The Observer*.[73] That Tsafendas was still being systematically mistreated at that time was confirmed by Breytenbach. Furthermore, in 1994, two unnamed former inmates told the *Sunday Tribune* that Tsafendas was 'beaten and brutalised time and time again for his assassination of Dr Verwoerd'.[74] Advocate George Bizos said that 'the information I got from Alex Moumbaris and others [fellow prisoners] regarding Tsafendas's treatment in prison was enough to make one throw up.'[75]

The Observer distributed the Price article widely to its syndication clients overseas, where it prompted a shocked response by alerting human rights groups to the continued plight of apartheid's opponents.[76] It could not have come at a worse time for the South African government, just six weeks after the Soweto uprising began and coinciding with claims that the South African military were torturing prisoners in Namibia.[77] Moving swiftly to repair the damage to its seriously battered image, the government denounced the article as 'a travesty of the truth' and invited *The Observer* to send a legal expert to South Africa, where it promised that he would receive 'complete freedom to investigate the alleged facts contained in Price's story'. The newspaper nominated Louis Blom-Cooper, QC, chairman of Britain's Howard League for Penal Reform, a member of the home secretary's advisory council on the penal system and one of the founders of Amnesty International. The Vorster government rejected his nomination without saying why and sent *The Observer* a list of the lawyers it would accept.[78]

The Observer found it absurd that the South African government should not only reject its nominee, but then seek to have one of its own choices carry out the investigation, and promptly rejected the proposal. 'If the South Africans are so keen to let the world know they have nothing to hide in their country, why do they persistently refuse entry visas to our reporters?' the newspaper asked.[79] Accusing the government of seeking merely to score publicity points against *The Observer*, the editor added, 'We found it difficult at first to believe in all the barbarities described by Mr Price. South Africa's subtle evasions since then have now persuaded us that they must have something very serious to hide.'[80]

On 28 September 1976, at the height of the Namibian controversy when South African troops were accused of giving electric shocks and water tortures to its prisoners, David Bloomberg visited Tsafendas in prison, his first visit to his ex-client since January 1968. This was something neither *The Observer*'s nominee, nor any lawyer or Western journalist had managed. Bloomberg had long ceased representing Tsafendas and thus had no right of access to him. Indeed, after the trial he had gone into municipal politics in Cape Town and served as mayor of that city from 1973 to 1975.[81] His tenure was not without controversy, however, and the European media and human rights groups accused him of using his position to propagandise for apartheid on at least two occasions.[82]

Bloomberg's visit to Tsafendas lasted 25 minutes from 2.15 pm to 2.40 pm. He was accompanied by a lieutenant and a prison warder throughout his meeting and some of those 25 minutes were taken up in conversation with these officials.[83] Four days later, on 2 October, Bloomberg released an account of his visit to the media in which he described Price's allegations as a 'diatribe' and 'without foundation'. He said he found Tsafendas to have aged, but that he was still 'alert, has a sound memory, is personable, reasonably well-informed and not without a sense of humour'. While Tsafendas 'remembers having spoken to Price briefly on occasions', he 'firmly denies' that he suffered any ill-treatment. Bloomberg said, 'Tsafendas spends his days reading, mainly the Bible, helping with gardening and has added Afrikaans to the many languages he speaks.'[84] According to Bloomberg, the prison officials said they liked and had 'affection' for Tsafendas.[85]

Bloomberg also said:

> *I found Tsafendas in apparently good physical condition and seemingly far healthier than he was ten years ago. His major mental aberration, that he has a giant tapeworm, which dictates his life, remains dominant in his thought processes. However, apart from this obsession, he is mainly rational and one is able to carry on a reasonably intelligent conversation with him. I questioned him closely as to whether he had been ill-treated in any way. He had no hesitation in stating that he was completely satisfied with his treatment, cell conditions, exercise facilities and with the food given to him. He told me that he received the same*

rights and privileges as other maximum security prisoners and was perfectly happy in prison and had no desire to be released ...[86]

This description of Tsafendas as a contented man with no desire for release bears an inescapable resemblance to the way the lawyer described him eight years earlier, in 1968. Obvious questions hang over the references to gardening and exercise facilities and his alleged readiness to stay in prison. The truth is Tsafendas was allowed only one hour every day outside his cell and this was on very rare occasions. Even then, this was not for exercising or gardening, but to be 'exercised' by the warders. As for being happy with his living conditions, Bloomberg apparently failed to notice that Tsafendas was locked in a cell on death row or he simply chose to ignore it. Plus, Bloomberg's comment about Tsafendas spending 'his days reading, mainly the Bible' was disingenuous at the least, since the Bible was the only book in his possession.

Bloomberg claimed that he visited Tsafendas because he had 'retained an interest' in his 'mental condition and welfare' ever since the trial. The depth of his interest and concern for Tsafendas's welfare must be questioned, in view of the fact that he visited him only twice in his ex-client's 33 years in custody. Bloomberg could not seriously have expected that Tsafendas would declare, in front of his torturers, that they were torturing him. Back in 1966, when Tsafendas told him he was being beaten while in custody, Bloomberg had done nothing. Surely, Bloomberg did not think Tsafendas would have forgotten all about this and would now confide in him again, especially in front of his captors and torturers. Finally, if Bloomberg really cared about Tsafendas's wellbeing, he could have spent a little longer than what could have been no more than 20 minutes with him, and he might also have asked to see him, even for five minutes, without the presence of the warders, so he could ask for the truth about conditions. It goes without saying that Bloomberg did not reveal in his press statement that the visit lasted such a short time, or that he was accompanied by two prison officials when talking to Tsafendas.

Bloomberg later claimed he would have visited more often but the authorities made it 'difficult' for him.[87] This seems unlikely in view of the alacrity with which a visit was authorised after *The Observer*'s allegations and especially at the moment when the apartheid regime denied Blom-Cooper and any other European lawyer or journalist access to Tsafendas. Bloomberg was no longer Tsafendas's lawyer, in which case the government would have been required to approve a visit, which tends to suggest the state was confident he would not report anything unfavourable to the regime. What seems most likely is that this was a personal mission by Bloomberg to provide another service for apartheid at a difficult time for the regime and in the knowledge that his gesture would not be forgotten if ever he needed the assistance of the authorities.

Clear indications to Bloomberg's true intentions in visiting Tsafendas might be deduced from the following note, dated 7 October 1976, which he sent to a prison official, who assisted him with the Tsafendas visit:

> *Dear … (the name is censored)*
>
> *I would like to thank you very much indeed for the courtesy extended to me when I visited Tsafendas recently. I thought you might be interested to read the statements which I issued to the press following this visit, and I enclose herewith a copy of same. This has received prominence in the South African press and, hopefully, will be published in England as well.*
>
> *You might not have seen the article in the Argus, and I am enclosing a copy of that for you.*
>
> *Again, my grateful thanks to you for your co-operation and with kind personal regards …*[88]

The note clearly assumes that the official would be pleased that a rebuttal had been distributed of the torture claims made against the prison. That Bloomberg enclosed copies of his statement to the media and the *Cape Argus* article further suggests that a rebuttal of *The Observer's* claims using Tsafendas's words was the aim of his visit. As a leading lawyer and public servant, Bloomberg acted the part of stalwart defender of the regime, perhaps not in any officially sanctioned arrangement, rather as an individual who knew how to trim his sails to the prevailing political winds. Indeed, it was not long afterwards that the apartheid regime did in fact reward Bloomberg for his services over the years.[89]

Despite Bloomberg's best efforts, his statement on Tsafendas failed to quell the criticisms against South Africa concerning the treatment of prisoners and of Tsafendas specifically, as well as the continued application of hard-line apartheid. General van den Bergh, founder and now head of BOSS, the Bureau of State Security, South Africa's secret service, conceived a plan to make another attempt to refute the claims. He turned to Gordon Winter, a secret agent for BOSS, whose cover job was writing and reporting for *The Citizen,* a new, state-funded English-language government mouthpiece, to visit Tsafendas in prison and write a convincing denial of *The Observer* torture story.[90] Van den Bergh was one of the important figures behind the launch of *The Citizen* earlier that year which was intended to counter the liberal position of the long-established *Rand Daily Mail*.[91] Winter was the first journalist allowed to interview Tsafendas after the assassination. Until then, the South African authorities had refused permission to all those seeking permission. Like Bloomberg, Winter saw Tsafendas in the company of two prison officials – General Jannie Roux, the Deputy Commissioner of Prisons, and Brigadier Gerrie Visser, the Commanding Officer of Pretoria Central Prison. Confronted by this trio, Tsafendas denied being ill-treated. Winter took an immediate liking to Tsafendas, while also feeling sorry for him. It was when Winter briefly found himself alone with him that Tsafendas demonstrated how clearly he understood the situation which had been engineered. Winter whispered, 'Of course, you must have been ill-treated at *some* time, haven't you?' whereupon Tsafendas replied, 'You are obviously here to do a denial story for the new government newspaper, *The Citizen*, so what's that question supposed to mean?' Winter was stunned. Tsafendas had somehow deduced perfectly that his brief was to write a knockdown of *The Observer* story and that *The Citizen*, as the government's propaganda tool, would print it word for word.[92] Taken aback by Tsafendas's perspicacity, Winter had no choice but to come clean. He said, 'I can't write a completely one-sided story saying what a bed of roses you have in jail. I've got to put a few small niggles in to make it look credible.' Tsafendas nodded that he understood. When the officers returned, Winter asked Tsafendas if he had any complaints. Tsafendas smiled and addressing Brigadier Visser said, 'Yes, there was one warder who was always abusive and tormented me. One day when he pretended to spit in my tray of food, I complained to the Brigadier. And you reprimanded him severely, didn't you sir?' Flustered by Tsafendas's ruse, Visser said yes, that is what happened.[93] It was a clever reversal of power whereby Tsafendas placed the prison chief on the spot, forcing him to admit misconduct by his staff, even if the claim was only a pretended spitting. Tsafendas must have got great enjoyment from this small victory.

Winter's article in *The Citizen* of 20 October 1976 not only rebutted the claims made in *The Observer*, but was accompanied by photographs of Tsafendas outside his cell, talking to his warders. The photos were clearly intended to suggest he had the freedom to move within the prison precincts, that he had a good relationship with the warders and that he enjoyed the same rights as the other prisoners. In an attempt to convince his readers that Tsafendas nurtured no political animus against Verwoerd, Winter began his article with a statement he alleged was given to him by Tsafendas, namely, 'I SWEAR I didn't kill Dr Verwoerd for political reasons. The real reason was because he was known as "The Doctor". He was the top man in the country and to me he symbolized all doctors – people I've always wanted to kill.'[94] Winter went on to write two more articles for *The Citizen* about Tsafendas, the first of which mentioned that he had been a member of the South African

Communist Party in the late 1930s and early 1940s. This was something which Winter considered old news, but Van den Bergh was alarmed and ordered the journalist-agent to write a follow-up minimising Tsafendas's role in the party.

In the new article, Winter quoted General van den Bergh as saying:

> *It is true that Tsafendas joined the CPSA in the late 1930s, but he was completely ineffective as a member of the Party because he never really appreciated what Communism was all about. He was totally incapable of converting other people to the communist cause and that is why they merely used him to fill the ranks whenever a street procession was mounted. I can tell you that no person in South African history has ever been interrogated as much as Tsafendas.*[95]

In 1998, Winter told David Beresford of *The Guardian* newspaper in Britain why Van den Bergh was so upset:

> *Pretoria did not want there to be any suggestion whatsoever that Tsafendas was clever, or programmed, or politically affiliated in any way … H.J. van den Bergh was horrified when I wrote that story in The Citizen stating that Tsafendas had joined the South African Communist Party in Johannesburg in 1939, which H.J. van den Bergh then told me to water down by writing a follow-up article in which he [Van den Bergh] described Tsafendas as being an ineffective Red, and was just used as a crowd fodder in marches etc. All H.J. wanted the public to believe was that Tsafendas was totally mad and that if he managed to get out of Death Row he would definitely kill again.*[96]

Winter visited Tsafendas on several more occasions. He described him as 'a highly intelligent man, seriously highly intelligent, remarkably astute, charming and even witty'.[97] After Winter retired from BOSS and left South Africa, he admitted that the stories he wrote on Van den Bergh's instructions were propaganda, that Tsafendas was indeed tortured and that he was perfectly sane; he confessed that he had made up aspects of his articles in order to support the required picture of an insane person who killed Verwoerd without any political motivation.[98]

Winter's articles did not convince Western onlookers, least of all *The Observer*, which characterised the government's handling of the case as 'Pretoria propaganda', noting the 'extraordinary lengths' to which the government would go 'to score a dubious propaganda point'.[99] The inescapable question was: If Tsafendas was not tortured and the authorities had nothing to hide, why were the newspaper's nominated lawyer and reporters not allowed to see him, while Bloomberg and Winter were?

This was a time in South Africa when Van den Bergh was seen by many as a co-equal of the Prime Minister. Assessing the power politics of the day, the *South African Observer* wrote that Premier Vorster would have been 'unable to govern the country without having General van den Bergh at his elbow' with the National Party being 'a mere instrument in the hands of these two ambitious men'.[100] However, Van den Bergh's and Vorster's time as national leaders was quickly running out, although they did not then know it. Ironically, it was information secured through an official inquiry that led to their downfall.[101] When a Commission was set up in 1978 to investigate exchange control regulations, the Chairman and sole member, Judge Anton Mostert, discovered evidence of widespread government corruption, particularly at the Ministry of Information. The scandal was nicknamed Muldergate, combining a reference to Cornelius Mulder, the Minister of Information, and Washington's Watergate. The investigation pointed the finger directly at Van den Bergh and Vorster.[102] A major exposure was of efforts they had undertaken in 1976 to conceal their involvement by ordering information ministry bureaucrats to destroy all 'unnecessary documentation' that could link them to corrupt acts.[103]

What Judge Mostert discovered was evidence of collaboration between the information ministry and institutions controlled by Van den Bergh and Vorster to influence public opinion in favour of apartheid. Resisting government pressure, Judge Mostert disclosed that the Ministry of Information worked closely and secretly throughout the 1970s with Van den Bergh's BOSS.[104] The judge further found that, in 1973, Vorster secretly agreed to move R64 million from the defence budget to fund a series of propaganda projects. These included bribes for international news agencies, an attempt to buy the *Washington Star* for US$25 million and the spending of US$30 million to establish *The Citizen*.[105] In a statement that shocked the South African power establishment, Judge Mostert described Van den Bergh boldly as 'a sinister figure who saw himself as the power behind the throne of Prime Minister Vorster'.[106] Inevitably, for making his disclosures public, Judge Mostert was fired and the Commission of Inquiry was disbanded.[107] However, the cat was out of the bag.

On 29 September 1978, with the domestic political scene focused on the reported misuse of public money and pressures increasing from abroad for international sanctions against the republic, Vorster resigned, citing ill health.[108] He was given the position of state president. Vorster was succeeded by Defence Minister P.W. Botha, who happened to be a bitter enemy of Van den Bergh. As a result of Judge Mostert's revelations, the Erasmus Commission was appointed to carry out further investigations and, by June 1979, it issued no fewer than three reports implicating Vorster and Mulder, primarily for misleading Parliament about the secret funding of *The Citizen*. Humiliatingly for a man who once wielded immense power, Van den Bergh had his passport confiscated[109] and even signed a nationwide petition calling for his own prosecution.[110] However, it was the old Van den Bergh who appeared before the Commission in person. Accused of being a 'ruthless manipulator', he retorted that the inquiry was 'a big farce' and its report was 'full of lies'. He also boasted, or threatened, that he controlled a 'sinister network of agents' and that he would 'stop at nothing' to achieve his ends. Despite his boasts or threats, Van den Bergh was forced to resign as head of BOSS and Vorster as state president, the latter only eight months after taking up the post. Van den Bergh faded from public view, farming broiler chickens at Bronkhorstpruit, Pretoria.[111]

In December 1979, three years after Van den Bergh's failed propaganda war, Alexander Moumbaris escaped from the European section of the Pretoria Prison, where he had been held since 1973, and eventually ended up in France. At a press conference in Paris in January 1980 organised by the ANC, Moumbaris said that Tsafendas 'was being buried alive. The warders beat him several times a day. Although he is not a sane man, the treatment he is getting for his illness is non-existent. He told me – and this was corroborated – that he was often put into a straight-jacket and his testicles twisted by warders.'[112] Moumbaris later clarified his calling of Tsafendas as 'not a sane man'. He said, 'I couldn't say otherwise. This is what they thought. If they knew he was sane, they would have killed him and claimed he committed suicide. The only reason he was kept alive was because they thought he was insane.'[113]

Sometime in the mid-to-late 1970s, Father Minas Constandinou, a Greek Orthodox priest and friend of Tsafendas from Mozambique back in 1963, was appointed as chaplain to the Greek Orthodox prisoners in Pretoria. He immediately thought of visiting Tsafendas, but hesitated. Tsafendas was still the black sheep of the Greek community in Pretoria and the priest knew that such visit would not be welcomed by church members if it became known. In 1978, Marika died and Father Minas guessed that Tsafendas did not know about this since he had heard nothing of or from any family member since his arrest in 1966. The priest then decided to visit Tsafendas without mentioning it to anyone in the Greek community and to break the news of Marika's death because he believed he was entitled to know. He was also curious to see his old friend after so long but he did not plan regular visits, just to call, give him the news and see how things were with him. Thus, he became Tsafendas's first visitor since Gordon Winter two years earlier in 1976.[114] Even after 15 years, Tsafendas recognised Father Minas immediately but was surprised to see him

– cautious, perhaps even suspicious, of his old friend. Visitors and prisoners were separated by a glass panel, conversations were to be in English or Afrikaans and were openly monitored. However, these regulations were relaxed in the case of ministers of religion. Tsafendas and Father Minas began conversing in English and when they ascertained that no one was listening, they began talking in Greek.[115]

At the outset, both men were wary and hesitant. Tsafendas guessed there must be a specific reason for the priest's visit and asked him what it was. When Father Minas told him his stepmother was dead, Tsafendas sobbed bitterly. He asked for all the details of her death and wanted to know everything she had been doing since he last saw her. He seemed embarrassed that he was unaware of Marika's passing, although there was no way he could have known. It soon became obvious to the priest that his old friend was desperate to talk and the conversation veered onto how they had changed after all these years and Tsafendas asked about political developments in South Africa and around the world, as well as for news of his friends. Father Minas avoided asking Tsafendas about the assassination. He had never believed the tapeworm story or that his friend was insane, convinced it was a ploy to escape the gallows. Father Minas believed none of the characterisations of Tsafendas in court in 1966, but was curious to know if Tsafendas would display any of these in pretence of insanity. He was worried also that his long years in prison might have genuinely affected his mind. In fact, Tsafendas talked and acted exactly as he remembered. He was not as talkative as in the past, but the priest found no deterioration in his speech and quickly concluded that his mind was as sharp as ever. They spoke in Greek for the duration of the visit and, when the priest moved to leave, Tsafendas pleaded, 'Will you come again?' This was not something Father Minas had planned, but seeing the desperation for human contact in the eyes of the 60-year-old man, he made up his mind. 'I will come, Dimitri,' the priest said, 'I promise.'[116]

Father Minas kept his promise and it was during these encounters, so precious to Tsafendas, that much of his extraordinary life was subsequently revealed. At first, Tsafendas said little that was personal and their conversations mostly concerned current affairs, history and religion. In time, however, Tsafendas talked more widely, as if he had regained the use of a tongue stilled for some 30 years, opening up about his travels and adventures in Europe and the Middle East, as well as delivering his views on the politics of the day. It was at this point in their relationship that Father Minas finally asked him about the assassination and why he did it. Tsafendas frowned, clearly uncomfortable, then pointed with his finger to his stomach and said in Greek, 'It was the tapeworm, my Father, it was the tapeworm.' Their conversation could not be heard, but a warder was sitting in the room, observing. Tsafendas made the gesture to his stomach so obvious that the warder could not avoid seeing it. Father Minas was taken aback by Tsafendas's reaction. He did not believe him but came to the conclusion that, as long as he was in prison, Tsafendas would feel obliged to keep telling the tapeworm story. Still curious, many months later, while they were alone in the room, the priest asked again about the assassination. Tsafendas gave the same response and made the same gesture; Father Minas realised that he would never hear Tsafendas's version of the killing of Verwoerd as long as he was in prison and under threat of execution. He never raised the subject again.[117]

Over the following years and into the 1980s, the priest discovered aspects of his friend that he never knew, one being his extensive knowledge of classical literature. Tsafendas would name a book he admired, urge Father Minas to read it and then discuss it with him on a subsequent visit. The priest was not much of a reader and initially was not keen, but Tsafendas insisted, and soon they were discussing works of the highest literary merit. The first book was Tagore's *The Home and the World,* which was difficult to find. This was followed by Primo Levi's *If This is a Man,* a biography of Marcus Garvey and then the works of Brecht, Balzac, Dostoyevsky, Fanon and others. Father Minas soon realised that one of Tsafendas's major preoccupations was his hero, Paul Robeson. The priest had never heard of Robeson and, being in apartheid South Africa, found it difficult to unearth information about an international star who was black and a communist. Eventually, he discovered from an encyclopaedia that Robeson had died back in 1976. Tsafendas was deeply saddened to hear the news and he urged Father Minas to get hold of Robeson's records and listen to the songs. Curious by then, Father Minas searched far and wide but was unable to find a Paul Robeson album in all of apartheid South Africa.[118]

Another of Tsafendas's requests was to find out more about the death of Tennyson Makiwane, the anti-apartheid activist with whom Tsafendas had spent time in London. Tsafendas had heard through the prison grapevine that his one-time comrade was assassinated in 1980 and was deeply saddened, having so admired the young Makiwane's passion and dynamism. Tsafendas believed that Makiwane was assassinated by BOSS or some other South African security service, but as it turned out, he was executed by Umkhonto we Sizwe because of suspicions that he had become a police informer. Father Minas knew nothing of Makiwane and was unable to find any information about him, thus Tsafendas never learnt how he died but remembered his old friend with great affection to the end of his days.[119]

One of the most painful aspects of imprisonment for Tsafendas was losing touch with his family, and in particular, not seeing his nephews, by then in their mid-20s. He was disappointed that no one in the family had visited or written to him, but he did not hold it against them; he knew they were in a difficult position with the authorities and would feel safer if they were not associated with him. Tsafendas often expressed his sadness about this estrangement to Father Minas, so the priest decided to visit Bushia, who was now living in Pretoria. He asked her for photographs of her two children. Bushia was still very angry with Dimitri, but gave the priest a picture of her two children together with her sister Eleni's two children. She made it perfectly clear that this was all she would ever do for her half-brother and he should never ask her for anything else. When Father Minas handed the photograph to Tsafendas he did not name the youngsters but said simply, 'Have a look here.' Tsafendas seized the picture eagerly and within seconds began weeping inconsolably, gasping for breath and unable to speak. The warder, who had given permission for the priest to show the photograph, moved forward in alarm and with the help of the priest, slowly calmed the hyperventilating Tsafendas until the tears dried and he could talk again. All Tsafendas managed was to ask Father Minas if he could keep the picture. The priest looked at the warder, who nodded yes. Father Minas, who still had not made it known that he was visiting Tsafendas in prison, decided to call on Evangelia, Tsafendas's older half-sister, who also lived in Pretoria. He intended to ask if she would be willing to visit Tsafendas, but as soon as he mentioned Tsafendas's name, Evangelia stopped the conversation. She declared that she did not want to hear or discuss anything about her half-brother. Father Minas did not press her, nor did he mention that he was already visiting Tsafendas.[120]

During the early meetings between the priest and Tsafendas, much of the talk was about each other's lives and their recollections of the old days in Mozambique. However, one day, an incident occurred that changed the trajectory of their relationship. Tsafendas saw Father Minas talking to one of the warders. He asked the priest whether the prison staff wanted to know what they discussed. Father Minas replied seriously, 'Yes.' Tsafendas looked worried. 'What have you been telling them?' he asked the priest hesitantly. Father Minas was well aware that the warders believed Tsafendas was mad and that it was in his friend's interest that they should continue to do so. He smiled and told him 'I told them that you constantly talk about the tapeworm', that 'the tapeworm was hungry today' or that 'it did not let him sleep last night'. Tsafendas said nothing but gave him a restrained smile. The priest smiled quietly back. They had come a long way from Tsafendas gesturing wildly at the tapeworm supposedly in his stomach. In the new, freer atmosphere between them, Tsafendas became more talkative, even chatty, and asked Father Minas to read the day's newspapers before he came and tell him what was going on in the outside world. Tsafendas was still denied access to newspapers or radio and the only information he got was from warders if they felt disposed to tell him. Some of the new, younger warders were quite talkative and ignored the 'silent treatment' rule because they felt sorry for Tsafendas. Other topics of conversation between Father Minas and Tsafendas included the latter's life and travels before the assassination, but above all Tsafendas was interested in the current political situation in South Africa and around the world.[121]

Tsafendas remained under conditions of solitary confinement in the same cell on death row in Pretoria Maximum Security throughout the 1980s. The beatings and systematic tortures gradually lessened, but he was still brutalised and some of the warders continue to think it great fun to urinate or spit in his food. As older warders retired, some of their younger replacements would allow Tsafendas to leave his cell for a few minutes and talk briefly to other prisoners. Also, an inmate in Pretoria Maximum Security at that time was Professor Renfrew Christie, an anti-apartheid activist sentenced for giving the ANC important secret information on the apartheid government, including its nuclear development plans. One day in the early 1980s, Christie was exercising in the prison compound when some of the warders pointed to another prisoner and said, 'That is Tsafendas.' Christie got the impression that he was being invited to talk to Tsafendas. It was the first and last time in the 1980s that Christie saw Tsafendas outside his cell among other prisoners. He approached Tsafendas while the warders watched. Christie said:

> *I was left alone with Tsafendas for a very short time. He looked like a man who had been shocked; his face, his hair, were bleached grey/white and he was clearly a man who had been through immense stress. He was, and the best word to use is, a ghost. Neither of us was expecting this meeting. I don't know if I was identified, although I think he understood that I was there for my opposition to apartheid, and we had three sentences together, no more, as a greeting. He was a man sleep-walking and in great, great shock, distinctly distressed ...*
>
> *My sense is that these particular warders wanted to do him a favour and let him see some other person, but I cannot say what their motive was ... I believe that the warders who arranged this 'accident' were trying to do him a favour, to let him see some other person, and they picked me. Maybe they thought I was friendly, I don't know, but we said little more than, 'Hello. How are you?' Polite conversation and, of course, the warders were present and we could not say anything serious ... I cannot say that the person I met was insane in any way, I can say he was deeply, deeply stressed and he looked like a ghost, but that doesn't make him insane, that makes him someone who's been in solitary for 15 or 18 years or whatever the number is.*[122]

Father Minas's visits continued irregularly, once or, at most, twice a month, throughout the 1980s. Each time, before leaving, he always asked Tsafendas if he wanted anything and he always said 'No'. One day, sometime in the late 1980s, however, Tsafendas asked the priest to write to some of his friends on his behalf, saying he did not want to embarrass them or bring police attention to them by writing himself. He named four people: Father Nikola Banovic in Istanbul, John Michaletos in Athens, Manuel in Maputo and Patrick O'Ryan in Cape Town. The priest wrote to the addresses provided by Tsafendas and very soon received replies from all apart from Manuel. Each of them wanted to correspond directly with their friend and were not worried about it, but Tsafendas said it would be better if the priest continued to write the letters on his instruction. When Father Minas asked why, Tsafendas simply said, 'It would be better if you write them' and did not elaborate further. As for Manuel, Father Minas discovered that he was no longer living at the address provided by Tsafendas and attempts to locate him through contacts in Maputo were fruitless. Tsafendas never learnt what became of his life-long friend.[123]

Patrick O'Ryan wanted to come and visit Tsafendas and asked when he could do so. However, Tsafendas, through Father Minas, told him that it would be very expensive to travel to Pretoria just for an hour's visit. O'Ryan pressed his case, but Tsafendas remained adamant that he should not visit, at least for the time being. Tsafendas never explained his stance adequately to O'Ryan, but after Tsafendas's death, his old friend came to understand what the probable reasons were.[124]

On 10 September 1983, John Vorster died from a blood clot in the lung at age 66. Although he had left office in disgrace four years earlier, Vorster had been unable to stay away from politics entirely. In 1980 he condemned anyone who opposed apartheid as 'no friend of the country, of the Afrikaner or of the white man'. As for power-sharing between black and white, he rejected the idea 'in whatever form' even shortly before his death.[125]

With Vorster gone and P.W. Botha at the helm, South Africa came under pressure as never before from anti-apartheid fighters inside the country and from critics overseas demanding an end to its racist rule. At the same time, a massive international campaign began for the release of political prisoners, pre-eminently Nelson Mandela. The government's response to these increased pressures was to behave as before, even more so. Home-based freedom fighters were met by both military force and by state terrorism in the form of death squads, like in Vlakplaas. In South Africa's prisons, torture was widespread, including even of children, some as young as 14. Opponents of apartheid were not the only government victims. Like the Nazis, the authorities targeted men in the military who they suspected might be homosexual. Under the infamous Aversion Project of Dr Aubrey Levin, government medics attempted to 'cure' gay soldiers of their homosexuality.[126] Treatments included chemical castrations and electric shock treatment. As many as 900 draftees, aged 16 to 24, were forced to undergo 'sexual reassignment' surgery, being deprived of their manhood against their will.[127] During these dark times, Tsafendas was not forgotten. Writing in the London *Independent* newspaper, John Carlin described him as 'the sanest human on the planet' and revealed that a graffiti painted on the wall of a busy Johannesburg street read 'Forget Mandela. Release Tsafendas'.[128] In the ANC's office in Zambia, a picture of Tsafendas was given a place of honour.[129] In 1986, 20 years after the assassination of Verwoerd and while apartheid still ruled the roost, Tsafendas's name resurfaced in the media. On 6 June, KOOS, a recently formed band, released a song entitled 'Tsafendas'. It began with a voice purporting to be that of Tsafendas, supposedly narrating his movement in the House of Assembly before the assassination. The same year, two daring South Africans, Matthew Krouse and Robert Colman, wrote and staged a musical satire entitled *Famous Dead Man,* the 'dead man' being Verwoerd. Sexually and linguistically outspoken, the show contained a representation of the assassination in which Tsafendas was portrayed as angry and insane. The play ran successfully for three months in Johannesburg, but when it moved to Durban, Verwoerd's daughter, Anna Boshoff, protested to the government and Home Affairs Minister Stoffel Botha banned the play. An appeal by Krouse and Colman was rejected.[130] Father Minas watched the play and liked it a lot. He hastened to tell Tsafendas, but found to his surprise that his friend showed not the slightest interest in the play or how it portrayed him. Some years later, Tsafendas told Father Minas he was not interested because he did not care what people thought about him or how they presented him; his conscience was clear about who he was and what he had done, he said.[131]

Father Minas visited the prison for several years and Tsafendas spoke freely to him about everything except the assassination. Sometimes, however, Verwoerd's name cropped up and Tsafendas would smile, lift his right hand and make a stabbing motion. It seemed clear to the priest that Tsafendas was proud of what he had done. These gestures and the two times when Tsafendas pointed to his stomach were the only allusions to the assassination during the priest's visits in the 1980s. Towards the end of that decade, Father Minas was transferred to Cape Town and did not visit Tsafendas again in Pretoria.[132]

In June 1989, Tsafendas was the subject of another article in *The Guardian,* which reported that although he was now 71, he was still on death row and still being tortured. David Beresford, the article's author, made the widely noted point that instead of being detained in a psychiatric hospital, as the law required for the mentally ill, he had been kept in a maximum security prison, and worse than that, on death row.[133] Correctional Services denied that Tsafendas was mistreated and insisted that he had always been well looked after. However, in 1994, ANC spokesman Carl Niehaus said that he was told by warders that Tsafendas was indeed tortured.[134]

In 1989, a young Greek Orthodox priest, Father Michalis Visvinis, arrived in Pretoria from Greece and took over prison visiting duties from Father Minas. He did not know of Tsafendas or that his predecessor had visited him until he talked to the local Greek community, all of whom, including Tsafendas's family, asserted that Verwoerd's assassin was perfectly sane and that he had made up the tapeworm story. The priest, knowing that Tsafendas did not have any visitors, decided he must see this notorious prisoner himself and, when he did so, the two developed a good relationship. Visiting on a regular basis over the next three to four years, Father Michalis mostly let Tsafendas talk, since his need for human contact was so obvious. At first, he was sceptical of Tsafendas's stories from his past, but then he heard him describe in detail places he had visited in Athens in 1947–49 and in 1961. Father Michalis had lived in Athens before South Africa and some of the cafés and other places Tsafendas described were indeed those he knew in the Greek capital. Through discussions with other Greeks, Father Michalis confirmed the truth in everything he heard from Tsafendas.[135]

As Verwoerd's 1966 assassination receded into history and Tsafendas grew older and frailer, the prison authorities began to relax the rules around him. It was at this juncture that a new person entered his life and showed him a compassion and understanding he had not known for decades. Rika Nikolatos, a social worker, then in her 50s and chairperson of the Hellenic Orthodox Ladies Association (HOLA), decided to visit Tsafendas after hearing from Father Michalis of his emotional needs. Nikolatos was a cousin of Dr Costa Gazidis, a member of the South African Communist Party and the Pan Africanist Congress who had been imprisoned for four years in the 1960s for anti-apartheid activities. Gazidis had not met Tsafendas but had heard about him from people who did know him, and looked upon him as a revolutionary hero. Nikolatos knew about Tsafendas from other local Greeks, but all that she heard from them was negative. Nikolatos ignored their protests and visited Tsafendas, and found a hugely intelligent man, deprived of intellectual sustenance and rendered desolate, most of all because of his rejection by his own family. Sometimes alone, sometimes with Father Michalis or later with another priest, Father Spiros Randos, Nikolatos visited Tsafendas until his death,[136] maintaining until she died that Tsafendas was 'completely sane'.[137]

As Nikolatos gained Tsafendas's confidence, he told her a lot about his early life, especially his political activities, but he made no mention of the assassination and she never asked about it. In the more relaxed conditions of the later years, Nikolatos brought newspapers, books and magazines, and Tsafendas devoured their contents at great speed, particularly crosswords, to which he became addicted and highly adept. Realising how deeply stricken Tsafendas was by his family's abandonment, Nikolatos got in touch with his three half-sisters to see if they were open to visiting him. Bushia and Evangelia dismissed the idea out of hand, but Eleni Vlachopoulos was ready to listen. Nikolatos told her how happy Tsafendas would be, especially the nephews he was so desperate to see. Eleni spoke to her husband Nick and he agreed that she should go. Their decision was angrily opposed by other family members, especially Evangelia and their older brother Victor, as well as many of their Greek friends. Nick contemplated going, too, but decided against it out of guilt. He recalled his close friendship with Tsafendas before the assassination and was now deeply embarrassed that he had not gone to see him in all those years. He told his wife that he was 'ashamed' and he would not be able to look Tsafendas in the face. Neither Nick nor Eleni ever did visit Tsafendas, but on a few occasions, Eleni asked Nikolatos to take Greek food she had prepared for him.[138]

Nikolatos also cooked food for Tsafendas and discussing supplies one day led to an incident which momentarily shocked her. Nikolatos told him she planned to bring something from Eleni. Tsafendas replied that she should bring an extra portion and tell the guards that he had asked for it to feed the worm. Nikolatos was astounded. She considered Tsafendas entirely sane and in all her years of visiting, he had never mentioned the tapeworm. On reflection later, she concluded that Tsafendas, ever-wary even in his new relaxed environment, was reminding the warders that he was still insane.[139]

On 10 April 1989, the South African Prisons Service publicly announced that Tsafendas was seriously ill, without elaborating further.[140] Tsafendas's main medical issue was his knees, which had been the target for warders' batons over many years. He was in continual pain, often unable to walk and forced to remain in bed as the authorities refused to provide him with a wheelchair. His heart was showing signs of weakness too. In September 1989, Tsafendas was transferred to the low-security Zonderwater Prison in Cullinan, just outside Pretoria, a decision most likely prompted in great part by the negative publicity generated by David Beresford's article in the *Guardian* three months earlier about Tsafendas's condition in prison and the deterioration in his health. South Africa was changing drastically and it was apparent that the collapse of apartheid was imminent. On 15 October 1989, some prominent anti-apartheid activists were set free after 26 years behind bars. They included Ahmed Kathrada, Jeff Masemola, Raymond Mhlaba, Wilton Mkwayi, Andrew Mlangeni, Elias Motsoaledi, Oscar Mpetha, Billy Nair and Walter Sisulu. On 11 February 1990, Nelson Mandela was also released after 27 years of imprisonment.

Tsafendas followed these developments with rising excitement. He knew that apartheid was ending, but he told Nikolatos that he did not expect any favours from a democratic government, expecting instead to die in prison. There was a difference between expectation and hope, however, and Tsafendas repeatedly expressed the hope that he would be released one day. He often quoted the Latin saying *dum spiro spero* ('While I breathe, I hope').[141]

By now, Tsafendas was being allowed to associate with other prisoners. Despite the easing of some rules, the authorities diligently followed the laws of apartheid that remained and Tsafendas was no exemption to the rule. Sometime in the early 1990s, a chief of the Shangaan tribe, the ethnic group to which Tsafendas's birth mother belonged, turned up at Zonderwater Prison and asked to see Tsafendas. He had been one of the children Tsafendas taught English and History all those years ago and the little boy had never forgotten him. However, since the chief spoke very little English, and the law stated that prison visitors must speak in a language known to the guards – either English or Afrikaans – the prison authorities declared that they could not allow the visitor from Mozambique to meet his old teacher.[142] The chief was the first person who was not either a lawyer, journalist, priest or social worker, to attempt to meet Tsafendas during his 28 years of imprisonment. In its dying throes, apartheid made sure that such a humane gesture would not take place.

Chapter 14

Justifying the Deed

In late 1993, Tsafendas suffered a stroke and was transferred from Zonderwater Prison to the Pretoria Central Prison's hospital. He was 75 years old and had spent 23 years in solitary confinement, most of them under severe psychological and physical torture. Back in Pretoria Central Prison, Tsafendas's treatment was the complete opposite of the previous 22 years he had spent there. To begin with, he was in a hospital not a cell, and for the first time in detention he was accorded dignity, respect and dedicated health care. Tsafendas was placed in a communal ward and was allowed to exercise in the courtyard at the same time as other prisoners. After years of solitary confinement, he was thrilled to interact with his fellow inmates. Most of the warders were genuinely appalled that he had been imprisoned for so many years under such barbaric conditions, while others guessed that he would be released soon and wanted to make a good impression on him. Despite the effects of the stroke, Tsafendas socialised freely with the other prisoners and his outspoken, jokey and friendly personality made him popular, even with the white inmates. The prisoners were curious about his past and he spent hours talking about it, though always careful not to reveal anything that might jeopardise his safety.[1]

Tsafendas spent the next few months between the prison hospital and the detention wing. Tsafendas's best friend among the prisoners was Hugo van der Merwe, an Afrikaner but an opponent of apartheid. A large, strong man with the reputation of a tough guy, Van der Merwe became Tsafendas's personal carer-cum-bodyguard. He helped him shave and bathe and made sure his personal needs were met. These included newspapers and magazines, which he paid for because Tsafendas was penniless.[2] Another inmate Tsafendas met at the time was Dimitris Skoularikis, a young Greek-South African sentenced to life imprisonment for a triple homicide. Like everyone else, Skoularikis had heard of the tapeworm and assumed Tsafendas was insane. However, when they conversed in Greek several times, he realised that Tsafendas was not only perfectly sane, but highly intelligent. They became quite close and, suspecting that Tsafendas was play-acting, he asked him one day, 'How is the tapeworm, Mr Tsafendas?' Smiling, Tsafendas replied, 'I don't have one. They [pointing to the prison guards] think I have one.'[3]

Nikolatos remained a frequent visitor, as well as Father Michalis. They were permitted to bring Tsafendas treats and gifts such as sweets, biscuits, newspapers and magazines. On one of her visits, Nikolatos gave Tsafendas a transistor radio. He was delighted. He spent many hours listening to news bulletins and to music, often remarking how much easier his jail time would have been if he had been allowed a radio during the first 28 years of his incarceration. He did complain though that it consumed a lot of batteries.[4] 1994 was a historic year for South Africa. The country's first-ever democratic election was held on 27 April with the participation of all citizens. The ANC surged to power with a commanding 62.65% of the vote and Nelson Mandela became president. It marked the end of apartheid. During the early 1990s, before the election, a major issue in the ongoing negotiations between the then government and the ANC was the release of political prisoners. Deeply involved in this process was the largest legal non-governmental organisation in the country, Lawyers for Human Rights. Jody Kollapen, a young lawyer at the time and subsequently a High Court judge, was heading up the Lawyers for Human Rights' Political Prisoner Release Programme as its national projects director. Kollapen and his colleagues visited jails throughout the country, explaining to prisoners who may have committed a crime with a political motive that they could apply for amnesty and assisting them in doing so. Many were set free as a result of the process, but Tsafendas was not approached because there was uncertainty about whether his crime was politically motivated. However, shortly after the April election, Kollapen received a call from the Governor of Pretoria Central Prison, saying, 'Look, there's a man here and perhaps you should come and visit him.'[5]

Like many South Africans, Kollapen had long suspected that Tsafendas was perfectly sane and was curious to talk to him. When he visited the prison, he found Tsafendas on his bed, surrounded by other prisoners, laughing and telling stories and clearly in very high spirits. For some time, Kollapen just sat there listening. He noted that Tsafendas was talking clearly and thinking logically, with nothing to suggest he was insane or unable to follow a conversation for more than 15 minutes as the trial court was told 28 years ago. Finally, Kollapen made a move and introduced himself, naming the organisation he represented. Tsafendas appeared surprised. 'Do you know who I am?' he asked.

> 'I know who you are and we all know who you are. You're a very famous man,' Kollapen replied.
>
> Tsafendas appeared to be flattered and said, 'Well, you know I killed Verwoerd.'
>
> 'Yes, I know. I went to his funeral,' Kollapen said with a smile.

Tsafendas did not find this funny and appeared uneasy, even worried. Could this lawyer's visit mean trouble for him, particularly since he had heard him talking as a 'normal' man? Finally and hesitantly, he asked, 'Well, why did you go to his funeral? He was your friend?'

'No,' Kollapen said, 'he wasn't my friend.' The lawyer explained that on the day of Verwoerd's burial in Pretoria, he was a young boy and when he and other local kids saw a lot of women, all dressed in black, walking towards the cemetery, they followed them out of curiosity. The police were there in large numbers but they allowed the boys to go through the crowd to the front, where they watched troops march and counter-march with military precision. This was something they had never seen before and they were transfixed. They had no idea that the funeral they were watching was that of the slain Prime Minister. Once Kollapen told his story, Tsafendas relaxed.[6]

Kollapen then explained to Tsafendas that the purpose of his visit was to assess his current situation. Recalling the visit, Kollapen said:

> *The authorities certainly did not regard him as someone who should be in prison. Without them expressing a view on what he did, the view was that he did not belong in prison. If he had committed a crime ... in any event he had served his time, and given where the country was at the time, trying to achieve reconciliation, trying to create a value system where people could say, 'Look, this is not about revenge,' and given that everyone understood the suffering he had gone through, there was a sense that he should not be here.*[7]

Tsafendas was delighted to hear this entirely unexpected news of a possible release and Kollapen was pleased to find him perfectly sane, lucid and logical in their conversations. Detecting in Tsafendas a deep need for companionship, Kollapen visited him several times in the prison hospital and spent many hours talking with him, not about the legal aspects of the case or his possible release, but about normal, everyday topics. Kollapen took advantage of his visits to ask other prisoners how Tsafendas was treated and received the unanimous answer that he was treated well and indeed was popular with authorities and inmates alike. He did not doubt this, as he had seen it with his own eyes. Although deeply grateful to Kollapen, Tsafendas was careful to confide nothing significant about the assassination. All his conversations with Kollapen were straightforward and matter-of-fact except once when Tsafendas described in vivid detail the story Tom Tuff had told him about the tapeworm, presenting it as his own experience.[8] Obviously, Tsafendas had no intention of dropping his guard with someone he had just met, no matter how good and kind he seemed to be.

It was at this time that the new prison authorities and the ANC government, aware of the appalling conditions in which Tsafendas was kept during the apartheid years and believing that he should be imprisoned no longer, began to consider amnesty. Many political prisoners were then benefitting from ANC amnesties, so the prison authorities arranged for him to be examined by a state-appointed physician and a psychiatrist. Tsafendas, suspicious of the doctors and unsure of what the future held for him, did not drop his guard. They found him to be suffering from cerebral atrophy[9] and as expected, schizophrenia as well, and in a joint report recommended that he be moved to a mental hospital.[10] Kollapen supported the idea of amnesty for Tsafendas and followed developments closely.

Mandela at the time was due to grant amnesty to a number of political prisoners and it was widely rumoured that Tsafendas would be among them. ANC spokesman Carl Niehaus said that Tsafendas, like all the political prisoners, should be considered for amnesty and release. In a public statement, he said:

> *The conditions under which he's been kept for the last twenty-eight years are absolutely appalling. We feel he was never correctly psychologically evaluated at the time of his trial, and the matter never treated the way it should have been. We're not justifying his crime all those years ago, but we don't know whether Tsafendas himself was even capable of knowing whether what he did was wrong or right. I personally have been worried about him for a long, long time, and now that the political scenario has changed, Tsafendas's situation can no longer continue.'*[11]

Sometime in early 1994, Father Minas, then in Cape Town, returned for a few days to Johannesburg and, upon hearing from Nikolatos about Tsafendas's health problems, visited him. For the priest, it was to be a defining meeting during which Tsafendas admitted that the tapeworm was a fiction and talked at length about his motives for assassinating Verwoerd. Father Minas had not seen Tsafendas since the late 1980s and found him in high spirits about the downfall of apartheid and the possibility of his getting amnesty. In such a jovial atmosphere, the priest felt it was safe to ask, 'How is the tapeworm, Dimitri?' Smiling with wide-eyed innocence, Tsafendas inquired, 'What tapeworm, my Father?' Father Minas, pretending to be taken aback, exclaimed, 'The tapeworm, Dimitri, the tapeworm,' and pointed to Tsafendas's stomach, just as Tsafendas had done in the high-security section years previously. Dropping the jokey dialogue but still smiling, Tsafendas said, 'I don't believe I have a tapeworm, my Father.' He then pointed to the warders and said, 'They think I have one.' He added, 'You have known me for 30 years, Father, did I ever give you the impression that I am insane?' Father Minas had never believed Tsafendas had a tapeworm but was pleasantly surprised to hear him admitting as much. A few moments later, Tsafendas told Father Minas lightly, 'If I believed I had a tapeworm, I would have gone to a gastroenterologist, not to a psychiatrist.'[12]

Tsafendas, relaxed and witty as in the old days in Mozambique, explained how he first heard the tapeworm story from Tom Tuff in the 1940s, and how he had taken possession of the tale and used it up to his arrest in 1966. He insisted that he had never told the police that the tapeworm had anything to do with the assassination. He admitted that he pretended to be mad while in police custody because he 'couldn't take the pain [of torture] any more'. He did not go into detail about how he used the tapeworm after his arrest or how he pretended to be mad, but said simply that his aim was to stop being tortured or even murdered. He said that he was ready to die for what he did, but he was afraid of an 'undignified death'. He was certain that the police would hang him in his cell and claim he committed suicide, that he was crazy and had no political motive for killing Verwoerd. He appeared to be embarrassed that he had used the tapeworm to escape death but avoided going into detail. This was the first time Father Minas had heard Tsafendas talk in such depth about his feelings, fears and motivations and though he was always certain he was quite sane, he was astonished by the details that his friend volunteered and by his knowledge of mental illness.[13]

Tsafendas told the priest that it was not at all difficult to convince his defence team and others who examined him that he was insane. Firstly, he had done it before and knew what to do, but more importantly, 'it was easy because everyone wanted to find me mad, both the government and my defence team,' he told his friend. He even gave advice to Father Minas of what to do if he ever wanted to convince someone that he was insane. 'You need two things,' he told him, 'a family history of mental instability and a childhood trauma' in his life. Like a lecturer, he explained that one of the commonest ways to simulate insanity was to pretend to hear voices, but that this was tricky because nowadays, psychiatrists could easily deduce if a person was lying. He said the only time he was caught pretending to be insane was in the United States when he had claimed to hear voices coming from the radiators. The memory seemed to amuse Tsafendas and he soon had the priest laughing along with him at his insanity antics. However, he also made a serious point about mental status and the law. It was too late when he discovered that US Immigration Law denied entry visas to insane persons and because of that, he was not allowed to stay. However, he said, he learnt his lesson from that and never made the same mistake again.[14]

Finally, Father Minas asked what prompted him to kill Verwoerd. Tsafendas took a deep breath. He told the priest exactly what he told the police 28 years earlier: that he considered Verwoerd to be a dictator and a tyrant, and he believed that because he was the 'brains behind apartheid', his 'removal' would be a stepping stone towards the collapse of racist rule. After finally opening up to Father Minas, Tsafendas talked at length about the assassination, but he always called it an 'execution'. He refused to use the word assassination and always corrected the priest when he did. He maintained consistently that his act was justifiable because of the reasons he had outlined earlier.[15]

Father Minas was still based in Cape Town, but was now spending more time in Johannesburg, so he visited Tsafendas regularly in the prison hospital. Invariably, they talked about the past, but also about current affairs. Once, Tsafendas, appearing unusually diffident, asked the priest if he would mail some letters for him or lend him the money to post them himself. He said he would use the hospital as a return address so the priest would not have to deal with any replies. Father Minas agreed readily to give him the money but asked why his friend was suddenly prepared to write letters himself. Tsafendas explained that in the 1980s, the prison censors read all of his letters and since they considered him to be a lunatic, they expected to see evidence of his insanity, such as references to the tapeworm. If he had written such letters in the past, they would have thought that he had gone insane.[16]

Another new visitor at the time for Tsafendas was Father Spiros Randos, the Greek Orthodox assigned as prison chaplain and a good friend of Father Minas. The new priest developed a good relationship with Tsafendas, who talked freely about his life but did not confide in him as he did with Minas, probably because he did not know him from the past. As to the assassination, as with the two other priests, he repeated that he had hoped to bring about a change of policy. The tapeworm was never mentioned. Father Spiros quickly formed the impression that Tsafendas was perfectly sane, witty and often sarcastic, even about himself, and the possessor of an extraordinary memory.[17]

In 1993, Father Ioannis Tsaftaridis, a Greek Orthodox priest from Zante, Greece, arrived in South Africa. A young 24-year-old, he heard the Tsafendas' story from Nikolatos, the other priests, as well as the local Greeks. Father Minas told Father Ioannis a great deal about Tsafendas, but he did not tell him everything, eschewing confidences his friend had entrusted to him. The young priest was nevertheless puzzled that his confrere and mentor should speak so passionately in defence of a man who had killed. After all, Father Minas was a priest and killing was a serious sin. Equally strange was that while the highest authorities stated that Tsafendas was insane, Father Minas, Father Michalis and Nikolatos insisted that he was perfectly sane. Father Minas agreed to take his young colleague on his next visit to the prison hospital.[18]

The two priests visited Tsafendas in early 1994 and found him, just as Kollapen had, surrounded by fellow prisoners, leading them in a series of South African songs, some of them revolutionary anthems from the worst years of apartheid. One was 'Ndodemnyama we Verwoerd', written in the 1950s by Vuyisile Mini, a prominent member of the ANC and Umkhonto we

Sizwe, who was hanged in 1964 for his anti-apartheid activities. The song, written in isiXhosa, contained the lyrics 'Pasopa nantsi 'ndondemnyama we Verwoerd' ('Look out, Verwoerd, here are the Black people'), an obvious warning to the architect of apartheid; it was a very popular anti-apartheid anthem throughout the years of the struggle. Although the lyrics were in isiXhosa and Tsafendas did not speak the language, he was able to sing the song perfectly and would later perform it for the priests.[19]

Fathers Minas and Ioannis did not interrupt the singing, but watched quietly. When Tsafendas spotted his visitors, he greeted them happily, delighted to see a friendly new face. When Father Minas introduced Father Ioannis to Tsafendas, he said, 'This is one of the greatest Greek heroes of our century. One day history will recognise him as such.' Tsafendas looked around and behind him, playfully in search of the big hero. 'I am so honoured to meet you, Mr Tsafendas,' Father Ioannis said nervously and shook his hand. Recognising the young priest's shyness, Tsafendas patted his back, shook his own head and said, 'That is Father Minas's nonsense. I am not a hero.' Tsafendas then chatted to the young priest, asking him about his life and where he was from. Soon, the priest and Tsafendas discovered that they had a common interest in poetry. Two of Tsafendas's favourite poets were from Zante. They were Dyonisios Solomos, whose poem 'Hymn to Liberty' became the Greek national anthem in 1865, and Andreas Kalvos. Father Ioannis was deeply impressed by Tsafendas's ability to quote so many of the poets' works. A few years later, Father Ioannis, who later became Bishop of the Greek Orthodox Church in Mozambique and then was given the same office in Zambia and Malawi, began a PhD at the University of Johannesburg about Solomos, partly inspired by Tsafendas's admiration for him and their conversation that day.[20]

This common interest apart, Tsafendas took to his new visitor immediately. While talking about music, Tsafendas happily showed the priests the radio Nikolatos had given him. Although there was music aplenty, that which was provided by the various radio stations was not to Tsafendas's taste. He told them he wanted to listen to 'revolutionary music', 'partisan songs', 'Greek music' and, of course, Paul Robeson. He explained how badly he had missed the music he liked in solitary and let them into his technique of singing songs to himself. Father Ioannis said he would get him a Walkman Compact Disc player so that he could listen to his preferred music whenever he liked. Father Minas had to explain to Tsafendas what a Walkman and CDs were.[21]

Excited to talk to someone who had been in Greece recently, he bombarded the priest with questions about the country's recent history and the current state of affairs there. He was aware of the 1967 coup and the seven-year rule that followed, but he knew almost no details. He also asked his visitor about his life and his own political views. Father Ioannis, scholarly and well-read, patiently answered all of Tsafendas's questions. After a while, Father Minas interrupted. 'Dimitri,' he said, 'we are here because Father Ioannis wanted to meet you and hear your story, not to tell his story or Greece's history. I'll get you a historical book to read if you like, but now tell us about Mozambique and Egypt, your childhood.' He also urged Tsafendas to elaborate on specific incidents in his life, such as his arrests and torture by the Portuguese and his participation in the Greek Civil War. Minas had asked his fellow priest not to mention the assassination and generally to let Tsafendas do the talking. This suited the shy Father Ioannis and he listened as Tsafendas talked about his life. Father Ioannis was deeply impressed and although he was desperate to ask about the assassination, he refrained. Father Minas occasionally interrupted to ask questions, all of which Tsafendas answered. When they left, Tsafendas asked the young priest to visit him again and Father Ioannis agreed readily.[22]

Father Ioannis did buy a Walkman, but, unsurprisingly perhaps, found no CDs of Paul Robeson or communist songs in the record stores of Johannesburg or Pretoria. Since he needed to go to Greece, he gave Nikolatos the Walkman and some CDs of modern Greek music to pass on. Tsafendas was delighted with the Walkman, but the CDs were not to his taste and he gave them back to Nikolatos with a request for old Greek or Cretan music. Nikolatos was dismayed that Tsafendas should return someone's gifts. Tsafendas argued that it was better not to listen to music at all than to listen to something one did not like and that it would be better to give the CDs to someone who would appreciate them. Despite her disappointment, Nikolatos got back to Father Ioannis and the priest began scouring the record shops of Athens and Zante. After much searching, he discovered a Paul Robeson CD, which he mailed to Nikolatos along with five or six discs of Tsafendas's preferred Greek music, plus a collection of Greek partisan songs. Tsafendas could not have been happier, but his hearing was deteriorating and it was becoming difficult for him to listen to the music.[23]

One of the CDs Father Ioannis sent was of the famous Cretan singer, Nikos Xilouris, known as the archangel of Crete, who died in 1980. Xilouris had become famous during the 1970s, so the imprisoned Tsafendas had never heard of him, but he fell in love with his voice immediately and quickly learnt to sing most of his songs. One of them was a musical version of Erotokritos, the 17th-century romantic epic by Vintsentzos Kornaros and the most famous of all Cretan poems. Tsafendas knew the poem well, having learnt it from his grandmother when he was a boy in Egypt. He was not aware that it had become a song and he listened to it time and again, memories of Egypt and his grandmother and Aunt Artemis flooding into his mind. Events he thought he had forgotten came back to him and he wept often. However, the song that became Tsafendas's absolute favourite was another traditional Cretan epic, 'Pote tha kani Xasteria' ('When Will the Sky Be Clear?'), a revolutionary anthem from the 18th century. It was written during the Cretan struggle for freedom from the Ottoman occupation and the lyrics were sung by a rebel who wondered when the sky would be clear so that he could take up his gun and fight the Turks. The song had become popular as a protest song during the military dictatorship in Greece between 1967 and 1974. Tsafendas was deeply moved by the powerful lyrics and often wept as he listened, humming or singing along.[24]

Although the CD player and the radio gave Tsafendas a great deal of happiness, he used them so much that he was always in need of batteries. Nikolatos brought replacements regularly and other prisoners would often give him some. The Walkman became very popular in the hospital ward and many of the inmates wanted to borrow it. Tsafendas was always happy to lend it out as long as the borrowers used their own batteries! At Tsafendas's request, Nikolatos also brought food and sweets for other prisoners, especially those whose families lived far away or had abandoned them, as his own family had done. He told Nikolatos to say the food and sweets came from their families. The warders saw nothing wrong with this and allowed the deception to continue.[25]

Sometime in late May or June of 1994, Father Ioannis returned to South Africa from Greece and visited Tsafendas with Father Minas. Delighted to see Ioannis again, Tsafendas seized the priest's hand in both of his and thanked him repeatedly for the Walkman and the CDs, explaining how much happier his life had become with the music. He said it had given him 'some years' (a Greek way of saying it had added extra years to his life).

With Tsafendas's effusive thanks over, Father Minas took out of his pocket a newspaper cutting. It was from the 15 May issue of the *Sunday Tribune*, which contained an article headlined, 'Amnesty for Tsafendas'. The story highlighted a statement by ANC spokesman Carl Niehaus suggesting just such a possibility for South Africa's most famous prisoner. The priests told Tsafendas that there was much discussion about him in the media and amnesty seemed a very possible outcome. Tsafendas was not so optimistic. There was nothing he desired more, he said, but he feared the government would never approve such a move for fear of alienating Verwoerd's supporters.[26]

Father Minas had also brought a cutting from an Afrikaner newspaper that contained a photograph of Verwoerd. Upon seeing it, Tsafendas made the identical spitting gesture he had made 28 years earlier when he saw Verwoerd's photo before the assassination. Then, he looked around and when he was certain no one was looking, he smiled and made a stabbing gesture. Turning to young Father Ioannis, Tsafendas said, 'Verwoerd was a dictator and a tyrant who oppressed his people. People were like slaves. He created apartheid. Do you know what apartheid was?' Father Ioannis said quietly, 'Of course, Mr Tsafendas.' Tsafendas shook his head and said, 'You can't know its real extent because you did not live here. Even if you had lived here, you would not have been able to tell of its real extent unless you had lived with coloureds and blacks. People were like slaves, they were only living to serve the whites. Verwoerd did that. He was a monster, almost as bad as Hitler. I call him 'Hitler's best student' because he copied some of Hitler's Nuremberg Laws and applied them to the blacks here. Do you know the Nuremberg Laws?' Father Ioannis, slightly embarrassed, said quietly again, 'Of course, Mr Tsafendas.' Tsafendas went on, 'Verwoerd would have done to the blacks what Hitler did to the Jews if he did not need them to serve the whites.'[27]

Tsafendas then launched into a monologue lasting several minutes on how Verwoerd used race theory to propel himself to near absolute power, earning the title the 'architect of apartheid' in the process. Tsafendas's grasp of the political building blocks leading to Verwoerd's career success was seen as extraordinary by both priests. Even Minas, though was always sure Tsafendas had killed Verwoerd because of his policies, didn't know he was so well informed about the Prime Ministers' life and political ascendancy. Father Ioannis, ignoring his fellow priest's admonition not to mention the assassination, asked, 'Why did you do it Mr Tsafendas?' Tsafendas repeated what he had told the police and Father Minas; however, this time, Tsafendas did not stop there but sought passionately to explain to the young priest how he found it within himself to kill Verwoerd. He said he could never have killed an ordinary person, but he would have had no hesitation in killing someone like Verwoerd. 'Verwoerd,' he said, 'was not an ordinary man but a dictator and a tyrant', the 'monster who created apartheid', 'an evil person'.[28]

Tsafendas said what he did was 'an act of profound moral principle', justifiable because Verwoerd was a dictator and tyrant. He explained that he had the 'chance to kill the monster who created apartheid', that it was his 'social responsibility', indeed his 'duty', to accept the chance, and that he would have regretted it all his life if he had not acted on it. He quoted Frantz Fanon at length, highlighting his revolutionary hero's argument that violence in the de-colonisation struggle was not just necessary but legitimate. He urged the priests to read the works of the political thinker he most admired. Again, Tsafendas referred to the assassination as 'the execution' and labelled it 'tyrannicide' and he reiterated his mantra that Verwoerd was 'the brains behind apartheid' and that he hoped 'things would change' and apartheid would sooner or later collapse without him.[29]

Father Minas interjected, 'Well, it did not collapse, Dimitri, it took almost another 30 years to collapse.' Tsafendas looked unhappy and did not reply. The priest said it was a very long shot to expect apartheid to collapse without

Verwoerd, to which Tsafendas replied that though he did not expect it to collapse overnight or within a couple of years, he sadly did not expect it to last another 28 years either. Father Ioannis then asked whether he regretted killing Verwoerd since apartheid took so long to collapse. Passionately, Tsafendas declared: 'No, no, no, not even for a moment, never, never.' Seized by emotion, his face contorted, he fiercely defended his action: 'I did the right thing. He was a dictator, he created apartheid; it was him who did everything. You did not live then to see how it was, people were like slaves ... Verwoerd had taken away their dignity.'[30]

Calming down, Tsafendas conceded he had miscalculated the longevity of apartheid, but reiterated that he never wished he had not acted. Verwoerd within his reach, failing to act would have made him not only a coward, but in effect, an accessory to Verwoerd's crimes, Tsafendas said. Father Minas, taken aback by the frankness with which Tsafendas talked about the killing, disagreed both with the deed and Tsafendas's justifying arguments and did not hide his viewpoint. Angered by this, Tsafendas demanded to know what he would have done if he had the chance to kill Verwoerd. Boldly, Minas replied, 'I would never have used violence or killed someone, Dimitri, to bring about political change.' Tsafendas retorted that if everybody thought like that, apartheid, colonialism and other dictatorships around the world would continue to exist. The priest smiled and nodded. Clearly unhappy with this response and reluctant to let the matter drop, Tsafendas raised the issue of sinning by omission, that if he had not acted, his guilt would have equalled that of Verwoerd, because any person who was aware of a crime and failed to intervene, or worse allowed it to continue when he had the power to end it, was as guilty as the criminal himself. Minas agreed with the second part of his friend's argument, but disagreed with the first, reiterating that it was wrong to kill a human being, however, he behaved. Tsafendas then put this question to the priests: 'Every day, you see a man you know committing a very serious crime for which millions of people suffer. You cannot take him to court or report him to the police because he is the law in the country. Would you remain silent and let him continue with his crime or would you do something to stop him? You are guilty not only when you commit a crime, but also when you do nothing to prevent it when you have the chance.'[31]

The priests replied that they would have wanted to stop the crime but would not kill to stop it. Tsafendas said, 'Then you would have been as guilty as Dr Verwoerd.' The argument dragged on, with the priests stressing the immorality of murder while Tsafendas produced arguments, counterarguments and examples from history to support his case. Tsafendas reminded Minas that many states killed people, legally and scientifically, under the constitutionally accepted laws of capital punishment. Minas said this was wrong too and that 'no one should have such power'. Tsafendas disagreed with the death penalty in normal circumstances but argued that it was applied correctly at the Nuremberg Trials and in the case of Adolf Eichmann and that it should have applied to all Nazi criminals.[32]

Hesitantly, Father Minas reminded him that he had killed a man and that it was a mortal sin, no matter who the person was and what he had done. Father Minas then asked another hard question: Had he thought about Verwoerd's children and the fact that he took their father away from them? Tsafendas lowered his head and said nothing. An awkward silence ensued; it was the first time Tsafendas appeared lost for an answer. Father Minas was about to change to some random, mundane question when Tsafendas raised his head and said slowly, 'I have thought of that, my Father, I really have.' Looking directly at the priest, he set out his view: It was sad that he had to deprive the children of their father, they were 'collateral damage' and there was nothing he could have done about it; also, the children were old enough at the time to know who their father was and what he was doing; if they were of the 'correct' mind, they would have acknowledged that, for most South Africans, their father was a tyrant. Minas asked if he would apologise to Verwoerd's children were he ever to meet them. Tsafendas replied that he would not, that to do so would be hypocritical since he was not sorry for what he had done and believed it to be the right thing. He argued that the children should understand that the 'execution' was justifiable. This prompted Minas to ask what he meant by 'justifiable'. Tsafendas argued that killing Verwoerd was justifiable on moral grounds, that as a tyrant, to assassinate him counted as tyrannicide, the killing of an unjust ruler for the common good. He reminded them that in ancient Greek it was the people's duty to remove a tyrant from power, even by killing him. Minas, a little hesitantly again, said, 'Yes, Dimitri, but we are not in ancient Greece, and being a Christian it is a sin to kill anyone, no matter who it is.'[33]

Tsafendas then replied that tyrannicide was an act whose morality had been upheld by philosophers and theologians down the ages, including such influential Christian theologians as Thomas Aquinas, John of Salisbury, Benjamin Franklin and Dietrich Bonheoffer. The priests were unaware of these positions, the only name they knew being Benjamin Franklin, but still insisted that killing someone was wrong. For Tsafendas, the lynching of Benito Mussolini and the killing of Reinhard Heydrich during the Second World War were both examples of modern-day tyrannicide. He then asked the priests if they would have killed Hitler to prevent the war and Father Minas said 'No', that the only justifiable reason to kill was in self-defence.[34]

When Father Ioannis asked Tsafendas if he would have killed Hitler, Tsafendas said 'Yes' without hesitation. The priest then asked if he could travel back in time whether he would have killed Hitler or Verwoerd as babies so that they would never grow up to become monsters. 'No,' said Tsafendas, adding that if he could travel back in time, he would try to veer the babies away from those influences that made them turn towards evil,[35] justifying his answer with a quote from Rousseau that 'all people are good by nature, but corrupted by society'.[36] Although he disagreed, Father Minas was impressed by his friend's cogent and methodical reasons for Verwoerd's assassination, as well as his arguments for the morality behind the act and his principled belief that to do nothing would have made him complicit in Verwoerd's own crimes.[37]

Father Ioannis asked why he stabbed the Prime Minister in Parliament, knowing full well that he could not possibly escape. Tsafendas explained how he had been unable to get a firearm, which was why he decided to use a knife, and that he did not care what would happen to him, that one should accept the loss of personal freedom or even one's life, if such an act would bring about beneficial social or political change. He went on to quote Andreas Kalvos from his poem, 'Eis Samon' (To Samos): 'Those who feel fear's unbending hand weighing on them may bear the yoke of bondage. Freedom demands virtue and courage ...'[38]

When Minas said that to kill someone without an escape plan was not very clever, Tsafendas's face darkened momentarily, then, speaking calmly, elaborated on his initial plan to shoot Verwoerd, then flee and take refuge in the *Eleni*; when he failed to get hold of a gun, he considered using a knife, though fully aware that in such a case there would be no escape; he struggled with the problem in his mind for two or three days before deciding to go ahead because he did not care what would happen to him. He had no wife or children or responsibility for anyone who might suffer from his action. He alone would pay the price and he was willing to do so. When Father Minas likened his action to a suicide mission and suggested he could have planned it better, Tsafendas, clearly unhappy again, replied with calm restraint that he was forced to act when he did because he was hired on a temporary basis and he might not find a gun in time. Minas said it was surely madness to kill Verwoerd knowing he would be captured. Tsafendas was now clearly angry with Minas's comments, particularly his characterisation of his act as madness. Speaking slowly and heavily, he turned to Minas and said, 'If I don't burn, if you don't burn, if we don't burn, how will the light vanquish the darkness?' He paused then added '... my Father?' making clear that the poet's question applied to the priest, too. Minas did not reply, aware that he had hurt his friend more than he realised and, importantly, that Tsafendas's political convictions were much greater than he had imagined. Tsafendas, smiling, then lightened the mood by pointing out that the words were not his, but a verse from Nazim Hikmet's poem, 'Like Karem (Kerem Gibi)'.[39]

When Minas asked if he had planned in advance to use the tapeworm to escape the death sentence, Tsafendas insisted that was never his intention, that what he wanted was to claim 'political responsibility' for his act. Father Ioannis then returned to the tapeworm. As he had done with Father Minas, Tsafendas explained that because he 'could not take the torture anymore' and fearing he would be murdered in his cell, he used the tapeworm. He insisted that he was not afraid to die, but he did not wish an 'undignified death' where he was murdered by the police who would then claim he was insane and had committed suicide.

Tsafendas appeared reluctant, clearly out of embarrassment, to elaborate further to the priests about the tapeworm and how exactly he used it after the assassination, but he talked proudly and happily about his Saint Peter act. Laughing loudly, he repeated what he had said to convince the Portuguese he was Christ's number one apostle and chuckled with delight as he mimicked their reactions.[40]

Father Minas then asked him how he considered his act in retrospect, since he had failed to bring down apartheid, lost his freedom and endured many years of torture. Tsafendas remained silent for a few seconds and then, clearly disappointed, said, 'I hoped things would change … I had the chance to kill this monster … if I had not done it, I would have regretted it all my life.' When Father Minas suggested Tsafendas had acted in a lost cause, he replied, 'There is no such thing as a lost cause, my Father. Any cause can be won … no cause or battle is ever lost until it is fought. If you fight, you always have a chance to win …' He then quoted Jean-Paul Sartre as saying, 'A lost battle is a battle one thinks one has lost.' He insisted that this was a battle he had won because although apartheid did not die immediately, it was never as strong afterwards as during Verwoerd's time. Besides, if the act had no other positive result, it meant Verwoerd was punished for his crimes. 'Look at Vorster, look at Botha,' Tsafendas told the priests. 'Just like Verwoerd, they were responsible for the enslavement of 20 million people and for the death and torture of thousands and they were not punished for their crimes. At least Verwoerd got what he deserved.'[41]

After hearing Tsafendas's explanation, Father Ioannis said he felt strongly that the world should know the truth about the tapeworm and all other aspects of his actions that had been covered up or distorted by the insanity defence. He said that the true story of the assassination should be disseminated worldwide and everyone should know that he was not a madman but a hero. Tsafendas appeared unimpressed. He shook his head and urged him not to do so. He said he did not care about being a hero because he had only done his duty, and seeking to get glory from it would undermine the value of his action. He said, 'When you do a good thing, you can't go around advertising it. You do it because it is the right thing to do, not to be applauded by the others. Do a good thing and then throw it into the sea[42] ... I believed it was my duty to do it when I had the chance and I did it.' Ioannis reminded him that posthumous fame and how people were remembered was of primary importance for ancient Greeks. Tsafendas replied, 'But we are not in ancient Greece, my Father,' then, looking at Minas, 'and I am not an ancient Greek, I am a modern one.' He told the priests he did not care about posthumous fame, he had done his duty and his conscience was clear. Anyway, he said, he did not agree with the ancient Greek philosophy; he believed that being happy in life was more important than how you would be remembered after death. Better, he said, to live a happy life and be forgotten afterwards than to live a miserable life and be hailed as a hero when you were dead.[43]

Father Ioannis insisted that it was an injustice that he was regarded insane. Father Minas was disturbed by his colleague's persistence and gestured to him to drop his argument. Tsafendas noticed the signal and said, 'It is all right,' but he insisted that they should not reveal his thoughts to anyone; he repeated that his conscience was clear and he did not care how people perceived him. Tsafendas then raised another reason for keeping quiet, the possibility that white racists might kill him if they found out that he was not mad after all but had killed Verwoerd for political reasons. He was convinced that he had remained alive all these years because everyone thought he was insane. Tsafendas also expressed the belief that one day the world would recognise that his deed, 'the execution', was a political act and not a mindless one, as it had been presented. Ioannis doubted the sincerity of Tsafendas's last two excuses, but, seeing the agitation on Minas's face, he dropped the subject.[44]

In private, the priests disagreed about what to do with Tsafendas's story. Father Ioannis argued that it should be told for Tsafendas's benefit, but Father Minas wanted to respect his wish for silence. Minas also argued that as priests, they should not reveal what they heard, a suggestion which his colleague opposed since the discussion had not been under the seal of confession. Father Minas was also concerned that revelations about Tsafendas's past actions and motives made while his amnesty was being discussed could damage his chances of freedom. Father Ioannis agreed and, for the time being dropped the subject.[45]

Privately, Father Minas wondered if Tsafendas carried out the assassination as he did, without any possible escape, because of guilt over his conduct during the Second World War. The priest had the impression that Tsafendas was ashamed of his lack of enthusiasm for a fighting role in the war and for pretending to be mad to avoid seaborne action. Minas wondered if the assassination, essentially a sacrificial gesture, was a way of redeeming himself for his cowardice. Ioannis did not see it that way and Minas conceded that it was only speculation, plus Tsafendas never said anything to support such a theory. However, Minas maintained that he would not be surprised if one day he heard that such was the case.[46]

Immediately after Nelson Mandela and the ANC won the elections, they began a campaign to rid the country of all vestiges of apartheid. The name of the once mighty Verwoerd, visible on many streets and public buildings, began to disappear. Mandela became president on 10 May 1994 and at the first meeting of his cabinet on 23 May, it was decided to 'throw the architect of apartheid out of the precincts of Parliament', as Reuters reported. In mid-June Verwoerd's marble bust was removed from the main auditorium of the H.P. Verwoerd Building, leaving just a brass plaque stating that the bust had been donated by his widow. Verwoerd's name was also stripped from the façade of a tower block opposite Parliament which housed ministers' offices. Mrs Betsie Verwoerd asked that the discarded relics be given to her family.[47] Soon afterwards, a statue of Verwoerd in Bloemfontein was taken down and a plaque in his honour was removed from Stellenbosch University; Hendrik Verwoerd Drive in Johannesburg was renamed Bram Fischer Drive and the H.F. Verwoerd Dam was renamed the Gurier Dam; Verwoerdburg was renamed Centurion.[48]

That is not to say that Verwoerd was removed from the minds of South Africans. When Media24 organised a nationwide survey in 1999 to determine who had the greatest influence on South African affairs during the 20th century, Verwoerd placed third, behind Nelson Mandela and F.W. de Klerk.[49] Support for the idea of apartheid persisted among some South African whites who argued that, harsh as it was, the policy formed a bulwark against Communism, which was then taking root in some independent African nations.[50] As late as 2004, an SABC poll for the '100 Greatest South Africans of All Time' placed Verwoerd 19th with 50,000 votes. Tsafendas was not named in this survey.[51]

During Tsafendas's time in the Pretoria Prison hospital, the staff were polite and kind, always allowing his visitors to bring gifts or treats and letting them stay beyond the official time. Nikolatos and Kollapen remained regular visitors. However, in late 1994, Father Ioannis returned to Greece and did not visit him again in the Pretoria Prison hospital; nor did Father Minas, who returned to his post in Cape Town. One who did visit Tsafendas regularly at this time was Hugo van der Merwe. One day, Van der Merwe went to see Jody Kollapen in the Lawyers for Human Rights offices as he knew the lawyer was visiting Tsafendas. He told Kollapen, 'Look, you know ... keep an eye on him, because he's a good old man.' Kollapen assured Van der Merwe that he was looking after Tsafendas and fully intended to keep on doing so.[52]

At this time, the government and the prison authorities were examining Tsafendas's case. Jody Kollapen and Alex Moumbaris, Tsafendas's one-time fellow prisoner in Pretoria, were among those who supported the idea of granting him amnesty and releasing him from prison. However, there were problems. Several members of the ANC and the new government privately recognised Tsafendas as a hero of the anti-apartheid struggle, but they were not ready to say so publicly. This was the much-touted era of forgiveness and reconciliation and some influential figures feared that to free the man who had murdered the god of many white South Africans would seriously set back those efforts. Another problem was the belief that Tsafendas could be in serious danger from racist whites if he was given his freedom. After much debate on the issue, the government, in June 1994, accepted the prison authority's recommendation to transfer Tsafendas to a mental institution. Officially, he was not given amnesty, simply released to a hospital for humanitarian reasons because of his health. The government saw this as the perfect solution as it sought to do the right thing for a man it believed did not belong in prison, without dangerously upsetting any whites. Thus it was the ideal balancing act. For someone to qualify for amnesty, that person had to prove that his crime was political. The official version held by apartheid, that Tsafendas was insane, was generally accepted by most South Africans, although many who knew the details of how apartheid operated and others in the struggle movement had serious doubts. The new government could easily have discovered the truth about Tsafendas simply by looking at the police records and of course by talking to him as well as to people who knew him. However, this did not happen for fear of a violent white reaction should Tsafendas be given amnesty.[53]

On 1 July, the correctional services minister, Dr Sipho Mzimela, ordered that Tsafendas's release and transfer to a hospital should be effected 'as soon as possible'.[54] When Tsafendas was informed he would be leaving, and aware that he was losing his hearing, he gave the radio and some CDs to fellow prisoners. He intended to keep the Walkman, but eventually, he gave it to a recently appointed warden who had been admiring the player and asking about it. As for the Greek CDs, since no one was interested in them, he gave them back to Nikolatos.[55]

On 5 July, Tsafendas was taken from the prison hospital to Sterkfontein Psychiatric Hospital in Krugersdorp, a gold-mining town about an hour's drive from Pretoria. The move was authorised by the then Minister of Health, Dr Nkosazana Dlamini-Zuma.[56] Tsafendas had spent 28 years in prison, making him the longest-serving prisoner in South African history. Arriving at the hospital, Tsafendas wondered if this was not another prison. Uniformed personnel at the entrance looked like prison officers and the gate could easily have been the entrance to a prison compound. The hospital was surrounded by a fence, doors were covered by metal grills, there were bars at the entrance and some of the windows had bars that any jail would be proud of. Expecting white-suited hospital medics, he saw security guards who could pass for warders and the living quarters appeared more like prison cells than hospital accommodation. Tsafendas was taken to Ward 12B, which author Henk van Woerden described as 'a barrack-like building divided into a number of dim, echoing rooms'. At the end of a long corridor was a vestibule and a small reception office, which, Van Woerden said, 'smelled of Lysol and old meals and of something unpleasant and difficult to identify'. The staff had no idea who Tsafendas was or that he had killed Verwoerd.[57]

Tsafendas was deeply unimpressed and his suspicions grew when he met Dr Merryl Vorster, the forensic psychiatrist in charge of his care. She was tall, with blonde hair cut short and dressed in what Tsafendas thought was a somewhat manly fashion. He thought she looked mean and more suited to being a prison warder or even a Nazi concentration camp guard. Then there was her surname and he wondered if she was related to the former Prime Minister.[58] Tsafendas had a difficult time at Sterkfontein, especially at the beginning. The hospital was seriously understaffed and the nurses were unable to look after all of the patients. What bothered him in particular was the noise, which was almost constant, with patients shouting or screaming, or simply talking loudly. Although he now had access to books, it was hard to find the tranquillity needed to read them. He mused how in prison he was tortured but also enjoyed long hours of quiet, something he became accustomed to over the many years spent there; in Sterkfontein, he was not tortured physically, but the noise seriously disturbed his peace of mind. The transfer also impacted visits. Sterkfontein was about an hour away from Pretoria, therefore more difficult for visitors to reach, and new regulations had been introduced for those wishing to see him. Because of concern for his safety, potential visitors needed permission from the ministry of health, the office of the Attorney-General and Dr Vorster. These rules, however, did not apply to Nikolatos because she was a registered social worker.

Jody Kollapen had expected Tsafendas released into society. Though disappointed, he believed the psychiatric hospital would be an improvement on prison and continued visiting him there. Confronted with the problems of access, he wrote to the Minister of Health, Dr Dlamini-Zuma, on 6 October 1994:

> *As you are probably aware, Mr Tsafendas is one of South Africa's more well-known prisoners and for many years was held under trying conditions within the South African prison system. The writer did visit*

> *Mr Tsafendas on a few occasions when he was still being held by the Department of Correctional Services at the Pretoria prison hospital. On those occasions I personally found that I was able to effectively communicate with him and the time we had spent together was certainly productive in attempting to understand him, as well as in attempting to provide some type of companionship to him. I was informed at those times he received no other visitors and it was certainly my intention to continue visiting with him.*
>
> *He is seventy-six-years old and might not have many years ahead of him. It is with this in mind that I attempted to arrange to visit him at the Sterkfontein hospital. I made telephonic contact with the Superintendent, Dr Botha, and was informed that before permission for a visit could be granted I had to seek consent from the Department of Health, the office of the Attorney-General as well as from the doctor who was presently treating Mr Tsafendas. I must say that this came as a total surprise to me as during the times that I had visited him in Pretoria I did not experience such problems in gaining access to him. In particular, Mr Tsafendas was held in a communal hospital ward with ten to fifteen other prisoners and even during my visits with him we were often joined by other prisoners in our discussions.*
>
> *I believe that the requirements that have been imposed (and I am not certain on whose authority they emanate from) are unreasonable and effectively make access to Mr Tsafendas unnecessarily difficult.*
>
> *I believe, given the suffering the man has endured over the years, it certainly would be cruel if visits to him are dealt with in the fashion I have described. I trust that you will look into this matter in order to facilitate easier access to visiting Mr Tsafendas. I certainly believe that the interests of the patient as well as the interests of society do not warrant the type of conditions that have been imposed.*[59]

The Minister replied promptly, granting him unlimited access, and Kollapen began seeing Tsafendas again on a regular basis. He was saddened to see that the move had affected Tsafendas negatively. The lively, jokey, outspoken and talkative man of the prison hospital had, in a few months in Sterkfontein, become taciturn, depressed and moody, scarcely recognisable as the Tsafendas of old. Both his physical health and his morale had deteriorated markedly. Kollapen was convinced that Tsafendas should be released from the psychiatric hospital to live the last years of his life as a free man. He promptly embarked on a mission to achieve such an outcome. On 24 November 1994,

Kollapen wrote a striking memorandum to the new, democratically elected regional government of Gauteng, pleading for Tsafendas's unconditional release. He stated:

> *... he [Tsafendas] was the only State President's patient who was not held in a mental institution but in a prison and we have no doubts whatsoever that the reasons for that were purely political and were based on inflicting the maximum amount of suffering upon the man who killed the so-called architect and grandmaster of apartheid ...*
>
> *It remains my belief that Mr Tsafendas should not die a lonely man in an institution but should spend the last years of his life in the company of people he knows and perhaps trusts ... In summation, I believe that the man has served his debt to society (if he owed a debt at all in the first place). His age and disposition certainly do not warrant him being held in an institution and if it was possible to release him either to family or into an old age institution run by the State, this might be the best approach to follow at the present time.*[60]

Kollapen's plea prompted the government at both local and national levels to reconsider Tsafendas's case. The amnesty issue resurfaced and one idea raised was to release Tsafendas on purely humanitarian grounds without reference to amnesty, which would have raised the question of the assassination. The government was in favour, but there was a problem: Where would Tsafendas go upon release and who would care for him? He was 76 and unable to walk unaided. He spent his waking hours in a wheelchair and, though he spoke and thought clearly, he was incapable of looking after himself physically.[61]

Kollapen insisted Tsafendas be released to his family or to individuals who were willing to look after him. However, the question of Tsafendas's care proved a huge problem for the young lawyer. Since Verwoerd's assassination, Victor Tsafantakis had removed his name from all official or quasi-official publications to avoid being contacted regarding Tsafendas. The family had also appointed a lawyer to represent them, and all inquiries, from journalists or others, regarding their half-brother went through him. No outsider had managed to talk to the family since the assassination. Kollapen contacted members of the Greek community who got in touch with some of Tsafendas's family who lived in Pretoria. Victor had died by then, leaving only his three half-sisters. However, at the time, only Evangelia was in Pretoria as Bushia and Eleni were away on holiday in Greece. Evangelia had never enjoyed a good relationship with Tsafendas and when asked if she would look after her half-brother upon his release, she refused point blank. For one thing, she said, she was too old. At 74, she lived alone with occasional help from a domestic worker; her husband Charles had died several years earlier. As for Bushia and Eleni, since they were out of the country at the time, neither was contacted by Kollapen, and Evangelia never apparently mentioned the issue to them.[62]

After his setback with the family, Kollapen again contacted the Greek community in Pretoria. Nikolatos suggested that Tsafendas should be admitted to Agios Nektarios, an old people's home in Johannesburg run by the Greek Orthodox Church of South Africa. Father Michalis Visvinis supported the idea and agreed to have Tsafendas moved there. However, the decision was not his, but that of the councils of the Greek communities in Pretoria and Johannesburg and mostly of the Reverend Pavlos Ligris, Archbishop of the Greek Orthodox Church in South Africa since the 1960s. Although the Archbishop was instinctively conservative in his political views, he was sympathetic towards Tsafendas and often asked the visiting priests, 'How is that poor man doing?'[63]

Upon hearing from Nikolatos about Tsafendas's proposed release, the Archbishop agreed without hesitation to have him housed and cared for in Agios Nektarios. However, the elected representatives of the councils had to agree too. The issue became an instant talking point among Pretoria's and Johannesburg's Greeks. Commercial leaders warned the Archbishop that such a move would attract negative publicity to the community and there was a very real possibility that Afrikaners would boycott their businesses. Worse, they feared that Afrikaners who had not forgotten the assassination might attack Greeks and their properties, as had happened in 1966. Other opponents of the move said that Tsafendas's presence in the care home and the probable constant presence of journalists would upset others living in the home.[64]

Aris Papageorgiou, Pretoria's council president, favoured giving shelter to Tsafendas, but he was one of few on the board and even fewer in the wider Greek community who felt this way. With a vast majority of Greeks opposed to the idea, Archbishop Pavlos reversed his position. Nikolatos was furious when she heard of the Archbishop's change of heart and tried desperately to convince him that the business people were wrong. Fathers Michalis, Spiros, Ioannis and Minas supported her. They were fighting a losing battle, however, and the Archbishop and the council ruled that Tsafendas would not be admitted to the old-age home.[65]

Disappointed but undeterred, Kollapen decided to give another try with the family, hoping they might change if the request came from a high official level, rather than from a young lawyer working for an organisation they had probably never heard of. Accordingly, Kollapen wrote to the regional government, asking it to intercede with Tsafendas's family. He considered that if the government 'were to approach the family, their response might well be different'.[66] A government representative duly contacted the family, but the response remained the same. With no private party available to care for him and the government unwilling to accept him in any of the state's institutions, Kollapen conceded defeat and accepted that Tsafendas would remain in Sterkfontein. On reflection, Kollapen concluded that the old man would be happier with the care he was receiving from people who knew him than in a new institution where nobody wanted him. He continued visiting Tsafendas and inquired about taking him out of the hospital for a day. However, bureaucratic difficulties and Tsafendas's fragile health prevented this from ever taking place.[67]

Tsafendas had often spoken to Kollapen of his regard for Archbishop Tutu, admiring his resistance to apartheid. He believed he was exactly what a priest should be, on the side of the people, not the government; he said this often to the priests who visited him in prison. Where Tsafendas disagreed with Tutu was with regard to the Archbishop's criticism of Communism. Kollapen was told by the hospital staff that Tsafendas had written to Tutu asking if he would visit him, but the Archbishop had not done so. On 15 December 1994, Kollapen wrote to Tutu, as follows:

> *... in a few of my visits that I have had with him he has often expressed the desire to speak with you ... In addition, staff informed me that he has informed them that he has written to you with regard to visiting him.*
>
> *I know that you have a busy schedule and that you probably receive numerous requests which make inroads into your time, but I wish to appeal to you that if, when you are next in the Johannesburg area and if you can find the time to pop in and say hello to him, he would really appreciate it. He is now 77 years old, not in the best of health and I understand reliably from doctors who are treating him that his time on earth is limited. I have no doubt that a visit by yourself to him will certainly be the highlight of his life and in this context I appeal to you to see whether it is at all possible for you to schedule a visit to him at the Sterkfontein Hospital into your busy schedule. If you are able to do so I would be obliged if your offices could make contact with me with regard to a possible date and time, where after I will ensure that all the necessary logistical and administrative arrangements are made at the hospital for such visit.*[68]

However, Archbishop Tutu did not manage to visit Tsafendas. Sometime in 1995, Tsafendas suffered another stroke which left him with a paralysed arm. Unable to shave or use the toilet unaided, he was now heavily dependent upon the nurses and this he found deeply embarrassing. He always asked for a male nurse when he needed the bathroom. The staff rarely offered to help, though they knew his needs, and so he was forced to ask, a dependence he hated. In his practical and clear-headed way, Tsafendas did not blame the staff. He told Father Minas the nurses' jobs were the worst in the world, requiring them to deal with so many people, often elderly and with mental problems, to clean them, to clean up after them, to feed them and dress them. He characterised the nurses as 'heroes' and said he could never have done their jobs for all the money in the world.[69]

Van Woerden described the smell in the hospital as 'the rotten sweetness of uncared-for teeth and unwashed armpits, mixed with the odours of half-digested food rising from the bowels and through the pores of the skin'. He called it 'the smell of old, unwashed men'.[70] Tsafendas was well aware of the odour; he knew that he, too, smelled because he was dirty, but he could do nothing about it since he could no longer wash himself. He had to ask again and again to be washed or shaved but there simply were not enough workers to look after everyone. Tsafendas would tell the priests and Nikolatos when they visited, 'Stay away from me, I smell.' Nikolatos often asked the staff to wash him and they always said 'yes', but rarely did. Sometimes, she would wash or shave Tsafendas herself. Nikolatos also gave him a bottle of perfume, but Tsafendas had never liked colognes and scents; after a few reluctant applications, he decided that the perfume mixed with his body smell produced an odour that was even worse than his normal one. Thus, he gave the perfume to another patient.[71]

Unsurprisingly, Tsafendas's behaviour changed and his morale plummeted after entering Sterkfontein. When Nikolatos first met him, although he was in prison, Tsafendas was lively, pleasant and scrupulously polite. Now, he was grumpy, difficult, unreasonable and sometimes plain rude. Once, Tsafendas shouted angrily at a nurse after she said she would attend to him 'later'; when she turned her back, Tsafendas grabbed a pillow from another patient and threw it at her. The nurse just looked at him and walked away. Tsafendas told Nikolatos that he had been asking this nurse all day to wash him and she had given him the same response each time. Nikolatos was aware of Tsafendas's frustrations, but she would scold him for his behaviour. She could scarcely believe how he had changed in less than a year.[72] Among those nurses who were more attentive to Tsafendas was an African he called 'the Strong Man'. One day, the nurse slapped Tsafendas good-humouredly on the back, then extended a hand and gave him an African palm-and-thumb greeting. Tsafendas described the Strong Man to his visitors as 'a really good chap. A very virtuous man, but strong.'[73]

Throughout his life, Tsafendas had managed to adjust to radically different environments and in Sterkfontein, he sought and found a measure of relief in the patients around him. His eventful past provided an endless series of real-life stories with which he entranced the many ward-mates who loved his company. As a man of ideas and strong opinions, he would also originate lively debates about politics, religion and history, his favourite subjects. Among these patients was Tsehla Mike Phahlane, also known as Mazurkie. Phahlane, three years older than Tsafendas, had been a famous jazz musician and critic and a leading crime reporter. Phahlane became one of Tsafendas's closest friends, one of the few the latter ever spoke to, albeit cautiously, about his life and the assassination. They had much in common, in particular their love for jazz, and he was the first person Tsafendas met during his time in detention who had heard of Paul Robeson! Phahlane, for his part, considered Tsafendas to be a South African hero for killing Verwoerd and every year on 6 September organised a party in the hospital to celebrate his friend's deed. At first, Tsafendas baulked, but Phahlane convinced him that he had nothing to fear, and somehow food and drink were found to mark the day. Phahlane had influence with some of the staff, as well as patients, and persuaded them to look after Tsafendas when he was not around.[74]

It was also due to Phahlane that Tsafendas celebrated his birthday for the first time in 29 years. Since 1966, 14 January had been like any other day in Tsafendas's life. He was the only person in prison who knew it was the day of his birth and invariably, he spent it alone in his cell. When Phahlane somehow learnt of the date, he organised a celebration to mark his 77th birthday in 1995, that took Tsafendas totally by surprise. Wheeled into a special room, he was met with Phahlane and a crowd of nurses and patients singing for him. Tsafendas sat with his mouth open throughout the song and then the tears came in a flood. Phahlane broke from the choir ranks when the song ended and hugged and kissed Tsafendas, who clung to him, choking and repeating, 'Thank you, thank you, thank you so much.' Phahlane then raised a glass and declared loudly, 'To my comrade Dimitri, the greatest hero of our beloved country.' He paused, then added … 'who had the courage to do what no one else had the courage to do.' Most of those present did not know about Tsafendas's past but raised their glasses and joined in the toast. However, some asked Phahlane afterwards and he told them who Tsafendas was, to their total surprise. Tsafendas rated the party the happiest event in his life since his arrest for the assassination. He cried a lot that night, but they were tears of joy. None of his regular visitors had ever asked about his birthday, not even Nikolatos or the priests, and when Tsafendas asked Phahlane how he had found out, the only answer he got was a wide smile.[75]

Phahlane frequently told Nikolatos and the patients that 'this man [Tsafendas] is the greatest South African hero of all … he is the sanest man in this country' and he urged her to work for his release. Tsafendas saw Phahlane as his best friend in the hospital, 'a great and caring man', and always asked

Nikolatos to bring something for him when she visited. When Tsafendas first introduced the two, Nikolatos shook Phahlane's hand and said, 'Very nice to meet you.' Tsafendas signalled that she should kiss him. Surprised and unsure, Nikolatos hesitated, but Tsafendas repeated the gesture and she then greeted Phahlane with a kiss on each cheek. Later, Tsafendas thanked Nikolatos for her warm gesture and explained that since Phahlane had been held for almost 20 years, he thought a kiss from a woman would cheer him up. After that, Nikolatos always greeted Phahlane with a warm embrace and the double kiss.[76] As Tsafendas had requested, she also brought him food. Ironically, it was her food gifts to the hospital patients that were later to cause a deep rift between Tsafendas and herself.

Dances were a social highlight of the patients' dull lives and the hospital organised these on a regular basis. Stuck in a wheelchair, Tsafendas could not perform on the floor, but sometimes a nurse or fellow patient would push him round in the chair in time to the music, and this he loved. He never missed a dance, clapping from the sides of the floor and urging the shyer patients to give it a try. The dances were one of the very few things that reminded him he was in a hospital, no longer a prison.[77]

The talk of amnesty had brought Tsafendas back into the national limelight and journalists were eager to speak to him. Sometime in late 1994 or early 1995, Liza Key, a film-maker and anti-apartheid activist decided to fulfil a long-held dream to make a documentary about Tsafendas. Thus, she visited Tsafendas in Sterkfontein where he was still interned in a ward for the criminally insane. She was accompanied by David Beresford of the British *Guardian* newspaper who had already written about Tsafendas in 1989 and was keen to follow up on the story. However, Tsafendas was suspicious of just about everyone and journalists were no exception. Although Key and Beresford made a good impression on him and he was flattered by their interest, he did not trust them and revealed little about his life or the assassination, certainly nothing like what he told the priests. Key took an immediate liking to Tsafendas and the feeling was mutual. She felt deeply sorry for the treatment she had received over the years and was distressed by his current situation, abandoned by his family and no one in the State concerned about him. Tsafendas, for his part, admired Key's strong personality and evident kindness. After this visit, it would be some months before Key and Beresford saw Tsafendas again.

In the meantime, curious about Tsafendas's past, Key visited the National Archives of South Africa and accessed his files, the first inquirer ever to do so. Among the documents were Tsafendas's statements to the police, which, to her great surprise, revealed that he had given clear and logical political reasons for the assassination. More than that, he made no mention of a tapeworm, indeed, she found the police were pressing him to say that a tapeworm had something to do with the assassination. Further exploration revealed that Tsafendas described in police statements by friends and acquaintances was a completely different person to the one portrayed at his trial and during the Commission of Enquiry.[78]

In October 1995, Key filmed her first interview with Tsafendas at Sterkfontein Hospital. Beresford accompanied her. Still interned in a ward for the criminally insane, Tsafendas was escorted across a courtyard by a guard to his seat in front of Key's camera. He was wearing a khaki hat pinned up at the edges and a striped dressing gown. He seemed remarkably cheerful and quite amenable to being interviewed although his hearing had markedly deteriorated since their first meeting. It soon became clear, that Tsafendas seemed able to hear 'better' when he was interested in what the other person had to say, while he was unable to hear about subjects he did not care about. Beresford scribbled on a piece of paper, 'Did you kill Verwoerd?' Tsafendas matter-of-factly replied, 'Yes, Hendrik Verwoerd was an immoral man and I decided to kill him. And I killed him". Key had hoped to tell Tsafendas about the discovery of the police statements in the National Archives but soon realised that they were not going to get a response out of him. He either could not hear or was not interested in talking about the documents that had kept him imprisoned for 28 years.[79] Nevertheless, he described in detail how he planned and carried out the assassination and even told them that he had used an anti-rust solution on the knife. He never told them that the tapeworm had anything to do with the assassination.[80] The pair revisited Tsafendas several times for the film. Key was certain that Tsafendas was perfectly sane, while Beresford thought that he was sane before he was imprisoned, but that now his mind had begun fraying. Their disagreement on this topic became a matter of friction between the two.[81]

Key was initially uncomfortable with Dr Vorster, but something the doctor said came to affect her deeply. At the end of Key's first visit, the psychiatrist told her, 'You are like everybody else. You come to see him once or twice and then forget about him.' Dr Vorster was angered by the attitude of some politicans and officials who had taken an interest in Tsafendas, then walked away, curiosity satisfied. 'No one cares about him,' the doctor told Key, who thereupon decided to prove her wrong. She made it her aim to visit Tsafendas at least once every two weeks, and true to her word, long after the documentary, indeed for the rest of his life, Key visit him regularly out of friendship and compassion. She always brought him chocolates and avocadoes and listened patiently to him talk about his life. Sometimes, she gave him photographs of people he knew, such as Patrick O'Ryan, who she met while making her film, or of places like Maputo, so he could see how they had changed. Often Tsafendas recognised people he had known and places he had been, but other times, too many years had passed since he last saw them. Frequently, he wept on recognising an old friend or companion and noting how much older they were now. Key also sometimes took friends with her to meet and talk to Tsafendas. The two developed a good friendship and Tsafendas, trusting her more and more, opened up about his past and the assassination. Key had no doubt that her new friend was perfectly sane and became determined, like Jody Kollapen, to help him. As for Dr Vorster, Key realised that she was in fact a truly compassionate person who cared deeply for Tsafendas.[82]

Shortly after completing *A Question of Madness*, Liza Key organised a screening of the film at Sterkfontein Hospital. On an improvised screen, she projected the documentary for Dimitri and about 20 of his fellow inmates. All in various states of drug-induced consciousness and slightly perplexed, they shuffled into the makeshift cinema and took their seats. Some eyes lit up briefly when they saw the cake and drinks laid out for refreshments afterwards, though other heads started nodding as soon as they took their seats. As with the priest's account of the play that featured him, Tsafendas seemed quite uninterested in the film of which he was the 'star'. As the documentary began to roll, the shuffling stopped and the entire audience, including Tsafendas, fell asleep. As the story of a man who changed the course of South African history unfolded all that was heard above the soundtrack and the buzzing of a trapped fly were the sounds of snoring, the odd mutterings and heavy breathing. Twenty minutes into the film, news footage of Hendrik Verwoerd explaining apartheid away as something that good neighbours always do, Dimitri opened his eyes, looked at the screen, said: 'I know that man' and went back to sleep.[83]

One person who never forgot Tsafendas was Alexander Moumbaris, who was still attempting to have him amnestied. He had lobbied all his friends in the ANC, especially Ronnie Kasrils, who had recruited him to the MK and who was now Deputy Minister of Defence in Mandela's government. In March 1996, Moumbaris, along with his wife Marie-Jose and his daughter Chloe, visited South Africa for the first time since his famous escape in 1979, as a personal guest of Nelson Mandela. With the help of Kasrils, he promptly arranged to see Tsafendas. Moumbaris and Marie-Jose travelled together to Sterkfontein Hospital, where they were met by Dr Vorster. Like Tsafendas, Moumbaris also thought the hospital seemed more like a prison: 'It was just like a prison, only the qualification was different.' Like Tsafendas, he thought Dr Vorster appeared 'hard' and not suited to care for people in need of compassionate attention. Moumbaris also got the impression that the psychiatrist and the hospital staff were disappointed that Minister Kasrils was not present as they had apparently expected. When Moumbaris suggested that the warders/nurses were more like security guards, Dr Vorster assured him that this was not so, but he remained unconvinced.[84]

Dr Vorster led the visitors to the building where the visit was to take place and a wooden door was unlocked by a uniformed guard. On the left was a room with a table and a few chairs and to the right, an office with a person in uniform; ahead of them was a grilled partition and door, just as in the South African prisons Moumbaris remembered. Soon, Tsafendas was brought in from beyond the grill. Moumbaris was shocked. His old friend had snow-white hair, walked with difficulty, stooping and uncertain; he had aged markedly and his face was so highly coloured that it was almost mauve. Deeply saddened, Moumbaris embraced the old man warmly, as did his companion, only to find that Tsafendas had no memory of him. 'Who are you all?' he wanted to know.[85] That Tsafendas did not recognise Moumbaris was hardly surprising, since 24 years had passed since they last saw each other.

Soon, Dr Vorster left, but a uniformed nurse stayed behind, apparently to observe or monitor Tsafendas's conversations with his guests. Moumbaris spoke in Greek, which the nurse certainly did not understand, but she did not intervene. Moumbaris recalled their time together in prison, but Tsafendas was vague. When Marie-Jose said she came from France, Tsafendas came to life and started speaking French to her, recounting his time in that country. Moumbaris mentioned that he had been born in Egypt and Tsafendas promptly switched to Arabic, but none of his visitors could speak the language. It was obvious that Tsafendas had serious hearing problems and his visitors had to shout to be understood. Sometimes they resorted to writing questions or observations.[86]

One question from Moumbaris that got through was about conditions in the hospital. Tsafendas replied, 'I am ignored.' He said the staff paid little attention to him and he struggled to meet his everyday needs. At one point, Moumbaris asked him, always in Greek, if there was anything he wanted. Tsafendas replied with emotion, 'My liberty.' Tsafendas said he received no regular visits, had no money and no spectacles, which he needed to read. He complained that his Concise Oxford Dictionary had been stolen by somebody he named as Ivan Ward, who used it to buy cigarettes. About the food, he had no complaints. 'I have plenty to eat and plenty clothes,' he said.[87]

At the end of the visit, Marie-Jose kissed Tsafendas on the cheek and embraced him warmly. 'Can I get you something? Is there anything you need?' she asked in French. Staring longingly at the window, Tsafendas replied in

French, 'I want to see the sea once again before I die ...' Marie-Jose hugged Tsafendas tightly again and he would not let her go. He had not been held by a woman for almost 30 years and he found long-forgotten comfort and warmth in her embrace. Marie-Jose could not hold back her tears and averted her head so that Tsafendas would not see her weeping. When her husband moved to embrace Tsafendas, Marie-Jose slipped quietly out of the room. Moumbaris asked Tsafendas in writing if there was anything he could do for him since he was well connected with the ANC and was going to meet Nelson Mandela. Tsafendas wrote in English: 'I want my freedom.' Moumbaris held Tsafendas in a farewell embrace and silently vowed to help him get his freedom.[88]

After the visit, Moumbaris wrote a report for the ANC, saying Sterkfontein seemed more like a prison than a hospital, and that Dr Vorster, in his view, was 'unsuitable to deal with patients who are frail and who have been submitted to the treatment that Tsafendas had inflicted upon him in the last thirty years'. About Tsafendas, he wrote, 'Clearly, he is lucid, capable of sustaining a conversation as long as it is done in a friendly way. Clearly, he needs human attention and affection. He needs care and to live as normal a life as possible. Living in these conditions, after thirty years of incarceration, is cruel and inhuman treatment.'[89]

A few days later, after he had dinner in Nelson Mandela's house as his official guest, Moumbaris met with George Bizos, who had defended him after his arrest in 1972. Moumbaris raised the issue of Tsafendas, hoping that Bizos might help because of his close relationship with Mandela and the ANC. However, Bizos only warned Moumbaris that, if Tsafendas was freed, his life could be at risk from fanatical Afrikaners who worshipped the memory of Verwoerd. Bizos insisted that the hospital was at present the best place for Tsafendas since at least there he was receiving care and protection. Moumbaris was not happy with the outcome and continued pressing for Tsafendas's release, though with no realistic results.[90]

As she had done at the Pretoria Prison Hospital, Nikolatos, at Tsafendas's request, would bring food for some of the patients who had been abandoned by their families. Again, following Tsafendas's instructions, she would tell them that the food came from their own people. One day, a female nurse told Tsafendas to stop asking Nikolatos to bring the extra food, saying if he wanted to be extravagant, it should be with his own money, not Nikolatos's. Tsafendas was furious and shouted at the nurse that he was acting for the benefit of the patients not for personal gain. The nurse retorted that he was creating false expectations among the patients, who might start asking to see their relatives. Besides, she said, Nikolatos could not go on bringing extra provisions forever and the whole situation could end in exposure. Tsafendas tacitly acknowledged that she had a point but he was angered by the nurse's tone and told her to 'stop patronising me'. The argument concluded with Tsafendas swearing at the nurse and telling her to 'get lost'.[91]

When Nikolatos heard about the dispute, she talked to the hospital staff who argued that the extra food could not be supplied indefinitely, especially since a day would come when Nikolatos would stop visiting and the patients would then be deeply disappointed. Nikolatos thereupon agreed to stop bringing food for other patients. Her decision angered Tsafendas, who declared that if Nikolatos would not bring anything for his friends, she should not come back to see him. Nikolatos was deeply upset by this and thought Tsafendas should have been more understanding. However, she continued to visit him and, although Tsafendas apologised for his behaviour, he refused to accept anything she brought him.[92]

Nikolatos was worried about Tsafendas's deterioration in health, especially over the last two years, when he had lost much of his physical capability. His mind was sharp, but he had aged noticeably, his hearing was very poor and with one arm paralysed, he could not walk, bathe, shave or use the toilet without assistance. Nikolatos sensed that he did not have much time left and his doctors did not disagree with her.[93]

Sometime in 1996, Henk van Woerden, a Dutch author and painter, visited Tsafendas with the intention of writing a book about him. Tsafendas was suspicious about this new visitor because of his origins, because he thought he had an 'untrustworthy face' and because he did not care for the way he dressed; in his view like an undercover police officer in a noir movie. In time, however, Tsafendas's instinctive hostility faded and, needing companionship, he chatted amiably enough with the writer, though careful never to reveal anything truly important about his life and thoughts.[94] Van Woerden did not tell Tsafendas that he planned to write a book about him, although he did say he was an author. He always brought a tape recorder and a camera, recording their conversations and taking photographs of Tsafendas. Tsafendas just assumed that, like Beresford and Winter, he was preparing a newspaper article. When it became apparent that Van Woerden knew a great deal about his background, Tsafendas was quietly gratified but also taken aback; it was another reason to be careful with this latest visitor.[95]

As for Van Woerden, he was impressed by Tsafendas and characterised him as 'a charming chatterbox, a survivor from the detritus of South African history'. For all his doubts, Tsafendas asked Van Woerden at the end of his first visit if he would visit him again. When the author said 'yes', he would come the next day, Tsafendas made him swear to do so. Van Woerden promised and was duly back at Sterkfontein the following day.[96] Indeed, the writer turned out to be the very opposite of the person Tsafendas had feared. He genuinely cared for Tsafendas and treated him accordingly, not merely as the subject for his literary endeavours, as Tsafendas had suspected.

Throughout their association, Van Woerden showed a lively concern for Tsafendas's welfare. On his first visit, he asked Matron Geyer if he could take Tsafendas for a walk in the garden. She replied, 'I'm afraid you'll find it difficult.' He had been seriously ill the previous year, she said, his hearing was poor and he cried a lot. When Tsafendas was brought in, he was wearing a T-shirt, jogging pants and ill-fitting slippers. He was not supposed to have sweet drinks, but when Van Woerden was given a Coca-Cola, Tsafendas asked, 'Do you mind?' and emptied the glass in one gulp. It was quickly apparent to Van Woerden that the old man badly needed a hearing aid and he raised the matter with a doctor. She replied that the money to get one was simply not available.[97]

During the few hours Van Woerden spent with Tsafendas, he heard stories of past adventures where a particular reference would take him on to a new country in a new era. After a mention of Marlene Dietrich, Tsafendas laughed and began to sing her most famous song, 'Falling in Love Again'. The next half-hour was spent singing songs such as 'Deep Purple', 'Jeepers Creepers' and 'I Can't Give You Anything But Love, Baby'. Snatches of Greek, Italian and Portuguese songs followed,[98] but, cautious as ever, he sang no communist or revolutionary numbers.

A few months later, on what was to be his last visit, Van Woerden brought Tsafendas a baglama, a small stringed Greek instrument, which he hoped would relieve his boredom. Tsafendas was dozing in a chair, clad in the blue, striped dressing gown which most of the patients wore, except his was back to front and looked absurd. He wore no slippers and his right leg was stretched out, with a bloodied bandage around the big toe. The sticking plaster holding the bandage had come loose and trailed under his chair. Conversation was impossible for the noise of the patients clustered around him, so Van Woerden and a male nurse lifted the 'disconcertingly heavy' Tsafendas into a wheelchair and moved him to a room next to the kitchen.[99]

Away from the din, Tsafendas immediately asked for chocolate. Van Woerden had none, but produced the instrument and strummed a little tune. Tsafendas admired the instrument and talked about his interest in the piano accordion, the organ and the bugle. The musical interlude ended when Tsafendas suddenly asked the name of South Africa's president. Told Nelson Mandela, he said he would like to speak to him, that he was a strong man. He then fell silent and Van Woerden decided this was the time to raise the assassination. On a pad, he scrawled, 'Do you remember Verwoerd?' According to his published account, Tsafendas responded verbally, 'I didn't know Hendrik Verwoerd personally. I had never spoken to him before.' Moving uneasily in his wheelchair, he stammered three times, 'I do regret,' then taking the pencil, wrote in block letters 'I REGRET WHAT HAPPENED.' He began to cry and Van Woerden held him, saying, 'Never mind, other times, not your fault.' Sobbing, Tsafendas said, 'A whole other time. I am not that kind of person. It was not in my nature. Besides, I was sick.' He then referred directly to the tapeworm.[100] It was clear that however much he liked Van Woerden, he could not trust a writer of Dutch origin, and a lifetime of cautious deception kicked in. He pointed to his stomach. Why hadn't the doctors removed the creature in there? 'It will not die. I am helpless against the dragon tapeworm. I cannot do anything, but they won't investigate. Too difficult and very complicated. At night when I sleep I see orgies, all imagination, visions.' When Tsafendas fell silent, Van Woerden remarked, 'Like a real Cretan,' and Tsafendas said, 'Yeah, nature, hereditary nature.' When they said goodbye, Tsafendas pulled Van Woerden close to him and, sobbing, pressed a kiss on his cheek and forehead.

In an interview in Carte Blanche Interactive in 2001, three years after the publication of his book, Van Woerden spoke more directly of Tsafendas's attitude towards Verwoerd. He said then that when he asked Tsafendas why he killed the Prime Minister, he replied, 'I didn't like the man, I dislike what he's doing to the country, I don't agree.' Van Woerden later stated that 'the records that I have looked at suggest without a doubt that at the time he murdered Verwoerd, he was completely *compos mentis*.'[101]

Father Minas Constandinou and Bishop Ioannis Tsaftaridis were surprised to read about Tsafendas's reaction to Van Woerden's question about the assassination as the author described it in his book and found it hard to believe. Neither of them had spoken to Tsafendas about that topic since 1994, but they could not believe he had changed his mind. His reference to the tapeworm convinced them that Tsafendas did not trust Van Woerden and that he had resorted to the old lie so as not to jeopardise any possibility of amnesty.[102]

In mid-1996, the Truth and Reconciliation Commission (TRC) hearings began. The TRC was a restorative justice body established after the abolition of apartheid which enabled victims of racial injustice to tell their stories and name their persecutors. Modelled on a court-like system, the Commission also allowed perpetrators of violence to give testimony and appeal for amnesty. The TRC was seen as a gesture towards peace and reconciliation and a crucial component in the transition to full democracy. Archbishop Desmond Tutu was appointed as chairman of the Commission, which was enough for Tsafendas to end his long admiration for Tutu. In his heart, he had forgiven the Archbishop for being anti-communist, but this new development, he considered, was a step too far.

Tsafendas disagreed profoundly with the process. He was shocked that criminals who had killed in the name of apartheid could receive amnesty and walk away free. He insisted to anyone who would listen that such people should receive the punishment they deserved. Mike Phahlane sided with Tsafendas. What angered Tsafendas particularly was that anti-apartheid fighters who had committed violent crimes also asked for amnesty. He found it absurd that those who had committed violent acts for apartheid and those who had committed violent acts against apartheid were put in the same category. He argued that the rebels' acts were completely different from those of the police or the security services, that they were acts of resistance against tyrants and thus morally justified; they should not, he insisted, be placed in the same category as crimes committed by the apartheid state. Anti-apartheid violence, he argued, was equivalent to anti-Nazi resistance during the Second World War and the activists who fought against the dictatorship in Greece. Denouncing the TRC process as 'absurd' and a 'disgrace', he said it was embarrassing that anti-apartheid rebels should seek amnesty for their brave acts against a dictatorship. 'Is this why people fought all these years,' he demanded, 'to go and ask for amnesty for doing the right thing? To be placed in the same category as apartheid's killers? Would the French ever have asked the rebels of 1789 to ask for amnesty? Was this why the Bastille fell?' 'The apartheid killers and torturers should be hanged, not pardoned', he used to say.[103]

Tsafendas's belief was shared by a large proportion of South Africa's population; it was also the opinion of Simon Wiesenthal, the Jewish Austrian Holocaust survivor who became a legendary Nazi hunter.[104] While the TRC was taking place, Jody Kollapen found himself at a conference in Vienna and met Wiesenthal there. Upon hearing that Kollapen was from South Africa, Wiesenthal, clearly surprised, asked him, 'What are you doing there in South Africa? You should hang these people!'[105]

Nikolatos disagreed, she believed that 'violence is violence, no matter where it comes from' and she supported the TRC philosophy. However, she stopped mentioning the hearings to Tsafendas because he became so upset. The hearings were a constant topic of debate in the hospital and most of the staff supported the idea. One day, exasperated after a heated argument with some white patients and staff, Tsafendas angrily demanded a nearby patient give him his walking stick, which he then brandished angrily at his opponents, though stopping short of violence. When Nikolatos suggested to him that he should apply for amnesty because the assassination qualified as a political act, an outraged Tsafendas refused even to discuss it. Efforts by Father Spiros to change his mind came to nothing. Tsafendas said he would rather die there in Sterkfontein than ask for amnesty for something he considered was the right thing to do. Essentially, he said, this would place him in the same category as the apartheid killers. His friends argued that the amnesty idea was part of a process of national reconciliation and forgiveness and that on a practical level it would give him the chance of the freedom for which he so longed. Tsafendas was adamant. He retorted that he did not want anyone's forgiveness or to reconcile with those who had tortured him and thousands of others. To ask for amnesty would be tantamount to admitting that he had done something wrong. He added that he would accept an unconditional amnesty, providing the process did not involve the TRC.[106]

In the event and without his knowledge, Tsafendas's own case came before the Commission in late 1996. The anti-apartheid activist and human rights lawyer, Mr Krish Govender, submitted that Tsafendas's circumstances should be 'reviewed and investigated'.[107] Govender said that the purpose of his submission was to discover how Tsafendas, as 'a State President's patient' could have spent 28 years on death row. He requested that 'all decisions, documents and material [regarding Tsafendas's case] be reviewed and investigated thoroughly' and that he 'should be visited by members of the TRC urgently to reassure him that mechanisms for justice for him are taking shape. The public needs to be reassured about his safety, well-being and state of mind, before something happens to him.'[108]

It was a reasonable request, given the way the legal system was known to operate during apartheid. However, Chief Justice Michael Corbett[109] rejected the suggestion as 'pointless and absurd'. Ignorant of the significant facts in Tsafendas's case, Justice Corbett considered the evidence presented to the court regarding his mental health overwhelmingly conclusive.[110] Nevertheless, as a result of Govender's request, Liza Key was asked by the TRC to make a submission on Tsafendas's behalf. Key discussed this with Tsafendas and told him that the reason was to not only put his story on the record but to appeal to the new government to help people in the same situation as himself. Tsafendas was happy for Key to go ahead.[111]

In the meantime, Key had continued working on her documentary film and was evaluating some of the documents she found in the National Archives of South Africa, including all the evidence collected by the Commission of Enquiry into Verwoerd's death. Crucial among these were Tsafendas's statements to the police after the assassination and documents which consisted mainly of interviews with people who knew Tsafendas. These portrayed a person with a long history of political activism and someone entirely different to the supine, confused and apolitical person described in court and by the Commission's report. Liza Key, who knew that Van Woerden intended to write a book about Tsafendas, gave him copies of some of the documents she found in the archives as well as other information she had collected for her film.[112] Van Woerden himself then visited the archives and accessed some of the documents there.[113]

Eager to question Tsafendas about all this new information and hoping to hear about the assassination and his previous political activities, Liza Key visited Tsafendas again in Sterkfontein in late October 1997. She was accompanied by David Beresford, his partner Ellen Elmendorp, a photographer, and his fifteen-year-old son Joris. Beresford and Key were shocked by whom he found, a grey-haired old man in a floppy, purple-coloured tracksuit and slippers made of towelling ensconced in an armchair on a sheltered veranda. He was gazing vacantly towards the hospital boundaries. In the year that had passed since Beresford last saw him, Tsafendas had gone markedly downhill. He was deeply fatigued and his hearing problems had worsened. It was a fact, however, that Tsafendas seemed able to hear 'better' when he was interested in what the other person had to say, while he was unable to hear about subjects he did not care about. Beresford quickly realised that he was not going to get anything out of him. However, Tsafendas happily talked to Joris, who was writing a high school essay about him. Some time later, Key took Joris again to Sterkfontein and he spoke to Tasfendas once more. Joris's essay eventually earned him a school award.[114]

Subsequently, on 6 November 1997, Beresford wrote in the *Guardian* about his experience with Tsafendas and Key's discovery of the interrogation transcripts. Beresford was the first person ever to publicise Tsafendas's crucial statement to the police that he had killed Verwoerd because he was 'so disgusted with the racial policy', thereby indicating for the first time that his act was seriously political. He also wrote, "Police interrogators, try though they did, never managed to get his admission that the worm talked to him, much less ordered the murder of the Prime Minister of the Republic of South Africa."[115] About two years later, Beresford wrote in Tsafendas's obituary in *The Guardian* 'Although there were attempts by police, during interrogation, to suggest to him that he believed a tapeworm had "ordered" him to carry out the killing, he never seems to have made the claim himself.'[116]

In early November 1997, a few days after Beresford's visit, Key made her submission to the TRC. She told the Commission that she "had become friends" with Tsafendas and that "it is in the capacity as a friend and a concerned citizen that I appeal to you. My concern relates to his treatment by the South African authorities since the assassination." Subsequently, Key referred to Tsafendas's sentencing and imprisonment saying that

> *"the decision to imprison Tsafendas – rather than place him in a mental asylum, as would have been appropriate – is, so far as I am aware, without precedence where a State President's patient is concerned. Even though the legal authority was there in the Mental Disorders Act, (the Act)*

> *itself evidently represents a human rights abuse. It was compounded further by the fact that he was placed in what was effectively death row. By the accounts of other prisoners, he was treated abominably there, not only being subjected to the sounds of the weekly proceedings in the human abattoir which was the gallows, but suffering personal abuse at the hands of warders who are alleged to have made a practice of urinating in his food and beating him up while trussed in a straight-jacket. The authorities were aware of his treatment, because an operation was mounted at one stage to cover it up with the connivance of the prison authorities and the help of an agent of the Bureau of State Security, Gordon Winter – masquerading as a newspaper reporter working for The Citizen."*[117]

Key then suggested to the Commission that it should investigate those with "responsibility for this treatment of him." Subsequently, Key gave some background on Tsafendas and also told the Commission that although brought up, like any other South African citizen, believing that Tsafendas was a madman and killed Verwoerd because he was ordered by a tapeworm, she had "discovered no evidence that it ordered him to kill Dr. Verwoerd, despite attempts by his interrogators to elicit that response from him." She concluded her submission by saying:

"It could be said that today Tsafendas stands at the bar of history. I do not think we wish to judge him, right or wrong. But it is important, I believe, to try and understand him if we are to understand ourselves, our country and our times. To some people, Tsafendas might seem a monster, a creature beyond human understanding, a Frankenstein. But I would remind you that the power of Mary Shelley's famous story of Frankenstein lay in the sense of humanity which the monster shared with mankind. I would, as a friend of Tsafendas, like to conclude by quoting the following words of Frankenstein's monster in Mary Shelley's novel: 'Am I to be thought the only criminal, when all humankind sinned against me?'"[118]

Eventually, the TRC, perhaps also influenced by Chief Justice Corbett's ignorant comments, took no action and the case did not proceed further.[119] Thus Tsafendas was condemned to spend the rest of his life in institutions while the tapeworm mythology continued unchecked for another 22 years.

Had the TRC searched the National Archives of South Africa and investigated official files in Portugal from 1997, it would have discovered bountiful testimony to the truth about Tsafendas and the assassination, evidence that lay unexposed for a further 20 years until recovered by the research for this book. The Commission's investigators also could have spoken to friends and acquaintances of Tsafendas then alive who had personal knowledge of the intelligent, politically committed person Tsafendas really was. Almost certainly, in light of this evidence, Tsafendas would have been released from Sterkfontein Hospital into a caring environment for old, sick men.

Van Woerden, in the meantime, unaware of Govender's and Key's submissions, began a personal mission to have Tsafendas released from the 'wretched institution' to which he had been confined for the last four years. Hoping that the old man might spend his remaining days in the relative comfort of a private clinic, Van Woerden wrote to TRC chairman Archbishop Tutu asking for some form of amnesty and reparation. Towards the end of 1998, Tsafendas was moved to a more comfortable section of Sterkfontein Hospital, possibly as a result of Van Woerden's and Key's interventions, but the only action by the TRC on his letter was to pass it to the ministry of health. In her reply to Van Woerden, Minister Dr Dlamini-Zuma expressed her belief that Tsafendas was receiving the necessary care and attention at Sterkfontein, adding that a private facility 'could not offer the secure environment required, as threats to his life are still a possibility'. She added that 'the State does not pay for patients in private institutions'.[120]

Tsafendas's health meanwhile was worsening rapidly. Not only was he subject to frequent bouts of pneumonia, it was discovered that he was suffering from chronic heart disease. Nikolatos's visits had become less frequent after their arguments but also because Tsafendas could scarcely communicate. One day in late 1998, Nikolatos received a telephone call from the Health Department, saying Tsafendas was very ill and likely to die. She was warned that in the event of his death, the media should not be informed and the news should become known only after he was buried. Nikolatos contacted Father Spiros, the Greek Orthodox chaplain, and they went together to see him, expecting this would be the last time. They stayed by his bedside for almost two days, but Tsafendas did not die.[121] By now, Tsafendas had changed his opinion about Dr Vorster. He thought she was 'a good doctor and a very nice lady'. He once told Nikolatos, 'She is the only one here who cares for me. She protects me.' He invariably referred to Dr Vorster as a 'lady' and came to her defence if other patients talked negatively about her.[122]

When Father Ioannis heard about Tsafendas, he asked Father Spiros to take him along on his next visit, which he did at Christmas 1998, a regular visiting and gift-giving time for the priest. Father Ioannis wept when he saw Tsafendas, a huddled figure in an invalid chair. He had been badly shaved, apparently by someone in a hurry, and cuts were visible on his jaw and cheeks. There was no resemblance to the proud, self-confident and talkative man he had met just four years ago. Indeed, he looked to have aged 10–12 years in four years. Tsafendas tried to speak but only high-pitched noises came from his mouth. However, he made a sign to the priests to take him from where he was surrounded by other patients and they followed his pointing finger to the corner of the room.[123] Tsafendas recognised Father Spiros, but not Ioannis. When Father Ioannis said he had visited him four years earlier, Tsafendas only shook his head, indicating that he did not remember him, or that he did not care. He appeared grouchy and ill-tempered, clearly frustrated by his inability to communicate. Father Spiros spoke about the Christmas gifts they had brought for him, but it was obvious Tsafendas was not interested. He signalled to the priests to stop talking and whispered in Greek, 'Come closer.' Father Spiros leaned towards him and as he did so, Tsafendas grabbed his hand and pulled it forcibly towards him. For a moment, Spiros thought he had gone mad and tried to pull away, but Tsafendas dragged him closer. 'Listen to me,' Tsafendas said. Realising he wanted to say something important, the priest placed his ear close to Tsafendas's mouth. With long pauses between the words, Tsafendas got out, 'I am dying, Father.' The priest shook his head, but Tsafendas squeezed his hand and said, 'Please ... listen to me.' Then looking also at Father Ioannis, he said, 'I beg you ... I want you ... to do something for me ... very important for me.' Father Ioannis also moved his head close.[124]

Tsafendas then said, 'Go to Cape Town and find Patrick O'Ryan ... he is a teacher.' Father Spiros immediately indicated he would do so, although he had no idea who O'Ryan was. He tried to say something, but Tsafendas squeezed his hand again. 'Listen, listen,' Tsafendas repeated urgently as if afraid something might happen to him before completing what he wanted to say. Between quiet sobs, Tsafendas said that when he died, the priests should go and find O'Ryan, and apologise to him on his behalf for putting him in a situation that required him to lie in court to save his [Tsafendas's] life. The priests had no idea what Tsafendas was talking about and Father Spiros asked exactly what O'Ryan had done. Tsafendas repeated, 'Listen, listen.' Spiros was confused and uncomfortable. Ioannis was surprised, but realised this was something very important for Tsafendas. 'We are listening Mr Tsafendas,' he assured him. Tsafendas repeated that O'Ryan had lied on oath to save his life. During his evidence at the summary trial, he told the priests that O'Ryan had mentioned the tapeworm, although he knew that this was something Tsafendas had invented to stop the Portuguese torturing him when he was in prison and did not really believe he had one. Tsafendas said he had never had the chance to apologise personally. He said he knew O'Ryan was very religious and considered lying to be a serious sin, thus it must have been extremely difficult for him to go through with his performance in court. Tsafendas said the only regret he had about killing Verwoerd was putting his best friend in such a difficult position.[125]

Puzzled and uncertain, Father Spiros asked Tsafendas to tell them more about O'Ryan. Tsafendas sensed that the older priest had doubts about the case and turned to Ioannis. 'Please,' he said, with tears in his eyes and struggling for breath, 'you must go ... find O'Ryan and tell him ... what I told you ...' Father Ioannis nodded acquiescence and said, 'We will go, Mr Tsafendas, I promise you.' Addressing both priests, Tsafendas shouted desperately, 'Swear to me that you will do it.' Father Ioannis responded immediately, 'I swear, Mr Tsafendas, I swear,' and reverently made the sign of the cross. Seeing Spiros hesitating, Tsafendas seized his hand and, howling rather than speaking, pleaded, 'Swear to me ... swear to me.' It was not that Father Spiros was reluctant to find O'Ryan or to swear, he was simply overwhelmed by the situation. Seeing Tsafendas close to hysteria, a nurse approached. Tsafendas waved her away but she asked Father Spiros what was going on. Before he could reply, Tsafendas turned again to Father Spiros. This time, the priest nodded and enunciated clearly, with his lips visible, 'I swear,' simultaneously tracing the sign of the cross above Tsafendas. The nurse, seeing Tsafendas talking, walked away.[126]

Relieved and less fraught, Tsafendas instructed the priests to wait until he had died. He said if they told him now, O'Ryan would come immediately to Sterkfontein and he could not bear to face him after what he had done to him. Besides, he said, he was a poor man with eleven children and it would be costly for him to travel from Cape Town. When the priests inquired how they would find O'Ryan, Tsafendas asked for paper. Father Spiros took out his notebook and handed it to him along with a pencil. By then, Father Ioannis was nervous, fearing the medical staff would remove them for upsetting their prisoner/ patient. Tsafendas wrote rapidly in the notebook, tore off the page and gave it to Father Ioannis. He wrote again in the notebook, which he then handed back to Father Spiros. What Tsafendas had written and given to the two priests was an address: 'Patrick O'Ryan, 9 Westminster Street, Lansdowne, Cape Town. Teacher at Bishop Lavis High School, Telephone: 989050.'[127]

Tsafendas then said, 'Thank you, thank you,' and bowed his head in gratitude. Seeing him crying, another nurse approached, but Tsafendas waved her away. Father Ioannis told him, 'We are going to tell the people about you,' but Tsafendas shook his head angrily and said, 'Just tell Patrick O'Ryan what I told you ... no one else.' As they were leaving, Tsafendas grabbed Ioannis's hand and tried to speak. The priest leaned down and told him in his ear, 'We will find Mr O'Ryan, Mr Tsafendas, and we will tell him. I swear to you.' Tsafendas then let his hand go. The priests blessed Tsafendas with the sign of the cross and kissed him before they left. They did not know it at the time, but they were never to see him again.[128]

The two clerics were deeply affected by their emotional meeting with Tsafendas and talked of nothing else when they left. Spiros had visited

Tsafendas on a few occasions but had never seen him so overwrought. Further, they were taken aback to learn that one of the key trial witnesses had lied to protect Tsafendas. The priests agreed that they would find O'Ryan and pass on Tsafendas's apology after his death. However, they disagreed strongly about the timing; Ioannis was determined that they should tell the world what they had learnt, that Tsafendas had acted from political motives and with political intentions and that he was not mad. Father Spiros disagreed. Like Father Minas, he believed they should respect Tsafendas's wish to say nothing. Their only duty, he believed, was to find O'Ryan and apologise on Tsafendas's behalf, nothing else. There was, however, one thing on which both agreed that evening, that, as Tsafendas himself had said, he did not have much time left.[129]

Nikolatos continued to visit Sterkfontein from time to time, but Tsafendas's memory was fragmenting badly and sometimes he failed to recognise her. On other occasions, he clearly remembered events from long ago, often episodes which made him weep, such as the death of little Elenitsa Banovic, the fact that he went for 22 years without seeing his father and particularly that he did not see him before he died, and that he had never met his biological mother after infancy. Liza Key also remained a regular visitor. Much of the communication with visitors was done by writing notes.[130]

In early October 1999, Tsafendas's health took another downward turn and he was transferred to a ward for patients with serious physical conditions, in his case pneumonia aggravated by heart disease. On Thursday, 7 October 1999, he died quietly. He was 81 years old and South Africa's longest-serving prisoner. He had spent the last 33 years of his life in prison or in the high security hospital. Taking in approximately two years in Portuguese prisons, this meant that he had been free for only 46 years of his life.

Chapter 15

An Unmarked Grave

At 4 pm on Thursday, 7 October 1999, Rika Nikolatos received a telephone call from the superintendent of Sterkfontein Hospital informing her that Tsafendas had died a few hours earlier. The superintendent asked her to inform his family and to make arrangements for the funeral, stressing that the government wanted everything done as discreetly as possible and the media should in no circumstances be informed. In fact, the authorities had been monitoring Tsafendas's health for some time and had decided what they would do long before he died. Most importantly, there were to be no announcements of his death or funeral arrangements until after the burial had taken place. Nikolatos acknowledged the news and told the superintendent that the Hellenic Orthodox Ladies Association would meet the funeral expenses.[1] The next 24 hours were telling, where sections of the Greek community struggled desperately to distance themselves as much as possible from the dead man.

Nikolatos contacted Archbishop Ioannis Zachariou first, who agreed immediately that Tsafendas should be buried by a priest in a Greek Orthodox ceremony. Though only appointed in 1998, the Archbishop was aware of the polarising feelings towards Tsafendas among South African-resident Greeks, especially the businessmen, but Nikolatos and the priests who visited him had spoken highly of him and he saw no problem with the funeral. In fact, the issue was discussed and settled by Nikolatos and the Archbishop a few months earlier when Tsafendas had almost died, and he agreed then on a Greek Orthodox funeral with HOLA paying the expenses.[2]

Next, Nikolatos called Tsafendas's former prison visitor, Father Michalis Visvinis, still Bishop of Pretoria. Father Michalis was close to Tsafendas's half-sisters and she asked him to tell them of Dimitri's death. Eleni was in Greece on holiday while Katerina and Evangelia were at home. All three said they were saddened by the news; however, Katerina and Evangelia wanted nothing to do with the funeral and would not even send flowers, while Eleni wanted to attend, but could not make it back in time.[3]

Some hours after Nikolatos's conversation with the Archbishop, he called her back to say that he had changed his mind and decided it would be better if Tsafendas were not buried by a Greek Orthodox priest after all. The reasons for his change of heart were that Tsafendas was not a Greek Orthodox Christian but a member of a small sect known as the Christian Church, that they were not certain if he had ever been baptised and that he had shown no remorse for killing Verwoerd. Nikolatos was furious. Quickly she deduced, and the Archbishop later admitted, that he had been pressured by leading Greeks in Pretoria and Johannesburg who feared that a Greek Orthodox funeral would attract hostile attention to their community. The Greek leaders argued that 'for 30 years we have been trying to remove any association of Tsafendas from our community', and they feared the reaction of white South Africans to the revival of this link.[4]

Seeking to convince the Archbishop on theological grounds, Nikolatos argued that although Tsafendas was a member of the small sect, he considered himself a true Christian and believed all Christians to be one in faith, whatever the names of their churches. Nikolatos further assured the prelate that Tsafendas had indeed been baptised as a Greek Orthodox Christian, thereupon he agreed, provided it took place far from Pretoria. Though buoyed by this victory, Nikolatos knew the battle was only half-won when she came under intense personal pressure to dissociate the Greek community from Tsafendas's funeral rites. What hurt her deeply were lobbying calls from friends and long-time acquaintances who knew how much she cared about Tsafendas.[5]

Somehow, the news of Tsafendas's death leaked to the media and immediately became front-page news. Interest in Verwoerd's assassin and his family revived and relatives in Pretoria hastily went into seclusion, remaining in their homes for days on end, staying away from work and refusing to answer their telephones. Journalists besieged Bushia's house and she had to leave the constantly ringing telephone receiver off the hook. She was strongly reminded of the painful days after Dimitri's arrest in 1966, but what angered her now was the media's portrayal of her half-brother as insane and lacking any political motive.[6]

Nikolatos's next task was to find a priest willing to conduct the funeral, and so she contacted Tsafendas's old friend, Father Michalis. While he was willing to act as celebrant, like the Archbishop, he thought the ceremony should take place in Krugersdorp, near the hospital where Tsafendas died, and therefore led by a priest from that area. This, he thought, would draw attention away from Tsafendas's relatives in Pretoria.[7] So, Nikolatos got in touch with Father Dimitrios Vergitsis, the Greek Orthodox Church priest for East Rand. Father Dimitrios had never met Tsafendas, but had heard about him from his colleagues who visited him, and personally considered him a hero of the anti-apartheid struggle. Without hesitation, he told Nikolatos he would be honoured to conduct Tsafendas's funeral at Saint Andrew's (Agios Andreas), his church in Krugersdorp.[8]

The matter finally appeared settled, but only hours later, Archbishop Ioannis Zachariou had another change of heart and decreed that Tsafendas should not be buried by a Greek Orthodox priest. Under tremendous pressure from Pretoria and Johannesburg's Greeks, he accepted that their businesses might be boycotted by whites, even subjected to violence by furious Afrikaners, as had happened in 1966. Nikolatos tried to change his mind again, but this time the Archbishop held firm; he said he was only trying to do his best for the Greek community as a whole.[9]

On hearing this, Father Dimitrios telephoned the Archbishop, but he remained unmoved and sought to persuade the priest to withdraw. Technically, Father Dimitrios did not need the Archbishop's assent to conduct the service, but he faced the possibility of suspension if he defied his superior. Archbishop Ioannis stressed that it was not known for certain whether Tsafendas had been baptised as Greek Orthodox. Father Dimitrios said whether he was or not, he would still bury him, citing a clause in the constitution of the church, which allowed a Greek Orthodox priest to bury a non-Greek Orthodox person. Sternly, the Archbishop reminded the young priest that Tsafendas was a murderer. Father Dimitrios replied that only God could be the judge of Tsafendas's guilt concerning the assassination and that even criminals deserved a Christian burial. He reminded the Archbishop that the first person who entered heaven with Christ was a thief and that God alone could judge Tsafendas's motives at the time.[10]

Father Dimitrios had scarcely put the telephone down when he received a call from Ioannis Theophanopoulos, the Greek ambassador to South Africa. The ambassador asked him to withdraw from the funeral, using the now well-worn argument of probable negative effects on the Greek community. The priest replied that his sacerdotal duties included conducting funerals, that only God could judge Tsafendas and he was more than willing to lead his funeral rites. Whether he was a criminal or a hero, Tsafendas was a human being and deserved a dignified burial. Despite the pressure, Father Dimitrios refused to discuss the matter further.[11]

The pressure did not end there and the next person to call Father Dimitrios was Andreas Argyrou, president of the Greek community in Krugersdorp. He went as far as to suggest that white South Africans might burn down his church in Krugersdorp if the funeral went ahead. Dimitrios replied that his church was just a building while the real church was composed of people. Argyrou warned him that if anything happened to the Greeks in South Africa he would be solely responsible. Dimitrios acknowledged this statement, then having briefly considered and instantly dismissed the idea of using another distant church, began preparations for the funeral, to take place at his church on Monday, 11 October 1999.[12]

Having spent much of Thursday, the day of Tsafendas's death, fighting off pressures from various quarters, Father Dimitrios received a new call from

Archbishop Ioannis Zachariou on Friday, 9 October. By now, the Archbishop accepted that he could not change the priest's mind; his new suggestion was that the process be accelerated and the funeral held the next day, Saturday. He feared that the longer the delay the more dangerous the situation would become for the Greek community, including Tsafendas's family. Having dismissed warnings by the Archbishop, the ambassador and Greek community leaders of possible violence, Father Dimitrios, for his own peace of mind, informed the Krugersdorp police of the situation. Three cars were dispatched immediately to his house and he was given a personal bodyguard who accompanied him everywhere.[13]

When Patrick O'Ryan and his family heard the news, they were deeply saddened. They had always hoped they would see their old friend again. For his part, Patrick was invaded by guilt that he had never visited the man he considered one of the best friends he ever had. During the first few years of Tsafendas's incarceration he had not dared even to think of visiting him. Then as time passed, finding the money for travel to Pretoria proved impossible for a poor man like him with a large family. Tsafendas himself had said he should not visit, though O'Ryan suspected this was out of consideration for his financial position. Now, having never visited him for one reason or another, O'Ryan felt obliged to attend his friend's funeral. He bought aeroplane tickets for himself and his wife Louisa to travel on Sunday from Cape Town to Johannesburg and made arrangements to spend Sunday evening at the home of one of their church's members. Learning later that the funeral had been brought forward, O'Ryan changed his tickets, at extra cost, for very early the next day.[14]

On the morning of 9 October 1999, St. Andrew's Church in Krugersdorp was packed. Unlike normal funerals, however, the vast majority congregated were policemen, either in uniform or plain clothes, and journalists.[15] Mourners totalled three, Patrick and Louise O'Ryan and Akis Apergis, a Greek anti-apartheid activist and member of the South African Communist Party. Apergis was in South Africa when the assassination took place and though he had never met Tsafendas, he had heard much about him and had always considered him to be a hero of the anti-apartheid struggle.[16]

Father Dimitrios arrived at the church escorted by three police cars. When the hearse pulled in with Tsafendas's coffin, a police dog leapt inside to check for explosives. The police then ordered the evacuation of the church while sniffer dogs and their police handlers searched each nook and cranny and everyone waited outside. When journalists complained to Father Dimitrios about allowing dogs in his church, he explained the necessity, ever conscious of the possible violence he had been warned about by the Archbishop and many others. When the search ended, Father Dimitrios was allowed into his church, followed by a congregation of about a hundred.[17] The number of mourners had grown to six. In addition to the O'Ryans and Apergis, there was an unidentified man who said he had become a good friend of Tsafendas when he was hospitalised in Sterkfontein, Aron Mabe from the PAC and Gagi Mohane, a member of the ANC. Mabe and Mohane were attending in their private capacities, not as representatives of their organisations, they said. One of them, though, speaking on behalf of both, told the journalists, 'We are burying a human being whom we believe to have been a hero.'[18]

Conspicuously absent were Rika Nikolatos, who was seriously ill, Father Minas Constandinou, who could not get away from his pastoral obligations in Cape Town, and Father Ioannis Tsaftaridis, who was in Greece. When he heard the news, Father Minas had contacted Father Nikola Banovic in Istanbul and informed him of Tsafendas's death. During their conversation, Father Nikola confirmed everything that Tsafendas had told Father Minas about his time in Istanbul.[19] Liza Key, one of the few who had become close to Tsafendas and cared compassionately for him during his final years, was also out of the country and unable to attend the funeral. However, she sent a large wreath of lilies and a plaque to be placed on his coffin which read: 'Dimitri Tsafendas 1918–1999: Displaced Person, Sailor, Christian, Communist, Liberation Fighter, Political Prisoner, Hero: Remembered By His Friends.'[20] Few descriptions could have fitted Tsafendas better.

In his eulogy, Father Dimitrios said that God would judge Tsafendas and his deed and that He alone had the right to do so. At one point, Apergis shouted, 'Tsafendas was a hero, he was not mad,' and the unidentified man repeated the words. Several journalists nodded 'yes, yes' or mouthed agreement. When the church service was over, Tsafendas's coffin was carried to the cemetery, which was close to Sterkfontein Hospital. Father Dimitrios conducted the graveside service, pouring oil on the coffin in a gesture of re-anointment in the faith. Apergis was among the men who lowered the coffin into the grave, then covered it with soil. Louise and Patrick O'Ryan wept quietly. Although nothing untoward happened at the funeral, the police maintained their guard on Father Dimitrios for another three days.[21] No headstone was ever erected to mark Tsafendas's burial place and, years later, it was unidentifiable from the tangled mass of weeds and grass in the area.

Writing shortly after the funeral in the *Mail & Guardian*, John Matshikiza, a prominent South African actor/director, anti-apartheid activist, journalist and poet, described Tsafendas as 'an unsung hero' and South Africa's 'greatest political assassin', and declared his certainty that he had found a place in heaven. Matshikiza, who was a friend of Mike Phahlane and had spoken to him about Tsafendas, had also seen the transcripts of Tsafendas's interrogation; just as Beresford and Key had done earlier. He wrote that Tsafendas had never mentioned the tapeworm during his police interrogation despite his interrogators' prodding. He concluded his article as follows, 'Any warrior who would be prepared to strike a blow against it [apartheid] would be entitled to a place in heaven. For 33 years we ignored Tsafendas. He had embarrassed us by getting straight to the point, while we were still justifying our pain. Last Saturday, he was buried quietly in Krugersdorp. Ten people, mostly members of the Greek community, were in attendance. The politicians and the humble victims of apartheid for whom he had struck the most awesome blow in the fight for freedom, chose to stay away.'[22]

A few months after the funeral, Father Ioannis Tsaftaridis returned to South Africa from Greece. He was devastated by Tsafendas's death and deeply disappointed that he had not been able to see him again or attend the funeral. One of the first things he did upon his return was to discuss with Father Spiros Tsafendas's last wish; that they should contact Patrick O'Ryan and apologise to him on Tsafendas's behalf. He was ready and eager to fulfil this mission. However, Father Spiros had been diagnosed with cancer and was often in hospital receiving treatment. When it became apparent that he would not be able to make the journey to Cape Town, he suggested to his colleague asking Father Minas, who lived in Cape Town, to take his place. Sometime in the early 2000s, Ioannis met with Father Minas at the latter's Cape Town residence. When Ioannis told his colleague about Tsafendas's last wish, Minas was fascinated and immediately agreed to go with his colleague and see O'Ryan.[23]

The O'Ryans were surprised when the two priests turned up on their doorstep, although Patrick immediately realised that this must have something to do with Tsafendas. Why else would two Greek Orthodox priests visit him? The priests confirmed they were on an errand concerning Tsafendas but did not go into detail in front of Louise because Tsafendas had specifically said to speak to Patrick and no one else. For almost an hour, the four of them exchanged memories about Tsafendas, talk which often brought Patrick to tears. He praised Tsafendas as the 'kindest man I ever met', who frequently bought food and toys for his family, and characterised him as a 'fanatic about politics'. At one point, Louise left the room and Father Minas hurriedly told Patrick the reason for their visit, to express Tsafendas's heartfelt sorrow over his friend's discomfort as a witness at his trial. For a few seconds, O'Ryan was speechless and turned his head to look out of the window. Then the tears came in a flood. Louise rushed back into the room followed by two grandchildren. She looked at the priests, who said nothing. When Patrick could speak, he asked his wife softly to leave with the children. Then looking at the priests and, shaking his head in remorse and disappointment, he said between sobs, 'He should never have felt this, never, never…'[24]

O'Ryan then told the priests how deeply he regretted never visiting Tsafendas. When Father Minas reminded him that Tsafendas had specifically asked him not to visit (Father Minas himself had written the necessary letters), Patrick dismissed this out of hand; no matter what Tsafendas had said, he should still have gone. O'Ryan then told how Tsafendas confided to him about the tapeworm more than 30 years ago. He confirmed everything that Tsafendas had already told the priests about the tapeworm, including its origins with Tom Tuff. He said he had never told anyone, not even his wife, that the tapeworm was a fiction.[25]

As for Tsafendas's concern about O'Ryan's religious principles, he said it was true his court appearance was the only time he had ever lied. However, his faith told him that God would forgive him for this transgression because he had committed it for a righteous cause. He told the priests that when Tsafendas's lawyers first mentioned the tapeworm, he was unsure if they saw it as a weapon in Tsafendas's defence or as the joke that it had become in his own home. He then remembered that Tsafendas had used the tapeworm as a way out of trouble when he was arrested by the Portuguese police and he guessed that his friend might be using it in that way once more. The aspect of his police statement that he most regretted was telling them that he believed Tsafendas was not insane. At that point, he had not guessed that Tsafendas might be trying to fake madness. Recalling the many stories Tsafendas had told him about himself and his life, Father Minas found that O'Ryan confirmed everything. Although the priest had never doubted Tsafendas, he noted with pleasure the confirmation of even the slightest detail by O'Ryan. As for Father Ioannis, the way O'Ryan spoke about Tsafendas made him an even greater hero than he already considered him. He now had no doubt that the truth about Tsafendas should be told to the world and that the people should stop believing apartheid's lies. In the car ride to Father Minas's house, both priests acknowledged how profund that meeting with O'Ryan was, indeed the most dramatic moment in their lives. The image of O'Ryan breaking down and weeping inconsolably after they told him why they had come would live in their memories for ever.[26]

Back in Minas's house, a lively dispute developed between the two priests over what they should do now. Father Ioannis argued strongly for revealing the truth about the tapeworm and Tsafendas as a politically minded person. Minas was adamant that they should not. The issue became a major bone of contention, constantly argued over, sometimes with the participation of Father Spiros. Ioannis wanted to contact a journalist to publish the truth about Tsafendas. Spiros opposed such a move on the grounds that Tsafendas had asked them specifically not to do so. Minas wavered but tended to agree with Spiros. Father Ioannis argued that Tsafendas had spoken as a humble man who did not want to be glorified, but that the right thing to do, especially now that he was dead, was to correct the historical record and honour his memory. Eventually, Ioannis accepted Spiros's stance, at least for the time being. Spiros was suffering from terminal cancer and Ioannis did not want to upset him.[27]

A few months after Tsafendas's death, and a year after its publication in Holland, Henk van Woerden's *A Mouthful of Glass* was published in English and in Afrikaans; it was the first book ever written about Tsafendas. Widely praised by critics and in the press, it won the Alan Paton award for non-fiction in South Africa. To write the book, Van Woerden had used some documents found in the South African National Archives, Liza Key's notes, videos, documents and interviews with Tsafendas, along with meetings he had with Tsafendas near the end of his life.[28] Tsafendas never got to see the book and did not even become aware of it.[29]

Around the same time, Liza Key's documentary on Tsafendas, *A Question of Madness*, was shown on SABC3. It was highly acclaimed by critics in South Africa and around the world. It was also shown on BBC in England. It was the first time Tsafendas had ever been filmed for television. Tsafendas's three half-sisters and their families watched it together. They were shocked to see how sick and aged Dimitri looked and deeply saddened to hear him talk of how he was ill-treated in prison. The children berated their parents for never visiting Tsafendas and the sisters, for the first time, wept for their half-brother. Eleni taped the documentary to watch again sometime, but never found the strength to do so. For several weeks, she suffered serious depression as she agonised over Dimitri's sufferings, but mostly out of remorse for never visiting him in prison.[30]

The book and the documentary sparked an immediate renewal of public interest in Tsafendas. Two plays followed soon after – *Living in Strange Lands: The Testimony of Dimitri Tsafendas* by Dr Anton Krueger and Renos Spanoudes as Tsafendas in 2001, and *I.D.* by the Cape Town-born Shakespearean actor, Sir Antony Sher, who also portrayed Tsafendas, in 2003. Both were very successful and critically acclaimed, especially the two actors who played Tsafendas.

As time passed and memories of apartheid began to fade, Father Ioannis grew increasingly unhappy that most of the world still considered Tsafendas to be a lunatic who killed a Prime Minister because of a tapeworm. Several times, he urged his two priest friends to change their opinions about telling the truth to the world, but to no avail. In 2004, Father Spiros died of cancer and Father Ioannis intensified his efforts to persuade Father Minas. Of course, he could have acted alone at any time, but he did not wish to upset the priest who was not only his colleague but his mentor, and it was Minas who knew more about Tsafendas than anyone. Whatever Ioannis tried, Minas was unwilling to speak publicly about Tsafendas.[31]

In 2011, Father Ioannis Tsaftaridis was appointed Bishop of the Greek Orthodox Church in Mozambique and began living in Maputo. He was conducting his own research into Tsafendas's past, out of personal interest, mostly by talking to people, usually Greeks, who had met him. They included contemporaries from the days of his youth, such as Ira Kyriakakis and Andreas Babiolakis. What became immediately apparent to Ioannis from these conversations was that, just as he had heard from Minas, Spiros and Tsafendas himself, his friend was a political animal, a communist and a committed supporter of the independence of Mozambique. As well as his political activities in Mozambique in the 1930s and later the 1960s, Ioannis began to hear about his voluntary activities, that he gave free history and English lessons to poor Mozambican children and that he campaigned in the rural areas for independence from Portugal. None of the many people he talked to who knew Tsafendas personally gave the slightest credence to suggestions that he was insane; on the contrary, most described him as highly intelligent.[32]

On 22 October 2013, Christian Martins, Eastern Cape MP for the ANC, made a request to the National Heritage Council of South Africa to declare Tsafendas's and Verwoerd's graves as heritage cites. He said that 'homage should be bestowed upon Dimitri Tsafendas, a hero and martyr for the cause of the South African people'.[34] One who expressed disagreement with the proposal was David Bloomberg. In a statement to the *Cape Times*, Bloomberg expressed his 'astonishment' at such an 'outrageous request', reiterating the claim that Tsafendas was a schizophrenic without any political motive whatsoever.[35] In seeking to refute a claim by Martins that Tsafendas 'changed the course of post-war South African history', Bloomberg contradicted a similar statement he had himself made 16 years earlier. Asked by Liza Key in 1997 whether he believed Tsafendas had 'changed the course of history in South Africa', Bloomberg said, 'He certainly changed the course of history of that time. I have no doubt that the eventual outcome would have been the same with the passage of time, that one couldn't suppress the majority of the people of South Africa for all time … probably in retrospect, I think Tsafendas may have hurried things a little …'[36]

Researching Tsafendas's past was not the only thing Ioannis did to bring the truth into the light. Now the bearer of high ecclesiastical office, Bishop Ioannis made use of public ceremonies to proclaim Tsafendas as an idealist and a national hero, at least twice. The first took place when he laid the foundation stone for the church of Saint Dionysius, also a Greek Orthodox missionary centre, at Murakela village in Nangoma Murumbi, north Mozambique. The date was 9 October 2015, two days after the 16th anniversary of Tsafendas's death. Recalling the date for the congregation, the Bishop apostrophised Tsafendas as 'the man who killed apartheid' and 'a modern Greek hero who wanted to set the people of South Africa and Mozambique free'. He was, Ioannis said, 'a humble man, a man of dignity, an idealist concerned about the sufferings of others'. Bishop Ioannis described Verwoerd's killing as an act of tyrannicide, and then in words Tsafendas would have loved, declared him 'the Greek Che Guevara', detailing his political activities in Mozambique, South Africa, Greece and Britain.[37]

The next public occasion came nine days later when Bishop Ioannis led a memorial service for Tsafendas at the Greek Orthodox Church in Maputo. Advance press notices and posters in the city hailed Tsafendas as 'The Idealist' and this was how the Bishop characterised him at the service, namely, 'an idealist who removed a tyrant … a freedom fighter who struggled for the independence of Mozambique and against apartheid'. He said, 'Tsafendas was not an ordinary man, but a man who gave up his life for a principle and for the good of his fellow citizens. His actions were borne out of selflessness and for the public good.' Noting that Tsafendas 'never got the recognition he deserved', Ioannis pointed out that 'he did not care that he was never hailed a hero.' The Bishop quoted Tsafendas as saying, 'Do a good thing and then throw it in the sea,' that is, 'when you do a good thing, don't go around advertising it'. He concluded by calling on the people of South Africa and Mozambique to acknowledge Tsafendas's heroic efforts on their behalf 'and stop believing apartheid's lies'.[38] Bishop Ioannis later asked the Mozambican government to name the street in front of the Greek Orthodox Church in Maputo 'Dimitri Tsafendas Street'.[39] The request is still under consideration by the government.

Bishop Ioannis was not the only Bishop of the Greek Orthodox Church who was deeply impressed by Tsafendas. Bishop Seraphim Kykkotis, a one-time Archbishop of Johannesburg and Pretoria (2001–10), never met Tsafendas, but heard much to his credit from the priests who visited him and Greeks who knew him socially. They all said the same thing, that Tsafendas was politically committed, passionate against apartheid and a heartfelt supporter of independence for Mozambique; they were also convinced that he was perfectly sane and pretended lunacy to escape the gallows. In his 2013 book about Nelson Mandela *Αναφορές στο Νομπελίστα Νέλσον Μαντέλα* [*Anafores sto Nobelista Nelson Mandela*], Bishop Seraphim described Tsafendas as 'a Greek soul, a brave Cretan who raised in his stature the dignity of humanity against apartheid'. He described the killing of Verwoerd as 'heroic'. He concluded that 'people in his time called [Tsafendas] a murderer, while others thought that he was crazy … However, his motives were absolutely pure: he was a selfless fighter for people's dignity who acted only out of love, to protect people's rights.'[40]

Epilogue

On 23 April 2018, Tsholofelo Masilo, Judge Jody Kollapen's registrar in the High Court in Pretoria submitted to the office of the Minister of Justice of South Africa, Advocate Tshililo Michael Masutha, a report. Titled, 'Report in the Matter of Dr Verwoerd's Assassination', it consisted of three hardback volumes totalling 2,192 pages and 861,803 words, accompanied by a 16GB USB that contained all the evidence gathered by the author for this research. Along with the report and the evidence, the following letter/request by Advocate George Bizos, Professor John Dugard, Krish Govender, Advocate Dumisa Ntsebeza and Judge Zak Yacoob was also submitted to the Minister.

RE: REQUEST TO RE-EVALUATE THE HISTORICAL RECORD FOLLOWING THE ASSASSINATION OF DR HF VERWOERD

The death of Prime Minister HF Verwoerd on 6 September 1966 was no doubt a significant event in the history of South Africa and one that would have long-term consequences for the people of South Africa. Dr Verwoerd was killed by Dimitri Tsafendas, a Portuguese national of Greek descent, in the House of Assembly at a time when Tsafendas was employed there as a messenger.

At the trial of Tsafendas in the Cape Supreme Court he was found unfit to stand trial on the ground that he suffered from schizophrenia. The court found that Tsafendas had no political motive for killing Verwoerd. These conclusions were confirmed by a subsequent Commission of Enquiry. Arising out of this, Tsafendas was declared a State President's patient and was detained first in prison, then in a mental institution until his death in 1999. For most of his incarceration he was subjected to cruel and inhumane treatment by the prison authorities. He died a sad and lonely death in a mental institution.

There were understandable reasons why it was in the interests of the apartheid regime not to seriously dispute that Mr Tsafendas was schizophrenic and to ignore weighty evidence that he was not mentally ill, but that Mr Tsafendas's actions were in fact wholly politically motivated. First, the apartheid regime wished to have people believe that no sane person could kill or even want to kill an outstanding leader as Verwoerd was projected to be. Second, the Minister of Justice and Police, John Vorster, would have been embarrassed that a communist who had made his strong opposition to apartheid publicly known passed the security clearance that allowed him to work as a messenger in the House of Assembly and gave him the opportunity to kill Verwoerd. To avoid accountability for this lapse in security, it would have been considered wiser for Vorster and the National Party to portray Tsafendas as an insane person. Third, a full-blown criminal trial would have had the inevitable effect of placing the national and international spotlight on the excesses of the system of apartheid – something the regime of the day would have preferred to avoid.

Consequently, the apartheid regime embarked on a cover-up in which the trial, the subsequent Commission of Enquiry and media were carefully orchestrated to present Tsafendas as an insane person. This succeeded to a large measure as the dominant discourse that emerged and still prevails is that Mr Tsafendas was mentally ill and his actions were not even remotely political. It is equally understandable that Mr Tsafendas adopted the correct strategy in which he too feigned insanity. Otherwise, he would undoubtedly have been sentenced to death.

A recent study by Harris Dousemetzis of Durham University in England reveals the full extent of the cogent evidence that the regime ignored. It shows convincingly that Mr Tsafendas was not a schizophrenic who believed that his actions were determined by a tapeworm. In fact, the study compellingly demonstrates that he was a man with a deep social conscience who was bitterly opposed to apartheid and viewed Verwoerd as the prime architect of this policy. Tsafendas told the police after the assassination that he killed Dr Verwoerd because he was 'disgusted with his racial policies' and hoped that 'a change of policy would take place'. The killing of Verwoerd was therefore a political assassination and not the act of an insane man.

The study also shows that Tsafendas was a highly politicised person. He was arrested several times in his home country of Moçambique by the Portuguese police for promoting Communism and denouncing colonialism. The Portuguese security police – PIDE – had a file on Tsafendas dating back to 1938, when he was 20 years old, and kept a careful watch over him when he was exiled for 12 years from Moçambique on account of his political activities. He fought in the Greek Civil War with the communists and he was imprisoned in Portugal for his pro-communist and anti-colonialist activities. In London he became a member of the British Anti-Apartheid Movement and associated with Tennyson Makiwane, the ANC's representative in England. He was a member of the South African Communist Party from 1937 to 1942 and was later refused admission to South Africa for this reason. Shortly before the killing of Verwoerd, Tsafendas characterised a possible assassination of Dr Verwoerd as morally justifiable on the grounds that he was a dictator and a tyrant who oppressed his people. Tsafendas repeated this notion about thirty years later while he was at a psychiatric hospital. These are but some features of the study all of which are fully substantiated. They powerfully militate against the conclusion that the actions of Tsafendas on 6 September 1966 were those of an individual ignorant of the scope and consequences of his actions.

Dousemetzis's study is painstakingly thorough and is based on an examination of some 12,000 pages of documents in the South African National Archives, as well as those of Portugal and the United Kingdom. It is supported by interviews with 137 persons, 69 of whom knew Tsafendas personally. The study collaborated closely with several relevant South African and international legal experts, including the signatories to this letter. We are in full agreement with the study, the conclusions it reaches as well as the reasons advanced in support of it.

In addition, a wide spread of experts in fields relevant to this research was also contacted on an ongoing basis, including lawyers, judges, psychologists, psychiatrists, academics, retired high-ranking police officers and former secret agents. Further, to examine the diagnosis of schizophrenia, the study collaborated closely with the forensic psychiatrist, Professor Tuviah Zabow, the former head of the forensic psychiatry unit at Valkenberg Hospital, former professor of psychiatry at the University of Cape Town and chairman of the College of Psychiatrists of South Africa.

The study also consulted with the following noted psychiatrists and psychologists: Professor Alban Burke, head of the Department of Psychology at the University of Johannesburg; Professor Kirk Heilbrun, forensic psychologist and professor of psychology at Drexler University, USA; Professor Phillip Resnick, forensic psychiatrist and director of the Division of Forensic Psychiatry at Case Western Reserve University School of Medicine, USA; and Professor Robert L. Sadoff, clinical professor of psychiatry and director of the Center for Studies in Social-Legal Psychiatry at the University of Pennsylvania, former president of the American Academy of Psychiatry and the Law as well as of the American Board of Forensic Psychiatry. Collectively they represent some of the best minds in the field of psychiatry and psychology.

This overview is provided both as a glimpse into the study and how it was conducted as well as to disavow any notion that the study is anything other than a carefully considered and well-researched body of work on a matter of great significance to South Africa.

We are also convinced that much of this evidence was available to the state. In normal course, and had not the insanity plea and finding suited the regime's purposes, it would have challenged the insanity plea. Our experience is that the state has never yet so docilely accepted an insanity plea without more in a case in which without insanity, the crime would have been vicious murder without extenuating circumstances if not treason.

At present, South African history records Tsafendas as the insane killer of Dr Verwoerd who had no political motive for his act. This is as inadequate as it is incorrect and this is borne out by the study.

South African history, in proper recognition of the generations who preceded us as well as those to come, should record in its annals an accurate account of the killing of Dr Verwoerd, which recognises that Tsafendas was motivated to kill him by reason of his deep opposition to apartheid and was indeed a freedom fighter and a hero. This must be acknowledged by a revision and a correction of this event in history. This is necessary in order that what occurred is properly recorded and that the distortion of it by the apartheid government is laid bare. It is not about being vindictive or vengeful but simply about recording our painful history with the accuracy that our commitment to the truth and reconciliation requires.

In our submission, the study is so thoroughly and painstakingly done that we would have no hesitation in recommending that the Minister may well accept its findings and conclusions and act thereon. On the other hand, we fully accept and understand that the Minister may wish to subject the study to an independent assessment. We hardly seek to be prescriptive in this regard. What is of interest to us is the course of action that the South African government, once it is satisfied with regard to the study and its findings, may elect to take. Again this area falls squarely within the discretion of the government as advised by the Minister, but may we suggest a few options for consideration and they would include:

> a public acknowledgement of the acceptance of the study and its findings; and the appropriate steps to revise the curriculum of schools and other institutions of learning to correct the teaching and learning of the killing of Verwoerd. This is not an exhaustive list of possible actions but are merely suggestions and we remain willing to work with you and the government on these.

Finally, in order to assist you in this process, we attach a copy of the report by Mr Dousemetzis. We are confident that you will find that it raises a convincing case for a re-evaluation of the death of Dr HF Verwoerd. Mr Dousemetzis has indicated his willingness and availability to assist by way of clarification, if required, of any matter dealt with in the research undertaken by him.

Kindly acknowledge receipt and do advise us of your consideration at your earliest convenience.

***

Advocate George Bizos commented that the author's report is 'of major historical importance for South Africa and as to our understanding of Verwoerd's assassination'.[1] He described the evidence gathered and presented by this report, proving that Tsafendas was not insane but politically motivated in killing Dr Verwoerd, as 'overwhelming and unquestionable'.[2] He also characterised this report as 'monumental', describing it as 'a mammoth enquiry into the steps taken by the government to declare him mad and to cover up his treatment. It's absolutely amazing what the government did.'[3]

Professor John Dugard had this to say about the Tsafendas case and the report:

> *Many South Africans suspected that there was a political cover-up in the Tsafendas case. The apartheid regime had two reasons for portraying Tsafendas to be insane. First, the regime wished to suggest that no one in his right mind could kill such a wonderful leader as Hendrik Verwoerd. Secondly, there was the security aspect. The security apparatus, led by the Minister of Justice and Police, John Vorster, wished to avoid accountability for allowing a political revolutionary to be employed in a position close to the Prime Minister. So it was that the media and the legal proceedings were manipulated to present Tsafendas as a mentally deranged person dictated to by a tapeworm.*
>
> *This research confirms that there was a cover-up. It shows convincingly that Tsafendas was a political revolutionary, whose assassination of Dr Verwoerd was motivated by a hatred of Dr Verwoerd and all he stood for. He was not an insane killer but a political assassin determined to rid South Africa of the architect of apartheid. Political assassinations seldom achieve their goal and this was no exception. But at least South African history should know the truth about Tsafendas. Dousemetzis has done South Africa a service by correcting the historical record.*[4]

When asked whether Verwoerd would have been prosecuted by the International Court of Justice for his apartheid policies, if he were alive today, Professor Dugard said:

> *In today's legal language he would have been accused of committing a crime against humanity, because in 1973 the United Nations promoted the UN convention on the prohibition of the crime of apartheid. So apartheid was defined as a crime against humanity in 1973. And clearly, Verwoerd, as the main architect of apartheid, would have been categorised as a criminal, yes. So if he had been brought before the court, he would have been charged with a crime against humanity ... Leaders of the National Party used to be very careful about trouble in Africa,*

> *because most African states had signed the convention, and there was always the fear that they might be prosecuted for a crime against humanity. But, in fact, that never happened to anyone. There were lots of people who should have been prosecuted but never were ... Well, that would be a purely political decision [to prosecute Verwoerd]. It would depend upon how popular South Africa was. I mean, Netanyahu has not been prosecuted. He is just as bad. Netanyahu is probably worse.*[5]

Justice Zak Yacoob said he agreed '100%' with all of the report's findings and added:

> *The historical record shows that Comrade Tsafendas killed Verwoerd, that he pleaded insanity at the trial, his plea was upheld and he was, consequent to his plea, confined at the pleasure of the relevant authority. If he had spoken the truth, he would have been sentenced to death, so the tactic was a very good one in the circumstances. History does not record that he pretended to be insane to save his life. This is well brought out in the research. The research shows conclusively that he did a deliberate courageous anti-apartheid act but pretended insanity at the trial; understandably so. I think the research speaks for itself.*[6]

The following day, Mr Solly Mapaila, the first deputy General-Secretary of the South African Communist Party, made a similar request to the Minister on behalf of his party:

> *We hereby request that the Minister assesses and considers the new evidence, based on research by Mr Harris Dousemetzis, on the assassination of Prime Minster Hendrik Verwoerd and that the act be classified as politically motivated.*
>
> *Currently, court records characterise Mr Dimitri Tsafendas as having suffered from schizophrenia and indicate that the assassination of Prime Minister Verwoerd was due to his mental instability, which the research now proves beyond reasonable doubt to be incorrect. We attach herewith the research summary and records including the details of Mr Harris for further inquiries in this regard.*
>
> *We have further interfaced with the legal fraternity which agrees with Mr Harris's research. We agree with the thrust of their submissions too based on the evidence collated by Mr Harris and also plead for your careful consideration.*

Given the bad treatment Mr Tsafendas endured during his period of incarceration it is only fair that we put the record straight and renew his human value despite the act he committed.

Prior to the assassination, Mr Tsafendas had an extensive and impressive political record, with a demonstrable history of anti-colonialist activism and pro democracy. He was also an active member of the British Anti-Apartheid Movement. There is, therefore, no doubt that he was a conscientious man and his actions were politically motivated. We deem it important to correct this record.

Trusting that our request will be considered expeditiously and favourably as we express our continued high regards.

Solly Mapaila told the author about Tsafendas:

The majority of our people in the country have relied, not exclusively but in the main, on the information from the apartheid treaty about Tsafendas, which sought to deal away with the discourse that the liberation movement or the political actors at the time, whether on behalf of the liberation movement or on behalf of their own conscience, could actually take political action against the apartheid treaty. Which is what Tsafendas did. So, they did not want to create an impression that somebody can respond to the might of oppression and Tsafendas not only responded to this might, he hit them hard. He hit the main force, the principal force and the principal instigator of the apartheid system.

So, with that he was politically astute and correct in the actual identifying of the real problem and he decided to sort it out the best way he could and I think any other black person who has political conscience with that access could have actually done it, knowing that he will pay the ultimate price for it and I'm quite convinced that Tsafendas had a clear conscience that he will die on the side of the people by his actions and he was brave enough. In fact, I regard him as a hero and a warrior for his bravery to confront the might of apartheid systems, right in its Parliament and actually dealt with Verwoerd. So, the apartheid regime created this impression that this was a lunatic, a madman, who one day decided to kill the Prime Minister of the country at the time, not knowing what he was doing because he was a lunatic. Obviously only fools really believe this stupid idea throughout history.[7]

Professor Renfrew Christie told the author:

> *I was in my final year of high school when Tsafendas carried out his political assassination of Verwoerd. My own view is that he was perfectly sane, he was, after all, a member of the South African Communist Party. My own interpretation of the events is that this was a fully legitimate, politically motivated part of the armed struggle. Remember, Nelson Mandela had been sentenced for armed struggle just two years before, two or three years and there was a legitimate armed struggle going on against one of the great evils of the 20th century and the greatest architect was Hendrik Verwoerd. So, the person that killed Verwoerd was a member of the Communist Party, the South African Communist Party and, in alliance with the ANC, were in an armed struggle. I think his basic motives are perfectly obvious; he carried out an armed struggle and killed the tyrant and that is, I think, how he should be remembered, as a hero. I think it is very peculiar that the new South Africa has accepted the crooked old South Africa's interpretation of Tsafendas.*
>
> *In the time of reconciliation and settlement, I think a lot of the heroism of the armed struggle got whitewashed and papered over and forgotten. There's a sustained pressure out of Western Europe, and even now, we get people who paint art works about the settlement and about Mandela the 'peacemaker' and we get people coming to stress how important was the non-violent struggle in liberating the country. And it sometimes has a Cold War flavour, that the ANC was aligned with the Communist Party and was supported by the Soviets whereas the West were not democrats in South Africa for 40 years, the West fought against democracy for 40 years. So, there's an attempt to hide the armed struggle and to play up the side of Nelson Mandela, the 'peacemaker' rather than Nelson Mandela, the 'armed struggler'. In fact, and in the actual history, there was 30 years of armed struggle. The latter-day attempt to ignore it and to say we would have had a peaceful settlement anyway and capitalism would naturally have reformed, is a continuation of Cold War thinking. The fact remains that the West armed, even after sanctions, secretly armed apartheid and they did it, not only because they were racists, although there was deep racism in places like Brazil and America, they did it because they wanted forced labour for mining gold and diamonds and uranium.*[8]

Denis Goldberg told the author that Tsafendas's statements to the South African police after his arrest, 'clearly shows that he was politically motivated [in killing Verwoerd] and not insane ... the man is determined to kill the Prime Minister because of the racism ... [Tsafendas] has a clear political opinion about racism'. Goldberg always had doubts about Tsafendas's supposed insanity, believing that such a declaration would be the obvious course of action for the state. This would enable them to claim that 'only an insane person would kill this brilliant Prime Minister'. As for Tsafendas being a communist, it would have been seriously embarrassing for the security authorities and the police if it was known that Tsafendas had been in the South African Communist Party and politically active elsewhere. 'They would never have admitted that a communist did it,' Goldberg told the author. 'They had made a decision, they're not going to have a proper trial, they want Tsafendas declared insane and unfit to stand and that was their decision. So, we lock him away until the government says it's okay to release him or never and the answer was never, until he died.' Goldberg said while he did not agree with political assassinations, he could not condemn this one. Regarding Tsafendas, he said, 'I have no problem with him.'[9]

Krish Govender said that the 'society should recognise the hero-ism of Tsafendas and his place in history should be in the category of a freedom fighter and he should be honoured'.[10] Ronnie Kasrils characterised Dousemetzis's report to the Minister regarding Verwoerd's assassinaiton as 'incredible' and said that 'the powers of the day sought to portray Tsafendas as a crazy man, and what we now can see and the country needs to know is that the man was motivated with good intentions and that he was a communist'. Kasrils also said that Tsafendas should have been pardoned back in 1994, but instead, 'what we have is an invisible man. We have an unmarked grave at Sterkfontein ... his name should be on the wall of Freedom Park.'[11]

The question is sometimes asked whether Dr Verwoerd's assassination changed the course of history in South Africa, hastening the end of apartheid. When the author put this proposition to Ahmed Kathrada, he replied, 'There is no doubt about that.' He added that he did not agree with political assassinations, but he could not condemn Tsafendas's action.[12] High Court Judge Jody Kollapen told the author that 'the interesting thing is, that if he [Tsafendas] was found not to be insane then the trial would have to proceed, right. Then, there's a real risk – given his early arrest for distributing pamphlets, etc. – that you're putting on trial, then, not only Dimitris Tsafendas, you're putting on trial on the international stage the entire system of apartheid.'[13]

For his actions against apartheid, Alexander Moumbaris received the award of Grand Companion of O.R. Tambo and a Sabotage Campaign medal, but he always regretted that he could not do more for Tsafendas. His efforts to get Tsafendas released came to nothing and Moumbaris was deeply saddened that Tsafendas died a lonely death in a psychiatric hospital. He believed that no one in the history of South Africa had been treated so unfairly and in 2003 he created a web page headed 'Dimitri Tsafendas. Remembering a Revolutionary.

Homage to Dimitri Tsafendas. Hero and Martyr of the Cause of the South African People.' Moumbaris declared: 'I regret not having done better for him to get out of there [the hospital where he died]. He deserved a better liberty than the one he got.'[14] He described Tsafendas as 'a brave revolutionary, the bravest man I ever met'. Moumbaris's wish is that South Africa should formally acknowledge that 'Tsafendas was a revolutionary and not a lunatic, and that in executing Verwoerd, he was committing not an insane act but a brave political one'.[15]

Helen Suzman told Liza Key about the assassination's impact:

> *I do think the assassination of Verwoerd changed the course of history in South Africa, because nobody was quite as sure as he was of the policy of separate development. I mean, he was steeped in it. It was religion to him. But the others all had doubts. I mean there was no doubt that Vorster was determined to maintain white domination, but that was a different thing. It wasn't based in any philosophy the way Verwoerd's was. Nobody had the same certitude that he had.*[16]

The question of Tsafendas's sanity was never an issue with the many people who knew him before the assassination. Not a single friend or acquaintance accepted that he had suddenly gone mad and believed he had a tapeworm in his stomach. Fellow opponents of apartheid saw Tsafendas as a hero who committed a noble and selfless act. Even those who disagreed with his political ideas and abhorred the assassination acknowledged that he was a sane and deeply political person who acted for the benefit of the oppressed in South Africa. What is extraordinary is that the world came to believe Tsafendas was insane when, with the benefit of hindsight, the facts might suggest that it was Verwoerd who was thus afflicted.

It was Verwoerd who saw himself after being shot by David Pratt as a martyr for the cause of apartheid and came to believe that his life was saved by God's intervention and that this was proof of God's support for apartheid. [17] He believed that the Bible gave sanctions for racial separation[18] and that apartheid was divinely inspired.[19] He believed that the minority whites should rule because blacks were not civilised, although the whites were quite happy to 'civilize, protect, help and teach democracy' to them.[20] He defended apartheid by claiming that the minority whites should rule South Africa as a form of self-protection, arguing that 'apartheid is based on the principle that only in this way can the weak be protected from the strong, and the minority be made to feel safe'. Against all the evidence of history and science, he proclaimed that South Africa was empty until the Europeans arrived.[21] He even declared that Africans should be grateful that the whites had not wiped them out, as happened to most of the indigenous people of North America.[22] Verwoerd's views on race were so extreme as to call into question the balance of his mind. He considered blacks to be uncivilised entities who could never aspire to be anything better than labourers and thus should never 'gaze at the green pastures of European society'.[23] He banned marriages between different races to protect the 'purity' of whites, once telling his wife, 'I will not be responsible for the bastardisation of the Afrikaner people.'[24] Finally, he was so delusional as to believe, or at least to claim, that 'a vast number' of blacks supported apartheid, while the rest simply failed to understand that his policies were beneficial to them and for their own good![25]

Tsafendas was the antithesis of Verwoerd. His eminently rational anti-racist beliefs, which came to be widely accepted as standard morality, were based on his profound conviction that all people were equal, regardless of colour. Contrary to Verwoerd, he believed that individuals should marry whomever they wanted, a belief he demonstrated personally with girlfriends who were variously black, white, Jewish, Christian and Muslim. In contrast to Verwoerd's clampdown on black education, he believed learning was the route out of poverty and taught children voluntarily in Turkey and Mozambique. He campaigned for a Mozambique that would be 'governed by the natives of that Province, be they white or black'.[26] He regarded South Africa as 'occupied' by fascist rulers typified by Verwoerd, who, in Tsafendas's eyes, was the 'brains behind apartheid'[27] and not the 'real representative of all South African people'. He wanted to see 'a government that would represent all South African people' and hoped that by killing him, a 'change of policy would take place'.[28]

These were different times, in a God-fearing nation, where human rights did not constitute the moral benchmark that they do today. However, by any standard of social injustice, which of these two men's opinions and actions would suggest insanity? How profoundly ironic that Verwoerd's bizarre notions were never seriously questioned, while the sane and moderate views of Tsafendas saw him demonised as that of a mindless person.

Bertolt Brecht, whose works Tsafendas much admired, once wrote about death thus: 'There are many ways to kill. One can stab a knife into someone's belly, take away one's bread, not heal one from a disease, stick one in a bad apartment, work one to death, drive one to commit suicide, send one off to war, etc. Only a few of these things are forbidden in our country.'[29] Ironically, Tsafendas chose the only method that was outlawed by apartheid; all the other forms of death, as categorised by Brecht, took place frequently in South Africa as a routine result of apartheid racist policies.

After 1994, many of the lies of apartheid began to unravel, such as the death of activist Ahmed Timol being exposed as murder and not suicide as claimed by the police. However, Tsafendas continued to still be widely considered a simple schizophrenic lacking any political motivation. This is not entirely surprising, given that his case was presented in court and by the Commission of Enquiry in a manner that would make such a conclusion inescapable. Nevertheless, there were many who knew perfectly well how apartheid operated and that any form of official inquiry would always return a verdict that the government wanted, especially when the architect of apartheid himself was a victim. Surely, in these circumstances, there should always have been doubt about Tsafendas's proclaimed guilt and state of mind. Was there ever any possibility of the regime admitting that Verwoerd was assassinated by a dedicated communist with a long list of political activities in his background? Or that the nation's much-vaunted security service had failed to prevent such a person not only entering the country but securing a job in Parliament with access to the Prime Minister? It is intriguing to speculate on the consequences had the 'big lie' not succeeded: Vorster and Van den Bergh would have been publicly disgraced and apartheid itself would have gone on trial; Tsafendas would have become a hero of the anti-apartheid struggle and Verwoerd's image and status irrevocably shattered.

It is regretful that Tsafendas lies in an unmarked grave while the world's history books still refer to him as a deranged messenger who killed Verwoerd because of a tapeworm. It is all the more significant that this view prevailed after the doctors who examined him testified at his summary trial that Tsafendas had insisted to them that the tapeworm had nothing to do with the assassination. The reporting by the media of the time, much of it pro-apartheid, and the flippant attitude to the tapeworm held by many ordinary South Africans and the subsequent manipulation of history ensured that this characterisation prevailed. We should remember that Father Minas and Bishop Ioannis wanted to tell the world the truth about Tsafendas and his motive. It was Tsafendas who urged them to remain silent, arguing that his conscience was clear and he had done what he believed to be right; he believed it was his 'social responsibility' to stop a mass crime from being committed, namely the continuation of apartheid. He believed that by 'advertising' his action, this would undermine it and rob it of its value and validity.

This book is not an attempt to glorify Tsafendas nor to canonise him as a saint or hero of the struggle against oppression. It seeks simply to set out the facts about Tsafendas and the assassination. Whether Tsafendas should be considered a hero of the anti-apartheid struggle is a subjective question dependent upon each person's values and opinions, particularly whether or not a political assassination is justifiable. What is essential is that the historical record be corrected and the truth disclosed in full concerning Tsafendas's life, his political views and his motives. It is then up to the individual to decide whether Tsafendas is a hero or not.

On November 8, 2018, *The Man Who Killed Apartheid* was launched at the Apartheid Museum in Johannesburg in co-operation with the Ahmed Kathrada Foundation. The speakers were Judge Jody Kollapen, who gave the keynote address; Neeshan Balton, Executive Director of the Ahmed Kathrada Foundation; Maggie Davey of Jacana Media; Reneva Fourie, member of the Central Committee of the SACP; Attorney Krish Govender; and Minister of Justice and Correctional Services Michael Masutha.

Judge Jody Kollapen said that the book "is about a search for the truth" and that it is important because South Africa needs to know the truth about such a major historical event. He said that Tsafendas "was incensed about what Verwoerd did and he was prepared to risk his life" and that he had personally discovered that Tsafendas never lost his militancy even towards his last days.

Reneva Fourie said:

"Our first Deputy General-Secretary, comrade Solly Mapaila, is out of the country and had requested that I stand in for him. He deemed it essential that the SACP be represented at this very important occasion -the launch of a book that makes such a significant contribution to our history. We are here feeling guilt while simultaneously feeling elation. Harris did what we failed to do... Today, one day and a month after the passing of Dimitri Tsafendas, 19 years ago, the work of Harris Dousemetzis empowers us to affirm that Dimitri was a comrade, our comrade... we formally endorsed the submission to Minister Mike Masutha that the historical records be rectified. His presence here today provides us with assurance that every effort will be made in this regard... As the SACP we undertake to repair the tombstone and to ensure that the 20th Anniversary of comrade Dimitri Tsafendas' passing is appropriately commemorated."

Minister Masutha, who had volunteered to attend the event and to speak, described the book launch as "a moment to celebrate the truth" about Tsafendas. He said:

"Tonight we're here to celebrate the truth. Only the truth will set you free ... Indeed, the story that is being told tonight is one of a man who may have killed a man, but I believe in the depth of his mind he was not a killer. He did not want to kill a human being. He wanted to kill a system. It is unfortunate that the system personified itself in a human being."

Minister Masutha added that at the time, it would have suited the apartheid state to conceal the truth as it would have been to its detriment to admit that a Communist had been in service inside parliament. Thus they misportrayed him. Attorney Kris Govender highlighted the book's importance to South Africa's history for "revealing the truth" about Tsafendas and Dr. Verwoerd's assassination. He also conveyed to the audience the following message from Judge Zak Yacoob:

"This publication shows how hard work and attention to detail reveal truth to conquer powers of evil that seeks to hide it."

At the end of the event, in a private conversation with the author and Advocate George Bizos, Minister Masutha said that his legal team, headed by Mr. Prince Maluleke, had finished reading the Report and evaluating the accompanying evidence. Asked by the author whether they agreed with the findings, Mr. Maluleke said, "We wouldn't have been here if we did not agree." Subsequently, Minister Masutha and Mr. Maluleke told the author and Advocate Bizos that they were going to explore ways to take the matter further. However, Minister Masutha took no further action regarding the case as he was soon after replaced as Minister of Justice by Ronald Lamola. In 2019, a revised version of *Living in Strange Lands*, which incorporated some of the new evidence presented in this book, entitled *Strange Lands*, opened in South Africa with Spanoudes starring again as Tsafendas. Both the play and Spanoudes received critical acclaim. In Apil 2020, Advocate Dumisa Ntsebeza submitted to Minister Lamola the same report and the evidence that had been submitted to Minister Masutha. The submission was accompanied by another letter from Bizos, Dugard, Govender, Ntsebeza and Yacoob, which asked Minister Lamola to advance the matter. Their letter said:

Dr. Dousemetzis collaborated with us in the evaluation of the evidence he gathered; we endorsed his findings, which proved that Tsafendas killed Verwoerd for political reasons and not because of a tapeworm. We asked the Minister, once he had read the Report and evaluated the evidence, to make an announcement accepting the Report's findings and take the appropriate steps to revise the curriculum of schools and other institutions so that children would be taught the truth about Tsafendas... we respectfully ask you to advance this matter, which seems to have become somewhat becalmed. Although we and Minister Masutha have agreed with the Report's findings, we understand that you might want to examine the Report and the evidence yourself... Today, Tsafendas still lies in an unmarked grave. Tsafendas did what he considered it to be his duty towards South Africa - we believe the time has come for South Africa to do her duty to him and at least publicly recognise his political motivation. We respectfully suggest that this overdue acknowledgement of a true hero will augur positively in every respect for our government at this difficult time.

A similar request was simultaneously submitted to the Minister by Mr. Solly Mapaila on behalf of the Communist Party. On October 9, 2021, His Grace Ioannis Tsaftaridis, Archbishop of Zambia and Malawi and Deputy of the Orthodox Diocese of Mozambique, and liaison between the Inter-parliamentary Assembly on Orthodoxy and the Pan African Parliament, held a memorial service in Maputo, Mozambique, to honour Tsafendas and his memory. The ceremony, which was part of the wider celebrations for the 200th anniversary of the Greek Revolution against the Ottomans, was held at the premises of the Greek Orthodox Cathedral of the Archangels Michael and Gabriel in Maputo.[30] The Archbishop's invitation characterized Tsafendas as a "'tragic' Hero of Freedom, who fought for the national liberation of Mozambique and the freedom of the people of South Africa from the regime of racial discrimination (apartheid)."[31] Among those who were invited and attended the ceremony were Mr. Eneas Comiche, the President of the Municipal Council, representatives of the Government of the Republic of Mozambique, members of the Diplomatic Corps in the country, and representatives of other religions and churches. The event attracted wide media coverage and it was broadcasted by national channels such as the TVM, Tv Miramar, and Stv.[32] The ceremony opened with the reading of a message by His Beatitude the Pope and Patriarch of Alexandria and All Africa Theodoros II who characterized the event as a "wonderful initiative" and stated that:

"Morally speaking, the act of an assassination may not be justified, but Tsafendas' act escapes the narrow ethical boundaries as it is a deeply political act, with the essential and substantive meaning of the term. It is an act orbiting around the symbolic level and contains the desperate feelings of a people who have suffered. Dimitrios Tsafendas, in spite of the attempts to tarnish his personality and his characterization as allegedly 'insane,' was a real fighter for human rights, a missionary of freedom and a true martyr who experienced during the most part of his life unspeakable tortures... The demand of the Peoples for peace, equality and self-determination is universal and timeless and Tsafendas served these values to the end. Each one of us, we have a sacred duty towards Dimitrios Tsafendas, towards this Greek citizen and freedom fighter, to restore his memory and to place him on the pedestal he deserves."[33]

The Patriarch's message was extremely important because it marked the first time that the head of the Greek-Orthodox Church in all Africa officially recognized Tsafendas not only as a freedom fighter, but also as a hero. Archbishop Ioannis then, in his speech, told his distinguished guests that people "should never forget Tsafendas's titanian sacrifice for freedom" and added:

"Tsafendas deeply loved his continent, Africa and its people, who suffered for their passions and fought for a better day. But he mainly loved his motherland, Mozambique.... where he has been on the forefront of the national liberation struggle of the Mozambican people from colonial powers, encouraging all Mozambicans of the local communities, regardless of race or color, to join forces in the National Liberation Front. Tsafendas was one of the pioneers of the Mozambican national liberation movement and was repeatedly imprisoned by the Secret Services of the Colonial Power for his revolutionary ideas and actions. However, his passion for freedom motivated him to continue the Struggle untouched... The culmination of Tsafendas' struggles and political action was the taking of the life of the then South African Prime Minister Hendrik Frensch Verwoerd, also known as the 'Architect of Apartheid'. It is a revolutionary act that was not directed against a man but against an inhuman and dirty system ... It is our duty to keep the memory of this freedom fighter alive, not to forget his sacrifice, martyrdom and humiliation he experienced in prison, but above all not to forget that Tsafendas remained free even behind bars, because no one can be deprived of the freedom of mind and soul."[34]

Messages were also sent and read during the ceremony by the South African Communist Party and prominent anti-apartheid activists. Solly Mapaila, the First Deputy Secretary-General of the SACP hailed Tsafendas in his message as "a great hero of the South African people," "a people's hero of our liberation struggle," and "a devoted socialist revolutionary." Mapaila said that the SACP "fully recognized" Tsafendas's "revolutionary contributions" and has committed to "erect a proper tombstone and a memorial for him; this process was disrupted in 2020 by the Covid-19 pandemic." He added that

"Tsafendas was the most decisive revolutionary of his contemporaries. He attacked and killed not only the pivot symbol of apartheid system but the real architect of racial segregation ideology in South Africa, Hendrik Verwoerd's apartheid policy. Tsafendas was a great man of courage who absorbed so much pain to protect his comrades, he sacrificed so much to protect the SACP. We owe it to him and the many revolutionaries of his high calibre consciousness that today we enjoy certain freedoms because of their contributions. We will never forget his enduring legacy and huge sacrifices for our freedom."[35]

Krish Govender said in his message that Tsafendas "will be remembered as the courageous communist freedom fighter who made his way into SA and struck a powerful blow against the might of the apartheid parliament in Cape Town, by driving a knife into the heart of the architect of apartheid, Hendrik Verwoerd, the Prime Minister of the evil racist regime, in full view of the world knowing that he will be captured, tortured and executed. ... It is hope that one day SA will find the heart to properly remember and commemorate the life of this unique and courageous martyr."[36]

Ronnie Kasrils said in his message that Tsafendas was "motivated by political ideals and morality" and that "is only just and right that he should be remembered as a man who sought freedom and justice for the oppressed and honoured as a freedom fighter."[37] Alexander Moumbaris said, "He is the bravest man I have met. He was a tyrannicide (Τυραννοκτόνος)."[38] Finally, Judge Zak Yacoob said in his message,

"Our worthy comrade Tsafendas was imprisoned and died in the course of his undeniably valiant struggle against the injustice and the crime against humanity: Apartheid. The death of that criminal Prime Minister represented an immeasurable step forward in our struggle. We salute and thank Comrade Tsafendas. We also repeat our often stated request and urge our government to ensure that his untold courage is correctly recorded in history."[39]

At the end of the ceremony, Archbishop Ioannis announced that he will erect a bust of Tsafendas that would be placed in the forecourt of the Greek-Orthodox church in Maputo and asked the President of the Municipal Council of Maputo that the name "Dimitris Tsafendas" be given to a street in Maputo. The SACP and FRELIMO support both initiatives.[40] Tsafendas did what he considered to be his duty towards South Africa and Mozambique; let us hope that one day Mozambique and South Africa will do its duty towards him.

Notes

Chapter 1: The Deed

[1] Demetrio Tsafendas statement to Major Rossouw, 11 September 1966, K150, Report of the Commission of Enquiry (COE) into the circumstances of the death of the late Dr the honourable Hendrik Frensch Verwoerd, (*hereafter cited as* K150), Vol. 1, File: Verklaring van Demetrio Tsafendas. National Archives of South Africa (hereafter cited as NASA); Minas Constandinou, author interview.

[2] A.J. Harrison statement to the COE, 5 October 1966. K150, Vol. 6, File 3, NASA.

[3] Maurice Klein's testimony to the COE, 25 October 1966. K150, Vol. 10, File: Uittreksels uit Getuienis, NASA; Constandinou author interview.

[4] Johannes Joachim Jurgens Scholtz, *Dr Hendrik Frensch Verwoerd* (Johannesburg: Perskor-uitgewery, 1974), p. 313.

[5] Adriaan Nicolaas Pelzer, ed., *Verwoerd Speaks: Speeches 1948–66* (Johannesburg: APB Publishers, 1966), p. 83.

[6] Dimitris Tsafendas in *A Question of Madness*, 1997; Constandinou author interview.

[7] Constandinou and Ioannis Tsaftaridis, author interviews.

[8] Nelson Mandela, *Long Walk to Freedom* (London: Abacus, 2013 [1994]), p. 512.

[9] Constandinou and Tsaftaridis, author interviews.

[10] Edward Furness statement to the police, 12 October 1966. K150, Vol. 12, File: Verklarings, NASA.

[11] Tsafendas's statement to Major Rossouw, 19 September 1966. K150, Vol. 1, File: Verklaring van Demetrio Tsafendas, NASA.

[12] Constandinou and K. Pnefma, author interviews.

[13] Demetrio Tsafendas statement to Major Rossouw, 11 September 1966. K150, Vol. 1, File: Verklaring van Demetrio Tsafendas, NASA; Frank Walter Waring statement to the police, 9 September 1966. K150, Vol. 12, File: Verklarings, NASA.

[14] George Oliver, 'I have something to do, said the assassin', *Rand Daily Mail*, 7 September 1966: 1.

[15] Constandinou, author interview.

[16] K. Pnefma, author interview.

[17] Constandinou and K. Pnefma, author interviews.

[18] Constandinou, author interview.

[19] *Rand Daily Mail*, 'Unsaid speech was expected to set new SA foreign policy', 7 September 1966: 7.

[20] *The New York Times*, 'Dr Verwoerd: Relentless advocate of apartheid', 7 September 1966: 16.

[21] Vic Alhadeff, *A Newspaper History of South Africa* (Cape Town: Don Nelson, 1985), p. 107.

[22] *Sunday Times* (Johannesburg), 'Lift delay spared window', 11 September 1966.

[23] *The New York Times*, 'Unafraid of assassins, Dr Verwoerd said in 1962', 7 September 1966: 16.

[24] Dr Aubrey Radford's statement to the police, 19 September 1966. K150, Vol. 12, File: Verklarings, NASA.

[25] *TIME*, 'South Africa: Death to the architect', 16 September 1966: 38.
[26] Paul van der Merwe statement to the police, 8 September 1966. K150, Vol. 12, File: Verklarings, NASA; 'O assassinato do Dr Verwoerd', *O Primeiro de Janeiro*, 7 September 1966: 2; Gerald Shaw, *Believe in Miracles: South Africa from Malan to Mandela – and the Mbeki Era* (Newlands: Ampersand Press, 2007), p. 57; *The Canberra Times*, 'Dr Verwoerd assassinated in Parliament House', 7 September 1966: 1.
[27] Frank Walter Waring statement to the police, 9 September 1966. K150, Vol. 12, File: Verklarings, NASA; Willem L.D.M. Venter statement to the COE, 19 October 1966. K150, Vol. 12, File: Verklarings, NASA; *The Australian*, 'Dr Verwoerd stabbed', 7 September 1966: 1; Chris Barron, *Collected South African Obituaries* (Parklands: Penguin Books, 2005), p. 336; Jonathan Stephenson, 'Jonathan Stephenson on a Cape Town Incident', *Fortnight*, No. 159 (1978), p. 27; Shaw, *Believe in Miracles*, p. 57.
[28] *Daily Express*, 'Assassination', 7 September 1966: 2; *Deutsche Zeitung*, 'Sudafrikas Ministerprasident Dr Verwoerd im Parliament von einem Weiben erstochen', 7 September 1966: 1; *Rand Daily Mail*, 'Desperate fight to reach killer, save Prime Minister', 7 September 1966: 2; *Washington Post*, 'Dr Verwoerd slain at his Parliament desk', 7 September 1966: 1.
[29] Shaw, *Believe in Miracles*, p. 57.
[30] Feliz George Miles statement to the police, 7 October 1966. K150, Vol. 2, File: 1, NASA.
[31] Dr Aubrey Radford's statement to the police, 19 September 1966. K150, Vol. 12, File: Verklarings, NASA; Paul van der Merwe statement to the police, 8 September 1966. K150, Vol. 12, File: Verklarings, NASA; *Daily Dispatch*, 'Dr Verwoerd assassinated,' 7 September 1966: 1.
[32] Johannes Joachim Jurgens Scholtz, *Die Moord op Dr Verwoerd* (Cape Town: Nationale Boekhandel BPK, 1967), p. 42.
[33] *Daily Dispatch*, 'Dr Verwoerd assassinated'; *The Cape Argus*, 'Crowed at the hospital', 6 September 1966; *The Chronicle* (Bulawayo), 'Dr Verwoerd killed', 6 September 1966: 1.
[34] *Daily Dispatch*, 'Dr Verwoerd assassinated'; *The Chronicle* (Bulawayo), 'Dr Verwoerd killed'.

Chapter 2: After the Deed

[1] Dirk Kotze Genis statement to the police, 24 October 1966. COE, K150, Vol. 3, File: Afskrif van vorm Z 204, NASA.
[2] Constandinou and Tsaftaridis, author interviews.
[3] Dr Kossew's report on examination in case of alleged assault or other crime, 6 September 1966. K150, Vol. 6, File: 3, NASA.
[4] Mandela, *Long Walk to Freedom*, p. 495.
[5] Major Rossouw's testimony to the Commission of Enquiry, 14 October 1966. K150, Vol. 10, File: Uittreksels uit Getuienis, NASA.
[6] Dirk Kotze Genis statement to the police, 24 October 1966. K150, Vol: 3, File: Afskrif van vorm Z 204, NASA.
[7] David Goodman, *Fault Lines: Journeys into the New South Africa* (Berkeley and Los Angeles: University of California Press, 1999), pp. 154–5.
[8] Dr T.A. Darby statement re: Demitrio Tsafendas. G.S.H. NO. 65/014-181, 6 September 1966. K150, Vol. 12, File: Verklarings Demitrio Tsafendas, NASA.

[9] The most flagrant case was that of anti-apartheid activist Steve Biko, who died on 12 September 1977 after serial beatings by the police. Two doctors, Ivor Lang and Benjamin Tucker, who saw him five days before his death, when he was suffering from a traumatic brain injury, reported that they saw no evidence of abnormality. The security forces claimed that his death was the result of injuries received in a scuffle and this was accepted at the official inquest. Biko was the 21st person to die in a South African prison over 12 months. It took eight years of intense pressure before the South African Medical Council (SAMDC) took disciplinary action. On 30 January 1985, the Supreme Court ordered the SAMDC to hold an inquiry into the conduct of the doctors who treated Steve Biko. In his judgment, Judge President of the Transvaal, Justice W.G. Boshoff, said that there was prima facie evidence of improper or disgraceful conduct on the part of the doctors. Dr Lang was then stripped of his medical qualifications (Lionel J. Nicholas, 'Psychological sequelae of political imprisonment during apartheid', *South African Journal of Psychology*, Vol. 44, No. 1 (2014): 20).

[10] Dr Isaac Sakinofsky in correspondence with the author, 30 March 2016.

[11] *Cape Times*, 'Suspect's jaws broken', 7 September 1966.

[12] Constandinou, author interview.

[13] John D'Oliveira, *Vorster – The Man* (Johannesburg: Ernest Stanton Publishers, 1977), p. 180.

[14] Born in Transvaal in 1912, he joined the police in 1932 and served as Deputy-Commissioner of the CID from 1964 to 1968, before becoming Commissioner of the police in 1972 (International Magazine Services photo archive, n.d.).

[15] *Cape Times*, 'Suspect's jaws broken'.

[16] Goodman, *Fault Lines*, pp. 154–5.

[17] *The New York Times*, 'Assassination stirs concern among leaders of Black Africa', 7 September 1966: 17; *Pretoria News*, 'Sports cancelled as mark of respect for Dr Verwoerd', 7 September 1966.

[18] *Washington Post*, 'Dr Verwoerd stabbed to death at his desk in Parliament', 7 September 1966: 8.

[19] *Die Welt*, 'Dr Verwoerd ermordet', 7 September 1966: 1; *The Canberra Times*, 'Stock Exchange numbed', 7 September 1966: 1; *The New York Times*, 'London stocks fall after Dr Verwoerd assassination', 7 September 1966: 69; *Sunday Times* (Johannesburg), 'Assassination shakes market', 11 September 1966: 24.

[20] *Cape Times*, 'Dr Verwoerd film in city', 8 September 1966; *Daily News*, 'Durban Indians pay tribute in prayer', 8 September 1966: 3.

[21] *The Herald* (Melbourne), 'Murder shocks world', 7 September 1966: 2.

[22] Lionel Davis, author interview.

[23] Mandela, *Long Walk to Freedom*, p. 513.

[24] Louise O'Ryan in *A Question of Madness*, 1997. This part is available in the rushes.

[25] Chris Barron, 'Stanley Uys: Veteran journalist who tracked the rise and fall of the Nats', *Sunday Times*, 19 January 2014.

[26] Mary Eintracht and K. Pnefma, author interviews.

[27] Eintracht, Fotini Gavasiadis and K. Pnefma, author interviews.

[28] K. Pnefma, author interview.

[29] Eintracht, Gavasiadis and K. Pnefma, author interviews.

[30] Eintracht and K. Pnefma, author interviews.

[31] Marika Tsafantakis statement to the police, 7 September 1966. K150, Vol. 12, File: Verklarings Demitrio Tsafendas, NASA.

[32] We cannot know for certain whether Tsafendas's characterisation of Jesus as a revolutionary was his own inspiration or whether he was adopting the idea of others. Certainly, a Colombian Roman Catholic priest, Father Camilo Restrepo (1929–66), a socialist, university professor and member of the National Liberation Army of Colombia, had declared that 'If Jesus were alive today, he would be a guerrillero.' Similar views, that Jesus was a revolutionary and the first communist, were expressed by philosophers such as Robert Eisler and Karl Kautsky. The likelihood is that Tsafendas's expression was his own, since he had been using it since at least 1961, before Father Restrepo was widely known.

[33] K. Pnefma, author interview.

[34] Antony Michaletos, author interview.

[35] George Bizos author interview; George Bizos in *Live and Let Live*, 2007.

[36] *To Vima*, 'Από παιδί ήταν ανισόρροπος ο δολοφόνος του Φερβέρντ', 9 September 1966: 1.

[37] Mary Vasilakou author interview.

[38] *Acropolis*, 'Ολόκληρον το Νοτιοαφρικόν Έθνος εκήδευσε τον πρωθυπουργό του', 17 September 1966: 1.

[39] *Natal Mercury*, 'The face of Demitri Tsafendas', 8 September 1966: 5; *Rand Daily Mail*, 'Boyhood days of Tsafendas', 8 September 1966: 2.

[40] William Mare Volbrecht statement to the police, 3 October 1966. K150, Vol 3, File Verklaring deur Majoor Venter, NASA. *Rand Daily Mail*, 'Boyhood days of Tsafendas'.

[41] *Rand Daily Mail*, 'Boyhood days of Tsafendas'.

[42] *Rand Daily Mail*, 'Assurances for Greeks', 14 September 1966.

[43] *The Herald* (Melbourne), 'Don't touch the Greeks', 9 September 1966: 9.

[44] *Pretoria News*, 'City Greek café hit by bullet', 7 September 1966: 1; *The Times* (London), 'Attacks on Greek shops', 7 September 1966: 1.

[45] *Kathimerini*, 'θλίψις εις την Ελληνικήν παροικίαν του Γιοχάνεσμπουργκ', 7 September 1966: 1; Andreas Babiolakis, Nick Papadakis and Costas Poriazis, author interviews.

[46] Constandinou, Reuben O'Ryan and Tsaftaridis, author interviews.

[47] *The Australian*, 'Murder shocks world, but some leaders are glad', 8 September 1966.

[48] *The Globe and Mail*, 'Assassination condemned by friend and foe alike', 7 September 1966: 3; *The Herald* (Melbourne), 'Murder shocks world', 7 September 1966: 2.

[49] *Le Courrier d'Afrique*, 'A eleicao do sucessor', 9 September 1966: 3.

[50] *Pretoria News*, 'Shock news on BBC', 6 September 1966: 1; *Umtali Post*, 'BBC reports the death', 6 September 1966: 1.

[51] *The Times* (London), 'BBC News criticized', 7 September 1966: 1.

[52] *The Herald* (Melbourne), 'Murder shocks world'.

[53] Albie Sachs author interview.

[54] *The Guardian*, '"Stinking" quotation by BBC', 9 September 1966: 11; *The Times* (London), 'BBC news criticized'.

[55] *The Stage*, 'BBC drops further behind in September', 20 October 1966: 10.

[56] *Private Eye*, 'Dr Verwoerd: A nation mourns', 17 September 1966: cover.

[57] *Daily Express*, 'Epitaph for a fanatic', 7 September 1966: 2; '*The Times* (London), Jubilation at news in Nigeria', 7 September 1966: 1; *The Herald* (Melbourne), 'How Africa took the news', 7 September 1966: 1; *Washington Post*, 'London Conference shocked by slain', 7 September 1966: 8.
[58] *TIME*, 'South Africa: Death to the architect'.
[59] *Kathimerini*, 'Ατομον ελληνικής καταγωγής εδολοφόνησε τον Φέρβειρντ', 7 September 1966: 1.
[60] *The New York Times*, 'Johnson decries assassination; Rights leaders echo dismay', 7 September 1966: 16; *Washington Post*, 'London Conference shocked by slain'.
[61] John F. Burns, 'Acid general is key to Pretoria scandal', *The New York Times*, 1 April 1979: 10; Gordon Winter, *Inside BOSS: South Africa's Secret Police* (Harmondsworth: Penguin Books, 1981), p. 34.
[62] TRC, *Report: Volume Two*, p. 16, 195.
[63] John F. Burns, 'Pretoria scandal testimony reveals talk of murder', *The New York Times*, 18 May 1980: 3; Richard Leonard, *South Africa at War: White Power and the Crisis in Southern Africa* (Westport: Lawrence Hill and Company, 1983), p. 124; Clifford Luyt, 'The killing fields: South Africa's human rights record in southern Africa', *Social Justice: A Journal of Crime, Conflict and World Order*, Vol. 16, No. 2 (1989): 110; *Rand Daily Mail*, 5 June 1979; TRC, *Report: Volume Two*, p. 18.
[64] James Sanders, *Apartheid's Friends: The Rise and Fall of South Africa's Secret Service* (London: John Murray, 2006), pp. 34–5.
[65] International Defence and Aid Fund, *BOSS: The First Five Years* (London: International Defence and Aid Fund, 1975), p. 15.
[66] Philip H. Frankel, *An Ordinary Atrocity: Sharpeville and Its Massacre* (New Haven and London: Yale University Press, 2001), pp. 194–5.
[67] Like Dr Verwoerd, Van den Bergh simply blamed the communists. There was another significant link between these two powerful men. Just as Verwoerd believed his life had been saved by divine intervention, Van den Bergh credited God with performing a similar service for him. He told the best-selling British author, Frederick Forsyth: 'I was standing alone once on the High Veldt when a great storm came up. I knew the land was riven with iron ore deposits and lightning strikes would be often and dangerous. So I took shelter under a large *mwataba* tree. There was an old kaffir standing nearby, also sheltering. The storm raged with biblical intensity. The thunderbolts poured out of the sky and the thunder was enough to deafen me. The tree was struck and split down the middle, its core a smoking ruin. The old kaffir was struck and at once electrocuted. But the storm passed and the sky cleared and I was not touched. And it was then when I knew that the hand of God was upon me.' Expressing his personal view, Forsyth declared that the man he described as 'master of one of the most brutal secret police forces in the world', was 'mad as a frog' (Frederick Forsyth, *The Outsider: My Life in Intrigue* (London: Bantam Press, 2015), pp. 334–5).
Van den Bergh thought that God was helpful in other ways. In 1963, John Harris, an anti-apartheid revolutionary and member of the African Resistance Movement, planted a bomb which exploded in Johannesburg railway station. Van den Bergh said that sometime later, he was sitting in his car wondering who might have placed the bomb when suddenly the name John Harris came into his mind. He had never heard the name before. God, he believed, had whispered it in his ear (Henry R. Pike, *A History of Communism in South Africa* (Primrose Hill, Germiston: Christian Mission International

of South Africa, 1985), p. 405). Professor Dan O'Meara said Van den Bergh personified 'the most paranoid and the most vicious tendencies in Afrikaner nationalism' (Dean O'Meara, *Forty Lost Years: The Apartheid State and the Politics of the National Party 1948 –1994* (Randburg: Ravan Press, 1996), p. 211), while Helen Suzman described him in Parliament as 'South Africa's own Heinrich Himmler' (Winter, *Inside BOSS*, p. 26; Debates of the House of Assembly, 8 December 1978).

[68] David Beresford, author interview.

[69] Gordon Winter's correspondence with David Beresford, 8 September 1998. Liza Key's personal collection; Constandinou and Tsaftaridis, author interviews.

[70] Terry Bell & Dumisa Buhle Ntsebeza, *Unfinished Business: South Africa, Apartheid and Truth* (London and New York: Verso Books, 2003), pp. 56–7; Terry Bell, Beresford, Constandinou, Liza Key and Tsaftaridis, author interviews; Gordon Winter's correspondence with David Beresford, 8 September 1998. Liza Key's personal collection.

[71] *Cape Argus*, '180-day prison for Tsafendas', 7 September 1966: 1.

[72] South African Police report regarding the activities of Dimitrio Tsafendas in Mozambique and Rhodesia, 12 September 1966. K150, Vol. 3, Sub file: 1/5, NASA.

[73] Memorandum of the Special Branch of the British South African Police in Salisbury regarding Demitrio Tsafendas, 9 September 1966. K150, Vol. 12, File: Verklarings Demitrio Tsafendas Demitrio Tsafendas, NASA.

[74] *Cape Argus*, 'Killer was a lone worker', 7 September 1966 (late edition): 1.

[75] Dominique Lapierre, *A Rainbow in the Night: The Tumultuous Birth of South Africa* (Cambridge: Da Capo Press, 2009), p. 126.

[76] Lapierre, *A Rainbow in the Night*, p. 126.

[77] Report of the COE, chapter IID, paragraph 12, December 1966. RP 16/1967. Pretoria.

[78] Secret telegram from SA Embassy, Lisbon to Secretary of Foreign Affairs, Cape Town, 7 September 1966. K150, Vol. 7, File: 09/04 Suspect Persons Demetrio Tsafendas, NASA.

[79] Top secret letter of the head inspector of PIDE in Lisbon to the Subdirector of PIDE in Mozambique regarding Demitrio Tsafendas, 08/09/1966. PIDE/DGS, SC, CI (2) 6818, NT 7461, PNA. Arquivo National da Torre do Tombo, Portugal (hereafter cited as ANTT).

[80] Vertaling. Information: Demitrio Tsafendas or Demetrio Tsafandakis, 7 September 1966. K150, Vol. 6, File: 3, NASA; PIDE report: Information: Demitrio Tsafendas or Demetrio Tsafandakis, 7 September 1966. PIDE/DGS, SC, CI (2) 6818, NT 7461, PNA. ANTT.

[81] Vertaling. Information: Demitrio Tsafendas or Demetrio Tsafandakis, 7 September 1966. K150, Vol. 6, File: 3, NASA; PIDE report: Information: Demitrio Tsafendas or Demetrio Tsafandakis, 7 September 1966. PIDE/DGS, SC, CI (2) 6818, NT 7461, PNA. ANTT.

[82] Secret Criminal Record nº 10.415 of Demitrios Tsafantakis. 25 August 1951. PIDE/DGS, SC, CI (2) 6818, NT 7461, PNA. ANTT.

[83] Confidential Report of the Police Body of the Province of Mozambique regarding Demetrio Tsafendas. No: 726/694/PI, 3 May 1955. PIDE/DGS, SC, CI (2) 6818, NT 7461, PNA. ANTT.

[84] South African Police report regarding the activities of Dimitrio Tsafendas in Mozambique and Rhodesia, 20 September 1966. K150, Vol. 3, Sub file: 1/5, NASA; Report of the Commission of Enquiry into the circumstances of the death of the late Dr the honourable Hendrik Frensch Verwoerd, chapter IIC, paragraph 19, December 1966. RP 16/1967. Pretoria.

[85] PIDE confidential report regarding Demetrio Tsafendas: no: 2707/64/SR, 25 November 1964. SR. PIDE/DGS, SC, CI (2) 6818, NT 7461, PNA. ANTT.
[86] Vertaling. Information: Demitrio Tsafendas or Demetrio Tsafandakis, 7 September 1966. K150, Vol. 6, File: 3, NASA; PIDE report: Information: Demitrio Tsafendas or Demetrio Tsafandakis, 7 September 1966. PIDE/DGS, SC, CI (2) 6818, NT 7461, PNA. ANTT.
[87] Secret telegram from SA Embassy, Washington, to Secretary of Foreign Affairs, Cape Town, 9 September 1966. K150, Vol. 4, Sub file: 1/8, NASA.
[88] Grafton State Hospital report regarding Demetrios Tsafandakis, n.d. Demitrio Tsafendas Mediese Leer A125, NASA.
[89] *Ibid.*
[90] A.J. Harrison letter to the COE, 5 October 1966. K150, Vol. 6, File 3, NASA.
[91] Johannes Jacobus Botha statement to the police, 15 September 1966. K150, Vol. 12, File: Verklarings Demitrio Tsafendas, NASA.
[92] Johannes Jacobus Botha's statement to the police, 3 October 1966. K150, Vol. 12, File: Verklarings Demitrio Tsafendas, NASA.
[93] Christoffel Johannes van Vuuren statement to the police, 13 September 1966. K150, Vol. 12, File: Verklarings Demitrio Tsafendas, NASA; Christoffel Johannes van Vuuren statement to the police, 14 September 1966. K150, Vol. 12, File: Verklarings Demitrio Tsafendas, NASA.
[94] I have not been able to establish for a fact whether Tsafendas ever visited the Soviet Union. The likelihood is that he was being vexatious with the priest once he realised he was an apartheid supporter and anti-communist.
[95] Father Hanno Probst statement to the police, 9 September 1966. K150, Vol. 12, File: Verklarings Demitrio Tsafendas, NASA; Father Hanno Probst statement to the COE, 13 October 1966. K150, Vol. 12, File: Verklarings Demitrio Tsafendas, NASA; Christoffel Johannes van Vuuren statement to the police, 13 September 1966. K150, Vol. 12, File: Verklarings Demitrio Tsafendas, NASA.
[96] Kenneth Heugh Ross statement to the police, 7 September 1966. K150, Vol. 12, File: Verklarings Demitrio Tsafendas, NASA.
[97] Robert Harpur Smith statement to the police, 7 September 1966. K150, Vol. 12, File: Verklarings Demitrio Tsafendas, NASA.
[98] Jacobus Johannes Borman statement to the police, 3 October 1966. K150, Vol. 12, File: Verklarings Demitrio Tsafendas, NASA.
[99] Edward Charles Furness statement to the police, 12 October 1966. K150, Vol. 12, File: Verklarings Demitrio Tsafendas, NASA.
[100] Report of the COE, chapter II B, paragraph 32, December 1966. RP 16/1967. Pretoria.
[101] South African Police report regarding the activities of Dimitrio Tsafendas in Mozambique and Rhodesia, 20 September 1966. K150, Vol. 3, Sub file: 1/5, NASA.
[102] Cleanthes Alachiotis, Nikolaos Billis, Nikolas Kambouris, Georgios Kantas, Emanuil Mastromanolis and Michalis Vasilakis, author interviews.
[103] Costas Michaletos statement to the police, 10 September 1966. K150, Vol. 12, File: Verklarings, NASA.
[104] Letter of the Director of PIDE to the Mr Director-General for Political Affairs and Internal Administration regarding John Machletos, 16 November 1966. PIDE/DGS, SC, CI (2) 6818, NT 7461, PNA. ANTT.

[105] Esperanza Theron statement to the police, 24 September 1966. K150, Vol. 12, File: Verklarings Demitrio Tsafendas, NASA.
[106] Robert Harpur Smith statement to the police, 7 September 1966. K150, Vol. 12, File: Verklarings Demitrio Tsafendas, NASA.
[107] Report of the COE, chapter IIC, paragraph 33, December 1966. RP 16/1967. Pretoria.
[108] Thelma Beryl Suddes statement to the COE, 22 October 1966. K150, Vol. 12, File: Verklarings Demitrio Tsafendas, NASA.
[109] Johannes Christoffel Broodryk statement to the COE, 24 October 1966. K150, Vol. 12, File: Verklarings Demitrio Tsafendas, NASA.
[110] South Africa History Online (n.d.) 'Rowley Israel Arenstein'. Available at: https://www.sahistory.org.za/people/rowley-israel-arenstein, accessed on 12 September 2015.
[111] Report of the COE, chapter XI, paragraphs 4 and 5, December 1966. RP 16/1967. Pretoria.
[112] Report of the COE, chapter IIA, paragraph, 16 December 1966. RP 16/1967. Pretoria.
[113] PIDE report: Information: Demitrio Tsafendas or Demetrio Tsafandakis, 8 September 1966. PIDE/DGS, SC, CI (2) 6818, NT 7461, PNA. ANTT.
[114] South African Police report regarding the activities of Dimitrio Tsafendas in Mozambique and Rhodesia, 12 September 1966. K150, Vol. 3, Sub file: 1/5, NASA.
[115] *Die Landstem* telegram. n.d. K150, Vol 5, NASA.
[116] *O Primero de Janeiro,* 'O assassinio do primeiro-ministro Sul-Africano', 8 September 1966.
[117] Piet Bester Burger testimony to the COE, 13 October 1966. K150, Vol. 10, File: Uittreksels uit Getuienis, NASA; Fred Feinauer statement to the police, 3 October 1966. K150, Vol. 12, File: Verklarings Demitrio Tsafendas, NASA; Feliz George Miles statement to the police, 7 October 1966. K150, Vol. 2, File: 1, NASA; Petrus Robert Samuel Schuin testimony to the COE, 13 October 1966. K150, Vol. 10, File: Uittreksels uit Getuienis, NASA; Sydney William Wiehand testimony to the COE, 5 October 1966. K150, Vol. 10, File: Uittreksels uit Getuienis, NASA.
[118] Jamie Miller, *An African Volk: The Apartheid Regime and its Search for Survival* (New York: Oxford University Press, 2016), p. 29.
[119] Bell and Ntsebeza, *Unfinished Business: South Africa, Apartheid and Truth,* p. 28; Ivor Wilkins & Hans Strydom, *Broederbond: The Super-Afrikaners* (London: Corgi Books, 1979), p. A290.
[120] *TIME,* 'South Africa: The security man', 23 September 1966: 34–7,
[121] Sipo Elijah Mzimela, 'Nazism and apartheid: The role of Christian churches in Nazi Germany and apartheid South Africa' (PhD thesis, New York University, 1980), p. 155; Floris Albertus van Jaarsveld, 'The Afrikaner's idea of his calling and mission in South African history', *Journal of Theology for Southern Africa,* Vol. 19 (1977): 17.
[122] Christoph Marx, *Oxwagon Sentinel: Radical Afrikaner Nationalism and the History of the Ossewabrandwag* (Berlin: Lit Verlag, 2011), p. 559; Wilkins and Strydom, *Broederbond,* p. 107.
[123] South Africa's New Prime Minister. Telegram of Sir H. Stephenson from Cape Town to the Foreign Office. 20 September 1966. South Africa. Assassination of Dr Verwoerd, Prime Minister of South Africa. PREM 13/1211. BNA.
[124] *TIME,* 'South Africa: The security man'; *The New York Times,* 'South African aide defends jailing law', 12 June 1965: 7.
[125] D'Oliveira, *Vorster,* pp. 157–8.

[126] During his time as Prime Minister, Vorster failed to manage apartheid with the same deft hand as Verwoerd, but simultaneously turned South Africa into a virtual police state. His tenure was marked by a stream of deaths in detention, numerous bannings, an increase in prison terms and widespread reports of torture and violations of human rights. Despite his fierce reputation, South Africa deteriorated from a halcyon era of economic growth and white control into a state of rudderless instability and uncertainty. After 12 years as head of government, Vorster retired in 1978 and was succeeded by P.W. Botha. Vorster accepted the honorary position of state president. However, only eight months later, he resigned in disgrace over what became known as Muldergate, a scandal centred on the Ministry of Information. Inquiries revealed that Vorster, General van den Bergh, Information Minister Cornelius Mulder and Eschel M. Rhoodie, secretary of the Department of Information, were involved in widespread corruption. Despite the scandal, Vorster remained an influential figure behind the scenes in South African politics. In September 1983, he was hospitalised for the second time in a month suffering from a lung infection. His condition worsened after he developed a blood clot in one of his lungs and he died on 10 September 1983 at 67.
[127] *The Canberra Times*, 'Coins honour Verwoerd', 23 September 1966: 6.
[128] *Daily Dispatch*, 'Premier's killing full inquiry', 15 September 1966: 1; *The Cape Argus*, 'Judge will probe Dr V's death', 14 September 1966: 1.
[129] John Dugard, author interview.
[130] *Ibid.*
[131] Gordon Winter in *A Question of Madness*, 1997; Gordon Winter's correspondence with David Beresford, 8 September 1998. Liza Key's personal collection.
[132] Luli Calinicos, author interview.
[133] D'Oliveira, *Vorster*, p. 180.
[134] Henry R. Pike, *A History of Communism in South Africa* (Germiston: Christian Mission International of South Africa, 1985), 461; Gordon Winter, 'Tsafendas was ineffective Red – Van den Bergh', *The Citizen*, 26 October 1976.

Chapter 3: The Son of an Anarchist

[1] Constandinou, Antony Michaletos, K. Pnefma and Mike Vlachopoulos, author interviews.
[2] Demetrio Tsafendas statement to Major Rossouw, 11 September 1966. K150, Vol. 1, File: Verklaring van Demetrio Tsafendas, NASA.
[3] *Dagbreek*, 'Kleurlingmoeder in haglike omstandighede', 11 September 1966; Constandinou, author interview.
[4] Hazel Goldstein, 'Tsafendas timid and puny as a boy', *Rand Daily Mail*, 14 September 1966.
[5] Born on 21 October 1891. Michalis Tsafantakis birth certificate. Personal collection of Mike Vlachopoulos.
[6] Interview by Mr T.I. Potgieter, Senior Magistrate, with Mr Demitriou Tsafendas at the Pretoria Central Prison on 20 October 1987. Correctional Services. File 80/0043, A123, Dimitrio Tsafendas, Vol. 1, NASA; K. Pnefma, author interview.
[7] Eintracht, Antony Michaletos and K. Pnefma, author interviews.
[8] Eintracht and K. Pnefma, author interviews.
[9] K. Pnefma and Vlachopoulos, author interviews.
[10] Goldstein, 'Tsafendas timid and puny as a boy'; K. Pnefma, author interview.

[11] Antony Maw statement to the police, 7 September 1966. K150, Vol. 4, Sub file: 1/8, NASA; Antony Michaletos, author interview; K. Pnefma and Vlachopoulos, author interviews.
[12] Demetrio Tsafendas statement to Major Rossouw, 11 September 1966. K150, Vol 1, File: Verklaring van Demetrio Tsafendas, NASA.
[13] K. Pnefma, author interview.
[14] *Ibid.*
[15] Antony Maw statement to the police, 7 September 1966. K150, Vol. 4, Sub file: 1/8, NASA; Costas Maroudas author interview.
[16] Antony Maw statement to the police, 7 September 1966. K150, Vol. 4, Sub file: 1/8, NASA; Helen Grispos, Ira Kyriakakis and K. Pnefma, author interviews.
[17] K. Pnefma, author interview.
[18] Antony Michaletos and K. Pnefma, author interviews.
[19] K. Pnefma, author interview.
[20] K. Pnefma and Vlachopoulos, author interviews.
[21] Antony Michaletos, K. Pnefma and Vlachopoulos, author interviews.
[22] Antony Michaletos and K. Pnefma, author interviews.
[23] Demetrio Tsafendas statement to Major Rossouw, 11 September 1966. K150, Vol. 1, File: Verklaring van Demetrio Tsafendas, NASA; Antony Maw statement to the police, 7 September 1966. K150, Vol. 4, Sub file: 1/8, NASA.
[24] Michalis and Marika Tsafantakis marriage certificate. Private collection of Mike Vlachopoulos.
[25] Eintracht, Antony Michaletos and K. Pnefma, author interviews.
[26] *Ibid.*
[27] *Ibid.*
[28] K. Pnefma, author interview.
[29] Eintracht, Antony Michaletos and K. Pnefma, author interviews.
[30] Eintracht, author interview.
[31] Nikola Banovic, author interview.
[32] Constandinou, author interview.
[33] Eintracht, Antony Michaletos and K. Pnefma, author interviews.
[34] Antony Michaletos, author interview.
[35] Eintracht and Antony Michaletos, author interviews.
[36] Vlachopoulos, author interview.
[37] K. Pnefma, author interview.
[38] Vlachopoulos, author interview.
[39] Constandinou and Antony Michaletos, author interviews.
[40] K. Pnefma, author interview.
[41] *Ibid.*
[42] Costas Michaeletos statement to the police, 10 September 1966. K150, Vol. 12, File: Verklarings Demitrio Tsafendas, NASA.
[43] Demetrio Tsafendas statement to Major Rossouw, 11 September 1966. K150, Vol. 1, File: Verklaring van Demetrio Tsafendas, NASA.
[44] K. Pnefma, author interview.
[45] *Ibid.*
[46] Banovic, Constandinou and K. Pnefma, author interviews.
[47] Constandinou, author interview.

[48] K. Pnefma, author interview.
[49] *Ibid.*
[50] Marika Tsafantakis statement to the police, 7 September 1966. K150, Vol. 12, File: Verklarings Demitrio Tsafendas, NASA.
[51] Grispos, Kyriakakis and K. Pnefma, author interviews.
[52] Constandinou, author interview.
[53] Grispos, Kyriakakis and K. Pnefma, author interviews.
[54] Tsafendas's family statement to the COE, 21 October 1966. K150, Vol. 10, File: Excerpts from testimony, NASA.
[55] K. Pnefma, author interview.
[56] Babiolakis and Kyriakakis, author interviews.
[57] Kyriakakis, author interview.
[58] K. Pnefma, author interview.
[59] Grispos, author interview.
[60] Kyriakakis, author interview.
[61] Grispos, author interview.
[62] K. Pnefma, author interview.
[63] *Ibid.*
[64] Demetrio Tsafendas statement to Major Rossouw, 11 September 1966. K150, Vol. 1, File: Verklaring van Demetrio Tsafendas, NASA.
[65] Costas Michaeletos statement to the police, 10 September 1966. K150, Vol. 12, File: Verklarings Demitrio Tsafendas, NASA.
[66] Marika Tsafantakis statement to the police, 7 September 1966. K150, Vol. 12, File: Verklarings Demitrio Tsafendas, NASA; Eintracht and K. Pnefma, author interviews.
[67] Middelburg primary school report regarding Demitrios Tsafandakis, 17 December 1963. K150, Vol. 4, Sub file: 1/7, Departement van immigrasie, NASA.
[68] William Mare Volbrecht statement to the police, 3 October 1966. K150, Vol 3, File Verklaring deur Majoor Venter, NASA.
[69] *Rand Daily Mail*, 'Boyhood days of Tsafendas'.
[70] Demitri Tsafendas in *A Question of Madness*, 1997; Babiolakis and Constandinou, author interviews.
[71] William Mare Volbrecht statement to the police, 3 October 1966. K150, Vol. 3, File: Verklaring deur Majdor Venter, NASA.
[72] Constandinou, author interview.
[73] K. Pnefma, author interview.
[74] Reyner van Zyl's testimony on Tsafendas's summary trial, 18 October 1966. K150, Vol. 10, File: Trial, NASA.
[75] Constandinou, author interview.
[76] Dimitris Tsafendas in *A Question of Madness*, 1997; Constandinou, author interview.
[77] K. Pnefma, author interview.
[78] Kyriakakis, author interview.
[79] Grispos and K. Pnefma, author interviews.
[80] Eintracht, Kyriakakis and K. Pnefma, author interviews.
[81] Babiolakis, Kyriakakis and K. Pnefma, author interviews.
[82] K. Pnefma, author interview.
[83] *Ibid.*
[84] *Ibid.*

[85] Antony Michaletos, Irene Michaletos and John Michaletos, author interviews.
[86] Report of the COE, chapter IIA, paragraph 11, December 1966. RP 16/1967. Pretoria.
[87] Demetrio Tsafendas statement to Major Rossouw, 11 September 1966. K150, Vol. 1, File: Verklaring van Demetrio Tsafendas, NASA.
[88] Detailed information for a Memorandum regarding Demetrio Tsafendas by Attorney-General W.M. van den Berg, 3 October 1966. K150, Vol. 1, File: VDSO 17/64, Subject: Beweerde Omkopery, NASA.
[89] Demetrio Tsafendas statement to Major Rossouw, 11 September 1966. K150, Vol. 1, File: Verklaring van Demetrio Tsafendas, NASA.
[90] K. Pnefma, author interview.
[91] Detailed information for a Memorandum regarding Demetrio Tsafendas by Attorney-General W.M. van den Berg, 3 October 1966. K150, Vol. 1, File: VDSO 17/64, Subject: Beweerde Omkopery, NASA.
[92] Babiolakis, Grispos and K. Pnefma, author interviews.
[93] Detailed information for a Memorandum regarding Demetrio Tsafendas by Attorney-General W.M. van den Berg, 3 October 1966. K150, Vol. 1, File: VDSO 17/64, Subject: Beweerde Omkopery, NASA.
[94] K. Pnefma, author interview.
[95] Babiolakis and Papadakis, author interviews.
[96] *Ibid.*
[97] K. Pnefma, author interview.
[98] Constandinou, Papadakis and K. Pnefma, author interviews.
[99] K. Pnefma, author interview.
[100] Kyriakakis and K. Pnefma, author interviews.
[101] Constandinou, Papadakis and K. Pnefma, author interviews.
[102] K. Pnefma, author interview.
[103] *Ibid.*
[104] *Ibid.*
[105] Marika Tsafantakis statement to the police, 7 September 1966. K150, Vol. 12, File: Verklarings Demitrio Tsafendas, NASA.
[106] Babiolakis, Mary Eintracht, Grispos and Kyriakakis, author interviews.
[107] Kyriakakis, author interview.
[108] Antonis Chaldeos, *The Greek Community in Mozambique* (Athens: self-published, 2015), pp. 64, 194; Evangelos Mantzaris, author interview.
[109] Chaldeos, *The Greek Community*, 2015: 64, 194; Mantzaris, author interview.
[110] Constandinou, author interview.
[111] *Ibid.*
[112] *Ibid.*
[113] *Daily Worker*, '"I am at home," says Robeson at reception in Soviet Union', 15 January 1935.
[114] Banovic, Constandinou and Tsaftaridis, author interviews.
[115] Babiolakis, Constandinou, Grispos, Kyriakakis and K. Pnefma author interviews.
[116] *Ibid.*
[117] Constandinou, author interview.
[118] Babiolakis, Constandinou, Grispos, Kyriakakis and K. Pnefma author interviews.
[119] *Ibid.*

[120] Babiolakis, Constandinou, Grispos, Kyriakakis, Papadakis, K. Pnefma and Poriazis, author interviews.
[121] Babiolakis, Constandinou, Grispos, Kyriakakis and K. Pnefma author interviews.
[122] Grispos, author interview.
[123] Babiolakis, Constandinou and Grispos, author interview.
[124] Babiolakis, Grispos, Kyriakakis and K. Pnefma, author interviews.
[125] Kyriakakis, author interview.
[126] Eintracht and K. Pnefma, author interviews.
[127] Confidential Report of the Police Body of the Province of Mozambique regarding Demetrio Tsafendas. No: 726/694/PI, 3 May 1955. PIDE/DGS, SC, CI (2) 6818, NT 7461, PNA. ANTT.
[128] Grispos, Kyriakakis and K. Pnefma, author interviews.
[129] Constandinou, Maroudas, Antony Michaletos and K. Pnefma, author interviews.
[130] *Ibid.*
[131] *Ibid.*
[132] *Ibid.*
[133] *Ibid.*
[134] Banovic, Constandinou, Eintracht, Grispos, Kyriakakis, Antony Michaletos and K. Pnefma, author interviews.
[135] K. Pnefma, author interview.
[136] *The history of the person who inflicted the fatal wounds to the late Dr Verwoerd* drafted by Col. McIntyre, 3 October 1966. K150, Vol. 3, Subject: Leer W.D. 10/10/4102 der Stafendas, NASA.
[137] Antony Maw statement to the police, 7 September 1966. K150, Vol. 4, Sub File: 1/8, NASA.
[138] Constandinou, author interview.
[139] Babiolakis, Eintracht, Grispos, Kyriakakis and K. Pnefma, author interviews.
[140] Report of the COE, chapter IIA, paragraph 13, December 1966. RP 16/1967. Pretoria.
[141] Demetrio Tsafendas statement to Major Rossouw, 11 September 1966. K150, Vol. 1, File: Verklaring van Demetrio Tsafendas, NASA.
[142] Demetrio Tsafendas statement to Major Rossouw, 11 September 1966. K150, Vol. 1, File: Verklaring van Demetrio Tsafendas, NASA; Eintracht, author interview.
[143] Home Affairs Department report regarding Demitrio Tsafendas, 1 October 1966. K150, Vol. 1, Sub file: 1/2, NASA.
[144] Vlachopoulos, author interview.
[145] Marika Tsafantakis statement to the police, 7 September 1966. K150, Vol. 12, File: Verklarings Demitrio Tsafendas, NASA; Secret Criminal Record nº 10.415 of Demitrios Tsafantakis. PIDE/DGS, SC, CI (2) 6818, NT 7461, PNA. ANTT; Confidential Report of the Police Body of the Province of Mozambique regarding Demetrio Tsafendas. No: 726/694/PI, 3 May 1955. PIDE/DGS, SC, CI (2) 6818, NT 7461, PNA. ANTT.
[146] Constandinou, author interview.
[147] Goldstein, 'Tsafendas timid and puny as a boy'; *Rand Daily Mail*, 'Boyhood days of Tsafendas'.
[148] Babiolakis and K. Pnefma, author interviews.
[149] Marika Tsafantakis statement to the police, 7 September 1966. K150, Vol. 12, File: Verklarings Demitrio Tsafendas, NASA; Kyriakakis and K. Pnefma, author interviews.
[150] Babiolakis and Constandinou, author interviews.

[151] K. Pnefma, author interview.
[152] PIDE confidential report regarding Demetrio Tsafendas: no: 2707/64/SR, 25 November 1964. SR. PIDE/DGS, SC, CI (2) 6818, NT 7461, PNA. ANTT; *The Cape Argus*, 'Brainwashed in jail held man told Argus', 7 September 1966: 3.
[153] COE report regarding visit to family members of Demitrio Tsafendas, Pretoria, 21 October 1966. K150, Vol. 12, Sub file: 5, Subject: Algemeen, NASA.
[154] K. Pnefma, author interview.
[155] Babiolakis, Eintracht and K. Pnefma, author interviews.
[156] Grispos, author interview.
[157] Report of the COE, chapter IIA, paragraph 17, December 1966. RP 16/1967. Pretoria.
[158] K. Pnefma, author interview.
[159] Report of the COE, chapter IIA, paragraph 17, December 1966. RP 16/1967. Pretoria.
[160] Kyriakakis and Antony Michaletos, author interviews.
[161] Babiolakis, author interview.
[162] Antony Michaletos, author interview.
[163] Report of the COE, chapter IIA, paragraph 16, December 1966. RP 16/1967. Pretoria.
[164] Eintracht, Grispos, Kyriakakis and K. Pnefma, author interviews.
[165] Secret Criminal Record nº 10.415 of Demitrios Tsafantakis. PIDE/DGS, SC, CI (2) 6818, NT 7461, PNA. ANTT; Confidential Report of the Police Body of the Province of Mozambique regarding Demetrio Tsafendas. No: 726/694/PI, 3 May 1955. PIDE/DGS, SC, CI (2) 6818, NT 7461, PNA. ANTT.
[166] Report of the COE, chapter IIA, paragraph 16, December 1966. RP 16/1967. Pretoria.
[167] Secret Criminal Record nº 10.415 of Demitrios Tsafantakis. PIDE/DGS, SC, CI (2) 6818, NT 7461, PNA. ANTT.
[168] Top Secret Letter of the Head Inspector of PIDE in Lisbon to the Subdirector of PIDE in Mozambique regarding Demitrio Tsafendas, 8 September 1966. PIDE/DGS, SC, CI (2) 6818, NT 7461, PNA. ANTT.
[169] Letter of the Director of PIDE to the Ministry of Foreign Affairs, 4 November 1961. PIDE/DGS, SC, CI (2) 6818, NT 7461, PNA. ANTT.
[170] Kyriakakis, author interview.
[171] PIDE report regarding Demitrios Tsafandakis or Demitrio Tsafendas, 15 October 1953. SR. PIDE/DGS, SC, CI (2) 6818, NT 7461, PNA. ANTT.

Chapter 4: Tsafendas and Verwoerd in South Africa

[1] Pieter W. Grobbelaar, *This Was a Man* (Cape Town: Human & Rousseau, 1967), p. 9.
[2] O'Meara, *Forty Lost Years*, p. 92.
[3] Grobbelaar, *This Was a Man*, pp. 13–15.
[4] Dioné Prinsloo, 'Dr H.F. Verwoerd as Hoofredakteur van *Die Transvaler*', *Kleio*, Vol. 13, No. ½ (1981): 5.
[5] Christoph Marx, 'Hendrik Verwoerd and the Leipzig School of Psychology in 1926'. *Historia*, Vol. 58, No. 2 (2013): 92; Johannes D. Froneman, 'HF Verwoerd's student years: Cradle of his political career and thought', *Koers*, Vol. 65, No. 3 (2000): 401.
[6] Marx, 'Hendrik Verwoerd and the Leipzig School of Psychology in 1926', p. 92.
[7] Paul Gilroy, 'After the great white error … the great black mirage', Paper presented at a conference titled 'The burden of race? "Whiteness" and "Blackness" in modern South Africa', University of the Witwatersrand, 5–8 July 2001, p. 36; Brian Lapping, *Apartheid: A History* (London: Grafton Books, 1986), p. 106; Marx, 'Hendrik Verwoerd and the Leipzig

School of Psychology in 1926', p. 92; Freda Troup, *South Africa: An Historical Introduction* (Harmondsworth: Penguin Books, 1975), p. 318.

[8] Froneman, 'HF Verwoerd's student years', p. 406; Grobbelaar, *This Was a Man*, pp. 20–3.

[9] Jan Botha, *Verwoerd is Dead* (Cape Town: Books of Africa, 1967), p. 34; Suzanne Cronje, *Witness in the Dark: Police Torture and Brutality in South Africa* (London: Christian Action, 1964), p. 1; Patrick Jonathan Furlong, *Between Crown and Swastika: The Impact of the Radical Right on the Afrikaner Nationalist Movement in the Fascist Era* (Hanover and London: Wesleyan University Press, 1991), p. 80; Marx, 'Hendrik Verwoerd and the Leipzig School of Psychology in 1926', p. 93; Martin Meredith, *In the Name of Apartheid: South Africa in the Post-War Period* (London: Hamish Hamilton, 1988), p. 70; Alister Sparks, *The Mind of South Africa* (London: Heinemann, 1990), p. 163; Frank Welsh, *A History of South Africa* (Great Britain: Harper Collins, 2000), p. 448.

[10] Froneman, 'HF Verwoerd's student years', p. 406; Grobbelaar, *This Was a Man*, pp. 20–3.

[11] Marx, 'Hendrik Verwoerd and the Leipzig School of Psychology in 1926', p. 92; Roberta Balstad Miller, 'Science and society in the early career of H.F. Verwoerd', *Journal of Southern African Studies*, Vol. 19, No. 4 (1993): 637.

[12] Alban Burke, 'Mental health care during apartheid in South Africa: An illustration of how "Science" can be abused', in J.T. Parry, ed. *Evil, Law and the State: Perspectives on State Power and Violence* (Amsterdam and New York: Rodopi B.V, 2006), p. 1.

[13] Froneman, 'HF Verwoerd's student years', p. 406; Grobbelaar, *This Was a Man*, pp. 20–3; *The New York Times*, 'Dr Verwoerd: Relentless advocate of apartheid'.

[14] *The New York Times*, 'Dr Verwoerd: Relentless advocate of apartheid'.

[15] R. Italiaander, *The New Leaders of Africa* (Englewood Cliffs, New Jersey: Prentice Hall, 1961), pp. 105–106.

[16] O'Meara, *Forty Lost Years*, p. 93.

[17] Henry Kenney, *Architect of Apartheid: HF Verwoerd – An Appraisal* (Johannesburg: Jonathan Ball Publishers, 1980), p. 26.

[18] C.J. Beyers, ed., *Dictionary of South African Biography, Vol. 4* (Pretoria: HSRC Press, 1981), p. 731; Dean Foster, 'Race and racism in South African psychology', *South African Journal of Psychology*, Vol. 21, No. 4 (1991): 205.

[19] *Robert Michael Citino, Germany and the Union of South Africa in the Nazi Period (New York: Greenwood Press, 1991), pp. 77–78*; Jocelyn Hellig, 'German Jewish immigration to South Africa during the 1930s: Revisiting the charter of the SS *Stuttgart*', *Jewish Culture and History*, Vol. 11, No. ½ (2009): 124–5.

[20] Barbara Henkes, 'Shifting identifications in Dutch-South African migration policies (1910–1961)', *South African Historical Journal*, Vol. 68, No. 4 (2016): 641–69.

[21] Dunbar T. Dunbar, *The Rise of Afrikanerdom* (Berkley: University of California Press, 1975), p. 64.

[22] Brian Bunting, *The Rise of the South African Reich* (London: International Defence and Aid Fund for South Africa, 1986 [1968]), pp. 60–1; Furlong, *Between Crown and Swastika*, pp. 61–4; Troup, *South Africa*, p. 318; Stanley Uys, 'Dr Hendrik Frensch Verwoerd, Prime Minister of South Africa', *Africa South*, January–March 1959, p. 1.

[23] Hellig, 'German Jewish immigration to South Africa', p. 124–38; Nathaniel Weyl, *Traitor's End: The Rise and Fall of the Communist Movement in Southern Africa* (New Rochelle, NY: Arlington House, 1970), p. 112.

[24] Alan Paton, *South African Tragedy: The Life and Times of Jan Hofmeyr* (New York: Scribner, 1965), p. 194.

[25] Wilkins & Strydom, *Broederbond*, p. 3.
[26] Douglas Booth, *The Race Game: Sport and Politics in South Africa* (London: Frank Cass Publishers, 1998), p. 38; William Fryre, *In Whitest Africa: The Dynamics of Apartheid* (Englewood Cliffs, New Jersey: Prentice-Hall INC., 1970), p. 100.
[27] Alex Callinicos, *South Africa: Between Reform and Revolution* (London: Bookmarks, 1995), p. 30.
[28] Martin Burger, 'Dr Verwoerd of South Africa: Architect of doom' (London: A Christian Action pamphlet, 1961), p. 4; William Henry Vatcher, *White Laager: The Rise of Afrikaner Nationalism* (London: Pall Mall Press, 1965), p. 61.
[29] Alexander Hepple, *Verwoerd* (Harmondsworth: Penguin Books, 1967), p 45.
[30] *Newsweek*, 'The champion of apartheid', 11 April 1960, p. 55.
[31] Paton, *South African Tragedy*, p. 201.
[32] Emil Solomon Sachs, *The Anatomy of Apartheid* (London: Collet's, 1965), p. 239.
[33] David Bloomberg, *My Times: The Memoirs of David Bloomberg* (Simon's Town: Fernwood Press, 2007), p 149; Dean O'Meara, *Volkskapitalisme: Class, Capital and Ideology in the Development of Afrikaner Nationalism* (Cambridge: Cambridge University Press, 1983), p. 105; Vatcher, *White Laager*, p. 61.
[34] Hepple, *Verwoed*, p. 46; John Higginson, *Collective Violence and the Agrarian Origins of South African Apartheid, 1900–1948* (Cambridge: Cambridge University Press, 2014), p. 325; Gideon Shimoni, *Community and Conscience: The Jews in Apartheid South Africa* (Hanover, N.H.: Brandeis University Press published by University Press of New England, 2003), p. 14; Uys, 'Dr Hendrik Frensch Verwoerd', p. 1.
[35] Uys, 'Dr Hendrik Frensch Verwoerd', p. 3.
[36] Meredith, *In the Name of Apartheid*, p. 70.
[37] K. Pnefma, author interview.
[38] Demetrio Tsafendas statement to Major Rossouw, 11 September 1966. K150, Vol. 1, File: Verklaring van Demetrio Tsafendas, NASA.
[39] K. Pnefma, author interview.
[40] Demetrio Tsafendas statement to Major Rossouw, 11 September 1966. K150, Vol. 1, File: Verklaring van Demetrio Tsafendas, NASA; K. Pnefma, author interview.
[41] K. Pnefma, author interview.
[42] The name is fictitious as the witnesses do not remember her real name and Tsafendas never spoke about her.
[43] K. Pnefma, author interview.
[44] *Ibid.*
[45] *Ibid.*
[46] Vlachopoulos, author interview.
[47] Eintracht, author interview.
[48] Demetrio Tsafendas statement to Major Rossouw, 11 September 1966. K150, Vol. 1, File: Verklaring van Demetrio Tsafendas, NASA.
[49] Report of the Commissioner for Immigration and Asiatic Affairs regarding Demetrios Tsafandakis, 14 October 1941. K150, Vol. 3, File: W.D. 10/10/4102. Subject: Enquiry regarding Demetrios Tsafandakis, NASA.
[50] *Ibid.*
[51] Letter of the Deputy Commissioner of Police to the Police Commissioner regarding Demetrios Tsafandakis, 20 October 1941. K150, Vol. 3, File: W.D. 10/10/4102. Subject: Enquiry regarding Demetrios Tsafandakis, NASA.

[52] Burger, 'Dr Verwoerd of South Africa', 1961: 13; *Gloucestershire Echo*, '£15.000 libel claim result', 14 July 1943: 1; Hepple, *Verwoerd*, p. 215; Kenney, *Architect of Apartheid*, p. 64; Paton, *South African Tragedy*, pp. 292–3; *The New York Times*, 'Many of South Africa's leaders were pro-Nazi', 25 July 1985: 22; Uys, 'Dr Hendrik Frensch Verwoerd', p. 5; Vatcher, *White Laager*, p. 64.
[53] *Ibid.*
[54] Weyl, *Traitor's End*, p. 112.
[55] Ossewabrandwag (Ox Wagon Sentinel) was a pro-Nazi paramilitary organisation formed in February 1939, largely with 'true Afrikaner' members from the Broederbond. During 1940 and 1941 in the Witwatersrand area they were responsible for 25 bomb explosions aimed primarily at newspaper premises, cinemas, shops, railway lines, state buildings, electrical and telephone lines, electrical substations and pylons. Because of these activities, many Ossewabrandwag members were imprisoned during the war, including some who went on to have successful careers within the Nationalist Party.
[56] Dione Prinsloo, 'Dr H.F. Verwoerd en die Ossewa-Brandwag 1938–1952', *Kleio*, Vol. 17, No. 1 (1985): 74.
[57] Wilhelm J. Verwoed, *Verwoerd: Só Onthou ons Hom* (Pretoria: Protea Boekhuis, 2001), p. 47.
[58] David Beresford and Desmond Blow, author interviews, and Gordon Winter interview with Dr James Sanders on behalf of the author.
[59] *Die Transvaler*, 8 August 1941: 2; Mzimela, 'Nazism and apartheid', p. 101.
[60] John Hughes, *The New Face of Africa: South of the Sahara* (New York: Longmans, Green and Co., 1961).
[61] Botha, *Verwoerd is Dead*, p. 13; Moodie, *The Rise of Afrikanerdom*, p. 257.
[62] Vlachopoulos author interview.
[63] K. Pnefma, author interview.
[64] *Ibid.*
[65] Confidential Letter of the Lieutenant for the Deputy Commissioner of Witwatersrand Division to the Commissioner for Immigration and Asiatic Affairs, 12 June 1942. K150, Vol. 3, File: W.D. 10/10/4102. Subject: Enquiry regarding Demetrios Tsafandakis, NASA.
[66] K. Pnefma, author interview.
[67] Confidential Letter of the Lieutenant for the Deputy Commissioner of Witwatersrand Division to the Commissioner for Immigration and Asiatic Affairs. 12 June 1942. K150, Vol. 3, File: W.D. 10/10/4102. Subject: Enquiry regarding Demetrios Tsafandakis, NASA.
[68] Report of the COE, chapter IIA, paragraph 26, December 1966. RP 16/1967. Pretoria.
[69] Demetrio Tsafendas statement to Major Rossouw, 11 September 1966. COE, Vol. 1, File: Verklaring van Demetrio Tsafendas, NASA; Report of the COE, chapter IIA, paragraph 27, December 1966. RP 16/1967.

Chapter 5: Enter the Tapeworm

[1] Demetrio Tsafendas statement to Major Rossouw, 19 September 1966. K150, Vol. 1, File: Verklaring van Demetrio Tsafendas, NASA.
[2] Antony Michaletos, author interview.
[3] Henk van Woerden, *A Mouthful of Glass* (London: Granta Books, 2000), p. 141.
[4] Grafton State Hospital report regarding Demetrios Tsafandakis, n.d. Demitrio Tsafendas Mediese Leer A125, NASA.

[5] Demetrio Tsafendas statement to Major Rossouw, 19 September 1966. K150, Vol. 1, File: Verklaring van Demetrio Tsafendas, NASA.
[6] Translation of the PIDE report regarding Demitrio Tsafendas or Demetrio Tsafantakis, 7 September 1966. K150, Vol. 6, File: 3, NASA.
[7] A. Moumbaris, author interview.
[8] Grafton State Hospital report regarding Demetrios Tsafandakis, n.d. Demitrio Tsafendas Mediese Leer A125, NASA.
[9] A. Moumbaris, author interview.
[10] Grafton State Hospital report regarding D. Tsafandakis, n.d. Demitrio Tsafendas Mediese Leer A125, NASA.
[11] Demetrio Tsafendas statement to Major Rossouw, 11 September 1966. K150, Vol. 1, File: Verklaring van Demetrio Tsafendas, NASA; Report of the COE, chapter IIB, paragraph 2, December 1966. RP 16/1967. Pretoria.
[12] Grafton State Hospital report regarding Demetrios Tsafandakis, n.d. Demitrio Tsafendas Mediese Leer A125, NASA; Constandinou, author interview.
[13] Constandinou, author interview.
[14] *Ibid.*
[15] Grafton State Hospital report regarding Demetrios Tsafandakis, n.d. Demitrio Tsafendas Mediese Leer A125, NASA.
[16] It was founded in 1897 in Ireland by Scottish evangelist William Irvine.
[17] Banovic and Constandinou, author interviews.
[18] Grafton State Hospital report regarding Demetrios Tsafandakis, n.d. Demitrio Tsafendas Mediese Leer A125, NASA.
[19] The Grafton State Hospital report states that Tsafendas was released on a $1,000 bond, equivalent to about $16,000 today, a huge amount at the time. It is hard to think that Tsafendas could produce such a sum and the likeliest scenario is that it was donated by members of the Christian Church. However, what cannot also be discounted is that the amount was a typographical error and the real sum was $100.
[20] Grafton State Hospital report regarding Demetrios Tsafandakis, n.d. Demitrio Tsafendas Mediese Leer A125, NASA.
[21] Marika Tsafantakis's statement to the police, 7 September 1966. K150, Vol. 12, File: Verklarings Demitrio Tsafendas, NASA; Banovic, Constandinou and Vasilakis, author interviews.
[22] Constandinou, author interview.
[23] Grafton State Hospital report regarding Demetrios Tsafandakis, n.d. Demitrio Tsafendas Mediese Leer A125, NASA.
[24] *Ibid.*
[25] *Ibid.*
[26] Constandinou, author interview.
[27] Grafton State Hospital report regarding Demetrios Tsafandakis, n.d. Demitrio Tsafendas Mediese Leer A125, NASA.
[28] Constandinou, author interview.
[29] Eintracht and K. Pnefma, author interviews.
[30] Banovic, Constandinou and Tsaftaridis, author interviews.
[31] Constandinou, author interview.
[32] *Ibid.*

[33] Demetrio Tsafendas statement to Major Rossouw, 11 September 1966. K150, Vol. 1, File: Verklaring van Demetrio Tsafendas, NASA; Grafton State Hospital report regarding Demetrios Tsafandakis, n.d. Demitrio Tsafendas Mediese Leer A125, NASA.
[34] Constandinou, author interview.

Chapter 6: Redemption

[1] Report of the COE, chapter IIB, paragraph 12, December 1966. RP 16/1967. Pretoria.
[2] Demetrio Tsafendas statement to Major Rossouw, 11 September 1966. K150, Vol. 1, File: Verklaring van Demetrio Tsafendas, NASA.
[3] Report of the COE, chapter IIB, paragraph 12, December 1966. RP 16/1967. Pretoria.
[4] Demetrio Tsafendas statement to Major Rossouw, 11 September 1966. K150, Vol. 1, File: Verklaring van Demetrio Tsafendas, NASA; Banovic, author interview.
[5] Banovic, author interview; Constandinou, author interview; Eintracht, author interview; K. Pnefma, author interview.
[6] Banovic, author interview; Constandinou, author interview; Eintracht, author interview; K. Pnefma, author interview.
[7] The name is fictitious.
[8] Constandinou, author interview.
[9] Banovic, Constandinou, Eintracht, K. Pnefma and Vasilakis, author interviews.
[10] Constandinou, author interview.
[11] Detailed information for a Memorandum regarding Demetrio Tsafendas by Attorney-General W.M. van den Berg, 3 October 1966. K150, Vol. 1, File: VDSO 17/64, Subject: Beweerde Omkopery, NASA; Demetrio Tsafendas statement to Major Rossouw, 11 September 1966. K150, Vol. 1, File: Verklaring van Demetrio Tsafendas, NASA; Demetrios Tsafendakis Affidavit, November 1965. K150, Vol. 12, Sub file: 5, subject: Algemeen, NASA; Constandinou, author interview.
[12] Constandinou, author interview.
[13] Demetrio Tsafendas statement to Major Rossouw, 11 September 1966. K150, Vol. 1, File: Verklaring van Demetrio Tsafendas, NASA.
[14] Demetrios Tsafendakis Affidavit, November 1965. K150, Vol. 12, Sub file: 5, Subject: Algemeen, NASA.
[15] Constandinou, author interview.
[16] *Ibid.*
[17] *Ibid.*
[18] *Ibid.*
[19] Pierre L. van den Berghe, *South Africa: A Study in Conflict* (Berkeley: University of California Press, 1967), p. 115; Apartheid quickly began to give rise to a considerable body of literature, including Schalk Peinaar & Antony Sampson, *South Africa: Two Views of Separate Development*; N.J. Rhoodie & H.J. Venter, *Apartheid: A Socio-Historical Exposition of the Origin and Development of the Apartheid Idea*; Philippus Pistorius, *No Further Trek*; B.B. Keet, *The Ethics of Apartheid*; Eugene P. Dvorin, *Racial Separation in South Africa*, etc.
[20] Saul Dubow, *Apartheid 1948–1994* (Oxford: Oxford University Press, 2014), pp. 8–17; Study Commission on US Policy toward Southern Africa, *South Africa: Time Running Out - The Report of the Study Commission on U.S. Policy toward Southern Africa* (Berkeley: University of California Press, 1981), p. 41.
[21] Dubow, *Apartheid 1948–1994,* p. 2.

[22] Although Verwoerd discarded a leading journalistic role when he quit as editor of *Die Transvaler,* he maintained a significant presence on the commercial side of the publishing business. At the time of his death in 1966, he controlled two major companies which produced a Sunday paper, two dailies and several magazines. Over a time span of three years, his businesses secured government printing orders to the tune of £12 million (*The Globe and Mail,* 'Verwoerd created republic of white ascendancy', 7 September 1966: 3).
[23] Botha, *Verwoerd is Dead,* p. 13; Grobbelaar, *This Was a Man,* p. 39; Moodie, *The Rise of Afrikanerdom; The New York Times,* 'Dr Verwoerd: Relentless advocate of apartheid'; Uys, 'Dr Hendrik Frensch Verwoerd, Prime Minister of South Africa', p. 6.
[24] Colin Legum & Margaret Legum, *South Africa: Crisis for the West* (London and Dunmow: Pall Mall Press 1964), p. 24; Troup, *South Africa,* p. 318; Wilkins & Strydom, *Broederbond,* p. 197.
[25] Malan is often characterised as being primarily interested in nationalism, but he was also dedicated to segregation and other racialist legislation (William Beinart, *Twentieth Century South Africa* (Oxford: Oxford University Press, 2001), p. 146), and had referred to Jews as 'parasites' (John Higginson, *Collective Violence and the Agrarian Origins of South African Apartheid, 1900–1948* (Cambridge: Cambridge University Press, 2014), p. 322). He persisted in his anti-Semitism after the war, having described the situation in 1939 as one in which the 'Jewish question' 'hangs like a dark cloud over South Africa', and suggested that an organised cabal of Jews had 'robbed' Afrikaners of their heritage (Vatcher, *White Laager,* p. 61). However, he had no specific 'blueprint' for apartheid, which continued to develop from what had gone before, and to react to current circumstances (Daryl Glaser, *Politics and Society in South Africa* (London: Sage Publications, 2001), p. 97).
[26] James Barber, *South Africa in the Twentieth Century: A Political History – In Search of a Nation State* (Oxford: Wiley Blackwell, 1999), p. 140; G.V. Doxey, 'The South African problem: A conflict of nationalism', *International Journal: Canada's Journal of Global Policy Analysis,* Vol. 18, No. 4 (1963): 501; Dubow, *Apartheid 1948–1994,* p. 45; Jurgen Schadeberg, ed., *Nelson Mandela and the Rise of the ANC* (London: Bloomsbury Publishing Limited, 1990), p 33.
[27] Phil Bonner, Peter Delius & Deborah Posel, 'The shaping of apartheid', in Phil Bonner, Peter Delius & Deborah Posel, eds. *Apartheid's Genesis: 1935–62* (Braamfontein: Raven Press, 1993), pp. 24–5; Alex Callinicos. *Between Apartheid and Capitalism: Conversations with South African Socialists* (London: Bookmarks, 1992), p. 12; Henry Gibbs, *Twilight in South Africa* (New York: Jarrolds, 1949), p. 215.
[28] Hermann Giliomee, *The Afrikaners: Biography of a People* (London: Hurst and Company, 2011), p. 497.
[29] Dubow, *Apartheid 1948–1994,* p. 64; Giliomee, *The Last Afrikaner Leaders,* p. 52.
[30] William H. Worger, Nancy L. Clark & Edward A. Alpers, *Africa and the West: A Documentary History. Volume 2: From Colonialism to Independence, 1975 to the Present* (Oxford: Oxford University Press, 2010), p. 103.
[31] Italiaander, *The New Leaders of Africa,* p. 103.
[32] Kader Asmal, Louise Asmal & Ronald Suresh Roberts, *Reconciliation Through Truth: A Reckoning of Apartheid's Criminal Governance* (Cape Town: David Philip Publishers, 1996), p. 210.
[33] Constandinou, author interview.

[34] Demetrio Tsafendas statement to Major Rossouw, 11 September 1966. K150, Vol. 1, File: Verklaring van Demetrio Tsafendas, NASA.
[35] Report of the COE, chapter IIB, paragraph 17, December 1966. RP 16/1967. Pretoria.
[36] I am not in a position to know if Michaletos was a member of the sect or if he simply acted as a godfather.
[37] Demetrio Tsafendas statement to Major Rossouw, 19 September 1966. K150, Vol. 1, File: Verklaring van Demetrio Tsafendas, NASA; Banovic, Constandinou and K. Pnefma, author interviews.
[38] Demetrio Tsafendas statement to Major Rossouw, 11 September 1966. K150, Vol. 1, File: Verklaring van Demetrio Tsafendas, NASA.

Chapter 7: Exiled

[1] Demetrio Tsafendas statement to Major Rossouw, 11 September 1966. K150, Vol. 1, File: Verklaring van Demetrio Tsafendas, NASA.
[2] PIDE Confidential Report about Demitrio Tsafendas or Demetrio Tsafantakis, 13 November 1962. PIDE/DGS, SC, CI (2) 6818, NT 7461, PNA. ANTT.
[3] K. Pnefma, author interview.
[4] PIDE Confidential Report about Demitrio Tsafendas or Demetrio Tsafantakis, 13 November 1962. PIDE/DGS, SC, CI (2) 6818, NT 7461, PNA. ANTT.
[5] PIDE Confidential Report about Demitrio Tsafendas, 7 June 1955. PIDE/DGS, SC, CI (2) 6818, NT 7461, PNA. ANTT.
[6] PIDE Confidential Report about Demitrio Tsafendas or Demetrio Tsafantakis, 13 November 1962. PIDE/DGS, SC, CI (2) 6818, NT 7461, PNA. ANTT.
[7] PIDE Confidential Report about Demitrio Tsafendas, 7 June 1955. PIDE/DGS, SC, CI (2) 6818, NT 7461, PNA. ANTT.
[8] PIDE confidential report regarding Demetrio Tsafendas: no: 2707/64/SR, 25 November 1964. SR. PIDE/DGS, SC, CI (2) 6818, NT 7461, PNA. ANTT
[9] *The Cape Argus*, 'Brainwashed in jail held man told Argus', 7 September 1966: 3.
[10] Constandinou, author interview.
[11] PIDE confidential report regarding Demetrio Tsafendas: no: 2707/64/SR, 25 November 1964. PIDE/DGS, SC, CI (2) 6818, NT 7461, PNA. ANTT.
[12] *Ibid.*
[13] *The Cape Argus*, 'Brainwashed in jail held man told Argus'.
[14] Banovic, Constandinou, Eintracht, Nikolas Kambouris, Georgios Kantas, Kyriakakis, Grigoris Pouftis and Vasilakis, author interviews.
[15] Confidential Report of the Police Body of the Province of Mozambique regarding Demetrio Tsafendas. No: 726/694/PI, 3 May 1955. PIDE/DGS, SC, CI (2) 6818, NT 7461, PNA. ANTT.
[16] *Ibid.*
[17] Demetrio Tsafendas statement to Major Rossouw, 11 September 1966. K150, Vol. 1, File: Verklaring van Demetrio Tsafendas, NASA.
[18] Emanuel Tsabouniaris and Vasilakis, author interviews.
[19] Eintracht and K. Pnefma, author interview.
[20] Constandinou, author interview.
[21] Salim Badat, *The Forgotten People: Banishment under Apartheid* (Leiden and Boston: Brill, 2013), p. 11.
[22] Wilkins & Strydom, *Broederbond*, p. 197.

[23] Worger et al., *Africa and the West*, p. 103.
[24] PIDE confidential report regarding Demetrio Tsafendas: no: 2707/64/SR, 25 November 1964. PIDE/DGS, SC, CI (2) 6818, NT 7461, PNA. ANTT.
[25] PIDE confidential report regarding Demetrio Tsafendas: no: 2707/64/SR, 25 November 1964. PIDE/DGS, SC, CI (2) 6818, NT 7461, PNA. ANTT; Antony Maw statement to the police, 7 September 1966. K150, Vol. 4, Sub file: 1/8, NASA; Portuguese Security Police's report regarding Dimitrio Tsafendas dated 21 February1962, translated by the South African Department of Defence and sent to the COE on October 12, 1966. K150, Vol. 4, Sub file: 1/6, Department of Defence, NASA.
[26] Babiolakis, Eintracht, Grispos, Kyriakakis, George Liberopoulos, Nick Papadakis and K. Pnefma, author interviews.
[27] K. Pnefma, author interview.
[28] Grispos, author interview.
[29] Antony Maw's statement to the police, 7 September 1966. K150, Vol. 4, Sub file: 1/8, NASA.
[30] Antony Michaletos, author interview.
[31] PIDE Record of questions. 25 November 1964. PIDE/DGS, SC, CI (2) 6818, NT 7461, PNA. ANTT.
[32] Antony, John and Irene Michaletos, author interviews.
[33] Confidential Report of the Police Body of the Province of Mozambique regarding Demetrio Tsafendas. No: 726/694/PI, 3 May 1955. PIDE/DGS, SC, CI (2) 6818, NT 7461, PNA. ANTT.
[34] *Ibid.*
[35] Confidential Letter of the Director of PIDE to the Ministry of Foreign Affairs, no: 2.077- S.R., 3 May 1961. PIDE/DGS, SC, CI (2) 6818, NT 7461, PNA. ANTT.
[36] Confidential Report of the Police Body of the Province of Mozambique regarding Demetrio Tsafendas. No: 726/694/PI, 3 May 1955. PIDE/DGS, SC, CI (2) 6818, NT 7461, PNA. ANTT; PIDE confidential report regarding Demetrio Tsafendas: no: 2707/64/SR, 25 November 1964. PIDE/DGS, SC, CI (2) 6818, NT 7461, PNA. ANTT.
[37] *Diario Popular*, 'E conhesido em Lisboa o assassino do Dr Verwoerd', 9 September 1966; PIDE report regarding Tsafendas, 5 May 1956. PIDE/DGS, SC, CI (2) 6818, NT 7461, PNA. ANTT.
[38] PIDE report regarding Tsafendas, 5 May 1956. PIDE/DGS, SC, CI (2) 6818, NT 7461, PNA. ANTT.
[39] Neville Vincent, 'The shame of Portugal', *The Spectator*, 12 April 1962: 11. Available at: http://archive.spectator.co.uk/article/13th-april-1962/11/the-shame-of-portugal, accessed on 30 April 2016.
[40] PIDE report regarding Tsafendas, 5 May 1956. PIDE/DGS, SC, CI (2) 6818, NT 7461, PNA. ANTT.
[41] A vivid picture of conditions in the prisons was painted a few years later by an Amnesty International report. Neville Vincent, a prominent London barrister, was the author of the report and reported on the prisons in 1962, but there can be no doubt that conditions ten years earlier were just as bad, if not worse: 'Torture of political prisoners is common; men are brutally beaten; prisoners are kept in dungeons in practically permanent darkness in solitary confinement for long periods. People practically out of their minds are put in a room with yellow walls, painted blue round the top. They think the blue represents the outside world and take crazy running jumps at the walls with

dreadful consequences. I learnt of a case of a woman badly beaten, and then burnt all over with cigarette ends. However, the most common torture is The Statue. Prisoners are made to stand against a wall or post continuously for as long as seven days and seven nights; after two or three days their legs begin to swell, but if they fall down a guard is there to kick them until they stand up again. Throughout this period, the PIDE come and question the prisoner to obtain such information as they require. The cells are either grossly overcrowded, or, if you are in solitary confinement, the cell measures one metre by two metres; many of these are extremely damp, and the prisoners consistently complain about the cold in the winter' (Vincent, 'The shame of Portugal'. Available at: http://archive.spectator.co.uk/article/13th-april-1962/11/the-shame-of-portugal, accessed on 17 September 2016).

[42] Constandinou and Tsaftaridis, author interviews.

[43] Banovic, Constandinou and Tsaftaridis, author interviews.

[44] PIDE report regarding Tsafendas, 5 May 1956. PIDE/DGS, SC, CI (2) 6818, NT 7461, PNA. ANTT.

[45] Constandinou and Tsaftaridis, author interviews.

[46] PIDE report: Information: Demitrio Tsafendas or Demetrio Tsafandakis, 12 December 1964. PIDE/DGS, SC, CI (2) 6818, NT 7461, PNA. ANTT; PIDE report regarding Tsafendas, 5 May 1956. PIDE/DGS, SC, CI (2) 6818, NT 7461, PNA. ANTT.

[47] http://www.cmjornal.xl.pt/nacional/sociedade/detalhe/albergue_da_mitra_cedido_a_santa_casa.html, accessed on 22 October 2014.

[48] Babiolakis, Banovic, Constandinou and Poriazis, author interviews.

[49] Banovic, Constandinou and K. Pnefma, author interviews.

[50] Letter of the Director-General of the Economic and Consular Affairs of the Portuguese Ministry of Foreign Affairs to the Director of P.I.D.E regarding Tsafendas, proc. 518/15/55. 5 April 1961. PIDE/DGS, SC, CI (2) 6818, NT 7461, PNA. ANTT.

[51] Ochsensall Hospital report regarding Dimitri Tsafendas, 6 June 1955. K150. Vol. 4, File: 1, Sub file: 1/8, NASA.

[52] Dr Bieser's medical report on Tsafendas, Ochsenzoll Krankenhaus Hospital, 6 April 1955. K150, Vol. 4, Sub file: 1/8, NASA.

[53] Banovic and Efthimios Eleftheriadis, author interviews.

[54] Eleftheriadis, author interview.

[55] Dr Bieser's medical report on Tsafendas, Ochsenzoll Krankenhaus Hospital, 6 April 1955. K150, Vol. 4, Sub file: 1/8, NASA.

[56] Banovic and Eleftheriadis, author interviews.

[57] Constandinou, author interview.

[58] Dr Bieser and Dr Schmidt-Janssen report regarding Dimitri Tsafendas. K150, Vol. 4, File: 1, Sub file: 1/8, NASA; Father Efthimios Eleftheriadis author interview, 27 January 2011.

[59] Ochsensall Hospital report regarding Dimitri Tsafendas, 6 June 1955. K150, Vol. 4, File: 1, Sub file: 1/8, NASA.

[60] Eleftheriadis, author interview.

[61] Ochsensall Hospital report regarding Dimitri Tsafendas, 6 June 1955. K150, Vol. 4, File: 1, Sub file: 1/8, NASA.

[62] Eleftheriadis, author interview.

[63] PIDE report regarding Dimitri Tsafendas or Dimitrie Tsafandakis, 21 February 1962. K150, Vol. 4, Sub file: 1/6. Department of Justice, NASA.

[64] Banovic, author interview.

[65] Babiolakis, Banovic, Constandinou and Poriazis, author interviews.
[66] Letter of the Directorate-General of the Political and Civil Administration of the Overseas Ministry to the Director of the International and State Defence Police, 7 April 1958. PIDE/DGS, SC, CI (2) 6818, NT 7461, PNA. ANTT.
[67] Letter of Demetri Tsafendas to the President of the Portuguese Republic. (n.d. but according to the reply it was on March 1958) PIDE/DGS, SC, CI (2) 6818, NT 7461, PNA. ANTT.
[68] Letter of Demetri Tsafendas to the Interior Minister, 18 April 1956. PIDE/DGS, SC, CI (2) 6818, NT 7461, PNA. ANTT.
[69] PIDE report regarding Dimitri Tsafendas or Dimitrie Tsafandakis, 21 February 1962. K150, Vol. 4, Sub file 1/6. Department of Justice, NASA.
[70] Demetrio Tsafendas statement to Major Rossouw, 11 September 1966. K150, Vol. 1, File: Verklaring van Demetrio Tsafendas, NASA.
[71] Constandinou and Vaporidis, author interviews.
[72] *The Cape Argus*, 'Did he live in W. Germany?' 7 September 1966 (late edition): 2.
[73] Eleftheriadis, author interview.
[74] *Daily Dispatch*, 'He made a good impression', 8 September 1966: 1; *O Primeiro de Janeiro*, 'Tsafendas trabalhou como soldador em Frankforte', 8 September 1966.
[75] *Daily Dispatch*, 'He made a good impression'; *Daily Express*, 'The assassin', 8 September 1966: 2; *Natal Witness*, 'Tsafendas was so friendly', 10 September 1966; *O Primeiro de Janeiro*, 'Tsafendas trabalhou como soldador em Frankforte'.
[76] *Daily Dispatch*, 'He made a good impression'; *Natal Witness*, 'Tsafendas was so friendly', 10 September 1966; *O Primeiro de Janeiro*, 'Tsafendas trabalhou como soldador em Frankforte'.
[77] Callinicos, *South Africa: Between Reform and Revolution*, p. 46; Lawrence Elwin Neame, *The History of Apartheid: The Story of the Colour War in South Africa* (London: Pall Mall Press with Barrie and Rockcliff, 1962), p. 156; *The Canberra Times*, 'Dr Verwoerd, South Africa's "evil genius"', 25 May 1957: 6; *The New York Times*, 'Dr Verwoerd: Relentless advocate of apartheid'.
[78] O'Meara, *Forty Lost Years*, p. 111.
[79] Minister of Finance from 1958 to 1967; he assumed the role of acting Prime Minister on 6 September 1966, when Dr Verwoerd was assassinated. He remained in this post until 13 September when John Vorster became Prime Minister (Harris M. Lentz, *Heads of States and Governments since 1945* (London: Routledge, 1966), p. 698).
[80] A supporter of the Nazis, member of the Broederbond and of the Ossewabrandwag (E.J. Verwey, ed., *New Dictionary of South African Biography, volume 1* (Pretoria: HSRC Press, 1995), p. 237). He served as acting Prime Minister in 1958, the last governor-general and the first state president of the Republic of South Africa from 1961–67 (Verwey, *New Dictionary of South African Biography*, pp. 238–40).
[81] Hepple, *Verwoerd*, p. 134; Hughes, *The New Face of Africa*, p. 177; *The New York Times*, 'Dr Verwoerd: Relentless advocate of apartheid'; J.H. van Rooyen, 'The psychopath in South African criminal and mental health law', *Comparative and International Law Journal of Southern Africa*, Vol .9, No. 1 (1976): 1–56; Vatcher, *White Laager*, p. 125.
[82] Barber, *South Africa in the Twentieth Century*, p. 161; Bunting, *The Rise of the South African Reich*, p. 147; Sachs, *The Anatomy of Apartheid*, p. 7.
[83] *The New York Times*, 'Bad news from South Africa', 6 September 1958: 16.
[84] van den Berghe, *South Africa: A Study in Conflict*, p. 104.

[85] A.M. Bezdrop du Preez, *Winnie Mandela: A Life* (Cape Town: Zebra Books, 2003), p. 75; Kenneth W. Grundy, *South Africa: Domestic Crisis and Global Challenge* (Boulder: Westview Press, 1991), p. 8.
[86] Dean Foster, *Detention and Torture in South Africa: Psychological, Legal and Historical Studies* (London: James Currey, 1987), p. 19; Furlong, *Between Crown and Swastika*, p. 257.
[87] Hans Pienaar, 'Hendrik Verwoerd', in Human & Rousseau, *They Shaped our Century: The Most Influential South Africans of the Twentieth Century* (Cape Town: Human & Rousseau, 1999), p. 25.
[88] Demetrio Tsafendas statement to Major Rossouw, 11 September 1966. K150, Vol. 1, File: Verklaring van Demetrio Tsafendas, NASA.
[89] Eleftheriadis, author interview.
[90] *Ibid.*
[91] Secret telegram from SA Embassy, London to Secretary of Foreign Affairs, Cape Town, 9 September 1966. K150, Vol. 4, Sub file: 1/8, NASA.

Chapter 8: Teacher of English and Bomb-maker

[1] Secret telegram from SA Embassy, London to Secretary of Foreign Affairs, Cape Town, 9 September 1966. K150, Vol. 4, Sub file: 1/8, NASA.
[2] *Ibid.*
[3] Report of the COE, chapter IIB, paragraphs 28–30, December 1966. RP 16/1967. Pretoria.
[4] Report of the COE, chapter VI, paragraphs 18 and 20, December 1966. RP 16/1967. Pretoria.
[5] Banovic and Constandinou, author interviews.
[6] *Ibid.*
[7] Edward Charles Furness statement to the police, 12 October 1966. K150, Vol. 12, File: Verklarings Demitrio Tsafendas, NASA; Constandinou, author interview.
[8] Demetrio Tsafendas statement to Major Rossouw, 19 September 1966. K150, Vol. 1, File: Verklaring van Demetrio Tsafendas, NASA.
[9] Report of the COE, chapter IIB, paragraph 32, December 1966. RP 16/1967. Pretoria.
[10] Antony and John Michaletos, author interviews.
[11] Constandinou, author interview.
[12] *The Guardian*, 'Winding back', 30 September 1966: 10.
[13] Secret telegram from SA Embassy, London to Secretary of Foreign Affairs, Cape Town, 9 September 1966. K150, Vol. 4, Sub file: 1/8, NASA; Demetrio Tsafendas statement to Major Rossouw, 19 September 1966. K150, Vol. 1, File: Verklaring van Demetrio Tsafendas, NASA; Constandinou, author interview.
[14] Constandinou, author interview.
[15] Felix Bernheim's testimony on Tsafendas's summary trial, 19 October 1966. K150, Vol. 10, File: Trial, NASA.
[16] Constandinou, author interview.
[17] Secret telegram from the SA Embassy in London to the Secretary of Foreign Affairs, Cape Town, 9 September 1966. K150, Vol. 4, Sub file: 1/8, NASA.
[18] Constandinou, author interview.

[19] Secret telegram from SA Embassy, London to Secretary of Foreign Affairs, Cape Town, 9 September 1966. K150, Vol. 4, Sub file: 1/8, NASA; Report of the COE, chapter IIB, paragraph 33, December 1966. RP 16/1967. Pretoria.
[20] Demetrio Tsafendas statement to Major Rossouw, 11 September 1966. K150, Vol. 1, File: Verklaring van Demetrio Tsafendas, NASA.
[21] The Bishop of Johannesburg, *Report on South Africa* (London: Christian Action, 1960), pp. 3–4.
[22] Philip H. Frankel, *An Ordinary Atrocity: Sharpeville and Its Massacre* (New Haven and London: Yale University Press, 2001), p. 149.
[23] Report of the Commission Appointed to Investigate and Report on the Occurrences in the Districts of Vereeniging (namely, at Sharpeville location and Evaton) and Vanderbijlpark, Province of the Transvaal, 1960, p. 128, par. 209.
[24] Frankel, *An Ordinary Atrocity*, 194–5.
[25] Margaret Ballinger, *From Union to Apartheid* (Folkestone: Bailey Bros and Swinfen Ltd, 1969), p. 425.
[26] Mandela, *Long Walk to Freedom*, p. 281.
[27] Ian Loveland, *By Due Process of Law? Racial Discrimination and the Right to Vote in South Africa 1855–1960* (Oxford: Hart Publishing, 1999), p. 283; *The Illustrated London News*, 'South Africa: The issues appraised', 9 April 1960: 590.
[28] *The New York Times*, 'Dr Verwoerd: Relentless advocate of apartheid'.
[29] *TIME*, 'South Africa: The Sharpeville Massacre', 4 April 1960: 19.
[30] Italiaander, *The New Leaders of Africa*, p. 110.
[31] *The New York Times*, 'Dr Verwoerd: Relentless advocate of apartheid'.
[32] Truth and Reconciliation Commission (TRC), *Truth and Reconciliation Commission of South Africa Report, Volume Two* (Cape Town: Juta Books, 1998), p. 533; Dubow, *Apartheid 1948–1994*, pp. 77–8.
[33] Ambrose Reeves, *Shooting at Sharpeville: The Agony of South Africa* (London: Victor Gollancz Ltd, 1960), p. 101.
[34] Van den Berghe, *South Africa: A Study in Conflict*, p. 85.
[35] Rolf Jaster, 'A regional security role for Africa's frontline states', in Rolf Jaster, ed. *Southern Africa: Regional Security Problems and Prospects* (Aldershot: Gower Publishing, 1985), p. 45; Harold Rudolph, *Security, Terrorism and Torture: Detainees' Rights in South Africa and Israel: A Comparative Study* (Cape Town: Juta and Co Ltd, 1984), p. 4; *TIME*, 'South Africa. From mourning to action', 11 April 1960: 32.
[36] Madeleine Fullard, 'State repression in the 1960s', in South African Democracy Education Trust, *The Road to Democracy in South Africa, Volume 1 (1960–1970)*, (Cape Town: Zebra Press, 2004), p. 344.
[37] *Sunday Tribune*, 'Sex talk banned under emergency rules', 10 April 1960: 1.
[38] Ambrose Reeves, *South Africa: Let the Facts Speak* (London: Christian Action, 1962), p. 4.
[39] Meredith, *In the Name of Apartheid*, p. 89; Reeves, *Shooting at Sharpeville*, 101.
[40] Constandinou, author interview.
[41] Hein Marais, *South Africa: Limits to Change: The Political Economy of Transition* (Cape Town: University of Cape Town Press, 2001), p. 25.
[42] The Rand Show has been reported as the largest consumer exhibition in the world, outside of the United States. Coinciding with Easter festivities, it is both a culturally and socially significant show. First held in 1894 by the Witwatersrand Agricultural Society

and opened by Paul Kruger at Milner Park in Braamfontein, it still takes place today (Komane, 'Rand Show turns 121', *The New Age*, 1 April 2015).

[43] *Daily Mirror*, 'The day farmer Pratt called at No. 10', 12 April 1960: 5; *Evening Standard*, 'Death for gunman?' 11 April 1960: 1; Blow and Radsma, author interviews.

[44] CBS Archives, available at: http://www.cbc.ca/archives/entry/sharpeville-massacre-sparks-international-condemnation, accessed on 9 July 2016; *The Cape Argus*, 'Journalist to be freed – but must leave', 11 April 1960: 1; *The Star*, 'Canada angry over newsman's arrest', 11 April 1960: 3; *The Times* (London), 'Protest over journalist's arrest', 11 April 1960: 10.

[45] Alamy, 'Correspondent of the *Daily Herald* Myrna Blumberg is arrested'. Available at: http://www.alamy.com/stock-photo-correspondent-of-the-daily-herald-myrna-blumberg-is-arrested-69364057.html, accessed on 12 November 2016; 'Woman detained – Canadian released', *Daily Dispatch*, 13 April 1960: 1; 'Satisfactory', *Daily Express*, 12 April 1960: 1; 'Dr Verwoerd men hold woman reporter', *News Chronicle*, 12 April 1960: 1; 'South Africa not yielding on race', *The Chicago Daily Defender*, 13 April 1960: 3; 'Portrait of the week', *The Spectator*, 14 April 1960: 3; 'South Africa widens emergency rule', *Washington Post*, 12 April 1960: 6.

[46] *The Spectator*, 'Portrait of the week', 14 April 1960: 3.

[47] *The Chicago Daily Defender*, 'Rap South Africa for denying 1600 a trial', 7 July 1960: 3; Howard Johnson, 'And now he must be called "nameless"', *Daily Mirror*, 12 April 1960: 5; *The New York Times*, 'Press silence on Pratt ordered', 7 July 1960: 3; Richard Kasischke, 'Africa shields assassin's fate', *Washington Post*, 12 April 1960: 1.

[48] *News Chronicle*, 'Dr Verwoerd is whisked away for operation', 11 April 1960: 1.

[49] David Pratt's testimony in the Enquiry regarding his mental condition in *Regina vs. David Beresford Pratt*, 13 September 1960. *The State versus David Beresford Pratt*. 712-60, NASA.

[50] Blow, author interview.

[51] Botha, *Verwoerd is Dead*, p. 67.

[52] *The New York Times*, 'Dr Verwoerd: Relentless advocate of apartheid'.

[53] Kenney, *Architect of Apartheid*, p.186; J.J. Venter, 'H. F. Verwoerd: Foundational aspects of his thought', *Koers*, Vol. 64, No. 4 (1999): 428–29.

[54] *The New York Times*, 'Saboteurs strike in Johannesburg', 14 October 1961: 10.

[55] Leonard Ingalls, 'Luthuli assailed by South Africa', *The New York Times*, 27 October 1961: 8; *The New York Times*, 'Luthuli "stunned" by honour', 24 October 1961: 22.

[56] Mary Benson, *Chief Albert Luthuli of South Africa* (Oxford: Oxford University Press, 1963), p. 51; Albert Luthuli, *Let My People Go* (London: Collins, 1962).

[57] I am not in a position to know how and where Tsafendas got this document from.

[58] Demetrio Tsafendas statement to Major Rossouw, 11 September 1966. K150, Vol. 1, File: Verklaring van Demetrio Tsafendas, NASA.

[59] Burger, 'Dr Verwoerd of South Africa: Architect of doom', p. 11.

[60] Newell M. Stutlz & Jeffrey Butler, 'The South African general election of 1961', *Political Science Quarterly*, Vol. 78, No. 1 (1963): 87.

[61] Elizabeth Landis, 'The new order in South Africa', *Africa Today*, Vol. 8, No. 8 (1961): 4; F.W. de Klerk, *The Last Trek. A New Beginning* (London: Pan Books, 1999), p. 35.

[62] Giliomee, *The Afrikaners*, p. 525.

[63] Botha, *Verwoerd is Dead*, p. 63.

[64] Mandela, *Long Walk to Freedom*, pp. 305–06.

[65] Hendrik F. Verwoerd, *The Truth about South Africa* (Bloemfontein: National Party's Information Service, 1961), p. 5.
[66] Demetrio Tsafendas statement to Major Rossouw, 11 September 1966. K150, Vol. 1, File: Verklaring van Demetrio Tsafendas, NASA.
[67] *Ibid.*
[68] *Ibid.*
[69] van Woerden, *A Mouthful of Glass*, p. 76.
[70] Banovic, author interview.
[71] *Ibid.*
[72] *Ibid.*
[73] Banovic and Vaporidis, author interviews.
[74] Banovic, author interview.
[75] *Ibid.*
[76] *Ibid.*
[77] *Ibid.*
[78] *Ibid.*
[79] *Ibid.*
[80] *Ibid.*
[81] *Ibid.*
[82] *Ibid.*
[83] *Ibid.*
[84] Banovic and Vaporidis, author interviews.
[85] Banovic, author interview.
[86] *Ibid.*
[87] Banovic and Constandinou, author interviews.
[88] Banovic, author interview.
[89] *Ibid.*
[90] *Ibid.*
[91] Banovic, Constandinou and Vaporidis, author interviews.
[92] Banovic, author interview.
[93] Banovic and Constandinou, author interviews.
[94] Constandinou, author interview.
[95] Banovic, author interview.
[96] Demetrio Tsafendas statement to Major Rossouw, 11 September 1966. K150, Vol. 1, File: Verklaring van Demetrio Tsafendas, NASA; Banovic, author interview.
[97] Demetrio Tsafendas statement to Major Rossouw, 11 September 1966. K150, Vol. 1, File: Verklaring van Demetrio Tsafendas, NASA.
[98] Aris Tsafantakis, author interview.
[99] Alexandros, Maria and Michalis Tsafantakis, author interviews.
[100] Constandinou and Tsaftaridis, author interviews.
[101] Constandinou, Alexandros Tsafantakis, Maria Tsafantakis and Michalis Tsafantakis, author interviews.
[102] Constandinou and Tsaftaridis, author interviews.
[103] Demetrio Tsafendas statement to Major Rossouw, 11 September 1966. K150, Vol. 1, File: Verklaring van Demetrio Tsafendas, NASA.
[104] Seccao consular report regarding Dimitri Tsafendas, 10 February 1962. PIDE/DGS, SC, CI (2) 6818, NT 7461, PNA. ANTT.

105 Confidential PIDE report regarding Demetrio Tsafendas, No: 3.699-G.U, 13 November 1962. PIDE/DGS, SC, CI (2) 6818, NT 7461, PNA. ANTT.
106 Confidential PIDE report regarding Dimitro Tsafendas, 7 September 1966. PIDE/DGS, SC, CI (2) 6818, NT 7461, PNA. ANTT.
107 Marika Tsafantakis statement to the police, 7 September 1966. K150, Vol. 12, File: Verklarings Demitrio Tsafendas, NASA.
108 Eintracht and K. Pnefma, author interviews.
109 Constandinou and Eintracht, author interviews.
110 Dr Pegado's report regarding Dimitrio Tsafandakis, 6 April 1962. K150, Vol. 4, Sub file: 1/6, subject: Departement van Verdediging, NASA.
111 Constandinou, author interview.
112 Robert Harpur Smith statement to the police, 7 September 1966. K150, Vol. 12, File: Verklarings Demitrio Tsafendas, NASA.
113 Edward Furness's statement to the police, 12 October 1966. K150, Vol. 12, File: Verklarings, NASA.
114 *Ibid.*
115 Constandinou, author interview.
116 Dave Hann, *Physical Resistance. A Hundred Years of Anti-Fascism* (Winchester: Zero Books, 2013), p. 211.
117 Constandinou, Eintracht and K. Pnefma, author interviews.
118 Constandinou and Antony Michaletos, author interviews.
119 *Ibid.*
120 Constandinou, Eintracht, Grispos, Kyriakakis, Antony and John Michaletos, K. Pnefma and Tsaftaridis, author interviews.
121 Eintracht and K. Pnefma, author interviews.
122 Constandinou, Eintracht, Grispos, Kyriakakis, Antony and John Michaletos, K. Pnefma and Tsaftaridis, author interviews.
123 Eintracht, K. Pnefma and Vlachopoulos, author interviews.
124 Eintracht and K. Pnefma, author interviews.
125 *Ibid.*
126 Constandinou, John Michaletos and Tsaftaridis, author interviews.
127 Letter of a police agent to the Ministry of Interiors regarding Tsafendas's exile. 30 October 1962. PIDE/DGS, SC, CI (2) 6818, NT 7461, PNA. ANTT.
128 Report of the COE, chapter IIB, paragraph 40, December 1966. RP 16/1967. Pretoria.
129 Constandinou and Tsaftaridis, author interviews.
130 *Ibid.*
131 Demetrio Tsafendas statement to Major Rossouw, 11 September 1966. K150, Vol. 1, File: Verklaring van Demetrio Tsafendas, NASA.
132 *Ibid.*
133 It is not possible to state where Tsafendas obtained this literature, but it seems likely that he carried it from England the previous year or it was mailed to him by friends in the British Anti-Apartheid Movement.
134 Eintracht, Antony and John Michaletos, and K. Pnefma, author interviews.

Chapter 9: Back to Africa

1 Marika Tsafantakis statement to the police, 7 September 1966. K150, Vol. 12, File: Verklarings Demitrio Tsafendas, NASA; Antony and John Michaletos, author interviews.

[2] Kyriakakis, author interview.
[3] Antony and John Michaletos, author interviews.
[4] *Ibid.*
[5] South African Police report regarding the activities of Dimitrio Tsafendas in Mozambique and Rhodesia, 20 September 1966. K150, Vol 3, Sub file: 1/5, NASA.
[6] Constandinou, author interview.
[7] Antony and John Michaletos, author interviews.
[8] *Ibid.*
[9] *Ibid.*
[10] Eleni Vlachopoulos in *Live and Let Live*, 2007; Constandinou, Antony Michaletos, John Michaletos and K. Pnefma, author interviews.
[11] Constandinou, Gavasiadis, Antony Michaletos, John Michaletos and K. Pnefma, author interviews.
[12] *Ibid.*
[13] J.J. van den Berg statement regarding the 'Admission to the Republic of Demitrio Tsafendas', 20 September 1966. Report of COE, Vol. 4, Sub file: 1/8, NASA.
[14] John Michaletos, author interview.
[15] Report of the COE, chapter IIC, paragraph 1, December 1966. RP 16/1967. Pretoria.
[16] Eintracht, author interview.
[17] Eintracht and K. Pnefma, author interviews.
[18] Eintracht, author interview.
[19] K. Pnefma, author interview.
[20] *Ibid.*
[21] Eintracht and Gavasiadis, author interviews.
[22] K. Pnefma, author interview.
[23] Eintracht, Gavasiadis and K. Pnefma, author interviews.
[24] Memorandum about the application for permanent residence in terms of the Aliens Act from Demetrio Tsafendas, drawn up by the Secretary for Immigration, n.d. K150, Vol. 4, File: 1/7, Departement van immigrasie, NASA.
[25] Demitrio Tsafendas' medical certificate issued by Dr Been for the Aliens Act, 1937. K150, Vol. 4, File: 1/7, Departement van immigrasie, NASA.
[26] Memorandum about the application for permanent residence in terms of the Aliens Act from Demetrio Tsafendas, drawn up by the Secretary for Immigration, n.d. K150, Vol. 4, File: 1/7, Departement van immigrasie, NASA.
[27] *Ibid.*
[28] From 1948 to 1965 the National Party had handed down 55 major laws that restricted Black South Africans in everything in their everyday life (*TIME*, 'South Africa: Champagne for Whites', 5 November 1965: 42).
[29] Verwoerd wanted to turn South Africa into a white country by forcibly removing the majority of its black citizens. As a result, Black South Africans were forced to move to rural areas while people of Indian origin were threatened with deportation to India if they resisted removal. An important advantage for the whites was that the demarcation allowed them to take control of prosperous trading areas where blacks had been dominant (Chris Alden, *Apartheid's Last Stand: The Rise and Fall of the South African Security State* (Basingstoke: Palgrave Macmillan, 1996), p. 17; Edgar H. Brookes, *Apartheid: A Documentary Study of Modern South Africa* (London: Routledge and Kegan Paul, 1968), pp. 131, 137; John Dugard, *Human Rights and the South African Legal Order*

(Princeton, New Jersey: Princeton University Press, 1978), p. 80; Randolph Vigne, *Liberals against Apartheid: A History of the Liberal Party in South Africa.* (Houndsmills and New York: Palgrave, 1997), p. 100.)

30 Heinz Klug, 'Law before and after apartheid: Abel's socio-legal analysis', *Law and Social Inquiry,* Vol. 25, No. 2 (2000): 657–67.

31 Govan Mbeki, *Learning from Robben Island. The Prison Writings of Govan Mbeki* (London: James Currey, 1991), p. 9.

32 *The New York Times,* 'Dr Verwoerd: Relentless advocate of apartheid'; *TIME,* 'South Africa: God's man', 15 September 1958: 26.

33 Ronald Segal, *The Agony of Apartheid* (London: A Christian Action pamphlet, 1960), p. 2.

34 Mary Benson, 'The destruction of family life' in M.V. Friedmann, ed., *I Will Still Be Moved: Reports from South Africa.* London: Arthur Baker, 1963, p. 113–14; Keith Breckenridge, *Biometric State: The Global Politics of Identification and Surveillance in South Africa, 1850 to the Present* (Cambridge: Cambridge University Press, 2014), p. 138; Sol Dubula, *The Menace of Apartheid* (London: Peace and Socialism Publishers, 1965), p. 13.

35 Pienaar, 'Hendrik Verwoerd', p. 25.

36 Mbeki, *Learning from Robben Island,* pp. 5–6, 167; Immanuel Suttner, ed., *Cutting Through the Mountain: Interviews with South African Jewish Activists* (Viking Penguin: New York, 1997).

37 Mbeki, *Learning from Robben Island,* pp. 5–6, 167.

38 Rosalynde Ainslie, *Masters and Serfs: Farm Labour in South Africa* (London: International Defence and Aid Fund for South Africa, 1977), p. 8.

39 *Neues Deutchland,* 'Dr Verwoerd', 9 September 1966: 7.

40 Brookes, *Apartheid,* p. 51; Bunting, *The Rise of the South African Reich,* p. 260; Dubow, *Apartheid 1948–1994,* p. 55–6; Alex La Guma, *Apartheid: A Collection of Writings on South African Racism by South Africans* (New York: International Publishers, 1971), p. 46; Merle Lipton, *Capitalism and Apartheid: South Africa, 1910–1984* (Aldershot: Gower Publishing/Maurice Temple Smith, 1985), p. 24; O'Meara, *Forty Lost Years,* p. 73; Schadeberg, *Nelson Mandela and the Rise of the ANC,* p. 81; Pelzer, *Verwoerd Speaks,* pp. 83–4; Caroline Willems (ed.), *A Case for Change: Rights, Repression and Responses in South Africa* (Leeds: Leeds Education Development Centre, 1988), p. 16.

41 Sparks, *The Mind of South Africa,* p. 196.

42 *Newsweek,* 'The champion of apartheid', 11 April 1960: 55; *The Canberra Times,* 'Dr Verwoerd, South Africa's "evil genius"', 25 May 1957: 6.

43 *Corriere Della Sera,* 'L'apartheid', 8 September 1966: 1; *Daily Mirror,* 'Misunderstood says Dr Verwoerd', 12 April: 5; *The Chicago Daily Defender,* 'South Africa not yielding on race', 13 April 1960: 3; *The Star,* 'If people only realised that we are Christians', 12 April 1960.

44 Pelzer, *Verwoerd Speaks,* p. 426.

45 Ethel Khopung, *Apartheid: The Story of a Dispossessed People* (Dar es Salaam: Sharpeville Day Association Mbizana, 1972), p. 20.

46 *Newsweek,* 'Exploding South Africa', 11 April 1960: 50.

47 Botha, *Verwoerd is Dead,* p. 63.

48 Pienaar, 'Hendrik Verwoerd', p. 25.

49 Cronje, *Witness in the Dark,* p. 1; Peter Hain, *Sing the Beloved Country: The Struggle for the New South Africa* (Chicago: Pluto Press, 1996), p. 86.

50 Pienaar, 'Hendrik Verwoerd', p. 25.

[51] A Distinguished South African Lawyer (who for obvious reasons must remain anonymous), '*Verwoerd's Police State*' (London: A Christian Action Pamphlet, 1965), p. 4; Denis Herbstein, *White Lies: Canon Collins and the Secret War against Apartheid* (Oxford: James Currey, 2004), p. 75; Mandela, *Long Walk to Freedom*, p. 402; Robert Vassen, 'Detentions without trial during the apartheid era', available at: http://overcoming apartheid.msu.edu/sidebar.php?id=65-258-9&page=1, accessed on 7 March 2015.
[52] Herbstein, *White Lies*, p. 75; World Peace Council, *Apartheid is Built on Torture* (Helsinki: Information Centre of the World Peace Council, 1972), p. 14; Nelson Mandela Organization, 'Criminal Procedure Amendment Act No 96'. Available at: https://www.nelsonmandela.org/omalley/index.php/site/q/03lv01538/04lv01828/05lv01829/06lv01 920.htm, accessed on 16 August 2015; Harold Rudolph, *Security, Terrorism and Torture: Detainees' Rights in South Africa and Israel: A Comparative Study* (Cape Town: Juta and Co Ltd, 1984), p. 12.
[53] Bunting, *The Rise of the South African Reich*, p. 213.
[54] Myrna Blumberg, 'The Mafekeng affair', *Africa South*, April/June (1960): 39–46.
[55] Madeleine Fullard, 'State repression in the 1960s', in South African Democracy Education Trust, *The Road to Democracy in South Africa, Volume 1 (1960–1970)* (Cape Town: Zebra Press, 2004), p. 382.
[56] Tony Gifford, *Southern Africa's Record of International Terrorism* (United Nations Centre Against Apartheid. London: Anti-Apartheid Movement, 1981), pp. 5–6.
[57] Gifford, *Southern Africa's Record of International Terrorism*, 1981. p. 5–6.
[58] South African Institute of Race Relations. *A Survey of Race Relations in South Africa 1961* (Johannesburg: South African Institute of Race Relations, 1962), p. 61.
[59] Brookes, *Apartheid: A Documentary Study of Modern South Africa*, p. 187–92.
[60] *Sunday Tribune*, 'Apartheid ban on Louis Armstrong', 25 September 1960: 1.
[61] Annatjie Boshoff, *Sekretaresse vir die Verwoerds* (Cape Town and Pretoria: Human & Rousseau, 1974), p. 228; Kenney, *Architect of Apartheid*, p. 263.
[62] C. Mitson, 'South Africa's barbarous racial oppression makes Mississippi as mild as a Tea Party', *Morning Record*, 28 January 1965: 6.
[63] Robert Conley, 'Apartheid in sports', *The New York Times*, 15 October 1963: 64.
[64] Eintracht and K. Pnefma, author interviews.
[65] I do not know what Tsafendas did with the pamphlets and the rest of the anti-apartheid literature.
[66] Eintracht, Gavasiadis and K. Pnefma, author interviews.
[67] Nelson Mandela, 'Clear the obstacles and confront the enemy: Wither the Black Consciousness Movement? An assessment', in Mac Maharaj, ed., *Reflections in Prison: Voices from the South African Liberation Struggle* (Cape Town: Zebra Press, 2001), p. 49.
[68] Willems, *A Case for Change*, p. 22.
[69] Barber, *South Africa in the Twentieth Century*, p. 151–2; *TIME*, 'South Africa: Not guilty', 7 April 1961: 30.
[70] Eintracht and K. Pnefma, author interviews.
[71] *Ibid.*
[72] *Ibid.*
[73] Gavasiadis, author interview.
[74] Eintracht and Vlachopoulos, author interviews.
[75] George Bizos, author interview; George Bizos in *Live and Let Live*, 2007.
[76] Gavasiadis, author interview.

[77] Gavasiadis, author interview.
[78] Eintracht and Gavasiadis, author interviews.
[79] Hendrik Johannes van Loggerenberg statement to the police, 8 September 1966. K150, Vol. 12, File: Verklarings Demitrio Tsafendas, NASA.
[80] Gavasiadis, author interview.
[81] *Ibid.*
[82] Eleni Vlachopoulos in *Live and Let Live*, 2007.
[83] Eintracht, author interview.
[84] Eintracht and Gavasiadis, author interviews.
[85] K. Pnefma, author interview.
[86] Banovic, Constandinou and Eintracht, author interviews.
[87] Report by D.G. Gallard of City Engineering and Carron Limited regarding Demitrio Tsafendas to the Commission of Enquiry, 4 October 1966. K150, Vol. 6, File: 3, NASA.
[88] Gavasiadis, author interview.
[89] Eintracht, Gavasiadis and Mike Vlachopoulos, author interviews.
[90] COE report regarding a visit to family members of Demitrio Tsafendas, Pretoria, 21 October 1966. K150, Vol. 12, Sub file: 5, Subject: Algemeen, NASA; Eintracht, author interview; Gavasiadis, author interview; K. Pnefma, author interview.
[91] Gavasiadis and K. Pnefma, author interviews.
[92] Constandinou, author interview.
[93] Report by D.G. Gallard of City Engineering and Carron Limited regarding Demitrio Tsafendas to the Commission of Enquiry, 4 October 1966. K150, Vol. 6, File: 3, NASA.
[94] Report by N.F. Lubie of F.A. Poole PTY, Ltd regarding Tsafendas to the Report of the COE, 13 October 1966. K150, Vol. 6, File: 3, NASA.
[95] Albert Vercual statement to the COE, 25 October 1966. K150, Vol. 12, File: Verklarings Demitrio Tsafendas, NASA.
[96] K. Pnefma, author interview.
[97] Antonio Teixeira Da Silva statement to the police, 9 September 1966. K150, Vol. 12, File: Verklarings Demitrio Tsafendas, NASA.
[98] Nikolaas Jacobus Nel statement to the police, 9 September 1966. K150, Vol. 12, File: Verklarings Demitrio Tsafendas, NASA.
[99] Dr Been statement to the police, 30 September 1966. K150, Vol. 12, File: Verklarings Demitrio Tsafendas, NASA.
[100] Albert Vercueil statement to the police, n.d. K150, Vol. 12, File: Verklarings Demitrio Tsafendas, NASA; Albert Vercueil statement to the Commission of Enquiry, 25 October 1966. K150, Vol. 10, File: Trial transcripts, NASA.
[101] Demetrio Tsafendas statement to Major Rossouw, 11 September 1966. K150, Vol. 1, File: Verklaring van Demetrio Tsafendas, NASA.
[102] Report of the COE, chapter IIC, paragraph 11, December 1966. RP 16/1967. Pretoria.
[103] Nick Vlachopoulos statement to the police, 3 October 1966. K150, Vol. 12, File: Verklarings Demitrio Tsafendas, NASA; Gavasiadis, author interview.
[104] South African Police report regarding the activities of Dimitrio Tsafendas in Mozambique and Rhodesia, 20 September 1966. K150, Vol. 3, File: 1/5. Subject: Suid Afrikaanse Polisie, NASA.
[105] K. Pnefma, author interview.
[106] Demetrio Tsafendas statement to Major Rossouw, 11 September 1966. K150, Vol. 1, File: Verklaring van Demetrio Tsafendas, NASA.

[107] Colonel van Wyk's report regarding the activities of Dimitrio Tsafendas in Mozambique and Rhodesia, 20 September 1966. K150, Vol. 3, File 1/5. FILE Suid Afrikaanse Polisie, NASA; Grispos, author interview.
[108] Confidential Security Report of the Special Branch of the British South African Police in Umtali, Subject: Assassination of Dr Verwoerd. 10 September 1966. K150, Vol. 3, Sub file: 1/5, NASA.
[109] South African Police report regarding the activities of Dimitrio Tsafendas in Mozambique and Rhodesia, 20 September 1966. K150, Vol. 3, File: 1/5. FILE Suid Afrikaanse Polisie, NASA.
[110] Papadakis, author interview.
[111] Irini Michaletos, author interview.
[112] Confidential Security Report of the Special Branch of the British South African Police in Umtali, Subject: Assassination of Dr Verwoerd. 10 September 1966. K150, Vol. 3, Sub file: 1/5, NASA; Grispos, author interview.
[113] Demetrio Tsafendas statement to Major Rossouw, 11 September 1966. K150, Vol. 1, File: Verklaring van Demetrio Tsafendas, NASA; South African Police report regarding the activities of Dimitrio Tsafendas in Mozambique and Rhodesia, 20 September 1966. K150, Vol. 3, Sub file: 1/5, NASA; Papadakis, author interview.
[114] Irini Michaletos and Papadakis, author interview.
[115] Papadakis, author interview.
[116] Demetrio Tsafendas statement to Major Rossouw, 11 September 1966. K150, Vol. 1, File: Verklaring van Demetrio Tsafendas, NASA; Papadakis, author interview.
[117] Papadakis, author interview.
[118] South African Police report regarding the activities of Dimitrio Tsafendas in Mozambique and Rhodesia, 20 September 1966. K150, Vol. 3, File 1/5. FILE Suid Afrikaanse Polisie, NASA.
[119] Babiolakis, Papadakis and Poriazis, author interviews.
[120] *Ibid.*
[121] Unsworth, 'A play about assassination, a tapeworm and notions of madness', *Sunday Times*, 21 September 2003.
[122] Babiolakis, Papadakis and Poriazis, author interviews.
[123] Papadakis, author interview.
[124] Babiolakis, author interview.
[125] *Ibid.*
[126] PIDE confidential report regarding Demetrio Tsafendas: no: 2707/64/SR, 25 November 1964. SR. PIDE/DGS, SC, CI (2) 6818, NT 7461, PNA. ANTT; Andreas Babiolakis author interview, 19 March 2016; Papadakis, author interview.
[127] PIDE Record of questions, 25 November 1964. SR. PIDE/DGS, SC, CI (2) 6818, NT 7461, PNA. ANTT; Andreas Babiolakis author interview, 19 March 2016; Kyriakakis, author interview; John Michaletos author interview, 16 April 2016; Papadakis, author interview.
[128] Babiolakis and Papadakis, author interviews.
[129] Babiolakis, Constandinou, Poriazis and Tsaftaridis, author interviews.
[130] Babiolakis and Papadakis, author interviews.
[131] Tsaftaridis, author interview.
[132] PIDE confidential report regarding Demetrio Tsafendas: no: 2707/64/SR, 25 November 1964. SR. PIDE/DGS, SC, CI (2) 6818, NT 7461, PNA. ANTT; Vertaling. Information: Demitrio Tsafendas or Demetrio Tsafandakis, 7 September 1966. K150. Vol.

6, File: 3, NASA; PIDE report: Information: Demitrio Tsafendas or Demetrio Tsafandakis, 7 September 1966. PIDE/DGS, SC, CI (2) 6818, NT 7461, PNA. ANTT.
[133] PIDE confidential report regarding Demetrio Tsafendas: no: 2707/64/SR, 25 November 1964. SR. PIDE/DGS, SC, CI (2) 6818, NT 7461, PNA. ANTT; Andreas Babiolakis author interview, 19 May 2016; Kyriakakis, author interview; Papadakis, author interview; Costas Poriazis author interview, 5 April 2016.
[134] PIDE report about the Defendant: Demitrio Tsafendas or Dimitrius Tsafendakis, 19 January 1965. SR. PIDE/DGS, SC, CI (2) 6818, NT 7461, PNA. ANTT; PIDE report regarding Demitrio Tsafendas or Dimitrius Tsafendakis, 19 January 1965. K150, Vol. 12, File: Verklarings Demitrio Tsafendas.
[135] South African Police report regarding the activities of Dimitrio Tsafendas in Mozambique and Rhodesia, 20 September 1966. K150, Vol. 3, File 1/5. FILE Suid Afrikaanse Polisie, NASA.
[136] PIDE Record of questions, 25 November 1964. SR. PIDE/DGS, SC, CI (2) 6818, NT 7461, PNA. ANTT.
[137] PIDE confidential report regarding Demetrio Tsafendas: no: 2707/64/SR, 25/1125 November 1964/1964. SR. PIDE/DGS, SC, CI (2) 6818, NT 7461, PNA. ANTT.
[138] Constandinou and Tsaftaridis, author interviews.
[139] Ibid.
[140] Babiolakis, Papadakis and Poriazis, author interviews.
[141] PIDE report: Information: Demitrio Tsafendas or Demetrio Tsafandakis, 12 December 1964. PIDE/DGS, SC, CI (2) 6818, NT 7461, PNA. ANTT.
[142] Letter of Francisco Bartolomeu da Costa Lontrão to the Subdirector of the PIDE in Lourenço Marques, 19 January 1965. PIDE/DGS, SC, CI (2) 6818, NT 7461, PNA. ANTT.
[143] Alberto Henriques de Matos Rodrigues conclusion to the Subdirector, 23 January 1965. PIDE/DGS, SC, CI (2) 6818, NT 7461, PNA. ANTT.
[144] South African Police report regarding the activities of Dimitrio Tsafendas in Mozambique and Rhodesia, 20 September 1966. K150, Vol. 3, Sub file: 1/5, NASA; Report of the COE, chapter IIC, paragraph 19, December 1966. RP 16/1967. Pretoria.
[145] Vertaling. Information: Demitrio Tsafendas or Demetrio Tsafandakis, 7 September 1966. K150. Vol. 6, File: 3, NASA; PIDE report: Information: Demitrio Tsafendas or Demetrio Tsafandakis, 7 September 1966. PIDE/DGS, SC, CI (2) 6818, NT 7461, PNA. ANTT.
[146] Constandinou and Tsaftaridis, author interviews.
[147] South African Police report regarding the activities of Dimitrio Tsafendas in Mozambique and Rhodesia, 20 September 1966. K150, Vol. 3, File: 1/5. Subject: Suid Afrikaanse Polisie, NASA; Nick Vlachopoulos statement to the police, 3 October 1966. K150, Vol. 12, File: Verklarings Demitrio Tsafendas, NASA; Demetrio Tsafendas statement to Major Rossouw, 11 September 1966. K150, Vol. 1, File: Verklaring van Demetrio Tsafendas, NASA.
[148] K. Pnefma, author interview.
[149] Babiolakis, Papadakis and Poriazis, author interviews.
[150] Babiolakis and Poriazis, author interviews.
[151] *Ibid.*
[152] K. Pnefma, author interview.
[153] Babiolakis and K. Pnefma, author interviews.
[154] Babiolakis and Poriazis, author interviews.

[155] Demetrio Tsafendas statement to Major Rossouw, 11 September 1966. K150, Vol. 1, File: Verklaring van Demetrio Tsafendas, NASA; South African Police report regarding the activities of Dimitrio Tsafendas in Mozambique and Rhodesia, 20 September 1966. K150. Vol. 3, File: 1/5. FILE Suid Afrikaanse Polisie, NASA.

Chapter 10: Parliamentary Messenger

[1] Report of the COE, chapter IIC, paragraphs 23 and 24, December 1966. RP 16/1967. Pretoria.
[2] Esperanza Theron's statement to the police, 24 September 1966. K150, Vol. 12, File: Verklarings Demitrio Tsafendas, NASA; Constandinou, author interview.
[3] Michalis Michelis, 'Δημήτρης Τσαφέντας: Έκανα το Καθήκον Μου ... Εσείς;' ['Dimitris Tsafendas: I did my Duty ... You?'] Σχολιαστής [Sholiastis], Vol. 70 (1988): 14; Constandinou, author interview; Michalis Michelis author interview, 23 January 2016; Esperanza Theron statement to the police, 24 September 1966. K150, Vol. 12, File: Verklarings Demitrio Tsafendas, NASA; Report of the COE, chapter IIC, paragraph 33, December 1966. RP 16/1967. Pretoria.
[4] Cornelius Johannes Rudolph statement to the police, 7 September 1966. K150, Vol. 12, File: Verklarings Demitrio Tsafendas, NASA.
[5] *Sunday Times*, 'Assassin-man with a chip on his shoulder', 11 September 1966: 1, 8.
[6] *O Primeiro de Janeiro*, 'Algumas versoes sobre a vida de Tsafendas', 8 September 1966.
[7] Kyriakos Skordis statement to the police, 7 September 1966. K150, Vol. 12, File: Verklarings Demitrio Tsafendas, NASA.
[8] *Rand Daily Mail*, 'Tsafendas: in the eyes of a friend', 14 September 1966.
[9] South African Railways Confidential Medical Examination Certificate of Demitrio Tsafendas. K150, Vol. 7, File: S 83708, Tsafendas: D, NASA.
[10] Garnet Vincent Muller's statement to the police, 7 September 1966. K150, Vol. 12, File: Verklarings Demitrio Tsafendas, NASA.
[11] Johannes Jacobus Uys Aurets statement to the police, 7 September 1966. K150, Vol. 12, File: Verklarings Demitrio Tsafendas, NASA.
[12] Garnet Vincent Muller's statement to the police, 7 September 1966. K150, Vol. 12, File: Verklarings Demitrio Tsafendas, NASA.
[13] Charles Edwin Woods statement to the police, 19 September 1966. K150, Vol. 12, File: Verklarings Demitrio Tsafendas, NASA.
[14] *The Cape Times*, 'Tsafendas in brawl in canteen', 9 September 1966: 15.
[15] Christoffel Johannes van Vuuren statement to the police, 13 September 1966. K150, Vol. 12, File: Verklarings Demitrio Tsafendas, NASA.
[16] Alachiotis, Constandinou, Kambouris, Kantas, Tsaftaridis and Vasilakis, author interviews.
[17] Charles Edwin Woods statement to the police, 19 September 1966. K150, Vol. 12, File: Verklarings Demitrio Tsafendas, NASA.
[18] Jan Johannes Albertus Fourie statement to the police, 3 October 1966. K150, Vol. 12, File: Verklarings Demitrio Tsafendas, NASA.
[19] Demetrio Tsafendas's statement in the court regarding the incident, 14 May 1965. K150, Vol. 3, File: Afskrif van saak dossier Nyoni R.A.A. 14 May 1965, NASA; Demetrio Tsafendas statement to Major Rossouw, 11 September 1966. K150, Vol. 1, File: Verklaring van Demetrio Tsafendas, NASA; Johannes Jacobus Botha statement to the police, 15

September 1966. K150, Vol. 12, File: Verklarings, NASA; Alachiotis, Constandinou, Kambouris, Kantas, Tsaftaridis and Vasilakis, author interviews.
[20] Demetrio Tsafendas's statement to Major Rossouw, 11 September 1966. K150, Vol. 1, File: Verklaring van Demetrio Tsafendas, NASA.
[21] Johannes Jacobus Botha's statement to the police, 3 October 1966. K150, Vol. 12, File: Verklarings Demitrio Tsafendas, NASA.
[22] Christoffel Johannes van Vuuren statement to the police, 13 September 1966. K150, Vol. 12, File: Verklarings Demitrio Tsafendas, NASA.
[23] Demetrio Tsafendas' statement to the police regarding the incident, 7 May 1965. K150, Vol. 3, File: Afskrif van saak dossier Nyoni R.A.A. 14 May 1965, NASA; Nikolas Vergos' statement to the police regarding the incident, 14 May 1965. K150, Vol. 3, File: Afskrif van saak dossier Nyoni R.A.A. 14 May 1965, NASA.
[24] Christoffel Johannes van Vuuren statement to the police, 13 September 1966. K150, Vol. 12, File: Verklarings Demitrio Tsafendas, NASA.
[25] Father Hanno Probst's statement to the police, 9 September 1966. K150, Vol. 12, File: Verklarings Demitrio Tsafendas, NASA; Father Hanno Probst statement to the COE, 13 October 1966. K150, Vol. 12, File: Verklarings Demitrio Tsafendas, NASA.
[26] *Ibid.*
[27] Father Hanno Probst's statement to the COE, 13 October 1966. K150, Vol. 12, File: Verklarings Demitrio Tsafendas, NASA.
[28] Kenneth Heugh Ross statement to the police, 7 September 1966, K150, Vol. 12, File: Verklarings Demitrio Tsafendas, NASA.
[29] Robert Harpur Smith statement to the police, 7 September 1966. K150, Vol. 12, File: Verklarings Demitrio Tsafendas, NASA.
[30] Kenneth Heugh Ross statement to the police, 7 September 1966, K150, Vol. 12, File: Verklarings Demitrio Tsafendas, NASA; Robert Harpur Smith statement to the police, 7 September 1966. K150, Vol. 12, File: Verklarings Demitrio Tsafendas, NASA.
[31] Helen Dorothy Daniels statement to the police, 15 September 1966. K150, Vol. 1, File: VDSO 17/64, NASA.
[32] Demetrio Tsafendas statement to Major Rossouw, 11 September 1966. K150, Vol. 1, File: Verklaring van Demetrio Tsafendas, NASA; Peter Daniels's testimony on Tsafendas's summary trial, 18 October 1966. K150, Vol. 10, File: Trial, NASA.
[33] Helen Dorothy Daniels statement to the police, 15 September 1966. K150, Vol. 1, File: VDSO 17/64, NASA.
[34] Helen Dorothy Daniels statement to the police, 15 September 1966. K150, Vol. 1, File: VDSO 17/64, NASA; *The Post*, 'I jilted Tsafendas, says Coloured girl', 18 September 1966: 1; Constantaras and Dick, author interviews.
[35] I am not in a position to establish for certain why Tsafendas applied to be reclassified as a coloured person. He told the police that he did so in order 'to marry a Coloured woman named Helen Daniels'. However, according to Helen Daniels, Tsafendas appeared to have no interest in marrying her and made no attempt to establish a relationship with her. The Report of the Commission of Enquiry also stated that Tsafendas gave as a reason for his application that 'he regarded himself as a Coloured and that he wished to marry a Coloured'. Attorney General W.M. van den Berg stated in a memorandum that according to a statement in his possession, 'there was never any question of a marriage between him (Tsafendas) and the Coloured woman, Helen Daniels from Bellville South. Information from Home Affairs files indicated that

Tsafendas applied for reclassification because he wanted to apply for a business licence in a Coloured area.' Patrick O'Ryan testified that Tsafendas was 'favourable towards the Coloureds and sought repeatedly to be classified as a Coloured'. None of the witnesses interviewed by the author ever recalled Tsafendas talking about his application, thus it is not possible to determine for certain what his reason was. The likeliest explanation is Patrick O'Ryan's – that Tsafendas just wanted to live freely among other Coloureds.

36 Demetrio Tsafendas statement to Major Rossouw, 11 September 1966. K150, Vol. 1, File: Verklaring van Demetrio Tsafendas, NASA; Report of the COE, chapter IX, paragraph 1, December 1966. RP 16/1967. Pretoria.

37 Helen Dorothy Daniels statement to the police, 15 September 1966. K150, Vol. 1, File: VDSO 17/64, NASA; Peter Daniels's testimony on Tsafendas's summary trial, 18 October 1966. K150, Vol. 10, File: Trial, NASA; Elias Constantaras author interview, 11 April 2015.

38 Dick, author interview.

39 Helen Dorothy Daniels statement to the police, 15 September 1966. K150, Vol. 1, File: VDSO 17/64, NASA.

40 Department of Labour report regarding Demitri Tsafendas, 323/026034, n.d. K150, Vol. 1, Sub file: 1/2, NASA; *The history of the person who inflicted the fatal wounds to the late Dr Verwoerd* drafted by Col. McIntyre, 3 October 1966. K150, Vol. 3, Subject: Leer W.D. 10/10/4102 der Stafendas, NASA; Donald Neville Mackay statement to the police, 12 October 1966. K150, Vol. 12, File: Verklarings Demitrio Tsafendas, NASA; Demetrio Tsafendas statement to Major Rossouw, 11 September 1966. K150, Vol. 1, File: Verklaring van Demetrio Tsafendas, NASA.

41 Violet Irene Manning statement to the COE, 21 October 1966. K150, Vol. 3, File: 1/5. Subject: Suid Afrikaanse polisie, NASA; Constantaras, author interview.

42 Patrick O'Ryan testimony on Tsafendas's summary trial, 18 October 1966. K150, Vol. 10, File: Trial, NASA; Patrick O'Ryan in Liza Key's *A Question of Madness*, 1997. This part is available in the rushes; Constandinou, author interview.

43 Louisa O'Ryan's testimony on Tsafendas's summary trial, 18 October 1966. K150, Vol. 10, File: Trial, NASA; Patrick O'Ryan's testimony on Tsafendas's summary trial, 18 October 1966. K150, Vol. 10, File: Trial, NASA; Constandinou and Reuben O'Ryan, author interviews.

44 Donald Neville Mackay's statement to the COE, 12 October 1966. K150, Vol. 12, File: Verklarings Demitrio Tsafendas, NASA.

45 Constandinou, author interview.

46 Reuben O'Ryan, author interview.

47 Patrick O'Ryan in *A Question of Madness*, 1997. This part is available in the rushes; Constandinou, author interview.

48 Constandinou and Tsaftaridis, author interviews.

49 *Ibid.*

50 *Ibid.*

51 Demetrios Tsafendakis Affidavit, November 1965. K150, Vol. 12, Sub file: 5, Subject: Algemeen, NASA.

52 Shaw, *Believe in Miracles*, p. 58.

53 Hagios, author interview.

54 Richard Poggenpoel statement to the police, 15 September 1966. K150, Vol. 12, File: Verklarings Demitrio Tsafendas, NASA.

[55] Johannes Oosthuizen statement to the police, 12 October 1966. K150, Vol. 12, File: Verklarings Demitrio Tsafendas, NASA.
[56] Tsafendas's Marine Diamond Corporation application for Employment, 13 January 1966. K150, Vol. 6, File: 3, NASA.
[57] Carel van Heerden statement to the police, 4 October 1966. K150, Vol. 12, File: Verklarings Demitrio Tsafendas, NASA.
[58] Ralph Lighton's statement to the police, 17 September 1966. K150, Vol. 12, File: Verklarings Demitrio Tsafendas, NASA.
[59] Keith Terrence Bertram Martincich's statement to the police, 4 October 1966. K150, Vol. 12, File: Verklarings Demitrio Tsafendas, NASA.
[60] Gillian Claire Liebermann's statement to the police, 6 October 1966. K150, Vol. 12, File: Verklarings Demitrio Tsafendas, NASA.
[61] Constandinou and Tsaftaridis, author interviews.
[62] Statement by Dr I. Eisenberg regarding Demitrio Tsafendas, n.d. K150, Vol. 12, File: Verklarings Demitrio Tsafendas, NASA.
[63] Hulse's first name is not given in this statement to the police, but in Henk van Woerden's *A Mouthful of Glass* the name is given as John.
[64] Ralph Lighton statement to the police, 17 September 1966. K150, Vol. 12, File: Verklarings Demitrio Tsafendas, NASA; Hulse statement to the police, 28 September 1966, K150, Vol. 12, File: Verklarings Demitrio Tsafendas, NASA.
[65] Constandinou and Tsaftaridis, author interviews.
[66] Hepple, *Verwoerd*, p. 200.
[67] Elizabeth Groves statement to the police, 27 September 1966. K150, Vol. 12, File: Verklarings Demitrio Tsafendas, NASA.
[68] Jacobus Johannes Borman's statement to the police, 3 October 1966. K150, Vol. 12, File: Verklarings Demitrio Tsafendas, NASA.
[69] House of Assembly, Question no 17, 3 February 1967. K150, Vol. 12, File: Social Welfare and Pensions, NASA; Dr Ralph Kossew testimony at Tsafendas's summary trial, 18 October 1966: 88. K150, Vol. 10, File: Union of SA, NASA.
[70] British Embassy in Cape Town letter to the South African Police regarding Tsafendas, 14 September 1966. K150, Vol. 7, File: 09/04 Suspect Persons Demetrio Tsafendas, NASA.
[71] Constandinou and Tsaftaridis, author interviews.
[72] Dr Ralph Kossew's testimony at Tsafendas's summary trial, 18 October 1966: 88. K150, Vol. 10, File: Union of SA, NASA; House of Assembly, Question no 17, 3 February 1967. K150, Vol. 12, File: Social Welfare and Pensions, NASA.
[73] Ian James Boswell's statement to the police, 30 September 1966. K150, Vol. 1, File: VDSO 17/64, NASA.
[74] Gideon Cloete testimony at Tsafendas's summary trial, 19 October 1966. K150, Vol. 12, File: Union of South Africa, NASA.
[75] Pieter Geldenhuys statement to the police, 3 October 1966, K150, Vol. 1, Sub file: 1/1, Department of Labour, NASA.
[76] Wilhelmina Sophia de Vos statement to the police, 3 October 1966. K150, Vol. 12, File: Verklarings Demitrio Tsafendas, NASA.
[77] Alice Mary Theyser statement to the police, 27 September 1966. K150, Vol. 12, File: Verklarings Demitrio Tsafendas, NASA; *The Cape Argus*, 'Tsafendas seen as a bitter, withdrawn man', 7 September 1966.
[78] *The Cape Argus*, 'Tsafendas seen as a bitter, withdrawn man'.

[79] Herbert Summers statement to the police, 27 September 1966. K150, Vol. 12, File: Verklarings Demitrio Tsafendas, NASA.
[80] Mary Kathleen Scott's statement to the police, 15 September 1966. K150, Vol. 12, File: Verklarings Demitrio Tsafendas, NASA.
[81] Abrahams, Constantaras, Pamela and Panagiotis Peroglou, and Vamvarapis, author interviews.
[82] Constantaras, author interview.
[83] Report of the COE, chapter IIC, paragraph 75, December 1966. RP 16/1967. Pretoria.
[84] Vasilakis, author interview.
[85] Hughes, *The New Face of Africa*, p. 171; Richard Leonard, *South Africa at War: White Power and the Crisis in Southern Africa* (Westport: Lawrence Hill and Company, 1983), p. 164; Rob Nixon, *Homelands, Harlem and Hollywood: South African Culture and the World Beyond* (New York: Routledge, 1994), p. 43; *Washington Post*, 'Dr Verwoerd stabbed to death at his desk in Parliament', 7 September 1966: 8.
[86] John Daniel & Peter Vale, 'South Africa: Where were we looking in 1968?' in Philipp Gassert and Martin Klimke, eds., *1968 – Memories and Legacies of a Global Revolt* (Washington, DC: German Historical Institute, 2009), p. 140.
[87] Constandinou and Tsaftaridis, author interviews.
[88] Interview by T.I. Potgieter, Senior Magistrate, Pretoria with Demitriou Tsafendas at the Pretoria Central Prison on 20 October 1987. Correctional Services. File: 80/0043, A123, Dimitrio Tsafendas, Vol. 1, NASA; Constandinou and Tsaftaridis, author interviews.
[89] Piet Bester Burger testimony to the COE, 13 October 1966. K150, Vol. 10, File: Uittreksels uit Getuienis, NASA; Petrus Robert Samuel Schuin testimony to the COE, 13 October 1966. K150, Vol. 10, File: Uittreksels uit Getuienis, NASA; Sydney William Wiehand testimony to the COE, 5 October 1966. K150, Vol. 10, File: Uittreksels uit Getuienis, NASA.
[90] *Die Volksblad*, 'Dimitri Tsafendas. Nuwe feite oor bode onthul', 8 September 1966: 1.
[91] Michaelis Augustides statement to the police, 3 October 1966. K150, Vol. 3, File: Die 'Eleni', NASA.
[92] Peter Lambley, *The Psychology of Apartheid* (Athens: The University of Georgia Press, 1980), p. 241.
[93] John Patrick Leach testimony to the COE, 17 October 1966. K150, Vol. 3, Sub file: 1/5, Subject: South African Police, NASA.
[94] *Eleni* crew list, 18 July 1966, Greek Department of Maritime Labour, Office D; *Eleni* crew list, 24 July 1966. K150, Vol. 3, File: Die 'Eleni', NASA.
[95] Mastromanolis, author interview.
[96] Tsabouniaris, author interview.
[97] Vasilis Perselis and Vasilakis, author interviews.
[98] Alachiotis, Billis, Kambouris, Kantas, Mastromanolis, Pouftis and Vasilakis, author interviews.
[99] Demetrio Tsafendas statement to Major Rossouw, 11 September 1966. K150, Vol. 1, File: Verklaring van Demetrio Tsafendas, NASA; Mastromanolis, author interview.
[100] Vasilakis, author interview.
[101] Kambouris, author interview.
[102] Vasilakis, author interview.
[103] Alachiotis, Billis, Kambouris, Kantas, Mastromanolis, Pouftis and Vasilakis, author interviews.

[104] Aspiotis, Mastromanolis, Speis and Tsabouniaris, author interviews.

[105] Billis, Kambouris, Kantas, V. Perselis, Pouftis and Vasilakis, author interviews.

[106] Alachiotis, Billis, Kambouris, Kantas, V. Perselis, Pouftis and Vasilakis, author interviews.

[107] Report of the COE, chapter IX, December 1966. RP 16/1967. Pretoria.

[108] Demetrio Tsafendas statement to Major Rossouw, 11 September 1966. K150, Vol. 1, File: Verklaring van Demetrio Tsafendas, NASA; Mastromanolis, author interview; V. Perselis, author interview.

[109] Constandinou and Tsaftaridis, author interviews.

[110] Reuben O'Ryan, author interview.

[111] Fred Feinauer statement to the police, 3 October 1966. K150, Vol. 12, File: Verklarings Demitrio Tsafendas, NASA.

[112] Demetrio Tsafendas statement to Major Rossouw, 19 September 1966. K150, Vol. 1, File: Verklaring van Demetrio Tsafendas, NASA; Constandinou, author interview.

[113] Report of the COE, chapter IX, paragraph 5, December 1966. RP 16/1967. Pretoria.

[114] Brenda Nicholson's statement to the police, 12 September 1966. K150, Vol. 12, File: Verklarings Demitrio Tsafendas, NASA; Demetrio Tsafendas statement to Major Rossouw, 11 September 1966. K150, Vol. 1, File: Verklaring van Demetrio Tsafendas, NASA.

[115] Emanuil Mastromanolis statement to the police, 12 October 1966. K150, Vol. 3, File Die 'Eleni', NASA; Nicolas Mavronas statement to the police, 12 October 1966. K150, Vol 3, File Die 'Eleni', NASA; Demetrio Tsafendas statement to Major Rossouw, 11 September 1966. K150, Vol. 1, File: Verklaring van Demetrio Tsafendas, NASA; Mastromanolis and Tsabouniaris, author interviews.

[116] Demetrio Tsafendas statement to Major Rossouw, 11 September 1966. K150, Vol. 1, File: Verklaring van Demetrio Tsafendas, NASA.

[117] Nicolas Mavronas's statement to the police, 12 October 1966. K150, Vol. 3, File: Die 'Eleni', NASA; Mastromanolis, author interview.

[118] Fred Feinauer statement to the police, 3 October 1966. K150, Vol. 12, File: Verklarings Demitrio Tsafendas, NASA; Demetrio Tsafendas statement to Major Rossouw, 11 September 1966. K150, Vol. 1, File: Verklaring van Demetrio Tsafendas, NASA.

[119] Maria Kokkinidou statement to the police, 27 September 1966. K150, Vol. 3, File: Die 'Eleni', NASA; Peter Protoulis statement to the police, 28 September 1966. K150, Vol. 3, File: Leer W.D. 10/10/ 4102 oor Stafendas, NASA; Nichas and Protoulis, author interviews.

[120] Alachiotis, Billis, Kambouris, Kantas, Pouftis and Vasilakis, author interviews.

[121] *Ibid.*

[122] Mastromanolis, author interview.

[123] Kambouris and Vasilakis, author interviews.

[124] Reginald Robert Maile statement to the police, 27 September 1966. K150, Vol. 3, File: Die '*Eleni*', NASA.

[125] Harry Hall statement to the police, 6 October 1966. K150, Vol. 12, File: Verklarings, NASA.

[126] Rosamund Elizabeth Popkiss statement to the police, 9 September 1966. K150, Vol. 3, File: Afskrif van vorm Z 204, NASA.

[127] Demetrio Tsafendas statement to Major Rossouw, 11 September 1966. K150, Vol. 1, File: Verklaring van Demetrio Tsafendas, NASA; Constandinou and Tsaftaridis, author interviews.

Chapter 11: The Outbreak of Torture

[1] Constandinou, author interview.
[2] *The Cape Times*, 'Tsafendas: fear for life', 9 September 1966: 1; Constandinou, author interview.
[3] *Daily Dispatch*, 'Tsafendas in court', 9 September 1966: 1; *The Globe and Mail*, 'Dr Verwoerd's slayer appears for formal hearing in court', 9 September 1966: 4.
[4] *Daily Dispatch*, 'Tsafendas in court'.
[5] Constandinou and Tsaftaridis, author interviews.
[6] *Ibid.*
[7] *Ibid.*
[8] International Defence and Aid Fund, *South African Prisons and the Red Cross Investigation* (London: International Defence and Aid Fund, 1967), p. 43.
[9] Electrocution was a standard torture technique used by the apartheid police at that time with several anti-apartheid activists attesting to being treated the same way (Madeleine Fullard, 'State repression in the 1960s', in South African Democracy Education Trust, *The Road to Democracy in South Africa, Volume 1 (1960–1970)* (Cape Town: Zebra Press, 2004), p. 358–63; Torture in South Africa (extracts from the Report of the UN Special Committee on the policies of Apartheid of the Govt. Of the Republic of South Africa, /5825, 8 December 1964), *Transition*, No. 19 (1965): 17–22). In 1963, Isaac Tiale was handcuffed and subjected to electric shocks with a bag tied over his head until he lost consciousness twice. He was also tied into a straightjacket. (Torture in South Africa (extracts from the Report of the UN Special Committee on the policies of Apartheid of the Govt. Of the Republic of South Africa, /5825, 8 December 1964), *Transition*, No. 50 (1976): 5–7). Zollie Malindi was given the notorious helicopter treatment, where his hands and legs were tied behind his back and he was suspended in mid-air. He also got electric shocks heightened by the water-soaked suffocating bag (Fullard, 'State repression in the 1960s', 2004, pp. 358–63). About the same time, Ndovela Nxasana lost some of his hearing as a result of electric torture, and bones in his joints were broken by police clubs. MK fighters Laloo Chiba and Abdulhai Jassat were beaten and given electric shocks, and Mountain Qumbela was similarly tortured but also forced to hold agonising physical positions for long periods. Four years into the future, in 1970, the police would claim that James Thabiso Lenkoe, held like Tsafendas under the 180-day detention law, committed suicide by hanging himself with his own belt. There was clear evidence from autopsy results that electrical torture had been used during his detention (Hilda Bernstein, *South Africa: The Terrorism of Torture* (London: International Defence and Aid Fund, 1972), p. 30–1; Fullard, 'State repression in the 1960s', 2004, pp. 357–63; International Defence and Aid Fund, *'Resettlement' – The New Violence to Africans* (London: International Defence and Aid Fund, 1969), pp. 7–8; TRC, *TRC Report: Volume Two*, p. 539).
[10] Michelis, author interview.
[11] Ely Jacques Kahn. *The Seperated People: A Look at Contemporary South Africa* (New York: W.W. Norton & Company, Inc, 1968), p. 151.
[12] *The Globe and Mail*, 'Dr Verwoerd's slayer appears for formal hearing in court', 9 September 1966: 4.
[13] Goodman, *Fault Lines*, p. 155.

[14] House of Assembly Debates (Hansard), 6 and 7 September, 1966; *Personality*, 'The state funeral of Dr H.F. Verwoerd, Prime Minister', 29 September 1966: 19–24; *Scope*, 'The entire nation mourns ... and a critical world press passes caustic comments', 23 September 1966: 12–18; *The Canberra Times*, 'Dr Verwoerd buried in Heroes' Acre', 12 September 1966: 5; *The Cape Argus*, 'Magnificence for "quiet man"', 11 September 1966: 1 (late edition); *The New York Times*, '10,000 people attend funeral service', 11 September 1966; *The Times* (London), 'Hundreds file past grave of Dr Verwoerd', 12 September 1966: 7; *The Star*, 'Vast crowds pay last respects to Dr Verwoerd', 11 September 1966: 1.
[15] *The Cape Times*, n.d. 'State funeral on air in 11 languages.'; *The Illustrated London News*, 'The state funeral of Dr Verwoerd', 17 September 1966: 1; *The Star*, 'Vast crowds pay last respects to Dr Verwoerd.'
[16] *Die Vaderland*, 'Hy is weg, maar sy boodskap bly', 10 September 1966: 1.
[17] *Pretoria News*, 'Vorster: Police had no file on Tsafendas', 12 September 1966: 11.
[18] Report of the COE, chapter XI, paragraphs 4 and 5, December 1966. RP 16/1967. Pretoria.
[19] Fullard, 'State repression in the 1960s', p. 362.
[20] Constandinou, author interview.
[21] Demetrio Tsafendas statement to Major Rossouw, 11 September 1966. K150, Vol. 1, File: Verklaring van Demetrio Tsafendas, NASA.
[22] *Ibid.*
[23] *Pretoria News*, 'Suicide of Tsafendas rumoured', 12 September 1966: 1.
[24] Demetrio Tsafendas statement to Major Rossouw, 11 September 1966. K150, Vol. 1, File: Verklaring van Demetrio Tsafendas, NASA.
[25] *Ibid.*
[26] *Ibid.*
[27] *Ibid.*
[28] Constandinou, author interview.
[29] Constandinou, author interview; Tsafendas was not alone in suffering the window torture, it was a standard information-extracting/torture technique used by the police at that time. Several anti-apartheid activists, such as Abdullay Jassat and Tseliso Phofu, described being treated the same way. In 1971, police claimed that Ahmed Timol, a leading member of the South African Communist Party, opened a window and jumped to his death from the tenth floor of the John Vorster Square police station in Johannesburg, where he had been interrogated and brutalised.
[30] Constandinou, author interview.
[31] Maria Kokkinidou statement to the police, 27 September 1966. K150, Vol. 3, File: Die 'Eleni', NASA.
[32] Reginald Robert Maile statement to the police, 28 September 1966. K150, Vol. 3, File: Die 'Eleni', NASA; Edmund George Stollenkamp statement to the police, 7 October 1966. K150, Vol. 3, File: Die 'Eleni', NASA.
[33] Pouftis, Speis and Vasilakis, author interviews.
[34] Alachiotis, Billis, Kambouris, Kantas, Mastromanolis, Pouftis and Vasilakis, author interviews.
[35] Alachiotis, Aspiotis, Billis, Kambouris, Kantas, Mastromanolis, V. Perselis, Pouftis, Speis, Tsabouniaris and Vasilakis, author interviews.
[36] *Ibid.*
[37] *Ibid.*

[38] *Ibid.*
[39] Alachiotis, Billis, Kambouris, Kantas, Pouftis and Vasilakis, author interviews.
[40] Constandinou and Michelis, author interviews.
[41] *Ibid.*
[42] Constandinou, author interview.
[43] *Ibid.*
[44] Michelis, author interview.
[45] *Daily Dispatch,* 'Premier's killing full inquiry', 15 September 1966: 1; Dugard author interview; *Rand Daily Mail* 'Killing inquiry to be secret', 22 September 1966; *The Canberra Times,* 'South Africa: Assassination Inquiry', 23 September 1966: 5; *The Cape Argus,* 'Judge will probe Dr V's death', 1 September 1966: 1.
[46] David Beresford of the British *Guardian,* in an article in that newspaper marking the death of Tsafendas on 11 October 1999 which was headlined 'Demitri Tsafendas: Long-jailed assassin of South African premier', wrote 'There were attempts by police, during interrogation, to suggest to him that he believed a tapeworm had "ordered" him to carry out the killing (but) he never seems to have made the claim himself.' Beresford wrote the article based on documents found in Tsafendas's police file (David Beresford author interview, 11 April 2014). Tsafendas confirmed that the police tried to make him say that the tapeworm asked him to kill Verwoerd in discussions with Liza Key (who, like Beresford, had also accessed Tsafendas's police file), with Father Minas Constandinou and Bishop Ioannis Tsaftaridis. He insisted to these people that despite police pressure and torture, he always told the police that he had killed Verwoerd for political reasons, such as that 'a change of policy would take place' after his death. The documents found in the National Archives of South Africa confirm Tsafendas's story.
[47] Dr Harold Cooper's testimony on Tsafendas's summary trial, 17 October 1966. K150, Vol. 10, File: Trial, NASA.
[48] Demetrio Tsafendas statement to Major Rossouw, 19 September 1966. K150, Vol. 1, File: Verklaring van Demetrio Tsafendas, NASA.
[49] Babiolakis, Constandinou, Eintracht, Kyriakakis, Papadakis and K. Pnefma, author interviews.
[50] Memorandum to Maj. Rossouw re. Demitrio Tsafendas, 19 September 1966. K150, Vol. 6, File: 3, NASA.
[51] Constandinou, author interview; Michalis Michelis author interview, 12 December 2015.
[52] Constandinou and Michelis, author interviews.
[53] Constandinou, author interview.
[54] Gavin van den Berg, son of J.J. van den Berg, in *A Question of Madness,* 1997. This part is available in the rushes.
[55] *Pretoria News,* 'Suicide of Tsafendas rumoured.'
[56] Michelis, 'Δημήτρης Τσαφέντας: Έκανα το Καθήκον Μου ... Εσείς;' p. 14; Constandinou and Michelis, author interviews.
[57] Professor Adolf Johannes van Wyk's testimony on Tsafendas's summary trial, 19 October 1966. K150, Vol. 10, File: Trial, NASA.
[58] This is what Tsafendas conveyed to Father Minas Constandinou and Bishop Ioannis Tsaftaridis. Constandinou and Tsaftaridis, author interviews.
[59] G. Bizos, author interview.
[60] Dugard, author interview.

[61] Marius A. Diemont, *Brushes with the Law* (Cape Town: Human & Rousseau, 1995), p. 132; Dugard, author interview.
[62] Van Zyl, author interview.
[63] David Bloomberg, 'Yes to South Africa', *The New York Times*, 23 May 1965: xi.
[64] Wilfrid Cooper in *A Question of Madness*, 1997.
[65] Gavin Cooper, *Under Devil's Peak: The Life and Times of Wilfrid Cooper, an Advocate in the Age of Apartheid* (Kenilworth: Burnet Media, 2016).
[66] David Bloomberg, *My Times: The Memoirs of David Bloomberg* (Simon's Town: Fernwood Press, 2007), pp. 74–5.
[67] Cooper, *Under Devil's Peak*, p. 101; Wilfrid Cooper in *A Question of Madness*, 1997.
[68] Bloomberg, *My Times*, p. 76.
[69] *Ibid.*
[70] Bloomberg, *My Times*, pp. 76–7.
[71] Report of the Commission of Inquiry into the Responsibility of Mentally Deranged Persons and Related Matters, p. 17. *Pretoria: Government Printer. 1967.*
[72] David Bloomberg in *A Question of Madness*, 1997. The part is available in the rushes; Bloomberg, *My Times*, p. 82.
[73] G. Bizos and Dugard, author interviews.
[74] Bloomberg, *My Times*, pp. 80–1.
[75] Jacobus Andreas Johannes Erasmus's testimony on Tsafendas's summary trial, 20 October 1966. K150, Vol. 10, File: Trial, NASA.
[76] Dr J.W. MacGregor's testimony on Tsafendas's summary trial, 18 October 1966. K150, Vol. 10, File: Trial, NASA.
[77] Constandinou, author interview.
[78] Dr Aubrey Zabow's testimony on Tsafendas's summary trial, 18 October 1966. K150, Vol. 10, File: Trial, NASA
[79] Constandinou, author interview.
[80] Peter Lambley, *The Psychology of Apartheid* (Athens: The University of Georgia Press, 1980), p. 273.
[81] Dr Harold Cooper's testimony on Tsafendas's summary trial, 17 October 1966, p. 20. K150, Vol. 10, File: Trial, NASA.
[82] Professor Adolf Johannes van Wyk's testimony on Tsafendas's summary trial, 19 October 1966. K150, Vol. 10, File: Trial, NASA.
[83] David Bloomberg author interview, 6 April 2014.
[84] Medical Bulettin of Dimitrio Tsafendas, 6 June 1955. K150, Vol. 4, File: 1, Sub file: 1/8, NASA.
[85] Dr Isaac Sakinofsky's testimony at Tsafendas's summary trial, 18 October 1966, p. 132. K150, Vol. 10, File: Trial, NASA.
[86] Bloomberg, *My Times*, 2007, pp. 80–1; *The Cape Argus*, 'Tsafendas: Question to Court', 6 October 1966: 1.
[87] *The Cape Argus*, 6 October 1966: 1, 'Tsafendas: Question to Court.'
[88] Dr Isaac Sakinofsky's testimony at Tsafendas's summary trial, 18 October 1966, p. 132. K150, Vol. 10, File: Trial, NASA.
[89] Dimitris Tsafendas in Liza Key's documentary *A Question of Madness*, 1997; Constandinou, author interview.
[90] Dr Hendrik Muller's testimony on Tsafendas's summary trial, 18 October 1966. K150, Vol. 10, File: Trial, NASA.

[91] Van Zyl, author interview.
[92] Constandinou, author interview.
[93] Dimitri Tsafenda in Liza Key's *A Question of Madness*, 1997.
[94] Cooper, *Under Devil's Peak*, 2016, pp. 106–07.
[95] Eintracht, author interview; Gavasiadis, author interview.
[96] Patrick O'Ryan in Liza Key's documentary *A Question of Madness*, 1997. This part is available in the rushes; Constandinou and Tsaftaridis, author interviews.
[97] Patrick O'Ryan in Liza Key's documentary *A Question of Madness*, 1997. This part is available in the rushes; Constandinou and Tsaftaridis, author interviews.
[98] James Johnston statement to the police, 6 October 1966. K150, Vol. 12, File: Verklarings Demitrio Tsafendas, NASA.
[99] Bloomberg, *My Times*, 2007, pp. 81–2.
[100] Jacobus Andreas Johannes Erasmus testimony on Tsafendas's summary trial, 20 October 1966. K150, Vol. 10, File: Trial, NASA.
[101] Adolph Johannes van Wyk testimony on Tsafendas's summary trial, 20 October 1966. K150, Vol. 10, File: Trial, NASA.
[102] Bloomberg, *My Times*, 2007, 88–9; Diemont, *Brushes with the Law*, 1995, pp. 132–3.
[103] Kahn, *The Seperated People*, 1968, pp. 148, 16

Chapter 12: A Verdict is Arranged

[1] K. Pnefma, author interview.
[2] Eintracht, author interview; Gavasiadis, author interview.
[3] K. Pnefma, author interview.
[4] Eintracht, author interview; Gavasiadis, author interview.
[5] Eintracht, author interview; K. Pnefma, author interview.
[6] Eintracht, author interview.
[7] Eintracht, author interview; Gavasiadis, author interview.
[8] David Bloomberg, *My Times: The Memoirs of David Bloomberg* (Simon's Town: Fernwood Press, 2007), pp. 83–4; D'Oliveira, *Vorster – The Man* (Johannesburg: Ernest Stanton Publishers, 1977), p. 208; Beaumont M. Shoeman, *Die Sluipmoord op Dr Verwoerd* (Pretoria: Strydpers Bpk, 1975), p. 4.
[9] Eintracht, author interview; K. Pnefma, author interview; K. Pnefma, author interview.
[10] 'Tsafendas mentally disordered defence contends as trial starts', *Pretoria News*, 17 October 1966: 1.
[11] Dr Harold Cooper's testimony on Tsafendas's summary trial, 17 October 1966. K150, Vol. 10, File: Trial, NASA.
[12] Bloomberg, *My Times*, 2007, pp. 88–9.
[13] Dr Harold Cooper's testimony on Tsafendas' summary trial, 17 October 1966. K150, Vol. 10, File: Trial, NASA.
[14] Professor Kirk Heilbrun author interview, 16 January 2017.
[15] Detailed information for a memorandum regarding Demetrio Tsafendas by Attorney-General W.M. van den Berg, 3 October 1966. K150, Vol. 1, File: VDSO 17/64, Subject: Beweerde Omkopery, NASA.
[16] Gilliam Clare Lieberman statement to the police, 6 October 1966. K150, Vol. 12, File: Verklarings, NASA.
[17] Ralph Lighton's statement to the police, 17 September 1966. K150, Vol. 12, File: Verklarings, NASA.

[18] 'Assassin – man with a chip on his shoulder', *Sunday Times*, 11 September 1966: 1, 8.
[19] Peter G. Bourne, *Fidel: A Biography of Fidel Castro* (New York: Dodd Mead, 1986), p. 101.
[20] Ashley and McAskill, 'History will be my judge', *The Guardian*, 1 March 2003; 'Bush: History will ultimately judge ... I am a contented man', CNN, 25 April 2013.
[21] Demetrio Tsafendas statement to Major Rossouw, 19 September 1966. K150, Vol. 1, File: Verklaring van Demetrio Tsafendas, NASA.
[22] Eintracht, author interview; K. Pnefma, author interview.
[23] 'She prayed in the dock for Tsafendas', *The Cape Argus*, 22 October 1966: the date of the publication of this article is uncertain, but it seems most likely to be 22 October 1966.
[24] K. Pnefma, author interview.
[25] K. Pnefma, author interview.
[26] Irene Michaletos author interview, 21 June 2016.
[27] Dr Hendrik Muller testimony on Tsafendas's summary trial, 18 October 1966. K150, Vol. 10, File: Trial, NASA.
[28] Dr Ralph Kossew testimony on Tsafendas's summary trial, 18 October 1966. K150, Vol. 10, File: Trial, NASA.
[29] House of Assembly, Question no. 17, 3 February 1967. K150, Vol. 12, File: Social Welfare and Pensions, NASA.
[30] Professor Alban Burke author interview, 4 April 2016.
[31] Van Zyl, author interview.
[32] Peter Daniels testimony on Tsafendas's summary trial, 18 October 1966. K150, Vol. 10, File: Trial, NASA.
[33] Helen Dorothy Daniels statement to the police, 15 September 1966. K150, Vol. 1, File: VDSO 17/64, NASA.
[34] Helen Dorothy Daniels statement to the police, 15 September 1966. K150, Vol. 1, File: VDSO 17/64, NASA.
[35] Marle Daniels's testimony on Tsafendas's summary trial, 18 October 1966. K150, Vol. 10, File: Trial, NASA.
[36] Patrick O'Ryan testimony at Tsafendas's summary trial, 18 October 1966. K150, Vol. 10, File: Trial, NASA.
[37] Patrick O'Ryan in Liza Key's documentary, *A Question of Madness*, 1997. This part is available in the rushes; Constandinou and Tsaftaridis, author interviews.
[38] Constandinou and Tsaftaridis, author interviews.
[39] Marle Daniels testimony on Tsafendas's summary trial, 18 October 1966. K150, Vol. 10, File: Trial, NASA.
[40] Owen Smorenberg's testimony on Tsafendas' summary trial, 18 October 1966. K150, Vol. 10, File: Trial, NASA.
[41] Owen Smorenburg's statement to the police, 6 October 1966. K150, Vol. 3, File: Leer W.D. 10/10/ 4102 oor Stafendas, NASA.
[42] Jacobus Johannes Bornman statement to the police, 3 October 1966. K150, Vol. 12, File: Verklarings, NASA.
[43] Father Hanno Probst's statement to the police, 9 September 1966. K150, Vol. 12, File: Verklarings, NASA. Father Hanno Probst's statement to the COE, 13 October 1966. K150, Vol. 12, File: Verklarings, NASA.
[44] Colonel van Wyk's report regarding the activities of Dimitrio Tsafendas in Mozambique and Rhodesia, 20 September 1966. K150, Vol. 3, Sub file: 1/5, NASA.

[45] Demetrio Tsafendas statement to Major Rossouw, 11 September 1966. K150, Vol. 1, File: Verklaring van Demetrio Tsafendas, NASA.
[46] 'Dr Verwoerd: Key witness found', *Daily Dispatch*, 12 October 1966: 1.
[47] 'Dr Verwoerd Inquiry: Important witness traced', *The Cape Times*, 12 October 1966: 1.
[48] Christoffel Johannes van Vuuren statement to the police, 13 September 1966. K150, Vol. 12, File: Verklarings, NASA.
[49] Johannes Jacobus Botha statement to the police, 15 September 1966. K150, Vol. 12, File: Verklarings, NASA.
[50] Jan Johannes Albertus Fourie statement to the police, 3 October 1966. K150, Vol. 12, File: Verklarings, NASA.
[51] Christoffel Johannes Van Vuuren statement to the police, 14 September 1966. K150, Vol. 12, File: Verklarings, NASA.
[52] Cleanthes Alachiotis author interview, 29 September 2010; Nikolas Kambouris author interview, 17 January 2014; Georgios Kantas author interview, 11 January 2012; Michalis Vasilakis author interview, 17 March 2016.
[53] Dr Isaac Sakinofsky's testimony at Tsafendas's summary trial, 18 October 1966, p. 132. K150, Vol. 10, File: Trial, NASA.
[54] PIDE report: Information: Demitrio Tsafendas or Demetrio Tsafandakis, 8 September 1966. PIDE/DGS, SC, CI (2) 6818, NT 7461, PNA. ANTT.
[55] Adriaan Nicolaas Pelzer, ed., *Verwoerd Speaks: Speeches 1948–66* (Johannesburg: APB Publishers, 1966), p. 494.
[56] Banovic, author interview; Constandinou, author interview.
[57] Dr Isaac Sakinofsky in correspondence with the author, 30 March 2016.
[58] Dr Bieser and Dr Schmidt-Janssen report regarding Dimitri Tsafendas. K150, Vol. 4, File: 1, Sub file: 1/8, NASA.
[59] Gillian Claire Liebermann's testimony on Tsafendas's summary trial, 18 October 1966. K150, Vol. 10, File: Trial, NASA.
[60] Gillian Clare Lieberman's statement to the police, 6 October 1966. K150, Vol. 12, File: Verklarings, NASA.
[61] Carel Sebastiaan van Heerden statement to the police, 5 October 1966. K150, Vol. 12, File: Verklarings, NASA.
[62] Reyner van Zyl's testimony on Tsafendas's summary trial, 18 October 1966. K150, Vol. 10, File: Trial, NASA.
[63] Peter Lambley, *The Psychology of Apartheid* (Athens: The University of Georgia Press, 1980), pp. 272–3.
[64] Ibid, pp. 272–3.
[65] Van Zyl, author interview.
[66] Lambley, *The Pyschology of Apartheid*, p. 239.
[67] Van Zyl, author interview.
[68] Professor Alban Burke author interview, 4 April 2016.
[69] Keith Terrence Bertram Martincich's statement to the police, 4 October 1966. K150, Vol. 12, File: Verklarings, NASA.
[70] Hulse statement to the police, 28 September 1966. K150, Vol. 12, File: Verklarings, NASA.
[71] Ian James Murdock Boswell statement to the police, 30 September 1966. K150, Vol. 1, File: VDSO 17/64, NASA; Pieter Geldenhuys statement to the police, 3 October 1966. K150, Vol. 1, Sub File: 1/1, Department of Labour, NASA.

[72] Owen Smorenberg statement to the police, 6 October 1966. K150, Vol. 3, File: Leer W.D. 10/10/ 4102 oor Stafendas, NASA.
[73] Albert Vercual statement to the COE, 25 October 1966. K150, Vol. 12, File: Verklarings, NASA.
[74] Jacobus Johannes Bornman statement to the police, 3 October 1966. K150, Vol. 12, File: Verklarings, NASA.
[75] 'He made a good impression', *Daily Dispatch*, 8 September 1966: 1; 'The assassin', *Daily Express*, 8 September 1966: 2; 'Tsafendas was so friendly ...', *Natal Witness*, 10 September 1966; 'Tsafendas trabalhou como soldador em Frankforte', *O Primeiro de Janeiro*, 8 September 1966; 'Tsafendas seen as "mystery man"', *The Daily News*, 8 September 1966: 17.
[76] Van Zyl, author interview.
[77] James Johnston's testimony on Tsafendas's summary trial, 18 October 1966. K150, Vol. 10, File: Trial, NASA.
[78] James Johnston statement to the police, 6 October 1966. K150, Vol. 12, File: Verklarings, NASA.
[79] Gideon Jacobus Cloete testimony at Tsafendas's summary trial, 19 October 1966. K150, Vol. 10, NASA.
[80] Gerald Shaw's testimony on Tsafendas's summary trial, 19 October 1966. K150, Vol. 10, File: Trial, NASA.
[81] Fred Feinauer statement to the police, 3 October 1966. K150, Vol. 12, File: Verklarings, NASA.
[82] Shaw, *Believe in Miracles*, p. 64.
[83] Felix Bernheim's testimony on Tsafendas's summary trial, 19 October 1966. K150, Vol. 10, File: Trial, NASA.
[84] It is incontestable that, during apartheid, some lawyers, judges and doctors 'conspired with the security police to keep torture and murder under wraps' (Sydney Kentridge quoted in George Bizos, *No One to Blame? A Personal Account of Inquests into Some Deaths in Detention under Apartheid* (Cape Town: David Philip Publishers, 1998), p. vii). Less well known is that some handwriting experts were collaborators, too. On 15 July 1976, Mapetla Mohapi, aged 25, a former official of the South African Students' Organisation and of the Black People's Convention, was arrested near East London. Three weeks later, Mohapi was dead. The police claimed he had committed suicide in his cell and had left a note of his intention. After comparing the note with other samples of Mohapi's hand, K. Landman, a South African handwriting expert, gave as his professional opinion that the note was without a doubt in Mohapi's handwriting. This opinion was disputed by two internationally renowned graphologists, who declared the note a forgery (For more about the case see: Shireen Motala, *Behind Closed Doors* (Johannesburg: South African Institute of Race Relations, 1987). By coincidence, Wilfrid Cooper, Tsafendas's advocate, was also the advocate for Mohapi (Motala, *Behind Closed Doors*, pp. 34–5).
[85] 'He wrote to the British Premier ...', *The Cape Argus*, 19 October 1966: 1–2.
[86] Dr Abraham Aubrey Zabow's testimony on Tsafendas's summary trial, 19 October 1966. K150, Vol. 10, File: Trial, NASA.
[87] Dr James William MacGregor's testimony on Tsafendas's summary trial, 19 October 1966. K150, Vol. 10, File: Trial, NASA.

[88] Dr James William MacGregor's testimony on Tsafendas's summary trial, 19 October 1966. K150, Vol. 10, File: Trial, NASA.
[89] Dr James William MacGregor's testimony at Tsafendas's summary trial, 19 October 1966. K150, Vol. 10, File: Trial, NASA.
[90] Jacobus Andreas Johannes Erasmus' testimony on Tsafendas' summary trial, 20 October 1966. K150, Vol. 10, File: Trial, NASA.
[91] Professor Adolf Johannes van Wyk's testimony on Tsafendas's summary trial, 19 October 1966. K150, Vol. 10, File: Trial, NASA.
[92] Bloomberg, *My Times*, 2007, p. 98.
[93] Cooper, *Under Devil's Peak*, 2016, p. 123.
[94] George Bizos author interview, 5 April 2016; Dugard, author interview.
[95] Dugard, author interview.
[96] Advocate George Bizos author interview, 6 April 2016.
[97] Bloomberg, *My Times*, 2007, p. 98.
[98] Judge Beyers' verdict on Tsafendas's summary trial, 20 October 1966. K150, Vol. 10, File: Trial, NASA.
[99] Owen Smorenberg's testimony on Tsafendas's summary trial, 18 October 1966. K150, Vol. 10, File: Trial, NASA.
[100] Patrick O'Ryan testimony on Tsafendas's summary trial, 18 October 1966. K150, Vol. 10, File: Trial, NASA.
[101] Patrick O'Ryan testimony on Tsafendas's summary trial, 18 October 1966. K150, Vol. 10, File: Trial, NASA
[102] Dr James William MacGregor's testimony on Tsafendas's summary trial, 19 October 1966. K150, Vol. 10, File: Trial, NASA.
[103] Israel Maisels, *A Life at Law: The Memoirs of I.A. Maisels, QC* (Johannesburg: Jonathan Ball Publishers, 1998), p. 105.
[104] Prof. Lamont's psychiatric report on David Beresford Pratt in *Regina vs. David Beresford Pratt*, 26 September 1960. *The State versus David Beresford Pratt*. 712-60, NASA; 'Judge rules Pratt is mentally disordered', *The Cape Argus*, 26 September 1960: 2.
[105] Prof. Lamont's report about David Pratt: Accused reaction to information gleaned from documents, friends, relatives and employees in *Regina vs. David Beresford Pratt*, 26 September 1960. *The State versus David Beresford Pratt*. 712-60, NASA; 'Judge rules Pratt is mentally disordered', *The Cape Argus*, 26 September 1960: 2.
[106] 'No trial for David Pratt', *Daily Dispatch*, 27 September 1960: 1; 'Pratt will not stand trial: mentally disordered', *The Cape Argus*, 26 September 1960: 1; 'Assailant of Dr Verwoerd found mentally unfit', *The New York Times*, 27 September 1960; 'Pratt is unfit to plead', *The Star*, 1 October 1960: 1.
[107] Eintracht, author interview; Gavasiadis, author interview.
[108] 'Tsafendas: I was a communist', *The Post*, 30 October 1966: 1.
[109] Detailed information for a Memorandum regarding Demetrio Tsafendas by Attorney-General W.M. van den Berg, 3 October 1966. K150, Vol. 1, File: VDSO 17/64, Subject: Beweerde Omkopery, NASA.
[110] 'Amazing liar says Utar', *Rand Daily Mail*, 18 October 1966.
[111] Benjamin Pogrund, *War of Words: Memoir of a South African Journalist* (New York: Seven Stories Press, 2000), p. 168.
[112] Maisels, *A Life at Law*, 1997, p. 319.
[113] Pogrund, *War of Words*, 2000, pp. 173–4.

[114] 'Perjury in State case alleged', *Rand Daily Mail,* 21 October 1966: 4–5; For more details about the case see Pogrund, *War on Words: Memoirs of a South African journalist,* 2000.
[115] Denis Goldberg author interview, 12 April 2016.
[116] Banovic, author interview; Father Efthimios Eleftheriadis author interview, 27 January 2011; Antony Michaletos, author interview; John Michaletos author interview, 16 April 2016; K. Pnefma, author interview; Alexandra Vaporidis author interview, 23 August 2014.
[117] 'Pelser asks public to accept verdict', *Pretoria News,* 20 October 1966.
[118] 'Mad killer can still stand trial if cured', *The Cape Times,* 21 October 1966: 1.
[119] 'Assassination probe begins', *Rand Daily Mail,* 5 October 1966: 1.
[120] Bishop, *An accidental good,* p. 7.
[121] Sitze, *The Impossible Machine,* p. 157
[122] Dugard, author interview.
[123] Report of the COE, chapter I, paragraph 4, December 1966. RP 16/1967. Pretoria.
[124] 'Killing inquiry to be secret', *Rand Daily Mail,* 22 September 1966; 'South Africa: Assassination Inquiry', *The Canberra Times,* 23 September 1966: 5.
[125] Dugard, author interview.
[126] Gerald Friedman & Jeremy J. Gauntlett, *Bar, Bench and Bullshifters. Cape Tales 1950–1990* (Cape Town: Siber Ink, 2013), pp. 8–9.
[127] Friedman & Gauntlett, *Bar, Bench and Bullshifters,* 2013, p. 73; Francois Marais quoted in Geni.com. Available at: www.geni.com/people/Jacques-Theodore-Van-Wyk/6000000008317660124, accessed on 15 June 2015.
[128] Dugard, author interview; Friedman & Gauntlett, *Bar, Bench and Bullshifters,* 2013, pp. 8–9.
[129] Dennis Davis & Michelle le Roux, *Precedent and Possibility: The (Ab)use of Law in South Africa* (Cape Town: Double Storey Books, 2009), p. 25.
[130] Marinus Wiechers, 'South West Africa: The decision of 16 July 1966 and its aftermath', *The Comparative and International Law Journal of Southern Africa,* Vol. 1, No. 3 (1968): 408.
[131] 'A eleicao do sucessor', *Le Courrier d'Afrique,* 9 September 1966: 2.
[132] Dugard, author interview.
[133] Davis and Le Roux, *Precedent and Possibility,* 2009, p. 18.
[134] Ellison Kahn, 'Constitutional and administrative law: The general election of 1966', *Annual Survey of South African Law,* (1966): 3.
[135] Report of the COE, chapter IID, paragraph 18, December 1966. RP 16/1967. Pretoria.
[136] Report of the COE, chapter III, December 1966. RP 16/1967. Pretoria.
[137] Major Daniel Jacobus Rossouw testimony to the COE, 14 October 1966. K150, Vol. 10, File: Uittreksels uit Getuienis, NASA.
[138] Report of the COE, chapter IIC, paragraph 86, December 1966. RP 16/1967. Pretoria.
[139] Report of the COE, chapter IIC, paragraph 58, December 1966. RP 16/1967. Pretoria.
[140] Report of the COE, chapter IIC, paragraph 65, December 1966. RP 16/1967. Pretoria.
[141] Wilhelmina Sophia de Vos statement to the police, 3 October 1966. K150, Vol. 12, File: Verklarings, NASA.
[142] Dugard, author interview.
[143] Bunting, *The Rise of the South African Reich,* p. 76; 'Premier's brother drops a bombshell', *Sunday Times,* 19 March 1967.

[144] 'Premier's brother drops a bombshell', *Sunday Times*.
[145] Jaap Marais, *Die Era van Verwoerd* (Pretoria: Aktuele Publikasies, 1992), p. 208.

Chapter 13: A State-President's Patient

[1] Dimitris Tsafendas in Liza Key's *A Question of Madness*, 1997; Constandinou, author interview.
[2] Dean Foster, 'On racism, virulent mythologies and fragile threads', in L. Nicholas, ed., *Psychology and Oppression: Critiques and Proposals* (Johannesburg: Skotsville Publishers, 1993), p. 68.
[3] Barbara Hutton, *Robben Island: Symbol of Resistance* (Johannesburg: Mayibuye Books, 1994), pp. 36–7.
[4] Fran Lisa Buntman, *Robben Island and Prisoner Resistance to Apartheid* (Cambridge: Cambridge University Press, 2003), pp. 3, 5, 19.
[5] Hutton, *Robben Island*, 1994, p. 50.
[6] Dominique Lapierre, *A Rainbow in the Night: The Tumultuous Birth of South Africa* (Cambridge: Da Capo Press, 2009), p. 124.
[7] Lapierre, *A Rainbow in the Night*, 2009, p. 124.
[8] Ahmed Kathrada, *Memoirs* (Cape Town: Zebra Press, 2004), pp. 228, 338.
[9] Noel Solani & Noor Nieftagodien, 'Political imprisonment and resistance in South Africa: The case of Robben Island, 1960–1970', in South African Democracy Education Trust, *The Road to Democracy in South Africa, Volume 1 (1960–1970)* (Cape Town: Zebra Press), pp. 391–7.
[10] Moses Dlamini, *Robben Island, Hell-Hole: Reminiscences of a Political Prisoner* (Nottingham: Spokesman, 1984), pp. 28–41; Solani and Nieftagodien, 'Political imprisonment and resistance in South Africa', 2004, pp. 391–7.
[11] Kathrada, *Memoirs*, 2004, p. 220.
[12] Lapierre, *A Rainbow in the Night*, 2009, p. 124.
[13] Kathrada, *Memoirs*, 2004, p. 221; Lionel Davis, author interview.
[14] Lionel Davis, author interview.
[15] Constandinou and Tsaftaridis, author interviews.
[16] Constandinou and Tsaftaridis, author interviews.
[17] Constandinou and Tsaftaridis, author interviews.
[18] Constandinou and Tsaftaridis, author interviews.
[19] Constandinou and Tsaftaridis, author interviews.
[20] Kathrada, 2004: 221.
[21] Tsafendas's transfer order from Robben Island to Central Prison, Pretoria. 3 February 1967. Demitrio Tsafendas Mediese Leer A125, NASA.
[22] For conditions of prisoners on death row and life in Pretoria Maximum Security Prison, the ironically so-called 'Beverly Hills', see Breyten Breytenbach's memoir *The True Confessions of an Albino Terrorist*; Jeremy Cronin's poem 'Death row' in his collection *Inside and Out*; Tim Jenkins's *Escape from Pretoria*; Hugh Lewin's memoir *Bandiet: Seven Years in a South African Prison*; and Raymond Suttner's memoir *Inside Apartheid's Prison*.
[23] Goldberg, a civil engineer, was one of apartheid's most dogged opponents. His Rivonia conviction earned him 20 years in prison, but he re-joined the fight, working with the ANC, immediately upon his release in 1985.

[24] The South African-born Kitson graduated in mechanical engineering from Howard College, Durban, then served as a sapper with the South African army in the Second World War, gaining expertise in bomb-making. Angered by the Sharpeville massacre, he became a bomb instructor for the ANC's military wing. Available at: www.theguardian.com/world/2011/jan/17/david-kitson-obituary, accessed on 8 July 2017.
[25] Herbstein, 'David Kitson obituary', *The Guardian*, 17 January 2011.
[26] Suttner, *Cutting through the Mountain*, p. 62.
[27] John de St Jorre, 'I was glad that cancer got me out of Vorster's jail', *The Observer*, 1 December 1968: 7.
[28] Albie Sachs, 'The violence of apartheid', An International Defence and Aid Pamphlet, Christian Action Publications, London, 1970, p. 1.
[29] Beresford, 'Dr Verwoerd's insane killer being brutalised on SA death row: Cell next to gallows for 71-year old prisoner', *The Guardian*, 9 June 1989: 12; Constandinou, author interview; Ledwaba, 'My ANC: We were put close to the gallows', *News 24*, 7 January 2012; Thornycroft and Lee, 'Amnesty for Tsafendas?', *Sunday Tribune*, 15 May 1994.
[30] Thornycroft and Lee 'Amnesty for Tsafendas?', *Sunday Tribune*, 15 May 1994.
[31] Ledwaba, 'My ANC: 'We were put close to the gallows', *News 24*, 7 January 2012.
[32] de St Jorre, 'I was glad that cancer got me out of Vorster's jail', *The Observer*, 1 December 1968: 7.
[33] Dimitri Tsafendas in Liza Key's *A Question of Madness*, 1997.
[34] Tsafendas did not forget the warder's name, but the witnesses to whom he mentioned it could not remember it.
[35] Dimitris Tsafendas in *A Question of Madness*, 1997; van Woerden, *A Mouthful of Glass*, p. 133.
[36] Constandinou, author interview.
[37] Alex Moumbaris author interview, 7 March 2010; 'Horror in black and white', *The Observer*, 1 August 1976: 17.
[38] Breytan Breytenbach, *The True Confessions of an Albino Terrorist* (London and Boston: Faber and Faber, 1985), p. 145.
[39] 'World's first heart transplant', *The Cape Times*, 4 December 1967: 1.
[40] David Bloomberg letter to Brigadier Coetzee, 26 January 1968. Correctional Service. Demitrio Tsafendas, File no: 80/0043, A123, Vol. 1, NASA.
[41] David Bloomberg in Liza Key's *A Question of Madness*, 1997.
[42] David Bloomberg, *My Times: The Memoirs of David Bloomberg* (Simon's Town: Fernwood Press, 2007), p. 102.
[43] David Bloomberg letter to Brigadier Coetzee, 26 January 1968. Correctional Service. Demitrio Tsafendas, File no: 80/0043, A123, Vol. 1, NASA.
[44] de St Jorre, 'I was glad that cancer got me out of Vorster's jail', *The Observer*, 1 December 1968: 7.
[45] This was conveyed to A. Moumbaris by these three witnesses. A. Moumbaris author interview, 27 January 2018.
[46] Lambley, *The Psychology of Apartheid*, p. 273.
[47] Lambley, *The Psychology of Apartheid*, pp. 272–3.
[48] Professor Barend D. van Niekerk was a prominent South African law professor, passionate human rights activist and outspoken critic of apartheid.

[49] Member and strong supporter of the National Party, he was one of the judges in the Treason Trial but had to withdraw when the defence argued there was a conflict of interest and he could be prejudiced because he had represented the government in 1954. He was a lawyer for the police when Harold Wolpe sought a court interdict to eject the police from a meeting of the Congress of the People (Mandela, *Long Walk to Freedom*, pp. 29–30). He was later the judge in John Harris's trial, who found Harris guilty and the prisoner was hanged (David Beresford, *Truth is a Strange Fruit. A Personal Journey Through the Apartheid War* (Johannesburg: Jacana Media, 2010), pp. 326–41).
[50] Letter to Helen Suzman from Professor Barend D. van Niekerk of Wits referring to the 'cruellest' treatment being meted out to Dimitri Tsafendas in jail, 9 April 1971. Helen Suzman Papers 1944–2009. Mb2.10.1.5. University of the Witwatersrand.
[51] Letter to Helen Suzman from A.M. Towert informing her that Tsafendas is held in the 'execution block' at Central Gaol, Pretoria, 16 May 1971. Helen Suzman Papers 1944–2009. Mb2.10.1.5. University of the Witwatersrand.
[52] Letter from Helen Suzman to Prof. B.D. van Niekerk of Wits who had written to her saying that 'Tsafendas is being subjected to the cruellest possible treatment', 5 May 1971. Helen Suzman Papers 1944–2009. Mb2.10.1.6. University of the Witwatersrand.
[53] A. Moumbaris, author interview.
[54] *Ibid.*
[55] *Ibid.*
[56] Breyten Breytenbach in *A Question of Madness*, 1997.
[57] Nankin, author interview.
[58] Marwick, author interview.
[59] *The Spectator*, 'Tsafendas was the thorn in Verwoerd's side', 14 February 1976: 32.
[60] Ned Chailet, 'Tsafendas', *The Times* (London), 19 February 1976: 13.
[61] B.A. Young, 'Tsafendas: Almost free', *The Financial Times*, 21 February 1976: 10.
[62] Buzenzer, author interview.
[63] Lambley, *The Psychology of Apartheid*, 1980, p. 241; Dr Peter Lambley author interview, 28 May 2015.
[64] Lambley, *The Psychology of Apartheid*, pp. 240–2.
[65] *Ibid.*
[66] Lambley, author interview.
[67] John Stuart Kane-Berman, *Soweto: Black Revolt, White Reaction* (Cape Town: Ravan Press, 1978).
[68] Dugard, author interview.
[69] Chris Martin, 25 October 2013. Available at: http://www.christianmartin.co.za/index.php?option=com_content&view=article&id=93:request-to-declare-gravesites-of-hf-DrVerwoerd-and-dimitri-tsafendas-as-historically-heritage-sites&catid=36:articles&Itemid=62, accessed on 12 July 2015; Michalis Michelis's author interview, 12 December 2015; A. Moumbaris, author interview.
[70] Elisabé Brink, Sue Krige, Steve Lebelo, Gandhi Malungane & Dumisani Ntshangase, *Soweto: 16 June 1976* (Cape Town: Kwela Books, 2010), p. 9; David Harrison, *The White Tribe of Africa: South Africa in Perspective* (Berkley and Los Angeles: University of California Press, 1981), 143; Kane-Berman, *Soweto*, pp. 27–8; Helena Pohlandt-McCormick, "I Saw a Nightmare ...: Violence and the Construction of Memory (Soweto, June 16, 1976)." *History and Theory*, Vol. 39, No. 4, Theme Issue 39: "Not Telling": Secrecy, Lies, and History (Dec., 2000), pp.25–8.

[71] Ian Mather, 'Horror in black and white', *The Observer*, 1 August 1976: 17.
[72] *The Observer*, 'South Africa's evasions', 11 November 1976.
[73] Mather, 'Horror in black and white'.
[74] Peta Thorneycroft and Peta Lee, 'Amnesty for Tsafendas?' *Sunday Tribune*, 15 May 1994.
[75] G. Bizos, author interview.
[76] Bloomberg, *My Times*, p. 122.
[77] *The Guardian*, 'Pretoria troops in rape of Namibia', 30 August 1976; *The Guardian*, 'International inquiry demanded into Namibia atrocities', 31 August 1976: 2.
[78] *The Observer*, 'South Africa's evasions'.
[79] *The Observer*, 'Pretoria propaganda', 19 December 1976: 8.
[80] *The Observer*, 'South Africa's evasions'.
[81] Bloomberg, *My Times*, pp. 158–61.
[82] The first, in 1974, was when he gave his enthusiastic support to a proposal by Hilgard Muller, South Africa's Foreign Minister, that Cape Town be twinned with Nice, on the French Riviera. Bloomberg later claimed opportunistically that he saw the twinning with Nice as possibly providing 'a basis for a clandestine, second-tier diplomatic relationship in the event of formal ties between the two countries being suspended' (Bloomberg, *My Times*, 2007, pp. 177). Although himself Jewish, Bloomberg did not appear concerned that his opposite number in Nice, the fascist and now disgraced Mayor Jacques Medecin, was a fanatical anti-Semite and a Holocaust denier. Despite opposition, the twinning arrangement came into effect on 6 July 1974, bringing criticism upon South Africa and Bloomberg from politicians, trade union officials and civil rights workers around the world (Bloomberg, *My Times*, 2007, pp. 167–8; 'Protest in Nice at twinning with Cape Town', *The Times* (London), 8 July 1974: 4).
The second controversy came a few months later when Bloomberg was accused by the Western press and the British government of using diplomatic sleight of hand to promote the apartheid government at the expense of Britain. A flotilla of the British Royal Navy anchored in Table Bay on 16 October 1974 and Bloomberg invited the fleet commander, Vice-Admiral Henry Leach, and his senior officers to lunch at City Hall. In an impromptu speech, Mayor Bloomberg referred to the many links between the city and Britain's fighting ships (Bloomberg, *My Times*, 2007, p. 199). The British government was not pleased and Foreign Secretary James Callaghan accused Bloomberg of 'manipulating the visit' and giving it 'a badge of respectability'. He said the British government had 'nothing in common with the policies of apartheid and racialism, which are repugnant to us' and he ordered all British ships that needed to call at Cape Town to refuse hospitality in future. The London *Times* said Bloomberg and the South African government had 'turned the operation into a propaganda exercise, saying that the visit is a demonstration of Britain's good will towards the Republic' ('Callaghan apology in Navy visit dispute', *The Times* (London), 25 October 1974: 1). Bloomberg responded that the city council was 'not politically structured or motivated' and his invitation 'was not a clandestine attempt to influence foreign relations'. He described the affair, which received wide international press coverage, as 'an absurd incident' (Bloomberg, *My Times*, 2007, pp. 200).
[83] Bloomberg, *My Times*, p. 102.
[84] *The Cape Argus*, 'Tsafendas is no broken man – Bloomberg', 2 October 1976: 1.
[85] Bloomberg, *My Times*, p. 102.

[86] *The Cape Argus*, 'Tsafendas is no broken man – Bloomberg'.
[87] David Bloomberg in *A Question of Madness*, 1997. The part is available in the rushes.
[88] David Bloomberg letter to unnamed prison official, 7 October 1976. Correctional Service. Demitrio Tsafendas, File no: 80/0043, A123, Vol. 1, NASA.
[89] In the late 1980s, Bloomberg found himself in serious trouble when he was accused, along with casino magnate Sol Kerzner, of bribery, corruption, fraud and perjury. The charges concerned efforts by Bloomberg and Kerzner to secure a gambling monopoly in Transkei. Bloomberg subsequently left South Africa, lived for several years in Britain, then moved permanently to Switzerland. Seeking to reinvent himself in a 2007 memoir, *My Times*, he penned a self-portrait of a liberal-minded politician who valiantly fought the evils of apartheid. To this day, Bloomberg's portrait hangs in the Town Hall of Cape Town.
[90] Gordon Winter in *A Question of Madness*, 1997; Winter, *Inside BOSS*, pp. 477–9.
[91] James Sanders, *Apartheid's Friends: The Rise and Fall of South Africa's Secret Service* (London: John Murray, 2006), p. 99.
[92] I cannot state exactly how Tsafendas knew about *The Citizen*, the government's new mouthpiece, since he was being held incommunicado, but it is possible that he learnt about *The Observer* article from the warders. When advised that a journalist was to visit him, an astute man like Tsafendas would quickly put two and two together and conclude that the newsman had been sent to knock down the English newspaper's story. The fact that Bloomberg had earlier visited him about the same subject would have strengthened his belief that such was Winter's real mission.
[93] Gordon Winter in *A Question of Madness*, 1997; Winter, *Inside BOSS*, pp. 477–9.
[94] Gordon Winter, 'Why I killed Verwoerd', *The Citizen*, 20 October 1976: 1.
[95] Winter, 'Tsafendas was ineffective Red – Van den Bergh', *The Citizen*, 26 October 1976.
[96] Gordon Winter's correspondence with David Beresford, 8 September 1998. Liza Key's personal collection.
[97] Gordon Winter in *A Question of Madness*, 1997; Winter, *Inside BOSS*, pp. 477–9.
[98] Gordon Winter in *A Question of Madness*, 1997; Winter, *Inside BOSS*, pp. 476–9; Beresford, author interview and Winter interview with Dr James Sanders on behalf of the author.
[99] *The Observer*, 'Pretoria propaganda', 19 December 1976: 8.
[100] International Defence and Aid Fund, *BOSS: The First Five Years*, p. 15.
[101] Gavin Cawthra, *Brutal Force: The Apartheid War Machine* (London: International Defence and Aid Fund for Southern Africa, 1986), p. 38.
[102] Lindsay H. Smith, *Anatomy of Apartheid* (Germiston: Khanya Publishers, 1979), p. 43; *The Globe and Mail*, 'Secret life of Pretoria', 6 April 1979: 6.
[103] James Sanders, *South Africa and the International Media, 1972–1979: A Struggle for Representation* (New York: Routledge, 1999), p. 62.
[104] John F. Burns, 'Pretoria scandal testimony reveals talk of murder', *The New York Times*, 18 May 1980: 3; William A. Hachten & Anthony C. Giffard, *The Press and Apartheid: Repression and Propaganda in South Africa* (Madison, Wisconsin: The University of Wisconsin Press, 1984), pp. 243–4.
[105] Hachten & Giffard, *The Press and Apartheid*, pp. 250–1, 275.
[106] John F. Burns, 'Acid general is key to Pretoria scandal', *The New York Times*, 1 April 1979: 10; *The Globe and Mail*, 'Secret life of Pretoria'.
[107] *The Globe and Mail*, 'Secret life of Pretoria'.

[108] Joseph B. Treaster, 'John Vorster, former South African Prime Minister, dies at 67', *The New York Times*, 11 September 1983.
[109] Nicholas Ashford, 'The revelations of Dr Rhoodie', *The Spectator*, 17 March 1979: 8.
[110] *The New York Times*, 'South African General signs petition for his own prosecution', 4 February 1979: 5.
[111] Benjamin Pogrund, *How Can Man Die Better … Sobukwe and Apartheid* (London: Peter Halban, 1990), p. 17.
[112] Roger Omond, 'South Africans demand POW status', *The Guardian*, 22 January 1980: 7.
[113] A. Moumbaris, author interview.
[114] It is not clear what the rules were regarding prison visits for Tsafendas, but the issue seems redundant in retrospect since nobody ever visited him. Requests by Desmond Blow, David Beresford and other journalists for the British newspapers, *The Guardian* and *The Observer*, through the 1960s, 1970s, 1980s and 1990s were routinely refused. Gordon Winter was the only journalist who was ever allowed to visit Tsafendas in prison.
[115] Constandinou, author interview.
[116] *Ibid.*
[117] *Ibid.*
[118] *Ibid.*
[119] *Ibid.*
[120] *Ibid.*
[121] *Ibid.*
[122] Christie, author interview.
[123] Constandinou, author interview.
[124] *Ibid.*
[125] Treaster, 'John Vorster, former South African Prime Minister, dies at 67'.
[126] It is worth mentioning here that apartheid South Africa was not the only country which considered homosexuality to be a mental disease which could be cured. The American Psychiatric Association listed homosexuality as a psychiatric condition and young men troubled about their sexuality were often advised to consult a psychiatrist or a psychologist. It was only in the early 1970s that such attitudes began to change. As late as 1979, known gay foreigners arriving in the United States were required to submit to psychiatric examinations by the Public Health Service on the basis that they were the likely possessors of 'psychopathic personalities' (Charalampos Dousemetzis, 'The presidency of Jimmy Carter and the emerging politics of gay rights and evangelical religion', PhD thesis, Durham University, 2018). As for South Africa, Dr Levin's Aversion project, which started in 1971, continued until the late 1980s (Robert Kaplan, 'The Aversion Project: Psychiatric abuses in the South African Defence Force during the apartheid era', *South African Medical Journal*, Vol. 91, No. 3 (2001): 216–7.
[127] Kaplan, 'The Aversion Project', 216–7.
[128] John Carlin, 'Empires of delusions', *The Independent*, 27 November 1994.
[129] Michelis, 'Δημήτρης Τσαφέντας: Έκανα το Καθήκον Μου … Εσείς;'
[130] Matthew Krouse, 'The key to Tsafendas', *Mail & Guardian*, 25 June 1999.
[131] Constandinou, author interview.
[132] *Ibid.*
[133] David Beresford, 'Dr Verwoerd's insane killer "being brutalised" on SA Death Row: Cell next to gallows for 71-year-old prisoner', *The Guardian*, 9 June 1989: 12.
[134] Thornycroft and Lee, 'Amnesty for Tsafendas?'

135 Michalis Visvinis, author interview.
136 Costa Gazidis and Visvinis, author interviews.
137 Costa and Janet Gazidis, author interviews.
138 K. Pnefma, author interview.
139 Constandinou, author interview.
140 *The Times* (London), 'Assassin ill', 10 April 1989: 10.
141 Constandinou and Tsaftaridis, author interviews.
142 Jody Kollapen memorandum regarding Dimitrio Tsafendas. 24 November 1994. Tsafendas's file in the Lawyers for Human Rights collection (AL3183). South African History Archive (hereafter cited as SAHA); Constandinou, author interview.

Chapter 14: Justifying the Deed

1 Visvinis, author interview.
2 Judge Jody Kollapen author interview, 16 April 2015.
3 Dimitris Skoularikis author interview, 26 April 2015.
4 Constandinou, author interview.
5 Jody Kollapen, author interview.
6 *Ibid.*
7 *Ibid.*
8 *Ibid.*
9 Cerebral atrophy is shrinkage of the brain which occurs as part of the ageing process, often causing short-term memory loss.
10 Inigo Gilmore, 'Verwoerd's killer is moved to a mental unit', *The Times* (London), 1 July 1994: 13.
11 Thornycroft and Lee, 'Amnesty for Tsafendas?'
12 Constandinou, author interview.
13 *Ibid.*
14 *Ibid.*
15 *Ibid.*
16 *Ibid.*
17 Spiros Randos, author interview.
18 Tsaftaridis, author interview.
19 Constandinou and Tsaftaridis, author interviews.
20 *Ibid.*
21 *Ibid.*
22 *Ibid.*
23 Tsaftaridis, author interview.
24 Tsaftaridis, author interview.
25 Constandinou, author interview.
26 Constandinou and Tsaftaridis, author interviews.
27 *Ibid.*
28 *Ibid.*
29 *Ibid.*
30 *Ibid.*
31 *Ibid.*
32 *Ibid.*
33 *Ibid.*

[34] *Ibid.*
[35] *Ibid.*
[36] *Ibid.*
[37] Constandinou, author interview.
[38] Tsaftaridis, author interview.
[39] Constandinou and Tsaftaridis, author interviews.
[40] *Ibid.*
[41] *Ibid.*
[42] 'Do a good thing and then throw it into the sea' is an old Greek adage.
[43] Constandinou and Tsaftaridis, author interviews.
[44] *Ibid.*
[45] *Ibid.*
[46] Constandinou, author interview.
[47] Brendan Boyle, 'Verwoerd's bust removed from parliament', *Reuters*, 17 June 1994.
[48] A.J. Christopher, *The Atlas of Apartheid* (London and New York: Routledge, 1994), p. 232; Dubow, *Apartheid 1948–1994*, p. 3; Jacqueline Audrey Kalley, *Apartheid in South African Libraries: The Transvaal Experience* (Lanham: The Scarecrow Press, Inc, 2000) p. 113; David M. Matsinhe, *Apartheid Vertigo: The Rise in Discrimination against Africans in South Africa* (Farnham: Ashgate Publishing Ltd, 2013), p. 181; Dickson A. Mungazi, *The Tragedy of Apartheid in South Africa: Hendrik F. Verwoerd and Dimitri Tsafendas Meet at the Crossroads* (Kearney: Morris Publishing, 2006), p. 114; Leslie Witz, *Apartheid's Festival: Contesting South Africa's National Past* (Bloomington, Ind: Indiana University Press, 2003), p. 244.
[49] Human & Rousseau, *They Shaped our Century: The Most Influential South Africans of the Twentieth Century* (Human & Rousseau, 1999).
[50] Uriel Abulof, *The Mortality and Morality of Nations* (New York: Cambridge University Press, 2015), p. 280.
[51] Brian Tangang Fobi, 'The engineers of history: Hendrik Verwoerd, George Wallace, and the power of historical memory' (PhD thesis, Yale University, 2014), pp. 11–14.
[52] Kollapen, author interview.
[53] Kathrada and A. Moumbaris, author interviews.
[54] *Agence France-Presse*, 'State to release former premier's assassin', 30 June 1994; Gilmore, 'Verwoerd's killer is moved to mental unit'.7
[55] Constandinou, author interview.
[56] Tsafendas's order for removal, 5 July 1994. Demitrio Tsafendas Mediese Leer A125, NASA.
[57] van Woerden, *A Mouthful of Glass*, pp. 125–6; *The Times* (London), 'Times 2 Books', 30 August 2000.
[58] Constandinou, author interview.
[59] Letter of Jody Kollapen of Lawyers for Human Rights to the Minister of Health, 6 October 1994. Tsafendas's file in the Lawyers for Human Rights collection (AL3183). SAHA.
[60] Memorandum of Jody Kollapen of Lawyers for Human Rights, 24 November 1994. Tsafendas's file in the Lawyers for Human Rights collection (AL3183). SAHA.
[61] Kollapen, author interview.
[62] Kollapen and K. Pnefma, author interviews.
[63] Kollapen and Visvinis, author interviews.

[64] Constandinou and John Michaletos, author interviews.
[65] Papageorgiou and Visvinis, author interviews.
[66] Memorandum of Jody Kollapen of Lawyers for Human Rights, 24 November 1994. Tsafendas's file in the Lawyers for Human Rights collection (AL3183). SAHA.
[67] Kollapen, author interview.
[68] Letter of Jody Kollapen of Lawyers for Human Rights to Archbishop Desmond Tutu, 15 December 1994. Tsafendas's file in the Lawyers for Human Rights collection (AL3183). SAHA.
[69] Constandinou, author interview.
[70] Van Woerden, *A Mouthful of Glass*, p. 134.
[71] Constandinou, author interview.
[72] John Michaletos, author interview.
[73] Van Woerden, *A Mouthful of Glass*, p. 137.
[74] Constandinou and Selepe, author interviews.
[75] Constandinou, John Michaletos and Selepe, author interviews.
[76] Constandinou, author interview.
[77] Van Woerden, *A Mouthful of Glass*, p. 125; Constandinou, author interview.
[78] Beresford and Liza Key, author interviews.
[79] Key, author interview.
[80] Dimitris Tsafendas in *A Question of Madness*, 1997; Beresford and Key, author interviews.
[81] Beresford and Key, author interviews.
[82] Key, author interview.
[83] *Ibid.*
[84] Report to the ANC about our visit to Dimitri Tsafendas by A. Moumbaris, 15 March 1996. A. Moumbaris 's personal collection; A. Moumbaris, author interview.
[85] *Ibid.*
[86] Report to the ANC about our visit to Dimitri Tsafendas by A. Moumbaris, 15 March 1996. A. Moumbaris 's personal collection.
[87] *Ibid.*
[88] Report to the ANC about our visit to Dimitri Tsafendas by A. Moumbaris, 15 March 1996. A. Moumbaris 's personal collection; Alexander and Marie-Jose Moumbaris, author interviews.
[89] Report to the ANC about our visit to Dimitri Tsafendas by A. Moumbaris, 15 March 1996. A. Moumbaris 's personal collection.
[90] A. Moumbaris, author interview.
[91] Kyriakakis, author interview.
[92] *Ibid.*
[93] *Ibid.*
[94] Constandinou, author interview.
[95] *The Times* (London), 'Times 2 Books'.
[96] Van Woerden, *A Mouthful of Glass*, pp. 134–5.
[97] Van Woerden, *A Mouthful of Glass*, pp. 126–7, 141.
[98] Van Woerden, *A Mouthful of Glass*, pp. 137–40.
[99] Van Woerden, *A Mouthful of Glass*, pp. 147–50.
[100] Van Woerden, *A Mouthful of Glass*, pp. 150–1.

[101] Bronwyn Harris, 'Arranging prejudice: Exploring hate crime in post-apartheid South Africa', Race and Citizenship in Transition Series, Centre for the Study of Violence and Reconciliation (SWOP), University of the Witwatersrand, 2004, p. 28.
[102] Constandinou and Tsaftaridis, author interviews.
[103] *Ibid.*
[104] In 1969, Wiesenthal wrote *The Sunflower: On the Possibilities and Limits of Forgiveness,* where he described an experience he faced in the Lemberg concentration camp in 1943. Wiesenthal was asked by a dying Nazi soldier for forgiveness for burning down a house containing 300 Jews, most of whom he shot dead as they tried to flee from the blazing building. Wiesenthal remained silent as he listened to the account of this atrocity, then left the room without any words of forgiveness. Subsequently, Wiesenthal asks the reader what he would have done. His argument was that a man cannot forgive someone who has committed a crime against another person and that only the victim has the right to forgive.
[105] Kollapen, author interview.
[106] Constandinou and Tsaftaridis, author interviews.
[107] The request for Tsafendas's case to be re-investigated was one strand in a wide-ranging submission which Govender had put before the TRC concerning the conduct of the judiciary during the apartheid years. Entitled 'Injustice under Apartheid Judiciary,' it asked the Commission to scrutinise decisions taken by the judiciary under the apartheid regime and requested that all judges who were active before 1994 be held accountable for their conduct. The submission was entirely reasonable in that it highlighted a well-known fact, that the South African legal system had allowed itself to be co-opted by apartheid's repressive rulers. The TRC itself had already exposed inaccuracies and bias in some death inquests, including Steve Biko's, as well as flaws in the conduct of various Commissions of Inquiry, such as those into Sharpeville and Soweto.
[108] Liza Key letter to Dr Meryl Vorster, 14 October 1997. Personal collection of Liza Key.
[109] Notable in Justice Michael Corbett's career were two rulings he made which supported the apartheid government while contradicting international law. In 1991, he acted as co-chairman of the Convention for a Democratic South Africa (CODESA), which conducted negotiations between the apartheid government and leading anti-apartheid groups, including the ANC and the South African Communist Party (David Dyzenhaus, *Hard Cases in Wicked Legal Systems: Pathologies of Legality* (Oxford: Oxford University Press, 2010), p. 40). His term as chief justice was due to expire in 1993, but he stayed on for another year at the government's request, then Nelson Mandela asked him to remain in situ up to the end of 1996 (Ellison Kahn, 'Notes and comments: Retirement of Mr Justice Michael MacGregor Corbett, Chief Justice of the Republic of South Africa', *South African Law Journal,* Vol. 114 (1997): 209). The two decisions which cast opprobrium upon him in later years were his support for Appellate Division rulings concerning the provision of counsel for indigent accused and a state's responsibility for its agents. In the first, the court rejected the right to counsel of accused people who held no assets. This stood in flagrant opposition to the widely accepted view by human rights groups worldwide that poor people were entitled to have lawyers argue their case. The second issue focused on the abduction of people from Swaziland by South African security forces, a common practice at the time. Anti-apartheid activists were kidnapped and brought back to South Africa, where they were detained and tortured. Judge Corbett gave his formal support to a ruling that the state bore no responsibility for the

unauthorised acts of its agents, a position which ran counter to international law (John Dugard, 'The South African judiciary and international law in the apartheid era', *South African Journal on Human Rights*, Vol. 14 (1998): 118–20).
[110] Dyzenhaus, *Hard Cases in Wicked Legal Systems*, pp. 37–44.
[111] Key, author interview.
[112] *Ibid.*
[113] Van Woerden, *A Mouthful of Glass*, p. 158.
[114] Key, author interview.
[115] David Beresford, 'Inside Story: The madness that destroyed apartheid,' *The Guardian*, 6 November 1997: 6-7.
[116] David Beresford, 'Demitri Tsafendas: Long-jailed assassin of South African premier', *The Guardian*, 11 October 1999: 18.
[117] Liza Key's submission to the TRC. Personal Collection of Liza Key.
[118] *Ibid.*
[119] Key, author interview.
[120] Van Woerden, *A Mouthful of Glass*, p. 167.
[121] Van Woerden, *A Mouthful of Glass*, p. 144.
[122] Constandinou and John Michaletos, author interviews.
[123] Tsaftaridis, author interview.
[124] *Ibid.*
[125] *Ibid.*
[126] *Ibid.*
[127] *Ibid.*
[128] *Ibid.*
[129] *Ibid.*
[130] C. Gazidis and Key, author interviews.

Chapter 15: An Unmarked Grave

[1] Van Woerden, *A Mouthful of Glass*, pp. 152–3; Visvinis, author interview.
[2] Visvinis, author interview.
[3] *Ibid.*
[4] Constandinou and Demetrios Vergitsis, author interviews.
[5] Constandinou, author interview.
[6] K. Pnefma, author interview.
[7] Visvinis, author interview.
[8] Vergitsis, author interview.
[9] *Ibid.*
[10] *Ibid.*
[11] *Ibid.*
[12] *Ibid.*
[13] *Ibid.*
[14] Constandinou, author interview.
[15] Van Woerden, *A Mouthful of Glass*, pp. 154–5.
[16] Akis Apergis, author interview.
[17] Vergitsis, author interview.
[18] Van Woerden, *A Mouthful of Glass*, p. 154.
[19] Constandinou, author interview.

[20] Van Woerden, *A Mouthful of Glass*, p. 155.
[21] Apergis and Vergitsis, author interviews.
[22] John Matshikiza, 'Place in heaven for unsung hero', *Mail & Guardian*, 15–21 October, 1999: 4.
[23] Constandinou and Tsaftaridis, author interviews.
[24] *Ibid.*
[25] *Ibid.*
[26] *Ibid.*
[27] *Ibid.*
[28] Van Woerden, *A Mouthful of Glass*, pp. 157–9; Key, author interview.
[29] Constandinou, author interview.
[30] K. Pnefma, author interview.
[31] Constandinou and Tsaftaridis, author interviews.
[32] Tsaftaridis, author interview.
[33] Constandinou, Dimelas, Tsaftaridis and Visvinis, author interviews.
[34] *The Cape Times*, 'South Africans must "honour" Dr Verwoerd, Tsafendas', 22 October 2013; *News24*, 'Honour Verwoerd, Tsafendas – ANC MPL', 21 October 2013. Available at: https://www.news24.com/SouthAfrica/News/Honour-Verwoerd-Tsafendas-ANC-MPL-20131021, accessed on May 18 2014.
[35] David Bloomberg, 'I am astonished that the Eastern Cape ANC MPL, Christian Martins, has advanced ...' *The Cape Times*, 24 October 2013: 12.
[36] David Bloomberg in *A Question of Madness*, 1997.
[37] Michelas Dimelas, 'Ο πρώτος ναός στη μνήμη του Ελληνα «φονιά του απαρτχάιντ»' [The first church in memory of the Greek 'assassin of apartheid'], *Times of Change*, 2015. Available at: http://www.thetoc.gr/koinwnia/article/o-prwtos-naos-sti-mnimi-tou-ellina-fonia-tou-apartxaint, accessed on 21 October 2017; Tsaftaridis author interview.
[38] Press release of the Orthodox Metropolis of Mozambique, 18 October 2015; Tsaftaridis, author interview.
[39] Tsaftaridis, author interview.
[40] Serafim Kykkotis, Αναφορές στο Νομπελίστα Νέλσον Μαντέλα (Athens: Papasotiriou, 2013), p. 47.

Epilogue

[1] G. Bizos, author interview.
[2] *Ibid.*
[3] *Ibid.*
[4] Dugard, author interview.
[5] *Ibid.*
[6] Zak Yacoob, author interview.
[7] Solly Mapaila, author interview.
[8] Christie, author interview.
[9] Denis Goldberg, author interview.
[10] Monica Laganparsad, 'Verwoerd's killer a freedom fighter?' *Sunday Times*, 11 September 2016: 7.
[11] *Ibid.*
[12] Kathrada, author interview.

[13] Kollapen, author interview.
[14] Alexander Moumbaris, 'Dimitri Tsafendas: Remembering A Revolutionary,' *The Talking Drum*, www.Talkingdrum.com. Available at: https://archive.is/pYjSu#selection-205.0-205.110.
[15] A. Moumbaris, author interview.
[16] Helen Suzman in *A Question of Madness*, 1997.
[17] Johannes Joachim Jurgens Scholtz, *Dr Hendrik Frensch Verwoerd* (Johannesburg: Perskor-uitgewery, 1974), p. 153; *TIME*, 'South Africa: Death to the architect'; Vatcher, *White Laager*, p. 110.
[18] *The New York Times*, 'Symbol of apartheid: Hendrik Frensch Verwoerd', 17 March 1961; *The New York Times*, 'Dr. Verwoerd: Relentless advocate of apartheid', 7 September 1966: 16.
[19] Pelzer, *Verwoerd Speaks*, p. 92; *TIME*, 'South Africa: White man's God', 29 July 1957: 23
[20] Pelzer, *Verwoerd Speaks*, pp. 321, 494, 596.
[21] Pelzer, *Verwoerd Speaks*, p. 426.
[22] Botha, *Verwoerd is Dead*, p. 63.
[23] Bunting, *The Rise of the South African Reich*, p. 260; Dubow, *Apartheid 1948–1994*, pp. 55–6; Merle Lipton, *Capitalism and Apartheid: South Africa, 1910–1984* (Aldershot: Gower Publishing/ Maurice Temple Smith, 1985), p. 24; O'Meara, *Forty Lost Years*, p. 73; Schadeberg, *Nelson Mandela and the Rise of the ANC*, p. 81; Pelzer, *Verwoerd Speaks*, p. 83.
[24] Scholtz, *Dr Hendrik Frensch Verwoerd*, p. 171.
[25] Pelzer, *Verwoerd Speaks*, p. 161; *The Canberra Times*, 'Dr. Verwoerd, South Africa's 'evil genius', 25 May 1957: 6.
[26] Vertaling. Information: Demitrio Tsafendas or Demetrio Tsafandakis, 7 September 1966. K150. Vol. 6, File: 3, NASA; PIDE report: Information: Demitrio Tsafendas or Demetrio Tsafandakis, 7 September 1966. PIDE/DGS, SC, CI (2) 6818, NT 7461, PNA. ANTT.
[27] Babiolakis, Constandinou, Eintracht, Kyriakakis, Papadakis and K. Pnefma, author interviews.
[28] Demetrio Tsafendas statement to Major Rossouw. 11 September 1966. K150, Vol. 1, File: Verklaring van Demetrio Tsafendas, NASA.
[29] Bertolt Brecht, *Me Ti: Book of Interventions in the Flow of Things* (London: Bloomsburg Publishing, 2016).
[30] Marianne Thamm, 'Mozambique Honours Dimitri Tsafendas, while SACP Vows to Erect Tombstone,' *Daily Maverick*, 13 October 2021.
[31] Patriarcado de Alexandria E Toda A Africa Santa Diocese Grego Orthodoxade Mocambique, 'Convite,' 29 September 2021.
[32] Patriarcado de Alexandria E Toda A Africa Santa Diocese Grego Orthodoxade Mocambique, 'Press Release,' 10 October 2021.
[33] Message of His Beatitude the Pope and Patriarch of Alexandria and All Africa, Theodoros II to His Eminence the Archbishop of Zambia, 5 October 2021; Dimitris Psarras, 'Δεν θα ξεχάσουμε την τιτάνια θυσία του Τσαφέντα για την ελευθερία,' *Efsyn*, 18 October 2021.
[34] Message of His Beatitude the Pope and Patriarch of Alexandria and All Africa, Theodoros II to His Eminence the Archbishop of Zambia, 5 October 2021.
[35] Solly Mapaila statement on behalf of the SACP "In Honour of Our Great Unsung People's Hero Comrade Dimitri Tsafendas," 7 October 2021.

[36] Krish Govender, 'Statement for Tsafendas's Memorial Service: The Martyrdom of Dimitri Tsafendas,' 6 October 2021.

[37] Ronnie Kasrils' Statement for Tsafendas's Memorial Service, 6 October 2021.

[38] Nikos Konstandaras, 'The Slow Rehabilitation of A Tragic Hero,' *Kathimerini*, 18 October 2021.

[39] Zak Yacoob's Statement for Tsafendas's Memorial Service, 5 October 2021.

[40] Patriarcado de Alexandria E Toda A Africa Santa Diocese Grego Orthodoxade Mocambique, 'Press Release,' 10 October 2021.

Bibliography

Primary sources

Archival material

Correctional Services File 80/0043, A 123, Dimitrio Tsafendas, National Archives of South Africa, Pretoria.

Criminal Procedure Amendment Act No 96'. Available at: https://www.nelsonmandela.org/omalley/index.php/site/q/03lv01538/04lv01828/05lv01829/06lv01920.htm, accessed on 16 August 2015.

David Pratt's file at the National Liberal Club Archives, London, England.

Demitrio Tsafendas Mediese Leer, A124 and A125, National Archives of South Africa.

Demitrios Tsafantakis's file in Arquivo PIDE/DGS (physical location: PIDE/DGS, SC, CI(2) 6818, NT 7461), Arquivo National da Torre do Tombo, Portugal.

Demitrios Tsafantakis's file in Arquivo Antonio Oliveira Salazar (physical location: Arquivo Salazar, UL-46, cx. 843, pt.11), Arquivo National da Torre do Tombo, Portugal.

Helen Suzman Papers 1944–2009. Mb2.10.1.5, University of the Witwatersrand.

K150. Report of the Commission of Enquiry into the Circumstances of the Death of the Late Dr the Honourable Hendrik Frensch Verwoerd, National Archives of South Africa.

Mary Lindsay Cumming vs. David Beresford Pratt. 877/1953, National Archives of South Africa.

*Regina vs. David Beresford Pratt.*712-60. National Archives of South Africa.

Report of the Commission of Inquiry into the Responsibility of Mentally Deranged Persons and Related Matters, National Archives of South Africa.

Susan Diane Pratt. 6000/60. National Archives of South Africa.

Tsafendas's file in the Lawyers for Human Rights Collection (AL3183), South African History Archive.

Interviews

All interviews with witnesses were conducted and recorded personally by the author; except those with Gordon Winter, which were conducted and recorded by Dr. James Sanders on behalf of the author. All the interviewees who knew Tsafendas were interviewed on several occasions on an ongoing basis. Susie Cazenove and Dr. Isaac Sakinofsky were not interviewed face to face or by telephone, but corresponded with the author on several occasions; Dr. Sakinofsky very kindly answered all the questions sent to him. For each of the witnesses below the date given is the date of the last interview between the witness and the author.

Witnesses who met Tsafendas

Pamela Abrahams: She met Tsafendas in 1966 in Cape Town; 6 June 2016

Cleanthes Alachiotis: From the *Eleni*, he associated a lot with Tsafendas during the *Eleni*'s stay in Cape Town in July and August 1966; 29 September 2010.

George Ananiades: He met Tsafendas in 1963 in Lourenço Marques; 21 June 2016.

Pantelis Aspiotis: From the *Eleni*, he met Tsafendas in Cape Town in 1966; 6 June 2015.

Nick Augustides: Tsafendas's employer between July and September 1966; 19 February 2016.

Andreas Babiolakis: Grew up with Tsafendas in Mozambique and was a very close friend; 19 March 2016.

Nicola Banovic: A Greek Orthodox priest who became very close to Tsafendas, they initially met in Istanbul in 1961. Tsafendas lived in Father Banovic's house for four months and associated with him for another three; 21 August 2014.

David Beresford: *Guardian* journalist, he met Tsafendas in the mid-1990s in Sterkfontein hospital and wrote about him; 11 April 2014.

Nikolas Billis: From the *Eleni*, he associated a great deal with Tsafendas during the *Eleni*'s stay in Cape Town in July and August 1966; 12 June 2011.

David Bloomberg: Tsafendas's attorney in the summary trial; 4 June 2018.

Willie Burger: Tsafendas's lawyer at his summary trial; 9 April 2015.

Renfrew Christie: Anti-apartheid activist. He met Tsafendas in Pretoria Prison in 1980–81, where he was also imprisoned; 12 April 2016.

Minas Constandinou: A Greek Orthodox priest who met Tsafendas in Mozambique in 1963. He later visited him in prison and in hospital. They were extremely close and Tsafendas confided in him at length about his life; 6 February 2013.

Elias Constantaras: He associated with Tsafendas in Cape Town for several months in 1966; 11 April 2015.

Maggie Davey: She met Tsafendas in the mid-1990s at Sterkfontein hospital; 8 June 2018.

Joyce Dick: Helen Daniels's best friend. She met Tsafendas in 1965 in Cape Town; 6 August 2016.

Mary Eintracht: Tsafendas's cousin. They grew up together in Egypt and Mozambique and were very close; 9 October 2014.

Efthimios Eleftheriadis: A priest who met Tsafendas in Hamburg in the 1950s; 27 January 2011.

Mario Ferreira: He worked with Tsafendas at the Table Bay Power Station; 21 May 2019.

John Galanakis: He met Tsafendas in Beira in 1964; 22 May 2017.

Fotini Gavasiadis: One of Tsafendas's closest friends. She met him in Pretoria in 1963–64. She saw Tsafendas virtually every day for nine months in 1963–64, when they were flatmates and then neighbours while they also worked together; 19 May 2017.

Helen Grispos: She grew up with Tsafendas in Mozambique and met him again in Rhodesia in 1964. Her husband George Grispos was one of Tsafendas's best childhood friends. Her mother Sophia Gavadias was Tsafendas's step-mother's best friend in Lourenço Marques; , 22 January 2013.

Costas Hagios: He associated with Tsafendas for about two years, from 1965–66, in Cape Town; 14 July 2015.

Miltiades Kaldis: He met Tsafendas in Cape Town in 1965–66; 12 March 2016.

Nicolas Kambouris: From the *Eleni*, he associated a lot with Tsafendas during the *Eleni*'s stay in Cape Town in July and August 1966; 17 January 2014.

Georgios Kantas: From the *Eleni*, he consorted regularly with Tsafendas during the *Eleni*'s stay in Cape Town in July and August 1966; 11 January 2012.

Liza Key: Filmmaker and researcher. She met Tsafendas in Sterkfontein hospital in 1995 and subsequently visited him on several occasions. She made a documentary about him; 21 August 2018.

Judge Jody Kollapen: Anti-apartheid activist and High Court Judge in Pretoria. He met Tsafendas in prison in 1994 and tried to grant him amnesty; 5 April 2015.

Ira Kyriakakis: She grew up with Tsafendas in Mozambique and was a very close friend; 27 March 2015.

Dionisis Lallis: From the *Eleni*, he met Tsafendas in July and August 1966; 19 June 2015.

George Liberopoulos: He met Tsafendas in Lourenço Marques in 1963; 6 July 2014.

James Mange: He met Tsafendas in prison in the early 1980s; 8 April 2015.

Manolis Mastromanolis: From the *Eleni*, he associated a lot with Tsafendas during the *Eleni*'s stay in Cape Town in July and August 1966; 29 February 2016.

Nickolas Mavronas: From the *Eleni*, he sold Tsafendas the gun; 11 May 2019.

Antony Michaletos: Tsafendas's cousin and son of Artemis Michaletos, Tsafendas's aunt and his father's sister who brought him up in Egypt. He first met Tsafendas in 1951 in Lourenço Marques and got to know him well between 1963 and 1965 in Mozambique; 2 May 2016.

Irene Michaletos: She very closely associated with Tsafendas in Beira from 1964–65; 16 April 2016.

John Michaletos: Tsafendas's cousin and son of Artemis Michaletos, Tsafendas's aunt and his father's sister who brought him up in Egypt. He first met Tsafendas in 1951 in Lourenço Marques and got to know him between 1963 and 1965 in Mozambique; 16 April 2016.

Alexander Moumbaris: Anti-apartheid revolutionary, MK fighter and fellow prisoner in Pretoria Prison. He met Tsafendas in prison and later visited him at Sterkfontein hospital; 23 January 2018.

Marie-Jose Moumbaris: Anti-apartheid activist. She met Tsafendas in 1996 at Sterkfontein hospital; 27 June 2014.

Antonis Nichas: He associated with Tsafendas in Cape Town in 1966; 31 March 2016.

Jerome O'Ryan: Son of Patrick O'Ryan. He lived under the same roof as Tsafendas for five months in 1965; 15 April 2016.

Reuben O'Rya: Son of Patrick O'Ryan. He lived in the same house as Tsafendas for five months in 1965; 15 April 2016.

Stanley O'Ryan: Son of Patrick O'Ryan. He lived in the same house as Tsafendas for five months in 1965; 9 April 2015.

Nick Papadakis: He met Tsafendas in 1964 in Beira. They became good friends and they were also flatmates for two months; 30 January 2015.

George Petrakakis: He met Tsafendas in 1963 in Lourenço Marques; 15 May 2016.

Panagiotis Peroglou: He associated with Tsafendas in Cape Town in 1965–66; 6 June 2016.

Vasilios Perselis: From the *Eleni*, he associated with Tsafendas during the tanker's stay in Cape Town in July and August 1966; 14 January 2015.

Richard Poggenpoel: Tsafendas lived in his house in Cape Town in 1965; 30 July 2013.

Katerina Pnefma: Tsafendas's half-sister; 30 March 2015.

Michael Pnefma: Tsafendas's nephew. He met him in 1964; 30 March 2015.

Costas Poriazis: He met Tsafendas in 1965 in Beira; 5 April 2016.

Grigoris Pouftis: From the *Eleni*, he associated a lot with Tsafendas during the tanker's stay in Cape Town in July and August 1966; 28 November 2009.

Peter Protoulis: He met Tsafendas in Cape Town in 1966; 28 May 2016.

Spiros Randos: A Greek Orthodox priest who visited Tsafendas in Pretoria Prison Hospital and Sterkfontein hospital, Father Randos became close to him; 5 January 2004.

Isaac Sakinofsky: One of the psychiatrists who examined Tsafendas for the summary trial; 30 March 2016.

Dimitris Skoularikis: He met Tsafendas in prison in the early 1990s; 26 April 2015.

Ioannis Speis: From the *Eleni*, he met Tsafendas during the tanker's stay in Cape Town in July and August 1966; 12 July 2015.

Dimitris Stavrianos: From the *Eleni*, he met Tsafendas during the tanker's stay in Cape Town in July and August 1966; 18 January 2015.

Emmanuel Tsabouniaris; From the *Eleni*, he associated with Tsafendas during the tanker's stay in Cape Town in July and August 1966; 14 May 2016.

Ioannis Tsaftaridis: The Bishop of the Greek Orthodox Church in Zambia and Malawi. He visited Tsafendas at Pretoria Prison Hospital and at Sterkfontein hospital. Tsafendas told him much about his life; 23 January 2017.

Marina Tsichlakis: She met Tsafendas in Beira in 1964; 3 April 2015.

Evangelos Tsouroulis: President of the Greek community in Rhodesia in 1964 and of the Pan-Hellenic Association of Zimbabwe-Zambia-Malawi-Mozambique Greek Communities (PAZZIMMO). He met Tsafendas in Rhodesia in 1964; 16 January 2017.

Reyner van Zyl: The psychologist who examined Tsafendas for the summary trial; 10 April 2016.

Stratis Vamvarapis: He met Tsafendas between 1965 and 1966 in Cape Town; 31 May 2016.

Alexandra Vaporidis: She met Tsafendas in 1961 in Istanbul. Her husband, Father Agathagelos Vaporidis, was a close friend of Tsafendas; 23 August 2014.

Michalis Vasilakis: From the *Eleni,* he associated a lot with Tsafendas during the tanker's stay in Cape Town between July and August 1966; 17 March 2016.

Michalis Visvinis: A Greek Orthodox priest who regularly visited Tsafendas in prison for five years from 1989–94. They became very close and Tsafendas spoke extensively to him about his life; 11 July 2015.

Michael Vlachopoulos: Tsafendas's nephew, who met him in 1963; 30 March 2015.

Gordon Winter: Former BOSS agent, who met Tsafendas in Pretoria Prison in 1975; 19 August 2016.

Periklis Zouridis: He met Tsafendas in 1964 in Beira; 4 June 2016.

Witnesses who did not meet Tsafendas

Akis Apergis: Member of the Greek community in Johannesburg at the time of the assassination; 24 March 2015.

Barbara Bell: anti-apartheid activist; 10 April 2015.

Terry Bell: Anti-apartheid activist and journalist who co-authored *Unfinished Business: South Africa, Apartheid and Truth*; 10 April 2015.

Ioannis Bizos: Member of the Greek community in Johannesburg at the time of the assassination; 26 March 2015.

George Bizos: Human rights lawyer and anti-apartheid activist. His mother-in-law was one of the closest friends of Tsafendas's stepmother. Tsafendas's request to be represented by him was denied; 18 November 2017.

Desmond Blow: *Rand Daily Mail, Sunday Times* and *Sunday Express* journalist. He became very close to David Pratt after the latter's assault on Verwoerd; 23 February 2015.

Elizabeth Blow. Desmond's wife; 23 February 2015.

Graham David Blow: Desmond Blow's son who was named David by his father after David Pratt; 27 July 2016.

Alban Burke: Professor of psychology and head of the psychology department at the University of Johannesburg; 4 April 2016.

Stefan Bubenzer: Actor, who played Tsafendas in Will Tanner's play *Tsafendas* when it was performed in London in the 1970s; 12 June 2017.

Susie Cazenove: David Pratt's daughter; 24 November 2017.

Luli Callinicos: Historian and anti-apartheid activist, who lived in Johannesburg at the time of the assassination; 26 March 2015.

Mathys Carstens: He worked in the House of Assembly in 1966, but never met Tsafendas; 11 January 2019

Lionel Davis: An anti-apartheid activist, he was imprisoned on Robben Island while Tsafendas was held there; 8 April 2015.

John Dugard: Professor of law and judge at the International Court of Justice; 7 February 2016.

Judge Gerald Friedman: Retired Judge President, Cape High Court, 18 August 2016.

Costa Gazidis: Cousin of Rika Nikolatos. An anti-apartheid activist and social worker, he visited Tsafendas in prison and in the hospital; 10 April 2015.

Janet Gazidis: Wife of Costas Gazidis, who knew Nikolatos very well; 10 April 2015.

Denis Goldberg: Anti-apartheid activist, imprisoned in Pretoria Central Prison at the same time as Tsafendas, but he never met him; 12 April 2016.

Krish Govender: Former Durban State-Attorney and anti-apartheid activist. In 1996, he made a request in the TRC to examine Tsafendas's case; 12 May 2017.

Mike Grispos: Son of Helen and George Grispos. George Grispos was Tsafendas's schoolmate and childhood friend; 27 October 2016.

Maria Kasimatis: she lived in Lourenço Marques at the time of the assassination; 15 April 2016.

Ronnie Kasrils: Founding member of Umkhonto we Sizwe and former Minister for Intelligence Services; 16 May 2016.

Ahmed Kathrada: Anti-apartheid activist, he was imprisoned on Robben Island while Tsafendas was held there; 13 April 2016.

Ayten Kececi: Director of Limasollu Naci, 8 January 2016.

Jan-Ake Kjellberg: UN police officer and TRC investigator who handled Tsafendas's file in the TRC hearings; 11 August 2016.

Elias Kokkinos. From the *Eleni*, he was present in Venice when the crew was questioned; 30 August 2014.

Dr. Anton Krueger. Academic, playwright and author of *Living in Strange Lands;* 10 April 2015.

Peter Lambley: Psychologist and author of *The Psychology of Apartheid.* He knew some of those who examined Tsafendas and referred to his case in the book; 18 September 2013.

Adviye Vedia Limasollu: Wife of Limasollu Naci, owner of the college of the same name where Tsafendas worked while in Istanbul; 8 January 2016.

Tunc Limasollu: Son of Limasollu Naci, owner of the college with the same name where Tsafendas worked while in Istanbul; 8 January 2016.

Alan Lomas: he was involved with the case in 1966 and the Commission of Enquiry referred to him; 12 December 2014.

Dr. Evangelos Mantzaris: Academic, expert on trade unions in South Africa and of the Greeks of South Africa; 23 August 2017.

Saul Molobi: South Africa's Consul-General in Milan who took an interest in Tsafendas's case in the 1990s; 7 May 2015.

Solly Mapaila: First Deputy General-Secretary of the South African Communist Party; 24 March 2015.

Judge Robin Marais: Retired Judge and Judge Beyers' registar; 18 August 2016.

Costas Maroudas: He lived in Johannesburg at the time of the assassination. Son-in-law of Father Minas Constandinou and grandson of Father Bertolis, the priest who baptised Tsafendas and knew him throughout his life; 12 May 2015.

Tessa Marwick. Theatre director, who directed the play *Tsafendas* in 1976 in London; 11 June 2017.

Michael Meadowcroft: Former British MP with the Liberal Party and honorary president of the National Liberal Club; 2 February 2017.

Michalis Michelis: Journalist who extensively researched Tsafendas's case in 1987; 23 January 2016.

Abhilash Nair: Law academic; 23 November 2016.

John Nankin: Director, actor and stage designer. He did some research on Tsafendas in the mid-1970s for William Tanner's play *Tsafendas;* 13 September 2016.

Dumisa Ntsebeza SC. Anti-apartheid activist and advocate; 19 March 2017.

Akis Papageorgiou: President of the Greek Community of Pretoria in the early 1990s; 16 April 2015.

Emmanuel Perselis: From the *Eleni*, he was present in Venice when the crew was questioned; 30 November 2015.

Piers Pigou: International Crisis Group's Senior Consultant for Southern Africa and TRC Investigator; 7 April 2016.

Elizabeth Radsma: David Pratt's personal assistant and secretary; 9 January 2017.

Phillip Resnick: Forensic psychiatrist; 17 December 2016.

Albie Sachs: Retired Judge and anti-apartheid activist; 27 September 2016.

Robert L. Sadoff: Professor of clinical psychiatry and director of the Center for Studies in Social-Legal Psychiatry at the University of Pennsylvania, former president of the American Academy of Psychiatry and the Law, as well as the American Board of Forensic Psychiatry; 12 August 2015.

Emanuel Sakellaridis: *Eleni*'s former captain; 22 March 2014.

James Sanders: Author and researcher, specialising in South Africa; 4 June 2016.

Cheche Selepe; author and Mike Phahlane's friend; 9 April 2016

Dr. Aditya Sharma: Consultant psychiatrist, 12 October 2016.

Piet Swanepoel: former BOSS agent and Verwoerd's bodyguard; 6 April 2016.

Renos Spanoudes: Actor and drama teacher. He played Tsafendas in the play *Living in Strange Lands* and *Strange Lands*, 26 March 2015.

Guy Spiller: Filmmaker and director of *The Liberal and the Pirate*; 12 May 2016.

Dr. Arjun Thampy. Consultant psychiatrist.

Alexandros Tsafantakis; Tsafendas's nephew; 9 January 2016.

Aris Tsafantakis: Tsafendas's cousin; 13 April 2016.

Maria Tsafantakis: Granddaughter of Costas Kargakis, whose house Tsafendas stayed at in Crete. Maria taught him to make bombs; 9 January 2016.

Michalis Tsafantakis: Tsafendas's cousin. Tsafendas stayed at his parents' house in Crete in 1962; 9 January 2016.

Stelios Tsafantakis: Tsafendas's cousin. He was in Crete when Tsafendas visited the island in 1962; 9 January 2016.

Dimitris Vergitsis: Former Greek Orthodox priest who buried Tsafendas; 6 September 2015.

James J. Ward, Professor of History at the Cedar Crest College, Allentown, Pennsylvania, USA.

Zak Yacoob: Retired constitutional judge; 18 September 2017.

Professor Tuviah Zabow: Former professor of forensic psychiatry at the University of Cape Town and former head of the forensic psychiatry unit at Valkinberg hospital; 11 April 2016.

Dimitris Zitianelis: President of the Greek Community in Cape Town. He lived there at the time of the assassination;

Audio-visual materials

A Question of Madness by Liza Key (1997)

The Liberal and the Pirate by Guy Spiller (1999)

Live and Let Live by Manolis Dimelas (2007)

Government publications

Report of the Commission of Enquiry into the Circumstances of the Death of the late Dr The Honourable Hendrik French Verwoerd. R.PR.16/67. Pretoria, Government Printer, December 1966.

Report of the Commission of Inquiry into the Responsibility of Mentally Deranged Persons and Related Matters. R.PR. 69/1967. Pretoria: Government Printer, 1967.

Personal collections

David Bloomberg's personal documents regarding Tsafendas.

Desmond Blow's personal documents regarding David Pratt.

Liza Key's personal documents regarding Tsafendas.

Alexander Moumbaris's personal documents regarding Tsafendas.

Dr James Sanders's personal documents regarding Tsafendas.

Gordon Winter's personal documents regarding Tsafendas.

Newspapers and periodicals

Dagbreek

Daily Dispatch

Daily Mirror

Die Transvaler

Die Vaderland

Die Volksblad

Evening Standard

Kathimerini

Le Courrier d'Afrique
Natal Witness
News Chronicle
Newsweek
O Primeiro de Janeiro
Personality
Pretoria News
Rand Daily Mail
Scope
Sunday Tribune
TIME (Magazine)
The Australian
The Canberra Times
The Cape Argus
The Cape Times
The Citizen
The Chronicle (Bulawayo)
The Economist
The Illustrated London News
The Independent
The Globe and Mail
The Guardian (London)
The Herald (Melbourne)
The New York Times
The Observer
The Post
The Stage
The Spectator
The Star
The Sunday Times (Johannesburg)
The Sunday Times (London)
The Sunday Tribune
The Times (London)
The Washington Post
Umtali Post

Secondary Sources

Books and journal articles

A Distinguished South African Lawyer (who for obvious reasons must remain anonymous). *Verwoerd's Police State,* London: A Christian Action Pamphlet, 1965.

Abulof, Uriel. *The Mortality and Morality of Nations.* New York: Cambridge University Press, 2015.

Adam, Heribert. *Modernizing Racial Domination: South Africa's Political Dynamics.* Berkley: University of California Press, 1971.

Ainslie, Rosalynde. *Masters and Serfs: Farm Labour in South Africa.* London: International Defence and Aid Fund for South Africa, 1977.

Akinturk, Ayse Sule. 'The politics of English as a foreign language: The case of Turkey'. PhD thesis, Carleton University, Ottawa, Ontario, 2011.

Alden, Chris. *Apartheid's Last Stand: The Rise and Fall of the South African Security State.* Basingstoke: Palgrave Macmillan, 1996.

Alhadeff, Vic. *A Newspaper History of South Africa.* Cape Town: Don Nelson, 1985.

Asmal, Kader, Louise Asmal & Ronald Suresh Roberts. *Reconciliation Through Truth: A Reckoning of Apartheid's Criminal Governance.* Cape Town: David Philip Publishers, 1996.

Badat, Salim. *The Forgotten People: Banishment under Apartheid.* Leiden and Boston: Brill, 2013.

Baines, Gary. 'The master narrative of South Africa's liberation struggle: Remembering and forgetting June 16, 1976'. *The International Journal of African Historical Studies,* Vol. 40, No. 2 (2007): 283–302.

Ballinger, Margaret. *From Union to Apartheid.* Folkestone: Bailey Bros and Swinfen Ltd, 1969.

Barber, James. *South Africa in the Twentieth Century: A Political History – In Search of a Nation State.* Oxford: Wiley Blackwell, 1999.

Barron, Chris. *Collected South African Obituaries.* Parklands: Penguin Books, 2005.

Beck, Roger B. *The History of South Africa.* London: Greenwood Press, 2000.

Beinart, William. *Twentieth-Century South Africa.* Oxford: Oxford University Press, 2001.

Bell, Terry & Dumisa Buhle Ntsebeza. *Unfinished Business: South Africa, Apartheid and Truth.* London and New York: Verso Books, 2003.

Benson, Mary. *The Badge of Slavery (The Pass Laws of South Africa).* London: Christian Action Publications, 1960.

Benson, Mary. 'The destruction of family life' in M.V. Friedmann, ed. *I Will Still Be Moved: Reports from South Africa.* London: Arthur Baker, 1963.

Benson, Mary. *Chief Albert Lutuli of South Africa.* Oxford: Oxford University Press, 1963.

Beresford, David. *Truth is a Strange Fruit: A Personal Journey Through the Apartheid War.* Johannesburg: Jacana Media, 2010.

Bernstein, Hilda. *South Africa: The Terrorism of Torture.* London: International Defence and Aid Fund, 1972.

Beyers, C.J. ed. *Dictionary of South African Biography, Vol 4.* Pretoria: HSRC Press, 1981.

Bishop, Michael. 'An accidental good: The role of Commissions of Inquiry in South African democracy', *New York Law School Law Review,* 14 November 2014.

Bizos, George. *No One to Blame? A Personal Account of Inquests into Some Deaths in Detention under Apartheid.* Cape Town: David Philip Publishers, 1998.

Bloomberg, David. *My Times: The Memoirs of David Bloomberg.* Simon's Town: Fernwood Press, 2007.

Blumberg, Myrna. 'The Mafekeng affair', *Africa South,* April/June (1960).

Bonner, Phil, Peter Delius & Deborah Posel. 'The shaping of apartheid', in Phil Bonner, Peter Delius & Deborah Posel, eds. *Apartheid's Genesis: 1935–62.* Braamfontein: Raven Press, 1993, pp. 1–41.

Booth, Douglas. *The Race Game: Sport and Politics in South Africa.* London: Frank Cass Publishers, 1998.

Boshoff, Annatjie. *Sekretaresse vir die Verwoerds.* Cape Town and Pretoria: Human & Rousseau, 1974.

Botha, Jan. *Verwoerd is Dead.* Cape Town: Books of Africa, 1967.

Bourne, Peter G. *Fidel: A Biography of Fidel Castro.* New York: Dodd Mead, 1986.

Brecht, Bertolt. *Me Ti: Book of Interventions in the Flow of Things.* London: Bloomsburg Publishing, 2016.

Breckenridge, Keith. *Biometric State: The Global Politics of Identification and Surveillance in South Africa, 1850 to the Present.* Cambridge: Cambridge University Press, 2014.

Breytenbach, Breytan. *The True Confessions of an Albino Terrorist.* London and Boston: Faber & Faber, 1985.

Brink, Elisabé, Sue Krige, Steve Lebelo, Gandhi Malungane & Dumisani Ntshangase. *Soweto: 16 June 1976.* Cape Town: Kwela Books, 2010.

Brookes, Edgar H. *Apartheid: A Documentary Study of Modern South Africa.* London: Routledge and Kegan Paul, 1968.

Browett, John. 'The evolution of unequal development within South Africa: An overview', in David M. Smith, ed. *Living under Apartheid: Aspects of Urbanization and Social Change.* London: George Allen and Unwin, 1982, pp. 10–23.

Brunner, Edmund D. 'Problems and tensions in South Africa'. *Political Science Quarterly,* Vol. 70, No. 3 (1955): 368–86.

Bundy, Colin. (1994) 'At war with the future? Black South African youth in the 1990s', in Stephen John Stedman, ed. *South Africa: The Political Economy of Transformation.* Boulder and London: Lynne Rienner Publishers, 1994.

Bunting, Brian. *The Rise of the South African Reich.* London: International and Defence and Aid Fund for South Africa, 1986 [1968].

Buntman, Fran Lisa. *Robben Island and Prisoner Resistance to Apartheid.* Cambridge: Cambridge University Press, 2003.

Burger, Martin. *Dr Verwoerd of South Africa: Architect of Doom.* London: A Christian Action pamphlet, 1961.

Burke, Albun. 'Mental health care during apartheid in South Africa: An illustration of how "Science" can be abused', in J.T. Parry, ed. *Evil, Law and the State: Perspectives on State Power and Violence.* Amsterdam and New York: Rodopi B.V., 2006, pp. 1–8.

Callinicos, Alex. *Between Apartheid and Capitalism: Conversations with South African Socialists.* London: Bookmarks, 1992.

Callinicos, Alex. *South Africa: Between Reform and Revolution.* London: Bookmarks, 1995.

Cawthra, Gavin. *Brutal Force: The Apartheid War Machine.* London: International Defence and Aid Fund for Southern Africa, 1986.

Chaldeos, Antonis. *The Greek Community in Mozambique.* Athens: self-published, 2015.

Christopher, A.J. *The Atlas of Apartheid.* London and New York: Routledge, 1994.

Citino, Robert Michael. *Germany and the Union of South Africa in the Nazi Period.* New York: Greenwood Press, 1991.

Cooper, Gavin. *Under Devil's Peak: The Life and Times of Wilfrid Cooper, an Advocate in the Age of Apartheid.* Kenilworth: Burnet Media, 2016.

Cronje, Suzanne. *Witness in the Dark: Police Torture and Brutality in South Africa.* London: Christian Action, 1964.

Daniel, John & Peter Vale. 'South Africa: Where were we looking in 1968?', in Philipp Gassert & Martin Klimke, eds. *1968 – Memories and Legacies of a Global Revolt.* Washington, DC: German Historical Institute, 2009, pp. 137–46.

Davis, Dennis & Michelle le Roux. *Precedent and Possibility: The (Ab)use of Law in South Africa.* Cape Town: Double Storey Books, 2009.

De Beer, Cedric. *The South African Disease: Apartheid Health and Health Services.* Trenton, N.J.: South African Research Service, 1984.

Diemont, Marius A. *Brushes with the Law.* Cape Town: Human & Rousseau, 1995.

Dlamini, Moses. *Robben Island, Hell-Hole: Reminiscences of a Political Prisoner.* Nottingham: Spokesman, 1984.

Dousemetzis, Charalampos. 'The presidency of Jimmy Carter and the emerging politics of gay rights and evangelical religion', PhD thesis, Durham University, 2018.

Doxey, G.V. 'The South African problem: A conflict of nationalism'. *International Journal: Canada's Journal of Global Policy Analysis,* Vol. 18, No. 4 (1963): 501–12.

Dubow, Saul. *Apartheid 1948–1994.* Oxford: Oxford University Press, 2014.

Dubow, Saul. 'Racial irredentism, ethnogenesis and white supremacy in high apartheid South Africa', Public lecture at the University of the Witwatersrand, 15 October 2015.

Dubula, Sol. *The Menace of Apartheid.* London: Peace and Socialism Publishers, 1965.

Dugard, John. *Human Rights and the South African Legal Order.* Princeton, New Jersey: Princeton University Press, 1978.

Dugard, John. 'The South African judiciary and international law in the apartheid era'. *South African Journal on Human Rights,* Vol. 14 (1998): 110–26.

Duncan, Patrick. 'Toward a world policy for South Africa'. *Foreign Affairs*, Vol. 42, October (1963).

Du Preez Bezdrob, A.M. *Winnie Mandela: A Life*. Cape Town: Zebra Books, 2003.

Du Preez, Max. *Of Tricksters, Tyrants and Turncoats*. Cape Town: Zebra Press, 2008.

Dyzenhaus, David. *Judging the Judges, Judging Ourselves: Truth, Reconciliation and the Apartheid Legal Order*. Oxford: Hart Publishing, 2003 [1998].

Dyzenhaus, David. *Hard Cases in Wicked Legal Systems: Pathologies of Legality*. Oxford: Oxford University Press, 2010.

D'Oliveira, John. *Vorster – The Man*. Johannesburg: Ernest Stanton Publishers, 1977.

De Klerk, F.W. *The Last Trek: A New Beginning*. London: Pan Books, 1999.

De Klerk, Willem Abraham. *The Puritans in Africa: Story of Afrikanerdom*. London: Rex Collings, 1975.

En so Haber. 'Limasollu Naci Kimdir.' 23 May 2012. Available at: http://www.ensonhaber.com/limasollu-naci-kimdir-2012-05-23.html, accessed on 16 May 2015.

Fobi, Brian Tangang. 'The engineers of history: Hendrik Verwoerd, George Wallace, and the power of historical memory', PhD thesis, Yale University, 2014.

Forsyth, Frederick. *The Outsider: My Life in Intrigue*. London: Bantam Press, 2015.

Foster, Dean. *Detention and Torture in South Africa: Psychological, Legal and Historical Studies*. London: James Currey, 1987.

Foster, Dean. 'Race and racism in South African psychology'. *South African Journal of Psychology*, Vol. 21, No. 4 (1991): 203–10.

Foster, Dean. 'On racism, virulent mythologies and fragile threads', in L. Nicholas, ed. *Psychology and Oppression: Critiques and Proposals*. Johannesburg: Skotsville Publishers, 1993, pp. 55–81.

Frankel, Philip H. *An Ordinary Atrocity: Sharpeville and Its Massacre*. New Haven and London: Yale University Press, 2001.

Friedman, Gerald & Jeremy J. Gauntlett. *Bar, Bench and Bullshifters: Cape Tales 1950–1990*. Cape Town: Siber Ink, 2013.

Froneman, Johannes D. 'HF Verwoerd's student years: Cradle of his political career and thought'. *Koers*, Vol. 65, No. 3 (2000): 399–412.

Frye, William. *In Whitest Africa: The Dynamics of Apartheid*. Englewood Cliffs, New Jersey: Prentice-Hall INC., 1970.

Fullard, Madeleine. 'State repression in the 1960s', in South African Democracy Education Trust. *The Road to Democracy in South Africa, Volume 1 (1960–1970)*. Cape Town: Zebra Press, 2004, pp. 341–90.

Furlong, Patrick Jonathan. *Between Crown and Swastika: The Impact of the Radical Right on the Afrikaner Nationalist Movement in the Fascist Era*. Hanover and London: Wesleyan University Press, 1991.

Gibbs, Henry. *Twilight in South Africa*. New York: Jarrolds, 1949.

Gifford, Tony. *Southern Africa's Record of International Terrorism.* United Nations Centre Against Apartheid. London: Anti-Apartheid Movement, 1981.

Giliomee, Hermann. *The Afrikaners: Biography of a People.* London: Hurst and Company, 2011.

Giliomee, Hermann. *The Last Afrikaner Leaders: A Supreme Test of Power.* Cape Town: Tafelburg, 2012.

Gilroy, Paul. 'After the great white error ... the great black mirage', Paper presented at conference titled 'The burden of race? "Whiteness" and "Blackness" in modern South Africa', University of the Witwatersrand, 5–8 July 2001.

Glaser, Daryl. *Politics and Society in South Africa.* London: Sage Publications, 2001.

Goodman, David. *Fault Lines: Journeys into the New South Africa.* Berkeley and Los Angeles: University of California Press, 1999.

Grobbelaar, Pieter W. *This Was a Man.* Cape Town: Human & Rousseau, 1967.

Grundy, Kenneth W. *South Africa: Domestic Crisis and Global Challenge.* Boulder: Westview Press, 1991.

Hachten, William, A. & Anthony C. Giffard. *The Press and Apartheid: Repression and Propaganda in South Africa.* Madison, Wisconsin: The University of Wisconsin Press, 1984.

Hain, Peter. *Sing the Beloved Country: The Struggle for the New South Africa.* Chicago: Pluto Press, 1996.

Hann, Dave. *Physical Resistance: A Hundred Years of Anti-Fascism.* Winchester: Zero Books, 2013.

Harris, Bronwyn. 'Arranging prejudice: Exploring hate crime in post-apartheid South Africa'. *Race and Citizenship in Transition Series,* Centre for the Study of Violence and Reconciliation (SWOP), University of the Witwatersrand, 2004.

Harrison, David. *The White Tribe of Africa: South Africa in Perspective.* Berkeley and Los Angeles: University of California Press, 1981.

Harrison, Ronald. *The Black Christ: A Journey to Freedom.* Claremont: David· Philip Publishers, 2006.

Haysom, Nicholas. 'The Langa Shootings and the Kannemeyer Commission of Enquiry'. *Human Rights Quarterly,* Vol 8, (1986): 494–510

Hellig, Jocelyn. 'German Jewish immigration to South Africa during the 1930s: Revisiting the charter of the SS *Stuttgart*'. *Jewish Culture and History,* Vol. 11, No. ½ (2009): 124–38.

Henkes, Barbara. 'Shifting identifications in Dutch-South African migration policies (1910–1961)'. *South African Historical Journal,* Vol. 68, No. 4 (2016): 641–69.

Hepple, Alexander. *Verwoerd.* Harmondsworth: Penguin Books, 1967.

Herbstein, Denis. *White Lies: Canon Collins and the Secret War against Apartheid.* Oxford: James Currey, 2004.

Higgins, Rosalyn. 'International action and domestic jurisdiction', in Ronald Segal, ed. *Sanctions Against South Africa.* Baltimore: Penguin Books, 1964, pp. 85–94.

Higginson, John. *Collective Violence and the Agrarian Origins of South African Apartheid, 1900–1948.* Cambridge: Cambridge University Press, 2014.

Hughes, John. *The New Face of Africa: South of the Sahara.* New York: Longmans, Green and Co., 1961.

Human & Rousseau. *They Shaped our Century: The Most Influential South Africans of the Twentieth Century.* Cape Town: Human & Rousseau, 1999.

Hutton, Barbara. *Robben Island: Symbol of Resistance.* Johannesburg: Mayibuye Books, 1994.

International Defence and Aid Fund. *South African Prisons and the Red Cross Investigation.* London: International Defence and Aid Fund, 1967.

International Defence and Aid Fund. *'Resettlement' – The New Violence to Africans.* London: International Defence and Aid Fund, 1969.

International Defence and Aid Fund. *BOSS: The First Five Years.* London: International Defence and Aid Fund, 1975.

Inwood, Gregory J. & Carolyn Johns. 'Why study Commissions of Inquiry?', in Gregory J. Inwood & Carolyn Johns, eds. *Commissions of Inquiry and Policy Change: A Comparative Analysis.* Toronto: University of Toronto Press, 2014, pp. 3–19.

Italiaander, Rolf. *The New Leaders of Africa.* Englewood Cliffs, New Jersey: Prentice Hall, 1961.

Jaster, Rolf. 'A regional security role for Africa's frontline states', in Rolf Jaster, ed. *Southern Africa: Regional Security Problems and Prospects.* Aldershot: Gower Publishing, 1985, pp. 37–88.

Kahn, Ellison. 'Constitutional and administrative law: The general election of 1966'. *Annual Survey of South African Law,* (1966): 1–38.

Kahn, Ellison. 'Notes and comments: Retirement of Mr Justice Michael MacGregor Corbett, Chief Justice of the Republic of South Africa'. *South African Law Journal,* Vol. 114 (1997): 207–10.

Kahn, Ely Jacques. *The Separated People: A Look at Contemporary South Africa.* New York: W.W. Norton & Company, Inc, 1968.

Kalley, Jacqueline Audrey. *Apartheid in South African Libraries: The Transvaal Experience.* Lanham: The Scarecrow Press, Inc, 2000.

Kane-Berman, John Stuart. *Soweto: Black Revolt, White Reaction.* Cape Town: Ravan Press, 1978.

Kane-Berman, John. *South Africa's Silent Revolution.* Johannesburg: South African Institute of Race Relations. Southern Book Publishers, 1991.

Kaplan, Robert. 'The Aversion Project: Psychiatric abuses in the South African Defence Force during the apartheid era'. *South African Medical Journal,* Vol. 91, No. 3 (2001): 216–7.

Kathrada, Ahmed. *Memoirs.* Cape Town: Zebra Press, 2004.

Kenney, Henry. *Architect of Apartheid: HF Verwoerd – An Appraisal.* Johannesburg: Jonathan Ball Publishers, 1980.

Khopung, Ethel. *Apartheid: The Story of a Dispossessed People.* Dar es Salaam: Sharpeville Day Association Mbizana, 1972.

Kleyn, Leti, '"Even a footnote can be a tragic figure," Demitrios (Dimitri) Tsafendas (1918-1999) as literêre karakter', *South African Journal of Art History*, Vol. 29, Is. 4 (Jan. 2014), pp. 76-95.

Klug, Heinz. 'Law before and after apartheid: Abel's socio-legal analysis'. *Law and Social Inquiry*, Vol. 25, No. 2 (2000): 657–67.

Kykkotis, Serafim. *Αναφορές στο Νομπελίστα Νέλσον Μαντέλα*. Athens: Papasotiriou, 2013.

La Guma, Alex. *Apartheid: A Collection of Writings on South African Racism by South Africans*. New York: International Publishers, 1971.

Lambley, Peter. *The Psychology of Apartheid*. Athens: The University of Georgia Press, 1980.

Landis, Elizabeth. 'The new order in South Africa'. *Africa Today*, Vol. 8, No. 8 (1961): 4–6.

Lapierre, Dominique. *A Rainbow in the Night: The Tumultuous Birth of South Africa*. Cambridge: Da Capo Press, 2009.

Lapping, Brian. *Apartheid: A History*. London: Grafton Books, 1986.

Legum, Colin & Margaret Legum. *South Africa: Crisis for the West*. London and Dunmow: Pall Mall Press, 1964.

Lentz, Harris M. *Heads of States and Governments since 1945*. London: Routledge, 1966.

Leonard, Richard. *South Africa at War: White Power and the Crisis in Southern Africa*. Westport: Lawrence Hill and Company, 1983.

Lewin, Hugh. *Bandiet: Seven Years in a South African Prison*. London: Penguin Books, 1976.

Lipton, Merle. *Capitalism and Apartheid: South Africa, 1910–1984*. Aldershot: Gower Publishing/Maurice Temple Smith, 1985.

Lodge, Tom. *Sharpeville: An Apartheid Massacre and its Consequences*. Oxford: Oxford University Press, 2011.

Loveland, Ian. *By Due Process of Law? Racial Discrimination and the Right to Vote in South Africa 1855–1960*. Oxford: Hart Publishing, 1999.

Luthuli, Albert. *Let My People Go*. London: Collins, 1962.

Luyt, Clifford. 'The killing fields: South Africa's human rights record in southern Africa'. *Social Justice: A Journal of Crime, Conflict and World Order*, Vol. 16, No. 2 (1989): 89–115.

Maaba, Brown Bavusile. 'The PAC's war against the state', in South African Democracy Education Trust. *The Road to Democracy in South Africa, Volume 1 (1960–1970)*. Cape Town: Zebra Press, 2004, pp. 257–99.

Maisels, Israel. *A Life at Law: The Memoirs of I.A. Maisels, QC*. Johannesburg: Jonathan Ball Publishers, 1998.

Mandela, Nelson. 'Clear the obstacles and confront the enemy: Wither the Black Consciousness Movement? An assessment', in Mac Maharaj, ed. *Reflections in Prison: Voices from the South African Liberation Struggle*. Cape Town: Zebra Press, 2001, pp. 7–20.

Mandela, Nelson. *Long Walk to Freedom*. London: Abacus, 2013 [1994].

Marais, Hein. *South Africa: Limits to Change: The Political Economy of Transition*. Cape Town: University of Cape Town Press, 2001.

Marais, Jaap. *Die Era van Verwoerd.* Pretoria: Aktuele Publikasies, 1992.

Marx, Christoph. 'The Ossewabrandwag as a mass movement, 1939–1941'. *Journal of Southern African Studies,* Vol. 20, No. 2 (1994): 195–219.

Marx, Christoph. 'Hendrik Verwoerd's long march to apartheid: Nationalism and racism in South Africa', in M. Berg & S. Wendt, eds. *Racism in the Modern World: Historical Perspectives on Cultural Transfer and Adaptation.* New York: Berghahn Books, 2011, pp. 281–302.

Marx, Christoph. *Oxwagon Sentinel: Radical Afrikaner Nationalism and the History of the Ossewabrandwag.* Berlin: Lit Verlag, 2011.

Marx, Christoph. 'Hendrik Verwoerd and the Leipzig School of Psychology in 1926'. *Historia,* Vol. 58, No. 2 (2013): 91–118.

Matsinhe, David M. *Apartheid Vertigo: The Rise in Discrimination against Africans in South Africa.* Farnham: Ashgate Publishing Ltd, 2013.

Mbeki, Govan. *South Africa: The Peasants' Revolt.* London: Penguin Books, 1964.

Mbeki, Govan. *Learning from Robben Island. The Prison Writings of Govan Mbeki.* London: James Currey, 1991.

Meredith, Martin. *In the Name of Apartheid: South Africa in the Post-War Period.* London: Hamish Hamilton, 1988.

Michelis, Michalis. 'Δημήτρης Τσαφέντας: Έκανα το Καθήκον Μου ... Εσείς;' ['Dimitris Tsafendas: I did my Duty ... You?'] Σχολιαστής [Sholiastis], Vol. 70 (1988): 14–15.

Miller, Jamie. *An African Volk: The Apartheid Regime and its Search for Survival.* New York: Oxford University Press, 2016.

Miller, Roberta Balstad. 'Science and society in the early career of H.F. Verwoerd'. *Journal of Southern African Studies,* Vol. 19, No. 4 (1993): 634–61.

Moodie, Dunbar T. *The Rise of Afrikanerdom.* Berkley: University of California Press, 1975.

Motala, Shireen. *Behind Closed Doors.* Johannesburg: South African Institute of Race Relations, 1987.

Mungazi, Dickson A. *The Tragedy of Apartheid in South Africa: Hendrik F. Verwoerd and Dimitri Tsafendas Meet at the Crossroads.* Kearney: Morris Publishing, 2006.

Mzimela, Sipo Elijah. 'Nazism and apartheid: The role of Christian churches in Nazi Germany and apartheid South Africa', PhD thesis, New York University, 1980.

Neame, Laurence Elwin. *The History of Apartheid: The Story of the Colour War in South Africa.* London: Pall Mall Press with Barrie and Rockcliff, 1962.

Nicholas, Lionel J. 'Psychological sequelae of political imprisonment during apartheid'. *South African Journal of Psychology,* Vol. 44, No. 1 (2014): 18–29.

Nieftagodien, Noor. *The Soweto Uprising.* Johannesburg: Jacana Media, 2014.

Nixon, Rob. *Homelands, Harlem and Hollywood: South African Culture and the World Beyond.* New York: Routledge, 1994.

Okoth, Assa. *A History of Africa: African Nationalism and the De-Colonisation Process.* Nairobi: East African Educational Publishers, 2006.

O'Meara, Dean. *Volkskapitalisme: Class, Capital and Ideology in the Development of Afrikaner Nationalism.* Cambridge: Cambridge University Press, 1983.

O'Meara, Dean. *Forty Lost Years: The Apartheid State and the Politics of the National Party 1948-1994.* Randburg: Ravan Press, 1996.

Paton, Alan. *South African Tragedy: The Life and Times of Jan Hofmeyr.* New York: Scribner, 1965.

Paton, Alan. 'Dr Heinrich Verwoerd: A liberal assessment'. *Liberal Opinion,* December (1966): 3–6.

Pelzer, Adriaan Nicolaas, ed. *Verwoerd Speaks: Speeches 1948–66.* Johannesburg: APB Publishers, 1966.

Pienaar, Hans. 'Hendrik Verwoerd', in Human & Rousseau. *They Shaped our Century: The Most Influential South Africans of the Twentieth Century.* Cape Town: Human & Rousseau, 1999, pp. 22–6.

Pike, Henry R. *A History of Communism in South Africa.* Primrose Hill, Germiston: Christian Mission International of South Africa, 1985.

Pogrund, Benjamin. *How Can Man Die Better ... Sobukwe and Apartheid.* London: Peter Halban, 1990.

Pogrund, Benjamin. *War of Words: Memoir of a South African Journalist.* New York: Seven Stories Press, 2000.

Pohlandt-McCormick, Helena 'I saw a nightmare...: Violence and the construction of memory (Soweto, June 16, 1976)'. *History and Theory,* Vol. 39, No. 4 (2000): 23–44.

Posel, Deborah. *The Making of Apartheid 1948–1961.* Oxford: Clarendon Paperbacks, 1997.

Prinsloo, Dioné. 'Dr H.F. Verwoerd as Hoofredakteur van *Die Transvaler*'. *Kleio,* Vol. 13, No. 1–2 (1981): 5–19.

Prinsloo, Dioné. 'Dr H.F. Verwoerd en die Ossewa-Brandwag 1938–1952'. *Kleio,* Vol. 17, No. 1 (1985): 73–85.

Reeves, Ambrose. *Shooting at Sharpeville: The Agony of South Africa.* London: Victor Gollancz Ltd, 1960.

Reeves, Ambrose. *South Africa: Let the Facts Speak.* London: Christian Action, 1962.

Reeves, Ambrose. *South Africa – Yesterday and Tomorrow: A Challenge to Christians.* London: Victor Gollanz Ltd, 1962.

Rudolph, Harold. *Security, Terrorism and Torture: Detainees' Rights in South Africa and Israel: A Comparative Study.* Cape Town: Juta and Co. Ltd, 1984.

Sachs, Albie. *The Violence of Apartheid.* London: An International Defence and Aid pamphlet, Christian Action Publications, 1970.

Sachs, Emil Solomon. *The Anatomy of Apartheid.* London: Collet's, 1965.

Sagittarius [Rajat Neogy]. 'David Pratt is Dead'. *Transition,* No. 1 (1961), p. 27.

Sanders, James. *South Africa and the International Media, 1972–1979: A Struggle for Representation.* New York: Routledge, 1999.

Sanders, James. *Apartheid's Friends: The Rise and Fall of South Africa's Secret Service.* London: John Murray, 2006.

Schadeberg, Jurgen, ed. *Nelson Mandela and the Rise of the ANC.* London: Bloomsbury Publishing Limited, 1990.

Schoeman, Beaumont M. *Die Sluipmoord op Dr Verwoerd.* Pretoria: Strydpers Bpk, 1975.

Scholtz, Johannes Joachim Jurgens. *Die Moord op Dr Verwoerd.* Cape Town: Nationale Boekhandel BPK, 1967.

Scholtz, Johannes Joachim Jurgens. *Dr Hendrik Frensch Verwoerd.* Johannesburg: Perskor-uitgewery, 1974.

Schonteich, Martin & Henri Boshoff. *Volk, Faith and Fatherland: The Security Threat Posed by the White Right.* Pretoria: Institute for Security Studies, 2003.

Segal, Ronald. *The Agony of Apartheid.* London: A Christian Action pamphlet, 1960.

Shaw, Gerald. *Believe in Miracles: South Africa from Malan to Mandela – and the Mbeki Era.* Newlands: Ampersand Press, 2007.

Shimoni, Gideon. *Community and Conscience: The Jews in Apartheid South Africa.* Hanover, N.H.: Brandeis University Press published by University Press of New England, 2003.

Sitze, Adam. *The Impossible Machine: A Genealogy of South Africa's Truth and Reconciliation Commission.* Ann Arbor: University of Michigan Press, 2013.

Smith, Lindsay H. *Anatomy of Apartheid.* Germiston: Khanya Publishers, 1979.

Solani, Noel & Noor Nieftagodien. 'Political imprisonment and resistance in South Africa: The case of Robben Island, 1960–1970', in South African Democracy Education Trust. *The Road to Democracy in South Africa, Volume 1 (1960–1970).* Cape Town: Zebra Press, pp. 391–411.

South African Institute of Race Relations. *A Survey of Race Relations in South Africa 1961.* Johannesburg: South African Institute of Race Relations, 1962.

South Africa: House of Assembly (1961) *Debates,* 23–27 January 1961, col. 98.

South Africa: House of Assembly (1971) *Debates,* 21 April 1971.

South African History Online (n.d) *Rowley Israel Arenstein.* Available at: http://www.sahistory.org.za/people/rowley-israel-arenstein, accessed on 12 May 2015.

South African Law Journal. 'In Memoriam: Israel Aaron Maisels QC'. *South African Law Journal,* Vol. 112, No. 132. (1995): 132–5.

Sparks, Alister. *The Mind of South Africa.* London: Heinemann, 1990.

Stephenson, Jonathan. 'Jonathan Stephenson on a Cape Town Incident'. *Fortnight,* No. 159 (1978).

Study Commission on US Policy toward Southern Africa. *South Africa: Time Running Out – The Report of the Study Commission on U.S. Policy toward Southern Africa.* Berkeley: University of California Press, 1981.

Stutlz, Newell M & Jeffrey Butler. 'The South African general election of 1961'. *Political Science Quarterly,* Vol. 78, No. 1 (1963): 86–110.

Suttner, Immanuel. ed. *Cutting through the Mountain: Interviews with South African Jewish Activists.* New York: Viking, 1997.

The Bishop of Johannesburg. *Report on South Africa.* London: Christian Action, 1960.

Thompson, Leonard. *A History of South Africa.* New Haven and London: Yale University Press, 2001.

N.A. 'Torture in South Africa'. *Transition,* No. 19 (1965): 17–22.

N.A. '*Torture in South Africa*'. *Transition*, No. 50 (October 1975–March 1976): 52–7.

Troup, Freda. *South Africa: An Historical Introduction.* Harmondsworth: Penguin Books, 1975.

Truth and Reconciliation Commission. *Truth and Reconciliation Commission of South Africa Report, Volume Two.* Cape Town: Juta Books, 1998

Uys, Stanley. 'Dr Hendrik Frensch Verwoerd, Prime Minister of South Africa', *Africa South,* Jan–March (1959): 1–12.

Uys, Stanley. 'The Afrikaner establishment', in Shaun Johnson, ed. *South Africa: No Turning Back.* Bloomington and Indianapolis: Indiana University Press, 1989, pp. 206–40.

Van den Berghe, Pierre L. *South Africa: A Study in Conflict.* Berkeley: University of California Press, 1967.

Van Jaarsveld, Floris Albertus. 'The Afrikaner's idea of his calling and mission in South African history'. *Journal of Theology for Southern Africa,* Vol. 19 (1977): 16–26.

Van Rooyen, J.H. 'The psychopath in South African criminal and mental health law'. *Comparative and International Law Journal of Southern Africa,* Vol. 9, No. 1 (1976): 1–56.

Van Woerden, Henk. *A Mouthful of Glass.* London: Granta Books, 2000.

Vassen, Robert. 'Detentions without trial during the apartheid era', *South Africa: Overcoming Apartheid, Building Democracy.* Available at: http://overcomingapartheid.msu.edu/sidebar.php?id=65-258-9&page=1, accessed on 7 March 2015.

Vatcher, William Henry. *White Laager: The Rise of Afrikaner Nationalism.* London: Pall Mall Press, 1965.

Venter, J.J. 'H.F. Verwoerd: Foundational aspects of his thought'. *Koers,* Vol. 64, No. 4 (1999): 415–42.

Verwey, E.J. ed. *New Dictionary of South African Biography, volume 1.* Pretoria: HSRC Press, 1995.

Verwoerd, Hendrik F. *The Truth About South Africa.* Bloemfontein: National Party's Information Service, 1961.

Verwoerd, Wilhelm J. *Verwoerd: Só Onthou ons Hom.* Pretoria: Protea Boekhuis, 2001.

Vigne, Randolph. *Liberals against Apartheid: A History of the Liberal Party in South Africa.* Houndsmills and New York: Palgrave, 1997.

Visser, George Cloete. *OB: Traitors or Patriots?* Johannesburg: MacMillan South Africa, 1976.

Welsh, Frank. *A History of South Africa.* Great Britain: Harper Collins, 2000.

Weyl, Nathaniel. *Traitor's End: The Rise and Fall of the Communist Movement in Southern Africa.* New Rochelle, NY: Arlington House, 1970.

Wiechers, Marinus. 'South West Africa: The decision of 16 July 1966 and its aftermath'. *The Comparative and International Law Journal of Southern Africa,* Vol. 1, No. 3 (1968): 408–46.

Wilkins, Ivor & Hans Strydom. *Broederbond: The Super-Afrikaners.* London: Corgi Books, 1979.

Willems, C.N., N. West, R. Unwon & Eveleigh. *A Case for Change: Rights, Repression and Responses in South Africa.* Leeds: Leeds Education Development Centre, 1988.

Williams, Daniel K. 'Sex and the evangelicals: Gender issues, the sexual revolution and abortion in the 1960s', in A.R. Schafer, ed. *American Evangelicals and the 1960s.* Madison: University of Wisconsin Press, 2013, pp. 97–118.

Winter, Gordon. *Inside BOSS: South Africa's Secret Police.* Harmondsworth: Penguin Books, 1981.

Witz, Leslie. *Apartheid's Festival: Contesting South Africa's National Past.* Bloomington, Ind: Indiana University Press, 2003.

Worden, Nigel. *The Making of Modern South Africa.* Oxford: Wiley-Blackwell, 2000.

Worger, William, H., Nancy L. Clark & Edward A. Alpers. *Africa and the West: A Documentary History. Volume 2: From Colonialism to Independence, 1975 to the Present.* Oxford: Oxford University Press, 2010.

World Peace Council. *Apartheid is Built on Torture.* Helsinki: Information Centre of the World Peace Council, 1972.

About the Authors

Harris Dousemetzis is a tutor at the School of Government and International Affairs at Durham University, England and holds a PhD in politics (*The Presidency of Jimmy Carter and the Emerging Politics of Gay Rights and Evangelical Religion*) from the same university. He is also the author of the *Report to the Minister of Justice in the Matter of Dr. Verwoerd's Assassination.*

Gerry Loughran, author and journalist, spent many years in Africa as a foreign correspondent and as a senior executive of the Nation group of newspapers in Nairobi, Kenya. He was chef de bureau for United Press International in Beirut, Paris and Moscow before becoming foreign news editor in New York. Subsequently, he set up and ran Compass News Features, covering the developing world. He currently writes a weekly column in the *Sunday Nation.*

Index

#

100 Greatest South Africans of All Time 338
180-Day Detention Act (180-day detention law) 13, 159, 224, 432f
1943 general election 79
1948 general election 96
1966 World Cup 197-198
1994 elections 173, 324, 338
24th of July Avenue 36

A

A Flag Is Born 89
A History of South Africa (Webb) 283
A History of South Africa (Thompson) 283
A Mouthful of Glass vii, 370
A Question of Madness vii, xi, 349, 370
A. Di Summa Hospital 132
Abrahams, Kenneth 160
Abrahams, Pamela 197
Africa South magazine 119
African National Congress (ANC) 3, 18, 27, 32, 114, 118, 120-121, 134, 136, 160, 214, 284, 291, 302, 313, 317, 319-320, 324-326, 328, 331, 338-339, 349, 351, 367, 371, 374, 380, 442-443f, 451f
African Resistance Movement (ARM) 3, 228, 395f
Agincourt 135
Agios Nektarios old people's home 343
Alachiotis, Cleanthes 206-207, 219
Albee, Edward 230
Albergue da Mitra (Hostel Mitra) 104, 132
Alexandria 35, 37-40, 42, 52, 68, 95, 121, 387
Algiers 18-19
Aliens Act No. 1 of 1937 78
Aliens Office 109
Aliens Registration Act 78
Aljuba Prison 99, 103, 297
Almost Free Theatre 303
Amendments to the Criminal Procedure Act of 1944 278
American Academy of Psychiatry and the Law 375
American Board of Forensic Psychiatry 375
American Coast Guard 84-85
American Psychiatric Association 447f
American Reconstruction Mission 94, 98
American Revolution 90, 95
Amnesty International 306, 412f
Amsterdam 73
An Enemy of the People 59
An Experimental Study of the Blunting of Emotions 73
Anafores sto Nobelista Nelson Mandela (Αναφορές στο Νομπελίστα Νέλσον Μαντέλα) 372
Ananiadis, George 149
Anarchy (book) 55
Andrews, William H. 58
Anglican Mission School 48, 53

Anglo-American Fashions and Designers 111
Angola (ship) 102
Ankara 122
Anti-Apartheid Movement (boycott movement) 4, 22, 114, 118-119, 133-134, 155, 183, 261, 284, 374, 379, 419f
Anti-Semite and Jew 197
Anti-Slavery Society 114, 133
Aquinas, Saint Thomas 90, 183, 334
Arenstein, Rowley Israel 21, 28-29, 183
Argyrou, Andreas 365
Aristotle 44
Armstrong, Louis 160
Aspiotis, Panteleimon 202
Athens 28, 39, 91, 93, 98, 129-130, 202, 318, 320, 330
Atlantic Ocean 1, 26, 40, 83, 98, 295
Aucamp, Brigadier 11-13
Augustides, Mike 199-200, 305
Aurets, Johannes Jacobus Uys 184
Auschwitz 291
Australia ix, 18
Austria 121
Aversion project 318, 447f

B

Babiolakis, Andreas 51, 69, 172, 178-180, 371, 70, 164-165, 171-173, 366
Babiolakis, Giangos 179-180
Baker, Peter William Edward 240
Bakunin, Mikhail 56
Balkan War 1
Baltazar, Jose Lopez 178
Bangor, Maine 85
Banovic, Eleni ('Elenitsa') 5, 166, 362
Banovic, Nikola vii, 5, 122-130, 166, 280, 318, 367
Bantu Education Act 157
Baragwanath hospital 21, 117
Barbeau, Caroline 287
Barca d'Alva 99
Barclays Bank 204
Barling's Tea Lounge 196
Barnard, Christiaan 297
Baster, Brigadier 29
Bastille 3, 99, 355
Batista, Fulgencio 250
Baudoin, King 108
BBC 19, 370
Beatty, Warren 171, 250
Beeld, Die 213
Been, C. 155, 168
Beira 24, 170-171, 175-181, 195-196, 295
Beirut 121
Belgian Congo 156
Belgium 109, 215
Belgravia Café 192
Bella Ciao 161, 173, 211, 294
Ben Bella, Ahmed 163
Benjamin Franklin 90, 125, 334
Benjamin Franklin National Memorial 90
Benoni 187
Beresford, David xii, xiv, 79, 311, 319, 321, 347-348, 352, 357, 367, 434f, 447f
Berlin 67, 73
Berlin Olympic Games 1936 67
Berlin University 74
Bernheim, Felix 271
Bertolis, Father Elias 37, 60-61, 64-65
Bethsaida 177

Beyers, Justice Andries 229-231, 235-236, 238, 240, 245, 251, 254, 256, 268, 271-272, 275-277, 282, 288, 298
Bible 28, 86, 123, 174, 176, 283, 300-301, 304, 307-308, 382
Bieser, Dr 107
Biko, Steve 231, 393f, 451f
Billis, Nikolaos 206-207, 219
Bishop Lavis High School 189, 361
Bizos, George x-xii, xvi, 11, 17, 163, 229-230, 233, 275-276, 302, 306, 351, 373, 376, 386
Bizos, Antonis 11, 163
Black People's Convention 439f
Blair, Tony 250
Bloemfontein 278, 338
Blom-Cooper, Louis 306, 308
Bloomberg, Abe 230
Bloomberg, David viii, xiv, 230-236, 238-240, 246-247, 269-270, 275-276, 279, 298, 307-310, 312, 371, 445f-446f
Blow, Desmond xvi, 80, 441-442f
Blow Graham xiv
Boksburg Prison 21, 117
Boksburg 280
Bolivar, Simone 50-51, 53-54, 56, 125
Bonheoffer, Dietrich 334
Bornman, Jacobus Johannes 27, 194-195, 261, 269, 287
Boshoff, Anna 319
Boshoff, W.G. 393f
Bosporus 127
Boston 30, 87-89
Boston Psychopathic Hospital 26, 85, 88
Boswell, Ian 196, 269
Botha, Dr (Superintendent) 335
Botha, Johannes Jacobus 26, 185-186
Botha, Stoffel 319
Botha, P.W. 8, 312, 318, 336, 399f
Botswana 6
Brakpan 187
Bram Fischer Drive 338
Brazil 380
Brazilian Café 95
Brecht, Bertolt 59, 315, 383
Breytenbach, Breyten vii, 302, 306
Brindisi 132
Britannia Hotel 43
British Government 36, 445f
British Mining Supply Company 77-78, 80, 249
British Royal Navy 195, 445f
British Union of Fascists 134
Broederbond 31, 74, 96, 111, 407f, 414f
Bronkhorstpruit 313
Brunette, Donald B. 241, 256, 273
Brussels 108-109, 130
Brussels World Fair 108
Bulgaria 126, 129
Bulworth 171
Bureau of State Security (BOSS) viii, xiii, 32, 309, 311-313, 315
Burger, J.G. 8
Burger, Piet 199
Burger, Willie viii, 231-232, 246, 251
Burke, Alban x, xv, 247, 249, 255, 268, 375
Burundi 206, 286
Bush, George W. 250

C

Calais 112
Caledon Square police station 9, 11, 21, 26, 34, 209, 228, 236, 246, 278, 289, 291
Callinicos, Lulli 32

Canada ix, 18, 25, 81,83-85
Canoe Song 123, 166
Cape Argus 197, 309
Cape of Good Hope 83
Cape Times 7, 111, 263, 271, 371
Cape to Cairo Union 264
Cape Town xv-xvi, 1-2, 11, 12, 14, 18, 27-28, 31, 73-74, 80-81, 99, 117, 119, 130, 160, 183, 187, 190-192, 199-202, 204-207, 210, 213-214, 218, 232-234, 236, 245-246, 255, 267, 281, 286, 291, 295, 299, 304, 307, 318-319, 326-327, 338, 360-361, 366-368, 370, 388, 445-446f
Cape Town Bar 281
Cape Town City Council Power Station 261
Cape Town City Hall 446f
Caribbean 1, 114
Carte Blanche Interactive 354
Cascais Fort 103, 297
Cascais, Captain 133
Case Western University School of Medicine x, 375
Castro, Fidel 125, 163, 173, 202, 250
Cavafy, Constantine 39, 95
Caxton Hall 114
Center for Studies in Social-Legal Psychiatry and the Law x, 375
Centurion 338
Cerff, Major 231
Chai et Kiosk 62
Chaillet, Ned 303
Charleston, South Carolina 87
Chiba, Laloo 432f
Chief Inspector of PIDE in Lisbon 24
Christian Church 86, 91, 93, 95, 98, 105-106, 121, 124, 132, 166, 169, 187, 189-190, 192-193, 212, 214, 239, 270, 363, 408f
Christie, Renfrew 296, 317, 380
Christodoulou, Nikolaos 205
Church League of America 288
Church Street 163-164
Church Street cemetery 213
CIA 20
Cinderella Prison 280
Citizen, The 309-313, 358, 446f
City Engineering and Carron Limited 166
City Guns xv, 1, 26
City Tea Room 66
City Tramways 190, 192
Civil Rights Movement 59
Clark, Maud 7
Cloete, Gideon 196, 239, 270
Cockram, Mr 80
Coetzee, Floris 298
Coetzee, Christian Pieter 7
College of Psychiatrists of South Africa 375
Collins, Canon John 27, 134, 284
Colman, Robert 319
Cologne 118
Coloured People's Congress 160
Colpontoon 266
Commission of Enquiry into Dr Verwoerd's death viii, ix, 27, 31-32, 206, 214, 222, 245, 247, 263, 280-281, 283, 288-289, 303, 348, 356, 373-374, 384, 427f
Commission of Enquiry into the Sharpeville Massacre 281
Commission of Inquiry into Exchange Control Regulations 312
Commissioner for Immigration and Asiatic Affairs 53, 78, 80
Commissioner of Oaths Act and the Prisons Act 280

Commissioner of Police in Pretoria 78, 214
Commonwealth of Nations 121, 264
Comyn, Charles 304
Concise Oxford Dictionary 350
Congo 109, 186, 198
Congress of the People 162, 444f
Constandinou, Minas vii, 149-150, 280, 313-320, 326-338, 343, 345, 354, 362, 367-371, 384
Constantaras, Elias 197
Constitutional Court of South Africa x
Consulate of Spain in Jerusalem 122
Conte, Willie 67
Contis, Marika 170
Contis, Xenofon 170
Convention for a Democratic South Africa 451f
Cook, Captain 46
Cooper, Harold 233-235, 247-252, 254, 256, 260-262, 267, 269-271, 275, 299
Cooper, Gavin xv, 275
Cooper, Wilfrid xv, 231-232, 236, 238-240, 246-237, 251, 255-259, 261-262, 273, 275-276
Corbett, Michael 356, 358, 451f
Corday 99
Corinthia 98
Correctional Services (see also Department of Correctional Services) 319, 339, 341
Cosmopolitan Restaurant 66
Costa Do Sol 149
Council of Pretoria's Greek Community 343
Cox, Jack 48
Crete xiii, 21, 35, 37-39, 50, 130-132, 170, 330
Criminal Procedure Act 278
Cronin, Jeremy 231, 302
Cuba 1, 125, 167, 173, 184, 202, 295
Cuban Hat tea room 184
Cullinan 321

D

D. Spanos, Sucras., LDA 58
D'Artagnan 51
da Costa Lontrão, Francisco Bartolomeu 177
Da Silva, Antonia Texeira 168
Daily Dispatch 263
Daily Herald (London) 119
Daily Star (Toronto) 118
Daniels, Eddie 291
Daniels, Helen187-188, 239, 255-256, 422f
Daniels, (Helen's father) 188
Daniels, (Helen's mother) 188
Daniels, Merle 239, 256-257, 277, 427f
Daniels, Peter 239, 255-257, 261, 277
Daniels, Ralph 106
Danton 99
Darby, T.A. 12-13
Davis, Dennis 282
Davis, Lionel 14, 291
Davis, Sammy Jr 160
de Balzac, Honoré 44
De Fountotos, Maria Glinatsis 200
De Gama, Vasco 46
De Klerk, F.W. 338
de Matos Rodrigues, Alberto Henriques 178
de Vos, Wilhelmina 196, 255, 287
Deep Purple 353
Democratic Army of Greece (DSE) 28, 93-94, 96-98, 126, 131, 167, 202

Demons 45
Denmark 105
Department of Employment 196
Department of Immigration 29, 155
Department of Information 399f
Department of Psychology at the University of Johannesburg x, 375
Department of Social Welfare 195-196, 234, 254
Department of the Interior 98, 113, 168, 188, 227
Deputy Commissioner of Police, Witwatersrand Division 78
Dexameni 95
Dick, Joyce 188
Dickens, Charles 44
Diemont, Judge Marius 230
Dietrich, Marlene 353
Dimelas, Manolis vii, xiv
District Six 190
Division of Forensic Psychiatry at Case Western Reserve University 375
Dlamini-Zuma, Nkosazana Clarice 339-340, 359
Dönges, T.E. 13, 110
Dostoyevsky, Fyodor 45, 315
Dover 112-113
Doxiartis, Damaskinos 106, 280
Dr Verwoerd Award 194
Drexler University x, 375
Dugard, John x-xii, 32, 216, 233, 275
275, 281-282, 288, 373, 377, 386
Dukes, Sir Paul 120
Duncan, Graeme 282
Durban x, 27-29, 180-181, 183-185, 187, 190, 228, 255, 319, 443f
Durban Magistrate's Court 184, 249
Durban Men's Home 187
Durbanville 189
Durham University xv-xvi, 374
Durruti, Buenaventura 136
Dutch Reformed Church 31, 73
Dylan, Bob 15-16, 161

E

E.R. Carney Hostel 184
East African Airways 160
East Rand 364
Egypt 35-39, 41-44, 48, 53, 57, 107, 121, 131, 154, 215, 264, 291, 330, 350
Egyptian Consul in Johannesburg 76
Eichmann, Adolf 126, 334
Eintracht, Mary also see Vasilogiorgis, Mary 15, 40, 154
Eis Samon (*To Samos*) 335
Eisler, Robert 394f
Eleftheriadis, Efthimios 106-107, 280
Eleni (tanker) viii, xiii, 27, 200, 202-207, 218-221, 223, 227, 284-286, 335
Elgin Café 66
Ellis Island 87
Ellison, Ralph 169
Ennals, David 118, 120
Erasmus Commission of Inquiry 20, 312
Erasmus, Jacobus 234, 237, 240, 273-274
Eros 113
Erotokritos 330
Essop, Ismail 191
Ethiopia and Liberia v. South Africa 282
Ethiopia 19, 68

Europe 15, 18, 22, 25, 75, 79-80, 84, 87, 91, 94, 98, 100, 135, 150, 154-155, 158, 162, 165-166, 169, 180, 238, 244, 314, 380

F

F.A. Poole Engineering Pty. Ltd. 167, 249, 269
Fairbanks, Douglas 50
Falling in Love Again 353
Familiadis Community School 40
Famous Dead Man 319
Fanon, Frantz 173, 315, 333
Fatti's Building 161
Feinauer, Fred 204
Ferreira, Inspector Horacio 27, 175-176, 261
Ferreiras (a couple) 189
Figueira, Mário 102
Financial Times 304
Fischer, Bram 230
Fischer, Mr (Tsafendas's flat mate) 194
Fischia il Vento 173
Fisher, E.L. 7
Floka Café 95
Flynn, Bill 303
Forbes Border Post 170
Forsyth, Frederick 395f
Fort Napier Hospital 240
Founding Fathers 90
Fountain Café 66
Fountotos, Michalis 200, 205-206, 218, 220
Fourie, Jan Johannes Albertus 185
Fox-Pitt, Thomas 114-115
France viii, ix, xiii, 58, 98-99, 112, 215, 313, 350
Frankfurt 109, 111, 116, 199, 269
Franklin, Benjamin 89, 125, 328
Franco, General 69
Frankenstein 358
Fraser and Chalmers Ltd 185-186, 263
Fraserburg xvi
Freedom Charter 121, 161-162, 165
FRELIMO 173, 176, 179, 389
French Revolution 44, 55, 90, 99, 355
French Riviera 445f
Fries & Son 109-110, 155, 199
Fuad I (see also King of Egypt) 35
Furness, Edward 27, 134

G

Galanakis, George 180
Galleani, Luigi 55
Ganyile, Anderson 160
Gardener, David 134, 284
Garvey, Marcus 315
Gauteng xii, 342
Gavasiadis, Fotini 154, 163-168, 243
Gavasiadis, Markos 154, 163-164, 166
Gavasiadis, Nick 154, 166
Gazidis, Costa 320
Geldenhuys, Pieter Benjamin 196, 269
General Director of PIDE in Lisbon 176-177
Genis, Captian 9, 12
George I of Greece 206
German Embassy in Lourenço Marques 68
Germany 3, 44, 59, 73-75, 77-80, 134, 155-156, 159, 166, 201
East Germany ix
West Germany ix, 30, 105, 107, 109, 111, 116-118, 123, 126, 131, 197-198, 280

Germinal 58-59
Geyer, Matron 353
Ghost Squads 157
Goldberg, Denis xv, 153, 280, 295, 299, 302, 380-381, 442f
Goldman, Emma 56
Goldman, Leon 193
Gondola 170-177
Gondola Hotel 172, 175-176
Govender, Krish x-xii, 356, 359, 374, 381, 385-386, 388, 451f
Governor of Pretoria Central Prison 324
Grafton State Hospital ix, 25-26, 88-89, 408f
Grand Bazaar 123
Grand Companion of O.R. Tambo 381
Grand Parade Centre 233
Greco-Roman museum 39
Greece viii, ix, x-xi, 17, 28, 30, 40, 55, 90-91, 93, 95-96, 98, 105, 121, 131, 162, 167, 191, 201, 206, 244, 320, 328-331, 334, 337-338, 342, 355, 363, 367-368, 372
Greek Civil War 22-23, 28, 93, 95, 106, 114, 126, 130-131, 150, 169, 185, 200, 202, 214, 220, 264, 284, 330, 374
Greek Communist Party 28, 93, 200
Greek community of Beira 170, 172
Greek community of Cape Town 295
Greek community of Durban 184
Greek community in Krugersdorp 365
Greek community in Lourenço Marques 46, 49, 57, 64, 66-67
Greek community of Pretoria xiv, 154, 313, 320, 342-343
Greek community of South Africa 17-18, 163, 221, 303, 363-366, 368
Greek Ministry of Shipping viii, xv, 218-219
Greek National Day 41, 49
Greek Orthodox Church 40, 98, 106, 122, 202, 212, 329, 343, 364, 371-372, 387, 389
Greek Red Cross 98
Greek Revolution (Greek War of Independence) 40, 45, 55, 387
Greek-South African policeman 221-223, 228
Greyling, Cas 7
Grispos, George 51, 61-62, 67-68, 102, 169
Grispos, Helen *see* Kavadias, Helen 47, 169
Groote Schuur 2
Groote Schuur Hospital 8, 12, 193, 233, 236
Group Areas Act 274
Groves, Elizabeth Magdalena 194
Guardian, The xiv-xv, 79, 299, 311, 319, 321, 347, 357, 434f, 447f
Guevara, Ernesto (Che) 125, 372
Guilio Cesare 74
Gurier Dam 338

H

"H" Court in Johannesburg 78
H.F. Verwoerd Dam 338
H.F. Verwoerd Building 338
Haafe, Guenter 110, 269
Hagia Sophia 122
Hagios, Costas 192
Haiti 59
Halifax, Nova Scotia 83-84
Hall, Mr 207, 270

Hamburg 73, 104-107, 112, 235, 273
Hamburg University 73
Handel, George Frideric 160
Harding 117
Haron, Imam Abdullah 231
Harris case (electoral vote case) 230, 282
Harris, John 214, 228, 395f, 444f
Harrison, Tony 1-2, 26
Hartford, N.D. 197
Hartmann, Horst 110, 269
Havenga, Nicolaas 96
Health Department (South Africa's) 359
Hecht, Ben 89
Heilbrun, Kirk x, xv, 247, 375
Hellenic Orthodox Ladies Association (HOLA) 320, 363
Hendrik Verwoerd Drive 338
Henning, P.H. 240
Henry, King of England 135
Heraklion 35, 131-132
Heroes' Acre 213
Heydrich, Reinhard 334
Highgate Cemetery 113
Hikmet, Nazim 4, 126, 335
Hill, Joe 89
Himmler, Heinrich 396f
Hitler, Adolf 3, 67, 73, 75, 77, 79-80, 105, 111, 164, 332, 334-335
'Hitler's best student' 3, 17, 165, 190, 220, 246, 259, 287, 332
Hochst 111
Holiday, Antony 302
Holocaust 100, 355, 445f
Holy Land 122, 301
Holy Trinity Church 134
Hood, Robin 51
Hornsey 134
Hospital do Ultramar 25, 104, 177
House of Assembly 1-3, 32, 130, 192, 194, 198-199, 203-204, 216, 228, 271, 284, 319, 373
Howard College 443f
Howard League for Penal Reform 306
Hulse, Mr 194, 268, 429f
Human Zoo 108-109
Hurley, John 191
Hyde Park 113-114
Hymn to Liberty 329

I

I Can't Give You Anything But Love, Baby 353
i Galleanisti 55
I.D. 370
Ibsen, Henrik 59
If this is a Man 315
Immigration Act 87
Immorality Act 166
Imperial Airways 63, 66, 69-70
Independent Labour Organisation 157
India 59, 156, 420f
India 107
Indian Ocean 1, 183
Institute of Psychiatric Welfare of Lisbon 133
Instituto de Medicina Tropical 104
International Agency for Employment 157
International Aid and Defence Fund 20
International Brigades 68
International Court of Justice x, 282, 377
International Socialist League 58
International 58
Invisible Man 169
Irvine, William 408f

Iscor Iron and Steel Works 2, 78, 243
Isle of Wight 115-116
Italian embassy in Lourenço Marques 68
Italian Roman-Catholic priest 212

J

Jacobs, H.C.F. 210, 236
Japan 6
Jassat, Abdulhai 432-433f
Jeepers Creepers 353
Jenkins, Tim 302
Jericho 301
Jerusalem 122
Jessop, Tom 7
Jesus Christ 17, 40, 60, 124-125, 162, 177, 394f
Joe Hill (song) 89
Joffe, Mr 76
Johannesburg xv, 14, 18, 21, 58, 66, 69, 75-78, 80, 98, 117-118, 120-121, 131, 149, 155, 160, 162-163, 167, 183, 228, 233, 245, 249, 255, 263, 280, 311, 319, 326, 328, 330, 338, 343-344, 364-366, 372, 385, 395f, 433f
Johannesburg City Hall 76
Johannesburg Stock Exchange 14
John of Salisbury 90, 334
John Vorster Square police station 433f
Johnson, Jack 67
Johnston, James 239, 270, 277, 287
Jonathan, Leabua 6
Jones, Brutus 59
Jordan River 122
Joseph, Helen 153
Joubert, Gideon 14
Judson, Neville 305
Julius Caesar (Shakespeare's play) 179

K

Kalogirou, Antonis 183-184, 199
Kalvos, Andreas 329, 335
Kambouris, Nikolas 201-202, 206-207, 219
Kampala 20
Kantas, Giorgos 206-207, 219
Karageorgis, Ioannis (Jean) 206
Karanja 181-183
Kargakis, Costas xiii, xiv, 131-132
Karlsruhe 106
Kasos xiv, 200-201
Kasrils, Ronnie xv, 349-350, 381, 388
Kathrada, Ahmed xv, 291, 321, 381, 385
Katjivena, Ewald 19
Kautsky, Karl 394f
Kavadias, Sophia 169
Kavalieratos, Andrew 51
Keerom Street 246
Keevy, Lt. Gen. John 15, 18
Kemp, Stephanie 214
Kennedy, John F. 206, 288, 305
Kenya 19, 198
Kenya African National Union 19
Kerzner, Sol 446f
Key, Liza vii, xi, xv, 32, 347-349, 356-359, 362, 367, 370-371, 382, 434f
KGB 27
Kilimnos 205
King Baudoin 108
King, Martin Luther 20, 198
Kitharida xiii, 35, 131
Kitson, David 296, 299, 443f
Klein, Maurice 2
Kliptown 162

Kokkinidis, Costas 205, 218, 221, 285
Kokkinidou, Maria 205, 218, 221, 285
Kollapen, Jody x, xii, xvi, 324-326, 328, 338-344, 349, 355, 373, 381, 385
Komatipoort 152
Kornaros, Vintsentzos 330
Kossew, Ralph 11-12, 195-196, 234, 254-255
Kreipe, General Heinrich 131
Kroonstad 117
Kropotkin, Peter 56
Krouse, Matthew 319
Krueger (lawyer) 230
Krueger, Anton xvi, 370
Kruger Day 2262
Kruger, Paul 417f
Krugersdorp 339, 364-366, 368
Ku Klux Klan (KKK) 16, 135, 153, 160
Kuwait 218-219
Kykkotis, Seraphim 372
Kyriakais, Gerry 69, 71
Kyriakakis, Ira 47, 71, 149, 174, 371

L

Labour Party (British) 114, 134
Labour Party (South African) 58
Lagos 19
Lake Malawi 161
Lambley, Peter vii, 267-268, 299
Lamont, Austin 278
Landman, K 439f
Langa 117
Langa Inquiry 281, 288
Lansdowne 189, 361
Law Society of South Africa x
Lawyers for Human Rights 324, 338
le Roux, Michelle 282
Leach, Henry 445f
Lebanon 121-122
Lee, Stephen 302
Leipzig University 73
Lenin, Vladimir 55, 63, 125
Lenkoe, James Thabiso 432f
Lesotho 6
Let God's Blessing on Him Fall 110
Levi, Primo 315
Levin, Aubrey 318
Levy, Reuven 67
Lewin, Hugh 302
Liberal Party (British) xvi, 118
Liberal Party (South African) 118
Liberopoulos, George 149
Lieberman, Gillian Claire 193, 249, 265-266
Lighton, Ralph 193, 249
Ligris, Pavlos 343
Like Karem (*Kerem Gibi*) 4, 335
Limasollu Naci College xv-xvi, 126-127, 129-130, 199
Lisbon 24, 70, 99-102, 104, 107, 122, 132-133, 135, 137, 149, 174, 176-177, 197, 265
Live and Let Live vii
Liverpool 87
Living in Strange Lands The Testimony of Dimitri Tsafendas xvi, 370, 386
London xiv-xv, 4, 14, 16, 19, 22, 27, 113-115, 119, 133-134, 150, 153, 165, 169, 183, 215, 232, 271, 284, 303-304, 315, 319, 374
Longman's Chronicle of the 20th Century 283
Loock, Mrs 49
Louis XVI 99
Lourenço Marques xiii, 15-17, 28, 35-37, 39, 42-43, 45-46, 48-50, 52-57, 60-63, 65-70, 78, 81, 83,

93, 99-102, 122, 149-151, 155, 169, 171-172, 177-180, 184, 227, 244, 253, 264, 280, 291
Lourenço Marques Civil Administration 36, 63
Louw, Eric 118-119
Louw, P.A. 185
Love Can Open Prison Doors 252
Ludorf, Justive J.F. 299
Lumumba, Patrice 109, 161, 163
l'Università Popolare 36, 56
Lutheran Church 122
Luthuli, Albert 121, 159

M

Mabe, Aron 367
MacGregor, James William 233-235, 272-273, 278
Mackenzie, Myrna 119
Macmillan, Harold 115, 117, 119, 232, 271
Mafekeng, Elizabeth 159
Maforga 174
Maia, Augusto de Sousa 175
Mail and Guardian 367
Maile, Reginald Robert 218, 285
Maine 84
Makhatini, Johnny 18
Makiwane, Tennyson Xola 27, 114, 215, 284, 315, 374
Malan, Daniel Francois 96, 101, 110, 410f
Malatesta, Errico 55-56, 136
Malawi 329, 386
Malindi, Zollie 432f
Mandela, Nelson 3, 11, 14, 20, 122, 153, 159, 162, 173, 229, 291-292, 318-319, 321, 324, 326, 338, 349, 351, 353, 372, 380, 451f
Mandela A Biography 283
Mandela The Authorized Biography 283
Mandini 26-27, 185-187, 263
Mandini Store 186
Mangete 187
Mangete Catholic Mission 186
Mangete Reserve 27
Manning, Violet 189
Manuel 51, 67-70, 102, 149, 152, 318
Mapaila, Solly xiii, xv, 378-379, 385-386, 388
Maputo xiv, 318, 349, 371-372, 387, 389
Marandellas 168-169
Marangos, Stelios 170
Maria (Amelia's friend) 36-37, 39
Marie Antoinette 99
Marina 95-96
Marine Diamond Corporation 192-194, 249, 265-266, 268
Marine Jumper 91
Maritzburg 240
Mark Antony 179
Markram, J. 168, 227
Marshall Plan 94
Martincich, Keith 193, 268, 287
Martindale, J. 49
Martins, Christian 371
Marwick, Tess 303
Marx, Karl 111, 113, 125
Masemola, Jeff 321
Masilo, Tsholofelo xvi, 373
Massachussets 25, 85, 88, 90
Mastromanolis, Manolis (Emanuil) xiii, 201, 203-207
Masutha, Tshililo Michael xi, 373, 385-386
Matanzima, Paramount Chief Kaiser 213
Matshikiza, John 367
Matthews, John E. 299

Mavroleon Company 218
Mavronas, Nikolas 204-205, 219
Maw, Anthony 39, 102
Maximum Security Section, Pretoria Central Prison (also 'Beverly Hills') 300-302, 317, 320, 442f
Mbeki, Govan 156, 291
McDonald, A.C. 155
McLaren, Dorrian 304-305
Medecin, Jacques 445f
Medford 88
Media 24 338
Mein Kampf 73
Mental Disorders Act 246, 251, 298, 357
Meredith, Martin 283
Messiah (Handel's oratorio) 160
Messrs. Steers-Grove 98
Metropolitan State Hospital 85-86
Meyer, Izan 74
Meyer, Piet 74, 198
Mhlaba, Raymond 291, 321
Michaletos (née Tsafantakis), Artemis Diana 17, 37-42, 49, 52-53, 69-70, 93, 102, 149, 151-152, 170, 253, 280, 330
Michaletos, Costas (family friend) 28, 43
Michaletos Costas (teacher) 48
Michaletos, George (Tsafendas's uncle) 17, 48, 53, 93, 151-152
Michaletos, Irini (also Irini Contis) xiii, 170
Michaletos, John (Artemis's son and Irini's husband) xiii, 170
Michaletos, John (Tsafendas's friend, doctor) 28
Michaletos, John (Tsafendas's friend, teacher) 28, 93, 95-96, 98, 121, 129-130, 318
Michaletos, John (Tsafendas's godfather) 37, 48, 53
Michalis Tsafantakis Street 35
Middleburg Primary School 18, 48, 53
Mike's Outfitters 199, 202, 303, 305
Miles, Felix George 8
Miller, Arthur 230
Millin, Phillip 79
Milner Park 118, 417f
Mina al-Ahmadi 218-219
Mini, Vuyisile 328
Ministry of Information 312, 399f
Mitchell, Bernard 299
Mkwayi, Wilton 321
Mlambo, Johnson 292
Mlangeni Andrew 321
Mngqlikana, Lyttelon 211
Mohane, Gagi 367
Mohapi, Mapetla 231, 439f
Moires 131
Molotov–Ribbentrop Non-Aggression Pact 77
Montclair 184
Montreal 30, 83
Morrison, G. de V. 7
Moscow 27, 186
Moses 60
Mosley, Oswald 134-135
Mostert, Anton 312
Motsoaledi, Elias 321
Moumbaris, Alexander vii, xiii, 301-302, 306, 313, 339, 349-351, 381-382, 388
Moumbaris, Chloe 349
Moumbaris, Marie-Jose 349-351
Mozambican government 27, 372
Mozambique vii-ix, xvi, 5, 13-15, 17-18, 21-25, 27, 29-30, 35-38, 41-43, 48-49, 51, 53-56, 58, 61, 63, 66, 68-71, 78, 80-81, 83, 91, 98, 100-103-105, 107-108, 111,

121, 124, 129-130, 132-133, 136-137, 149, 154, 163, 166, 168, 170, 172-178, 180-181, 186, 190, 192, 195, 197, 204, 215, 224, 228, 250, 259, 261, 268, 280, 284, 295, 313, 316, 322, 327, 329-330, 371-372, 383, 386-389
Mozambique Channel 195
Mpetha, Oscar 321
Mulder, Cornelius 312, 399f
Muldergate 312, 399f
Muller, Hendrik 236-237, 254
Muller, Hilgard 7, 445f
Muller, Garnet Vincent 184
Munich 117, 121, 186, 249
Murakela 371
Murumbi, Nangoma 371
Mussolini, Benito 68, 172, 334
My Times 446f
Mzimela, Sipho 339

N

Nachtwey, Dr 107, 235
Naci, Limasollu xvi, 127-130, 155
Nair, Billy 321
Nairobi 19
Namaacha 35, 65
Namibia 306-307
Nankin, John 303
Naples 173
Natal 117, 160, 184
Natal Golf Open competition 160
National Archives (UK) ix, 375
National Archives of Portugal viii, 375
National Archives of South Africa viii, xi-xiv, 347-348, 356, 358, 370, 375, 434f
National Liberation Army of Colombia 394f
National Liberation Committee (NLC) 120
National Party 6, 17, 27, 30, 74, 79, 96, 110, 118, 134, 184, 187, 198-199, 213, 223, 230, 281, 312, 374, 377, 420f, 444f
National Socialist Movement 134
Native Commissioner's Court 157
Nazi Murder Mills 90
Nazis 17, 77, 79-80, 83, 91, 93, 96, 111, 134, 155, 164, 202, 318, 414f
Ndhlovu, Mr 281
Ndodemnyama we Verwoerd (*Beware, Verwoerd*) 328-329
Nektarios, Agios 343
Nel, Nikolaas Jacobus 168
Nelson House hostel 48-49
Netherlands 73
New Brunswick 83-84
New York 30, 56, 87-90
New York Post 119
New York Times 111, 121, 230
New Zealand 19
Nice 445f
Nichas, Antonis 205
Nicholson, Brenda Jessie 204
Niehaus, Carl 320, 326, 331
Nikolatos, Rika 320-321, 323, 326, 328-331, 338-340, 343, 345-347, 351-352, 355, 359, 362-365, 367
Nissiotis, Charles 77, 80, 150, 154, 245-246, 251-252, 254, 278
Nissiotis, Evangelia (née Tsafantakis) Evangelia (Vangela) xiii, 15, 41, 43, 45, 47, 51-52, 62, 64, 75-77, 80, 150, 154, 161-163, 244-245, 316, 321, 342-343, 363
Nixon, Richard 305
Nobel Peace Prize 121
No-Name Church *see* Christian Church
North Beach (Durban) 184

North Middlesex Cricket Club 134
Ntzebeza, Advocate Dumisa xi, xiii, 373, 386
Nuremberg Laws 3, 166, 332
Nuremberg Trials 334
Nxasana, Ndovela 432f
Nyanga 117
Nyasaland 169

O

O'Meara, Dan 396f
O'Neill, Eugene 59
O'Ryan, Enid 189-191, 193
O'Ryan, Louisa 189-191, 239, 257, 260-261, 366
O'Ryan, Patrick 189-194, 238-239, 247, 257, 260-261, 277, 318, 349, 360-361, 366-369, 428f
O'Ryan, Reuben 190, 203-204
Observer, The 306-311, 446-447f
Oceans 11 160
Ochsenzoll Krankenhaus Hospital 106, 235
Odyssey 39
Olivier, Laurence 160
Ontario 30
Oosthuizen, Johannes Christiaan 192
Oppenheimer, Harry 120
Oslo 121
Ossewabrandwag (OB) 21, 76, 79, 407f, 414f
Oswald, Lee Harvey 7, 210, 305
Othello 160
Ottoman Empire 40, 45
Owens, Jesse 67
Oxford University 73
Oyster Bay, Long Island 87

P

Padua 56
Palace of Versailles 99
Pan Africanist Congress (PAC) 3, 320
Panagia Church (Istanbul) 122
Papadakis, Nick 170-172, 177-180
Papageorgiou, Aris 343
Pappas, Peter 184
Pass Laws Act 117, 156-157
Paul Kruger Street 161
Pegado, Dr 133, 137
Peloponnese 95
Pelser, P.C. 280
Pennsylvania x, 90, 375
Pension, Gloria 170
Peroglou, Panagiotis 197
Perselis, Vasilis 203, 205
Persian Gulf 200
Peters, Miss 49
Petrakakis, Mr 149
Phahlane, Tsehla Mike (Mazurkie) xvi, 346-347, 355, 367
Philadelphia 90
Phillips, Norman 119-119
Piccadilly Circus 113
PIDE viii, 23-25, 27-28, 63, 70-71, 102-104, 108, 111, 137, 173-178, 180, 263, 374, 413f
Pietermaritzburg 117
Pilkington-Jordan, Attorney 282
Pinelands, Cape Town 207, 270
Piraeus 91, 93, 121, 130, 132
Place de Bastille 99
Place de la Concorde 99
Place de la Revolution 99
Plaka 94-95, 97
Plato 44
Pnefma, Gerry 165, 168-169, 179, 252-253

Pnefma (née Tsafantakis), Katerina (Bushia) xiii, 16, 36, 49, 56, 62, 64-65, 75, 80, 102, 154, 165, 168-169, 179-180, 243-244, 252-253, 316, 321, 342-343, 363-364
Pnefma, Mike xiii
Poggenpoel, Richard 192-193
Pogrund, Benjamin 280
Pokela, John Lyati 160
Polakis, Mr 179-180
Political Prisoner Release Programme 324
Popkiss, Rosamund 207, 304-305
Poriazis, Costas 179-180
Port Elizabeth 187
Port Said 37, 39
Portugal viii-ix, 13, 30, 63, 98-99, 104, 107-109, 116, 122, 130, 132-133, 137, 170, 173, 175, 189, 215, 250, 260, 297, 358, 371, 374-375
Portuguese Consulate-General (Jerusalem) 122
Portuguese East Africa 58
Portuguese Embassy in Rome 132
Portuguese Minister of the Interior 108
Portuguese Mission School 53
Post, The 279
Pote tha kani Xasteria 331
Potgieter (warder) 297, 300
Potgieter's assistant 297
Pouftis, Grigoris 206-207, 219
Pratt, David xiv, xvi, 5-7, 118-120, 153, 194, 228, 277-278, 382
President of the Portuguese Republic 108
Pretoria xvi, 2, 12, 14-15, 18, 21, 32, 66, 68, 77-78, 133, 151-155, 163-167, 178, 187, 213-215, 221, 227-228, 230, 234, 243, 245-246, 249, 252-253, 295-299, 311, 313, 316, 318-321, 325, 330, 339-343, 363-366, 372-373
Pretoria Central Prison 295-297, 299, 306, 310, 323-324
Pretoria Local Prison 302
Pretoria Central Prison Hospital 323, 325, 328, 338-339, 341, 351
Pretoria News 215, 228
Pretoria Railway Station 66
Price, Brian viii, 306-307
Prince Rwagasore 206, 286
Prince Street, Cape Town 189
Princippi Perfecto 137
Prisons Act 280
Private Eye 19
Probst, Hanno 27, 186-187, 261
Proclamation Hill Café 164
Progress College 75
Progressive Party 8, 299
Prophet Mohammed 60
Prostitute in Lourenço Marques 54, 67
Protoulis, Peter 205
Public Service Board 169

Q

Qumbela, Mountain 259, 432f
Queen Street, Durban 187
Quilemane 63

R

Rabkin, David 231, 302
Rabkin, Susan 231
Radford, Aubrey 6-8
Rand Daily Mail 18, 263, 280, 310
Rand Easter Show 118
Randos, Spiros 320, 328, 343, 355, 359-362, 368-371
Rebecca Street Cemetery 153

Referendum of 1960 in South Africa 121
Reformed Church pastor 300
Registrar of Births and Deaths in Lourenço Marques 65
Report in the Matter of Dr. Verwoerd's Assassination ix-xvi, 369, 373-378, 381, 386
Resnick, Phillip x, xv, 375
Restrepo, Camilo 394f
Rethmimnon 132
Rex v. Kennedy 233
Rhodes, Cecil John 264
Rhodesia 21, 23, 30, 73, 114, 154, 165, 168-169, 195, 198, 213, 224, 228, 243, 252, 263
Rhoodie, Eschel M. 399f
River Elbe 105
Rivonia Trial 153, 280, 295, 442f
Robben Island 14, 27, 289, 291, 293-297
Robeson, Paul 16, 59, 69, 89, 100, 103, 115, 123, 161, 165-166, 209, 211, 315, 329-330, 346
Robespierre (dog) 123
Robespierre (revolutionary) 99, 123
Rodrigues, Alberto Henriques de Matos 178
Roosevelt, President Franklin D. 88
Roper Hospital 87
Roquete, António Fernandes 102
Rorschach Personality Test 266-268
Rosamund Popkiss's daughter 304
Ross, Kenneth Heugh 27, 187
Rossouw, Daniel Jacobus 12, 214-218, 221, 223-224, 251, 285-286, 291
Rossouw, Mr (Department of Interior official) 188
Rousseau, Jean-Jacques 44, 335
Roux, Jannie 310
Royal Navy 195, 445f
Rua Andrade Corvo 37
Ruby, Jack 210
Rudman, Raymond Kirch 160
Rudolph, Cornelius Johannes 184
Russian Revolution 44, 55, 63, 90, 173

S

SABC3 370
Sabino, Joaquim Piçara 175
Sabotage Act 153, 212
Sacco, Nicola 55-56
Sachs, Albie 19, 160
Sachs, Solly 27, 134, 284
Sadoff, Robert L. x, xv, 247, 249, 375
Saint Andrew's Church 364
Saint Dionysius Church 371
Saint John, New Brunswick 83
Saint Peter 176-178, 241, 254, 336
Sakellaridis, George 17-18
Sakinofsky, Isaak viii, 13, 228, 234-237, 251, 263-265, 271
Salazar, Antonio de Oliveira 107, 136-137, 172, 263
Salisbury 169
Sampson, Anthony 283
Sanders of the River 161
Sanders, James viii, xiii, xvi
Sandip 59
Sarah 76-77
Sargent, Billy 134
Sartre, Jean-Paul 197, 336
Save 101
Scala Café 171
Scandinavia 105
Schinas, Eleni 39
Schmahmann, Samuel 48

Schmidt-Janssen, Dr 107
Schoeman, Barend J. 8
Schoombee, Elizabeth *see* Verwoerd, Betsie
Schuin, Piet 199
Scott, Mary 197
Scott, Robert Falcon 46
Seamen's Convalescence Home 87
Section 28 of the Mental Disorders Act of 1916 246
Sekukuhniland 117
Shackleton, Ernest 46
Shakespeare, William 44, 135, 179, 370
Shangaan 21, 35, 64-65, 322
Shangaan Chief 322
Sharpeville 117, 120
Sharpeville Commission 281, 288, 451f
Sharpeville Massacre 21, 33, 79, 117-118, 120-121, 198, 443f
Shaw, Gerald 7, 239, 271
Shelley, Mary 358
Sher, Antony 171, 370
Sideris, Peter 62-63, 66-67, 70
Sideris's daughter 66-67
Sideris's wife 66-67
Sisulu, Walter 153, 291, 321
Skordis, Kyriakos 184
Skoularikis, Dimitris xii, 323
Smith, Ian 213
Smith, Robert Harpur 27, 29, 187
Smorenberg, Owen 239, 261-262, 269, 272-273, 276-277
Sobukwe, Robert 291
Soho 113, 303
Solomos, Dyonisios 329
Somerset Hospital 233
Song of Freedom 59, 100, 103, 209, 211, 294
Song of the Plains 89
Songs of Free Men 89, 115
South Africa vii-xii, 2-5, 8, 11, 13-27, 30-33, 36, 44, 48, 53, 58, 66, 68-71, 73-81, 89, 91, 93, 96-98, 101-102, 104-106, 110-111, 113-114, 117-122, 124, 127, 129, 131-132, 134-136, 149-153, 155-163 165-168, 173, 180-181, 183, 186-187, 190-191, 195, 197-198, 201-203, 207, 211-213, 215-218, 220, 223-224, 227, 230, 234, 243-244, 249-250, 253, 255, 260-264, 276-278, 281-282, 284, 295-297, 299, 301-304, 306-307, 309, 311, 314-315, 317-318, 320-321, 324, 328, 331, 340, 343, 349, 353, 355, 357, 362, 365-368, 370-378, 380-383, 385-389, 399f, 420f, 445-447f, 451f
South African Air Force (SAAF) 295
South African Broadcasting Corporation (SABC) 4, 75, 121, 198, 213, 338
South African Communist Party (SACP) xiii, 3, 16, 21, 23, 32, 58, 66, 76, 111, 151, 167, 223, 279-280, 283-284, 295-296, 310-311, 320, 366, 374, 378, 380-381, 386, 388, 433f, 451f
South African Consulate in Cologne 118
South African Embassy in Lisbon 24, 137
South African Embassy in Washington 25, 191
South African government ix, 4, 14, 18-20, 27, 30, 32-33, 74-75, 111, 114, 117-121, 129, 134-136, 151, 153, 155, 158, 160, 162, 168, 187, 195, 198, 201-202, 213, 216-218, 220, 223-224, 228-231, 250, 279-282, 284-285, 288, 291-292, 302-303, 305-312, 317-319, 322,

324-325, 327, 331, 339, 342, 349, 356, 363, 373-377, 379, 381, 384, 386-389, 399f, 444-446f, 451f
South African Jewish Board of Deputies xvi
South African Medical Association 13
South African Military 306, 318
South African Observer 312
South African Office of the Commissioner for Immigration and Asiatic Affairs 53, 78
South African Police viii-ix, 9, 11, 15-18, 21-24, 26-31, 33, 43, 48, 57, 63, 70, 117-120, 134, 149, 159, 161, 195-197, 204, 211, 213, 215, 217-220, 222-223, 227-228, 232-235, 237-239, 243, 246-249,251, 253-257, 259-263, 265-271, 273-275, 277, 279-282, 284-287, 291, 306, 325, 327, 332-333, 336, 347-348, 355-357, 366-367, 374, 380-381, 383
South African press 20, 118, 309
South African Prisons Service 321
South African Railways 184
South African Rugby team 7
South African Security Police 9, 12, 23, 213-214, 221, 303, 439f
South African Students' Organization 439f
South West Africa 282
South West People's Organization (SWAPO) 19
Soviet Union ix, 27, 59, 61, 63, 77, 198, 397f
Soweto 305
Soweto Commission of Inquiry 288, 451f
Soweto uprising 305-306
Space Theatre Club, The 304
Spain 50, 68-69, 122
Spanish Civil War 44, 59, 68, 89
Spanos, Dimitris 57-63
Spanoudes, Renos 370
Spartacus 125
Special Branch of the British South African Police in Umtali 23
Speis, Ioannis 202
Spence, Reginald 193
SS *Benson* 87
SS *Eugene Livanos* 81, 83
SS *Hood Victory* 88
SS *John Holmes* 87
SS *Maria Nicolao* 88
SS *Pillory* 86
SS *Robin Locksley* 88
SS *Stuttgart* 74
St. Bernard's Home 88
St. Croix River 84
St. Nicholas's (Greek Orthodox Church) 106
St. Pancras Hospital 115-116, 271
Star, The 78
State of Emergency 117
Statue of Liberty 56
Stavrianos, Dimitris 202
Stellenbosch University 73-74, 338
Sterkfontein Psychiatric Hospital 339-341, 344-345, 347-349, 351-352, 355, 357, 359, 361-363, 367
Stokkiesdraai 2
Stollenkamp, Edmund George 218, 285
Stop List 15, 29, 113, 151, 155, 168, 183, 203, 214, 227
Stormjaers 20
Stowe, Harriet Beecher 44
Strange Lands 386
Strauss, J.G.N. 282
Strijdom, Johannes 74, 96, 110
"Strong Man" 345
Sub-Director of PIDE in Mozambique 24, 176-178

Suddes, Thelma Beryl 29
Summers, Herbert 197
Sunday Times (Johannesburg) xiv, 14, 79, 288
Sunday Tribune 306, 331
Suppression of Communism Act 29, 111, 121
Suttner, Raymond 302, 442f
Suzman, Helen xii, xv-xvi, 8, 299, 382, 396f
Swart, Charles 110, 213, 289
Swaziland 35, 301, 451f
Sweden 105
Switzerland 446f
Syria 122

T

Table Bay 291, 445f
Table Bay Power Station 188
Tagore, Rabindranath 58-59, 315
Tagus River 108
Tamburazis, Tamos 51
Tanner, William 303-305
Tapeworm ix, xi, 22, 26, 83, 85, 88-89, 92, 100, 103-107, 115-116, 132, 176, 190-191, 202, 216, 223-224, 229, 232, 236-240, 247-248, 252-254, 257-261, 265, 276, 279-280, 285, 288, 297-298, 303-304, 307, 314-316, 320-321, 323, 325-328, 336, 348, 354, 357-358, 360, 368-370, 374, 377, 382, 384, 386, 434f
Taurus mountain range 122
Teatro Gil Vicente 50, 59
Teatro Varieta 67
Tejo River 132
The Beatles 165
The Emperor Jones 59
The Fort 278
The Fort Napier Hospital 240
The Four Insurgent Generals 89
The Hague x, xii, 223, 282
The Home and the World 58-59, 315
The Jewish Problem Regarded from a Nationalist Point of View 75
The Psychology of Apartheid vii, 267
Thematic Apperception Personality Test 266, 268
Theophanopoulos, Ioannis 365
Theron, Esperanza 28-29
Theron, Johannes Andrias 280
Theron Trial 280
Theyer, Alice 196
Thomas Boydell Building 281
Thompson, Leonard 283
Thorpe, Jeremy 118, 120
Tiale, Isaac 432f
Tilliks 187
Times of Zambia 19
Times, The (London) 303
Tockar, Hymie 13
'Tool of the Nazis' 79
Toutountsoglou, Chief Officer John N. 205
Trades Hall 66
Trafalgar Square 113, 134, 165, 215
Transvaal 2, 48, 53, 74, 157, 280, 393f
Transvaler, Die 74-75, 78-79, 96, 410f
Treason Trial 162, 444f
Treatise of the Three Impostors 60
Trier 111
Trojan War 39
Troost, Mr. 258-259
Tropen Krankenhaus 105
Truth and Reconciliation Commission x, 354-359, 376, 451f

Tsabouniaris, Emanuel 200, 202, 205
Tsafantakis, Anna 150
Tsafantakis, Antonis 35-36, 38-39
Tsafantakis, (Captain) Dimitrios 35, 37-39, 41-42, 91
Tsafantakis, Giorgos 131
Tsafantakis (née Sakelis), Maria (Marika) 5, 15-16, 37-39, 41-43, 45-47, 49-52, 55-57, 63-66, 68-69, 76, 86, 124, 127, 133, 135-136, 149-151-154, 161-164, 166, 178, 244-245, 252, 313-314
Tsafantakis, Michalis (Tsafendas's father) xiii, 2, 5, 15, 21, 35-39, 41-51, 53-58, 60-65, 67-69, 71, 75-78, 80-81, 89, 91, 99, 101-103, 123-124, 130-131, 133, 135-136, 150-155, 184, 215, 244, 264, 291, 362
Tsafantakis, Michalis Captain 35, 37, 39, 41-43, 47, 50, 91, 94
Tsafantakis, Michalis (Tsafendas's nephew) 131, 166
Tsafantakis, Victor 14-15, 41, 43, 45-47, 51-52, 55, 64, 150-152, 161-163, 166, 243-245, 321, 342
Tsafantakis, Victoria 38, 41, 77
Tsafendas (play) 303-305
Tsafendas's dentist comrade 126, 129-130
Tsafendas's German girlfriend 106-107, 112
Tsafendas's Portuguese girlfriend 136
Tsafendas's Prison Service File 289
Tsafendas's Turkish girlfriend 126, 129-130
Tsaftaridis, Ioannis vii, xiv, 328-338, 343, 354, 359-362, 367-372, 384, 386-387, 389, 434f
Tuff, Tom 85-86, 88, 91-92, 100, 190, 229, 325, 327, 369
Turkey viii, 40, 122, 125-127, 129, 268, 280, 383
Tutu, Desmond 173, 344, 354, 359
Two by Twos *see* Christian Church
Tyrakis, George 131, 167

U

Umbilo 184
Umkhonto we Sizwe 120, 134, 295-296, 301-302, 315, 328, 349, 432f
Umtali 23, 169-170
UN Security Council 152
Uncle Tom's Cabin 44, 55, 58
Union Buildings 213
Union Movement (UM) 134
United Kingdom (also Britain) ix, 19, 75, 80, 93, 112-116, 133-134, 169, 195, 264, 306, 311, 372, 375, 445-446f
United Nations 152, 195, 377
United Party 27, 96, 110, 187, 230, 282
University of Cape Town x, xv, 291, 375
University of Johannesburg x, 255, 329, 375
University of Padua 36
US Army 96th General Hospital 87
US Consulate in Cape Town 191
US Immigration and Naturalization Service (INS) 86, 191
US Merchant Marine 86-88
US State Department 191
USA ix, 15, 18, 20, 25, 44, 55, 58-59, 73, 83, 87-91, 93-95, 101, 104, 109, 114-115, 169, 191, 198, 238, 288, 327, 375, 380, 416f, 447f
Uys, Stanley 14

V

Vaderland, Die 30, 213
Valkenberg Psychiatric Hospital x, 267, 299, 375
Vamvarapis, Stratis 197
Van den Berg, Attorney-General Willem 210, 235, 238-241, 246-251, 255-261, 264-266, 268-277, 279-280, 288, 427f
Van den Berg, J.J. 17, 151-152, 161, 227
Van den Bergh, General Hendrik ix, 14, 20-33, 117, 209, 212, 214-218, 221, 224, 227-230, 279, 309, 311-313, 384, 395-396f, 399f
Van der Merwe, C.V. 7
Van der Merwe, Hugo 323, 338
Van Heerden, Carel Sebastiaan 193, 266
Van Loggerenberg, Hendrik Johannes 164
Van Niekerk, Barend D. 299, 443f
Van Rensburg, Piet 293
Van Riebeeck, Jan 31
Van Vuuren, Christoffel Johannes 26, 186-187
Van Woerden, Henk vii, 340, 345, 352-354, 356, 359, 370, 429f
Van Wyk, Adolf Johannes 228, 235, 239-240, 272, 274-276
Van Wyk, Justice Jacques Theodore 223, 263, 281-282, 285-286, 288
Van Wyk, Lt. Col. P.J.P. 23, 30
Van Zyl, Reyner Johannes xvi, 233, 237, 255, 266-269, 273, 299
Vanzetti, Bartolomeo 55-56
Vaporidis, Agathagelos 280
Vasilakis, Michalis 201-202, 206-207, 219
Vauxhall Bridge Road 114
Venice 207, 220
Venter, W.L. 7
Vercoueil, Albert 167-168
Verghis, John 171, 179
Vergitsis, Dimitrios 364
Vergos, Nick (Nikolas) 26, 185-186, 26
Verwoerd, Betsie: 2, 8, 73–74, 79, 338
Verwoerd, Elize 14
Verwoerd, Hendrik Frensch vii-xv, 2-9, 12, 14, 16-20, 22-23, 25, 27-33, 44-45, 48, 57, 73-75, 78-80, 91, 96-97, 101, 110-111, 115, 117-120, 122, 131, 134-136, 149, 153, 156-160, 164-166, 172, 183, 187, 190, 192, 194-195, 198-199, 202-207, 210-211, 213-226, 228-233, 235, 241, 244, 246-253, 259, 261-265, 270-271, 273, 275, 279, 281-288, 291-294, 302-304, 306, 310-311, 315, 319-320, 324-329, 331-338, 340, 342, 346, 348-349, 351, 353-353, 356-358, 360, 364, 371-386, 388, 395f, 399f, 410f, 414f, 420f, 434f
Verwoerd, Wilhelm 12, 14
Verwoerd, Wilhelmus Johannes 73
Verwoerd's funeral 213, 230, 324-325
Verwoerdburg, Municipality of Lyttelton 338
Vicente, Gil 50
Virgílio, Francisco 175
Virgin Mary 40
Virginia 117
Visser, Gerrie 310
Visvinis, Father Michalis vii, xiv, 320, 323, 328, 343, 363-364
Vittorio 173
Vlachopoulos (Tsafantakis), Eleni 15, 43, 62, 66, 75, 80, 149-152,

154,161, 163, 165-167, 244-245, 316, 321, 342-343, 363, 370
Vlachopoulos, Mike xiii, 41, 80, 154
Vlachopoulos, Nick 15-16, 150-154, 161-166, 238, 243-246, 251-252, 254, 278, 321
Vlakplaas 318
Volbrecht, William Mare 18, 48
Voltaire 44
Vooruitsig Prison 211
Vorster, Dr Merryl 340, 348-351, 359
Vorster, J.D. 288
Vorster, Jacobus 31
Vorster, Johannes (John) Balthazar 14, 20, 23, 30-33, 159, 212-213, 217, 222-223, 229-230, 261-262, 281, 288-289, 305-306, 312-313, 318, 336, 373-374, 377, 382, 384, 399f, 414f
Voutselatos, George 36, 43, 53
Vulcan Iron Works, General Engineers 53, 249

W

Walker, Irene 49
Ward, Ivan 350
Waring, Frank Walter 7
Washington Star 312
Washington, DC 25, 191, 312
Waterkloof 295
Webb, Frank 283
Wechsler Bellevue Adult Intelligence Test 266
Weskoppies Hospital 234, 278
West 95th Street (New York City) 88
West End, Pretoria 163
Westminster Street, Cape Town 189, 361
White Terror 93
Whitecroft Mental Hospital 116
Wiehand, Sydney 199
Wiesenthal, Simon 355, 451f
Willemse, J. 249
William Rawbone and Co 2
Williams, Amelia 36-39, 42, 63-65, 98, 124
Willman, Chief Magistrate C. 210, 236
Winter, Gordon vii-viii, xiii, xvi, 32, 79, 309-313,
352, 358, 446-447f
Wisteria 87
Witwatersrand 78, 80,214, 407f
Witwatersrand Agricultural Society 416f
Wolfson, Mr. 76
Woods, Charles Edwin 185
Woodstock, Cape Town 196-197, 199
Worcestershire 87
World Court (also International Court of Justice) x, 223, 282, 377
World War Two xiv, 20, 22, 31, 75, 93, 106, 116, 131, 134, 154, 191, 201, 280, 284, 334, 337, 355, 443f

X

Xexenis, Ioannis 206
Xilouris, Nikos 330

Y

Yacoob, Zak x-xiv, 373, 378, 386, 389
Yellow Star Movement 16, 134-135, 153
Young, B.A. 304
Ysterplaat 295
Yugoslavia 121
Yutar, Percy 280

Z

Zabow, Aubrey 233-235, 237, 271-272
Zabow, Tuviah x, xv, 247, 249, 275
Zachariou, Ioannis 363-364, 366
Zafiriadis, Dimitris 201, 206-207, 219-220
Zambia 17, 19, 195, 253, 280, 319, 329, 386
Zante 328-330
Zeerust 117
Zeit, Die 159
Zoe 94-96
Zola, Emil 58-59
Zonderwater Prison 321-323
Zot Nit Keynmol (Song of the Warsaw Ghetto) 100, 294
Zululand 186
Zuma, Jacob 291

CPSIA information can be obtained
at www.ICGtesting.com
Printed in the USA
LVHW010320250523
747997LV00007B/95

9 781648 896965